Praise for B

"Best Places *are the best re*...

"Best Places *covers must-see portions of the West Coast with style and authority. In-the-know locals offer thorough info on restaurants, lodgings, and the sights.*"
—NATIONAL GEOGRAPHIC TRAVELER

"*. . . travelers swear by the recommendations in the* Best Places *guidebooks . . .*"
—SUNSET MAGAZINE

"*For travel collections covering the Northwest, the* Best Places *series takes precedence over all similar guides.*"
—BOOKLIST

"Best Places Northwest *is the bible of discriminating travellers to BC, Washington and Oregon. It promises, and delivers, the best of everything in the region.*"
—THE VANCOUVER SUN

"*Not only the best travel guide in the region, but maybe one of the most definitive guides in the country, which many look forward to with the anticipation usually sparked by a best-selling novel. A browser's delight,* Best Places Northwest *should be chained to dashboards throughout the Northwest.*"
—THE OREGONIAN

"*Still the region's undisputed heavyweight champ of guidebooks.*"
—SEATTLE POST-INTELLIGENCER

"*Trusting the natives is usually good advice, so visitors to Washington, Oregon, and British Columbia would do well to pick up* Best Places Northwest *for an exhaustive review of food and lodging in the region. . . . An indispensable glove-compartment companion.*"
—TRAVEL AND LEISURE

"Best Places Southern California *is just about all the inspiration you need to start planning your next road trip or summer vacation with the kids.*"
—THE FRESNO BEE

"Best Places Alaska *is the one guide to recommend to anyone visiting Alaska for the first or one-hundredth time.*"
—KETCHIKAN DAILY NEWS

"Best Places Northern California *is great fun to read even if you're not going anywhere.*"
—SAN FRANCISCO CHRONICLE

TRUST THE LOCALS

The original insider's guides, written by local experts

COMPLETELY INDEPENDENT

- No advertisers
- No sponsors
- No favors

EVERY PLACE STAR-RATED & RECOMMENDED

★★★★ The very best in the region

★★★ Distinguished; many outstanding features

★★ Excellent; some wonderful qualities

★ A good place

NO STARS Worth knowing about, if nearby

MONEY-BACK GUARANTEE

We're so sure you'll be satisfied, we guarantee it!

HELPFUL ICONS

Watch for these quick-reference symbols throughout the book:

FAMILY FUN

GOOD VALUE

ROMANTIC

EDITORS' CHOICE

BEST PLACES®

Southern California

The Best Restaurants, Lodgings, and Touring

Edited by
STEPHANIE AVNET YATES

EDITION

SASQUATCH BOOKS
SEATTLE

Printed in the United States of America
Published by Sasquatch Books
Distributed by Publishers Group West

Second edition
12 11 10 09 08 07 06 05 04 03   6 5 4 3 2 1

ISBN: 1-57061-375-3
ISSN: 1524-9255

Cover and interior design: Nancy Gellos
Interior composition: pdbd
Maps: Lisa Brower/Greeneye Design

SPECIAL SALES

Best Places® guidebooks are available at special discounts on bulk purchases for corporate,
club, or organization sales promotions, premiums, and gifts. Special editions, including personalized covers, excerpts of existing guides, and corporate imprints, can be created in large
quantities for specific needs. For more information, contact your local bookseller or Special
Sales, Best Places Guidebooks, 119 South Main Street, Suite 400, Seattle, Washington
98104, 800/775-0817.

SASQUATCH BOOKS

119 South Main Street, Suite 400
Seattle, Washington 98104
206/467-4300
books@sasquatchbooks.com
www.sasquatchbooks.com

CONTENTS

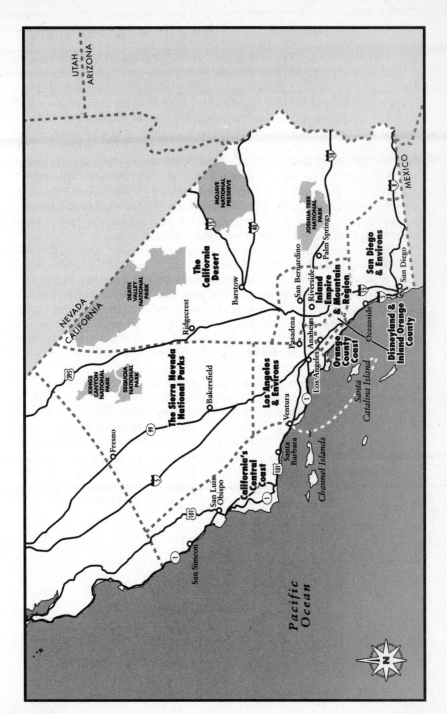

UTAH
ARIZONA

NEVADA
CALIFORNIA

MEXICO

The California Desert

MOJAVE NATIONAL PRESERVE

DEATH VALLEY NATIONAL PARK

Barstow

Ridgecrest

San Bernardino

JOSHUA TREE NATIONAL PARK

Riverside

Palm Springs

Inland Empire & Mountain Region

San Diego & Environs

San Diego

Pasadena

Anaheim

Oceanside

The Sierra Nevada National Parks

KINGS CANYON NATIONAL PARK

SEQUOIA NATIONAL PARK

Bakersfield

Los Angeles & Environs

Los Angeles

Orange County Coast

Disneyland & Inland Orange County

Fresno

Ventura

Santa Catalina Island

Santa Barbara

Channel Islands

California's Central Coast

San Luis Obispo

San Simeon

Pacific Ocean

N

Editor's Introduction

California is still the land of golden dreams. I confess I'm one for whom this larger-than-life state has never lost that ideal quality. When the sun shines a certain way—reflecting off the ocean, silhouetting a waving palm, or illuminating a desert landscape—I'm hooked all over again! It's my hope that within these pages you find your own connection to Southern California: For those of you who live nearby, a surprise in your own backyard; and for travelers from afar, an insider's key to the very best we have to offer. This guidebook covers a broad geographic area, so I hope you'll also read about the places you might not even be planning to visit (yet). Armchair travel can be just as rewarding as the kind that runs up the odometer.

I'd like to acknowledge the writers who helped me put this book together. The word "contributor" doesn't begin to convey the wealth of personal experience each brought to their own areas of expertise, and the passion I felt from each of them about the splendid region we are all lucky enough to call home.

I also want to express gratitude to my colleague Erika Lenkert, who had the challenge of creating the first edition of this book. She laid excellent groundwork for those of us who came after. I owe an equal debt of gratitude to the fine writers who contributed to that first edition—much of their work remains a vital part of this update, as well. I was also fortunate in being allowed to incorporate some of the excellent material found in other Best Places guides that cover California, and am grateful to those authors and editors for their hard work. Thank you Robin Kleven (editor of the Palm Springs destination guide) and Judith Babcock Wiley (editor of the Central California Coast destination guide).

My acknowledgements would not be complete without thanking the staff at Sasquatch Books, whose faith, patience, professional guidance, and personal dedication helped keep this book on track despite unforeseen challenges: Kate Rogers and Laura Gronewold, who were there at the beginning, as well as Suzanne DeGalan and Cassandra Mitchell, who joined the project in time to leave their mark in these pages, too.

The last—and most personal—thank you goes out to Bryan Yates, because the promise of reliving every one of these adventures with him is my constant inspiration.

—*Stephanie Avnet Yates*

About the Contributors

Born in Los Angeles, food and travel writer **ARLINE INGE** explored the tasty towns of New York and Paris before settling back in her hometown for good. Along the way, she worked as senior editor for magazines as diverse as *Cuisine, Bon Appetit,* and *Playgirl,* in addition to penning guidebooks to California, Spain, and Italy. Arline's mouthwatering food and travel articles have appeared in dozens of equally savory magazines, including *Chocolatier, Los Angeles, Westways, Architectural Digest,* in a weekly Internet dining column, and major newspapers nationwide. Arline diligently made the rounds of Los Angeles restaurants to help you navigate the L.A. dining scene.

Our resident Orange County expert is **DAVID LANSING,** a regular contributor to *National Geographic Traveler* and *Sunset* magazine. His award-winning essays and travel stories have also appeared in numerous magazines and websites, including *Westways, Los Angeles, Parenting, Orange Coast,* the *Los Angeles Times,* and Expedia.com. David makes his home in Newport Beach, though his passion for exploring lures him around the world. For Best Places®, David gives us his insider's look at Orange County's inland and coastal highlights.

JUDITH LAZARUS was born with wanderlust and a burning curiosity to discover the inside story of places far and near. Long the designated tour guide for visiting friends and family, she especially enjoys exploring Southern California. A freelance writer and editor for many years—covering topics from travel, recreation, health and fitness to theater, business and celebrities—Judith pinches herself every day because she now specializes in spa and lifestyle topics. She is the author of *The Spa Sourcebook, Stress Relief & Relaxation Techniques,* and www.AahSpa.com, and her articles have appeared in numerous newspapers, magazines and websites.

Former L.A. resident **CHERYL FARR LEAS** now calls Brooklyn, New York, home, but logs several bi-coastal jaunts each year. For Best Places®, she covered Los Angeles accommodations with a discerning eye and impeccable taste, leaving no duvet unturned. Cheryl's writing credits include major travel guidebooks to California, Hawaii, and New York City, as well as contributing articles about travel, real estate, spas, and other lifestyle topics to magazines that include *Variety, Travel & Leisure, Continental* (Continental Airlines' in-flight magazine), and *Bride's.*

MARIBETH MELLIN brought a wealth of experience to the San Diego chapter of this book. Over the past 25 years, she has covered San Diego for *San Diego* magazine, the *San Diego Union Tribune,* and the *Los Angeles Times.* An avid explorer, Maribeth has authored travel books to Mexico, Costa Rica, Argentina, Peru, Hawaii, and California, and received the prestigious Pluma de Plata prize for writing about Mexico. Maribeth is also the editor of our city guidebook, *San Diego Best Places.*

Native Angeleno **BONNIE STEELE** is the editor of *Valley Magazine,* a regional lifestyle magazine based in the San Fernando Valley, and *L.A. Brides,* a publication for area brides-to-be. In addition to contributing to several travel magazines and websites, Bonnie has co-authored a guide to her hometown. A frequent Best Places® contributor, Bonnie happily spent countless hours exploring Los Angeles and reporting back on worthwhile attractions, activities, and cultural pursuits around town.

KATHY STRONG is a Southern California native who's been splitting her time between the ocean and desert for the last 25 years. After owning and running a small B&B on the Central Coast, Kathy began writing travel guidebooks. Of the more than 20 she has published to date, most are about California; she's also authored guides to the Caribbean, Seattle and the spa industry. Kathy is a regular contributor to *Desert Magazine,* as well as various other leading magazines and newspapers. An enthusiastic road-tripper, Kathy explored the Inland Empire, desert national parks, and Sierra Nevada for this book.

A collectibles hound and pop history enthusiast, **STEPHANIE AVNET YATES** believes California is best seen from behind the wheel of a little red convertible. She has authored and/or edited several guidebooks to the Southland—including this book's companion guide, *Los Angeles Best Places*—and writes for various regional publications and websites. A California native, Stephanie spends her time exploring every corner of the Golden State. She used her local know-how to write the Central Coast chapter, along with sections on Palm Springs, Catalina Island, Big Bear and Lake Arrowhead, plus the Disneyland Resort.

About Best Places® Guidebooks

People trust us. Best Places® guidebooks, which have been published continuously since 1975, represent one of the most respected regional travel series in the country. Each guide is written completely independently: no advertisers, no sponsors, no favors. Our reviewers know their territory, work incognito, and seek out the very best a city or region has to offer. Because we accept no free meals, accommodations, or other complimentary services, we are able to provide tough, candid reports about places that have rested too long on their laurels, and to delight in new places that deserve recognition. We describe the true strengths, foibles, and unique characteristics of each establishment listed.

Best Places Southern California is written by and for locals, and is therefore coveted by travelers. It's written for people who live here and who enjoy exploring the region's bounty and its out-of-the-way places of high character and individualism. It is these very characteristics that make *Best Places Southern California* ideal for tourists, too. The best places in and around the region are the ones that denizens favor: independently owned establishments of good value, touched with local history, run by lively individuals, and graced with natural beauty. With this second edition of *Best Places Southern California* travelers will find the information they need: where to go and when, what to order, which rooms to request (and which to avoid), where the best music, art, nightlife, shopping, and other attractions are, and how to find the region's hidden secrets.

We're so sure you'll be satisfied with our guide, we guarantee it.

NOTE: *The reviews in this edition are based on information available at press time and are subject to change. Readers are advised that places listed may have closed or changed management, and, thus, may no longer be recommended by this series. The editors welcome information conveyed by users of this book. A report form is provided at the end of the book, and feedback is also welcome via email: bestplaces@ sasquatchbooks.com.*

How to Use This Book

This book is divided into eight major regions, encompassing San Simeon, Fresno, and Kings Canyon, and all destinations south to the Mexican border. All evaluations are based on numerous reports from local and traveling inspectors. Best Places® reporters do not identify themselves when they review an establishment, and they accept no free meals, accommodations, or any other services. Final judgments are made by the editors. **EVERY PLACE FEATURED IN THIS BOOK IS RECOMMENDED.**

STAR RATINGS Restaurants and lodgings are rated on a scale of zero to four stars (with half stars in between), based on uniqueness, loyalty of local clientele, performance measured against the establishment's goals, excellence of cooking, cleanliness, value, and professionalism of service. Reviews are listed alphabetically, and every place is recommended.

★★★★	The very best in the region
★★★	Distinguished; many outstanding features
★★	Excellent; some wonderful qualities
★	A good place
NO STARS	Worth knowing about, if nearby
UNRATED	New or undergoing major changes

(For more on how we rate places, see the Best Places® Star Ratings box below.)

PRICE RANGE Prices for restaurants are based primarily on dinner for two, including dessert, tax, and tip (no alcohol). Prices for lodgings are based on peak season rates for one night's lodging for two people (i.e., double occupancy). Peak season is typically Memorial Day to Labor Day; off-season rates vary but can sometimes be significantly less. Call ahead to verify, as all prices are subject to change.

$$$$	Very expensive (more than $100 for dinner for two; more than $200 for one night's lodging for two)
$$$	Expensive (between $65 and $100 for dinner for two; between $120 and $200 for one night's lodging for two)
$$	Moderate (between $35 and $65 for dinner for two; between $80 and $120 for one night's lodging for two)
$	Inexpensive (less than $35 for dinner for two; less than $80 for one night's lodging for two)

RESERVATIONS (for Restaurants only)
We used one of the following terms for our reservations policy: reservations required, reservations recommended, reservations not accepted, reservations not necessary.

ACCESS AND INFORMATION At the beginning of each chapter, you'll find general guidelines about how to get to a particular region and what types of transportation are available, as well as basic sources for any additional tourist information you might need. Also check individual town listings for specifics about visiting those places.

THREE-DAY TOURS In every chapter, we've included a quick-reference, three-day itinerary designed for travelers with a short amount of time. Perfect for weekend getaways, these tours outline the highlights of a region or town; each of the establishments or attractions that appear in boldface within the tour are discussed in greater detail elsewhere in the chapter.

ADDRESSES AND PHONE NUMBERS Every attempt has been made to provide accurate information on an establishment's location and phone number, but it's always a good idea to call ahead and confirm. If an establishment has two area locations, we list both at the top of the review. If there are three or more locations, we list only the main address and indicate "other branches."

CHECKS AND CREDIT CARDS Many establishments that accept checks also require a major credit card for identification. Note that some places accept only local checks. Credit cards are abbreviated in this book as follows: American Express (AE); Carte Blanche (CB); Diners Club (DC); Discover (DIS); Japanese credit card (JCB); MasterCard (MC); Visa (V).

EMAIL AND WEB SITE ADDRESSES Email and web site addresses for establishments have been included where available. Please note that the web is a fluid and evolving medium, and that web pages are often "under construction" or, as with all time-sensitive information, may no longer be valid.

MAPS AND DIRECTIONS Each chapter in the book begins with a regional map that shows the general area being covered. Throughout the book, basic directions are provided with each entry. Whenever possible, call ahead to confirm hours and location.

HELPFUL ICONS Watch for these quick-reference symbols throughout the book:

FAMILY FUN Family-oriented places that are great for kids—fun, easy, not too expensive, and accustomed to dealing with young ones.

GOOD VALUE While not necessarily cheap, these places offer you the best value for your dollars—a good deal within the context of the region.

ROMANTIC These spots offer candlelight, atmosphere, intimacy, or other romantic qualities—kisses and proposals are encouraged!

EDITORS' CHOICE These are places that are unique and special to Southern California, such as a restaurant owned by a beloved local chef or a tourist attraction recognized around the globe.

  ♿ Appears after listings for establishments that have wheelchair-accessible facilities.

INDEXES All restaurants, lodgings, town names, and major tourist attractions are listed alphabetically in the back of the book.

MONEY-BACK GUARANTEE Please see "We Stand by Our Reviews" at the end of this book.

READER REPORTS At the end of the book is a report form. We receive hundreds of reports from readers suggesting new places or agreeing or disagreeing with our assessments. They greatly help in our evaluations, and we encourage you to respond.

BEST PLACES® STAR RATINGS

Any travel guide that rates establishments is inherently subjective—and Best Places® is no exception. We rely on our professional experience, yes, but also on a gut feeling. And, occasionally, we even give in to a soft spot for a favorite neighborhood hangout. Our star-rating system is not simply a AAA-checklist; it's judgmental, critical, sometimes fickle, and highly personal. And unlike most other travel guides, we pay our own way and accept no freebies: no free meals or accommodations, no advertisers, no sponsors, no favors.

For each new edition, we send local food and travel experts out to review restaurants and lodgings anonymously, and then to rate them on a scale of zero to four. That doesn't mean a one-star establishment isn't worth dining or sleeping at—far from it. When we say that *all* the places listed in our books are recommended, we mean it. That one-star pizza joint may be just the ticket for the end of a whirlwind day of shopping with the kids. But if you're planning something more special, the star ratings can help you choose an eatery or hotel that will wow your new clients or be a stunning, romantic place to celebrate an anniversary or impress a first date.

We award four-star ratings sparingly, reserving them for what we consider truly the best. And once an establishment has earned our highest rating, everyone's expectations seem to rise. Readers often write us letters specifically to point out the faults in four-star establishments. With changes in chefs, management, styles, and trends, it's always easier to get knocked off the pedestal than to ascend it. Three-star establishments, on the other hand, seem to generate healthy praise. They exhibit outstanding qualities, and we get lots of love letters about them. The difference between two and three stars can sometimes be a very fine line. Two-star establishments are doing a good, solid job and gaining attention, while one-star places are often dependable spots that have been around forever.

The restaurants and lodgings described in *Best Places Southern California* have earned their stars from hard work and good service (and good food). They're proud to be included in this book—look for our Best Places® sticker in their windows. And we're proud to honor them in this, the second edition of *Best Places Southern California*.

LOS ANGELES AND ENVIRONS

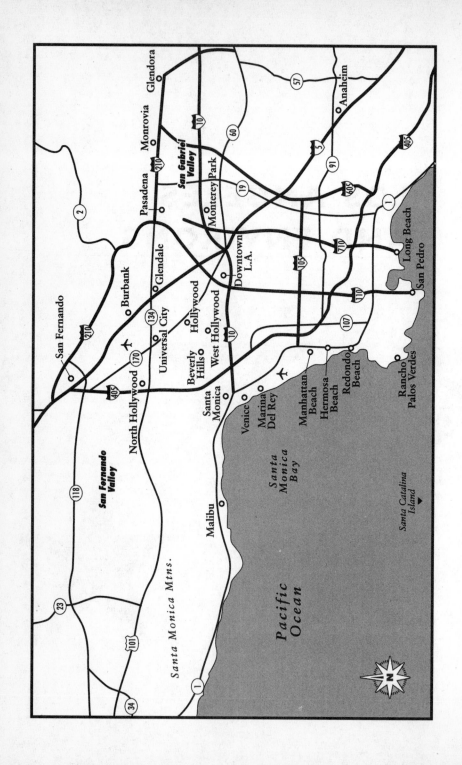

LOS ANGELES AND ENVIRONS

Los Angeles has been called La-La Land, Tinseltown, and "Nashville with a tan." For decades the city has been fodder for stand-up comics and talk show hosts. They've cracked wise about L.A.'s no-jacket-required atmosphere and about how everyone who lives here has a screenplay in the hopper and a stack of head shots in the desk drawer. Even Angelenos themselves seem to have a love-hate relationship with their city. They curse the smog and the traffic, and complain because it's almost impossible to get around without a car or find a place to park if you have one. They whine about the price of buying a home, and they grumble that instead of being a real city Los Angeles is a confusing jumble of disparate and self-contained communities sharing nothing but a nodding acquaintance and a clogged freeway system.

On the other hand, Angelenos enjoy their city because it is the uncontested entertainment capital of the world and the bandleader of pop culture. There are more things to do and see here—scattered over a greater variety of locales—than in any other metropolis anywhere on the planet. Many in Los Angeles are proud that more than 80 languages are spoken in this United Nations of a town and that there are lively ethnic enclaves at every turn. Los Angeles also has a local arts and culture scene that, in its edgy vibrancy, is quickly surpassing New York's. But what's the real draw?

The perpetually summery weather, which makes it possible to shoot movies year-round; the wide range of topography—mountains, rugged canyons, deserts, the blue Pacific nudging miles of incomparable coastline—which convinced turn-of-the-century filmmakers to migrate from the East Coast and establish their nascent companies here. Los Angeles remains wrapped in film industry magic and mythos so potent that even hardened denizens starting an hour-and-a-half commute on a warm afternoon in January feel a thrill of excitement when they spot a movie company filming up the street, or see Mel Gibson strolling through Beverly Hills, or realize the woman on the corner stool in Starbuck's lapping a latte is Meryl Streep. They temporarily forget that Los Angeles is strung out like a jack-o'-lantern's ragged teeth, with an overabundance of ugly strip malls and urban decay cramming the spaces in between; that it's full of industry, a working town, not as polished as its sister to the north or as venerable as its rival back east. But as the sun dissolves in a Technicolor tangerine puddle over the aquamarine sea, they remember for a moment that smog only makes the sunsets better.

ACCESS AND INFORMATION

Los Angeles is primarily served by **LOS ANGELES INTERNATIONAL AIRPORT (LAX)** (310/646-5252; www.lawa.org), which sits near the ocean just south of Marina del Rey and about 30 minutes from downtown or Hollywood. The smaller **BURBANK-GLENDALE-PASADENA AIRPORT** (2627 N Hollywood Wy; 818/840-8840 or 800/U-FLY-BUR; www.burbankairport.com) is in the San Fernando Valley, and—though it sees much less air traffic—is geographically as convenient to most of the L.A. area, excluding the beach communities.

Traveling to and from LAX or Burbank is a snap when you call one of the major **SHUTTLE SERVICES,** such as SuperShuttle (323/775-6600) or Prime Time (800/733-8267). **TAXIS** are in abundance and cost around $30 from the airport to downtown.

PARKING in Los Angeles is sometimes problematic, but not as challenging as in New York or San Francisco. Since this town is committed to car culture, valet parking is available practically everywhere, and it's relatively inexpensive at around $3–$5 a pop. Most of the city's meters have one- or two-hour time limits, and the meter readers are zealous. Meanwhile, in many parts of the city—Santa Monica and certain sections of West Hollywood, for example—parking is by residential permit only or restricted in one way or another (especially during rush hours). Read every sign carefully and stay within the guidelines; tickets and towing are such a part of life here that they're practically a rite of passage for new arrivals. The major hotels and most of the shopping malls have taxi stands, but cabs don't cruise in Los Angeles the way they do in Manhattan, so it's best to phone for one in advance.

The **MTA (METROPOLITAN TRANSPORTATION AUTHORITY,** 800/266-6883; www.mta.net) runs the buses. There aren't enough of them, and they're usually behind schedule, so incorporate extra time into your plans to allow for that. The MTA also operates L.A.'s new subway system, which consists of three lines: Red operates within the city; Blue heads north and south from downtown Los Angeles to "north" Long Beach; and Green travels east to west along the outer areas of Norwalk and the South Bay. The MTA system also includes the commuter light rail line Metrolink—what there is of it, and that doesn't go much of anywhere that you need to go. **AMTRAK** (800/USA-RAIL; www.amtrak.com) trains arrive and depart from downtown's exquisite Spanish Revival–style Union Station (800 N Alameda; 213/624-0171), and **GREYHOUND** (800/231-2222; www.greyhound.com) buses can be caught downtown (1716 E 7th St; 213/629-8401).

Visitors to Los Angeles certainly appreciate that when making vacation plans they usually don't need to factor in the **WEATHER.** Angelenos appreciate it, too. That's why they grumble so much when the mercury dips a bit in the winter months, or when the hot **SANTA ANA WINDS** intermittently blow from August through October. The **RAINY SEASON** occurs from January to March, but in non–El Niño years it doesn't rain very much. Compared to what's happening in the rest of the country during those months, the City of Angels is still a paradise, and winter is when Angelenos appreciate their city most. There is, however, a phenomenon in Los Angeles called **JUNE GLOOM**: because the marine layer of air is heavier during this month, the sun often doesn't appear before noon. Still, the **AVERAGE TEMPERATURE** during the summer is about 80 degrees, and about 70 degrees in the winter. If you're traveling to L.A., bring a jacket or a sweater no matter what the season, because most evenings are cool.

The people at the **LOS ANGELES CONVENTION AND VISITORS BUREAU (LACVB)** (800/366-6116; events hotline 213/689-8822; www.lacvb.com) are friendly and anxious to be of assistance. They maintain two walk-in **VISITORS CENTERS**: downtown (685 S Figueroa St), open Monday through Friday from 8am to 5pm, Saturday from 8:30am to 5pm; and in Hollywood, at the historic Janes House (6541 Hollywood Blvd), open Monday through Saturday from 9am to 5pm. Visit either and you can load up on brochures, maps, coupons, schedules, and advice from their helpful staff.

4

LOS ANGELES AREA THREE-DAY TOUR

DAY 1. A day in the heart of old Hollywood. Indulge in flannel cakes and golden-age atmosphere at **MUSSO & FRANK GRILL,** then spend the morning gazing at the stars on the **HOLLYWOOD WALK OF FAME,** and check out the stars' prints in the court-yard of **MANN'S CHINESE THEATRE.** Head to **HOLLYWOOD & HIGHLAND** for shopping and lunch at **WOLFGANG PUCK'S VERT** (323/491-1300), then explore the wonders of **GRIFFITH PARK** in time to watch the sun set beyond the city from the Griffith Park Observatory parking lot. Stop for an apéritif at **YAMASHIRO** (1999 N Sycamore Ave; 323/466-5125), then head down the hill to dine at Hollywood's renowned **PATINA,** where you're likely to see some of Hollywood's living legends as you indulge in celebrity chef Joachim Splichal's provocative fare. Catch a late flick at **LAEMMLE'S SUNSET 5,** or finish off the evening with a drink at the sexy **SKYBAR.**

DAY 2. A chic L.A. day. Have breakfast on the bougainvillea-draped patio at the **HOTEL BEL-AIR,** then head to Beverly Hills for a morning of browsing the **RODEO DRIVE** shops. After reinvigorating yourself with lunch at **SPAGO,** jump in the car and follow curvy **MULHOLLAND DRIVE** above the hills and stunning homes, winding your way to an afternoon at the Getty Museum at the **GETTY CENTER.** Return in time for dinner at celebrity-filled **MORTON'S**, and wind up the evening with a nightcap at **THE BEVERLY HILLS HOTEL'S POLO LOUNGE.**

DAY 3. Beach Life. If you aren't a registered guest, at least eat breakfast at the lovely **SHUTTERS ON THE BEACH.** From here walk to the **SANTA MONICA PIER** and take a ride on the antique carousel, then make a shopping stop at touristy **THIRD STREET PROMENADE.** Rent in-line skates or a bicycle and follow the beachfront path south to **VENICE BEACH** (about a half-mile jaunt along the 26-mile path). Return to your car and drive north on the Pacific Coast Highway for an afternoon at **ZUMA BEACH** in Malibu. Have a picnic lunch on the beach, then spend some time soaking up the sun. End your coastal day with dinner at Malibu's **GRANITA.**

Although the LACVB will provide information on the various cities-within-a-city that make up the L.A. metropolitan area, each separate municipality has its own dedicated visitor services. The **BEVERLY HILLS VISITORS BUREAU** (239 S Beverly Dr; 310/271-8174 or 800/345-2210; www.bhvb.org) is open Monday through Friday from 9am to 5pm. The **WEST HOLLYWOOD CONVENTION AND VISITORS BUREAU** (8687 Melrose Ave #M-26; 310/289-2525 or 800/368-6020; www.visit westhollywood.com) is open Monday through Friday from 8am to 6pm. The **HOLLYWOOD ARTS COUNCIL** (323/462-2355; www.discoverhollywood.com) distributes the magazine *Discover Hollywood.* This publication contains listings and schedules for the area's many theaters, galleries, music venues, and comedy clubs; the current issue is always available online. The **SANTA MONICA CONVENTION**

AND VISITORS BUREAU (310/393-7593; www.santamonica.com) is the best source for information about Santa Monica. Their Palisades Park walk-up center (1400 Ocean Ave) is located near the pier and is open daily from 10am to 5pm. And the **PASADENA CONVENTION AND VISITORS BUREAU** (171 S Los Robles Ave, Pasadena; 626/795-9311; www.pasadenacal.org) is open Monday through Friday from 8am to 5pm, Saturday from 10am to 4pm.

Los Angeles

The magic of Los Angeles lies not in any one particular site or attraction, but rather in just being here, absorbing its diverse and overwhelming atmosphere. Celluloid City's distinct neighborhoods and glorious beaches are clipped together like a film that showcases individual vignettes; drive (and you must drive) 10 minutes in any direction and the venue changes dramatically and immediately, which means you can submerge yourself in real-life versions of *Baywatch, Scenes from the Class Struggle in Beverly Hills, Melrose Place,* or *Swingers*—with less than a gallon of gas.

DOWNTOWN LOS ANGELES

Downtown is L.A.'s center for politics, finance, and performing arts. On weekdays expect crowded sidewalks and restaurants flush with office workers. However, weekend days are another story—that's when downtown's streets are, for the most part, left to visitors and the homeless. Two grand exceptions that remain active on the weekend are the fashion district and Broadway, the famed shopping boulevard catering to L.A.'s Spanish-speaking population. Bustling **GRAND CENTRAL PUBLIC MARKET** (bounded by 3rd and 4th Sts and Broadway and Hill Aves; 213/624-2378; www.grandcentralsquare.com) consists of an amazing square-block collection of stalls and stands full of produce, meats, fish, fowl, and multiethnic fast food, open daily from 9am to 6pm. Nearby is the ornate **BRADBURY BUILDING** (304 S Broadway Ave), Los Angeles's oldest commercial building, built in 1893 and one of the true marvels of Los Angeles architecture. Another worthy landmark, the **MIL-LENNIUM BILTMORE HOTEL** (506 S Grand Ave; 213/624-1011; www.millennium hotel.com), built in 1923, is looking extremely well for her age. The Crystal Ball-room and the newly remodeled lobby—a blend of Spanish rococo and Italian Renaissance—are wonders to behold. **ANGELS FLIGHT** (4th and Hill Sts), a funic-ular opened in 1901 to convey the rich to their Bunker Hill homes and recently restored to its former glory, offers a spectacular city view as the mini-railcar climbs to the pinnacle of Hill Street. However, Angels Flight is currently closed; call 213/626-1901 for the latest status. A visit to downtown Los Angeles wouldn't be complete without a stop at **EL PUEBLO DE LOS ANGELES** and **OLVERA STREET** to explore what the city was like when it was still a village, circa 1781. In the same locale are the Pico House Hotel and Plaza Church (circa 1822), as well as the Avila Adobe house (circa 1818). For those who want a more extensive and organized taste of historic downtown Los Angeles, **L.A. CONSERVANCY TOURS** (213/623-2489; www.laconservancy.org), led by very kindly and knowledgeable folk, offer a number of itineraries including "Marble Masterpieces," vintage movie palaces, and Little Tokyo.

While Los Angeles is rich with historic architecture, the City of Angels also boasts several new impressive structures. At the crest of First Street, between Hope and Grand, is the **WALT DISNEY CONCERT HALL**, future home of the Los Angeles Philharmonic. Scheduled to open in October 2003, the extravaganza of curved, billowing steel is designed by L.A. architect Frank Gehry and will be his first major Southern California building. Only blocks away, the **CATHEDRAL OF OUR LADY OF THE ANGELS** opened to much fanfare in 2002. Designed by Spanish architect Jose Rafael Moneo and executed by the L.A. offices of Leo A. Daly, the 122,000-square-foot cathedral has a seating capacity of 3,000, a 2.5-acre plaza, a cloister garden, and a residence for the archbishop.

LITTLE TOKYO is bounded by First, Second, Los Angeles, and San Pedro Streets, surrounding the New Otani Hotel. Within its boundaries is the **JAPANESE-AMERICAN CULTURAL CENTER** (244 S San Pedro St; 213/628-2725; www.jaccc.org), which offers rotating exhibitions and occasionally presents performances by Japan's Grand Kabuki Theatre group. **OLD CHINATOWN**, located along Broadway Avenue and Hill Street north of First Street, has a wide array of shops and restaurants, but it's comparatively small and caters less to tourists and more to its Chinese-American residents.

South of downtown lies **EXPOSITION PARK**, once filled with stately homes. While the years haven't been particularly kind to this neighborhood, the **UNIVERSITY OF SOUTHERN CALIFORNIA**, one of California's premier and most expensive private colleges, and the Exposition Park museum complex continue to lure visitors. These include the **CALIFORNIA SCIENCE CENTER** (700 State Dr; 323/SCIENCE; www.casciencectr.org), filled with interactive exhibits incorporating computers, virtual reality, and a space docking simulator; the **IMAX THEATER** (213/744-2014), where you can witness a space voyage or a Mount Everest expedition on a seven-story screen; the **NATURAL HISTORY MUSEUM** (900 Exposition Blvd; 213/763-3466; www.nhm.org); and the **CALIFORNIA AFRICAN-AMERICAN MUSEUM** (600 State Dr; 213/744-2060; www.caam.ca.gov), which explores the history, art, and cultural legacy of black people in the United States.

GRIFFITH PARK, stretching from L.A. to the San Fernando Valley and located between downtown and Hollywood, features the **GRIFFITH OBSERVATORY AND PLANETARIUM**, which was immortalized in the James Dean flick *Rebel Without a Cause*. The observatory is currently closed for expansion and restoration until 2005, but you can still enjoy amazing views of the city from its parking lot. Also within the park's boundaries are two other gems: **THE AUTRY MUSEUM OF WESTERN HERITAGE** (4700 Western Heritage Wy; 323/667-2000; www.autrymuseum.org) preserves both the mythology and the history of the Old West within its seven themed galleries. The **LOS ANGELES ZOO** (5333 Zoo Dr; 323/644-4200; www.lazoo.org) is now home to 2,000 creatures existing in simulated natural habitats, 78 endangered species among them.

BEVERLY HILLS AND THE WESTSIDE
In the geographic center of L.A.'s Westside—local jargon for the area between Hollywood and the beaches—is **BEVERLY HILLS**, a city jammed with fantastic places to eat and shop, but one of its most appealing activities is the 90-minute **BEVERLY HILLS ARTS AND ARCHITECTURE TROLLEY TOUR** (310/285-2438; Saturdays, May–December, $5 adults, $1 children under 12). The I. M. Pei–designed Creative Artists Associates (CAA) building with its lobby Lichtenstein, the venerated PaceWildenstein and Gagosian Galleries, as well as other important art and architecture sites in the area, are stops along the way. The tour concludes at the Richard Meier–designed **MUSEUM OF TELEVISION & RADIO** (465 N Beverly Dr; 310/786-1000; www.mtr.org), which offers special screenings and exhibitions; it also boasts a collection of more than 90,000 radio and television shows that may be heard or viewed on audio and video monitors in private carrels on the second floor.

West of Beverly Hills along Santa Monica Boulevard is **CENTURY CITY**, with its enormous hotels, magnificent theaters, towering office complexes, and the **CENTURY CITY WESTFIELD SHOPPINGTOWN**, which is one of the premier malls in L.A. Farther west, the **UNIVERSITY OF CALIFORNIA, LOS ANGELES (UCLA)** is in the charming community of Westwood. Any visit to the campus must include a stop at the handsome, Romanesque-style, red-brick **FOWLER MUSEUM OF CULTURAL HISTORY** (310/825-4361; www.fmch.ucla.edu). The museum possesses a permanent display of cultural objects from the world over. Featuring sculpture by artists such as Rodin, Calder, and Hepworth, the Franklin Murphy Sculpture Garden is near the Fowler and well worth the extra steps. To find the **UCLA HAMMER MUSEUM** (10899 Wilshire Blvd; 310/443-7000; www.hammer.ucla.edu), leave the UCLA campus via Westwood Boulevard and travel south to Wilshire Boulevard; the Hammer Museum is on the left. The most extraordinary feature of the museum, which opened in 1990, is its extensive collection of works by Honoré Daumier.

South of Beverly Hills, Westwood, and Century City in the Rancho Park area is the remarkable **MUSEUM OF TOLERANCE & SIMON WIESENTHAL CENTER** (9786 Pico Blvd, at Roxbury Dr; 310/553-8403; www.wiesenthal.com/mot), where visitors interactively explore the history of racism and the Holocaust. The community of West Los Angeles is home to the **MUSEUM OF JURASSIC TECHNOLOGY** (9341 Venice Blvd, near Robertson Blvd; 310/836-6131; www.mjt.org), a peculiar collection of what the curator and staff—all kidding aside—refer to as "natural" displays. The establishment is an ingenious hoax that takes itself utterly seriously, but it's also a crucial stopover for anyone with a sense of humor and a taste for the astonishing.

HOLLYWOOD AND WEST HOLLYWOOD
Hollywood is more a state of mind than a glamorous destination, but most visitors feel inclined to find that out for themselves. That said, there are a few worthy Tinseltown excursions. While Hollywood has done much in recent years to clean up, along the gritty length of Hollywood Boulevard, remnants of the golden age are still crammed in between kitschy souvenir shops and fronted by dubious-looking

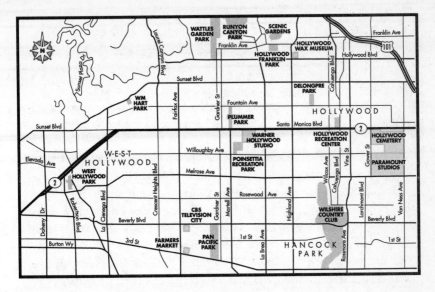

loiterers. However, one genuine attraction is the **HOLLYWOOD WALK OF FAME**, which runs along Hollywood Boulevard between La Brea Avenue and Vine Street, and then along Vine down to Sunset Boulevard. Along "the Walk," the names of luminaries and superluminaries in the film, radio, and television industries are commemorated by stars set in the polished mauve granite sidewalk. Another favorite is the recently renovated **MANN'S CHINESE THEATRE** (formerly Grauman's; 6925 Hollywood Blvd, near Sycamore Ave; 323/464-6266), where visitors may still match their hands and feet to the cement casts in the courtyard belonging to greats such as Clark Gable, Humphrey Bogart, Marilyn Monroe, Joan Crawford, Kirk and Michael Douglas, and Mel Gibson. Mann's merits alone make it a visit-worthy beacon of authentic Hollywoodness surrounded by a sea of schlock. The theater, with its murals, sparkling chandeliers, and carved-wood accents, was the site of countless Hollywood premieres in decades past; it remains pristine and is one of the most enjoyable spots in town to catch a flick. The famed theater, however, recently gained even more famous company with the debut of the new flashy **HOLLYWOOD & HIGHLAND** entertainment complex (6801 Hollywood Blvd, between Highland Ave and Orange Dr; 323/960-2331; www.hollywoodandhighland.com).

In addition to shops like Tommy Hilfiger (323/467-4199), Versace (323/464-7072), and Lather (323/962-6070), the multimillion-dollar complex also boasts fine dining at eateries like Wolfgang Puck's Vert (323/491-1300), a lively nightlife scene at the Highlands (323/461-9800), an additional six Mann's movie theaters, and the Renaissance Hollywood Hotel (323/856-1200). But perhaps its most impressive draw is the 3,500-seat Kodak Theatre (323/308-6363), which serves as the new

L.A. GOES TO THE MOVIES: CLASSIC FILMS AND LOCATIONS

Hollywood's first movie studio was established in 1911, and from the very beginning directors seeking film-worthy locations have found their inspiration literally outside the back door. The city continues to be an easy location for productions of all sorts—any day of the week you're sure to see hand-lettered signs directing crew members to shoots, or entire city blocks with temporarily restricted parking for "film production vehicles" only.

In the early days, it was as simple as using the nearby Cahuenga Pass as a rugged back-drop for American settlers, Spanish conquistadors, or cowboy-and-Indian brawls. As the years progressed, filmmakers began casting Los Angeles as herself. In the 1944 film noir classic *Double Indemnity*, Fred MacMurray races along the shadowy streets of the Holly-wood hills to Barbara Stanwyck's lavish mansion, allowing the viewer a detailed sense of what L.A.'s unspoiled World War II–era neighborhoods were really like. Roman Polanski's award-winning *Chinatown* (1974) re-creates 1930s Los Angeles with masterful accuracy, casting Faye Dunaway and Jack Nicholson in a Chandleresque mystery incor-porating the real-life intrigue of L.A.'s notorious battle for Owens Valley water rights. 1997's *L.A. Confidential* is that film's worthy successor in the L.A.-as-noir-landscape cat-egory, again re-creating the city's glamorous image and lawless underbelly (circa mid-'50s) for a murder mystery with Kim Basinger and Russell Crowe. And the ultimate SoCal beach movie is 1965's *Gidget*, an innocent romp that features Sandra Dee and James Darren frolicking amid surf-and-sand—the film's unbilled co-star is the classic Malibu beach scene that inspired countless restless teens to migrate west.

Sometimes individual landmarks make a lasting impression on the silver screen. In the 1955 James Dean classic *Rebel Without a Cause*, Dean (along with Natalie Wood and Sal Mineo) visits the Griffith Observatory for a dramatic knife brawl; later, this photo-genic art deco landmark provides a powerful backdrop for the film's climax. Remember

home of the Academy Awards, as well as other music and dance performances. The **EL CAPITAN THEATER** (across Hollywood Blvd at 6838; 323/467-7674; www.el capitantickets.com) is another of the grand old movie palaces, almost as famous as Grauman's/Mann's, and it's been recently restored to its original grandeur by Disney, which utilizes the theater to show its current films.

Some budgetary corners were obviously cut at the interactive **HOLLYWOOD ENTERTAINMENT MUSEUM** (7021 Hollywood Blvd; 323/465-7900; www.holly woodmuseum.com), but it does give visitors an education in pre- and postproduc-tion phases of movie and television filming. Visitors can "foley" (add sound effects to) and edit pieces of film and video, enjoy make-up demonstrations, view an exten-sive collection of props and costumes, and sprawl in the captain's chair on the bridge the merry-go-round operated by Paul Newman in *The Sting* (1973)? It's still an attraction on the Santa Monica Pier, housed in Charles Looff's stylized 1916 Hippodrome. Downtown's 1893 Bradbury Building, a historic and movie landmark, is on the corner of Broadway and Third. The building's ahead-of-its-time design, featuring an open central courtyard and dramatic five-story skylight, perfectly portrayed Ridley Scott's dark vision of the future in 1982's *Blade Runner*. Nearby, the stately Biltmore has been in countless pictures; a cinematic tidal wave turned the hotel's magnificent ballroom upside down in *The Poseidon Adventure* (1972). Downtown's most recent—and tallest—skyline addition is the distinctive office tower whose crown of lights drew the destructive force of unfriendly aliens in another disaster flick, 1996's *Independence Day*.

Los Angeles has always been a true silver screen diva, looking fabulous—and often stealing the scene. Some films capture the essence of the city as a whole. One of the most convincing is Robert Altman's superb *The Player* (1992), in which Tim Robbins's studio-exec character bounces from one Hollywood cliché to another—you'll see him on studio back lots, at power-lunch spot the Ivy restaurant, and even at desert-oasis resort Two Bunch Palms. The second-best portrayal of contemporary Tinseltown is Steve Martin's *L.A. Story* (1991), which takes an irreverent—but sometimes magical—look at the often-silly reality of living in L.A. Other choices for evoking a specific L.A. time and place include 1975's *Shampoo*, in which Warren Beatty takes us on a narcissistic tour of swinging '70s culture; *Valley Girl* (1983), an early Nicolas Cage flick—in a teen genre that also includes *Fast Times at Ridgemont High* and *Clueless*—pitting the Hollywood punk rock scene against suburban shopping-mall culture; *Pretty Woman* (1990), the Julia Roberts vehicle about finding happiness amid the rampant materialism of late-'80s Beverly Hills; and *Swingers* (1996), a low-budget sleeper portraying the Gen-X denizens of "Cocktail Nation" exploring Hollywood's nightspots.

—*Cheryl Farr Leas and Stephanie Avnet Yates*

of the starship *Enterprise*. Across the street from the museum, the recently reconstituted grand old **HOLLYWOOD ROOSEVELT HOTEL** (7000 Hollywood Blvd; 323/466-7000; www.hollywoodroosevelt.com) still reigns supreme at the corner of Sycamore Avenue. The open and airy upstairs gallery is lined with Hollywood yesteryear photos. L.A.'s latest historical attraction, the **HOLLYWOOD HISTORY MUSEUM** (1660 N Highland Ave; 323/464-7776), is located in the elegant deco-era Max Factor building and is devoted to the preservation and veneration of the film industry. Its four-story, 45,000-square-foot facility holds a Smithsonian-like collection of film memorabilia representing all eras and genres. A more current exploration of the film world is available with a tour of **PARAMOUNT STUDIOS** (5555 Melrose Ave; 323/956-5000; www.paramount.com), which is available on a limited basis. To the north and visible from all unobstructed mountain vistas, the **HOLLY-WOOD SIGN** is perhaps the town's most recognized landmark.

The community of **WEST HOLLYWOOD** stretches east to west from Fairfax Avenue to Robertson Boulevard and north to south from Sunset Boulevard to Melrose Avenue. The area along Santa Monica Boulevard and just north and south of it is sometimes referred to as "Boys Town" because it's packed with bars, restaurants, cafes, and shops that cater to Los Angeles's gay scene. Architecture mavens may want to stop at the **PACIFIC DESIGN CENTER** (8687 Melrose Ave, at San Vicente Blvd; 310/657-0800; www.pacificdesigncenter.com), near the border of Beverly Hills. Within this massive complex, constructed of brilliant green and blue glass, reside shops—many open to the public—showcasing the latest trends in home furnishings and design. The infamous **SUNSET STRIP** extends east to west along Sunset Boulevard from Laurel Canyon to Doheny Ave. Although the shops are très chic and ultra-expensive, numerous outdoor cafes are great for people-watching and star-sighting, and a lot of the club scene is located here.

SAN FERNANDO VALLEY

When most people think of the San Fernando Valley—known simply as "the Valley"—Frank and Moon Unit Zappa's satiric homage to Valley Girls often comes to mind. Thankfully, this northwestern region of Los Angeles County, which spreads from the Ventura County border to Glendale, has surmounted its claim to fame. What was once considered a bedroom community for neighboring Los Angeles is now a thriving business and entertainment-industry region, as well as a nice and relatively affordable place to live away from the hustle and bustle of the metropolis—if you can deal with the daily commute on gridlocked freeways. Though the Valley is often maligned as the lesser part of the Los Angeles basin, it could actually be considered the workaday heart of the entertainment industry, with Walt Disney Studios, Warner Bros., Universal Studios, NBC, CBS Studio Center, and DreamWorks SKG Animation all within its boundaries. With showbiz roots growing into a concrete jungle of opportunity, the Valley's creative community is growing rapidly, as are new strip malls and office buildings, which are popping up with regularity.

Back in the 1920s when Keystone Cops creator Mack Sennett outgrew his Silver Lake studio, he built a new facility near Ventura Boulevard and Laurel Canyon Boulevard. When he started calling the community "**STUDIO CITY**," the moniker stuck. With its location close to the surrounding studios and the L.A. side of the hill, today this area is widely considered the hippest neighborhood in the Valley—with some of the highest-priced real estate, especially south of Ventura Boulevard.

Movie mogul Carl Laemmle built his film studio back in 1915 on the site of a former chicken ranch and began giving behind-the-scenes studio tours himself, charging guests a quarter for a glimpse of the moviemaking process. Over the following years, Laemmle's early vision evolved into a massive hilltop attraction, featuring not only Universal Studios, the largest working film and television studio in the world, but a bustling promenade, Universal CityWalk, whose shops, restaurants, and movie theaters are frequented more by tourists and loitering teenagers than by locals. Though a small upscale community has sprung up in the vicinity, the only real reason to visit **UNIVERSAL CITY** is to see the phenomenally popular **UNIVERSAL**

STUDIOS HOLLYWOOD (1000 Universal Center Dr; 818/508-9600; www.universal studios.com), the number-one visitor attraction in Los Angeles County. Part behind-the-scenes studio tour and part theme park, its highlights include a tram tour where visitors learn a thing or two about moviemaking as they traverse the back lots and soundstages and meet the main star of *Jaws,* experience the sensation of an 8.3 earthquake, and get up close and personal with King Kong. Well-polished tour guides (most of them aspiring actors) spout interesting facts and stories about the studio. Other attractions include the "Back to the Future," "E.T.," and "Jurassic Park" rides, the interactive Nickelodeon Blast Zone, and live-action shows based on such Universal Pictures films as *Waterworld.* A virtual-reality attraction, "Terminator 2 3-D," was created by self-proclaimed King of the World James Cameron.

Within UNIVERSAL CITYWALK's (818/622-4455) minivillage of tourist attractions, some of the most popular venues are Wizards Magic Club and Dinner Theater (818/506-0066), which serves up dinner and a magic show; Gladstone's Universal (818/622-3474), a Valley outpost of the popular Malibu fish eatery; B. B. King's Blues Club (818/622-5464), which smolders with blues and barbecue; and Café Tu Tu Tango (818/769-2222), where all portions are served appetizer-size for sharing. All-Star Collectibles (818/622-2222) is filled with sports memorabilia, Wound & Wound Toy Co. (818/509-8129) features thousands of windup toys, and Quiksilver Boardrider's Club (818/760-6650) displays men's and women's surf wear.

Located just north of Universal City, NORTH HOLLYWOOD is best known for its trendy arts district, NoHo, which runs along Lankershim Boulevard between Chandler and Otsego. Lined with equity-waiver theaters like the El Portal Center for the Arts (5269 Lankershim Blvd; 818/508-4234) and Raven Playhouse (5233 Lankershim Blvd; 818/509-9519; www.ravenplayhouse.com), artist studios, coffeehouses, eclectic boutiques, and restaurants, this recently revitalized section of town is also the home of the ACADEMY OF TELEVISION ARTS AND SCIENCES COMPLEX (5220 Lankershim Blvd; 818/754-2800; www.emmys.tv), where TV fans can wander through the outdoor Hall of Fame Plaza to admire statues of their favorite television legends, including Bob Hope and Lucille Ball. Each June, NoHo celebrates the arts with its annual NOHO ARTS FESTIVAL, a street fair that includes musical performances, dancing, an arts and crafts show, and free performances at many area theaters.

Although Johnny Carson may have had reason to mock BURBANK during his years on *The Tonight Show,* today "beautiful downtown Burbank," as he dubbed it, is actually pretty neat—thanks to a renovation that transformed its main street, SAN FERNANDO ROAD, into a hip promenade lined with restaurants, bookstores, cafes, and movie theaters.

In addition to its newly revitalized downtown, Burbank seems to have a movie or television studio on every corner, with Disney, Warner Bros., and NBC all calling this busy city home. For a two-hour behind-the-scenes tour of where such shows as *E.R.* and *Friends* are produced, make a reservation for the WARNER BROS. STUDIOS VIP TOUR (4000 Warner Blvd; 818/972-TOUR; www.studio-tour.com). The Peacock Network also offers a tour; call NBC STUDIOS (3000 W Alameda Ave; 818/840-3537; www.nbc.com) for more information.

SPANISH ROOTS AND CHICANO CULTURE

When Mexican philosopher Octavio Paz described Los Angeles, he wrote: "At first sight, the visitor is surprised not only by the purity of the sky and the ugliness of the dispersed and ostentatious buildings, but also by the city's vaguely Mexican atmosphere, which cannot be captured in words or concepts." Paz's observation is not surprising, since from its earliest days as a sleepy pueblo founded by Spanish missionaries through its 20th-century explosion into bustling mega-metropolis, the area has maintained a Latin American flavor distinct from that of other American cities.

While that unique flavor has always seasoned the City of Angels with a subtle and spicy zest, after World War II the influx of Latin American immigrants swelled, the undercurrent of Hispanic culture underwent a renaissance, and the Latin community further evolved its uniquely Southern Californian culture. Mexican and other Latino immigrants became lost between two worlds—not blending completely into "white" North American culture, yet simultaneously ostracized by their countrymen for not being "real" Mexicans. Gradually, they came to embrace both American and Latin cultures and to blend them together in a new sensibility: Chicano culture.

As Chicano labor movements grew more vocal and visible in the 1970s, a sense of pride in their roots grew, and Chicanos (Americans born of Mexican parents) began to develop their own styles of dress, of speech, and of music, which frequently centered around such values as the strong family ties typical of their homeland, but also embraced such Angeleno values as love of the automobile. These new styles blended into a subculture all its own, finally earning respect from both Mexicans and Americans.

The emergence of Norteño and Banda music, both of which incorporate elements of American country-and-western and traditional Mexican music styles, has signaled the Chicano culture's emergence from the shadows. A huge success in Mexico, as epitomized by the late pop star Selena, these popular musical styles signaled the first time that cultural trends started by immigrants had trickled back home to alter the culture of the homeland.

As you travel through Southern California, notice the exaggerated sense of color to be found in Hispanic neighborhoods and throughout the city. Hear the soft cadences of Spanish spoken in the streets, smell the scents of Latin American cooking, and marvel at the wildly decorated "low-rider" cars on the roads beside you. For Los Angeles, once a sleepy Mexican town and now home to more than seven million Latinos, has not forgotten its roots—it has only modernized them.

—Sandow Birk

SANTA MONICA

Santa Monica's **BERGAMOT STATION** (2525 Michigan Ave; 310/829-5854; www.bergamotstation.com), formerly a trolley stop, is a one-stop gallery crawl with more than 20 of L.A.'s most notable galleries clustered around the Santa Monica Museum of Art (see Museums, below).

It's wonderful to stroll Santa Monica's Main Street shops and restaurants; however, the nearby **THIRD STREET PROMENADE,** stretching three blocks from Broadway to Wilshire, with its street performers, splendid variety of trendy shops and eateries, farmers markets, outdoor setting, and carnival atmosphere, is seducing even the diehards away from the previously favored shopping mecca. Kids prefer meandering through **PACIFIC PARK** (380 Santa Monica Pier, at the foot of Colorado Blvd off Ocean Ave; 310/260-8744; www.pacpark.com), located on the **SANTA MONICA PIER.** This family-oriented amusement park is a manageable size, with 12 child-friendly rides (as well as the respectable "West Coaster" for adults, which will incite a heart-stopping ripple or two), an arcade, unspectacular restaurants, and a captivating antique carousel that has been completely restored.

Also at the Santa Monica Pier is the interactive **UCLA OCEAN DISCOVERY CENTER** (1600 Ocean Front Walk; 310/393-6149; www.ocd.ucla.edu), which opened in 1997 and is the place where scrutinizing itty-bitty ocean critters in the microscope lab is the order of the day. The activity in the shark and ray tanks is absorbing, and so is the tidal pool display.

BEACHES

The **BEACHES** in Los Angeles are some of the best in the world, and the beaches in Malibu are the most famous in L.A. The **MALIBU LAGOON STATE BEACH** near the Malibu Pier is also known as Surfrider Beach, where, to quote the Beach Boys, "everybody's surfin' now." Members of the neoprene-and-sun-streaked-hair crowd travel here from the world over to hang ten on breakers that sometimes measure 11 feet high. Where Malibu Creek meets the sea is a protected wetlands, and the historic Adamson House is nestled within the lagoon's dunes. The most beautiful Malibu beach, however, is **ZUMA,** a vast stretch of flat sand that's also known for having the cleanest water. **SANTA MONICA STATE BEACH,** located at the end of Interstate 10, and **VENICE BEACH,** to the south, are the most popular in Los Angeles, although during the summer months it's hard to find parking and even the stiff sea breeze can't dispel the miasma of Coppertone. Of the two, Venice is the more fun, and that's because of **VENICE OCEAN FRONT WALK,** a low-rent version of the Third Street Promenade and in its own way just as satisfying. In summer it's mobbed with tourists and, admittedly, a lot of locals, who come to enjoy the musicians and other performers, scope out the stalls, shops, and cafes, and mingle with the freaks and scantily clad Rollerbladers. The beaches of the South Bay—**MANHATTAN STATE BEACH, HERMOSA CITY BEACH,** and **REDONDO STATE BEACH**—are popular among surfers, as well as beachgoers fond of the small-town ambience of these quintessential seaside neighborhoods.

THE SOUTH BAY

Strung along Los Angeles County's southern shores, in the figurative shadow of the "big city," several disparate communities provide a haven for urban escapees who eschew L.A. proper. Each community has developed a distinct personality, especially the three beach towns collectively known as the South Bay (Manhattan Beach, Hermosa Beach, and Redondo Beach). Daily life here revolves around the ocean, pleasant weather, and sparse parking, which has led to a laid-back walking-bicycling tradition. As Santa Monica Bay curves into its southern crescent, the Palos Verdes peninsula looms tall over the ocean. Once literally an island, "P.V." is now only figuratively one—a hard-to-reach enclave of affluent neighborhoods and breathtaking coastline.

Tucked away on the far side of Marina del Rey, the tiny bedroom community of **PLAYA DEL REY** might have surprised the unfortunate speculators who attempted at the end of the 19th century to turn the tiny lagoon into a full-blown tourist attraction. Between 1887 and 1917, an Asian-style entertainment pavilion, the 50-room Del Rey Hotel, an elegant boathouse, and grandstand seating for boat-race audiences all fell victim to wicked tides and furious storms that conspired to return the lagoon to marshland. Today's beachy cottages and ocean-view condos are built only on solid land, and the murky Ballona wetlands that isolate Playa del Rey from the ultra-developed Marina del Rey to the north are now a protected bird sanctuary. The neighborhood is funky and unspoiled, despite the inevitable higher rents that oceanfront real estate brings.

In the early 1950s surfing's popularity crested with a group of local kids called the Beach Boys, who spent their days catching waves and hanging out in **MANHATTAN BEACH,** and their nights recording what would become classic "surf music." Today the casual summer shacks that old-time surfers remember have been replaced with stellar ocean-view homes, and real estate prices edge steadily higher as the beach town takes on an upscale tone. Manhattan State Beach is as popular as ever, a wide white swath bordered by the Strand, a broad paved path crowded with walkers and skaters, and a steep hillside of homes boasting breathtaking views. The surfing is some of the best in the county, and volleyball nets stretch as far as the eye can see.

In Spanish, *hermosa* means "beautiful," and the tiny seaside community of **HERMOSA BEACH** is named for pristine **HERMOSA CITY BEACH**—2 miles of wide, pearly sand dotted with endless volleyball nets and lined by the Strand, a pedestrian and bicycle/skate path that stretches the entire length of the city. In the early 20th century, Hermosa Beach was a summer vacation spot for folks from Los Angeles, who built many opulent cottages and bungalows along the Strand, then a wooden boardwalk. In the 1920s, concrete replaced the wood, and today the homes on this prime real estate are small, expensive, and intimately close together. Many celebrities have lived here, including comedian Charlie Chaplin, filmmaker Warren Miller, and Ozzie and Harriet Nelson. If David and Ricky were boys today, they'd undoubtedly have skateboards and hang out around the Hermosa Pier, which is popular with anglers topside, and brave surfers—who thread their way between the pilings—underneath. Pier Plaza is a pedestrian-only block of Pier Avenue, lined with bars and restaurants known for raucous happy hours and party-all-night crowds.

MUSEUMS

Perched on a hillside in the Sepulveda Pass, the **GETTY CENTER** (1200 Getty Center Dr, just west of the San Diego Fwy, Brentwood; 310/440-7300; www.getty.edu) looms over the Westside. Home to the richly endowed J. Paul Getty Trust, it houses the Trust's research and education institute, a world-renowned art conservatory, and the **J. PAUL GETTY MUSEUM**. This massive edifice, opened in 1997, is also L.A.'s most expensive cultural landmark, clocking in at an astonishing $1 billion (and 14 years in the making). Architect Richard Meier created five two-story pavilions built of blindingly white travertine stone, glass, and steel. The centerpiece Robert Irwin–designed garden is itself a work of art. Illuminated manuscripts, drawings, sculpture, decorative arts, and photographs are displayed on the first levels; paintings occupy the second. The galleries display what is there to its best advantage with their electronically controlled skylights. To visit this art enclave on 110 acres of high and rocky chaparral with a 360-degree view of the Los Angeles basin, the Pacific, and the Santa Monica Mountains, guests park in the garage below (parking is $5) and take the brief tram ride from the parking area to the plaza. Here visitors enter the museum complex, composed of five galleries and an excellent gift shop. Admission is free.

The **SKIRBALL CULTURAL CENTER** (2701 Sepulveda Blvd, Brentwood; 310/440-4500; www.skirball.com), in its mountain location, is just a short distance from the Getty Center. The Moshe Safdie–designed complex has a chopped-from-rock feel and, like Meier's design for the Getty Center, achieves a beautiful cohesion between landscape and architecture. The center incorporates performance and conference facilities and a cafe, as well as an extensive and stimulating collection of historic art and artifacts tracing the Jewish experience. Youngsters will enjoy the chance to participate in the practice archaeological dig in the Discovery Center.

The **LOS ANGELES COUNTY MUSEUM OF ART (LACMA)** (5905 Wilshire Blvd near Fairfax Ave; 323/857-6000; www.lacma.org) presides over the midcity "Museum Row," and rivals the Getty as the cultural heart of Los Angeles. LACMA's permanent collections include pre-Columbian Mexican art, an expansive silver collection, mosaics, Indian and Southeast Asian Art, American and European paintings and sculpture, and one of the nation's largest holdings of costumes and textiles. The Pavilion for Japanese Art, with its fabulous permanent collection of paper art, pottery, kimonos, and much more, is well suited to its contemplative and Zen-influenced works. Curators are putting in extra effort to make LACMA cutting edge; there's now a new experimental gallery for children, the gift shop is one of the best of its kind in the metropolitan area, and on Friday nights there're often live jazz, blues, or classical music, a wine bar, and elegant eats under the portico. In a rare and commendable instance of historic preservation and reuse, the former May Company flagship department store—a Streamline Moderne gem a block away—has been transformed into the LACMA West annex.

LACMA may be the most imposing, but it's only one of several occupants of Museum Row. The **GEORGE C. PAGE MUSEUM OF LA BREA DISCOVERIES** (323/934-PAGE; www.tarpits.org), with its tar pits and 650 species of plants and animals, is just behind LACMA. A few blocks away, heaven awaits car aficionados at the **PETERSEN AUTOMOTIVE MUSEUM** (6060 Wilshire Blvd, east of Fairfax Ave;

323/930-CARS; www.petersen.org). In historically authentic displays, the fins and fenders of Cords, Caddies, and almost any other fantasy-based make and model gleam as they did when they first rolled off the assembly line.

Angelenos adore downtown's **MUSEUM OF CONTEMPORARY ART (MOCA)** (250 S Grand Ave, between 2nd and 3rd Sts; 213/626-6222; www.moca-la.org). Designed by the innovative Arata Isozaki and opened in 1986, the spacious and skylit galleries house a good permanent collection including works by Jackson Pollock, Robert Rauschenberg, Piet Mondrian, Andy Warhol, and the photographer Max Yavno. MOCA also presents a consistently impressive roster of fascinating traveling exhibitions, installations, and performance art. **THE GEFFEN CONTEM-PORARY** (152 N Central Ave; 213/626-6222), in Little Tokyo, is no less beloved, which is why, after a Frank Gehry overhaul, the former police warehouse reopened its doors. Previously dubbed the Temporary Contemporary, the satellite facility is charmingly located across from the LAPD horse barn, where members of the mounted force can often be seen grooming their trusty steeds.

On the other side of town the **SANTA MONICA MUSEUM OF ART (SMMOA)** (2525 Michigan Ave, west of Barrington Ave, Santa Monica; 310/586-6488; www. smmoa.org) is now an integral part of the Bergamot Station art complex. The museum has no permanent collection of its own, but in the 10,000-square-foot space, the long tradition of presenting mercurial and edgy exhibitions, multimedia installations, and performance art continues.

SHOPPING

Designer brands reign on fabled **RODEO DRIVE** in Beverly Hills, between Santa Monica Boulevard and Wilshire Boulevard, where all the right labels are represented within a three-block stretch. Elite department stores can be found here, too, such as Barneys New York (9570 Wilshire Blvd; 310/276-4400), Saks Fifth Avenue (9600 Wilshire Blvd; 310/275-4211), and Neiman Marcus (9700 Wilshire Blvd; 310/550-5900). Inland, still-trendy **MELROSE AVENUE,** between Robertson Boulevard and La Brea Avenue, features frocks and accoutrements for the young and painfully fashionable. However, ultrachic **RON HERMAN/FRED SEGAL** (8100 Melrose Ave, at Crescent Heights Blvd; 323/651-4129) is still the number-one retail outlet if you want to bump into real Hollywood royalty. A more mature and scattered version of trendy Melrose is nearby **LA BREA AVENUE,** where an interesting explosion of antique shops and vintage clothing stores line the avenue from Melrose Avenue to Wilshire Boulevard. Los Angeles's **THIRD STREET** (not to be confused with Santa Monica's Third Street Promenade) has several wonderful gift stores within a few blocks east of La Cienega Boulevard. Worthy stops include Free Hand (8413 W 3rd St, between Orlando Ave and La Cienega Blvd; 323/655-2607) and New Stone Age (8407 W 3rd St, between Orlando Ave and La Cienega Blvd; 323/658-5969), which both carry unusual pottery and jewelry, and Zipper (8316 W 3rd St, between Orlando and Sweetzer Aves; 323/951-0620), a top choice for affordable retro and modern gifts and housewares. **THE GROVE** (bordered by 3rd and Fairfax Sts, Stanley Ave, and CBS Studios) lets visitors stroll an outdoor shopping street anchored by Nordstrom on one end and the historic **FARMERS MARKET** on the other. In between, such brand-name shops as Banana Republic, Sur La Table, Barnes & Noble, and

Pottery Barn for Kids are set on a cobblestone street that looks straight out of Disneyland. A mini-Bellagio water show (set to music), numerous restaurants, and a multiplex movie theater round out the mall's offerings. The **BEVERLY CENTER** (8500 Beverly Blvd, at La Cienega Blvd; 310/854-0070) is a multilevel mall complete with Bloomingdales, Macy's, boutiques, a food court, and a multiplex movie theater. **ROBERTSON BOULEVARD** between Melrose Avenue and Third Street is the place to stroll designer boutiques and fashionable furniture stores. **CENTURY CITY WESTFIELD SHOPPINGTOWN** (10250 Santa Monica Blvd, between Century Park West and Ave of the Stars; 310/277-3898; www.westfield.com) is one of L.A.'s first malls and is completely outdoors. It's in a world of its own, with an excellent food court, a multiplex movie theater, and a superb selection of shops, including a Metropolitan Museum of Art Store (310/552-0905). The San Fernando Valley is known for its locally famous thoroughfare, **VENTURA BOULEVARD,** which is lined with shops, cafes, boutiques, and fine restaurants. Santa Monica's **MONTANA AVENUE** offers elite—and complete—shopping to match its clientele. **SANTA MONICA PLACE** mall (310/394-5451; www.santamonicaplace.com), a whirlwind of major department stores (Robinsons-May and Macy's) and specialty shops, is bounded by Second Street, Broadway, Fourth Street, and Colorado Avenue. The mall's front yard is the **THIRD STREET PROMENADE** (www.thirdst.com), a carnival of shops, tourist-oriented restaurants, movie theaters, and street performances.

Los Angeles has a wealth of great bookstores, and **BOOK SOUP** (8818 Sunset Blvd at Holloway Dr, West Hollywood; 310/659-3110; www.booksoup.com) is foremost among them. Despite its chaotic appearance when you first come through the door and become overwhelmed by the cornucopia of fiction, travel, memoirs, cookbooks, magazines, special-interest fiction, and nonfiction—and by hordes of customers bumping into each other in the narrow aisles—there's a method to this madness. Thousands of culinary titles stock the small storefront of **COOK'S LIBRARY** (8373 W 3rd St, between King's Rd and Orlando Ave, West Hollywood; 323/655-3141). **THE BODHI TREE** (8585 Melrose Ave at Westbourne Dr, West Hollywood; 310/659-1733) caters to New Agers, stocking volumes on holistic medicine, philosophy, astrology, alchemy, and the occult. **DUTTON'S BOOKS** (11975 San Vicente Blvd, between Bundy Dr and Montana Ave, Brentwood; 310/476-6263; www.duttonsbrentwood.com) offers an excellent collection of used and reference books as well as the latest fiction. **HENNESSEY + INGALLS** (1254 Third Street Promenade, Santa Monica; 310/458-9074; www.hennesseyingalls.com) has amassed one of the finest selections of art and architecture books in the country. They're well known for their sales and remainder tables and at any one time there may be as many as 4,000 titles marked down. At **SAMUEL FRENCH, INC.** (7623 Sunset Blvd at Stanley Ave, Hollywood; 323/876-0570; www.samuelfrench.com), an institution for actors in Los Angeles, every play that's ever been published is neatly arranged in alphabetical order on the floor-to-ceiling shelves. There's also a trove of publications on filmmaking, directing, how to prepare for auditions, and how to secure an agent, as well as film- and music-industry directories that many people in the area consider to be as sacred as the Bible.

PERFORMING ARTS

Ticketmaster (323/381-2000; www.ticketmaster.com) offers tickets to almost every concert, performance, and event in town, including, during the Jewish high holidays, passes to the larger and more popular synagogues. **THEATER ALLIANCE LEAGUE** (213/688-2787), an association of live theaters and producers in Los Angeles, operates the Internet-only discount ticket service **WEBTIX**. Log on to www.theatrela.org, where you can peruse the selection of same- or next-day tickets, all offered at half price. You can also sign up for e-mail alerts.

MUSIC: Founded in 1919 and now under the auspices of the brilliant and engaging director Esa-Pekka Salonen, the **LOS ANGELES PHILHARMONIC** (323/850-2000; www.laphil.org) is one of the world's most acclaimed orchestras. During its 26- to 30-week winter program, which opens each October, it's in residence at the Los Angeles County Music Center's Dorothy Chandler Pavilion (135 N Grand Ave, near West Temple St; 213/972-7211; www.musiccenter.org). During its 12-week summer season, the Philharmonic plays under the stars at the spectacular Hollywood Bowl (2301 N Highland Ave, north of Hollywood Blvd, south of the Hollywood Fwy; 323/850-2000; www.hollywoodbowl.org). The Philharmonic's repertoire includes critically acclaimed interpretations of the classics, as well as the cutting-edge **GREEN UMBRELLA CONCERTS** performed by their New Music Group. During the winter season, the Philharmonic's renowned Celebrity Recital Series is incorporated into the program at the Dorothy Chandler. During summer, these recitals become the **VIRTUOSO SERIES** and a component of the program at the Hollywood Bowl.

In 2003, when construction of the new **WALT DISNEY CONCERT HALL** (adjacent to downtown's Music Center) is scheduled for completion, the Philharmonic will leave the Dorothy Chandler Pavilion and take up residence there. The new facility, with a seating capacity of more than 2,300, is a Frank Gehry & Associates design and is itself a symphony of stainless-steel panels, bearing an alarming resemblance to a series of toppling drive-in movie screens. In addition, there will be a 38,000-square-foot urban arts park at the hall, designed to entice families to come early and enjoy the arts complex.

The Dorothy Chandler Pavilion is also where the **LOS ANGELES OPERA** (213/972-8001; www.laopera.org) resides. The company, which has traditionally included a large stable of young talent, debuted in 1986 with the world's foremost tenor, Placido Domingo, as the lead in Verdi's *Otello*. In 1995 Domingo assumed the position of artistic director and principal guest conductor, and he still functions frequently as both a performer and a conductor. The season, which begins in October, includes standards as well as rarely staged works. Peter Hemmings, who served a long tenure as managing director of the London Symphony Orchestra, is the company's general director.

The final resident of the Dorothy Chandler Pavilion is the country's number-one professional chorus, the **LOS ANGELES MASTER CHORALE** (213/972-7282; www.lamc.org). Their repertoire ranges from classical to Broadway to pop. Presided over by Musical Director Grant Gershon, they occasionally perform at the Hollywood Bowl and often accompany the Philharmonic.

The recently restored and renovated Deco Revival **WILTERN THEATER** (3790 Wilshire Blvd at Western Ave; 213/380-5005) presents a diverse program of performances, which have included the Dance Troupe of Lyon, Harry Connick Jr., and Yo-Yo Ma. Other terrific venues for enjoying an extensive array of performances include the hillside **JOHN ANSON FORD THEATER** (2580 Cahuenga Blvd, next to the Hollywood Fwy; 323/461-3673), the **GREEK THEATER** (2700 Vermont Ave in Griffith Park; 323/665-1927); the **UNIVERSAL AMPHITHEATER** (100 Universal City Plaza near Lankershim Blvd, Universal Studios; 818/622-4440); the **UCLA CENTER FOR THE PERFORMING ARTS** (Royce Hall, 405 Hilgard Ave on the UCLA campus in Westwood; 310/825-4401); the **SHRINE AUDITORIUM** (665 W Jefferson Blvd west of S Figueroa St; 213/749-5123); and the **SANTA MONICA CIVIC AUDITORIUM** (1855 Main St at Pico Blvd in Santa Monica; 310/393-9961).

DANCE: Los Angeles doesn't have a resident ballet company like San Francisco or New York, but check out the schedules for the Wiltern Theater, the Music Center, and UCLA Center for the Performing Arts; all present dance events featuring small local or touring companies.

THEATER AND COMEDY: The **AHMANSON THEATER** and the **MARK TAPER FORUM** (www.taperahmanson.com) combine with the Dorothy Chandler Pavilion (see Music, above) to form downtown's Los Angeles Music Center trinity. (The completion of Walt Disney Concert Hall will add a fourth component to the Music Center complex.) The incomparable Gordon Davidson is artistic director for both. The Ahmanson Theater was recently renovated to improve sight lines, enhance acoustics, and move the mezzanine closer to the stage. With its 1,600- to 2,000-seat capacity, it has been—since 1967—home to grand and glitzy musicals, revivals, and dramas. More than 50 productions at the Ahmanson have received prestigious and coveted Los Angeles Drama Critics Circle Awards. The thrust stage at the Mark Taper Forum is only one of the reasons this little jewel is just about the most popular and certainly the best place in L.A. to see theatrical productions. Since its inception more than 30 years ago, the Taper has presented consistently knockout productions of dramatic and comedic plays. The Taper is now viewed as an off-Broadway venue, since many of the plays originally produced here have moved to Broadway, where they've garnered both commercial success and critical acclaim. The **GEFFEN PLAYHOUSE** (10880 Le Conte Ave, near Westwood Blvd); 310/208-5454; www.geffenplayhouse.com), in Westwood near UCLA, mounts a diverse selection of productions, which in previous years has included Sir Ian McKellen's *Acting Shakespeare* and Steve Martin's *Picasso at the Lapin Agile*. The art deco **PANTAGES THEATER** (6233 Hollywood Blvd, Hollywood; 323/468-1779) books major Broadway productions, such as *The Lion King* and *The Producers*. Opened in 1930, the Pantages's gilded, ornate lobby is probably the boulevard's architectural highlight.

Richard Pryor got his start at **THE COMEDY STORE** (8433 W Sunset Blvd, a block east of La Cienega Blvd, West Hollywood; 323/656-6225; www.thecomedy store.com); so did Jim Carrey, Rosanne, and David Letterman. Pauly Shore's mom, Mitzi, is the owner/proprietor. They all come back now and then and join the new talent. The **LAUGH FACTORY** (8001 Sunset Blvd at Crescent Heights Blvd, Los

Angeles; 323/656-1336) is another Sunset venue that often showcases big-name performers. The wildly outrageous Groundlings troupe, appearing regularly at the **GROUNDLING THEATRE** (7307 Melrose Ave, near Poinsettia Pl, Los Angeles; 323/934-4747; www.groundlings.com) is one of the best improv groups in the city. Alumni include Jon Lovitz, Phil Hartman, Julia Sweeney, Chris Kattan, and Pee-wee Herman. **THE IMPROV** (8162 Melrose Ave, west of Crescent Heights Blvd, Los Angeles; 323/651-2583; www.improvclubs.com/hollywood/hollywood.htm) is extremely popular and usually packed. The Improv was the humble beginnings for big names like Jerry Seinfeld and Richard Lewis. Occasionally, one of the bigger names in the comedy pantheon drops in to check out the new competition, or to test the yuk power of new material.

FILM: The AFI (American Film Institute) **LOS ANGELES INTERNATIONAL FILM FESTIVAL** (323/856-7600), which runs for two weeks every October, is the best and the biggest of the Los Angeles celluloid showcases. Its focus is broad and multicultural, and it premieres the work of many emerging directors. The **LOS ANGELES INDEPENDENT FILM FESTIVAL**, which highlights the works of independent filmmakers, begins in June at Los Angeles's Laemmle's Sunset 5 and other theaters around Hollywood. **OUTFEST: THE LOS ANGELES GAY AND LESBIAN FILM FESTIVAL** runs for 10 days in mid-July and features films by, about, and for gays and lesbians. Its main venue is the Directors Guild of America (DGA) theater (7920 Sunset Blvd, Los Angeles, 2 blocks west of Fairfax Ave; 213/480-7065; www.outfest.org). Also screening at the DGA each April is the **CITY OF LIGHTS/CITY OF ANGELS FILM FESTIVAL**, presenting a selection of French-language films (310/289-2000).

The **NUART THEATER** (11272 Santa Monica Blvd, between Sepulveda Blvd and Sawtelle Ave, Santa Monica; 310/478-6379) is L.A.'s best art house, offering screenings of the work of dare-to-be-different filmmakers, as well as cult classics such as *Eraserhead* and *The Rocky Horror Picture Show*. Other excellent art-film venues include **AMERICAN CINEMATHEQUE**, which specializes in retrospectives, tributes, and infrequently screened films at Hollywood's restored historic Egyptian Theater (6712 N Highland Ave, Hollywood; 323/466-3456; www.egyptiantheatre.com); and **SILENT MOVIE THEATER** (611 N Fairfax Ave, Los Angeles; 323/655-2520; www.silentmovietheatre.com), a recently refurbished local treasure that screens silent greats with live organ accompaniment. Recently saved from the wrecking ball, the wide-screen **CINERAMA DOME** (6360 W Sunset Blvd; 323/464-4226; www.arclightcinemas.com) is now a part of the ArcLight Cinemas, which feature state-of-the-art movie theaters and reserved seats. To find out where the movie you want to see is currently playing and to charge tickets, call AOL MovieFone (777-FILM, in all area codes; www.moviefone.com).

NIGHTLIFE

BARS: A lot of negative things can be said about the City of Angels, but no one has ever complained about a shortage of fabulous watering holes. If you plan to make a night of it with a rambling pub crawl, a car is a must, and so is a designated driver, because the DUI laws are strict in these parts and the LAPD deals harshly with offenders. Also bear in mind that where there are cocktails, there's the singles scene—often young enough to make you wonder whether this town really is composed of nothing but twentysomethings.

In the Silver Lake–Los Feliz area, the warm and pleasantly shabby atmosphere at **AKBAR** (4356 Sunset Blvd, near Fountain Ave; 323/665-6810) is a good place to go on cold nights. It's mostly populated by the area's arty crowd of all sexual persuasions, and if you appreciate Britpop and electronica, the jukebox is awesome. As the name suggests, tiki style still dominates at **TIKI-TI** (4427 Sunset Blvd, near Fountain Ave, Los Feliz; 323/669-9381). The tropical drinks are served in coconut shells, and wearing an aloha shirt isn't unforgivable. **THE DERBY** (4500 Los Feliz Blvd, near Hillhurst Ave, Los Feliz; 323/663-8979; www.the-derby.com) caters to swinging Gen-Xers mixed with some of the town's hottest veteran dancers. It's swanky, with private booths; there's usually live swing music on Saturdays, and swing dance lessons are available. The Derby also showcases jazz and blues music. What can be said about **THE DRESDEN ROOM** (1760 N Vermont Ave, north of Hollywood Blvd, Los Feliz; 323/665-4294), where Marty and Elayne Roberts still perform their '60s lounge act? The mixed crowd at the bar is usually five deep, and that speaks for itself. **DEEP** (1707 N Vine St, Hollywood; 323/462-1144), on the corner of Hollywood and Vine, features a provocative setup of two-way mirrors and clear Plexiglas ceilings where patrons can ogle impossibly attractive, scantily clad hotties—of both genders—writhing in a suggestive cabaret. **THREE CLUBS** (1123 N Vine St, north of Santa Monica Blvd, Hollywood; 323/462-6441) is smart and supertrendy. It has a dress code and a doorman to assure that everyone adheres to the requisite hipness. **THE ROOM** (1626 N Cahuenga Blvd, north of Sunset Blvd, Hollywood; 323/462-7196) is tough to find but worth the trouble once you've negotiated the ratty alley where it's hiding. The interior is sexy, the jukebox is solid, and the DJ spins an eclectic variety of music. The **LAVA LOUNGE** (1533 N La Brea Ave, north of Sunset Blvd, Los Angeles; 323/876-6612) is a groovy favorite tucked into an aging strip mall. Inside, hipsters rock to blues and surf. On the cusp of Hollywood, the funky **FORMOSA CAFE** (7156 Santa Monica Blvd at Formosa Ave; 323/850-9050) remains as popular now as it was more than 50 years ago with the Hollywood and celebrity set, young and old. **MOLLY MALONE'S** (575 S Fairfax Ave, north of Wilshire Blvd, Los Angeles; 323/935-1577) is cozy and intimate during the week. Weekends it jumps because there's a dance floor and live bands.

Bars with a view are generally more refined than the town's favored Hollywood haunts. The **STANDARD LOUNGE** (8300 Sunset Blvd, West Hollywood; 323/650-9090), where the terminally hip come to sip martinis and mingle on the Astroturf-covered pool deck, falls into that category, as does **SKYBAR** (8440 W Sunset Blvd, West Hollywood; 323/848-6025) at the oh-so-trendy Mondrian Hotel, which is very good for star-gazing—both the human and the astral kind —if you can get past the doorman (or slip into the bar through the hotel before 8pm).

The perennially cool **WHISKEY BAR** (1200 N Alta Loma Rd at Sunset Blvd, West Hollywood; 310/657-0611) in the Sunset Marquis Hotel & Villas has no view, but is known as the Strip's less-self-conscious be-seen cocktail lounge. **BAR MARMONT**'s (8171 W Sunset Blvd, west of Crescent Heights Blvd, West Hollywood; 323/650-0575) retro-glamorous decor almost justifies the hefty cost of a cocktail.

Cross into the boundaries of Beverly Hills and the cocktail scene becomes instantly more refined. Such is the case at hotel lounges such as the **FOUR SEASONS** (300 S Doheny Dr at Burton Wy; 310/273-2222) and the **REGENT BEVERLY WILSHIRE** (9500 Wilshire Blvd at Rodeo Dr; 310/275-5200). **NIC'S MARTINI LOUNGE** (453 N Canon Dr, north of Brighton Wy; 310/550-5707) is a popular spot for martinis infused with spiced fruits.

On the Westside in Venice, **CANAL CLUB** (2025 Pacific Ave, at the corner of Venice Blvd; 310/306-6266), with its marine-flavored, ultramodern decor, is a favorite spot for cosmos and sushi; and **CHEZ JAY** (1657 Ocean Ave; 310/395-1741), with its dark interior and the vintage tunes blaring from the box, attracts a large crowd of Santa Monica regulars. In Marina del Rey, the singles mecca of Los Angeles, **BAJA CANTINA** (311 E Washington Blvd; 310/821-2252) is certainly doing its part to keep the singles scene alive. The place is usually packed with suntanned hard bodies talking fast and munching tortilla chips. The bar at **HOTEL CASA DEL MAR** (1910 Ocean Wy, Santa Monica; 310/581-5533) attracts the thirtysomething crowd who come to enjoy cocktails in an elegant oceanfront setting.

Downtown, check out **THE GRAND AVENUE SPORTS BAR** in the Biltmore Hotel (506 S Grand Ave; 213/612-1532) or **ENGINE COMPANY NO. 28,** in a converted 1912 firehouse (644 S Figueroa St; 213/624-6996). Rooftop libations are on the menu at the newly open **STANDARD HOTEL LOUNGE** (550 S Flower St, Los Angeles; 213/892-8080), where skyline views are almost as enticing as the beautiful people who come here to see and be seen.

CLUBS: Los Angeles is at its best after dark, with many exciting dance and/or music clubs to choose from. In addition to the entries provided here, check out L.A.'s free publication *LA Weekly* (available at cafes, bars, and markets), or go online at www.losangeles.citysearch.com, www.localmusic.com, or www.holly woodmonsters.com, for the complete word on what's happening in L.A.'s frenetic and fluid club scene. The heaviest concentration of clubs is in Hollywood and adjacent areas, so it's easy to hit more than one in an evening.

The recently remodeled **CRUSH BAR** (1734 N Cahuenga Blvd, north of Hollywood Blvd, Hollywood; 323/463-SOUL; www.thecrushbar.com) features '60s Motown and '70s and '80s chart-toppers. The **PALACE** (1735 N Vine St, above Hollywood Blvd, Hollywood; 323/462-3000), in an old movie theater, has been pulling in hipsters of all ages for years with DJs spinning techno, house, and hip-hop and frequent concerts as well. **CIRCUS** (323/462-1291), which is usually called the Big Top, and **ARENA** (323-462-0714) share the same address (6655 Santa Monica Blvd, 2 blocks east of Highland Ave, Hollywood), have multiple dance floors, and offer a broad variety of salsa, techno, disco, and hip-hop. Both cater to both the straight and the gay crowds. The **CATALINA BAR & GRILL** (1640 N Cahuenga Blvd, Hollywood; 323/466-2210) is a classy joint in the old sense of the phrase and one of the best places in the city for straight-ahead jazz. Many of the greats—Shirley Horne, Miles, and Ella, to name only a few—have put in an appearance or two at this one. **DORSCIA** (665 N Robertson Blvd, West Hollywood; 310/652-6364), in the former LunaPark space, draws celebrity scenesters and too-sexy-for-my-shirt models of both sexes who come to hit the dance floor and check out the lounge scene down-

THAT'S THE TICKET

Attending the taping of a television show may seem like a touristy thing to do, but it can actually be a lot of fun—you get a rare glimpse into the nitty-gritty production process, and see your favorite actors (or preview the stars of tomorrow) in a surprisingly intimate setting. Tickets are always free, so the best way to obtain tickets for your favorite show is to contact an official ticket outlet (see below) as far in advance as possible. Once you have the tickets in hand, show up at the studio at least an hour early so you'll be sure to get a seat. Remember when planning that you may be required to remain in the theater for several hours, and children under 10 are rarely allowed.

Keep in mind that most television production seasons run only from August through March, but game and talk shows are frequent exceptions. Tickets for NBC's (year-round) taping of **THE TONIGHT SHOW WITH JAY LENO** can be requested in advance by sending a self-addressed, stamped envelope to NBC, 3000 W Alameda Boulevard, Burbank, CA 91523 (818/840-3537; www.nbc.com). You can also go down to the studio the morning of the taping and stand in line for available seats. **AUDIENCES UNLIMITED** (100 Universal City Plaza, Bldg 153, Universal City, CA 91608; 818/506-0043; www.tvtickets.com) distributes tickets for most of the top sitcoms, including *Friends, Will & Grace, Everybody Loves Raymond,* and many more. **TELEVISION TICKETS** (323/467-4697) distributes tickets for talk and game shows, including *Jeopardy!*

—*Stephanie Avnet Yates*

stairs. Jennifer Lopez, Jimmy Smits, and other celebrity owners celebrate Latin music and dance at the **CONGA ROOM** (5364 Wilshire Blvd, Los Angeles; 323/938-1696; www.congaroom.com). **HOUSE OF BLUES** (8430 Sunset Blvd, West Hollywood; 323/848-5100; www.hob.com), with its hydraulic stage, kitschy Louisiana ambience, and nightly first-rate jazz, rock, hip-hop, and blues acts, is hard to beat. **THE ROXY** (9009 W Sunset Blvd, West Hollywood; 310/276-2222) and **WHISKEY A-GO-GO** (8901 Sunset Blvd, West Hollywood; 310/652-4202; www.whiskeyagogo.com) are cornerstones along the Sunset Strip. Both preview up-and-comers and new music by the seasoned. Today, the **VIPER ROOM** (8852 Sunset Blvd, West Hollywood; 310/358-1880; www.viperroom.com) has also become a favorite live music venue on the Strip, often attracting big-name performers for secret, late-night concerts. The **JAZZ BAKERY** (3233 Helms Ave, behind Venice Blvd, Los Angeles; 310/271-9039; www.jazzbakery.com) is located around back of the old Helms Bakery, now the Antique Guild. The sound system is excellent and it's another great spot for straight-ahead jazz from big names and new talent. **MCCABE'S** (3101 Pico Blvd, Santa Monica; 310/828-4403 or 310/828-4497; www.mccabes.com) has a 150-seat theater where everyone who's anyone has played, and many of them pop back in to make surprise appearances and deliver acoustic performances. The most interesting and intense entrant in the Los Angeles jazz scene is the **WORLD STAGE** (4344 Degnan Blvd, in the Crenshaw area; 323/293-2451). Sunday and Thursday nights there are jazz jams, and you might see a Marsalis brother playing next to today's nobody. If Charlie Parker were still alive this is where he would hang. It's not the best neighborhood, but there's safety in numbers, so go with a group. **THE MAYAN** (1038 S Hill St, between Olympic and 11th Sts, Los Angeles; 213/746-4287), in the old Mayan vaudeville palace downtown, offers dance music as eclectic as its patrons.

PARKS

GRIFFITH PARK (Entrances along Los Feliz Blvd at Riverside Dr, Vermont Ave, and Western Ave; 323-913-4688), adjacent to Hollywood, is L.A.'s answer to New York's Central Park. Located in the lovely and rugged hills that straddle Los Feliz and Burbank, it's the ideal spot for a picnic or hike. The parking lot of the Griffith Observatory and Planetarium (see Downtown, above) is the preferred spot from which to scan the city's vast landscape (smog permitting); however, the observatory itself is currently closed for expansion and restoration through 2005. Griffith Park's northern hills are crisscrossed with more than 250 miles of bridle paths; **HORSES** can be rented from the Los Angeles Equestrian Center (480 Riverside Dr; 818/840-8401), or the Bar S Stables (1850 Riverside Dr; 818/242-8443). One of the dinner rides departing from Sunset Ranch Hollywood Stable (3400 N Beachwood Canyon Dr; 323/469-5450), sauntering through a section of the park and concluding at the Mexican restaurant Viva Fresh in Burbank, is a wonderful way to spend an evening.

   RUNYON CANYON PARK (2000 N Fuller Ave, at the dead end, Hollywood; 213/473-7070) is something of a surprise to visitors and to Angelenos alike. Once you're inside the iron gates, hiking up any of several serpentine mountain trails that commence about 50 yards beyond, it's a different world. Coyote and rattler sightings are common, the silence is soothing, the view from Inspiration Point at the summit is unparalleled, and all this is just a few blocks north of frantic Sunset Boulevard. With more than 180 acres of grounds, a polo field, hiking trails, and ideal picnicking spots, **WILL ROGERS STATE HISTORIC PARK** (1501 Will Rogers State Park Rd, off Sunset Blvd, Santa Monica; 310/454-8212) is an easy pastoral escape at the cost of $3 per car. **PALISADES PARK** (Ocean Ave between Colorado Ave and Adelaide Dr, Santa Monica), a slim stretch of grass and palm trees fronting the Pacific Ocean, is a prime spot for watching the sunset, jogging, or taking in the sea air. The ethereal oasis known as the **SELF-REALIZATION LAKE SHRINE** (17190 Sunset Blvd, before Sunset Blvd dead-ends at the Pacific Ocean, Pacific Palisades; 310/454-4114) hints that this town does have a sense of spirituality. The Buddhist/cosmopolitan retreat, with its Zen lake, bridges, pastoral expanses, and meditators, is one of the city's most soothing and beautiful parks.

SPECTATOR SPORTS

In the past Los Angeles hasn't exactly been known for its spectator sports. Maybe that's because most L.A. fans lack the kind of team loyalty and enthusiasm you'll find in sporting towns like Chicago or New York. Or maybe it's because the City of Angels doesn't even have an NFL football team. (In 1995, the Los Angeles Raiders made a hasty retreat back to Oakland, while the Rams made St. Louis their new home.) Whatever the case, that may all be changing. When the $300 million Staples Center (adjoining the Los Angeles Convention Center) opened in 1999 as the new home of such teams as the **LOS ANGELES LAKERS**, the **LOS ANGELES KINGS**, the **LOS ANGELES SPARKS**, and the **LOS ANGELES CLIPPERS**, fans came out in droves to experience the new sporting venue. To celebrate their new stadium, the Los Angeles Lakers brought home the World Championship in 2000, 2001, and 2002, and a new generation of basketball fans was born. Tickets for all four teams are available from Ticketmaster (213/480-3232; www.ticketmaster.com). In the meantime, there has been talk of trying to bring a professional **FOOTBALL** team to Los Angeles. Gridiron fans otherwise have the option of taking in a UCLA Bruins or USC Trojans game or cheering on one of the city's newest teams: the L.A. Avengers, who play arena football at the Staples Center. And, of course, **BASEBALL** fans can always enjoy a day of America's favorite pastime at Dodger Stadium in Elysian Park. For ticket information, call 323/224-1448 or log on to www.dodgers.com.

FESTIVALS AND SPECIAL EVENTS

Los Angeles exploits any excuse for a party and hosts a variety of fairs, tournaments, shows, and festivals throughout the year. In January there's the **GREATER LOS ANGELES AUTO SHOW** (213/741-1151; www.laautoshow.com) at the Convention Center; a raucous celebration of Chinese New Year that consists of a street carnival and the **GOLDEN DRAGON PARADE** (Chinese Chamber of Commerce; 213/617-0396); and **JAPANESE NEW YEAR** (213/628-2725) in Little Tokyo, in which part of the revelry includes a seemingly endless line dance that winds through the area's shops as a good-luck blessing. The **ACADEMY AWARDS** (310/247-3000; www. oscars.org) are televised in late February. During the weekend before Easter, there's the annual **BLESSING OF THE ANIMALS** (213/625-5045) on Olvera Street, downtown. The best place for **EASTER SUNRISE SERVICES** (323/850-2000) is the Hollywood Bowl. In May comes the **LOS ANGELES/CALIFORNIA SCIENCE FAIR** (213/744-7400) at the California Science Center, where fanciful inventions abound, and the **CINCO DE MAYO** (213/625-5045) celebration on Olvera Street, celebrating Mexico's defeat of the French—a guaranteed blast, although parking is problematic. The **VENICE ART WALK** (310/392-WALK), one of L.A.'s most enjoyable events, commences at Westminster Elementary School (1010 Abbott Kinney Blvd); go and you will have the opportunity to sample the fare of L.A.'s finest chefs while touring the studios of more than 50 artists. The **PLAYBOY JAZZ FESTIVAL** (323/850-2000) at the Hollywood Bowl in June offers an excellent lineup of jazz greats and emerging jazz artists. In August, check out **NISEI WEEK** (213/687-7193) in Little Tokyo and rejoice in everything Japanese. In October, celebrate **HALLOWEEN** in West Hollywood—L.A.'s answer to New Orleans's Mardi Gras and Halloween in New York's East Village. In November, the best ways to celebrate **DÍA DE LOS MUERTOS** (Day of the Dead, November 1; 213/651-4741) are the parades and other festivities on Olvera Street. November is also the occasion for the **"VIVE LE BEAUJOLAIS" WINE FESTIVAL** (323/651-4741) at the Pacific Design Center. It's hosted by the French-American Chamber of Commerce, chichi, and très amusant. The **HOLLYWOOD CHRISTMAS PARADE** (323/469-8311) takes place the Sunday after Thanksgiving. Attending it is a good way to inaugurate the holiday season. In December, you may want to visit **ART EXPO** (213/741-1151) at the Los Angeles Convention Center to see acres—literally—of art in every medium by prominent, emerging, and unknown U.S. artists. Dress warmly for the **CHRISTMAS BOAT PARADE** (310/821-0555) in Marina del Rey, which usually occurs the two weekends before Christmas. **LAS POSADAS** (213/623-5045) on Olvera Street is a nightly Christmas celebration that includes a traditional candlelight march. One of the most beloved holiday traditions in the Southland is the annual **LOS ANGELES COUNTY HOLIDAY MUSIC PRO-GRAM** (213/972-7211) on Christmas Eve day. It happens downtown in the Dorothy Chandler Pavilion (see Music, above) at the Music Center, and it's free.

RESTAURANTS AND LODGINGS BY NEIGHBORHOOD

Downtown Los Angeles

RESTAURANTS

Cafe Pinot / ★★☆

700 W 5TH ST, DOWNTOWN; 213/239-6500 Joachim Splichal's downtown outpost brings life to an otherwise dead-after-dark neighborhood with this spin-off of Pinot Bistro in Sherman Oaks. Situated right next to the downtown public library, the shoe-box glass atrium restaurant has an upward view of downtown's shining towers and a patio view of the library's garden. The food is Splichal lite, which is to say that his eccentric, delicious European-California cooking commands somewhat more down-to-earth prices here. Expect a signature menu that might include a three-mustard-crusted rotisserie chicken with fries, crispy Peking duck breast with braised salsify and apricots, or roasted wild striped bass with chanterelle mushroom ravioli. *$$; AE, MC, V; no checks; lunch Mon–Fri, dinner every day; full bar; reservations recommended; www.patinagroup.com; at S Flower St.* &

Cicada / ★★

617 S OLIVE ST, DOWNTOWN; 213/488-9488 Friends thought Adelmo Zarif was slightly off when he moved his successful West Hollywood restaurant a block from Pershing Square five years ago. But that was before the current downtown renaissance brought us Staples Center and the Disney Concert Hall. Zarif set up shop in the historic, ornate Oviatt Building in a magnificent space that had been an elegant haberdashery. By adding gold leaf to the ceiling—all 15,000 square feet of it—he gave a warm glow to the beautiful space, both upstairs and down. The room is indeed the star, from the spectacular split staircase to the glass cabinets filled with prized wine and spirits. The food from executive chef Daniel Rossi's kitchen is Northern Italian. Typical of his creative cooking are a novel asparagus-crusted grilled salmon and his wildly popular linguine with lobster in a spicy tomato sauce. Zarif himself oversees the substantial wine list, divided almost evenly between California and Italy, and diners should seek his counsel with confidence on lesser-known Italian bottles as well as after-dinner grappas. *$$$; AE, DC, MC, V; no checks; lunch Mon–Fri, dinner Mon–Sat; full bar; reservations recommended; www.cicadarestaurant.com; between 6th and 7th Sts.* &

Ciudad / ★★

445 S FIGUEROA ST, DOWNTOWN; 213/486-5171 The powerhouse team behind L.A.'s Border Grill and its resulting TV show/cookbook empire—Susan Feniger and Mary Sue Milliken—channeled their pan-Latin passions into Ciudad ("city" in Spanish), part of the new wave of downtown destinations. The restaurant's colorfully upscale yet distinctly urban vibe provides the perfect backdrop for a menu featuring bold flavors and indigenous ingredients from across the Latin world—Havana, Rio de Janeiro, and Buenos Aires to Lisbon and Barcelona—in both authentic dishes and invented interpretations. Here, amid juicy sherbet pastel walls and retro-cool Klee-like murals, memorable dishes include Honduran ceviche with tropical fruit accents; Argentine rib-eye stuffed with jalapeños and whole garlic; and citrus-roasted Cuban-style chicken served with Puerto Rican fried rice and plantains. The cocktail menu is inspired and extensive, inviting the uninitiated to sample kicky concoctions—the trendy mojito is here, along with excellent sangría, and a full premium rum menu. Between 3 and 7pm on weekdays, come for *cuchifritos,* traditional snacks served at the bar; you might just make a meal from selections like sweet-savory pork-stuffed green tamales, *papas relleno* (mashed potato fritters stuffed with oxtail stew), plantain gnocchi in tomatillo sauce, and more. Ciudad is also a stop on the Music Center shuttle route and the restaurant offers transportation to Staples Center. *$$–$$$; AE, MC, V; no checks; lunch Mon–Fri, dinner every day; full bar; reservations recommended; www.millikenandfeniger.com; corner of 5th St.* &

La Serenata de Garibaldi / ★★

1842 E 1ST ST, BOYLE HEIGHTS (AND BRANCHES); 323/265-2887 A highly regarded family-run restaurant, La Serenata de Garibaldi serves some of the finest—and most authentic—regional Mexican cuisine in Los Angeles. This is the original Serenata, which has handed down its family recipes to the two other similar Westside establishments. Menu highlights include two handmade moles—poblano (sweet and complex) and Oaxacan (black and spicy)—which are great with everything from enchiladas to chicken and fish or pork. Beef medallions arrive in *molcajete* sauce, which has plenty of spice from its mix of peppers, fresh-roasted tomatoes, onions, and chunks of avocado. For dessert, you can't go wrong with the simple fresh strawberries or guavas in cream, or the house special *tres leches* cake, an unusually moist treat made with regular, condensed, and evaporated milks. There's also a stylish branch with hacienda decor in Santa Monica (1416 4th St; 310/656-7017). That makes number three, after the casual La Serenata Gourmet (10924 W Pico Blvd, West Los Angeles; 310/441-9667) adjacent to the Westside Pavilion. *$; AE, DC, DIS, MC, V; no checks; breakfast, lunch Sat–Sun, dinner every day; full bar; reservations recommended; between Mission and Soto Sts.* &

McCormick & Schmick's / ★★

633 W 5TH ST, DOWNTOWN (AND BRANCHES); 213/629-1929 This downtown mainstay features seafood, done both traditionally and California-style, in a setting right out of downtown San Francisco. Those with a piscatorial bent can usually be found crowding the bar, feasting on an impressive selection of Washington oysters on the half shell—Dungeness Bays, Olympias, Samish Bays, Quilcenes, Eagle Creeks, and Snow Creek Belons. They're just the start of an encyclopedic seafood menu that runs from steamed Manila clams in garlic and white wine broth, Penn Cove or Emerald mussels steamed with garlic and herbs, and traditional oyster stew to fine popcorn rock shrimp, very good Dungeness crab cakes, one of the best *salades niçoises* around, and a particularly rich clam chowder. There's much more, some of it on the line between creative and utterly wild-eyed—ling cod with pesto and sun-dried tomatoes, and white Alaskan king salmon pan-fried with Moroccan black barbecue sauce. Popular with downtown suits at lunchtime, the restaurant sees a smaller dinner crowd of late workers and theater-bound culture vultures. Additional locations include Beverly Hills (2 Rodeo Dr; 310/859-0434); Pasadena (111 N Los Robles Ave; 626/405-0064); and El Segundo (2101 Rosecrans Ave; 310/416-1123). *$$; AE, MC, V; no checks; lunch, dinner every day; full bar; reservations required; www.mccormickandschmicks.com; between Hope and Grand, in the Library Towers.* &

Pacific Dining Car / ★★★

1310 W 6TH ST, DOWNTOWN; 213/483-6000 / 2700 WILSHIRE BLVD, SANTA MONICA; 310/453-4000 A refuge for serious carnivores as well as lovers of big, tannic red wines, the Pacific Dining Car has been serving excellent steaks for 80 years. The restaurant owes its name to the front room, a faux train car, while the other rooms have a more clubby style; all are ideal venues for the red-meat renaissance. The beef is USDA Prime Eastern corn fed, dry aged on the premises, cut by PDC's own butcher and then cooked as simply as possible over high-heat mesquite charcoal to sear in the juices. Add the requisite baked potato, french fries, mashed potatoes, or rice, plus steamed spinach, creamed spinach, or broccoli hollandaise, and you've got yourself a good, old-fashioned dining experience. Alternatively, you can fake it with lime chicken or Maine lobster. The wine list has more than 400 beef-friendly choices. Perhaps best of all, the original downtown location is open 24 hours a day, 7 days a week, and even at breakfast there are some great steak options. Weekday happy hour in the cozy bar features fine hors d'oeuvres like baby back pork ribs, broiled chicken wings, and shrimp. The Santa Monica location closes at 2am. *$$$; AE, DC, MC, V; no checks; breakfast, lunch, dinner every day; full bar; reservations recommended; www.pacificdiningcar.com; at Witmer St (downtown); at Princeton St (Santa Monica).* &

Philippe the Original / ★★☆

1001 N ALAMEDA ST, CHINATOWN; 213/628-3781 Philippe, the city's oldest restaurant, dates back to 1908, and it looks it. There's sawdust on the floor, pickled eggs and pig's feet on the counter, and open jars of horseradish-laced mustard on the communal long tables. At just about any time of day, Philippe's is filled with the most remarkable assortment of customers—postal and railroad workers from the neighborhood, residents of Chinatown and East L.A., lawyers from downtown, Music Center performers, tourists, politicos and police from the Civic Center, and down-and-outers from local crevices. They all have one thing in common: a hunger for Philippe's fabled French-dipped sandwich, especially the lamb.

A crisp French roll is filled to bursting with roasted beef, pork, ham, or lamb, dipped in real, rich meat drippings and accompanied by your choice of creamy old-fashioned coleslaw, potato or macaroni salad, and perhaps a bowl of Philippe's soup of the day (don't miss the navy bean on Thursday). Coffee, which for years was five cents a cup, is still only a dime. Worth the trip! *$; Cash only; breakfast, lunch, dinner every day; beer and wine; reservations not accepted; www.philippes.com; at Ord St.* &

Seoul Jung / ★★

930 WILSHIRE BLVD, DOWNTOWN; 213/688-7880 This restaurant in downtown's Wilshire Grand Hotel is an unusually lovely space, with several large dining areas and smaller, elegant private rooms, all geared toward the celebration of Korean barbecue. The tables are marble, with a grill built into the center of each to accommodate that country's grill-intensive cuisine. Along with the various barbecue selections, which include tenderest beef rib-eye, you get salad, rice, soup, and side dishes in many small bowls, including several versions of kimchee, the fermented cabbage-based dish that defines Korean cuisine. Diners grill the meats themselves, and then roll them in lettuce leaves with assorted vegetables and condiments. Portions are substantial, but begin with an appetizer of *pa jun*, a briny, pizza-size pancake of seafood, including baby shrimp and calamari, mixed with scallions and strips of red and green bell pepper—a very satisfying dish. Korean Hite beer is a perfect match with any of the dishes. *$$; AE, DC, DIS, JCB, MC, V; no checks; lunch Mon–Fri, dinner every day; full bar; reservations recommended; corner of Figueroa and 7th Sts.* &

Water Grill / ★★★★

544 S GRAND AVE, DOWNTOWN; 213/891-0900 Widely acclaimed as the finest American seafood restaurant in Southern California, the Water Grill is a realm in which fish aren't so much consumed as they are venerated. There is a fine oyster and caviar bar, all shining brass and cool marble, offering fine Iranian and Caspian ocetra and beluga caviars and at least seven kinds of expertly chosen oysters. The menu proper is a celebration of the American approach to seafood—white chowder flavored with Manila clam and apple-smoked bacon; crisp Maryland soft-shell crabs atop vine-ripened tomatoes and spinach; king salmon, cured in house and flavored with a hint of citrus; rare bluefin tuna, hand cut into tartare with avocado and green peppercorns. There is an "American" bouillabaisse containing monkfish, sculpin, prawns, mussels, and clams. Tender Alaskan halibut is line caught and served with crushed Yukon gold potatoes; roasted Arctic char comes with artichokes and crayfish; black sea bass is poached in ginger and lime. The wine list is rich with lighter whites, the sort of wines that naturally marry with the flavors of the sea. Service here is quite formal, but the friendly and knowledgeable wait staff is never off-putting. *$$–$$$; AE, MC, V; no checks; lunch Mon–Fri, dinner every day; full bar; reservations recommended; www.watergrill.com; at 4th St.* &

Yang Chow / ★★

819 N BROADWAY, CHINATOWN (AND BRANCHES); 213/625-0811 Yang Chow has long been the place to go for well-nigh-perfect versions of the top 100 Chinese dishes. Although the menu does offer sea cucumber (served with either brown sauce or shrimp eggs), generally you won't find the way-out dishes that some Chinese restaurants list only on their Chinese-language menus. This is accessible Sichuan and Mandarin cuisine with such delicacies as spicy Sichuan wontons, which are soft, hot and sweet in a broth the color of a fire engine; cold noodles tossed with shredded chicken and warm-cool sesame sauce; steamed pork dumplings; hot and sour soup; or the dish that most people think of when Yang Chow comes up in conversation—the slippery shrimp. These are wonderful plump shrimp in a crisp batter under a sweet-sour-hot sauce. One bite and you're hooked. The same menu is offered at two other locations: in Pasadena (3777 E Colorado Blvd; 626/432-6868) and Woodland Hills (6443 Topanga Canyon Blvd; 818/347-2610). *$; AE, DC, MC, V; no checks; lunch, dinner every day; beer and wine; reservations recommended; www.yangchow.com; between Alpine and College Sts.*

LODGINGS

Figueroa Hotel / ★★☆

 939 S FIGUEROA ST, DOWNTOWN; 213/627-8971 OR 800/421-9092 The enchanting, Spanish-style Figueroa is emblematic of downtown L.A.'s flowering. Built in 1925 as a YWCA, this 12-story, 285-room hotel is an oasis in a spit-shined corner of downtown, a hop away from the Staples Center. Owner Uno Thimansson's artistic vision, eye for detail, and thoughtful management style make the Figueroa the magical spot that it is—but the gentrification of the district and the Metro line, which can whisk you to Hollywood and Universal Studios inside 20 minutes, helps a lot. This is squarely a budget hotel, and one with a funky edge. But stunning architecture, gorgeous multiethnic interiors, a professional staff, and low, low rates make this our favorite low-priced accommodation in the city. The grand lobby is a glorious sight, with stenciled beam ceilings, Southwestern tile floors, Navajo textiles, and towering palms in Moroccan and Balinese pots. The carefully decorated rooms carry on the Southwest Gothic theme, where terra-cotta, sponge-painted walls, wrought-iron beds, Indian cotton draperies, and Mexican-tiled baths come together in a beautifully exotic cheap-chic style. Rooms contain minimal amenities (most have unstocked fridges), but beds are firm and textiles fresh. Out back, a large landscaped patio enjoys blooming succulents, a terrific mosaic-tiled pool and whirlpool, and the festive Veranda Bar. A lobby cafe serves casual meals, and less than a block away is the Original Pantry Cafe, whose we-never-close policy lets you dig into killer breakfasts at any hour. *$$; AE, DC, JCB, MC, V; no checks; unofig@aol.com; www.figueroahotel.com; at Olympic Blvd.* &

Hilton Checkers / ★★★

535 S GRAND AVE, DOWNTOWN; 213/624-0000 OR 800/423-5798 Built in 1926, this lovely member of the Hilton chain feels more like a European boutique hotel than a downtown business hotel. With just 188 rooms and suites, it's more intimate and personal than most downtown chains, with a high level of service. Guest rooms are tastefully decorated in a restrained, somewhat traditional style that's given a lighter California vibe thanks to a beige, taupe, and cream color scheme. All of the rooms—which are restful and elegant, although some are on the small side—feature nicely made beds, a marble bath with terry robes, three two-line phones, a generous marble-topped work desk, and a coffeemaker. On site is a small fitness center and a terrific rooftop pool and whirlpool deck, whose tremendous views of the surrounding skyscrapers make it one of the best after-dark perches in downtown Los Angeles. The elegant dining room is no longer the destination restaurant that it was when renowned chef Thomas Keller (now of Napa's French Laundry) was behind the stove, but it's still a temple of elegant California-continental cuisine. Serving an impressive collection of Cognacs, single-malts, and ports, the Lobby Bar is popular with a well-heeled after-work crowd as well as for authentic English teatime. *$$$$; AE, DC, DIS, MC, V; no checks; www.checkers hotel.com; between 5th and 6th Sts.* &

Millennium Biltmore Hotel Los Angeles / ★★★☆

506 S GRAND AVE, DOWNTOWN; 213/624-1011 OR 800/245-8673 Downtown's oldest and grandest hotel seamlessly blends modern luxury with period appeal. Since 1923, this Italian–Spanish Renaissance beauty has been a favorite of globe-trotting royalty, U.S. presidents, and international celebrities, including the Beatles. Now owned by Millennium Hotels, this icon of old-world luxury sparkles more than ever. The dazzle begins the moment you enter the soaring lobby and galleria, with their fantastic hand-painted frescoes and bas-reliefs. Off the lobby is the stunning Gallery Bar, whose gorgeous terra-cotta tile helped to snag it recognition from *Los Angeles* magazine as one of the best—and sexiest—cocktail lounges in town. Extra-wide halls lead to 683 large guest rooms that aren't quite as stunning, but still suitably historic and appealing. Bathrooms tend to be small, but they boast rich, peach-toned marble and plush robes. The club level features newly renovated rooms, a private lounge serving complimentary continental breakfast, and butler service. A vintage treasure is the art deco health club, with whirlpool, steam, sauna, and a gorgeous, Roman-style, Pompeii-replica pool. A wide range of additional on-site services suit business and leisure travelers alike. A handful of on-site restaurants includes Sai Sai for superb Japanese, Smeraldi's for casual Italian-accented California cuisine, the romantic Rendezvous Court for afternoon tea, and a state-of-the-art sports bar. *$$$$; AE, DC, DIS, E, JCB, MC, V; checks OK; biltmore@ mhrmail.com; www.millennium-hotels.com; at 5th St.*

The Standard, Downtown LA / ★★★☆

550 S FLOWER ST, DOWNTOWN; 213/892-8080 This new-in-2002 outpost of Andre Balazs's swank West Hollywood neo-motel has transformed downtown into a hip destination once again. The Standard's signature Generation Y-targeted cheap-cool style and tradition-busting attitude has been successfully replicated in an atomic-age tower originally constructed in 1956 to house the headquarters of Superior Oil. Don't miss the fabulous 15-time-zone clock (an original feature) in the sleek-meets-eye-popping chic lobby. Designer Shawn Hausman has adorned the stainless steel and Carrara marble space with a multiplatform electric-pink sectional sofa by Vladimir Kagan that says "wow!" A DJ sets a perpetual party scene. Other fabulous public spaces include a 24-hour restaurant, a combo barbershop–cigar lounge, and a Jetsons-cool electric-blue AstroTurfed roof deck with a pool, pool toys, and private cabanas with heated vibrating waterbeds; no wonder the celebs can't stay away. The 207 guest rooms are equally stylish; features include ultra-modern platform beds dressed with oversize down pillows and fluffy duvets; 14-foot work desks that are both beautiful and functional; large-screen TVs, CD stereos, and free high-speed connectivity for laptop jockeys; and sexy lighting for setting the mood. Opt for one of the larger rooms, worth the price of admission for the giant foot sculpture in the bathroom alone. The staff is suitably sexy, too. *$$–$$$; AE, DC, DIS, MC, V; no checks; downtownla@standard.com; www.standardhotel.com; at 6th St.* &

Westin Bonaventure Hotel & Suites / ★★★

404 S FIGUEROA ST, LOS ANGELES; 213/624-1000 OR 800/228-3000 No hotel so divides Angelenos like this love-it-or-hate-it city-within-a-city, whose five cylindrical black-glass towers have starred in dozens of feature films (not to mention countless proms). Opened in 1977, L.A.'s largest hotel (1,354 rooms) feels fresh and contemporary after a $35 million renovation. Twelve glass elevators rise 35 stories, from the 6-story atrium lobby to the L.A. Prime steakhouse and its famous revolving cocktail lounge. Crowds amble through six levels of shopping and dining, a 9,000-square-foot spa, and a running track. (Guests also have access to an 85,000-square-foot fitness center adjacent to the hotel.) The more than 20 dining choices include a slate of Asian restaurants; the microbrew-pouring Bonaventure Brewing Co.; the top-notch Bonaventure Chowder Bar; and the hotel's very own Krispy Kreme. Outdoors, a deck as big as a football field boasts a heated lap pool. The pie-sliced guest rooms are on the small side, but streamlined contemporary furnishings and floor-to-ceiling windows maximize comfort and views. The divine Heavenly Bed is a huge selling point. Guest office suites are great for businessfolk, with a wet bar, executive workstation, fax machine, and terry robes. Tower Suites have a living room, an extra half-bath, minifridge, microwave, coffeemaker, robes, and two TVs—ideal for families or execs in need of intimate meeting space. *$$$$; AE, DC, DIS, JCB, MC, V; no checks; labon@westin.com; www.westin.com; between 4th and 5th Sts.* &

Beverly Hills and the Westside

RESTAURANTS

Asia de Cuba / ★★☆

8440 SUNSET BLVD (INSIDE THE MONDRIAN HOTEL), WEST HOLLYWOOD; 323/848-6000 The international see-and-be-seen crowd reaches terminal velocity at this hot spot in the Sunset Strip's scene-central Mondrian hotel. As the hotel's dining room, the restaurant serves traditional breakfasts and lunches, but the real fun starts at night when the eye-candy diners trickle in for an eclectic Chino-Latino menu that created a stir some half dozen years ago when the restaurant took Manhattan by storm. After starting with one of 16 exotic tropical house cocktails—or a selection from the specialty rum and sake menus—try *tunapica* (Spanish ahi tartare), Chinese five-spice seared foie gras, or dumplings with Cuban black bean filling. Each dish—all served family style and sized for sharing—features Asian and Latin flavors playing colorfully off each other, like chiles rellenos stuffed with tofu and red curry, then fried golden brown. At Asia de Cuba, table placement is everything: sit inside and you're in the center of the action, surrounded by a nonstop din and energetic bustle; on the twinkle-lit patio dotted with 6-foot-tall terra-cotta pots, you'll find seclusion and privacy. *$$–$$$; AE, DC, DIS, MC, V; no checks; breakfast, lunch, dinner every day; full bar; reservations required for dinner; between La Cienega Blvd and Olive St.* &

The Belvedere / ★★★

9882 SANTA MONICA BLVD (INSIDE THE PENINSULA BEVERLY HILLS HOTEL), BEVERLY HILLS; 310/788-2306 The Belvedere, under longtime executive chef Bill Bracken, draws locals and guests alike with its lovely, formal setting and colorful and creative California cuisine with Asian highlights. The dining room is where power players meet for breakfast over granola and oatmeal brûlée or more exotic frittatas and the like. Bracken offers eclectic dishes at lunch and dinner, from miso-poached sweetbreads with Sichuan-pepper-infused cherry syrup to truffle-roasted veal chateaubriand with wild mushrooms. But despite his wide range, he's known for straightforward prime beefsteaks and roasts. Popular with the lunch bunch is his $16 hot dog made from chicken and foie gras. And for those who simply can't decide, he recommends an assemble-it-yourself tasting menu called Small Bites, where you can try out some of his temptations in miniature form. Same goes for the dessert menu. Patio seating allows diners to enjoy the property's lushly landscaped hotel grounds—and is much in demand by smokers. *$$$; AE, DC, DIS, MC, V; no checks; breakfast, lunch, dinner every day; full bar; reservations recommended; www.peninsula.com; between Wilshire Blvd and Lasky Dr.* &

Casa Antigua Cantina / ★★

12217 WILSHIRE BLVD, LOS ANGELES; 310/820-2540 This is not your typical "L.A. Mexican" restaurant; Casa Antigua is pioneering gourmet Mexican cooking here as served in fine Mexico City restaurants and upper-class homes. Urbane chef Denis Jean-Louis Ferrari applies sophisticated cooking techniques to the varied regional cooking styles of Mexico. The restaurant, which opened in 2002, transformed the veteran '60s-style Bicycle Shop Cafe into a dimly lit hacienda, with live music in the up-front bar and decorative Mexican wood- and metalwork brightening up a cavernous dining space beyond. What to order? It's hard to go wrong, with friendly waiters just rarin' to advise you on moles and chiles used in many of the prime beef, poultry, and seafood delicacies. Popular dishes include an appetizer of little quesadillas filled with the woodsy-tasting corn fungus *cuitlacoche*, a Mexican delicacy; for a main course, sweet, mild red snapper is served in the corn husk where it was steamed. Portions are generous, so you may want to share starters and/or desserts like *crepas de cajeta con nuez*, delicate crepes lavished with rich goat's milk caramel. In addition to margaritas served on the rocks, there's a reasonably priced wine list. *$$; AE, CB, DC, DIS, MC, V; no checks; lunch, dinner every day; full bar; reservations recommended; info@casaantigua.com; www.casaantigua.com; 1 block west of Bundy Dr.* &

Celestino Italian Steak House / ★★★

8908 BEVERLY BLVD, WEST HOLLYWOOD; 310/858-5777 When indefatigable restaurateur Celestino Drago announced a new steak house toward the end of the

'90s, his sanity was called into question, since Italian cooking is not dominated by hunks of beef. But Celestino Italian Steak House proves that Italian cooking has more in common with the Atkins diet than might be expected. He's created an homage to meat, a great-looking room with lots of buzz, built around a type of beef called Piedmontese that has half the calories, a quarter of the fat, and all of the taste. This rather miraculous meat is served up as beef tartare and offered grilled in rib-eye, porterhouse, New York strip, and filet mignon form. We're not quite sure what chef Drago rubs on his steaks before grilling them, but we suspect it might make even old shoes taste great! The steaks come with a choice of six sauces, along with side dishes like creamed spinach, roasted potatoes, and, in case you've forgotten that you're in an Italian restaurant, sweet and sour baby onions and eggplant caponata. And yes, there is pasta—plus a risotto flavored with marrow that's a delicious form of excess, a dish for those who like their flavors as robust as a winter in Tuscany. *$$–$$$; AE, MC, V; no checks; dinner every day; full bar; reservations recommended; www.celestinodrago.com; between Robertson Blvd and Doheny Dr.* &

Chaya Brasserie / ★★★
Chaya Venice

8741 ALDEN DR, WEST HOLLYWOOD; 310/859-8833 / 110 NAVY ST, VENICE; 310/396-1179 Expect to see celebrities at these Cal-French bistro/ brasseries with major Japanese touches, brought to California by a venerable restaurant family from Tokyo. Inside the warehouselike setting of Chaya Brasserie, you'll find some of the most creative grill food around. Though the menu shifts with the seasons, executive chef Shigefumi Tachibe has certain classic preparations that travel from menu to menu (and to both Chayas): seaweed salad with ginger-soy rice wine vinaigrette, Hawaiian tuna tartare, Cantonese chicken rolls, spinach and roasted garlic ravioli, chicken Dijon with pommes frites, sesame-crusted whitefish, grilled Moroccan lamb chops, and sliced roasted venison with black peppercorn sauce. The menu at the sister restaurant Chaya Venice veers more toward seafood and Pacific Rim dishes but features much the same cooking style and an always-packed sushi bar. You won't find warehouse decor there, but a more elegant Japanese-influenced dining room. It's a choice spot for Santa Monica's handsome crowd. *$$; AE, DC, JCB, MC, V; no checks; lunch Mon–Fri, dinner every day; full bar; reservations recommended; www.thechaya.com; east of Robertson Blvd (Brasserie); corner of Main St (Venice).* &

Crustacean / ★★

9646 LITTLE SANTA MONICA BLVD, BEVERLY HILLS; 310/205-8990 Crustacean, in true Hollywood fashion, comes with its own subtitle: "Euro-Asian Cuisine." The owners, three generations of women, are Vietnamese, but this is not traditional Viet-namese cooking or even standard Asian fusion. It's the personal cuisine of Helene An, who was reared in a Hanoi culture that was both Vietnamese and French. Her affluent family's three chefs—French, Vietnamese, and Chinese—taught her how to cook, and the results are yours for the tasting at this nostalgic, camera-ready rendi-tion of '30s colonial Hanoi. The dramatic entrance brings you past a floor-to-ceiling aquarium into the bar, where another aquarium beneath the floor, 80 feet long and filled with brightly colored koi, is the glass-topped pathway winding into the dining room. Seafood may well be the best way to go here, from lemongrass-scented Asian bouillabaisse and lobster in tamarind sauce to whole roasted Dungeness crab with garlic sauce. House specialties, such as An's giant tiger prawns and potent garlic noodles, are created in the "secret kitchen," a separate area where recipes are kept under wraps. *$$$; AE, DC, MC, V; no checks; lunch Mon–Fri, dinner Mon–Sat; full bar; reservations recommended; between Rodeo and Roxbury Drs.* &

Delmonico's Seafood Grille / ★★☆

9320 W PICO BLVD, WEST LOS ANGELES; 310/550-7737 / 260 E COLORADO BLVD, PASADENA; 626/844-7700 Reserve one of the high-walled wood booths at this upscale San Francisco–style seafood eatery and you'll enjoy a little privacy along with strategic views of the comings and goings. The restaurant's primary attraction is its wide selection of fresh, cooked-to-order fish. The Boston clam chowder appeals to anyone with a preference for thick and creamy, as does the spicy *zuppa la pescatore,* whose fresh shellfish is served in a broth with respectable zing. Grilled swordfish is a generous, tender portion in a light rum glaze, accompanied by crisp crab pancakes. If you don't feel like seafood, you'll find just as good selections of pasta, steak, veal, and chicken, the last three of which come with a side of addictive garlic mashed potatoes. *$$$; AE, MC, V; no checks; lunch Mon–Fri, dinner every day; full bar; reservations recommended; www.delmonicos.com; between Beverly Dr and Doheny (West L.A.); in the Paseo Colorado mall (Pasadena).* &

Four Oaks / ★★☆

2181 N BEVERLY GLEN BLVD, LOS ANGELES; 310/470-2265 Four Oaks is one of Los Angeles's most unabashedly romantic restaurants, hidden in Beverly Glen's tree-shaded canyon. In the parking lot, twinkle lights blanket the trees in every direction; on your way in, glance through the kitchen windows, where the staff labors over some of the best modern French-California cooking in Southern California. Walk through the door, and you're in Provence—especially if you opt for the sylvan pleasures of the outdoor patio. Dishes are of exceptional focus and clarity: flavors are never hidden away beneath excessive sauces or embellishments. You'll find some typically French dishes here, like delectable veal sweetbreads with grilled foie gras and skate wings fillet with truffled mushroom duxelles. More eclectic treats include lobster spring rolls accompanied by passion fruit–mint dip enlivened by wasabi mustard; bourbon-marinated pork-loin fillet with brown sugar apple rings; a delicious calamari stuffed with vegetables; and roast venison fillet with intense lingonberry sauce. The very French dessert menu presents difficult choices. When in doubt, order the sampler of tarts, mousses, and soufflés. A spectacular treat is the chef's special *Menu du Cuisinier Gourmand* prepared for the whole table. The three-course Sunday brunch includes some of the restaurant's most popular entrees. Four Oaks is a place to dazzle that special someone, and it usually works. *$$$; AE, MC, V; no checks; lunch Tues–Sat, dinner Tues–Sun, brunch Sun; full bar; reservations required; www.fouroaksrestaurant. com; about 2 miles north of Sunset Blvd.* &

Gardens / ★★☆

300 S DOHENY DR (INSIDE THE FOUR SEASONS HOTEL), LOS ANGELES; 310/273-2222 While breakfast here is power dining at its cell-phone-wielding best, Gardens is also a top choice for an elegant dinner, with chef Conny Andersson in the kitchen, excellent service in the dining room, and—thanks to generous space between the richly appointed tables—one of the most tranquil atmospheres in town. More like a European salon than a garden, the restaurant serves a rather small but carefully chosen menu. Expect dishes to change with the seasons; recent selections include lobster and avocado cucumber roll; tableside-seared Hudson Valley foie gras; and sea scallops alongside a salad of spinach, basil, and artichoke. Also count on richly conceived vegetable accompaniments: truffle flan and caramelized fennel with lobster vinaigrette dress up an already luscious butter-poached Maine lobster, while cheese soufflé and potato gratin, wild boar bacon, braised greens, and orange-honey-glazed carrots augment the rack of lamb. Pastry chef Donald Wressell has won the Grand Prix of pastry making, so look forward to sweets of a divine order, like hot passion fruit tart or warm devil's food pudding cake with pistachio ice cream. *$$$; AE, DC, DIS, JCB, MC, V; no checks; breakfast, lunch, dinner every day, brunch Sun; full bar; reservations recommended; www.fourseasons.com; just north of Burton Wy.* &

The Grill on the Alley / ★★☆

9560 DAYTON WY, BEVERLY HILLS; 310/276-0615 Here's a classic American restaurant with hearty, straightforward fare. Awash in woods, brass, and leather, this old-boys'-club spot is the choice of power-dining businessfolk, who feast here on huge plates of well-prepared steaks and chops and suck down perfectly mixed martinis. Although the ambience is heavy on testosterone, the classic grill tempts both sexes with traditional renditions of fresh oysters, plump crab cakes, a generous Caesar salad, and juicy porterhouse or New York steaks, with such tasty side dishes as creamed spinach, fried onions, steamed vegetables, and shoestring potatoes. Sunday night is prime rib night, and the restaurant hosts year-round clambakes. But any night is right to sample the delicious homemade rice pudding or the hot fudge brownie sundae. If the surroundings seem familiar, it might be because this restaurant served as the inspiration for the popular Daily Grill chain. *$$$; AE, DC, DIS, MC, V; no checks; lunch Mon–Sat, dinner every day; full bar; reservations required; off Wilshire Blvd.* &

Il Cielo / ★★

9018 BURTON WY, BEVERLY HILLS; 310/276-9990 Romance oozes through every room, patio, and garden at Il Cielo (the sky). Pasquale Vericella took this red-brick house on a tree-shaded street and created *un ambiente d'amore* in each of the four sweetly shaded areas. There's a front patio facing Burton Way; a rear patio complete with arbors, bowers, and a trickling lion's-mouth fountain; plus two interior rooms. Celebrities are especially fond of the place because they can slip in through the rear entrance just off the parking lot (Frank Sinatra was a regular). The food is Southern Italian and pleasantly light; especially good are tomato-and-basil bruschetta, porcini mushroom risotto, chicken Bolognese, *branzino al forno* (whole baked sea bass, filleted tableside), and heart-shaped lobster ravioli. *$$–$$$; AE, CB, DC, DIS, MC, V; checks OK; lunch, dinner Mon–Sat; full bar; reservations recommended; at N Wetherly Dr.* &

Kate Mantilini / ★★☆

9101 WILSHIRE BLVD, BEVERLY HILLS; 310/278-3699 Classic American cuisine is the focus at this eatery, where comfort foods like meat loaf, chicken potpies, crab cakes, and garlic rotisserie chicken reign supreme in a dining room marked with high ceilings, wooden booths, an open kitchen, and an enormous colorful mural of '40s-era boxers. In addition to seafood, steaks, sandwiches, and salads, there's a large selection of healthy alternatives, from skinless chicken breasts to turkey burgers. Winning side orders, including broccoli with hollandaise sauce, fresh sautéed spinach with garlic and Parmesan cheese, and huge baked potatoes with all the fixings, are meals in themselves. Such daring choices as frogs' legs and calf's brains—once the favorite of famed director Billy Wilder—also grace the lengthy and diverse menu. For those in search of late-night dining, the restaurant stays open until 2am on weekends. *$$; AE, DC, MC, V; no checks; breakfast, lunch, dinner every day, brunch Sun; full bar; reservations accepted for 6 or more; at Doheny Dr.* &

La Cachette / ★★★

10506 LITTLE SANTA MONICA BLVD, CENTURY CITY; 310/470-4992 Chef/owner Jean Francois Meteignier was already a local star by the time he opened La Cachette (the hideaway) in 1994. During his 10-year stint at L'Orangerie, he was recognized for four years running by the *Zagat Survey* for Best French Cuisine. Meteignier's lighter style of modern French cooking, favoring stocks and reductions over cream and butter, is served in two rather formal softly lit white dining rooms with comfortable banquettes and impressionist reproductions. Your meal might begin with foie gras with rhubarb-strawberry chutney and honey-ginger sauce, Maine lobster salad, or warm artichoke hearts with white truffle oil dressing. Representative main courses include roasted rack of lamb with a snappy tapenade and Dijon mustard, seared Alaskan black cod with orange and horseradish jus, and venison whose cabernet sauce is enriched with a touch of dark chocolate and brandied cherries. Heavenly desserts include a chocolate tart with brandied cherries, as well as baked Alaska with a black currant sauce, crusty on the outside and filled with vanilla ice cream and raspberry sorbet. The selection of more than 250 French and California wines, some in half bottles, is worth the trip in itself. *$$$; AE, DC, MC, V; no checks; lunch Mon–Fri, dinner every day; full bar; reservations recommended; www.lacachetterestaurant.com; between Beverly Glen Blvd and Overland Ave.* &

Lawry's the Prime Rib / ★★☆

100 N LA CIENEGA BLVD, BEVERLY HILLS; 310/652-2827 Lawry's is cooking from the very heart of America: a well-loved restaurant launched in 1938 and predicated on the simple pleasures of prime rib of beef carved tableside from a cart in the old English tradition. It's also a restaurant straight out of central casting, with a serving staff that's real friendly and who make sure your portion of beef is cooked the way you like it. With only three items on the menu, it's not hard to choose: it's either prime rib with Yorkshire pudding, lobster, or fish, including salmon and halibut—all of which include green salad dressed with Lawry's bottled Sherry French. Creamed spinach, creamed corn, and spuds both baked and mashed, slathered with creamery butter, arrive on the side. The prices are right, and everyone leaves with a satisfied smile. *$$; AE, MC, V; no checks; dinner every day; full bar; reservations recommended; east side of La Cienega Blvd, north of Wilshire Blvd.* &

Matsuhisa / ★★★☆

129 N LA CIENEGA BLVD, BEVERLY HILLS; 310/659-9639 Eating at Matsuhisa is an experience akin to having never eaten before—that is to say, having never *really* eaten before. We've never had anything as visually tempting and exciting to the palate as the little mouthfuls that chef Nobu Matsuhisa—who receives equal raves for his New York restaurant and six others worldwide—creates here. His encyclopedic menu, complete with annotations, covers virtually every type of fish available through local Japanese markets, along with some shipped in from Asia. Though the selection is overwhelming, what catapults each and every morsel into the realm of otherworldly gastronomy are Matsuhisa's delicate and perfectly balanced sauces. Whatever accompaniment your fish comes swimming in or braised with, it's invariably a perfect marriage, allowing the subtle flavors of the sea to harmonize with creative combinations from the earth. Try the shrimp in zingy pepper sauce, black cod in a miso sauce that redefines that trendy glaze, squid pasta, and the dish that may well exemplify Nobu's culinary approach —sea urchin wrapped in a *shiso* leaf and cooked tempura style. Make your reservations early, for Matsuhisa is popular with hard-core foodies and L.A. celebs—though the biggest names are often ushered through to private dining rooms. Matsuhisa also has a smaller version, Nobu, in Malibu (3835 Cross Creek Rd; 310/317-9140). *$$$; AE, MC, V; no checks; lunch Mon–Fri, dinner every day; beer and wine; reservations required; www.nobumatsuhisa.com; north of Wilshire Blvd.* &

Mr. Chow / ★★☆

344 N CAMDEN DR, BEVERLY HILLS; 310/278-9911 Mr. Chow is actually more famous for its celebrity clientele than for its upscale Chinese food. In fact, we've never been here when there wasn't an A-lister (L. L. Cool J, Goldie Hawn, Joe Pesci, Seal) dining beside us. Fortunately for everyone, mirrors are strategically placed along the walls so that rubbernecking is kept to a minimum. Considering the prices, it's fair to argue you're paying for more than great dim sum. Regardless, the quality is good, the style is rather '80s moderne, and the atmosphere is about as enjoyably insider-Hollywood as you can get. Bankable selections include delicious house-made garlic noodles—which on occasion the chef makes before diners' eyes—the absolutely sumptuous gambler's duck (crispy, ginger-laced duck atop steaming pancakes with plum sauce), and buttery black pepper lobster. Order for yourself instead of letting the waiter choose for the table (usually a more expensive gambit), and the combined food and scene will make it well worth the price. *$$; AE, DC, MC, V; no checks; lunch Mon–Fri, dinner every day; full bar; reservations required; north of Wilshire Blvd.* &

Nic's (and the Martini Lounge) / ★★☆

453 N CANON DR, BEVERLY HILLS; 310/550-5707 Larry Nicola (previously of Silver Lake's L.A. Nicola and downtown's Nicola) is the mastermind and chef behind Nic's restaurant and the adjoining Martini Lounge in Beverly Hills—perhaps his best endeavor yet. The lovely, lively restaurant, with fresh flowers everywhere, dramatic fiberglass lamps, and striking collectible contemporary art on the walls, is the backdrop for Nicola's seasonal American menu, with such temptations as gnocchi with morels and champagne cream, pan-seared filet mignon with blueberries, and the classic Nic's oysters sautéed with walnuts and garlic. A strong chocolate theme runs throughout the exceptional desserts, such as Nic's chocolate martini—shaved chocolate with crème de cacao, chocolate liqueur, and vodka served, of course, in a martini glass. As the name suggests, the bar may be the best place in town for a classy, retro cocktail—especially when live music jazzes up the room on Thursdays through Saturdays. *$$$; AE, DC, DIS, MC, V; no checks; dinner Mon–Sat; full bar; reservations recommended; www.nicsbeverlyhills.com; between Santa Monica Blvd and Brighton Wy.* &

Nouveau Café Blanc / ★★★☆

9777 LITTLE SANTA MONICA BLVD, BEVERLY HILLS; 310/888-0108 Though Chinois-trained chef/owner Tommy Harase is one of L.A.'s extremely talented chefs, his restaurant magically remains one of Beverly Hills's best-kept secrets. Harase opened his first place, Café Blanc, in East Hollywood and later relocated to this spare spot, where he continues to create his very personal version of French-Japanese cuisine. Nouveau Café Blanc is small (just 24 seats) and straightforward, with an all-white decor, a few pieces of art, and a sprinkling of fresh flowers. The only change over the years is the addition of a small but diverse wine list, all reasonably priced and selected to match Harase's cooking. His fragrant, intense soups and sorbets offer proof of his talents, and all of his food is light and clean, with pure yet delicate flavors. No one does better lobster or foie gras, both of which are often found on his seasonal, multicourse prix-fixe menus. If the coffee "jello," a delicate, flavorful confection infinitely better than its name can convey, is on the menu, take our advice: order it. *$$$; AE, DC, MC, V; no checks; lunch, dinner Tues–Sat; beer and wine; reservations recommended; between Wilshire Blvd and Linden Dr.* &

Peppone / ★★☆

11628 BARRINGTON CT, BRENTWOOD; 310/476-7379 Gianni Paoletti, the original chef and partner at Santa Monica's Valentino, went off on his own and has run Peppone now for some 30 years. It's a Hollywood insider hangout, with a large following of celebrities who are lured by both the food and the comfortable booths in a dark, romantic setting. Paoletti's Italian cuisine—from fresh artichokes in olive oil, garlic, and broth to pork-loin scaloppine, calf's liver Venetian style, and homemade tiramisu—is a tribute to his flamboyant character and passionate love of wine and food. The wine list is nothing short of spectacular, and very reasonably priced, owing to the great volume and foresight of Paoletti's purchases, with great French, Italian, and California wines from major vineyards and vintages. Peppone is popular among Westside locals but not widely known beyond, which keeps the crowds under control. *$$$; AE, DC, MC, V; no checks; dinner every day; full bar; reservations required; www.peppone.com; south of Sunset Blvd.* &

The Restaurant at Hotel Bel-Air / ★★★

 701 STONE CANYON RD, BEL AIR; 310/472-1211 There's no lovelier setting in Los Angeles than the secluded Hotel Bel-Air, surrounded by 12 acres of glorious gardens with a rustic stream. Some go for the formality of the dining room; others prefer the romance of the bougainvillea-draped garden terrace, with its heated stone floor. Named L.A.'s Most Romantic Restaurant by *Saveur* magazine in 2002, this elegant establishment serves a Mediterranean-inspired French-California cuisine to the hotel's international celebrity clientele and discerning L.A. diners. Most popular dishes on its eclectic menu include a lavish version of tortilla soup, pistachio-crusted rack of lamb, and delicate lemon soufflé pancakes. Dedicated gourmets will appreciate the restaurant's Table One, a private dining spot just off the kitchen, where six to eight diners can watch the chef prepare their seven-course dinner. There's nightly entertainment in the adjacent wood-paneled bar, and the hotel puts on a glorious afternoon tea. *$$$; AE, DC, DIS, JCB, MC, V; no checks; breakfast, lunch, dinner every day, brunch Sun; full bar; reservations recommended; about 1 mile north of Sunset Blvd.* &

Ruth's Chris Steak House / ★★★

224 S BEVERLY DR, BEVERLY HILLS; 310/859-8744 The constant crowds here are further proof (as if any is needed) that steak is back in a big way. A prime contender for the title of Best Steak House in Los Angeles, this Beverly Hills branch of a New Orleans beef eatery serves prime Midwestern, perfectly selected beef—New York strip, porterhouse, T-bone, rib-eye, filet mignon—all of which are masterfully cooked (and served in butter unless you request otherwise). The à la carte menu includes what many say are the best side dishes of any steak house in town, including terrific spinach, fries, and onion rings. For those who can still manage another bite, there's bread pudding for dessert, either chocolate or regular. *$$; AE, CB, DIS, MC, V; no checks; dinner every day; full bar; reservations required; www.ruthschris.com; south of Wilshire Blvd.* &

Spago / ★★★★☆

176 N CANON DR, BEVERLY HILLS; 310/385-0880 What Daniel is to New York, Spago is to Los Angeles. Ever since designer Barbara Lazaroff and superstar chef (and then-husband) Wolfgang Puck unveiled their Xanadu-like dining room in April 1997, it's been Los Angeles's defining restaurant and the hottest reservation around. Executive chef Lee Hefter, a veteran of Puck's Granita in Malibu, oversees the eclectic menu, which includes his widely loved roasted beet and goat cheese "layer cake"; delicious skate and shrimp with artichokes; and duck, either roasted Cantonese style with sweet-sour plums and ginger, or as a honey-lacquered breast with foie gras. Meats include tandoori-style grilled lamb or succulent caramelized veal chop. This is also where Puck explores his Austrian roots with selections called "Wolfgang's Childhood Favorites." If you've never tried *Wiener-schnitzel vom Kalb mit Kartoffeln und Vogersalat* (Wiener schnitzel with warm potato and mâche) or *Rindgulasch mit Spätzle* (beef stew with spaetzle), this is the place to do it. Austrian memoirs continue through the dessert menu, where *Kaiserschmarr* soufflé (pancakes) and *Apfelstrudel* (apple strudel) are likely to be listed along with delights such as a bittersweet chocolate glazed tart with caramel crème fraîche or a hot nectarine cobbler with caramel ice cream. *$$$–$$$$; AE, DC, DIS, MC, V; no checks; lunch Mon–Sat, dinner every day; full bar; reservations required; www.wolfgangpuck.com; north of Wilshire Blvd.* &

LODGINGS

Avalon Hotel / ★★★

9400 W OLYMPIC BLVD, BEVERLY HILLS; 310/277-5221 OR 800/535-4715 Headquartered in a 1949 apartment complex that Marilyn Monroe once called home, this 86-room gem radiates only-in-L.A. panache. Designer Kelly Wearstler has fused impeccable mid-20th-century style—Eames chairs, Noguchi tables, George Nelson bubble lamps—with nubby textiles, bold sherbet hues, and her own clean-lined designs. The result is a wildly successful retro-modern look that's at once fresh, fashion forward, and playfully nostalgic. The hotel fills a trio of period apartment houses. The '50s-style main building is the place to be for scenesters, while rooms in the Canon building, many of which have kitchenettes and/or patios, are quieter. All guests have easy access to the facilities, which include a sunny courtyard with a figure-eight pool and built-in cabanas, a fitness room, and an Atomic Age restaurant/bar named one of 2002's 50 best hotel restaurants by *Food & Wine*. Every room is spacious and restful, with comforts to satisfy even design-blind travelers: 27-inch TV with VCR, CD player, fax, high-speed connectivity, Frette linens, terry robes, and cool Philosophy toiletries. Rooms 240 through 244 include giant furnished terraces at no extra charge. Located in a lovely, leafy residential area, the Avalon is more laid-back and attitude-resistant than other chic boutiques. Still, expect a beautiful-people clientele from the fashion, advertising, and music worlds. *$$$$; AE, DC, JCB, MC, V; no checks; www.avalonbeverlyhills.com; at Canon Dr.* &

Beverly Hills Hotel & Bungalows / ★★★★

9641 SUNSET BLVD, BEVERLY HILLS; 310/276-2251 OR 800/283-8885 No hotel so embodies Hollywood glamour—and the 90210 zip code—like this one. Built in 1912, the legendary pink palace and its 12-acre grounds have hosted a slew of famous guests, from Rudolph Valentino to Elizabeth Taylor (who spent six of her honeymoons here) to Raquel Welch (reportedly "discovered" while lounging poolside) to John and Yoko to . . . you get the picture. L.A.'s most famous retreat was restored to its original glory in the early '90s, complete with banana-leaf wallpaper, vivid pink and moss hues, and flowering gardens. The 203 large, lavishly adorned rooms, suites, and bungalows are done in a swanky late-deco style. Modern amenities include two-line phones, CD players, VCRs, fax machines, bathrooms often large enough to live in, and butler service. Many rooms feature private patios, whirlpool tubs, kitchens, and/or dining rooms. Some—including all 21 bungalows—have private entrances. The Olympic-size pool and its in-demand cabanas—decked out with TV, fax, and direct-dial phones—continue to be ground zero for high-profile Hollywood. Afternoon tea is served in the Sunset Lounge, while the Fountain

Coffee Shop specializes in simple home cooking (refreshing in a luxury hotel). Don't miss the Dutch apple pancakes in the iconic Polo Lounge, still a haven for power brokers. *$$$$; AE, DC, JCB, MC, V; no checks; reservations@beverlyhillshotel. com; www.beverlyhillshotel.com; at Rodeo Dr.* &

Century Plaza Hotel & Spa / ★★★

2025 AVE OF THE STARS, CENTURY CITY; 310/277-2000 OR 800/228-3000 In early 2001, this high-profile hotel emerged from a monster renovation that added a smart new lobby, a signature restaurant, an all-new pool, and L.A.'s largest and grandest spa. Each stylishly contemporary, super-comfortable room features Westin's blissful Heavenly Bed; warm fruitwood furnishings; gorgeous textiles; a sizable work desk; and big closets holding terry robes. The sleek bathrooms are some of the city's best, with lustrous Italian tile, generous glass countertops, and a wealth of mirrors that make the large space feel even bigger. Westin Guest Office rooms add a multifunction printer/fax, an ergonomic desk chair, glare-free task lighting, a coffeemaker, late checkout, and more, for just a few dollars extra. And thanks to the crescent shape of the 727-room hotel, virtually all rooms are blessed with cityscape views. At an impressive 30,000 square feet, Spa Mystique—winner of *Self* magazine's 2002 Best Day Spa award—rises above its hotel-spa status with an epic menu of traditional and Asian treatments; hydrotherapy features; and a cutting-edge fitness center. The hotel's restaurant Breeze boasts a high-style interior and a California grill menu that emphasizes fresh seasonal ingredients. Service is less than personal at this mammoth, always-bustling hotel, but all the amenities you could want are at hand. *$$$$; AE, DC, DIS, E, JCB, MC, V; checks OK; www.westin.com; south of Olympic Blvd.* &

Four Seasons Hotel Los Angeles at Beverly Hills / ★★★★

300 S DOHENY DR, LOS ANGELES; 310/273-2222, 210/786-2227 OR 800/819-5053 The intimate, elegant Four Seasons is an excellent choice for guests in search of a world-class experience from a small-scale hotel. As expected from a hotel catering to a distinctively demanding—and impressively loyal—clientele, this 16-story beauty is known for its amenities and impeccable service. With 285 rooms and suites, it's actually not at all intimate—but it seems so, from the flower-filled, marble-dressed lobby to the cozy, Florentine-inspired restaurant to the overall residential feeling. The traditionally styled, pastel-hued guest rooms feature extra-stuffed Sealy mattresses with sumptuous linens and pillows, VCRs, CD players, desk-level inputs with high-speed access, unfurnished balconies with French doors, and superb bathrooms with abundant counter space and a vanity TV. The splendid fourth-floor deck has urban panoramic views, an inviting lap pool, a magical above-the-city ambience, a poolside grill, and a view-endowed fitness center. Additional amenities include a pampering, 4,000-square-foot spa with sauna and steam, a high-tech business center, a terrific bar notable for ace martinis, complimentary limo service within a 5-mile radius, the gorgeous Weatherly Garden for unforgettable weddings, and unparalleled concierge service. The elegant and justifiably acclaimed Gardens restaurant (see review) offers a seasonal menu in a casual-meets-formal indoor/outdoor setting. *$$$$; AE, DC, DIS, E, JCB, MC, V; no checks; www.fourseasons.com; at Burton Wy.* &

Hotel Bel-Air / ★★★★

701 STONE CANYON RD, BELAIR; 310/472-1211 OR 800/648-4097 The Hotel Bel-Air is L.A.'s most romantic and exclusive hotel, and probably its best. Stunning mission-style architecture, pastoral ambience, and superb amenities give even locals reason to pony up for an ultra-expensive—but unparalleled—escape. With just 92 rooms and suites spread over 11½ magically manicured acres, the hotel has the air of a golden-age-of-Hollywood fantasy estate—one where white swans float in glassy ponds, fountains bubble at every turn, and cobbled paths wind past lush bougainvillea, azaleas, and birds-of-paradise. Shaded arcades, wrought-iron details, and intimate courtyards heighten the enchantment and romance, as do the sweetly appointed guest rooms. Each is unique—some have whirlpool tubs, many have private patios and wood-burning fireplaces—but all boast faultless country French decor and high-tech amenities that include VCRs, CD players, and dedicated fax lines. Service is beyond reproach—you won't ever hear "no" here. The pool is heated to 82°F year-round and fully attended. The well-equipped gym is always open. Don't be surprised if you spot world dignitaries or high-profile celebs lounging in the wood-paneled bar or dining in the consistently excellent Restaurant at Hotel Bel-Air; it's one of the cognoscenti's L.A. favorites, especially for Sunday brunch. *$$$$; AE, DC, DIS, E, JCB, MC, V; checks OK; reservations@hotelbelair.com; www.hotelbelair.com; a mile north of Sunset Blvd.* &

Hotel Del Capri / ★☆

10587 WILSHIRE BLVD, WESTWOOD; 310/474-3511 OR 800/44-HOTEL Hugely popular with a repeat clientele, this homey, older motel complex is an affordable oasis sandwiched between Westwood's chic high-rise condos. The low-rise main building surrounds a sunny, nicely landscaped courtyard with pool; there are also rooms in an adjacent tower. The spacious, well-tended rooms are short on high-tech amenities (think old-style push-button phones, fluorescent bathroom lighting) but perfectly comfortable nonetheless. More than half are one- and two-bedroom suites with a living room, sleeper sofa, and kitchenette. Owned by the same family since 1954, the Del Capri is well known for its friendly staff, who gladly assist with travel plans or arrange for a free shuttle to UCLA or Westwood Village. There's no on-site dining or room service, but a simple yet satisfactory complimentary continental breakfast can be delivered to your room or served poolside, and more than 30 restaurants have delivery arrangements with the hotel. Although there's no laundry service, coin-op machines are available; parking is free. Discounts off the already-low rates abound, so inquire about price breaks for AAA members, seniors, UCLA grads, military members, and the like. *$$; AE, DC, E, MC, V; checks OK if mailed in advance; www.hoteldelcapri.com; at Westholme Ave.*

Maison 140 / ★★☆

140 S LASKY DR, BEVERLY HILLS; 310/281-4000 OR 800/432-5444 Outfitted in an audaciously sexy Franco-Mandarin style by hot hotel designer Kelly Wearstler, Maison 140 breaks all design rules with a brazen and glorious East-meets-modern mix of art, color, and design. A lipstick-red door is the only hint to what lies within, where narrow black-on-black hallways lead to colorful rooms that are the ultimate in Valley of the Dolls chic. Most rooms are pied-à-terre tiny—best for short stays and light packers. Smart design uses available space well: platform beds have drawers underneath, and TVs are wall-mounted to free up floors and countertops. Every room features a stunning blend of chinoiserie textiles and wall coverings, original 1930s details, '60s-modern accents, and found objects from around the globe, from baroque headboards to Asian figure lamps. Luxury touches include Frette linens, CD player, and kimono-style robes; bathrooms have been beautifully redone. The Grande King rooms have no space problems, and even feature VCRs and good workstations. Facilities are limited to a seductive lounge, Bar Noir (whose signature cocktail is the champagne-and-Chambord French Kiss, *naturellement*), and a fitness room. Continental breakfast is included, and valet and concierge services are available. The residential location couldn't be better, with Beverly Hills's Golden Triangle a walk away. *$$$; AE, DC, JCB, MC, V; no checks; www.maison140beverlyhills.com; between Wilshire and Santa Monica Blvds.*

Peninsula Beverly Hills / ★★★★

9882 S SANTA MONICA BLVD, BEVERLY HILLS; 310/551-2888 OR 800/462-7899 This refined award-winner is the Hotel Bel-Air's only serious contender for L.A.'s finest hotel. A secluded, gardenlike oasis in the heart of Beverly Hills, the gracious property is impeccable from end to end. Formality begins in the elegant, cobbled crescent drive and continues through the marbled lobby and the English-garden-reminiscent Living Room—where afternoon tea is the best in town—then proceeds into the clubby mahogany-paneled bar, popular with CAA agents and their clients. Done in a lavish French Renaissance style, the 196 guest rooms are large and luxury laden, with beautifully made beds wearing Frette, bedside controls for everything (lighting, climate, "Do Not Disturb," and so on), executive work desks with fax, big Italian marble baths with large soaking tub and separate shower, VCRs, Bose radios, and 24-hour personal valets. Villa suites also feature gas fireplaces, kitchens, CD players, and individual security systems. Amenities are even more impressive: the 3,500-square-foot spa and fitness center is one of L.A.'s finest, with hydrotherapy treatments and high-tech cardio machines. The divine fifth-floor garden features a 60-foot lap pool; a whirlpool spa; cabanas with TV, fax, and Internet access; and cafe serving spa cuisine. The Belvedere is one of L.A.'s most celebrated restaurants (see review). *$$$$; AE, DC, DIS, E, JCB, MC, V; checks OK; pbh@peninsula.com; www.peninsula.com; at Wilshire Blvd.* &

Raffles L'Ermitage Beverly Hills / ★★★☆

9291 BURTON WY, BEVERLY HILLS; 310/278-3344 OR 800/800-2113 Stellar service and unparalleled in-room features make this forward-thinking hotel a shining star. It's serene and intimate, with 124 enormous, superbly decorated rooms done in a spare, Japanese *ryokan*-inspired minimalist style that traditionalists may find too austere. The custom maple furniture is mostly built-ins, from the low platform bed to the armoire hiding the bulk of the incomparable technology: 40-inch TV, CD/DVD player, Bose tuner and speakers, and fax/printer/copier. An all-in-one bedside "smart" control panel remembers your lighting and climate preferences. Five three-line phones include a cell you can tote around town. The work desk is large, seating is copious and comfortable, carpeting is Berber, and fabrics tend to tailored silk. The enormous bathrooms feature a soaking tub, a shower for two, cotton and terry robes, and more towels than you could use in a week. The beyond-impeccable service includes flexible check-in/checkout and a refreshing philosophy that eschews nickel-and-diming. Freebies include local and 800 calls and CD and DVD lending. There's a rooftop fitness center—whose staff is always ready with bottled water—a petite but lovely pool with cabanas, and the RafflesAmrita Spa for personal pampering. The small, very beautiful restaurant Jaan (Sanskrit for "bowl") garners consistent praise for its stellar Indochine fusion cuisine. *$$$$; AE, DC, JCB, MC, V; no checks; info@lermitagehotel.com; www.lermitagehotel.com; west of Doheny Dr.* &

St. Regis Los Angeles / ★★★★

2055 AVE OF THE STARS, CENTURY CITY; 310/277-6111 OR 877/ST-REGIS
Everything is just right at this smashing ultra-luxury hotel, from the gracefully appointed, almost masculine lobby to the sumptuously detailed accommodations and superb service. Rooms are larger than most competitors', and boast trendproof traditional-goes-contemporary decor in rich tobacco and creamy mustard hues, a sitting area, an executive leather-top work desk, and floor-to-ceiling windows with balconies and panoramic views. California kings give tall folks an extra foot of length, and everybody benefits from 300-count Frette linens and bedside controls for everything. The state-of-the-art phone system can link you to anyone from in-room dining to the airlines in one touch. Additional perks include VCRs, DVD and CD players, and high-speed connectivity. The marble-and-mahogany baths boast deep soaking tubs and separate showers. Set back from Century City's main drag, the tower is serene and ultra-elegant—not jeans-and-T-shirts territory (although the unflappable staff is unlikely to blink no matter what you wear). Off the wood-paneled, Oriental-carpeted lobby is the St. Regis Bar (modeled after New York's landmark King Cole Bar), presided over by a stunning Goya-inspired mural. Encore restaurant sets a magnificent scene for indoor/outdoor Provençal dining. There's a classic European spa; a view-endowed health club featuring plasma TV screens with email access; and fully wired poolside cabanas. Grand Luxe guests also benefit from round-the-clock butler service. *$$$$; AE, DC, DIS, E, JCB, MC, V; checks OK; www.stregis.com; between Santa Monica and Olympic Blvds.* &

W Los Angeles / ★★★

930 HILGARD AVE, WESTWOOD; 310/208-8765 OR 877/946-8357 Capitalizing on the boutique-hotel craze, corporate giant Starwood (the folks behind Westin and Sheraton) has done a terrific job of reinventing the chain hotel for a lively, style-conscious crowd. The former Westwood Marquis has built-in advantages: an all-suite configuration, two gorgeous acres of greenery, and great '60s architectural detailing.

The open, fluid lobby feels like a stage set, with concrete floors and polished fixtures, offset with sumptuous textiles—plush velvet, hammered silks—in rich colors. The garden features a pool and cabanas set up for massages and wired for Web surfing. The Away Spa is feng shui perfection, inspiring relaxation at every turn. All 258 spacious suites boast clean-lined furnishings in rich African wood, accented with grays and plums, plus Westin's celestial Heavenly Bed, the ultimate in hotel-bed comfort. Extras include a monster work/dining table; two 27-inch TVs; two CD players; a VCR; and the best minibars in town, complete with Gummi Bears and Slinkies. Bathrooms are spacious but otherwise unremarkable. Nuevo Latino restaurant Mojo is a superchic scene, while Whiskey Blue, the bar from nightlife impresario Rande Gerber (Mr. Cindy Crawford), is even hotter. The beautiful staff is well intentioned but far shy of faultless. Still, we'd stay here again in a Hollywood minute. *$$$$; AE, DC, DIS, JCB, MC, V; checks OK; www.whotels.com; north of Wilshire Blvd.* &

Hollywood and West Hollywood

RESTAURANTS

Ago / ★★★

8478 MELROSE AVE, WEST HOLLYWOOD; 323/655-6333 With Robert De Niro, Ridley Scott, Miramax's Weinstein brothers, and other heavy hitters backing this supertrendy Italian restaurant, it's no surprise that it's an industry hangout. In fact, the stylish split-level dining room, with its open kitchen, brick wood-burning oven, and sleek bar, offers the perfect balance of visible yet intimate dining—a plus for the high-profile crowd who like a little of both. But executive chef (and partner) Agostino Sciandri, formerly of Toscana, and his inventive Italian cuisine are what truly make this restaurant a favorite. While Sciandri's fare melds influences from Tuscany, Emilia-Romagna, and Liguria, his straightforward execution is sublime in such dishes as baby artichoke salad drizzled with olive oil and topped with shaved Parmesan or his herbed Tuscan chicken with spinach and perfect roast potatoes. And the man knows how to do risotto; the wild mushroom variation is respectfully al dente and pure heaven. But the veal ravioli with wild mushroom sauce and grilled salmon topped with a smart lemon-caper sauce are also good enough to ease the pain of the sure-to-be-hefty dinner bill. The dessert tray varies from day to day. If there's tiramisu, take it. *$$$; AE, DC, MC, V; no checks; lunch Mon–Fri, dinner every day; full bar; reservations recommended; at La Cienega Blvd.* &

Alto Palato / ★★

755 N LA CIENEGA BLVD, WEST HOLLYWOOD; 310/657-9271 While this modern trattoria's high ceilings, colorful artwork, and sleek two-level design are in keeping with the neighborhood's fashionable art galleries and boutique furniture stores, the cuisine at Alto Palato is strictly classic Italian. Chef Fredy Escobar delivers some of the best pizza this side of Rome; try one slice of his crisp, thin-crusted, wood-fired pies and you'll be a believer. Purists love the Margherita pizza's zesty sauce, fresh tomatoes, and smoke-infused crust; others may love the smoked salmon and goat cheese version. There's life beyond designer pizza, though, and it comes in such dishes as owner Danilo Terribili's own family recipe for chicken cacciatore in a fragrant white wine vinegar, rosemary, garlic, and anchovy sauce. Come in on a Wednesday night for live jazz and authentic regional cooking, a sliced roasted veal shank with white polenta from the Piedmont, wild boar stew in Chianti sauce from Tuscany, and other delicacies you'd be hard-pressed to find outside Italy. With the regional menu, you get 40 percent off the price of your wine. *$$–$$$; AE, DC, MC, V; no checks; dinner every day; full bar; reservations recommended; www.alto-palato. com; between Melrose Ave and Santa Monica Blvd.* &

Angelini Osteria / ★★★

7313 BEVERLY BLVD, LOS ANGELES; 323/297-0070 Lovers of fine Italian cooking who revered the now-closed Rex il Ristorante can enjoy more affordable osteria cooking by Rex's superstar chef Gino Angelini. His chic, airy little box of a storefront, though crowded and noisy, is packin' 'em in. Even the two narrow blond wood dining bars at the back of the room, designed for solo customers, are willingly occupied by couples, thankful just to get in on a busy night. Angelini Osteria serves food that is light, yet rich with flavorful Italian cheeses, old-country meat ragus, and the freshest vegetables and salad greens. Start with an antipasto of red beets and creamy burrata cheese, or try the very Italian primi of warm tripe with tomatoes and cuttlefish. Continue with a small pasta course of delectable ravioli stuffed with Swiss chard and ricotta, or the tantalizing lasagne verde with a rich beef and veal ragu. If the *branzino* (Italian striped sea bass) is on the menu, try this juicy whole fish roasted in sea salt. For a rare treat, order the thinly sliced *fegato alla veneziana* (calf's liver with caramelized onions). Other menu standouts include grilled Sonoma duck breast, veal chop alla Milanese, and Saturday night's special *porchetta*, a gargantuan leg of pork from the wood burning oven, sliced tableside. The beauty of chef Angelini's light nueva cucina is that even after three courses, you'll still have room for the most popular house dessert, *crustata di marmellata*—a lattice-crust tart filled with luscious fruit jam. *$$–$$$; AE, DC, MC, V; no checks; lunch Tues–Fri, dinner Tues–Sun; beer and wine; reservations recommended; north side of Beverly Blvd at Poinsettia St.* &

Arnie Morton's of Chicago / ★★☆

435 S LA CIENEGA BLVD, LOS ANGELES (AND BRANCHES); 310/246-1501 Morton's is generally considered to be the best steak house in Chicago, and the L.A. outposts of the national chain are equally reputed. The kitchen of namesake Arnie Morton—father of Hard Rock owner Peter Morton (who owns a different style of Morton's, on Melrose in West Hollywood)—serves truly outstanding cuts of meat, along with expertly prepared cocktails and appropriately paired wines in a masculine (leather, brass, wood) setting. But perhaps the most enjoyable aspect of a redmeat rendezvous here (aside from the dinner itself) is the wait staff's four-minute presentation, during which they wheel out a cart teeming with Saran-wrapped cuts of beef and explain each one and its optional preparations. (Usually there's an enormous, squirming lobster in there, too.) The overwhelming—and unintentionally humorous—display falls somewhere between a flight attendant's safety instructions and a QVC sales pitch. Invariably, though, the result is an excellent huge cut of beef, perfectly prepared; it's served with heaping portions of spuds, spinach, and corn.

Expect to pay handsomely for the honor of inhaling all this protein, and to leave very well fed. A second Morton's of Chicago, with evening shuttle service to Staples Center, serves an identical menu downtown (735 S Figueroa St; 213/553-4566); and the brand new Burbank outpost is convenient to studios and valley residents (3400 W Olive Ave; 818/238-0424). *$$$; AE, DC, MC, V; no checks; dinner every day; full bar; reservations recommended; www.mortons.com; 1 long block north of Wilshire Blvd.* &

Cobras & Matadors / ★☆

7615 W BEVERLY BLVD, LOS ANGELES; 323/932-6178 In the south of Spain, where tapas were born, they don't usually make a whole meal of these tempting little appetizers. But the groups of otherwise hip twentysomething diners who crowd around Cobras & Matadors' brown-paper-covered tables could care less. They just keep on ordering little plates of olive-oil-rich octopus morsels, tiny fried fish, tortilla (the Spanish egg and potato pie), lentils with ham, mushrooms and polenta, and iron pots of mussels with chorizo—about 20 possible selections in all. There are a few main courses, mostly meats, on the single-sheet menu, but when they come already cut up for sharing, it's hard to tell them from tapas. Count on ordering at least four little plates per person for the table. If you need more, just reorder. Despite the constant hugger-mugger of this jammed little storefront, the wait staff is patient and quick on the trigger. The space—formerly home to sleek Boxer—still eschews a liquor license, but welcomes BYO for a modest corkage fee. If you purchase from the restaurant-owned Spanish wine shop next door, you'll have the perfect accompaniment to your meal and won't pay for corkage. *$$; MC, V; no checks; dinner every day; no alcohol; reservations recommended; at Stanley Ave.* &

Dan Tana's / ★★

9071 SANTA MONICA BLVD, WEST HOLLYWOOD; 310/275-9444 Dan Tana's remains one of L.A.'s most favored Italian restaurants, still going strong in its fourth decade. At a restaurant so steeped in tradition, it's not surprising that chef Neno Mladenovic has been in the kitchen over 15 years. But with the exception of a classic Caesar salad, steaks considered by many to be L.A.'s finest, and traditional veal dishes, food isn't the thing at Tana's as much as the New York speakeasy atmosphere, which attracts a celebrity-heavy clientele out for an old-fashioned meal and a good time. Chianti bottles hang in groups of three from the high ceiling, and basketball jerseys from former Los Angeles Lakers Magic Johnson, Vlade Divac, and Jerry West, framed and autographed, hang on the walls. The bar is packed and noisy, and there's always a wait for a table. Service is professional—more than a few of the waiters have been here nearly since opening day—if a bit rushed. Don't leave without sharing a rich, creamy tiramisu. *$$$; AE, DC, DIS, MC, V; no checks; dinner every day; full bar; reservations required; between Doheny Dr and Robertson Blvd.* &

Dar Maghreb / ★★

7651 SUNSET BLVD, WEST HOLLYWOOD; 323/876-7651 The name means "Moroccan house," and dining here is very much like being invited into the home of a wealthy Moroccan. Once you enter through the strikingly ornate and massive brass doors with intricate Islamic designs, you're greeted by a host clad in a *djellaba,* the traditional Moroccan garment. It's an opulent setting, complete with atrium and fountain; long, narrow dining rooms with high ceilings; and belly dancers who undulate through the restaurant to the strains of loud music. Salmon, *m'choui* (lamb shoulder), and duck are often available as specials, and can be incorporated into the regular menu, which features a seam-splitting six-course prix-fixe dinner, eaten primarily with your fingers. Highlights include *b'stilla*—an airy pastry filled with chicken, almonds, and eggs, topped with powdered sugar and cinnamon—lemon chicken with olives, several vegetable "salads" scooped up with dense Moroccan bread, and savory couscous. An overflowing basket of fruit serves as dessert, but most diners are too stuffed to do more than nibble a few token grapes. *$$$; DC, MC, V; no checks; dinner every day; full bar; reservations recommended; www.dar maghrebrestaurant.com; east of Fairfax, on the corner of Stanley Ave.* &

Diaghilev / ★★☆

1020 N SAN VICENTE BLVD, WEST HOLLYWOOD; 310/854-1111 When a special occasion calls for a big night out, make a reservation at this elegant eatery named after famed Russian impresario Serge de Diaghilev and located in the Wyndham Bel Age hotel. Gracious Dimitri Dimitrov will greet you like a long-lost relative, whisking you through the ornate dining room to a table adorned with fine china and stemware. As piano and harp music plays in the background, you and your companions can get in the opulent mood with a taste of caviar and a shot of fine vodka while you decide what to select from the Franco-Russian menu. Start with the borscht, made with either red or yellow beets and served with flaky *pirozhki,* or a traditional Russian appetizer like the beef-and-rice-stuffed cabbage rolls, then move on to such main courses as chicken Kiev with black truffles and a rich port wine sauce, or a sautéed fillet of sturgeon with caviar. While an evening at this exquisite establishment can be expensive, it offers a refined dining experience not often found in Los Angeles. *$$$; AE, DC, DIS, JCB, MC, V; no checks; dinner Tues–Sat; full bar; reservations required; just south of Sunset Blvd.* &

The Ivy / ★★☆
The Ivy at the Shore / ★★☆

113 N ROBERTSON BLVD, LOS ANGELES; 310/274-8303 / 1541 OCEAN AVE, SANTA MONICA; 310/393-3113 Attracting everyone from big-shot Hollywood agents to big-name celebrities, this trendy restaurant is a longtime Hollywood hangout, where Julia Roberts has been known to drop by for the fantastic (though ridiculously priced) chopped salad and Tori Spelling is said to prefer the lime chicken. Aside from the fanfare and the constant parade of arriving Rolls-Royces and Mercedes sedans, the atmosphere is charming, especially along the front outdoor patio, where a white picket fence encloses comfy chintz seating and schmoozing power diners. The American fare is just as its clientele likes it: diverse and expensive, with such selections as sweet and spicy corn chowder, signature crab cakes, homey meat loaf, blackened shrimp, or Southern-style crisp fried chicken. The sitcom star at the table next to you may skip dessert, but if your goal isn't to share dress sizes with Calista Flockhart, try the pecan and praline square topped with ice

cream and butterscotch or fudge sauce, the warm and gooey fruit crumbles, or the homemade chocolate chip cookies. The restaurant's sister eatery, Ivy at the Shore, offers a similar country-inn-like ambience, though chances are you'll have to settle for views of the Pacific instead of celebrity sightings. *$$$; AE, CB, DC, DIS, MC, V; no checks; lunch, dinner every day, brunch Sun; full bar; reservations recommended; south of Beverly Blvd (the Ivy); near Colorado Ave (the Ivy at the Shore).* &

Jitlada / ★★★

5233½ SUNSET BLVD, HOLLYWOOD; 323/667-9809 For more than 25 years, Jitlada has been home to some of the best, most authentic, and spiciest Thai food to be found in the City of Angels. Though in a dicey section of Hollywood, it's the favorite of the local Thai community, who eschew many of the slicker places around town in favor of the great food served here in two drab, incongruously furnished rooms within a mini-mall. This is spicy stuff, to be sure; the brave or foolish can even request extra chiles, while the saner might want a Thai beer (Amarit or Singha) to cool the fire. Of course, they've got excellent versions of *mee krob* and Thai toast, but try the curry or the Thai-style catfish in chili sauce. *$; AE, DIS, MC, V; no checks; lunch, dinner Tues–Sun; beer and wine; reservations not necessary; between Western and Normandie Aves.* &

La Bohème / ★★

8400 SANTA MONICA BLVD, WEST HOLLYWOOD; 323/848-2360 An unlikely mix of Left Bank Paris and a Tuscan country villa, Bohème is the work of Kozo Hasegawa, one of Japan's flashiest restaurateurs. To make the otherwise cavernous room a bit more intimate, torches glow inside the enormous fireplace, and tapestries and fabrics drape the walls. Tables set well apart fill the middle of the floor, and a row of curtained, wood-paneled leather booths lines the wall across from the fireplace. Upstairs, a narrow, catwalklike construction holds more tables, and a dumbwaiter at one end carries up drinks from the ground-floor bar. The feeling is dramatic and theatrical, a bit like where the Addams Family might go to celebrate a special occasion. The menu sometimes leans toward bizarre combinations of ingredients, but if you stick to simple dishes, such as a zesty classic Caesar salad, fresh oysters, crisp fried calamari, delicately seared tuna tataki, filet mignon, or the chef's signature warm chocolate soufflé cake, you'll find happiness in the midst of one of L.A.'s more eccentric settings. *$$$; AE, DC, DIS, MC, V; no checks; dinner every day; full bar; reservations recommended; www.calendarlive. com/cafelaboheme; between La Cienega Blvd and Sweetzer Ave.* &

Le Dome / ★★★

8720 SUNSET BLVD, WEST HOLLYWOOD; 310/659-6919 Power lunch is such a way of life at this restaurant that magazines have actually published guides to which producers and which agents sit where on a regular basis. Le Dome functions as a French bistro, with a menu that's heavy with salads for the perennially diet-conscious regulars along with some very substantial bistro dishes for those who could care less if they fit into a designer dress come Oscar night. Despite the celeb-heavy crowd, the cooking is pleasantly egalitarian—cassoulet, tender leg of lamb, a healthy grilled chicken, fine french fries, hearty calf's liver, warm duck salad, a memorable tarte Tatin. There's a view of the city spread out like a string of pearls against the neck of night. Or something like that. *$$; AE, CB, DC, MC, V; no checks; lunch Mon–Fri, dinner Mon–Sat; full bar; reservations required; south side of Sunset Blvd, west of La Cienega Blvd.* &

Les Deux Café / ★★

1638 N LAS PALMAS AVE, HOLLYWOOD; 323/465-0509 Wander through Grant's parking lot in an unprepossessing section of Hollywood and you'll find the unmarked front entrance to this ultrahip French bistro, where proprietress Michele Lamy serves up French fare to Hollywood top directors and stars who rarely jaunt east of La Cienega. Guests dine on the charming garden patio, which embodies casual glamour and romance, or indoors in the woodsy 1902 Craftsman house dining room. While most of the clientele is here for the scene and the occasional live entertainment, the cuisine shouldn't be overlooked. Don't miss such starters as osetra caviar with delicate fingerling potatoes, or the alluring foie gras terrine with fig compote. Entrees such as a saffron-laced bouillabaisse, *loup de mer en papillote* with artichokes and tomato concassée, or succulent rack of lamb will make it easy to forget who's at the table next to you. For dessert, try some of the delicate ice creams and sorbets—rose petal ice cream, for one—or a rich little pot de crème or dreamy fruit tart. Or order the sinfully delicious chocolate fondant with ice cream. *$$$; AE, MC, V; no checks; lunch Mon–Fri, dinner Mon–Sat; full bar; reservations recommended; at Sunset Blvd.*

L'Orangerie / ★★★☆

903 N LA CIENEGA BLVD, WEST HOLLYWOOD; 310/652-9770 Housed in gleaming multimillion-dollar quarters on La Cienega and lapped in the formality of truly upscale fine dining rooms, L'Orangerie is the most opulent and certainly the most formal and expensive French restaurant in Los Angeles. The decor is country-garden romantic, with a center atrium courtyard, sumptuous floral displays, and trellises, and you'll be glad you dressed up and brought your special-occasion manners. Acclaimed for years for its classic French cuisine, the restaurant surprised many when its newest chef, Christophe Emé, vowed to bring back the nouvelle approach: cutting out butter and cream in favor of natural juices and emulsions. But Emé's menu still features such riches as Petrossian caviar with blinis and lemon coulis ($105), or escargots from Burgundy with traditional garlic-parsley sauce. There are beautifully plated and interesting combinations, like rotisserie veal chop with morels, roasted squab with macaroni gratin, and grilled tuna with clams and asparagus. The nightly prix-fixe six-course Menu Royale might feature a main course of prized Kobe beef. And old-timers will be happy to note that L'Orangerie's signature starter of egg and caviar served in the egg shell, as well as the beloved thin apple tart dessert, still grace the menu. The wine list features 500 selections from France and the United States. *$$$; AE, MC, V; no checks; dinner Tues–Sun; full bar; reservations recommended; www.orangerie.com; south of Santa Monica Blvd.* &

Lucques / ★★★☆

8474 MELROSE AVE, WEST HOLLYWOOD; 323/655-6277 Take Caroline Styne, former manager of trendy Jones Hollywood, and Suzanne Goin, the executive chef from Campanile, mix them in a romantically minimalist space-with-patio that used to be the carriage house for the Harold Lloyd estate, and the result is Lucques, a restaurant that intentionally eschews Hollywood flash to focus on serving intensely flavored food with staying power. Every meal at Lucques (say Luke with a French accent) begins with the dark, pungent Provençal olives that give the place its name and arrive with other savory nibbles soon after you sit down. The menu features the sort of casually satisfying and inventive French-Mediterranean food that matches the SoCal lifestyle to perfection—a heavenly soup of tomato confit with crème fraîche; a clever warm salad of suckling pig and peaches; half a grilled chicken dressed up with corn flan, figs, arugula, and proscuitto; ricotta ravioli with summer squash, Gruyère, and almond pesto. The cooking is rich enough to discourage dessert, but at least try something to share, like the nutty meringue-cream dacquoise updated with the refreshing tang of rhubarb compote. There's even a cheese course with each selection, served at its peak of ripeness. Here's a restaurant that stays open late, so you can drop in for a light bar menu after 10pm. The scene crackles in what has been, since opening night, a restaurant of the moment. *$$–$$$; AE, MC, V; no checks; lunch Tues–Sat, dinner Tues–Sun; full bar; reservations required; east of La Cienega Blvd.* &

Morton's / ★★⯪

8764 MELROSE AVE, WEST HOLLYWOOD; 310/276-5205 From hosting the *Vanity Fair* Oscars party to Madonna's post–MTV Music Video Awards bash, this restaurant is a Hollywood powerhouse, especially on Monday nights, when the showbiz crowd arrives in full force. Owned by Hard Rock Cafe co-creator Peter Morton and his twin sister, Pam (their father is Arnie Morton, as in Arnie Morton's of Chicago steak houses), this stunning restaurant boasts high ceilings with skylights, big paintings, and lots of greenery—though chances are you'll be too busy watching the action to appreciate the decor. The classic American grill food is top-notch, starting with an impeccable Caesar salad, or better yet the heavenly endive salad, or a spicy shrimp and black bean quesadilla, then moving on to such entrees as the health-conscious free-range lime chicken with crisp shoestring potatoes, a well-prepared filet mignon, or grilled Alaskan halibut with fennel, fava bean, and white corn fricassee. Desserts are divine, with diners currently swooning over the rich banana beignets. *$$$; AE, DC, DIS, MC, V; no checks; lunch Mon–Fri, dinner Mon–Sat; full bar; reservations recommended; at Robertson Blvd.* &

Musso & Frank Grill / ★★⯪

6667 HOLLYWOOD BLVD, HOLLYWOOD; 323/467-7788 Everyone from F. Scott Fitzgerald to Frank Sinatra has dined and drank (and often been drunk) at this classic Hollywood landmark restaurant. Dating back to 1919, Musso & Frank is reminiscent of bygone glamorous dining with its enormous dining room of dark wood, red booths, and career waiters, many of whom have been around since the Kennedy era. Though the retro restaurant serves breakfast all day, if you come for its famous flannel cakes (pancakes) you must do so by 3pm. The novella-length menu features every old-fashioned dish imaginable, from shrimp cocktail, short ribs, chicken potpie, and an open-face prime rib sandwich to steak, grilled liver and onions, creamed spinach, macaroni and cheese, and peas and carrots. Unfortunately, prices are at a premium for nostalgic dining and everything is served à la carte. But when all's said and done, it's worth the expense. The food may not be the best in town, but the atmosphere—and, some argue, the martinis—are definitely contenders. *$$; AE, DC, MC, V; no checks; breakfast, lunch, dinner Tues–Sat; full bar; reservations recommended; east of Highland Ave.* &

Off Vine / ★★

6263 LELAND WY, HOLLYWOOD; 323/962-1900 Tucked into a side street and enclosed by a towering wooden fence, this Craftsman-style bungalow stands out as a beacon of country charm in the midst of gritty Hollywood street life. It's a favorite luncheon option for nearby Paramount Pictures employees, but the only clue to the oasis within is the valet out front and the parade of sunglasses-sporting movers and shakers on their way in and out. On a typical sunny California day, lunch or brunch on the bougainvillea-curtained porch or patio is L.A. at its most civilized. Despite the Hollywood connection, you don't have to be "somebody" get friendly, attentive service. In the evening, diners gather inside at tables dispersed within the little house that's accented by hardwood floors, cheerful art, and a blazing fireplace. The unpretentious but extensive menu features favorite foods like house-made soups, a Chinese chicken salad large enough to feed a small family, filet mignon with shiitake mushroom–cabernet sauce, and vegetarian lasagne; for dessert, choose between chocolate, raspberry, and Grand Marnier soufflés. *$$; AE, DC, DIS, MC, V; no checks; lunch Mon–Fri, dinner every day, brunch Sat–Sun; beer and wine; just east of Vine St, south of Sunset Blvd.* &

Orso / ★★

8706 W 3RD ST, WEST HOLLYWOOD; 310/274-7144 Although it's overlooked by many, this noisy, affable, and very reasonably priced restaurant is popular with celebs who linger on the surprisingly intimate and romantic outdoor patio concealed behind a set of stucco walls and an almost overwhelming forest of ficus trees. The Northern Italian menu includes crisp-as-a-cracker pizzas, classic pastas (no one makes a better farfalle with smoked salmon), and pride-of-the-house seafood. An added bonus: Orso is very popular during the day with internists from Cedars-Sinai hospital across the street. If you choke on a chicken bone, there'll be lots of physicians to give you a Heimlich and then send you a bill for it. *$; AE, MC, V; no checks; lunch, dinner every day; full bar; reservations required; www.orsorestaurant.com; 2 blocks east of Robertson Blvd.* &

The Palm / ★★★

9001 SANTA MONICA BLVD, WEST HOLLYWOOD; 310/550-8811 / 1100 S FLOWER ST, DOWNTOWN; 213/763-4600 For the movers and shakers of Hollywood, especially those exuding testosterone, this sawdust-strewn traditional New York steak house is the place to go for prime, aged, Eastern corn-fed beef or for lobsters from the cold waters off Nova Scotia. There are also thick lamb and veal chops, chicken dishes, a number of salads, and pastas, along with legendary baked potatoes and fried onions. The scene continues to be absolutely frantic and lots of fun, due largely to the studiously rude waiters serving oversize portions of everything.

Lobsters, served grilled, cost about as much as a new Volkswagen Beetle . . . and are often larger. *$$$; AE, CB, DC, DIS, MC, V; no checks; lunch Mon–Fri, dinner every day; full bar; reservations recommended; www.thepalm.com; east of Doheny Dr (West Hollywood); corner of 11th St (downtown).* &

Pinot Hollywood / ★★☆

1448 N GOWER ST, HOLLYWOOD; 323/461-8800 Pinot Hollywood, like Disneyland, consists of several discrete but shared worlds and an array of attractions to help you feel jolly. The restaurant, the natural evolution of Joachim Splichal's Patina in midtown and his Pinot Bistro in Studio City, is divided between the warm, bright dining room and the power-lunch patio. In the back, sprawling across several rooms, is the Martini Bar and lounge that's popular with the Johnny Depp/Jennifer Aniston–wannabe crowd. Though much of the menu is light and casual (delicately grilled ahi with baby artichokes, goat cheese terrine with grilled ratatouille, herb-crusted John Dory with pea pods), this is a true bistro, with all the solidity that that implies. You could pretend to be on the Left Bank in a snowstorm as you tuck into dense, cold-weather dishes such as French onion soup with a cheese topping as thick as a brick or roasted leg of lamb with flageolets. But you can also choose to dine as though you were in Cannes on a warm summer's evening, on artichoke ravioli or three-mustard-crusted rotisserie chicken with fries. For dessert, in addition to a creamy tiramisu, there're a nice light trio of ice creams and sorbet and a sinfully memorable chocolate croissant pudding. *$$; AE, CB, DC, DIS, MC, V; no checks; lunch Mon–Fri, dinner Mon–Sat; full bar; reservations required; www. patinagroup.com; southeast corner of Sunset Blvd and Gower St.* &

Zankou Chicken / ★

5065 SUNSET BLVD, HOLLYWOOD (AND BRANCHES); 323/665-7845 If the old Armenian saying "Anyone can learn to cook, but you must be born knowing how to roast" is true, the Lebanese-Armenian family behind Zankou was gifted at birth. Zankou is truly the temple of roasted chicken—and you'll find dozens of birds slowly spinning on rotisseries, cooking to crisp-skinned perfection. Though fowl is king here, its palace is anything but regal. There's no option but to enjoy tender, fall-off-the-bone meat in the charmless dining room in a Hollywood mini-mall. The ramekin of garlic paste, which can be slathered on the juicy fowl or used as a dip, will surely spice things up. But be warned: you'll be sweating the stuff for days. Zankou also offers a smattering of typical Middle Eastern dishes such as hummus, tahini, and shawarma, all quite good and dirt-cheap. Three other branches offer the same wonderful food but with a more limited menus: Glendale (1415 W Colorado Blvd; 818/244-1937), Pasadena (1296 E Colorado Blvd; 626/405-1502), and Van Nuys (5658 Sepulveda Blvd; 818/781-0615). *$; Cash only; lunch, dinner every day; no alcohol; reservations not necessary; corner of Normandie Ave.* &

LODGINGS

The Argyle / ★★★

8358 SUNSET BLVD, WEST HOLLYWOOD; 323/654-7100 OR 800/225-2637

 If you like art deco, you'll love the Argyle. This 15-story 1929 Streamline Moderne tower was California's first all-electric apartment building, home to Bugsy Siegel, Charlie Chaplin, Errol Flynn, and John Wayne long before it was listed on the National Register of Historic Places and appeared in such films as *The Player*. Today, accommodations are generally small but extremely well furnished with period pieces and Italian reproductions that suit the architectural vernacular perfectly. Especially chic are the oval scalloped beds, credenzas that electronically lift the TV at the touch of a button, and deco-tiled baths. Management understands its entertainment-industry clientele perfectly and has added modern luxuries like CD players, VCRs, two-line phones, fax machines, and plush robes. Only 20 of the 64 rooms are queen-bedded standards, so call early or plan on splurging for a suite, some of which feature living and dining rooms, second bathrooms, whirlpool tubs, and/or steam showers. Amenities include a small but well-equipped gym with sauna; a small but memorable terrace pool with fabulous plaster palm trees; a round-the-clock concierge; and valet and butler services. The sexy restaurant and lounge, Fenix, draws the Sunset Strip's best-dressed crowd for martinis and sunset views. *$$$$; AE, DC, DIS, MC, V; checks OK; reserve@argylehotel.com; www.argylehotel.com; 2 blocks west of La Cienega Blvd, near Kings Rd.* &

Chateau Marmont / ★★★★

8221 SUNSET BLVD, HOLLYWOOD; 323/656-1010 OR 800/242-8328

This magnificent Norman castle has been the preferred refuge of Hollywood's left-of-center set since 1929. The funky Sunset Strip hostelry is steeped in more Hollywood history than any other L.A. hotel—yes, than even the Beverly Hills Hotel. Everyone from Greta Garbo to Robert De Niro has been in residence. Roman Polanski spent his last days in the United States holed up here, and John Belushi overdosed here. Now under the guiding hand of boutique hotelier extraordinaire Andre Balazs, the Chateau is more hip—and more exclusive—than ever. The discreetly unflappable staff is used to catering to the whims of its creative guests, so service is fluid and faultless—you won't want for anything. Still, the Chateau isn't for everybody; it's immaculately kept and eternally chic, but unarguably odd. No two of the 60 antique-filled accommodations, which run the gamut from standard rooms to bungalows, are alike. All have VCRs, many have fireplaces and CD stereos, and suites have kitchens and dining areas. The vibe is surprisingly unpretentious, casual, and residential; if it wasn't, Mick Jagger wouldn't feel comfortable making deals in the gorgeous lobby, lunching in the splendid garden cafe or intimate restaurant, or lounging by the brick-decked pool. Around the corner, trendy Bar Marmont serves cocktails to the in crowd. *$$$$; AE, DC, MC, V; no checks; chateaula@aol.com; www.chateaumarmont.com; east of Crescent Heights Blvd.*

Hollywood Roosevelt Hotel / ★★

7000 HOLLYWOOD BLVD, HOLLYWOOD; 323/466-7000 OR 800/950-7667 The legendary Roosevelt has been somewhat dowdy for decades—but no more. On the eve of its 75th anniversary, Hollywood's oldest hotel is poised for a spectacular comeback, just like the freshly reinvented Hollywood Boulevard blocks that surround it. Now under the guiding hand of the former general manager of Beverly Hills's ultrahip Avalon, it's hoping to attract an A-list clientele to its heart-of-Tinseltown location once again with a stylish remake, set to be complete in 2003. It's got the history for it: built in 1927, the Roosevelt hosted the first Academy Awards in 1929; the original sketch for "Oscar" was scrawled on a ballroom napkin during the ceremony; and the benevolent ghosts of Montgomery Clift and Marilyn Monroe are said to roam the halls. Expect a blend of original art deco detail and clean-lined modernism, sprinkled with a fair dusting of golden-age-of-Hollywood glamour, in the 335 redressed guest rooms (done by the chic Hong Kong–based, feng shui–minded Team HC Limited design firm). The Olympic-size pool will remain, as will the famous Cinegrill cabaret (albeit in a new space); new additions are set to include a 3,000-square-foot day spa, a new restaurant and bar, and a whole new level of luxury service. $$$; AE, DC, DIS, E, MC, V; checks OK; reserve@hollywoodroosevelt. com; www.hollywoodroosevelt.com; east of La Brea Ave. &

Le Montrose Suite Hotel / ★★★

900 HAMMOND ST, WEST HOLLYWOOD; 310/855-1115 OR 800/776-0666 This all-suite hotel is West Hollywood's best-kept secret. A quick phone call or visit to the Web site almost always yields bargain rates and value-added package deals. The 132 attractive, contemporary-style suites feel more like comfy apartments than generic hotel rooms. Junior and executive suites are spacious split-level studios, while larger suites are full one- and two-bedroom apartments. Each has a living room with gas fireplace, a very nice bathroom, a dining area, a private balcony (sorry, no views), and a minifridge; all but the junior suites also have a basic kitchenette (more suited to making coffee or plating takeout than cooking a full meal). Additional amenities include multiline and cordless phones, fax/printer/copier, high-speed connectivity, CD player, Nintendo, turndown, and 24-hour concierge and room service. On the rooftop you'll find a heated pool, a whirlpool spa, and a lighted tennis court; there's also a good all-day restaurant, an exercise room with sauna, and coin-op laundry. Don't be surprised if you spot a few famous faces or Hollywood power brokers in the halls; the luxury-level comforts, attentive service, and excellent location—on a quiet apartment-residential street two blocks from the bustling Sunset Strip—make Le Montrose very popular with industry folks in the know. $$$; AE, DC, DIS, E, JCB, MC, V; no checks; front desk@lemontrose.com; www.lemontrose.com; south of Sunset Blvd. &

Magic Castle Hotel / ★★

7025 FRANKLIN AVE, HOLLYWOOD; 323/851-0800 OR 800/741-4915 This little apartment-style hotel boasts a great location: in the Hollywood foothills just blocks from Hollywood Boulevard, but out of the touristy fray. What's more, its bargain-basement rates are a better bargain than ever now that the hotel has been freshly renovated. Situated around a very cute courtyard with a heated pool, rooms and suites still aren't stylish, but everything is extremely well kept. Each unit has a big bath and a furnished patio, plus a fully outfitted kitchen—with full-size appliances, microwave, coffeemaker, toaster, and dish-ware for four—in all but the few smallest units (which have a minifridge). Friends and families have a choice between a king and a sofa bed, two kings, or two queens; be sure to register your preference when booking. Underground parking, coin-op laundry, and a friendly front-desk staff (who also offer a grocery shopping service if you want your pantry stocked before you arrive) heighten the already excellent value. High-speed Internet access is an additional plus for laptop toters. Another big perk, especially for magic fans: hotel guests have access to the exclusive Magic Castle (www.magiccastle.com), one of the world's legendary sleight-of-hand houses; ask for details when booking. *$–$$; AE, DC, DIS, E, MC, V; no checks; info@magic castlehotel.com; www.magiccastlehotel.com; between La Brea and Highland Aves.*

Mondrian / ★★☆

8440 SUNSET BLVD, WEST HOLLYWOOD; 323/650-8999 OR 800/525-8029 Hotelier Ian Schrager helped to revitalize the Sunset Strip with this ultrachic—and very entertaining—boutique hotel, the product of his partnership with outré French designer Philippe Starck. This celebrity magnet is as pretentious as can be, and not as smartly designed as other Schrager-Starck hotels, like Miami's Delano. Still, if you want the best shot at having Hugh Grant or Shakira as a fellow guest, this is the place to stay. A young, model-beautiful staff works the gauzy hotel-as-theater lobby, where dressed-to-kill hipsters meet in stylized nooks or dine and deal at superhot Asia de Cuba. But the real scene is outdoors, where the brilliantly designed teak decking boasts queen-size lounge beds and a gorgeous infinity pool; at sunset it's reborn as Skybar, still L.A.'s hottest watering hole. Hotel guests are guaranteed admission (early-to-bedders beware: it's hard to shut out the din). The 238 white-on-white rooms seem like an afterthought, with interiors a bit too IKEA-like to be called luxurious. On the upside, most are spacious, and all have VCRs, CD players, and fresh orchids; some have kitchens and/or whirlpool tubs. All the services are available, but the staff (generally hired on looks first, experience second) sometimes falls down on the job. Still, the eye candy is unparalleled. *$$$$; AE, DC, DIS, MC, V; checks OK; mondrian@ianschragerhotels.com; www.ianschragerhotels.com; 2 blocks east of La Cienega Blvd, at Olive Dr.* &

Renaissance Hollywood Hotel / ★★★

1755 N HIGHLAND AVE, HOLLYWOOD; 323/856-1200 OR 800/HOTELS-1 New as of December 2001, this attractive new high-rise is part of the brand-new Hollywood & Highland development that has revitalized Hollywood Boulevard. It's set back from the boulevard, just like the bulldozed Holiday Inn it replaced—but that's where the similarities stop. A high-style blend of fashion-forward modernism and whimsical mid-20th-century touches has resulted in a look that blessedly surpasses the chain standard. Shapely modern furniture, bold hues, and an exciting collection of modern art—including works by such famous Southern California–based artists as Ed Ruscha, Charles Arnoldi (who painted the undulating 55-foot abstract that graces the lobby), and photographer Richard Ross—grace the public spaces and the guest rooms; midcentury buffs will love the Eames archive photos in the hallways. All 637 rooms are bright and playful, accented with vivid pastels; 21st-century twists include cordless phones and high-speed Internet access. Restaurant Twist boasts a sleek sushi bar as well as eclectic California cuisine, while the Lobby Lounge serves appetizers and cocktails. Other facilities include a nice terrace-level pool, a state-of-the-art fitness center, and a whopping 50,000 square feet of meeting space. More than 70 top-flight retailers, from Banana Republic to Louis Vuitton, fill the adjacent complex. Inquire about money-saving packages that include tickets to Universal Studios. *$$$; AE, DC, DIS, E, JCB, MC, V; no checks; info@renaissancehollywood. com; www.renaissancehollywood.com; a ½ block north of Hollywood Blvd.* &

The Standard, Hollywood / ★★☆

8300 SUNSET BLVD, WEST HOLLYWOOD; 323/650-9090 Über-hotelier Andre Balazs's shagadelic neo-motel is a futuristic stunner for the under-35 "it" crowd. A former retirement home, the Standard now commands a scene worthy of an Austin Powers movie: the groovy shag-carpeted lobby features a front-desk staff dressed like space-age cheerleaders and rock-and-roll lab techs, and a DJ spinning ambient sounds nightly. Look beyond the silver beanbag chairs, Warhol-print curtains, and Tang-orange bathrooms, and the guest rooms are little more than motel-standard. But they do provide such Internet-generation extras as cordless phones, high-speed connectivity, VCRs, CD players, and minibars, complete with sake, licorice whips, and condoms. If you don't mind staying in a ground-level room facing perpetually noisy Sunset Boulevard, try a budget room for just $99 a night; you'll pay more for a larger room and/or to overlook the electric-blue AstroTurf pool deck. Nonsmokers beware: there are no designated nonsmoking rooms, and this crowd loves to light up. On site is Rudy's Barbershop for cuts, piercings, and tattoos; a 24-hour coffee shop that transcends the shallow trappings by serving very good and affordable food; and a hugely popular bar that makes the Standard feel more like a red-hot club scene than a midprice hotel. *$$–$$$; AE, DC, DIS, MC, V; no checks; hollywood@standardhotel.com; www.standardhotel.com; at Sweetzer Ave.* &

Sunset Marquis Hotel & Villas / ★★★☆

1200 N ALTA LOMA RD, WEST HOLLYWOOD; 310/657-1333 OR 800/858-9758 Built in 1963, this Mediterranean-style compound is the original rock-and-roll boutique hotel. Smart, talented general manager Rod Gruendyke is dedicated to knowing what his guests want, and his crackerjack staff is ready to meet any demand—which is why everyone from Elle MacPherson to Metallica makes this their preferred L.A. lodging. (They also like the state-of-the-art recording studio, where Aerosmith, among others, has laid down tracks.) The main building features 108 suites, while 12 detached multiroom villas dot 3½ acres of mature gardens, interrupted only by bubbling fountains, cobbled pathways, and a wonderful brick-decked pool with cabanas. Rooms were recently remade in a smart, comfortable, modern style, with gorgeous clean-lined furniture in mahogany and metal, Noguchi Akari lamps emitting soft, sensual light, marble countertops, VCRs, CD players, and luxe fabrics in olive, chocolate, and beige. The Spanish-style villas have their own butlers, alarm systems, and fab bathrooms; a few also have saunas, whirlpools, and private pools. Both the restaurant and high-profile Patio Café feature excellent California cuisine with a Pacific Rim edge. Adorned in velvet and kilims, the sexy

Whiskey Bar is the original insiders' cocktail lounge. An exercise room with sauna is on site. *$$$$; AE, DC, DIS, E, JCB, MC, V; checks OK; www.sunsetmarquis hotel.com; south of Sunset Blvd.* &

Wyndham Bel Age Hotel / ★★★

1020 N SAN VICENTE BLVD, WEST HOLLYWOOD; 310/854-1111 OR 877/999-3223 This excellent all-suite hotel just off the Sunset Strip is West Hollywood's best value for those who want it all: a prime location, maximum comforts, and a reasonable price. Once owned by the Ashkenazy brothers, L.A.'s art-collecting hoteliers, the Bel Age features a surprisingly fabulous collection of original art adorning both public spaces and guest rooms. The extralarge, recently renovated suites are terrific, boasting somewhat masculine contemporary interiors in a soothing palette of gray, navy, maroon, and gold. Luxuries include pillowtop mattresses dressed in plush bedding; a king-size sleeper sofa; a TV with VCR; a CD player; two-line phones; an excellent work desk with an ergonomically correct Herman Miller desk chair and high-speed connectivity; and a wet bar. The nice bath has generous counter space and luxury robes. Two restaurants are on the premises: opulent, old-world Diaghilev, with Franco-Russian cuisine that consistently draws critical raves (see review); and La Brasserie, offering California-Tuscan all-day dining and Monk-inspired jazz on Friday and Saturday nights. Additional amenities include a gorgeous rooftop pool and whirlpool spa with a monster deck and fabulous city views; a new exercise room; a sculpture garden for private events; a salon; a knowledgeable and friendly staff, including a concierge; room service; and valet service. *$$$; AE, DC, DIS, JCB, MC, V; checks OK; www.wyndham.com; south of Sunset Blvd.* &

Mid-City

RESTAURANTS

Alex / ★★★☆

6703 MELROSE AVE, LOS ANGELES; 323/933-5233 A welcome addition to L.A.'s burgeoning fine-dining scene, British-born chef/owner Alex Scrimgeour's eponymous restaurant has taken over the large bright room made famous by Michel Richard's Citrus. After a thorough remodel inside and out, Alex's main dining room has new drama with dark beams, generous armchairs, and stained glass concealing the old open kitchen. By day, diffused light from a stretched canvas of ceiling bathes the room; by night, candlelight invites romance. A menu of true delicacies starts with dishes like duck leg confit, silken cauliflower soup with truffle shavings, or veal sweetbreads with asparagus and morels and puff pastry. Main course fish dishes—such as John Dory with mascarpone polenta and sea bass wrapped in pancetta—are delicate yet wreathed in flavor, while beef lovers can luxuriate in aged prime steaks, and risotto addicts can savor a cheesy wild mushroom–truffle version. At lunchtime, standouts include succulent lobster presented three ways—ravioli, poached tail, and grilled claw—along with goat cheese soufflé accompanied by caramelized pear and bacon on a bed of greens. The dessert menu features crispy tarte Tatin or the signature triple chocolate marquise. Not one to be left behind, chef Alex has joined the trend-setting superstar chefs on both coasts with his own whopping luncheon burger with bacon and brie ($18). *$$$; AE, DC, MC, V; no checks; lunch Tues–Fri, dinner Tues–Sat; full bar; reservations recommended; at Citrus Ave.* ♿

Authentic Cafe / ★

7605 BEVERLY BLVD, LOS ANGELES; 323/939-4626 Chef Roger Hayot's highly eclectic American-Southwestern-Asian cafe is a casual and colorful eatery near CBS Television City, so it's a fine spot for people-watching, meeting, and greeting. For years there's been a communal table, popular with single diners, and an eating counter where you can watch the goings-on in the kitchen. Hayot has just added an intimate lounge, serving small plates along with the drinks. Favorites like sweet corn tamales, chicken dumplings, powerfully spicy tortilla soup, and jerk pork chops, all at modest prices, keep lines outside especially on weekends. Brunch sidesteps the same old stuff with such in-demand entrees as *chilaquiles* (scrambled eggs, cheese, chiles, and tortillas) and the knockout grilled chicken salad. *$–$$; AE, MC, V; no checks; lunch Tues–Sun, dinner every day, brunch Sat–Sun; full bar; reservations not accepted; north side of Beverly Blvd, east of Fairfax Ave.* ♿

Campanile / ★★★½

624 S LA BREA AVE, LOS ANGELES; 323/938-1447 Thanks to the married team of owner/chefs Mark Peel and Nancy Silverton, Campanile continues to be one of L.A.'s finest dining spots. It's situated in a landmark building from the 1920s, once owned by Charlie Chaplin, with high ceilings and a striking bell tower (*campanile* in Italian). The spacious divided dining room is ideal for the rustic California-Mediterranean cuisine that landed Campanile on the map—grilled prime rib with black olive tapenade and flageolet beans, braised veal short ribs with horseradish mashed potatoes, yellowtail with Sungold tomatoes and the Sardinian caviar *bottarga,* and—on Thursday nights—the world's most expensive grilled cheese sandwiches, worth every penny. With a wine list the size of an L.A. phone book, making a choice can be tough but rewarding; the list showcases selections from California, Italy, Spain, and France and features small wine producers from around the world. Don't leave without at least sampling a dessert such as warm brioche with sautéed peaches, nectarines, and creamy sabayon sauce, or tangy nectarine lattice pie with mascarpone ice cream. Silverton's La Brea Bakery next door, known for single-handedly revolutionizing Los Angeles's bread scene, provides the crunchy breads for the restaurant. *$$$; AE, DC, DIS, MC, V; no checks; lunch Mon–Fri, dinner Mon–Sat, brunch Sat–Sun; full bar; reservations recommended; www.campanilerestaurant.com; between Wilshire Blvd and 6th St.* ♿

Flora Kitchen / ★

460 S LA BREA AVE, LOS ANGELES; 323/931-9900 Rivaling the enticing aromas streaming from the kitchen of this bright little cafe are the floral scents wafting in from the adjoining Rita Flora flower shop. Patrons can actually chow down on healthful salads and sandwiches among the flowers in the shop or eat in the adjacent main cafe, which boasts a deli-style glass case chock-full of homemade salads—from penne with grilled vegetables to Tuscan beans with ahi. Wherever you stake out a table, Flora Kitchen serves up some downright yummy fare, like salads, home-made soups, sandwiches grilled on La Brea Bakery bread, crab cakes, and hearty lasagne. The artsy Mediterranean-style cafe is also a great breakfast spot, where you can bring a good book and linger over a monster-size cappuccino and fresh-baked scones. When breakfast is done, the antique shops and boutiques of La Brea Avenue are the lure just up the street. *$; AE, MC, V; no checks; breakfast, lunch, early dinner Mon–Sat, brunch Sun; beer and wine; reservations not accepted; at 6th St.* &

Harold & Belle's / ★★

2920 W JEFFERSON BLVD, LOS ANGELES; 323/735-9023 OR 323/735-9918 A class act in a working-class neighborhood, Harold & Belle's has been serving down-home Southern cooking to the affluent African-American community for three decades. The original Harold has passed away, but Harold Jr. and his wife, Denise, continue the tradition, welcoming guests into dimly lit dining rooms, each intimate, cozy, and graced with fresh flowers. The understated, elegant ambience is certainly part of the draw, but the food—well, let's just say it offers more comfort than your favorite easy chair, and there's plenty of it. We're talking good old hold-on-to-your-heart, down-home Southern cooking: fried chicken coated in peppery, snappingly crisp batter; filé gumbo, a tasty mix of shrimp, crab, sausage, chicken, and ham in a spicy Creole sauce; plus traditional Creole standbys such as crawfish and shrimp étouffées, jam-balaya with red beans and hot sausage, and enormous po' boy sandwiches. Con-sidering the sometimes-dicey-after-dark neighborhood, some folks feel more comfortable coming for lunch, but valet parking is provided in the evening. *$$; AE, DC, MC, V; no checks; lunch, dinner every day; full bar; reservations recommended; between Western and Crenshaw Aves.* &

Jar / ★★★

8225 BEVERLY BLVD, LOS ANGELES; 323/655-6566 If you like Campanile, you'll also like Jar. Former Campanile chef Suzanne Tracht—who so successfully com-bined European tradition with Asian flair at the much-missed Jozu—has brought her wondrous comfort food to this smart though somewhat unlikely setting. A spare pastel decor, with lettuce-green contemporary plastic chairs, is hardly what you'd expect for a meat-and-potatoes restaurant, not even as sophisticated a version as this is. But one bite of Tracht's melt-in-your-mouth braised lamb shank with buttery mashed potatoes, her crispy lemongrass chicken, or her perfectly broiled prime steaks, and all is forgiven. Tracht's main courses come without much adornment, but her mix-and-match side orders, such as pea tendrils with garlic, water spinach with garlic and chiles, or duck fried rice, are treats in themselves. Though there are enticing first courses like honey fried quail, braised pork belly with pickled savoy cabbage, and freshest fried Ipswich clams, you might prefer a lighter starter like an old-fashioned iceberg lettuce wedge with blue cheese dressing, or a French bean salad with shiitakes and Parma ham. After all, you'll need room for an irresistible dessert like strawberry pie with whipped crème fraîche, homey banana cream pie, or ginger sticky cake with lemon curd. A late-night bar menu is served Monday through Saturday beginning at 10pm, and live jazz is featured on Monday nights.

$$$; AE, CB, DC, MC, V; no checks; lunch Mon–Fri, dinner every day; full bar; reservations recommended; www.thejar.com; at Harper Ave. &

The Little Door

8164 W 3RD ST, LOS ANGELES; 323/951-1210 An L.A. hot spot that's so "in" it can't be bothered with a sign, this exclusive French-Mediterranean restaurant, with many polished French servers, is nearly as dazzling as its celebrity roster and its twentysomething and wannabe-twentysomething patrons. Ensconced behind heavy wooden doors—which are anything but little—the main dining area is actually a romantic canopy-covered courtyard, lit mostly by candlelight, a plus for smokers. The sounds of the gurgling fountain and the heavenly aromas coming from the kitchen make you long to be in love and bring that special someone here. The Little Door uses organic produce whenever possible and turns out a menu of popular regional favorites such as delicate tuna tartare, flavorful pistou soup, grilled salmon steak, sautéed scallops, and lamb tagine with peaches and almonds. Wine buffs are wowed by the extensive selection, many offerings available by the glass. *$$$; AE, MC, V; no checks; dinner every day; beer and wine; reservations required; east of La Cienega Blvd.* &

Locanda Veneta / ★★☆

8638 W 3RD ST, LOS ANGELES; 310/274-1893 Inside Locanda Veneta it's hard not to be struck by an overwhelming sense that you're in Venice. On a warm summer's evening you can feel the breeze flowing in through the windows, smell the green olive oil being poured over the carpaccio, and hear the sizzle of roast lamb (served in a mustard and walnut sauce). Close your eyes (or, alternatively, drink enough pinot grigio) and you'll imagine hearing the songs of the gondoliers and the slap of the waves in the great lagoon. The menu is both simple and select, yet it's the sort of menu that bulges with meat, pasta, and seafood dishes you must try. By all means, order the *polpettine di anatra e pollo* (chicken and duck dumplings) and the spaghetti with oven-roasted tomatoes, spinach, and mixed lentils. Old-timers who remember when you had to be "somebody" to get a reservation in this intimate place will be glad to hear the restaurant has become quite welcoming. *$$; AE, MC, V; no checks; lunch Mon–Fri, dinner every day; beer and wine; reservations required; www.locandaveneta.com; west of San Vicente Blvd.* &

Mimosa / ★★

8009 BEVERLY BLVD, LOS ANGELES; 323/655-8895 While most restaurants claiming to be bistros are really bistro poseurs that serve lighter fare, Mimosa is the real thing—more or less. Here tables are cramped into a bright and cheery space where guests tend to focus on the flavorful French country cooking instead of scanning to see who's sitting nearby. Sidewalk seating is especially appealing to true French expats who still can't get over California's antismoking laws. A statement on the menu has always read, "No truffles, no caviar, no bizarre concoctions." This still goes for the new owner/chef Jean-Pierre Bosc, who, while adding his own bistro favorites, is keeping his former partner's standouts, like the thin-crusted tarte flambée, knockout macaroni and cheese with prosciutto, a classic charcuterie platter with large pickle jars of house-made cornichons and black olives, and the very best braised veal daube in town. Thursday, Friday, and Saturday are bouillabaisse nights. For dessert, there's floating island and wonderful fruit tarts, besides a cheese plate that varies from day to day. *$$; AE, CB, DC MC, V; no checks; dinner Tues–Sat; beer and wine; reservations required; www.mimosarestaurant.com; west of Fairfax Ave.* &

Patina / ★★★★

5955 MELROSE AVE, HOLLYWOOD; 323/467-1108 Most epicureans deem Patina the best fine dining experience in town. Chef Joachim Splichal's flagship restaurant comes with a variety of givens: it's a given that the service will be some of the most professional in town, that each eclectic dish will be artfully presented and prepared, and that even in this image-obsessed town the most important attraction here will be the cooking. Over the years the menu has demonstrated Splichal's whimsy with dishes such as a corn blini "sandwich" filled with marinated salmon; soufflé of grits with Herkimer cheddar and an apple-smoked bacon sauce; New York duck liver with blueberry pancakes and blueberry sauce; and red bell pepper soup with a tiny bacon, lettuce, and tomato sandwich on the side. Along with the playful additions, however, are a variety of classic Splichalian dishes such as a roast chicken for two with crackling crisp skin hiding deliciously tender meat beneath. It is carved ceremoniously tableside, as are the roast beef and a Scottish salmon baked in a salt crust. For those who can't make up their minds, there's a prix-fixe menu that changes regularly. The wine list bubbles with creativity, listing enough standards to please regular folks and enough obscure vintages to keep oenophiles happy. A recent remodel completely remade Patina's former collection of cramped dining rooms into airy, contemporary settings with warm overtones and a small patio. *$$$–$$$$; AE, MC, V; no checks; lunch Fri, dinner every day; full bar; reservations required; www.patinagroup.com; west of Vine St.* &

Pink's Famous Chili Dogs / ★★

709 N LA BREA AVE, LOS ANGELES; 323/931-7594 In a town where the hamburger is king, the hot dog usually gets the short end of the bun, but not at this homage to the wiener. A gritty indoor-outdoor stand that grew up around the late Paul Pink's 10-cent hot dog cart, Pink's has been serving frankfurters for more than half a century to fanatics frantic to shovel in specialties like the foot-long jalapeño dog topped with a sort of iridescent orange chili, or the heartburn-inducing double-bacon burrito-dog. There's always a crowd lined up in front, hungrily waiting for red-hot goodness, served steaming for under $3. *$; Cash only; lunch, dinner every day; beer and wine; reservations not accepted; north of Melrose Ave.*

Sonora Cafe / ★★★☆

180 S LA BREA AVE, LOS ANGELES; 323/857-1800 Sonora Cafe was a favorite in downtown Los Angeles before owner Ron Salisbury (who also owns the El Cholo restaurants) relocated it to a massive space on La Brea Avenue. Sonora still serves up some of the best Southwest cuisine around, with a rich variety of gourmet Mexican-influenced dishes. Duck is a specialty of the house, from the lunch-only duck tacos with duck confit in whole wheat tortillas to the evening entree of Long Island duckling glazed with a tequila-pomegranate sauce. Other favorites include oven-roasted mussels on a sizzling fajita tray and double-cut smoked pork chop with a sweet potato tamale and ancho chile barbecue sauce. The signature dessert is Sonora's Southwest Sundae: a gourmet banana split, laid out as artistically as a sand painting and topped with chocolate sauce and *cajeta* (a caramel sauce made from sugar and goat's milk). Sonora's dining room is comfortable, spacious, and a step above casual, while the splendid bar area is the prime spot for sampling one of the city's finest selections of tequila, mescal, and a superb array of top-shelf margaritas. *$$; AE, DC, MC, V; no checks; lunch Mon–Fri, dinner every day; full bar; reservations recommended; at 2nd St.* &

Tahiti / ★★

7910 W 3RD ST, LOS ANGELES; 323/651-1213 The tropical decor of this stylish restaurant celebrates its namesake with fun island overtones—from a thatched-hut patio to a decidedly South Pacific rest room—that are just one step away from being over the top. Fortunately, the cuisine of chef/owner Tony Di Lembo (a former co-owner of Indigo) is far better than any found in the unimpressive restaurants of French Polynesia. His eclectic, exotic menu combines Italian, Asian, and Pacific Rim cuisines and features such lovely starters as giant chicken and spinach pot stickers (which come with a spicy-minty dipping sauce), a scrumptious Thai grilled shrimp and papaya salad, and an unusual rendition of crab cakes, packed with tender crab meat and crisp angel hair pasta. Main courses tend to be anticlimactic after the appetizers, but there's enough choice to entice you: shrimp pad thai rice noodles, thin-crusted baby artichoke and rosemary potato pizza, and spicy Jamaican jerk-style redfish. Diners looking for a bit of romance should ask for a candlelit table on the patio—squint a little and you could be in Bora Bora. For even more intense island flavor and outrageous tropical drink concoctions, drift into the restaurant's lively Tiki Lounge. *$$; AE, MC, V; no checks; dinner every day; full bar; reservations recommended; www.tahitirestaurant.biz; west of Fairfax Ave.* &

Versailles / ★★☆

10319 VENICE BLVD, CULVER CITY (AND BRANCHES); 310/558-3168 Garlic lovers gather at Versailles, where they often wait in line for a table to order the signature Cuban chicken. Sure, there are other dishes available at this casual, dark, and dive-ish Havana-style restaurant, some of them very good— especially seafood and pork—but the half bird marinated in garlic and citrus is a must, especially on your first visit. Like many other dishes, it's served with rice, black beans, and chewy fried plantains. Portions are huge and prices are amazingly low. And the pungent scent of garlic fills the air, since virtually every table has at least one order of the chicken. There are other Cuban places in town, but this is the closest you can get to Havana and its food. Versailles has been such a success that it now has three other locations serving the same succulent dishes: Mid-city (1415 S La Cienega Blvd; 310/289-0392), Encino (17410 Ventura Blvd; 818/906-0756), and Manhattan Beach (1000 N Sepulveda Blvd; 310/937-6829). *$; AE, MC, V; no checks; lunch, dinner every day; beer and wine; reservations not accepted; between Motor and Overland Aves.* &

LODGINGS

Carlyle Inn / ★★

1119 S ROBERTSON BLVD, LOS ANGELES; 310/275-4445 OR 800/322-7595 One of L.A.'s best-value finds is this four-story hotel just south of Beverly Hills. A clever, modern design has created a pleasing courtyard and a sense of seclusion from a safe and attractive but busy retail neighborhood. Thirty-two good-size, fresh-feeling rooms feature smart faux-deco furnishings, new beds, VCR, coffeemaker, minibar, and terry robes; architectural prints lend an additional touch of class. Suites are only slightly larger than standard rooms, but have a pull-out sofa. Connecting rooms also suit families well. Views are nonexistent—but at these prices, you'll happily do without. Ask for a room away from Robertson Boulevard for maximum quiet. Amenities include dry cleaning and laundry service, an exercise room, a sundeck with whirlpool, and the pleasant, slate-tiled courtyard—an excellent place to enjoy the generous breakfast spread and weekday hors d'oeuvres. A conscientious manager keeps the property in racing form. Your fellow guests are likely to be businessfolk who know a good value when they see one—and keep coming back. *$$; AE, DC, DIS, MC, V; no checks; info@carlyle-inn.com; www.carlyle-inn.com; at Pico Blvd.* &

Élan Hotel Modern / ★★

8435 BEVERLY BLVD, LOS ANGELES; 323/658-6663 OR 888/611-0398 Situated on a decidedly unhip stretch of Beverly Boulevard, this hotel with a silly moniker is nevertheless one of L.A.'s best boutiques. It has transcended its retirement-home roots very successfully, even using key design elements from the original 1969 facade to set the stage for 21st-century style. Uncluttered and surprisingly plush guest rooms feature extra-high ceilings, custom blond-wood furnishings, luxuriant fabrics like mohair and chenille, and divine beds (with cushioned headboards, goose-down comforters, and Egyptian cotton linens). In-room comforts enhance the luxury: VCR, cotton robes, coffeemaker with Wolfgang Puck grounds, minibar including nonalcoholic beverages, high-speed Internet access, and double-paned windows to ensure quiet. Bathrooms continue the smart design and have the best bath towels in the city, bar none. Shoppers will love the direct sight lines to the Beverly Center, which is within walking distance. On the downside, there's nothing resembling a view from any room, the safe and central-to-everything neighborhood is not exactly L.A.'s most picturesque, and there's no pool or restaurant; but in this town, for less than $200 a night—continental breakfast included—those sacrifices are easy to live with. An exercise room is on site, and room service and an extensive video library are available. *$$$; AE, DC, DIS, MC, V; no checks; info@elanhotel.com; www.elanhotel.com; 2 blocks east of La Cienega Blvd.* &

Hotel Sofitel Los Angeles / ★★★

8555 BEVERLY BLVD, LOS ANGELES; 310/278-5444 OR 800/521-7772 This French-owned hotel is an oasis of European elegance at the chaotic corner of La Cienega and Beverly Boulevards, across the street from the Beverly Center. Soothing classical music erases all big-city angst the moment you step into the tranquil, marbled lobby. The swirling staircase may be more for show than for use (most guests take the elevator), but it is a grand introduction to the 311 rooms, all decorated in an exceptional French-country style that surpasses the chain-hotel norm. Distressed furnishings and gorgeous Pierre Deux fabrics in bright country colors create a cozy and inviting Provençal ambience. Rooms are large enough to hold a king or two doubles, deep closets accommodate large suitcases, and big bathrooms offer pretty tile, good lighting, generous counter space, and terry robes. Premium Plus rooms feature a separate work area with a second TV, while suites add CD players and furnished balconies. French-country appointments add personality to the big, well-outfitted fitness center. The rooftop sundeck features a good-size pool, but traffic noise makes relaxation a challenge. Regardless, it's the little extras—cold Evian at check-in, a fresh-baked baguette upon checkout—that keep guests returning again and again. Gigi, a very Parisian brasserie, serves traditional bistro fare and provides room service. *$$$–$$$$; AE, DIS, E, MC, V; no checks; sofitel_losangeles@accor-hotels.com; www.sofitel.com; at La Cienega Blvd.* &

The San Fernando Valley

RESTAURANTS

Barsac Brasserie / ★

4212 LANKERSHIM BLVD, NORTH HOLLYWOOD; 818/760-7081 With its close vicinity to the studios, this dining establishment is an industry hangout often filled with studio suits doing business deals over above-average California-French-Italian fare. To take advantage of seasonal ingredients, the menu here changes every three months. Start with the grilled eggplant rolls covered with goat cheese, sun-dried tomatoes, black olives, and feta cheese, and then move on to a warm seafood salad with salmon, giant scallops, and tiger shrimp. Choose from a tempting pasta menu or try an entree of lamb shank braised in red wine or delicate pan-fried sand dabs with shallots, tomatoes, orzo, and zucchini. The open kitchen facing the busy dining room makes it impossible to savor a quiet meal, but the studio crowd makes people-watching (and sipping a great martini) almost as much fun as eating. *$$; AE, DC, MC, V; lunch Mon–Fri, dinner Mon–Sat; full bar; reservations recommended; just north of Universal Studios.* &

The Bistro Garden at Coldwater / ★★★

12950 VENTURA BLVD, STUDIO CITY; 818/501-0202 Set in a formal European winter garden with skylights, latticework, and ficus trees, the Bistro Garden's dining room oozes romance. Executive chefs Harry Klibingat and Karl Rohner stick to the expected classics, such as French onion soup au gratin, roast rack of lamb with rosemary jus, and filet mignon with three-peppercorn sauce; but they also exercise their agility with more modern entrees like sesame-crusted salmon with soy and wasabi, or chicken curry with mango chutney, chopped bananas, almonds, and shredded coconut. The menu changes with the seasons, but one thing remains a Bistro Garden standard: the decadent chocolate soufflé, baked to order and served with mounds of freshly whipped cream. On most evenings, the mahogany bar area, with live piano music, teems with the business crowd who relax over martinis after a long day at the office or sip wine spritzers as they entertain clients. Just next door, BG To Go has several tables and an outdoor patio, where you can eat more casual fare like salads, rotisserie chicken, pasta, and chicken burgers— and even the famous chocolate soufflé—or grab something to go. *$$$; AE, DC, MC, V; no checks; lunch Mon–Fri, dinner every day; full bar; reservations recommended; www.bistrogarden.com; west of Coldwater Canyon Blvd.* &

Ca' del Sole / ★★☆

4100 CAHUENGA BLVD, NORTH HOLLYWOOD; 818/985-4669 This rustic Italian eatery transports diners to the Mediterranean with a vine-trellised terrace and countryside-inn atmosphere. The mouthwatering aroma of garlic and herbs wafting through the busy dining room helps the illusion. Waiters, many of whom are Italian, will encourage you to share such starters as crab cakes with stewed white kidney beans and tomatoes, or semolina dumplings baked with wild mushrooms and truffle-cream sauce. Pasta lovers enjoy the hearty bowls of freshly made pastas, including *bigoli alla Ca' del Sole,* a fragrant seafood pasta overflowing with lobster, clams, shrimp, and crab, or half-moon pumpkin raviolis accented with sage. The marinated corn-fed chicken with lemon zest and herbs and the wine-braised veal shank with saffron risotto are other popular choices. If you've left room for dessert, order the Italian ricotta cheesecake with pine nuts and fresh strawberry sauce, or the bread pudding with raisins soaked in grappa, served hot with vanilla sauce. *$$; AE, DC, MC, V; no checks; lunch Sun–Fri, dinner every day, brunch Sun; full bar; reservations recommended; www.cadelsole.com; between Lankershim Blvd and Moorpark St.* &

Café Bizou / ★★★

14016 VENTURA BLVD, SHERMAN OAKS (AND BRANCHES); 818/788-3536 This perennially packed restaurant and its two branches attract throngs of foodies with hearty portions of reasonably priced, delicious French-California fare. Order the delicate roasted monkfish with saffron risotto, a rich lobster sauce, and deep-fried carrots; sesame seed–crusted salmon perched on potato pancakes and mushrooms in a red wine sauce; steak au poivre; roasted chicken breast in a tangy balsamic vinegar sauce; or any other main course, and you'll find the bill still remarkably reasonable (and you can tack on a house salad or homemade soup, such as the velvety lobster bisque, for just $1). Café Bizou has a wine list, but if you bring your own bottle, the corkage fee is a modest $2. Tables are packed tightly together in unassuming and rather noisy dining areas—so forget about intimate conversation—but chances are you'll be so busy eating that it won't matter. Two other branches with the same menu but in more commodious surroundings than the Sherman Oaks original: Pasadena (91 N Raymond Ave; 626/792-9923) and Santa Monica (2450 Colorado Ave; 310/582-8203). *$$; AE, CB, DC, DIS, MC, V; no checks; lunch Mon–Fri, dinner every day, brunch Sat–Sun; full bar; reservations recommended; west of Costello Ave.* &

Dr. Hogly Wogly's Tyler Texas BBQ / ★

8136 SEPULVEDA BLVD, VAN NUYS; 818/782-2480 This authentic barbecue joint, located in a not-so-desirable part of town, may lack ambience, but all is forgiven the minute diners catch a glimpse of the juicy, megasize portions of barbecued and smoked meats served here. The unusual name was chosen by the original owner, Johnny Greene, who as a chubby little kid back in the early 1930s used to deliver groceries for a Piggly Wiggly market in Texas. But around these parts he's better known for launching this ultra-casual place offering barbecued chicken with enormous drumsticks straight out of *The Flintstones*. Barbecued beef ribs are also Flintstone-size, and they practically fall off the bone. Texas hot links have a spicy kick, and side orders include home-baked bread, barbecued beans, and fresh coleslaw. Career waitresses who greet you as "honey" or "doll" fit the kitschy atmosphere of vinyl booths and Formica tables. Save room for the pecan and sweet potato pie, and ask for your leftovers to go. *$; AE, CB, DIS, MC, V; no checks; lunch, dinner every day; beer and wine; reservations not necessary; south of Roscoe Blvd.* &

Inn of the Seventh Ray / ★★

 128 OLD TOPANGA CANYON RD, TOPANGA CANYON; 310/455-1311 Just because much of the cuisine in this ethereal canyon hideaway is organic and macrobiotic doesn't mean the food isn't delicious. Organic ingredients have always been used here, but the menu is not limited to the likes of veggie burgers or steamed vegetables with brown rice; you can depend on finding a juicy steak sandwich or mango-papaya duck, too. And the restaurant now features a special raw food four- or five-course dinner in which nothing is cooked, not even the lasagne (sliced eggplant subs for the pasta). Designed around an old church, Inn of the Seventh Ray is set high in the canyon, with towering oaks, flowering shrubs, and a babbling creek running through the outdoor seating area, creating a magical setting unparalleled by almost any in the Los Angeles area. On the seventh day, try the Inn's Sunday brunch. With more than 20 salads (two-thirds of which are vegan or macrobiotic), a bagel bar with spreads ranging from salmon to flavored cream cheeses, quiche, organic cereals, and chicken, fish, and vegetarian dishes, this feast is a great way to celebrate the weekend—naturally. *$$; AE, MC, V; no checks; lunch, dinner every day, brunch Sun; beer and wine; reservations recommended; just off Topanga Canyon Blvd, about 4 miles north of Pacific Coast Hwy.* &

Kushiyu / ★★★

18713 VENTURA BLVD, TARZANA; 818/609-9050 What sets this modest Japanese eatery apart from other neighborhood sushi haunts is its *kushiyaki*—tender skewers of chicken, beef, tuna, swordfish, scallops, quail eggs, mushrooms and onions, pork-wrapped asparagus, and more, which are grilled to perfection on the restaurant's imported kushiyaki grill. Though the swordfish skewers are a melt-in-your-mouth starter, they only inspire further exploration of the traditional Japanese fare, including *nabe* (pot-boiled dishes such as a seafood soup with huge portions of salmon), tempura, and inventive sushi such as the Tarzana roll, a delicate combination of white albacore sashimi, vegetables, and smelt eggs. Be sure to try the specials of the day; with fish deliveries three times a week, the seafood is always fresh. *$$; AE, MC, V; no checks; lunch Mon–Fri, dinner every day; beer and wine; reservations recommended; between Reseda and Tampa Blvds.* &

Market City Caffe / ★

164 E PALM AVE, BURBANK; 818/840-7036 There are few pleasures more satisfying than finding a nice table on the outdoor patio at the Market City Caffe and spending a long evening sipping a glass or two of pinot grigio while nibbling on dish after dish from the antipasto buffet (one of the best around, with a rich assortment of old Italian recipes). Located in the refurbished old downtown near Burbank's best shopping, this is a trattoria in the best meaning of the word—a casual, family-oriented sort of place where eating and drinking can be done at ease in comfort, and the cost doesn't cause indigestion afterward. They make quite a pizza, and the great bar at the other end of the patio—martinis on one side, antipasti on the other—certainly leaves little to be desired. *$; AE, DC, DIS, MC, V; no checks; lunch, dinner every day, brunch Sun; full bar; reservations recommended; www.marketcitycaffe.com; corner of San Fernando Blvd.* &

Max / ★★

13355 VENTURA BLVD, SHERMAN OAKS; 818/784-2915 When a noisy little Valley eatery—tucked into a restaurant row of local favorites—is jammed day and night with trendies who could afford to eat anywhere they want, it must be doing something right. And that has to be due to owner/chef André Guerrero's menu, cleverly balanced between mainstream California cuisine and Asian flavors—fusion in the best sense, without pushing the envelope. His baby back ribs are lavished in a hoisin-honey barbecue sauce but come with very American garlic mashed potatoes; sesame-crusted ahi marries happily with the sweetness of Thai peanut sauce; butterfish (black cod) is jazzed up with soy broth, ginger, and scallions and served over Asian sticky rice. Even the seared foie gras napoleon, combining the traditional French duck confit and slice of foie gras, is adorned with mango compote and tamarind. A couple of dishes you may not have seen before are among our favorites. Thai lemongrass-coconut soup with dumplings sets the tone for a savory meal to come. The trio of pork (a meat extravaganza with only a smidgen of veggies) is an upscale combo plate of pork tenderloin, baby back ribs, and braised bacon. In chic-ed up quarters that last housed Joe Joe's, the restaurant does crowd in its tables, but plans are afoot to help deaden the decibels. *$$–$$$; AE, CB, DC, MC, V; no checks; lunch Mon–Fri, dinner every day; beer and wine; reservations recommended; www.max restaurant.com; at Dixie Canyon Ave.* &

Mistral Brasserie / ★★★

13422 VENTURA BLVD, SHERMAN OAKS; 818/981-6650 Crystal chandeliers, wood-paneled walls, black-and-white tile flooring, and crisp linen tablecloths give this charming French bistro a warm and authentically Parisian feel. Owner Henri Abergel is a long-standing Valley restaurateur who once served as manager at the Valley's elegant, bygone La Serre. His cozy dining room attracts everyone from romancing couples to large birthday parties, as well as a slew of regulars who apparently can't go long without a fix of French chef Gilles Dirat's steak frites, served au poivre with garlic, parsley, and butter and accompanied by a salad. Onion soup gratinée, homemade rabbit pâté, and grilled entrecôte round out the traditional bistro menu, with chocolate soufflé the perfect selection to finish your night off right. And you can rely on Abergel to help you with his award-winning list of leading French and California wines. *$$$; AE, DC, MC, V; no checks; lunch Mon–Fri, dinner Mon–Sat; full bar; reservations recommended; between Coldwater Canyon Blvd and Woodman Ave.* ♿

Pinot Bistro / ★★★

12969 VENTURA BLVD, STUDIO CITY; 818/990-0500 With high-beamed ceilings, crisp white linen tablecloths, a checkerboard tile floor, and hutches displaying fine French china, this elegant-casual restaurant possesses all the comforts of a true French bistro. Thanks to owner Joachim Splichal of Patina and executive chef/partner Octavio Becerra, you can expect expert pairing of food and wine here. The cellar has more than 200 selections, and 20 wines are offered by the glass. A memorable dinner might begin with fresh oysters, or onion soup with perfectly caramelized onions in a beefy stock, topped with bubbling, golden-brown Gruyère, followed by such impressive main courses as braised lamb shank with Moroccan minestrone, oxtail ragout, or linguine with shellfish. Save room for the chocolate croissant bread pudding with a heady bourbon crème anglaise, a sinfully spectacular dessert that, along with practically everything on the menu, exemplifies why this dining room ranks at the top of food critics' lists. *$$$; AE, DC, DIS, JCB, MC, V; no checks; lunch Mon–Fri, dinner every day; full bar; reservations recommended; www.patinagroup.com; west of Coldwater Canyon Blvd.* ♿

Posto / ★★★

14928 VENTURA BLVD, SHERMAN OAKS; 818/784-4400 When renowned restaurateur Piero Selvaggio, owner of the *alta cucina* Santa Monica restaurant Valentino, added a humbler outpost called Posto in the Valley, he found a whole new audience for the Italian classics. The menu, with a Bolognese accent, features such satisfying standbys as osso buco and porcini risotto, as well as lighter entrees like monkfish in spicy tomato sauce, a mixed seafood grill, or grilled quail with rapini. Uncork a bottle of wine from the restaurant's impressive wine list, and sit back and enjoy the beautiful dining room and first-rate service. *$$–$$$; AE, DC, MC, V; no checks; lunch Mon–Fri, dinner Mon–Sat; full bar; reservations recommended; at Kester Ave.* ♿

Saddle Peak Lodge / ★★★

419 COLD CANYON DR, CALABASAS; 818/222-3888 A century-old hunting lodge in the mountains above Malibu Beach houses one of the grandest American restaurants in Southern California. Not far from where *M*A*S*H* was shot, this very manly hunting lodge is decorated with heads and horns and with fireplaces that blaze all year long. The modern American menu features in-season game—ostrich, boar, venison, elk, and more. Those who'd rather not eat Bambi and Thumper can choose from fine renditions of chicken, tuna, and salmon. Sunday brunch is memorable here, the beautiful drive into the hills rewarded by such delights as rabbit and potato hash with poached eggs and sage, or a roasted leg of lamb sandwich like none other. This is a breathtaking destination and a restaurant worth getting to an hour before your dinner reservation (when the days are long), so you can sit on the patio and watch the sun set over the Coast Range. *$$$; AE,*

DC, JCB, MC, V; no checks; dinner Wed–Sun, brunch Sun; full bar; reservations required; east of Malibu Canyon Rd. &

Sushi Nozawa / ★★☆

11288 VENTURA BLVD, STUDIO CITY; 818/508-7017 Located in a nondescript mini-mall, this tiny sushi restaurant (only 10 sushi-bar seats and five tables) has a word-of-mouth following that keeps it full at all times. The loyal patrons come for fresh, innovative sushi made by sushi master Kazunori Nozawa, whose sashimi, hand rolls, and nigiri combinations vary from day to day, depending on what fish is freshest. Devotees go for specials like the scallop roll, a creamy deviled-scallop concoction tightly wrapped with rice and toasted seaweed; jumbo crab hand rolls chock-full of sweet crab and sticky rice; tender soy-glazed octopus sprinkled with sesame seeds; thin slices of salmon layered with seaweed noodles; and ultrafresh, buttery hamachi. If you sit at one of the tables, you get a menu, but adventurers should opt for the sushi bar, where Nozawa generally doesn't tell you what he's bringing you (if you ask, he ignores you) but will tell you how to eat it, like "Eat this first" and "No soy sauce." Chef Nozawa prefers that you trust him to order for you, and he doesn't believe in making such ubiquitous fare as California rolls. But if you are game to try anything, this is one of the best places to go. $$–$$$; MC, V; no checks; lunch, dinner Mon–Fri; beer and sake; reservations not accepted; west of Vineland Ave. &

Tama Sushi / ★★★

11920 VENTURA BLVD, STUDIO CITY; 818/760-4585 From their early incarnations under the name Katsu on Hillhurst in Los Feliz, on Third Street midtown, and finally in Studio City (the man does move around), master sushi chef Katsu-san's little bento box restaurants were always acclaimed as some of the best in Los Angeles. After a recent fire at the Studio City jewel, Katsu renamed the restaurant Tama Sushi for his wife, Tama, but his cooked dishes and artistic sushi presentations remain much the same—perfect slices of richly flavored yellowtail (hamachi), silky sea bass (shiromi), blood-dark tuna (both maguro and the highly prized, fat-marbled toro), exquisitely oily mackerel (saba), jumbo clam (mirugai), and sea urchin (uni) that's like taking a bite out of the Mother Sea itself. The restaurant retains its gray-walled simplicity, but it now offers a full bar as well as the sake, beer, and wine of old. $$–$$$; AE, MC, V; no checks; lunch, dinner Mon–Sat; full bar; reservations recommended; 2 blocks east of Laurel Canyon Blvd. &

LODGINGS

Hilton Universal City & Towers / ★★☆

555 UNIVERSAL HOLLYWOOD DR, UNIVERSAL CITY; 818/506-2500 OR 800/HILTONS With its hilltop location just across the street from Universal Studios and extensive conference and ballroom spaces, this 24-story glass high-rise is perpetually bustling with tourists, business travelers, and conventioneers—so consider yourself warned. But complimentary tram service to the park means that it's hard for families to be better located, and after a day at the park, the oversize guest rooms—decorated in warm tones of burgundy and green and affording great views of the surrounding hills—are a welcome retreat. Rooms feature chain-standard amenities, although business travelers will appreciate two-line phones and round-the-clock room service. The club-level Tower Floors offer concierge service, a private lounge with complimentary snacks, and excellent views. There's no real reason to hang out in the bustling lobby, though its all-about-glass construction allows views of garden-filled courtyards with trickling fountains from virtually every angle. The pool and whirlpool spa make for pleasant lounging; an exercise room and an Avis car-rental desk are also on site. On the lobby level, everybody can sip cappuccino or cocktails in the Lobby Lounge, while a cafe-style restaurant offers all-day dining. *$$$; AE, DC, DIS, JCB, MC, V; checks OK; www.hilton.com; off Hwy 101.* &

Safari Inn / ★

1911 W OLIVE AVE, BURBANK; 818/845-8685 OR 800/782-4373 Used for exteriors in such films as *Apollo 13* and *True Romance,* this classic '50s motel underwent a complete renovation in recent years—though its retro-cool neon sign, a Burbank landmark, remains gloriously intact. From the outside the property looks like your basic two-story motor lodge, but everything else within is reinvented for today's traveler, from the keycard locks and IKEA-style furnishings to the colorful contemporary wall prints and bedspreads and the modern bathrooms. All rooms have coffeemakers, and a handful have a wet bar with microwave. Two suites have full kitchens, pull-out sofas, humongous closets, and a second TV in the bedroom, making them well suited to families; these book up way in advance, so reserve early if you want one. On site is a petite but pleasing heated pool, an elevated sundeck, an exercise room sporting all-new equipment, and guest laundry. Room service is available from the cute bistro at the Annabelle, the motel's charm-free but perfectly pleasant full-service sister hotel, as is laundry service. The neighborhood is quiet and pleasant, yet just down the street from the movie studios—great for visitors interested in studio tours and TV-show tapings. *$$; AE, DC, DIS, MC, V; no checks; www.anabelle-safari.com; at S Parish Pl, 5 blocks off Buena Vista St.* &

Sheraton Universal Hotel / ★★

333 UNIVERSAL HOLLYWOOD DR, UNIVERSAL CITY; 818/980-1212 OR 800/325-3535 Located on Universal Studios's back lot, this 442-room hotel caters to both tourists and business travelers, with well-outfitted rooms and every-15-minutes shuttle service to the theme park. The tasteful beige and gray lobby sets a sophisticated tone, but you'll feel fine ponying up to the front desk in shorts and sneakers. Done in a fresh contemporary style, guest rooms are rather corporate but plenty comfortable, with a work desk and in-room coffee among the extras; they're located in a 24-story smoked-glass tower, which overlooks the surrounding hills and the valley, and in a three-story wing with petite lanais that overlook the heated pool and whirlpool spa. It's worth it to spend the few extra dollars for a Club Level room, as the value-added extras include free local and 800 calls, plus complimentary continental breakfast and evening hors d'oeuvres. Special business rooms also feature a movable workstation with a fax/printer/copier. All the services are at hand, including room service (6am to midnight) and a 30,000-square-foot business center to accommodate sizable meetings—and you, too, if you just want to check your e-mail. The coffee-shop-style restaurant offers casual fare, and you'll find a coffee cart and a cocktail bar in the lobby. *$$$; AE, DC, DIS, JCB, MC, V; checks OK; sheraton.universal@sheraton.com; www.sheraton.com; off Hwy 101.* &

Sportsmen's Lodge Hotel / ★

12825 VENTURA BLVD, STUDIO CITY; 818/769-4700 OR 800/821-8511 A Valley landmark for more than 50 years, this 200-room hotel is really an upgraded California-style motel, with exterior hallways and an AstroTurf deck around the Olympic-size pool and whirlpool spa. While there's a definite retro-kitsch flavor here, the lush grounds—with waterfalls, wooden bridges, and a koi-filled lagoon with resident swans—set the place apart from most competitors in this category. Spacious rooms are decorated in a country-Colonial style in mauves and blues; they're otherwise unremarkable but perfectly comfortable. Studio suites provide extra space for families or travelers staying in town for a while, while the new Executive Business King rooms offer business-minded extras like two-line phones, fax machines, coffeemakers, and executive work desks. Free shuttle service to and from Universal Studios is a boon for families; also ask about theme park discount tickets, which are usually available. Free shuttle service to and from the Burbank Airport and Universal Studios as well as an on-site Enterprise car-rental desk mean that you can avoid the crowded airport rental counter. Food and beverage facilities include a coffee shop, a bar and grill, and a pub-like lobby bar. Other welcome facilities include an exercise room, a salon, and coin-op laundry, as well as valet service. *$$; AE, DC, DIS, JCB, MC, V; checks OK; information@slhotel.com; www.slhotel. com; at Coldwater Canyon Ave.* &

Santa Monica and Northern Beaches

RESTAURANTS

The Beach House / ★★☆

100 W CHANNEL RD, PACIFIC PALISADES; 310/454-8299 If you're not fortunate enough to have a friend who has great dinner parties at his beach house, dining at this casually elegant eatery is the next best thing. Restaurateur Liza Utter, former co-owner of La Cachette, has created a cozy, romantic room across from the beach with white walls, plenty of flickering candles, and wood shutters separating the dining room from the bustling bar area. Seaside fare is on the menu here—from jumbo bowls of clam and mussel steamers, seafood chowder, and lobster and brie quesadilla to lobster and rock shrimp pasta, but you'll also find other tempting dishes such as roasted beet salad and Beach House's famous buttermilk-battered fried chicken. There's an incredible bananas Foster and a beloved warm dark chocolate brownie à la mode, plus an extensive wine list. While you have to stand up to get a view of the Pacific, the staff of bronzed Adonises who must surely surf (and audition) by day is scenery enough. *$$$; AE, DC, MC, V; no checks; dinner Tues–Sun; full bar; reservations required; at Pacific Coast Hwy.* &

Border Grill / ★★☆

1445 4TH ST, SANTA MONICA; 310/451-1655 / 260 E COLORADO BLVD, PASADENA; 626/844-8988 Owned and operated by Susan Feniger and Mary Sue Milliken, the nationally famous duo known as the "Too Hot Tamales," Border Grill is large, colorful, and loud—and has some of the best Hispanic food north of the border. Feniger and Milliken began with a tiny version of Border Grill on Melrose in 1985, and then moved on to the larger City Restaurant before opening in 1990 this much larger Border Grill, which reflects their love of all things Latin. Architect Josh Schweitzer (Milliken's husband) designed the playful space to match their creative cuisine. There's a daily fresh ceviche, green corn tamales, and plantain empanadas among the appetizers. Signature entrees include the pescado Veracruzano—tender sea bass in a broth laden with rice, olives, and herbs—and sautéed rock shrimp with toasted ancho chiles, slivered garlic, and seared greens. The bar is well stocked with top tequilas, as well as an exotic, smoky mescal, and boasts an attractive social scene. *$$; AE, DC, DIS, MC, V; no checks; lunch Tues–Sun, dinner every day; full bar; reservations recommended; www.millikenandfeniger.com; north of Broadway (Santa Monica); in the Paseo Colorado mall (Pasadena).* &

Café del Rey / ★★

4451 ADMIRALTY WY, MARINA DEL REY; 310/823-6395 This marina-front restaurant has long been one of the prime reasons to head west for lunch or dinner. Executive chef David Lino continues retired Katsuo "Naga" Nagasawa's creative fusion-style cuisine, which incorporates French, Italian, and Pacific Rim elements, and is far more adventurous than fare at other nearby restaurants. Seafood is one of Lino's strengths: pan-fried blue crab cakes with leeks have a surprising pink grapefruit sauce, while black spaghetti is rich with lobster, shrimp, calamari, scallops, roast peppers, and mushrooms in a garlic soy sauce. The honey-cured Peking duck is roasted three times, slowly and at different temperatures, and served with a raisin-and-plum-wine sauce, mango chutney, and coriander-laced pancakes. Desserts are particularly noteworthy, especially if the raspberry napoleon brûlée is on the menu. The glassed-in wine display room is a good indication that wine is an important part of Café del Rey's appeal, and an impressive wine list—more than 300 bottlings—proves it. Sunday brunch is packed, but getting a table is worth the effort. *$$$; AE, CB, DIS, MC, V; no checks; lunch, dinner every day, brunch Sun; full bar; reservations recommended; www.cafedelrey.com; between Mindanao and Via Marina.* &

Chez Mimi / ★★

246 26TH ST, SANTA MONICA; 310/393-0558 Perched between Brentwood and Santa Monica, this exquisite spot is named for owner Micheline Hebert, nicknamed Mimi, the former chef/owner of Chez Hélène. Chez Mimi spreads over three cottages, each with its own fireplace, with lots of courtyard space for alfresco dining on temperate coastal nights—definitely the best and most romantic way to go here. Cuisine matches the decor—rustic French, with bouillabaisse and leg of lamb among the best main courses. And because Hebert hails from Montreal, she prepares a few Quebecois specialties as well, like *tourtière*—a hearty, spicy meat pie—and *chomeur,* an upside-down cake with caramel and raspberry. Her tarte

Tatin was honored as the best in town by a local French-language magazine. Service, mostly by French-accented waiters, is excellent, and the wine list is strong in both French and California selections. Whether you sit inside or out, you'll feel like you're dining in the countryside. *$$$; AE, CB, DC, DIS, MC, V; no checks; lunch Tues–Sat, dinner Tues–Sun; full bar; reservations recommended; south of San Vicente Blvd.* &

Chinois on Main / ★★★

2709 MAIN ST, SANTA MONICA; 310/392-9025 Wolfgang Puck's first foray into fusion is so well conceived that Chinois still rates as one of the best restaurants in town. Puck's business partner and former wife, Barbara Lazaroff, designed the dining room decor—it's an over-the-top Asian rendition, exploding with color and huge floral displays. While the menu changes constantly as new chefs rotate through the kitchen, some of the earliest creations are still the best—the whole sizzling catfish stuffed with ginger and topped with ponzu sauce; chicken salad of napa cabbage, baby lettuce, chicken, and fried wonton skins in a Chinese mustard vinaigrette; sautéed foie gras with marinated and grilled pineapple; and Shanghai lobster with spicy ginger sauce and crispy spinach. Grab one of the kitchen-counter seats in back and watch the chefs work their magic, or stake out one of the coveted tables along the front windows. But whatever you do, don't expect quiet conversation; the tables here are packed in tight, with a noise level that's usually deafening. *$$$; AE, DC, DIS, MC, V; no checks; lunch Wed–Fri, dinner every day; full bar; reservations required; www.wolfgangpuck.com; between Hill and Ashland Sts.* &

Granita / ★★

23725 W MALIBU RD, MALIBU; 310/456-0488 The isolated denizens of Malibu have their own high-profile Wolfgang Puck eatery, and the rest of us have a good excuse for a scenic drive along the coast. This Spago-by-the-sea fits right into the beach scene with a whimsical design that recalls Captain Nemo's submarine and *The Little Mermaid*. As a reminder that it is frequented by some of the best known beachfront estate holders in America, there's a stone near the entrance thanking Johnny Carson for his support—yes, Carson, along with a slew of celebrity neighbors, is a regular. The kitchen is open and bustling, and the food leans towards the well-loved Spago formula of designer pizzas and pastas. There's a wood-burning pizza oven that turns out Puck's longtime hit, the crisp, delicate potato galette with smoked salmon and dill cream, and a selection of inventive pizzas like baby artichoke with pecorino cheese. You can count on grilled double pork chops, prime steaks, and rack of lamb, but seafood dishes with their inventive vegetable accompaniments are the big draw. Chef Jennifer Naylor's Mediterranean training is reflected in preparations like seared scallops over mascarpone-porcini orzo, and daily fresh selections range seductively from Santa Barbara spot prawns or monkfish to Hawaiian opah. But Granita's most bountiful offering is its look and vibe—this ain't your typical beach shack by any stretch. *$$$; AE, MC, V; no checks; dinner Tues–Sun, brunch Sat–Sun; full bar; reservations recommended; www.wolfgangpuck.com; in Malibu Colony Plaza shopping center west of Pacific Coast Hwy.* &

The Hump / ★★☆

3221 DONALD DOUGLAS LOOP S, SANTA MONICA AIRPORT; 310/313-0977 Despite its peculiar name, the Hump, which sits atop Typhoon Restaurant at the Santa Monica Airport, serves some of Los Angeles's best sushi in a beautiful and unique room. Owner and history lover Brian Vidor designed and named this restaurant in homage to the Himalayan wartime route that American pilots nicknamed "the hump." The result is a sushi bar of remarkable quality, with a tarmac-front view and a spectacular setting designed by Steven Francis Jones (Spago, Chinois Las Vegas). The warm and elegantly artistic room sets the stage for great sushi prepared by master chef Shunji Nakao. Expect tuna, both big-eye and yellowfin, along with expensive (and worth it) *toro*. Luxuriate in unabashedly oily Japanese *iwashi* (sardines), the slippery crunch of jumbo clam, rich and buttery young yellowtail, addictive rock shrimp tempura, or quick-sautéed abalone. This is sushi so pure, it's astonishing. Great collection of hot and cold sakes. *$$–$$$; AE, DC, MC, V; no checks; lunch Mon–Fri, dinner every day; full bar; reservations recommended; www.typhoon.biz, south side of Santa Monica Airport, just off Bundy Dr.* &

JiRaffe / ★★☆

502 SANTA MONICA BLVD, SANTA MONICA; 310/917-6671 JiRaffe became an instant hit under the partnership between chefs Josiah Citrin (the Ji) and Raphael Lunetta (the Raffe), the young culinary team who were named among the 10 "Best New Chefs" by *Food & Wine* magazine. The pair separated in 1999, with Citrin heading off to open the more formal Melisse (see review). Now the light, airy two-story dining room, decorated with variations of the long-necked quasi-namesake (mostly gifts from satisfied customers), is overseen by Lunetta, who continues to serve excellent "rustic French/California" cuisine, explosively flavored yet not overly fussy. Signature dishes include a roasted rabbit appetizer; a crisp salad of roasted pears with mixed greens, hazelnuts, and imported cheese; and buttery salmon with parsnip purée, braised fennel, and balsamic *nage*. JiRaffe has a tasting menu, a vegetarian menu, and a chef's menu, the last especially good on Wednesdays after Lunetta has made his weekly trip to the local farmers market. At this sophisticated yet unpretentious operation, both the wine list and the menu are about quality rather than trends and flash. *$$$; AE, DC, MC, V; no checks; lunch Tues–Fri, dinner every day; beer and wine; reservations recommended; www.jirafferestaurant.com; corner of 5th St.* &

Joe's Restaurant / ★★★

1023 ABBOTT KINNEY BLVD, VENICE; 310/399-5811 This small, wildly popular restaurant in a remodeled old house combines the home-style cooking of chef/owner Joe Miller with a no-frills ambience. Miller, who enjoys culinary exploration and utilizing the region's access to fresh seasonal ingredients, puts an innovative spin on virtually everything he does. Fine examples are his signature porcini mushroom ravioli in a Parmesan cheese broth; slow-roasted wild salmon with chick-peas, fava beans and baked tomatoes; tender sirloin of lamb with beet risotto and grilled asparagus; and homey pork tenderloin whose accompanying mashed potatoes are jazzed up with wild mushrooms and roasted garlic jus. Charming desserts include lavender-scented crème brûlée with seascape strawberry phyllo tart, or chilled cherry soup with cherry sorbet. Chocoholics shouldn't miss the chocolate pudding and pistachio semifreddo torte. Anyone up for an all-out culinary adventure can embark on one of two four-course prix-fixe menus, offered nightly for $38 or $48 a person. If you think Joe's few small rooms are crowded at lunch or dinner, wait till you call for a brunch reservation! The green chile–turkey chorizo breakfast burrito and the thick brioche French toast with strawberry syrup, blackberries, and vanilla whipped cream keep the aficionados coming back. *$$$; AE, MC, V; no checks; lunch Tues–Fri, dinner Tues–Sun, brunch Sat–Sun; full bar; reservations recommended; www.joesrestaurant.com; between Main St and Westminster Ave.* ♿

Josie / ★★★⯪

2424 PICO BLVD, SANTA MONICA; 310/581-9888 If you've dreamed of having a personal chef serve you perfect meals in the comfort of your own dining room, you'll like Josie. Not that it's quiet or uncrowded—quite the opposite—but Josie's two low-key dining rooms, with artichoke-green walls and comfortable seating, do provide a welcome intimacy. After years as chef at Saddle Peak Lodge, chef and co-owner Josie Le Balch retains her reputation for great game cookery, and her venison and wild boar are mild and succulent. She balances the richness of game, rack of lamb, steaks, chicken, pork chops, and other prime meats with earthy vegetables like rapini, radicchio, savoy cabbage, grits, mushrooms, artichoke, and eggplant. Le Balch is equally adept at fish cookery, especially monkfish tagine with couscous, served in the traditional peaked Moroccan pot. Though each guest is greeted with a *lagniappe* of quiche, starters are not to be missed—summer's warm tomato tart with tiny egg tomatoes on a crispy pastry shell, a wild mushroom "sandwich" in an indulgent cream sauce topped with the lightest puff pastry, or delicate baked pear salad with Stilton and pecans, refreshed with the sheerest strips of crisp endive. Contributing wonderful pastries for appetizers as well as the desserts is pastry chef Jonna J. Jensen, whose trio of silken pots de crème in three flavors and ravishing blackberry crumble should remain on the menu forever. *$$$; AE, DC, MC, V; no checks; dinner Mon–Sat, full bar; reservations recommended; www.josierestaurant.com; corner of 25th St.* ♿

Lavande / ★★★

1700 OCEAN AVE, SANTA MONICA; 310/458-6700 With glorious views of the Pacific by day and an elegant pastel ambience after dark, Lavande brings the flavors of Provence to L.A. in a luxurious but straightforward menu weighted toward freshest seafood and prime beef. Chef Jeffrey Nimer manages to turn out delicious dishes with a minimum of butter, leaning instead to lighter sauce reductions, vinaigrettes, and olive oil. His roasted baby beet salad with peas and French feta cheese with a port reduction and his lobster and hearts of palm salad with blood-orange vinaigrette are refreshing starters. Seafood winners include grilled ahi with fennel-garlic purée and his generous bouillabaisse of scallops, shrimp, clams, mussels, and grouper. Besides nightly specials, there is a juicy grilled chicken and a tempting

Roquefort-crusted filet mignon, but you can also have your beef simply grilled. The extensive wine list is particularly strong in French bottles. *$$$; AE, DC, DIS, JCB, MC, V; no checks; breakfast every day, lunch, dinner Mon–Sat, brunch Sun; full bar; reservations recommended; where Pico meets the beach.* &

Melisse / ★★★★

1104 WILSHIRE BLVD, SANTA MONICA; 310/395-0881 Melisse is one of the most beloved fine dining restaurants in town, the creation of Josiah Citrin (formerly of Jackson's and then of JiRaffe), whose cooking has always had a casual, inexpensive edge to it in the past. Flouting the conventional wisdom that ultra-upscale dining doesn't work in L.A., he created a serious restaurant for grown-ups who demand service on fine china and linen. The formally dressed staff is practiced and smoothly well trained. The French-California menu offers overwhelming choices—along with à la carte dishes, there are always chef-composed prix-fixe menus that must be ordered for the entire table, with wine pairings on request. Should you order à la carte, appetizers run from sweet pea ravioli or sophisticated foie gras with caramelized cherries to a stunning warm mandarin tomato soup poured around a centerpiece of icy tomato sorbet. Main courses include pancetta-wrapped John Dory with a shellfish ragout, free-range chicken with fava beans, salmon with leeks, and rack of lamb with zucchini flowers. *$$$$; AE, MC, V; no checks; lunch Wed–Fri, dinner every day; full bar; reservations recommended; www. melisse.com; at 11th St.* &

Michael's / ★★★

1147 3RD ST, SANTA MONICA; 310/451-0843 Since the late '70s, Michael McCarty has done as much to define Cal-French cooking in Southern California as Alice Waters has at Chez Panisse in Northern California. The food, though no longer as cutting-edge, is still a fine sampling of the cuisine that moved Los Angeles beyond surf-and-turf, as currently interpreted by chefs de cuisine Christine Baria and Oliviet Rousselle. Michael's is a sublime place to go for American- and French-influenced dishes like whole lobster with watercress coulis and tomato confit, crisp duck breast with chanterelle flan, mission fig and braised savoy cabbage, seared wild king salmon with a wilted arugula salad, or a basic dry-aged prime New York steak with shallot butter and pommes frites. There's always an interesting seasonal tasting menu as well as à la carte. The setting is bright and beguiling, with a fine collection of paintings. There are few experiences more SoCal than a meal on the garden patio, where the sound of falling water easily drowns out the outside world. *$$$; AE, CB, DC, MC, V; no checks; lunch Mon–Fri, dinner Mon–Sat; full bar; reservations required; www.michaelssantamonica.com; just north of Wilshire Blvd.* &

One Pico / ★★

1 PICO BLVD (INSIDE SHUTTERS ON THE BEACH), SANTA MONICA; 310/587-1717 Consistently rated as one of the best hotel restaurants on the beach, this respectable California-style dining room boasts a large fireplace, an amazing ocean view, and a menu filled with what the restaurant calls classic American cooking. Here you'll find mussels with spicy coconut and lemongrass broth, house-smoked salmon with warm corn cakes and crème fraîche, a hearty rack of lamb, and Alaskan halibut with a tomato and fennel salad. Show up in time to sip a cocktail on the outside balcony while the sun sinks into Santa Monica Bay and the lights come alive on the Santa Monica Pier. There's live music seven nights a week in the lobby bar, which serves an inventive cocktail and martini menu as well as some signature appetizers. *$$–$$$; AE, MC, V; no checks; lunch, dinner every day, brunch Sun; full bar; reservations recommended; where Pico Blvd meets the shore.* &

Röckenwagner / ★★☆

2435 MAIN ST, SANTA MONICA; 310/399-6504 After years in a funky storefront on Abbott Kinney Boulevard in Venice, Hans Röckenwagner is now well established on Main Street in the Frank Gehry–designed Edgemar Center. The wood-accented interior with vaulted exposed ceilings is spacious to the point of being cavernous, though they cozied the room with whimsical decoration and have added a new WunderBar for tapas and 30 wines by the glass. While the menu changes, the chef's creative approach to California cuisine continues in such surefire dishes as roast lamb with a cinnamon red wine glaze, hazelnut-crusted halibut cheeks, spicy jumbo shrimp in black bean sauce, and broiled black cod with grilled jumbo asparagus and vegetable dumplings. Asparagus is a Röckenwagner passion, and in spring you can count on a white asparagus festival here. Every Tuesday Röckenwagner offers a *stammtisch*, or community-based dinner, served at an oversize table, where locals and anyone else who wants to can gather and order off the regular menu. Sunday brunch is popular here, and reasonably priced. *$$–$$$; AE, DC,MC, V; no checks; dinner every day, brunch Sun; full bar; reservations recommended; www.rockenwagner.com; south of Pico Blvd.* &

Union Restaurant and Bar / ★★☆

1413 5TH ST., SANTA MONICA; 310/656-9688 When you walk into Union—with its curving stairway, sleek hanging fountain, and contemporary supper-club air— you know you're there for a good time as well as a good meal. The spectacular setting, where culinary hot spots Bikini, Abiquiu, and lately Rix once reigned, offers subdued dining in a comfortable downstairs main room—but the happening place is upstairs in the roof garden next to the big, friendly bar. Executive chef James Grey doesn't try to dazzle with exotic ingredients, but shows what a skilled cook can do with mainstream American favorites and by enhancing quality meats and fish with delicious demi-glace, wine, or butter sauces. Vegetables fresh from the nearby farmers market threaten to steal the show: rosy duck breast slices sit atop rutabaga purée and bacon-braised brussels sprouts; a ragout of sweet corn, fava beans, and potatoes provides a foil for crispy, light cornmeal-crusted trout; delicate poached halibut is paired with tender baby artichokes, new potatoes, and roasted tomato; and earthy parsnip purée and a potato-onion tart sit alongside rack of lamb. Appetizers are straightforward—baby back ribs, fresh oysters, a rich blue cheese tart with poached pears and caramelized onions. It's hard to save room for dessert, but try, especially if the brown butter plum tart is on the menu. *$$–$$$; AE, CB, DC, MC, V; no checks; lunch Mon–Fri, dinner every day, full bar; reservations recommended; just south of Santa Monica Blvd.*

Valentino / ★★★★

3115 W PICO BLVD, SANTA MONICA; 310/829-4313 Deemed one of the primo Italian restaurants in the entire country, Sicilian-born chef/owner Piero Selvaggio's dining room has topped culinary charts since 1972 with sophisticated, swoon-inducing authentic contemporary Italian cuisine. Though a dinner here can add up to a moderate mortgage payment, it's the price many pay for perfection. The kitchen uses only the best ingredients, from fresh fish—both local and imported from Italy—to generous shavings of white truffles. Deep-pocketed regulars know to let the chef select the evening's meal, which might include several small courses such as delicate cuttlefish capellini, pappardelle tossed with broccoli and ricotta, a sublimely seasoned rack of lamb, and a risotto rich with white truffles (Selvaggio dubs this rice dish "the Lord's porridge"). Valentino's wine cellar has repeatedly been honored each year since 1981 with the Grand Wine Award from *Wine Spectator,* with 13,000 bottles ranging from $30 to $10,000. Guests are seated in a series of traditionally elegant dining rooms (including one with deep, intimate booths, plus the highly prized romantic patio), and the service is as practiced as you'd expect. *$$$–$$$$; AE, DC, MC, V; no checks; lunch Fri, dinner Mon–Sat; full bar; reservations recommended; www.valentinorestaurant.com; west of the 10 Fwy.* &

LODGINGS

Best Western Marina Pacific Hotel & Suites / ★★

1697 PACIFIC AVE, VENICE; 310/452-1111, 800/786-7789, OR 800/421-8151 The Venice Boardwalk isn't for those of you who desire pristine coastal beauty or uninterrupted peace and quiet, but this recently renovated hotel at the heart of the human carnival is a haven of smart value. The newly whitewashed four-story building is situated at Venice's most colorful crosswalk, just steps from the boardwalk and beach. A bright, contemporary lobby and freshly dressed halls adorned with artsy photos of local scenes and rock-and-roll legends lend the property a genuine Venice vibe. Motel-simple but nice-size rooms are dressed up with bright beachy colors and spanking new amenities like minifridges, two-line phones, and high-speed Internet access. Extras like fully equipped kitchens with microwave and dishwasher, dining areas, pull-out sofas, and fireplaces make the one- and two-bedroom suites a stellar deal. Good-value extras include free continental breakfast, free local phone calls, and complimentary shuttle to Santa Monica and Marina del Rey—great for vacationers who'd rather leave their car behind in the secured lot. Check www.mphotel.com for excellent-value packages. *$$; AE, DC, DIS, JCB, MC, V; no checks; mphotel@aol.com; www.mphotel.com or www.bestwestern.com; near Venice Blvd.* &

Cal Mar Hotel Suites / ★

220 CALIFORNIA AVE, SANTA MONICA; 310/395-5555 OR 800/776-6007 If you're trying to stretch your travel dollars, these garden apartments will deliver a big bang for your buck. The location alone makes this place a steal: the well-maintained Eisenhower-era complex, in an upscale residential neighborhood, is just two blocks from the beach and one block from Third Street Promenade dining and shopping. Each large, fully furnished one-bedroom apartment overlooks the heated pool and comes with one king or two twin beds, a complete kitchen, ceiling fans, cable TV, and cheap but comfortable mix-and-match discount furnishings, including a pull-out sofa in the living room (great for the kids). Don't expect much in the way of style, service, or modern amenities like microwaves and data ports, but retro pricing makes up for such deficiencies. Daily maid service and free access to a nearby gym is part of the deal, front-desk staff is friendly and attentive, a heated kidney-shaped pool is in the lush courtyard, and self-service laundry is on hand. Tip: The master suites offer the best value and quietest accommodations. *$$–$$$; AE, DC, DIS, MC, V; no checks; info@calmarhotel.com; www.calmarhotel.com; at 3rd St.*

Casa del Mar / ★★★★

 1910 OCEAN WY, SANTA MONICA; 310/581-5533 OR 800/898-6999 For the ultimate in beachy elegance, pull out your platinum card and book into this stunning resort, one of only two on-the-sand hotels in Santa Monica. (The other is sister Shutters, reviewed below.) This impeccably restored 1920s Renaissance Revival beach club bursts with period style. Its grand scale and striking, almost sexy beauty are evident from the moment you walk through the front door, where a curvaceous staircase leads to a mammoth living room dressed with rich wood paneling, damask-covered sofas, buttery leather, polished bamboo, and ocean views; an ivory-tinkling pianist and faultless martinis make it a hangout of choice among chic after-workers and hobnobbing Hollywood types. The U shape of the villa-like hotel awards ocean vistas to most of the guest rooms. Gauzy fabrics and sherbet colors accent a casually luxe style that evokes Grace Kelly–era European beach resorts (think Côte d'Azur). Beds are sumptuously made and the generous Italian marble bathrooms are some of the best in L.A., with oversize whirlpool tubs and separate showers; rubber duckies and turndown teddy bears add a touch of whimsy. The resort's restaurant, Oceanfront, has won deserved raves for its seafood-focused California menu, intimate setting, and spectacular views. There's a full-service spa and health club as well as a gorgeous Roman-style pool. Service is everything it should be. *$$$$; AE, DC, DIS, E, JCB, MC, V; information@ hotelcasadelmar.com; www.hotelcasadelmar.com; near Pico Blvd.* &

Casa Malibu Inn on the Beach / ★★☆

22752 PACIFIC COAST HWY, MALIBU; 310/456-2219 OR 800/831-0858 This modest but beautifully tended 1960s motel doesn't look like much from the street. But pass through the lobby to the charming, copa de oro–draped brick courtyard overlooking the motel's private white-sand beach and you'll feel the magic. More than half the rooms have ocean views, but even those facing the courtyard are quiet and offer easy access to sand and surf. The renovated quarters feature Mexican-tiled bathrooms, air-conditioning (not necessary), and VCRs as well as super-comfortable beds, good-quality plush towels, coffeemakers, and fridges; some also have fireplaces, kitchens, tubs (instead of shower only), and/or decks overlooking the sand. Suites have CD players. A furnished deck, fireplace, whirlpool tub, full modern kitchen, and gorgeous seaside style make the freshly redone Malibu Suite the best room in the house. The second-floor Catalina Suite (Lana Turner's favorite) boasts traditional furnishings and panoramic picture-window views. Friendly innkeepers Richard and Joan Page find true joy in making their guests happy. Guest laundry and a modest morning coffee-and-pastry spread are on hand; room service is available from a nearby restaurant. Book weekends well in advance, as this popular retreat fills up. Casa Malibu isn't for those who prefer more conformity in their accommodations, if that's you, choose the Malibu Beach Inn (see below) instead. *$$–$$$$; AE, MC, V; no checks; casamalibu@earthlink.net; www.casamalibu.com; next to Malibu Lagoon State Beach.*

Channel Road Inn Bed and Breakfast / ★★

219 W CHANNEL RD, SANTA MONICA; 310/459-1920 Built in 1910 by Texas oil baron Thomas McCall, this shingle-clad Colonial Revival house was moved to its current location, a block from the beach at the northernmost end of Santa Monica, in the 1970s. Now a gracious bed-and-breakfast, the beautifully restored home maintains a strong sense of history; McCall's own regal portrait hangs above the magnificent Batchelder-tiled fireplace in the antique-filled living room. It's an inviting spot for afternoon tea, hors d'oeuvres, or just curling up with a book. Guest rooms are spacious and individually decorated in a romantic late-Victorian style, with quality furnishings and modern niceties like phones, VCRs, plush terry robes, and spacious bathrooms. The innkeeper chose to sacrifice some rooms in order to expand baths, so most of the bathrooms are also on the generous side. "View" rooms offer extras like whirlpool tubs and/or fireplaces, but don't expect much from the promise of an ocean vista; your sliver of blue will be obscured by a busy street, wires, and rooftops. An expansive morning buffet is served in a bright breakfast room overlooking a bloom-filled patio and the hillside, home to a romantic hot tub. The staff is professional and attentive; what's more, this is one of the few kid-friendly B&Bs in Los Angeles. *$$$–$$$$; AE, MC, V; checks OK; info@channelroadinn. com; www.channelroadinn.com; just east of Pacific Coast Hwy.*

Georgian Hotel / ★★★

1415 OCEAN AVE, SANTA MONICA; 310/395-9945 OR 800/538-8147 A favorite love nest for Clark Gable and Carole Lombard, this 1930s hotel also coddled one of L.A.'s first Prohibition-era speakeasies. Today, the bold, beach-side art deco gem has been restored to its full grandeur, making it an excellent choice for those who want kicky retro style and a top-flight location at a moderate price. Awarded the Historic Hotels of America distinction, the 84-room Georgian stands across Ocean Avenue from the beach, just two blocks from the pier; a lovely wicker-furnished veranda offers gorgeous unobstructed views. Inside, expert restoration and a bold use of color highlight graceful archways, ornate moldings, and other original details, giving the whole place a lively golden-age-of-Hollywood glamour. The stylish guest rooms are an ideal blend of period and contemporary, with beautiful fabrics that include nubby naturals and hammered silk. Other perks include all-new mattresses dressed in goose-down comforters, ceiling fans, terry robes, two-line cordless phones, and desk-level inputs for laptop jockeys; suites have sleeper sofas and CD players. Front rooms can be a bit noisy, but the panoramas are spectacular; ask for a Malibu view (best from the fourth floor or higher) side room, or a quieter back-facing city-view room. The attentive staff is as happy to be here as you'll be. *$$$; AE, DIS, JCB, MC, V; no checks; reservations@georgianhotel.com; www.georgian hotel.com; north of Pico Blvd.*

Hotel Oceana / ★★★

849 OCEAN AVE, SANTA MONICA; 310/393-0486 OR 800/777-0758 Considering how easy it is to spend more than $300 on an average hotel room in this town, these vibrant luxury suites offer great value. A former apartment complex facing the ocean on the fringe of Santa Monica's loveliest residential neighborhood, the boutique-style Oceana combines the comforts of apartment living with the advantages of a full-service hotel. Decorated in a playful Matisse-goes-to-IKEA style, the extra-large suites are done in a parade of vivid yellows, reds, and blues with casual, comfortable, oversize furniture—perfect for the beach. Even the studios include a full-size kitchen, complete with microwavable pizzas and Häagen-Dazs pints in the freezer; a comfortable living room, large work desk, and dining area; a CD player and Sega Genesis game system; generous counter space and terry robes in the bathroom; and beds with pillowy headboards and Frette linens. Most suites have well-furnished lanais; ocean views are beautiful, but courtyard-facing apartments are quieter and cheaper. A concierge desk, valet and business services, a 24-hour fitness room, and round-the-clock room service are available, and a pool dominates the fetching courtyard. Oceana is an all-around excellent choice. Money-saving tip: Discounts are often available for the asking—but you do have to ask. *$$$$; AE, DC, DIS, MC, V; no checks; reservations_sm@hoteloceana.com; www. hoteloceana.com; south of Montana Ave.* &

Loews Santa Monica Beach Hotel / ★★☆

1700 OCEAN AVE, SANTA MONICA; 310/458-6700 OR 800/23-LOEWS This big, family-friendly beach hotel has always housed excellent facilities and emerged from a serious makeover in 2001 with a fresh, fun, California-casual look. Previous visitors will feel the difference the moment they enter the dramatic lobby, whose soaring eight-story atrium now has a breezy and playful vibe; walls were removed to make the space more loftlike and take maximum advantage of the spectacular ocean views. All clean lines and warm earth tones, the new guest rooms are stylish enough to please *Metropolitan Home* readers without being a turnoff to traditionalists. While some are on the small side, all are comfortable and user-friendly. But this hotel is really about the public spaces, including a terrific heated pool overlooking the ocean. The 6,000-square-foot fitness center and spa is an attraction in its own right, with a state-of-the-art gym, yoga and Pilates classes, and spa and salon services. The fireside lounge hosts a notable Visiting Artists Series, plus afternoon tea and light dining, while Lavande restaurant (see review) serves elegant California-Mediterranean cuisine along with fabulous vistas. A business center and all the services you'd expect from a hotel of this caliber are also on hand. *$$$$; AE, DC, DIS, MC, V; checks OK; loewssantamonicabeach@loewshotels.com; www. loewshotels.com.* &

Malibu Beach Inn / ★★☆

22878 PACIFIC COAST HWY, MALIBU; 310/456-6444 OR 800/4-MALIBU This pink-stucco, Spanish-style hotel on the sand is a fabulous choice for couples in search of a few nights of Malibu romance. Each room is built for two, with a private furnished balcony that extends virtually over the surf. Furnished in rattan and bamboo and decorated in a sea green and pale pink scheme that perfectly suits the style of the hotel, the rooms are attractively and efficiently designed. Modern amenities—minibar, wet bar, coffeemaker, VCR, Mexican-tiled bathroom—are neatly integrated, and little luxuries like plush robes are on hand. Most rooms also feature a Mexican-tiled gas fireplace, and many have two-person Soft Tub Jacuzzis on the oceanfront balcony. The open-air lobby maintains the Spanish theme, with a gurgling terra-cotta fountain, terra-cotta tiles, and an oceanfront patio—a perfect place to enjoy your free continental breakfast, or room service later in the day from the nearby Marmalade Cafe—with stairs leading to the sand. Rates include privileges at a neighboring health club. A Native American jewelry gallery is also on site. *$$$–$$$$; AE, DC, MC, V; no checks; reservations@malibubeachinn.com; www. malibubeachinn.com; next to Malibu Pier.* &

Sea Shore Motel / ★★

2637 MAIN ST, SANTA MONICA; 310/392-2787 This charming, family-run motel is Santa Monica's secret weapon in the budget wars. It's nothing more than your basic motel, but it's clean, is impeccably maintained, and boasts a ground-zero location on a cool shopping and dining street. It all adds up to a stellar bargain. The simple, smallish rooms have been renovated in the last few years; they feature terra-cotta tile floors, minifridges, telephones with voice mail and data ports, and granite countertops. Those with two double beds are roomy enough for small families or friends traveling on a shoestring, while the suite, with sitting room and microwave, is a phenomenal deal; book it as far in advance as possible. There's no view—rooms and a small sundeck overlook a tidy parking lot—but the beach is just two blocks away. A cheerful cafe on the premises is perfect for morning pastries and coffee. A laundromat is next door, and mealtime options abound. *$–$$; AE, DIS, MC, V; no checks; reservations@seashoremotel.com; www.seashoremotel.com; south of Ocean Park Blvd.*

Shutters on the Beach / ★★★★

1 PICO BLVD, SANTA MONICA; 310/458-0030 OR 800/334-9000 This exquisite on-the-sand hotel shares the spotlight with Casa del Mar as L.A.'s best beach resort. Gray-clapboarded Shutters exudes a contemporary Martha's Vineyard vibe, with a casual-chic lobby where Lichtenstein and Hockney artwork adorns the walls, wood-burning fireplaces cast a warm glow on cozy conversation pits, and a big balcony offers Santa Monica's finest ocean views. The gorgeous guest rooms continue the SoCal-goes-Cape-Cod theme, with lots of white sailcloth and blue cotton ticking, rich walnut furnishings, and floor-to-ceiling shuttered doors that open to the ocean breeze. More shutters divide the bedroom from the expansive marble bath, letting you bring the fabulous views all the way in. Rubber duckies in the oversize whirlpool tubs and nighttime storybooks on the

Frette-made beds add an irreverent touch that's just right. Food service is everything it should be, with One Pico for highly regarded New American food and blissful beach scenes (see review); Pedals Cafe for casual indoor-outdoor dining on fresh California fare; and the Lobby Lounge for afternoon tea and sunset cocktails. The magnificent pool and whirlpool area is Santa Monica's best, an activities center offers a beach-toy bonanza, and the modern health club features spa services. *$$$$; AE, DC, DIS, JCB, MC, V; checks OK; www.shuttersonthebeach.com; at Pico Blvd.* &

The Viceroy / ★★

1819 OCEAN AVE, SANTA MONICA; 310/451-8711 OR 800-622-8711 The rather stodgy, built-in-1969 Pacific Shore located a block from the beach has been reinvented as the hippest hostelry in town thanks to hot designer Kelly Wearstler and the hoteliers behind the fashion-forward Avalon and Maison 140. This is the most crowd-conscious of the Kor Group's hotels, and seems to be reveling in its Mondrian-like status as hotel of the moment. The theme is trad British colonial meets breezy SoCal midcentury modern, done in a prevailing color scheme of white, warm gray, and apple green; the result is cosmopolitan coastal, and lots of fun. The bright and airy lobby doubles as a vibrant cocktail lounge. It leads to 170 open, airy guest rooms that fuse clean lines and modern materials like Lucite with classical Regency-inspired detailing. Luxuries include glorious Frette linens, marble bath with soaking tubs and seated vanities, sitting areas, a CD/DVD player with surround sound, and high-speed Internet access. Outside is a glamorous patio with swaying palms, cocktail nooks with white vinyl wingbacks, and two petite swimming pools. A super-trendy party scene takes over on the weekends, so you should be in the mood. Despite its elbow-to-elbow seating and high volume, hip restaurant Whist is winning raves for its unfussy nouveau comfort fare. *$$$–$$$$; AE, DC, JCB, MC, V; no checks; info@viceroysantamonica.com; www.viceroysantamonica.com; 1 block north of Pico Blvd.* &

Westin Los Angeles Airport / ★★☆

5400 W CENTURY BLVD, LOS ANGELES; 310/216-5858 OR 800/937-8461 If you need a base in the LAX area, this attractive and recently renovated hotel is your best bet. What puts it a cut above the airport pack? The answer is Westin's own Heavenly Bed. Touted as "10 layers of heaven," from the custom pillowtop mattress to the fluffy down comforter and family of pillows, the Heavenly Bed lives up to its billing in every respect. This hotel is a great choice on other fronts as well. An attractive lobby leads to quality rooms with all the business-traveler-friendly conveniences, including two-line phones, a good-size work desk with ergonomically correct chair, coffeemakers with fixings from Starbucks, and 24-hour room service. Other handy services and facilities include a concierge, a business center with secretarial services, cell phone rentals, a rental-car counter, free airport shuttle, and conference facilities galore, plus a heated outdoor pool and a fitness center for letting off steam. Weekend rates, which can drop as low as $109—sometimes lower—are an especially good deal. *$$$; AE, DC, DIS, JCB, MC, V; checks OK; www.westin.com; east of Aviation Blvd.* &

The South Bay

RESTAURANTS

The Bottle Inn / ★★☆

26 22ND ST, HERMOSA BEACH; 310/376-9595 A local favorite, the Bottle Inn consistently garners awards for best Italian food, most romantic, and especially best wine list; owner Silvio Petoletti has been honored with *Wine Spectator* commendations for several years running. The restaurant is cozy, quiet, and friendly, located several blocks from the loud, bright center of town. Its rather dated, vaguely European decor has remained unchanged since the Bottle Inn opened in 1974. Surprisingly, it still works—largely thanks to the expert kitchen and exceptional wine list. Wine connoisseurs call ahead for the privilege of dining in the wine cellar, surrounded by great bottles. The menu is classic Italian with such favorites as veal piccata, chicken cacciatore, osso buco, fettuccine bolognese, minestrone soup, and seafood risotto, expertly prepared. Start off with the Bottle Inn's signature toasted Italian focaccia topped with mushrooms, prosciutto, and zucchini with béchamel, fontina, and melted mozzarella cheese, and the Italian wedding soup—flavorful chicken broth with beef dumplings, chicken, pasta shells, vegetables, and Swiss chard. If there's room for dessert, the house-made cannoli is a rare treat. *$$; AE, MC, V; no checks; lunch Mon–Fri, dinner every day; beer and wine; reservations recommended; between Hermosa Ave and the Strand.*

Cafe Pierre / ★☆

317 MANHATTAN BEACH BLVD, MANHATTAN BEACH; 310/545-5252 For years this modern bistro has been one of the South Bay's premier dining spots, and it continues to hold its own within the context of the laid-back beach community of Manhattan Beach, offering a smidgen of pretension along with its French-Italian cuisine. Picture windows open onto the sidewalk scene along busy Manhattan Beach Boulevard, making the cafe less romantic than you might expect from its name. Once seated, you can begin nibbling on marinated kalamata olives or a selection of fresh, crusty bread with gourmet dipping oils. Cafe Pierre serves excellent martinis, especially those made with fruit-infused vodkas (pineapple, strawberry, and more) from decorative jars adorning the bar. The restaurant also boasts a superior wine list. The menu, which combines straightforward bistro favorites with eclectic dishes, makes for mouthwatering reading, but those in the know stick with reliable standards: roasted salmon atop fennel mashed potatoes crowned with a crispy potato bird's nest; peppered filet mignon with either Cognac or Roquefort sauce, accompanied by a mound of pommes frites; or the house specialty, steamed mussels prepared three different ways. Ahi tuna tartare joins a list of more traditional starters like tender escargots and perfect French onion soup. *$$–$$$; AE, MC, V; no checks; lunch Mon–Fri, dinner every day; full bar; reservations recommended; just east of Highland Ave.* &

Caffe Pinguini / ★★☆

6935 PACIFIC AVE, PLAYA DEL REY; 310/306-0117 This small, nearly invisible trattoria might be the least obvious of Playa del Rey's assortment of taverns and comfort food joints, but devotees fill the casually elegant dining room every night. There's a pleasant European feel to the place, from the brick and wood patio enclosed with enormous palm fronds to simply set tables whose crisp linens are accented only by golden cruets of herb-infused olive oil in which to dip Pinguini's chewy, addictive bread. Recorded strains of vintage jazz and classic crooners waft through the restaurant. The menu is simple, but you can count on a subtlety of preparation many overzealous trattorias miss. A crisp arugula and radicchio salad is dressed with just enough balsamic vinegar; perfectly thin pizzas aren't weighed down with too many ingredients; pasta, such as the delectable tortellini stuffed with white truffles, are prepared al dente with economically applied sauces; and even the delicately flavored grilled chicken, fish, and veal picatta shine in their simplicity. You don't have to hear the owner's unmistakable Italian accent to know this is the genuine article. Try the homemade tiramisu. *$–$$; AE, MC, V; no checks; lunch Tues–Fri, dinner Tues–Sun; beer and wine; reservations recommended; at Culver Blvd.* &

Chez Melange / ★★

1716 PACIFIC COAST HWY, REDONDO BEACH; 310/540-1222 Located inside the modest Palos Verdes Inn, this well-regarded restaurant, despite its French name, has been presenting artful global cuisine so long that it's become a Redondo Beach institution. The menu may not be cutting-edge, but it does indeed present a mélange of dishes, moving seamlessly from Japanese to Cajun, Italian to Chinese, and keeping up to date with premium vodkas and a mouthwatering oyster-and-seafood bar. The decor has recently been updated for a comfortable contemporary look. During the day, a wide wall of picture windows makes the restaurant light and airy; at night, it feels decidedly more formal. Each meal begins with a basket of irresistible breads before you move on to American dishes and an array of international entrees such as Moroccan chicken with all the Middle Eastern accompaniments; a filet mignon carne asada platter; fish-and-chips; and fig and prosciutto pizza. Heart-healthy dishes are high on the chef's list, and there's an elegant vegetable plate. *$$; AE, DC, MC, V; no checks; breakfast, lunch, dinner every day; full bar; reservations recommended; www.chezmelange.com; between Palos Verdes Blvd and Prospect Ave.* &

Club Sushi / ★★

1200 HERMOSA AVE, HERMOSA BEACH; 310/372-5939 This place is to sushi what rock-and-roll is to the symphony—there's not a kimono in sight, and the sushi chefs are more likely to give you a high-five than a deferential bow. Situated at the ground-zero intersection of the raucous Hermosa scene, Club Sushi is high-tech, youth-oriented, loud, and beachy—it even has a half-price sushi happy hour daily (4 to 6pm). Crowds pack into an industrial-style space with exposed brick walls, small tables, shoulder-to-shoulder sushi-bar stools, and TV screens showing sportscasts muffled by the sounds of jazz, rock, and calypso music (live five nights a week). But Club Sushi is more than a hangout. It boasts a line of sushi chefs whose flashing hands churn out a mind-boggling amount of great sushi like garlic yellowtail sashimi, a terrific spicy tuna/asparagus tempura roll, and other special house creations. An added draw is the regular menu, which runs a surprising gamut from teriyaki chicken and traditional Japanese dishes to pizzas, pastas, burgers, and great steaks. *$–$$; AE, DC, MC, V; no checks; lunch, dinner every day; full bar; reservations not accepted for fewer than 6; www.clubsushi.com; at the corner of Pier Ave.*

Depot / ★★☆

1250 CABRILLO AVE, TORRANCE; 310/787-7501 Set in a restored train station, this big, welcoming eatery is a spin-off of Redondo Beach's Chez Melange (see review); chef/owner Michael Shafer serves an imaginative assortment of ethnic cuisines with a decided Asian influence and chopsticks on the table. Garlicky rock shrimp sausage with chile–goat cheese wontons, delicate Thai dumplings steamed in ale, or a rich ahi tuna and wasabi caviar tartare are all great ways to start your meal. Though daily specials like killer meat loaf with creamy mashers and pepper stew or Thai-barbe-cued New York steak with cashew rice make up a big portion of the menu, pasta dishes such as rock shrimp linguine and bow-tie pasta with house-smoked chicken, roasted corn, and chile cream sauce always hit the spot. The chef's spicy "Thai-dyed" chicken is a house specialty. While there is plenty for vegetarians, Depot also serves steaks and chops including a generous mixed grill. The wine list is sensibly priced, with plenty of wines by the glass and half bottles, and there's a goodly selec-tion of beers. For special occasions, gather a group of 8 to 12 friends and order the slow-roasted Chinese suckling pig, cooked with 100 cloves of garlic and served with such tasty side dishes as moo-shu pancakes, cashew rice, and spicy vegetable bowls. Aspiring gourmets might want to inquire about Shafer's cooking classes. *$$; AE, MC, V; no checks; lunch Mon–Fri, dinner Mon–Sat; full bar; reservations recom-mended; www.depotrestaurant.com; at Torrance Blvd.* &

Good Stuff / ★☆

1300 HIGHLAND AVE, MANHATTAN BEACH (AND BRANCHES); 310/545-4775 A mainstay of local casual dining, this popular crowd pleaser suits beachgoers, lunch-breakers, and families alike because there's something for everyone. Inside the gray clapboard corner restaurant you'll find brightly painted marine-themed murals and lifeguard memorabilia; picture win-dows let in the sunshine. On nice days the outdoor patio fills first for its view of M.B.'s human parade. Cheerful servers positively bounce through the restaurant, clad in casual sport togs and ferrying generous platters of food that's fresh, carefully prepared, and very affordable. The mile-long menu runs the gamut, featuring stand-outs like Santa Fe chicken omelet, cinnamon swirl French toast, a superb homemade veggie burger, turkey or tuna wrapped in gourmet tortillas, burritos and Mexican favorites, enormous main course salads, steaming hot pastas, and a selection of dinner-only prime rib, steak, ribs, fish, and chicken entrees. Other locations include one on the Strand near the Hermosa Beach pier (1286 The Strand; 310/374-2334), Redondo Beach (617 Pacific Coast Hwy; 310/316-0262), and West Los Angeles, with a much more limited menu (11903 West Olympic Blvd; 310/477-9011). *$; AE, DC, DIS, MC, V; no checks; breakfast, lunch, dinner every day; beer and wine; reser-vations not accepted; www.eatgoodstuff.com; at the corner of 13th St.* &

Kincaid's Bay House / ★★☆

500 FISHERMAN'S WHARF, REDONDO BEACH; 310/318-6080 This branch of the venerable San Francisco/Hawaii surf-and-turf chain lends a touch of class to the bustling Redondo Beach pier. A big cut above the usual wharfside eatery, this is an imposing, though informal, place with sleek, clubby decor, a huge mahogany bar, panoramic ocean views, and plenty of outdoor seating. Its open kitchen features a big hardwood spit-roaster turning out Kincaid's irresistible grilled and smoked seafood and meat. The menu offers Hawaiian-influenced dishes like char-sui pork skewers that are grilled over applewood to caramelize the sweet-tart honey-soy-hoisin marinade. Fresh fish from the Pacific Northwest and Hawaii are featured each day. You can't go wrong with the grilled salmon with a lemon-butter-vermouth glaze, served with garlic mashed potatoes and crispy waffle chips; other seafood specialties include wood-smoked prawns flavored with chipotle-ancho rub and Kincaid's signature barbecue hollandaise, plus crab-and-shrimp hash served with sherry-cream sauce. You'll catch a whiff of the pit-roasted prime rib on the way in. If that doesn't entice you, consider seasoned and buttered sirloin, or pan-seared venison flavored with blackberry and sage. For dessert there's a great chocolate soufflé and a real Key lime pie. *$$–$$$; AE, DC, DIS, MC, V; no checks; lunch Mon–Sat, dinner every day, brunch Sun; full bar; reservations recommended; www. kincaids.com; at the south end of Harbor Dr.* &

LODGINGS

Barnabey's Manhattan Beach / ★★

3501 SEPULVEDA BLVD, MANHATTAN BEACH; 310/750-0300 OR 888/239-6295 Step from laid-back Southern California into Merrie Olde England at this high-concept hostelry, which offers a pleasant surprise with dedicated attention, personal comfort and service, and romantic Victorian appeal. Located just a mile from the beach but a world removed, the hotel is shielded from busy six-lane Sepulveda Boulevard by privacy walls, abundant foliage, and a clever design that focuses attention on the lush interior courtyard. It's easy to play along with the Victorian theme when you're surrounded by dark wood paneling, ornate red gas lamps, quintessentially British gilt-framed oil paintings, and plenty of polished brass and frilly chintz. The 126 guest rooms have the rich aura of a turn-of-the-20th-century library, complete with lined bookshelves. They're also exceedingly comfortable, featuring hand-carved beds dressed in fluffy comforters, coffeemakers, two-line phones, and small but pretty bathrooms. Deluxe rooms sport a mantel-topped faux hearths and private balconies overlooking the wisteria-draped patio. There's a heated pool and whirlpool spa outdoors, and plus the Cambridge Club, an ornate Edwardian parlor serving cocktails and light fare for every meal. *$$–$$$; AE, DC, DIS, MC, V; no checks; www.barnabeyshotel.com; at Rosecrans Ave.* &

Beach House at Hermosa / ★★★

1300 THE STRAND, HERMOSA BEACH; 310/374-3001 OR 888/895-4559 Sporting a New England–reminiscent facade and oodles of beach-cottage luxury, this comfortable-chic retreat was built in 1998 on the South Bay's best beach, a half-hour south of Santa Monica. Time-share owners occupy the beautifully designed studio suites up to 90 days a year; otherwise, the units go to guests, who benefit from full resort services and five-star luxuries at a three-star price. Each studio is divided between a sleeping area—with a beautifully made king bed, terrific built-in work area, and its own TV—and a sunken living room with wood-burning fireplace, overstuffed sleeper sofa, entertainment center with five-disc CD player, furnished balcony or patio, and sleek "micro-kitchen" including stove top, microwave, and dishware. The rooms are furnished to feel like home, and everything is extra-plush and stylish. The big bathroom is a study in relaxation, with deep soaking tub, separate shower, and generous granite countertops. The hotel sits right on the Strand, offering immediate access to fabulous sand and surf. Rooms stay serene during the summertime carnival with quality construction that includes double-paned windows and "quiet" walls. The gracious staff has a respectful yet casual attitude that suits the property perfectly. Continental breakfast is included, and in-room spa services are available. *$$$–$$$$; AE, DC, DIS, JCB, MC, V; checks OK; info@beach-house.com; www.beach-house.com; at 14th St.* ♿

Inn at Playa del Rey Bed and Breakfast / ★★☆

435 CULVER BLVD, PLAYA DEL REY; 310/574-1920 This newish, 21-room B&B doesn't have the history behind it that sister Channel Road Inn does, but so what? The contemporary inn boasts better rooms, more luxury comforts, and a one-of-a-kind location—on the edge of the 350-acre Ballona Wetlands bird sanctuary—that gives it a feeling of total retreat. Distressed wood furnishings and antique beds lend the artfully decorated, amenity-laden rooms a sophisticated country-inn appeal. Luxuries include VCRs tucked away in handsome armoires, two-line phones, top-quality robes and linens, and gorgeous bathrooms; most have balconies as well. The ultimate in romance is the spacious View Suites, whose pièce de résistance is a two-sided fireplace that casts a heavenly glow on both your pillowy bed and the whirlpool tub for two. Guests can enjoy a soak under the stars in the garden hot tub and spectacular views from the bright and airy living room. A breakfast buffet features home-baked goods and gourmet hot dishes; refreshments are also laid out in the afternoon. Service is professional and impeccable. A swimmable beach is a walk away. While Playa del Rey is a half-hour drive from the city proper, it's ideal for those looking for quiet, a small-town vibe, or airport convenience. *$$$; AE, MC, V; checks OK; info@innatplayadelrey.com; www.innatplayadelrey.com; south of Jefferson Blvd.* ♿

The Portofino Hotel and Yacht Club / ★★☆

260 PORTOFINO WY, REDONDO BEACH; 310/379-8481 OR 800/468-4292 Built on a promontory jutting into the main King Harbor channel, this contemporary resort has a relaxed elegance that fits its yacht club personality and setting perfectly. The main level features an exquisite light-filled atrium lounge with cheerfully upholstered armchairs that invite you to sit before the marble fireplace and gaze oceanward through tall windows. Guest rooms are on three floors; views improve (and rates rise) as you ascend. Every room has a private balcony and floor-to-ceiling windows; those on the ocean-facing side have a panoramic view past the breakwater, while marina-side quarters spy on private yachts docked in the Portofino Marina as well as the massive Wyland whale mural adorning the concrete power plant on Harbor Drive. All are well outfitted with clean and bright French country furnishings that team broad plaids with richly colored florals and pale wood furniture. The rooms are modestly sized but provide every comfort, from coffeemakers to spacious work areas for business travelers; bathrooms are stocked with plush towels and luxury toiletries. On site is Breakwater, a jazzy surf and turf seafooder with a white-tablecloth waterside setting. All of King Harbor is within walking distance. $$$; AE, DC, DIS, MC, V; checks OK; www.hotelportofino.com; west of Harbor Dr. &

Pasadena and the San Gabriel Valley

Set in the foothills of the San Gabriel Mountains, the San Gabriel Valley, with its suburban landscape and laid-back Southern California lifestyle, is in stark contrast to the hustle and bustle of city living. What was once a rural area of orange, lemon, and walnut groves and ranches is today a largely residential region with a growing Asian and Hispanic population—an addition that has brought cultural diversity to the area. From the charming town of Pasadena, the San Gabriel Valley spans eastward, including such neighboring communities as San Marino, Arcadia, and Monrovia. Though you'll find turn-of-the-20th-century estates nestled on tree-lined streets and sprawling horse ranches with plenty of rugged terrain, much of the San Gabriel Valley is populated with boxy stucco homes and historic downtown sections that are hard to differentiate from city to city. New housing developments and up-and-coming businesses are forcing the region to expand haphazardly, but despite its commercial growth the valley still boasts vast expanses of picturesque countryside— from the hiking paths of Angeles Crest National Forest to equestrian trails in the neighboring foothills.

The crown jewel of the San Gabriel Valley, **PASADENA** is an oasis of style and culture. In the early 1900s, this onetime stretch of orange groves beneath the picturesque San Gabriel Mountains attracted wealthy East Coasters looking to escape harsh winters. But once the sun-seeking aristocrats arrived, many decided to stay. Elaborate Victorian mansions, Craftsman-style bungalows, and other lavish edifices soon sprang up around the rural community, and a sophisticated society with theater, museums, and elegant gardens quickly followed.

Today, this refined city possesses an air of old money, with its restored historic district and vast cultural offerings; and in contrast to neighboring Los Angeles's flashy community, it attracts more of a pearls-and-loafers crowd, who reside in lavish bungalows and drive Volvos.

Pasadena is perhaps best known for its January 1 **TOURNAMENT OF ROSES PARADE** and **ROSE BOWL** football game (626/449-7673; www.tournamentof roses.com), where the annual Big 10 versus Pac 10 football rivalry is played out. For the rest of the year the city's most popular draw is **OLD TOWN** (bordered by Arroyo Pkwy on the east, Pasadena Ave on the west, Walnut St on the north, and Del Mar on the south), a 20-block stretch of shops, restaurants, cafes, art galleries, and movie theaters. This bustling district, awash with restored buildings from the late 1800s, has in recent years attracted a whole new crowd to Pasadena, who come for the newly chic historic atmosphere, shopping, and restaurants and only later discover the historic city's museums and cultural attractions. Shoppers also flock to the recently opened **PASEO COLORADO** (280 E Colorado Blvd; 626/795-8891) for outdoor browsing amid 65 shops, dining, and moviegoing at Pacific 14 Theaters.

At the western end of Old Town, the **NORTON SIMON MUSEUM** (411 W Colorado Blvd; 626/449-6840; www.nortonsimon.org) offers an impressive collection of impressionist works by the likes of van Gogh, Renoir, Degas, and Monet. Farther east, the **PACIFIC ASIA MUSEUM** (46 N Los Robles Ave; 626/449-2742; www.pacasiamuseum.org), complete with Chinese-style garden and koi pond, celebrates Asian-inspired art from the Far East.

For a close-up look at Pasadena's early architecture, the **GAMBLE HOUSE** (4 Westmoreland Pl; 626/793-3334; www.gamblehouse.usc.edu) is the area's finest example of Craftsman style and is open for public viewing. Built in 1908 by famed architects Greene & Greene, the bungalow features amazing handcrafted teak woodwork, Tiffany glass, and many of the home's original furnishings.

The Rose Bowl may be best known for its annual namesake New Year's Day football game and as the home of UCLA football, but the stadium also hosts an amazing **FLEA MARKET** (626/577-3100; www.rgcshows.com/rosebowl.asp) on the second Sunday of every month, when the stadium parking lot is overflowing with collectibles, albums, antiques, furniture, carpets, and virtually everything else you can imagine.

For more information on the Pasadena area, call the **PASADENA CONVENTION & VISITORS BUREAU** (171 S Los Robles Ave; 626/795-9311; www.pasadena cal.com).

Set on the northwestern edge of the San Gabriel Valley, the suburban neighborhood of **LA CAÑADA–FLINTRIDGE** is known for rolling hills and rugged countryside, where avid equestrians reside on spacious ranches and gardeners come to swoon over the utterly romantic and pastoral **DESCANSO GARDENS** (1418 Descanso Dr; 818/949-4200; www.descansogardens.org). The stately 165-acre property features a California live oak forest—with an abundance of camellias and azaleas—that's straight out of *A Midsummer Night's Dream,* plus elaborate rose gardens, an iris garden, lilac garden, Japanese tea garden, art gallery, gift shop, cafe, and picnic area.

Founded in the early 1900s by railroad tycoon and art collector Henry Huntington, the exclusive neighborhood of **SAN MARINO** is the land of debutantes and blue bloods, with enough palatial estates to fill the pages of *Architectural Digest* well into the next decade. You could easily spend the day just driving around looking at fabulous homes, but make a point of stopping at **THE HUNTINGTON LIBRARY, ART COLLECTIONS, AND BOTANICAL GARDENS** (1151 Oxford Rd; 626/405-2100; www.huntington.org). Its more than 130 acres of beautifully landscaped grounds on the former estate of the city's founder are considered one of Los Angeles County's finest outdoor treasures. The library also boasts an impressive collection of rare books and artworks, including a Gutenberg Bible and Gainsborough's *The Blue Boy.*

One of the valley's oldest cities, the largely Hispanic community of **SAN GABRIEL** is the home of the **MISSION SAN GABRIEL ARCHANGEL** (428 S Mission Dr; 626/457-3035; www.sangabrielmission.org). Founded in 1771 on a spot intersected

PASADENA'S BUNGALOW HEAVEN

Long adored by "bungalowners" and architecture buffs, Pasadena's Bungalow Heaven is now a formally preserved slice of Southern California history. This charming neighborhood's nickname became its official designation in 1989, when determined preservationists succeeded in having a Landmark District created to encompass the 800-plus pre-Depression-era bungalows here.

Ironically, the bungalow, inexpensive to construct and often sold in kits, was never intended to be a lasting part of the landscape. Easterners had been drawn to the unspoiled beauty and hospitable climate of Pasadena (a Chippewa word meaning "crown of the valley") since Victorian times. In the early 20th century, Midwesterners looking for a warm, economical place to settle came in droves—hence the prevalence of street names like Madison, Michigan, Peoria, and Wabash. Their desire for affordable housing, coupled with the growing Arts and Crafts design movement, proved fertile ground for the growth of bungalow neighborhoods.

At the same time, many artists and architects were beginning to reject the stifling ornateness of Victorian style and to stress simplicity, organic motifs, and natural materials, along with a greater appreciation of—and interaction with—nature. The distinctive elements of the bungalow reflect these trends. Abundant windows, expansive porches, and limited indoor space all extend the living area outdoors. The widespread use of raw natural materials such as exposed beams, rough-hewn boulders, and simple clay tiles reflect a respect for nature and L.A.'s Spanish, Mexican, and Japanese heritage. Bungalow design spoke directly to the climate: there were overhanging eaves for daylight shading and lots of windows for pre-AC ventilation. Inside, the furniture style was often called mission because it resembled the stark simplicity of nearby Spanish missions.

North Mentor Avenue defines the western border of Bungalow Heaven; at number 775, don't miss the striking 1913 example of an airplane bungalow, whose wide lower gables resemble the spreading wings of a plane, topped with a second-story "cockpit." Over on North Michigan Avenue, notice the unusual entrance to number 875, a 1909 Craftsman whose front door passes right through the wide, lopsided brick chimney. Stroll these tree-lined blocks and choose your own favorites.

Bungalow Heaven—easily reached from the California 134 and Interstate 210 freeways—is centered around McDonald Park, between Lake and Hill Avenues north of Orange Grove Boulevard. The Bungalow Heaven Neighborhood Association conducts a house tour each April, but feel free to check out the neighborhood whenever you're in Pasadena. For more information, contact the BHNA (626/585-2172; http://home.earthlink.net/~bhna).

—*Stephanie Avnet Yates*

by three heavily trafficked trails leading new settlers into California, the mission was once one of the state's wealthiest, featuring a copper baptismal font that was a gift from the king of Spain. Though it has suffered extensive earthquake damage over the years and even had to close for a time because its structure was deemed unsafe, restorations have allowed it to reopen to the public for self-guided tours, guided tours by appointment, and mass twice daily on Sunday.

Glendale

RESTAURANTS

Cinnabar / ★★☆

933 S BRAND BLVD, GLENDALE; 818/551-1155 The neon signs outside tall windows cast a strange reddish hue over Cinnabar's eclectic dining room, and the faux-white-tiger-skin chairs and six-foot white parasols hanging upside down from the ceiling complete the uniquely exotic ambience. However, that just sets the mood for this out-of-the-ordinary dining establishment. Housed in an old Bekins warehouse, Cinnabar combines a casual atmosphere with elegant French/Pacific Rim fare. Chef Damon Bruner's menus emphasizes creative seafood, with such specialties as spicy lemongrass bouillabaisse chock-full of salmon, clams, lobster, rock shrimp, scallops, and rice noodles, or sesame-crusted farm-raised salmon with wasabi mashed potatoes and lobster curry sauce. Start with crisp spring rolls, or half a dozen oysters with an unusual sweet-spicy pickled ginger–sake granita. Save room for the homemade desserts, such as a delicious banana–chocolate mousse tart or chocolate fondue with rich warm Belgian chocolate. And be sure to pay homage to the ornate antique bar, a former Chinese shrine imported from a defunct Chinatown restaurant. You'll always find a prix-fixe vegetarian menu here, and many of the regular entrees are available as half orders—they're plenty big. *$$; AE, CB, DC, DIS, MC, V; no checks; dinner Tues–Sun; full bar; reservations recommended; 1 block north of Chevy Chase Dr.* &

Fresco Ristorante / ★★

514 S BRAND BLVD, GLENDALE; 818/247-5541 Set amid Glendale's strip of car dealerships, this restaurant has made a name for itself by serving inventive, reasonably priced Northern Italian fare with an emphasis on fresh ingredients. Owner/chef Antonio Orlando makes his breads, pastas, gelati, sorbetti, and pastries on the premises. Starters like corn crepes stuffed with duck in a port wine sauce pave the way for entrees like gnocchi with porcini mushrooms in a tomato sauce, smoked chicken and asparagus ravioli, and creamy lamb and mushroom risotto. Orlando also does a delightful thinly pounded and breaded veal chop with capers, garlic, and lemon in a light white wine sauce and other delectable meat, chicken, and fish dishes. And you can't go wrong with the garlicky Caesar salad, prepared for two tableside by tuxedo-clad waiters. The romantically lit dining room, bordered by Roman columns and archways and a glass-encased wine cellar, gives Fresco a feeling of elegance at affordable prices. There's live piano entertainment on Friday and Saturday nights. *$$; AE, DC, DIS,*

MC, V; no checks; lunch Mon–Fri, dinner Mon–Sat; full bar; reservations recommended; between Chestnut St and Colorado Ave. &

Pasadena

RESTAURANTS

Arirang / ★★☆

114 W UNION ST, PASADENA; 626/577-8885 In a rambling, warehouselike space just north of Colorado Boulevard in Old Town, Arirang is a Korean barbecue adventure raised to the level of, if not haute cuisine, at least highly sophisticated cooking. Most diners go for the various barbecue selections—marinated rib-eye steak, short ribs, pork, beef tongue, chicken, prawns, scallops, and the like, all of which arrive with the usual entourage of soup, rice, lettuce, raw garlic, sliced peppers, and sundry kimchees. But those who have been there and done that expand their horizons to include the remarkable panfried dumplings along with the spring onion pancake, the kimchee and pork pancake, the dazzling tartare steak, and the various hot pots of braised tripe and vegetables or sliced pork with salted cabbage. To wash it all down, there's OB Beer from Korea, as good as if not better than the fine beers of Japan. *$; AE, DC, DIS, MC, V; no checks; lunch Mon–Fri, dinner every day; full bar; reservations not necessary; south side of Union St, west of Fair Oaks Ave.* &

Arroyo Chop House / ★★★

536 S ARROYO PKWY, PASADENA; 626/57-PRIME In a modern-meets-Craftsman setting heavy with wood, glass, and brass, the pure-classic menu here starts with salads: there's a salad of mixed greens, a Caesar, a plate of sliced beefsteak tomatoes with sliced red onions (in the style of New York's Peter Luger's), a salad of spinach and hearts of palm, and the pride of the house—a chilled heart of iceberg lettuce (yes!) drenched in blue cheese dressing. Every one of the steaks are USDA prime—from the filet mignon through the rib-eye, porterhouse, New York strip, and the Delmonico cut—and seared to perfection in a high-temperature broiler (akin to the one pioneered at the Ruth's Chris chain) that seals in the meat's juices. The Chop House's old-money clientele appreciates this no-surprises high quality, presented by efficient and respectful servers who also know their way around the wine list. *$$; AE, CB, DC, V; no checks; dinner every day; full bar; reservations required; at California Blvd.*

Bistro 45 / ★★★

45 MENTOR AVE, PASADENA; 626/795-2478 The highly respected Bistro 45—regularly named one of the top restaurants in L.A. by *Wine Spectator*—took one of the fussiest spots in town and gave it an art-deco-at-the-end-of-the-decade look—very angular, very medium cool, very edge-of-decadence. The cuisine is basically California bistro, and it changes often. On any given day, the menu might include such pleasures as roasted citrus-marinated chicken breast with artichoke sauce and a crispy potato-Gruyère galette, or sautéed sea bass with shrimp sauce, truffled risotto, and roasted asparagus. Desserts are a major temptation here, especially the chocolate espresso praline cake with cocoa bean ice cream. The wine list is impressive and offers plenty of by-the-glass and half-bottle choices. Bistro 45's connoisseur wine dinners, generally built around a particular winery and often attended by the winemaker, are almost certainly the most popular in town. The waiters define the California style—affable and knowledgeable at the same time. The only attitude here is a good one. *$$; AE, DC, MC, V; lunch Tues–Fri, dinner Tues–Sun; full bar; reservations required; www.bistro45.com; south of Colorado Blvd.* ♿

Buca di Beppo / ★★

80 W GREEN ST, PASADENA (AND BRANCHES); 626/792-7272 Buca di Beppo is often compared to Carmine's in New York, as both are notable for red-sauce chow served in giant portions. The national Buca di Beppo chain is a Smithsonian of Italiana, with hundreds of photographs on the walls of gangsters, priests, pretty girls, grouchy mamas, and musicians. It's truly a place where you can revel in your Italian roots and chuckle at them at the same time. All the portions are for groups of four, which makes the prices—in the high teens—a terrific deal. And this is chow that sticks to your ribs—garlic bread, roasted peppers with garlic and anchovies, good pizzas as big as breadboards, rigatoni tossed with white beans and sausage, chicken cacciatore over garlic mashed potatoes, and linguine topped with an ocean of seafood. Hardly anyone leaves without a doggie bag. The same exuberant feasting goes on at these additional locations: Brea (1609 East Imperial Hwy; 714/529-6262), Encino (17500 Ventura Blvd; 818/995-3288), Redondo Beach (1670 S Pacific Coast Hwy; 310/540-3246), Santa Monica (1442 2nd St; 310/587-2782), and Universal City (1000 Universal Center Dr; 818/509-9463). *$; AE, MC; no checks; dinner every day; full bar; reservations recommended; www.bucadibeppo.com; southeast corner of DeLacey and W Green Sts.* ♿

Cafe Santorini / ★★☆

64 W UNION ST, PASADENA; 626/564-4200 Cafe Santorini sits in the same square as the AMC Multiplex in Old Town, with its entrance down a short alleyway. While the large upstairs room with bare brick walls and polished wood floors has a number of pleasant tables, they aren't nearly as popular as the tables outside. The upstairs patio is clearly the place to sit at Cafe Santorini, overlooking the crowds coming and going below. The thing to do here is to start with the meze platter, a bounty of stuffed grape leaves, spanakopita and *tiropita,* fried kibbee, tabbouleh, and feta cheese that's enough for a light meal for two. From there, things wander a bit—from a Caesar salad with salmon, a mushroom risotto with foie gras, an Armenian sausage pizza, and through a world of pastas. There's also a succulent souvlaki, a terrific oven-baked chicken with porcinis and a marsala wine sauce, and a Pacific seafood fricassee of shrimp, scallops, salmon, calamari, and mushrooms in a marinara sauce. Prices are right. And you can almost smell the Mediterranean in the air. *$–$$; AE, MC, V; no checks; lunch, dinner every day, brunch Sun; full bar; reservations recommended; www.cafesantorini.com; west of Fair Oaks Ave.*

Celestino Ristorante / ★★

141 S LAKE AVE, PASADENA; 626/795-4006 Celestino is the creation of chef Celestino Drago, L.A.'s impresario of Italian eateries (he's responsible for Drago, Celestino Steak House, and Il Pastaio). Here chef Drago (along with his brother Giacomino) is doing light, casual, relatively inexpensive fare. It's unlikely you'll find a better bruschetta this side of the Po River—wonderfully crisp bread, topped with just the right balance of garlic, tomato, and arugula. The less-traditional *arancine di riso* (literally, "little rice oranges") look like inverted ice cream cones filled with a dollop of beef stew, peas, and provolone. Pastas come in two forms— egg or durum wheat. Drago is a master of risottos, flavored with such combinations as red beets and goat cheese, porcini and mascarpone, lobster and peppers, or squid and scallops. Think of Celestino as a casual Italian cafe where you can find dishes that always satisfy, no matter what you're in the mood for. *$$; AE, MC, V; no checks; lunch Mon–Fri, dinner Mon–Sat; full bar; reservations recommended; www. celestinodrago.com; south of Green St.* &

Clearwater Seafood / ★★

168 W COLORADO BLVD, PASADENA; 626/356-0959 Clearwater is where you'll find New Wave seafood in a comfortably modernistic setting. Call it seafood for the new millennium: the freshest of fish cooked in a wide variety of ways, a good deal of heart-healthy Mediterranean ingredients thrown in for good measure, and a fair number of vegetarian dishes and salads, served in a setting complete with a dramatic outdoor patio. Oysters are whatever happens to be fresh and available—perhaps nothing more complex than Bluepoints from Long Island or Hama Hamas from Washington State. Though the menu changes regularly, expect a fine cioppino, a creamy clam chowder, the sweetest lobster tails, roasted halibut, crisp striped bass, ahi, mahimahi and the like. Prince Edward Island mussels and Hog Island Manila clams are steamed. This is easily some of the best seafood in Pasadena. *$–$$; AE, MC, V; no checks; lunch, dinner every day; full bar; reservations recommended; www.kingsseafood.com; southeast corner of Colorado Blvd and Pasadena Ave.* &

Crocodile Cafe / ★

140 S LAKE AVE, PASADENA (AND BRANCHES); 626/449-9900 The Crocodile Cafe is the sort of restaurant where you can drop by for a casual burger or where a sizable group can go for a jolly and affordable festive birthday celebration. What they do, they do very well—the black bean and sirloin chili soup is one of the best in town. The quesadilla is packed to overflowing with jack and ranchero cheeses and topped with salsa and guacamole. Pot stickers are filled with shrimp and veggies in a lime-ginger-soy dip. They make a classic hamburger here, oak-wood grilled, served with fries, and with or without grilled onions. The pizzas and calzones are variations on the Spago/California Pizza Kitchen style, with the barbecued chicken pizza a real standout. Of the large plates, the Cuban chicken breast is quite a feed—cinnamon-and-raisin-sweetened chicken with bananas and rice on the side. It's easy to get stuffed here for very little and have a heck of a good time in the process. You'll find more Crocodile Cafes in Old Town Pasadena (88 W Colorado Blvd; 626/568-9310), Burbank (201 N San Fernando

Blvd; 818/843-7999), Glendale (626 N Central Ave; 818/241-1114), and Santa Monica (101 Santa Monica Blvd; 310/394-4783). *$; AE, MC, V; no checks; lunch, dinner every day; full bar; reservations not necessary; www.crocodilecafe.com; near Green St.* &

DeLacey's Club 41 / ★

41 S DELACEY ST, PASADENA; 626/795-4141 DeLacey's is one of the most comfortable steak houses around. It's a manly establishment, heavy with wood, glass, and brass, with a fine TV bar where sports lovers gather, and spacious booths where an affectionate couple can gaze deep into each other's eyes over oysters Rockefeller or a perfect Caesar salad. Though DeLacey's is only about 15 years old, it smacks of early times. Service is the style you'd expect at Musso & Frank in Hollywood—efficient without being abrupt. The menu is classic—there's a whole section of dipped sandwiches (roast beef, pork, lamb), along with hot plate specials such as roast pork with applesauce, calf's liver and meat loaf, and a goodly selection of pastas. Spinach salad is served with a proper hot dressing, filet mignon is wrapped in bacon, lamb chops are double loin, the rib-eye steak melts in your mouth, and the prime rib comes as rare as you want it. *$$; AE, CB, DC, DIS, MC, V; no checks; lunch, dinner every day; full bar; reservations recommended; south of Colorado Blvd.* &

Derek's / ★★★☆

181 E GLENARM ST, PASADENA; 626/799-5252 The best way to approach dinner in this casually elegant Cal-American restaurant is to head straight for the chef's menu. It changes once a month, shifting with the seasons. A typical five-course menu might include appetizer and hot or cold soup of the day, followed by plumpest prosciutto-wrapped sea scallops, herb-crusted ahi tuna with house-made spinach ravioli and asparagus cream, and an impressively moist pork tenderloin main course. Diners might be invited to choose dessert from the regular menu, which typically lists a decadent chocolate-espresso bread pudding served warm with caramel sauce and crème anglaise. A lighter wine-poached pear tart with whipped crème fraîche and a grape cabernet sauce would be an equal temptation. Those who prefer à la carte might consider a sinfully rich starter of seared foie gras with caramelized mangos, the perfect rack of lamb with peppered gnocchi, or the roast Muscovy duck with trendy wasabi mashed potatoes, soy beurre blanc, and wild mushrooms. Derek's is hard to spot; even while driving down Glenarm, you might not notice it. But as an exercise in serendipity, it's worth sleuthing out. *$$; AE, MC, V; no checks; dinner Tues–Sat; full bar; reservations recommended; www.dereks.com; in a mini-mall on north side of Glenarm St, east of Arroyo Pkwy.* &

The Grill at the Ritz-Carlton Huntington Hotel & Spa / ★★★

1401 S OAK KNOLL AVE, PASADENA; 626/577-2867 Dining is more of an event than a meal in this elegant hotel restaurant. Wood-paneled walls, crystal sconces, seascape paintings, and a collection of antique carved ships create a sophisticated, clubby background for the menu of continental classics. Selections here, as refined as the setting, might include sautéed foie gras with a warm fig tart or a tropical crab salad to start, followed perhaps by perfectly poached Maine lobster with roasted corn cake and lobster bisque sauce, or roast veal loin with arti-choke–white bean ragout and serrano ham—all served by waiters whose profes-sionalism is quintessential Ritz-Carlton. A warm chocolate cake with liquid caramel center and banana ice cream is one highlight of the exquisite dessert menu. The chef offers both a three-course à la carte menu and a five-course tasting menu. An impres-sive wine list of more than 350 vintages ensures the perfect bottle to complement your meal. *$$$; AE, DC, DIS, JCB, MC, V; no checks; dinner every day; full bar; reservations required; www.ritzcarlton.com; exit 210 Fwy at Lake Ave and go south until it becomes Oak Knoll St.* &

Houston's / ★★

320 S ARROYO PKWY, PASADENA; 626/577-6001 Houston's is a burgeoning chain now numbering some two dozen, with restaurants in Southern cities like Atlanta, Dallas, and, yes, Houston. It's a good-looking steak house with an open kitchen and a menu that mixes burgers with barbecue. The beef choices, like the filet mignon, the New York strip, and the prime rib, are large enough to feed two people with ease. The thing to pacify your hunger pangs while you wait for your meal is the Chicago-style spinach and artichoke dip, a ridiculously caloric bowl of creamed spinach and artichoke hearts topped with melted cheese, accompanied by sour cream, salsa, and tortilla chips. Main courses go straight to the point—good, solid, culinary Americana. There's a fine hickory burger, and an intriguing firehouse-chili-topped Texas burger that's served only on Saturdays. And there's everybody's favorite dish, the barbecued ribs. The menu says "Our Knife and Fork Version," but that isn't really true: pick up the tender ribs with your fingers, and the meat absolutely drops off the bone. *$–$$; AE, MC, V; no checks; lunch, dinner every day; full bar; reservations recommended; www.houstons.com; south of Colorado Blvd.* &

Il Fornaio / ★★

1 COLORADO BLVD, PASADENA (AND BRANCHES); 626/683-9797 This outpost of the Il Fornaio chain is noisy in the way that restaurants filled with people having a very good time tend to be noisy. It's very much like being in Italy, with food to match: soft polenta with mushrooms and Parmesan, and an out-standing eggplant dish with goat cheese, sun-dried tomatoes, onions, capers, and balsamic vinegar. They make a fine Tuscan bean and barley soup, and a fantastic tomato soup with Tuscan bread. The pizza is crispy, crunchy, and thin-crusted, topped with the sort of stuff you might find in the Piazza Navona in Rome—moz-zarella, provolone, grilled eggplant, ricotta, red onions, garlic, and so forth. It works perfectly as an appetizer for two or as a main course for one, as does the focaccia bread stuffed with Gorgonzola, pine nuts, basil, and onions. Additional Southern California locations include Beverly Hills (301 N Beverly Dr; 310/550-8330), Santa Monica (1551 Ocean Ave; 310/451-7800), and Manhattan Beach (1800 Rosecrans Ave; 310-725-9555). *$; AE, MC, V; no checks; breakfast, lunch, dinner every day; full bar; reservations recommended; www.ilfornaio.com; west of Fair Oaks Ave.*

Julienne / ★★☆

2649 MISSION ST, SAN MARINO; 626/441-2299 Julienne is where affluent San Marino goes to eat out casually, and a major destination for the ladies who lunch. It's a beguiling setting with really terrific food, open for breakfast and lunch only. If you like, you can sit outdoors surrounded by flowers and watch (to quote T. S. Eliot), "the women come and go/talking of Michelangelo." As you might expect here, *les salades* abound—baby greens topped with warmed cornmeal-encrusted chèvre and herbed croutons; salade niçoise with seared ahi; Caesar julienne tossed with rosemary-spiked croutons and grilled chicken breast; and garden greens with sautéed crab cakes. Breakfast is a major treat as well, with fluffy omelets featuring delightful fillings, bread pudding French toast, great steel-cut oatmeal you can bite into, and inventive quiches. The restaurant also has a thriving takeout section, a major stop for Hollywood Bowl picnickers in summer. *$; AE, MC, V; checks OK; breakfast, lunch Mon–Sat; wine only; reservations recommended; near El Molino Ave.* &

Kingston Cafe / ★

 333 S FAIR OAKS AVE, PASADENA; 626/405-8080 The Kingston Cafe is several blocks south of the manic energy of Old Town's Colorado Boulevard, a renovated little house where you can enjoy a privacy and friendly service along with your good Jamaican meal. Dishes on the menu here offer a fine cross-section of that cuisine—many at the spicy end of the spectrum. The option is yours, but know that if you ask for a dish to be prepared hot, it will be blazing. Jerk chicken, the ubiquitous specialty of Jamaican restaurants, is titled Hot Flashes here and is so tender it falls right off the bone. Curried chicken is named Yellow Glow, and curried goat is Kingston Glow. The matrimony bread pudding is sweeter than most marriages, and holds together far better. *$; AE, DIS, MC, V; no checks; lunch, dinner Tues–Sat; beer and wine; reservations not necessary; west side of Fair Oaks Ave, south of Colorado Blvd.*

Kuala Lumpur / ★

69 W GREEN ST, PASADENA; 626/577-5175 At Kuala Lumpur, named for the capital of Malaysia, dishes are both familiar and exotic. The satay is as good as any in town—skewered beef, chicken, pork, or shrimp with a smooth peanut-chile sauce. The *puteri* roll is an ample Malaysian egg roll, very crisp, filled with just about everything in the kitchen. Spicy mango shrimp is stir-fried with mango, mango juice, chile sambal, garlic, and onions. The deep-fried pulau shrimp's flavor is tempered with a sauce of lemongrass, garlic, and shallots, a different flavor emerging with each bite. Spicy fish comes cooked in a tamarind sauce over broad noodles, a dish whose exotic flavor is hard to pinpoint and harder to forget. Try the chicken grilled in *ketjap*, a sweet soy sauce that has nothing to do with the red stuff—in spite of its familiar name. For dessert, sticky rice with mango covered in custard sauce, or fried banana with honey or custard will put out the fire in your mouth—although actually most dishes here can be ordered mild. *$; AE, MC, V; no checks; lunch, dinner Tues–Sun; beer and wine; reservations recommended; at DeLacey St.*

Marston's / ★★☆

151 E WALNUT ST, PASADENA; 626/796-2459 Marston's is not an old restaurant, but within a decade this sweet Craftsman bungalow near City Hall has become a Pasadena tradition. It's a cozy (read: small) place, so at lunchtime there's always a wait. Breakfast is a gala affair, ideal for those who like their first meal of the day big and sumptuous and could care less about cholesterol. The menu includes arguably the best French toast in town—two fat slabs of sourdough soaked in egg batter, rolled in cornflakes, and griddled to perfection; another fine choice is macadamia nut–blueberry pancakes. For lunch the best of the best is the Pasadena salad, an incredible mixture of spinach, avocado, candied pecans, chicken, scallions, and bacon in a slightly sweet dressing accompanied by a basket of crunchy cheese popovers. You might also consider the superb cobb salad, grilled chicken Caesar, grilled chicken breast club sandwich with black bean mayonnaise, "white lightnin' chili" with chicken, or grilled chicken and Gorgonzola melt. *$; MC, V; no checks; breakfast, lunch Tues–Sat; no alcohol; reservations not accepted; north side of Walnut St, east of Raymond Ave.* &

Mi Piace / ★★

25 E COLORADO BLVD, PASADENA (AND BRANCHES); 626/795-3131 Mi Piace is a phenomenon—a restaurant that's never without customers. The formula is simple—lots of good Italian comfort food freshened up with California touches, served in a cheerful setting at very reasonable prices. The room is warmly high-tech, with massive mirrors hanging from the back walls, an open kitchen, and a busy bar that separates the restaurant from the adjacent bakery. You can easily mix and match a meal of classic pasta, chicken, and veal dishes with cutting-edge carpaccios, risottos, and seafood, all made with state-of-the-art olive oils and balsamic vinegars. The pizzas are wonderful, too, with a good crunchy crust and enough toppings to satisfy even the most persnickety pizza lover. Other branches are in Burbank (801 N San Fernando Blvd; 818/843-1111) and Calabasas (4799 Commons Wy; 818/591-8822). *$; AE, MC, V; no checks; breakfast, lunch, dinner every day; full bar; reservations accepted for 4 or more; between Fair Oaks and Raymond Aves.* &

Parkway Grill / ★★★

510 S ARROYO PKWY, PASADENA 626/792-1001 Commonly regarded as the Spago of Pasadena and certainly one of the better restaurants in town, the Parkway Grill offers revisionist American fare with a California edge. When you enter, you overlook the open kitchen, where a bevy of chefs make pizzas and compose salads. The room itself is warm and welcoming, filled with a small forest's worth of plants and trees. Consider black bean soup with smoked pork; lobster crepes; marvelous pizzas topped with lamb sausage, grilled eggplant, clams, and scallops; smoked chicken and cilantro; spinach pasta with shrimp and asparagus; or a whole fried catfish with fresh ginger and lime soy dipping sauce, served with caraway rice and cucumber mint relish. Some diners come just for the mesquite-grilled filet mignon with red wine risotto, glazed carrots, and oven-dried tomatoes. A great finish is the crème brûlée napoleon, a crisp phyllo square layered with rich vanilla bean custard and caramel sauce. The wine list is known for its selections from the best of the small, choice California wineries, and there are 30 wines by the glass to encourage tasting. *$$; AE, MC, V; no checks; lunch Mon–Fri, dinner every day; full bar; reservations required; east side of Arroyo Pkwy, north of California Blvd.*

The Raymond / ★★

1250 S FAIR OAKS AVE, PASADENA; 626/441-3136 The Raymond is, in its own understated way, one of the most traditionally romantic spots in Southern California—a place that doesn't scream romance but subtly lets it get beneath your skin. It's actually the sort of atmospheric restaurant that makes guys feel rather comfortable—all that nice wood in a lovingly restored Craftsman-style California bungalow (formerly the caretaker's cottage at the Victorian-era Raymond Hotel), the kind of place that men who spend their weekends at Home Depot might like. The food is also special without being overly fussy—Long Island roast duckling with fresh pomegranate and cranberry sauce, soft-shell crabs with sliced oranges and toasted almonds, rack of lamb chops with fresh rosemary and garlic, and medallions of beef with Stilton cheese and port wine cream sauce. Tables are scattered throughout the house and quiet garden, with music, wonderful service, and soft lighting. She'll love it; he won't mind it. *$$; AE, MC, V; checks OK; lunch Tues–Fri, dinner Tues–Sun, brunch Sat–Sun; full bar; reservations recommended; www.mind spring.com/~theraymond; east side of Fair Oaks Ave, north of Pasadena Fwy.*

Shiro / ★★★

1505 MISSION ST, SOUTH PASADENA; 626/799-4774 Shiro is named for its chef, who first leaped to prominence with his fine cooking at Pasadena's long-departed Cafe Jacoulet. In the tradition of many of L.A.'s Cal-Asian restaurants, the room is high-ceilinged and noisy. The virtually all-seafood menu, printed daily, might consist of no more than six appetizers and six entrees plus a couple of specials. The Asian influence is manifested in dishes such as the superb Chinese ravioli filled with the most delicate shrimp-salmon mousse and nestled in a mild fennel sauce; the popular lobster spring roll; smoked salmon with masago roe on potato pancakes; California king salmon napped in a ginger-lime sauce; and Shiro's signature dish, a whole sizzling catfish (you can order either medium or large) served with sweet ponzu sauce. *$$; AE, DC, MC, V; no checks; lunch Tues–Thurs; dinner Tues–Sun; beer and wine; reservations recommended; south side of Mission St, west of Fair Oaks Ave.* &

Twin Palms / ★★

101 W GREEN ST, PASADENA; 626/577-2567 When it comes to re-creating the feeling of a bistro-cafe by the Mediterranean, there are few settings more dramatic or successful than Twin Palms. This is a Disneyland version of a cafe in Nice or Cannes, with an enormous tent billowing around the central patio. The cooking has evolved over the years from California-French to the California coastal cooking of Tony Zidar, who's given the menu his own fresh approach. Main courses include roast chicken and bacon brie crostada; herb-crusted filet mignon with potato leek gratin in port wine sauce; and Moroccan lamb atop eggplant–white bean purée. There are 450 seats here that are almost always full, especially on weekends when live bands fill the tent with jazz, rock, salsa, and reggae during dinner and late into the night. Come Sundays, Twin Palms puts on a wonderful buffet brunch. *$$; AE, MC, V; no checks; lunch, dinner every day, brunch Sun; full bar; reservations required; www.twin-palms.com; northwest corner of DeLacey and Green Sts.* &

Xiomara / ★★★

69 N RAYMOND AVE, PASADENA; 626/796-2520 Feisty proprietor Xiomara Ardolina has always flirted with Latin food and was exploring Asian twists on Cuban cuisine long before it became trendy; the restaurant's current New World/Pan-Asian menu reflects those culinary whims. Pasadena's "Restaurant Row" side street has grown up around Xiomara, which retains an intimate, semi-industrial (bare brick, fat support columns) ambience softened with mirrors and flickering votives. Against a subtle musical backdrop of jazzy vocalists and Latin-beat serenades, Xiomara's knowledgeable, friendly servers seriously want you to enjoy. They're quick to recommend the best-in-town mojito, the traditional Cuban mix of Florida cane sugar, rum, crushed mint, and chopped limes. Try not to get caught up in the menu, which lists each dish in excruciating detail ("spicy duck *ropa vieja* on a Colombian manchego cheese corn cake with marinated Cuban-style tomatoes and watercress")—the kitchen never sends out a loser. While most dishes celebrate meat and seafood, there's a surprisingly complex and richly satisfying poblano risotto with tangy tomatillo, cilantro, lime, and garlic. Leave room for the sinfully good signature dessert: chocolate bread pudding slathered with cool coffee custard sauce. *$$$; AE, MC, V; no checks; lunch Mon–Fri, dinner every day; full bar; reservations recommended; www.xiomararestaurant.com; between Colorado Blvd and Green St.* &

Yujean Kang's / ★★⚝

67 N RAYMOND AVE, PASADENA; 626/585-0855 There's a subtlety to Yujean Kang's cooking that one needs to be prepared for. It's quintessentially understated—so much so that it's hard to say whether the food is Chinese or Kangian. His menu changes with clockwork regularity, for there is a restless imagination at work here. Typical of his twists are tiny Chinese dumplings with hot chili oil, perhaps a quarter the size of the normal model—a bit like gnocchi filled with minced pork and garlic chives. Kang is fond of sweet and sour, a trait found in appetizers like fish with kumquats and passion fruit. His most talked-about soup, called Pictures in the Snow, is a brown stock with julienne of chicken, ham, and mushrooms, and a meringue floating island depicting a scene created out of vegetable bits. Additional offerings might include beef with oyster mushrooms, chicken with glazed cashew nuts, tea-smoked duck, and six novel prawn choices, including prawns with taro root purée. His cooking is very impressive, very personal, and often like nothing we've had before. And this is one Chinese restaurant where the desserts are a temptation. Try a warm Chinese kumquat polenta with ice cream and white chocolate sauce, or mandarin orange cheesecake. *$$; AE, DC, DIS, MC, V; no checks; lunch, dinner every day; beer and wine; reservations required; west side of Raymond Ave, north of Colorado Blvd.* &

LODGINGS

Artists' Inn & Cottage Bed & Breakfast / ★★

1038 MAGNOLIA ST, SOUTH PASADENA; 626/799-5668 OR 888/799-5668 An 1895 Victorian farmhouse and neighboring 1909 home form this beautifully and artistically restored inn, complete with flourishing rose garden and white picket fence. The public rooms are adorned with well-chosen antiques, original art, rich fabrics, and luxurious Oriental rugs. Each of the nine guest rooms has its own muse—either a particular artist or artistic period—that is reflected in the decor. For instance, the Van Gogh Room has been outfitted to replicate the tormented master's painting of his own bedroom, while the Expressionist Suite wears the bold, pure colors found in the works of Matisse, Picasso, and Dufy. B&B traditionalists will enjoy the 18th-century English Room, outfitted in frills and cabbage roses. Every room has a telephone and its own private bath, some with lovely period fixtures. Most rooms have TVs; if yours doesn't, the innkeeper is glad to provide one on request. The five rooms housed in the 1909 cottage have whirlpool tubs and fireplaces. A generous full breakfast is served every morning, and tea and home-baked sweets every afternoon; you're welcome to enjoy them on the old-fashioned porch overlooking the blooming gardens on sunny days. The quiet residential neighborhood is just minutes from Old Town Pasadena. *$$–$$$; AE, MC, V; no checks; artistsinn@artistsinns.com; www.artistsinns.com; west of Fair Oaks Ave and north of Mission St.*

The Bissell House Bed & Breakfast / ★★

201 ORANGE GROVE AVE, SOUTH PASADENA; 626/441-3535 OR 800/441-3530 Check into this Victorian mansion on Pasadena's Millionaire's Row, and it's not a far stretch to daydream that you're visiting a socialite friend at the dawn of the 20th century. The former home of Anna Bissell McCay (the Bissell vacuums heir), this B&B is set on a half-acre lot surrounded by 40-foot hedges that keep street noise to a minimum. The innkeepers add extra warmth to the elegant home, with its mahogany floors, antique-filled rooms, and sweeping veranda. Each of the six guest rooms is individually decorated in a frilly English style and has its own bathroom; no phones or TVs intrude on the period ambience. The Garden Room is utterly romantic, with an antique, hand-carved queen-size bed, floral chintz decor, and whirlpool tub for two. The Morning Glory, decorated in china blue and white, and the Prince Albert Room, with its double-corner leaded-glass window, boast claw-footed tubs. Gabled ceilings and tall windows that look out onto the exclusive neighborhood make the Rose Room an ideal spot for snuggling up with a good book. Rates include a full breakfast, plus afternoon tea and all-day wine and beverages. A small pool and spa just behind the house invite a dip in warm weather. *$$–$$$; AE, MC, V; no checks; info@bissellhouse.com; www.bissellhouse.com; at Columbia St.*

Hilton Pasadena / ★★

168 S LOS ROBLES AVE, PASADENA; 626/577-1000 OR 800/HILTONS This centrally located Pasadena hotel may be a Hilton, but its upscale interior design is more reminiscent of an Ethan Allen showroom than a standard chain hotel. From the stylish lobby with its glistening marble floors and slipcovered couches to the well-appointed rooms decorated in soft blues and greens, it does its best to be anything but generic. Each room features a "smart desk" with ergonomic chair, two-line phones, high-speed connectivity, and plenty of space to spread out. Located in an office-tower complex across from the Pasadena Convention Center and close to the Rose Bowl, the 14-story, 285-room lodging often doubles as home-away-from-home for both business travelers and traveling sports teams. On site is a decent California-style restaurant. *$$; AE, DC, DIS, JCB, MC, V; checks OK; www.hilton.com; south of Colorado Blvd.* &

Ritz-Carlton, Huntington Hotel & Spa / ★★★★

1401 S OAK KNOLL AVE, PASADENA; 626/568-3900 OR 800/241-3333 Set on 23 luxuriant acres in the San Gabriel foothills is one of California's most stunning resorts. Originally built in 1906, then reconstructed and reopened in 1991 as a Ritz-Carlton, it's the kind of place where once you check in, there's no reason to leave. Despite a wealth of luxury comforts—including a state-of-the-art 12,000-square-foot spa, salon, and fitness center with signature kur (mud-and-mineral based) body treatments, virtual-reality equipment, and eucalyptus steam—the spectacular grounds retain a timeless charm. Impeccable restorations include the rare covered Picture Bridge; the alluring Horseshoe and Japanese Gardens, designed in 1911–14; Southern California's first-ever Olympic-size pool; and more. The 418 guest rooms and suites are gorgeously outfitted in a traditional style that's softened by ultra-pretty English garden textiles and a wonderful palette of celadon, cream, and butter yellow. Luxuries include beautifully made feather beds dressed in Frette, high-speed connectivity, CD players, big marble baths, and plush terry robes. All the services you'll need are on hand, of course. The high-quality meal service includes an elegant high tea, divine alfresco dining, and the Grill, named one of America's 50 best hotel restaurants by *Food & Wine* magazine in 2002. Package deals abound, so ask. *$$$$; AE, DC, DIS, JCB, MC, V; checks OK; www.ritzcarlton.com; off 210 Fwy at Lake Ave.* &

Monrovia

RESTAURANTS

Devon / ★★★

109 E LEMON AVE, MONROVIA; 626/305-0013 Devon offers the most sophisticated contemporary cooking in the eastern San Gabriel Valley. The restaurant, a trio of storefronts in newly trendy historic downtown Monrovia, has seating at sidewalk tables or in one of two dining rooms with a view of the glassed-in wine cellar, known especially for its collection of older California cabernets, fine burgundies, and ports. Specials keep the menu flexible with soups rotated daily, so you might have a woodsy purée of mushroom one day, or an intense tomato-basil soup the next. Starters are creative and practically irresistible—steamed black mussels, smoked scallops, curried oysters, black bear ravioli. Yes, we said bear. Owners Richard and Gregory Lukasiewicz do dare to be different, so pan-roasted bear and caribou take their places on the menu alongside mainstays like prime dry-aged, rib-eye steak and at least two fresh fish selections. Even the delectable desserts push the envelope—caramelized peach slices with blue cheese ice cream, for instance. Devon's legendary wine list is extremely accessible, with 35 wines by the glass and many half bottles. *$$; AE, DC, MC, V; checks OK; lunch Tues–Fri, dinner Tues–Sun; full bar; reservations recommended; just east of Myrtle Ave.* &

La Parisienne / ★★

1101 E HUNTINGTON DR, MONROVIA; 626/357-3359 A friendly, homey place, La Parisienne is a genuine institution. Once you leave the traffic and mini-malls of Huntington Drive and enter this fine old wood-paneled room with flowers and French fabrics, it's not hard to believe, after a glass or two of wine, that you're in Lyon, eating at a pleasant little brasserie. Fare is both French classic and new at the same time. The right dishes are all here—escargots, mussels marinières foie gras, onion soup, duck *à l'orange,* delicate Dover sole (deboned tableside), and an authentic Friday-Saturday bouillabaisse. Snails, in particular, are a treat, richly flavored with garlic, parsley, and herb butter; mussels are perfectly cooked with shallots, parsley, white wine, and cream. The wine list of French and California selections is dazzling, with a number of good offerings by the glass. *$$–$$$; AE, DC, DIS, MC, V; no checks; lunch Mon–Fri, dinner every day; full bar; reservations recommended; www.laparisiennerestaurant.com; at Mountain Ave.* &

San Gabriel

RESTAURANTS

Tung Lai Shun / ★★

140 W VALLEY BLVD, SAN GABRIEL; 626/288-6588 Tung Lai Shun is a large, handsome restaurant on the ground floor of sprawling San Gabriel Square Shopping Center that serves the kind of cooking you'd find in the Islamic Chinese restaurants of Hong Kong and Taipei. That cuisine is marked by a love of breads, dumplings, lamb, mutton, and spices, so it's not surprising to find wonderful boiled lamb dumplings on the menu here, along with lamb pancakes, hot pots of lamb and pickled cabbage, lamb soup, Beijing-style ox tongue, and pan-fried beef dumplings with noodles. (Because it's an Islamic restaurant, there's no pork or alcohol on the menu.) The five-spice eggplant is spicy enough to raise a bit of a sweat on your upper lip, and the noodle dishes are more than sufficient for a main course. One item everyone orders is the sesame bread, a massive plate of soft bread that's steamed, then baked and topped with sesame seeds—insiders know to order the scallion-stuffed version. *$; MC, V; no checks; lunch, dinner every day; no alcohol; reservations not necessary; at Valley Blvd.* &

Monterey Park

RESTAURANTS

Empress Harbor / ★★

111 N ATLANTIC BLVD, MONTEREY PARK; 626/300-8833 Conventional wisdom has it that you may find better seafood next door at Ocean Star, but the dim sum is better at this SoCal branch of Hong King's hugely successful Harbor Village. Dim sum service here is done in true Hong Kong fashion; if you want something, you have to flag down one of the many dim sum carts pushed continuously through the aisles by ladies in traditional dress. Nonspeakers of Chinese may find themselves at a disadvantage, choosing items for their visual appeal and taking their chances. As you order, your table ticket is stamped, with the totals tallied at the end of the meal—plates range from $1.90 up to the three most expensive $5.50 plates—for very special beef tripe, squid, or Chinese vegetables. The roast pork filling in the steamed *cha siu bao* is rich with flavor, sweet yet subtle. The shrimp *har gow* and pork *shui mai* are well-nigh perfect, presented hot in their little steamers. If you feel up to venturing off the well-beaten dumpling path, try the boiled squid or the garlic spare ribs. *$; AE, MC, V; no checks; lunch, dinner every day; full bar; reservations recommended; northwest corner of Atlantic Blvd and Garvey Ave.* &

Lake Spring Shanghai / ★★★

219 E GARVEY AVE, MONTEREY PARK; 626/280-3571 Lake Spring is one of the few Shanghai-style restaurants this side of Hong Kong. The heavy, rich cooking of Shanghai stands in direct contrast to the lighter, simpler style found at most Cantonese eateries. One of the great delights of Shanghai cuisine is the hairy crabs that show up on the menu every autumn, filled with roe and served steamed, with ginger tea and vinegar sauce—a true delicacy. Far less delicate, though every bit as wondrous, are the many pork dishes served at this consistently jam-packed eatery—a large rump roast that could easily feed four; pemmican-like *ching chiang* cured pork; shrimp and shredded pork with bean curd soup; salted pork with bamboo-shoot casserole; shredded dry bean cake and pork; pepper-seasoned pork chops; vermicelli and ground pork; and so forth. Service here is efficient but impersonal; the staff rushes to serve mostly large parties in Lake Spring's ballroomlike dining room. *$$; MC, V; no checks; lunch, dinner every day; beer only; reservations recommended; east of Atlantic Blvd.*

Ocean Star / ★★★

145 N ATLANTIC BLVD, MONTEREY PARK; 626/308-2128 The dominant Hong Kong–style seafood palace in the San Gabriel Valley rambles through a series of large rooms, which can be reconfigured to hold parties of various sizes. On a good evening the main dining room is full, offering the opportunity to watch dozens of family groups convene for a fine feed of fresh-from-the-tanks lobster, crab, shrimp, abalone, oysters, clams, and a wide assortment of still-twitching fish. If there's a special on the lobster, by all means order it—"special" usually means half price. The deal often extends to shrimp as well, and there's hardly anything better than the platter of flamingo-pink shrimp fresh from the wok, lightly flavored with garlic. Pan-fried oysters with spicy salt are also remarkable; their crisp salty crust crackles when you bite into it. But don't just stick to the menu. Check out what others are eating and you might see unlisted dishes like stir-fried pea vines, or other intriguing preparations. *$$; MC, V; no checks; lunch, dinner every day; full bar; reservations required; northwest corner of Atlantic Blvd and Garvey Ave.* &

Long Beach and Harbor Area

San Pedro

South of magnificent Palos Verdes, the city of San Pedro is an often gritty, blue-collar port town; most of its residents work in the harbor, which has grown through the years to literally and figuratively dwarf any other interests in the city. The **SAN PEDRO PENINSULA CHAMBER OF COMMERCE** (390 W 7th St; 310/832-7272; www.sanpedrochamber.com) publishes visitor brochures and maintains an informative Web site. Learn about maritime history at the **LOS ANGELES MARITIME MUSEUM** (Berth 84, at the foot of 6th St; 310/548-7618), housed in a beautifully restored 1941 WPA Streamline Moderne building on the waterfront. Celebrating the maritime history of Southern California, the museum also offers sail training opportunities for youths at risk. A different kind of glimpse into maritime history is waiting at the SS *LANE VICTORY* (Berth 94, adjacent to the World Cruise Center; 310/519-9545; www.lanevictoryship.com), a 10,000-ton World War II cargo ship restored and operated by the Merchant Marines. This National Historic Landmark saw service through the Vietnam War and now operates as a working museum that offers guided ship tours, displays of memorabilia, and occasional all-day voyages. A particularly impressive harbor site is the soaring **VINCENT THOMAS BRIDGE**, San Pedro's answer to the Golden Gate. It crosses from San Pedro to Terminal Island, an uninviting industrial jungle of canneries, loading cranes, and a federal penitentiary. But it wasn't always this way—as you drive across, try to imagine the island circa 1899, as an appealing resort with its own pleasure pier and beach pavilions. The island was also home to a close-knit community of Japanese-American fishermen and their families, most of whom were removed for internment during World War II and never returned.

RESTAURANTS

Papadakis Taverna / ★★

301 W 6TH ST, SAN PEDRO; 310/548-1186 Papadakis is the best reason to head for San Pedro, assuming you're not a sailor. Every evening here runs with the efficiency—and predictability—of a Vegas-style production. Arriving women get a kiss on the hand from Papadakis brothers John or Tom, and then diners are shown to a table in this bright banquet room decorated with equal parts Aegean murals and football art (in deference to John Papadakis's glory days as a USC football legend). Start with a bottle of wine from a list that combines good California vintages with traditional Greek wines, and consider some mezes (small plates) to share such as spanakopita (spinach-filled phyllo pastries) or thick, satisfying tzatziki (garlic-laced cucumber and yogurt spread) with pita bread. Before long the lights dim, and any empty-handed waiter gets called upon to sing and dance through the aisles to traditional Greek music; as the evening wears on, these interludes grow more raucous. It's easy to make a complete meal of varied appetizer plates, or you can opt for grilled lamb, pork, citrus-laced fish, or other Mediterranean specialties. Plan on a relaxed pace—since your waiter might be otherwise engaged during the meal—and a festive party atmosphere best suited to groups and families. *$$; AE, DC, MC, V; checks OK; dinner every day; beer and wine; reservations recommended; papadakistaverna.com; at Centre St.* &

Long Beach

Formerly ranchland dating back to early Spanish land grants, the modern city of Long Beach was named during the real estate boom of the 1880s and conceived as a seaside resort community. But industry and commerce quickly took over, with the discovery of oil and the development of Long Beach Harbor (along with adjacent San Pedro) as the primary port of Los Angeles. Despite a devastating 1933 earthquake, downtown Long Beach enjoyed a steady prosperity throughout the first half of the 20th century, acquiring the nickname of "Iowa by the Sea" due to the many Midwest transplants who made their home here—and whose conservative, pragmatic culture still pervades the area. An aggressive downtown redevelopment plan that began in the 1970s has helped draw visitors back with new tourist attractions, an expensive waterfront Convention Center, and the small-town flavor of remarkably well-preserved residential neighborhoods. Visitor information and maps are available from the **LONG BEACH AREA CONVENTION & VISITORS BUREAU** (1 World Trade Center, Ste 300; 562/436-3645 or 800/4LB-STAY; www.visitlong beach.org). Each April the star-studded **TOYOTA LONG BEACH GRAND PRIX** (562/981-2600; www.longbeachgp.com) races through the streets around the Convention Center and harbor, attracting the likes of Jason Priestley and Paul Newman to burn some serious off-screen rubber, and Ashley Judd, who comes to cheer on her race-car driver husband Dario Franchitti.

Mention Long Beach to many people, and they're apt to associate the name with this city's biggest tourist attraction, and one that virtually saved it from bankrupt obscurity in the 1970s. Once the world's largest and most luxurious Atlantic ocean liner, the regal QUEEN MARY (located at the end of I-710; 562/435-3511; www. queenmary.com) sits permanently docked in Long Beach Harbor, open to visitors, diners, and overnight guests. Easy to dismiss as a tourist trap, the ship is really a living museum, the only surviving example of a particular kind of 20th-century elegance and excess that's hard to imagine until you actually stroll the gangways and grand salons of this splendid vessel. Vast teakwood decks, priceless interiors, and lavish staterooms once occupied by notables like Winston Churchill, the Duke of Windsor, and Greta Garbo all tell the story of a vanished era. Kiosk displays of historic photographs and memorabilia are everywhere, and guided tours take you from poop deck to pump room, passing through perfectly preserved crew quarters along the way. The ship is a must-see for nautical history buffs. Across the waterway is the **AQUARIUM OF THE PACIFIC** (100 Aquarium Wy; 562/590-3100; www.aquarium

ofpacific.org), which opened in 1998. City planners gave their all to the project, hoping that what worked in Baltimore and Monterey would reenergize the waterfront. Re-creating three separate regions of the Pacific, the Aquarium features animals native to tropical lagoons, coral reefs, the chilly Bering Sea, and temperate Baja waters. Kids and adults alike can learn little-known facts about sea creatures from sharks and sea lions to delicate sea horses and moon jellies; three-story-high tanks let you get nose-to-nose with these denizens of the deep. The waterfront also features aging **SHORELINE VILLAGE**, a shopping/dining/marina complex disguised as a 19th-century fishing village. Savvy crowds seem no longer enchanted by its kitschy theme, but it still makes a pleasant stroll if you're in the area, and it's also home to a 1906 Charles Looff carousel. Nearby Rainbow Harbor is where the **TALL SHIP** *American Pride* (714/970-8800; www.americanpride.com) is docked. A day sail aboard this three-masted, 130-foot schooner offers passengers a chance to help raise and lower the eight sails, take a turn at the helm, and experience the "romance of the high seas".

The **LONG BEACH MUSEUM OF ART** (2300 E Ocean Blvd; 562/439-2119; www. lbma.com) is situated on a prime waterfront knoll along Ocean Boulevard, in one of the several grand old mansions that still line this picturesque stretch. Built in 1912 as the summer home of New York philanthropist Elizabeth Milbank Anderson, the house was designed by the firm that built Los Angeles's landmark Chinese and Egyptian Theaters, and it functioned as a private social club and World War II officers' club before becoming the museum's home in 1957. In 1999, the home was restored to its original state and a complementary gallery annex was built on the property. In addition to its interest as an historic site, the museum is notable for its collection of 20th-century European modernists, post–World War II art from California, and the largest video art archive in the nation.

If you travel east of downtown Long Beach, you'll quickly find yourself in the neighborhood communities of **BELMONT SHORE** and **NAPLES,** whose quaint village feel and prewar bungalow-lined streets are in sharp contrast to the harbor district's industrial energy. East Second Street and East Broadway bisect Belmont Shore—known locally as "the Shore"—and provide hours' worth of strolling among antique and collectible shops, cafes, boutiques, and an increasing number of high-profile retailers like the Gap, Banana Republic, and Jamba Juice, happily coexisting alongside old-style hardware stores, barbershops, and delicatessens. The **BELMONT PLEASURE PIER** offers a romantic bayfront stroll; a bait-and-tackle shop, snack bar, and ice cream stand operate at the pier's end in summer. Naples is a manmade island community of picturesque canals, boardwalks lined with million-dollar homes, tiny sandy lagoons, and the romantic **GONDOLA GETAWAY** (562/433-9595; www. gondolagetawayinc.com). Since 1982 these authentic Venetian gondolas have been snaking through the canals, camping it up with experienced gondoliers ready to belt out an Italian aria at the drop of a straw hat. Passengers are encouraged to bring a beverage—the fee includes a nice basket of bread, cheese, and salami, plus wine glasses and a full ice bucket.

RESTAURANTS

Belmont Brewing Company / ★★☆

25 39TH PL, LONG BEACH; 562/433-3891 The best of the local brewpubs, this spot at the base of Belmont Pier features an outdoor patio with a million-dollar harbor view that takes in the *Queen Mary,* fiery sunsets, and the unusual multicolored street lamps that illuminate the pier after dark. The five respectable house brews include Top Sail (amber) and Long Beach Crude (porter), and the restaurant holds special dinners pairing beers with food. Within, you'll find an undersea theme, with a giant aquarium and murals featuring tropical fish against a turquoise background. But nearly everyone opts for the relaxing wind-shielded patio, with umbrellas for the midday sun and heat lamps to warm chilly evenings. Seated here, you can listen to the water lapping at the sand and enjoy food that goes a step beyond the usual tavern fare. There are plenty of appetizers, of course—favorites like crab cakes, fried calamari, and bruschetta as well as fresh ceviche and steamed artichokes. Pizzas, pastas, main-course salads, and sandwiches round out a menu that also features lots of seafood and delectable baby back ribs. *$; AE, DC, MC, V; no checks; breakfast Sat–Sun, lunch, dinner every day; beer and wine; reservations not accepted; www. belmontbrewing.com; west of Ocean Blvd.* &

Delius / ★★★

 3550 LONG BEACH BLVD, LONG BEACH; 562/426-0694 You might not expect an ambitiously conceived concept restaurant located in a mini-mall close to the freeway to last, but Louise and Dave Solzman's Delius has been going strong since 1996. Serving just one seating each evening, Delius offers a prix-fixe dinner according to a menu that changes weekly and reflects British-born chef Louise's excellent culinary sense. Despite its out-of-the-way location a 10-minute drive from downtown Long Beach, Delius creates an intimate romantic ambience insulated from the world outside. Once you enter the richly furnished, Victorian-flavored lounge and dining rooms, heavy velvet draperies enclose you in intimate surroundings where tables are set with a full complement of flatware for each course and stemware for every carefully chosen wine. Cocktails are at 6:30pm, and dinner begins at 7:15pm. The seven-course extravaganza includes hors d'oeuvres, soup, appetizer, first course, entree, fruit and cheese, and dessert. Menus have featured crab-and-shrimp-stuffed zucchini flowers, sautéed halibut on penne pasta with porcini sauce, rosemary-and-feta-stuffed filet mignon, grilled chicken with Indian mango chutney, and chipotle crab cakes with ginger-cilantro butter. A harpist entertains on Fridays, and the restaurant really pulls out the stops for frequent winemaker and holiday dinners. Delius recently installed a plush wine bar, which opens at 4pm and serves substantial appetizers. *$$$; DC, DIS, MC, V; checks OK; dinner Tues–Sat; beer and wine; reservations required; www.deliusrestaurant.com; between Wardlow Rd and 36th St.* &

The Madison Restaurant & Bar / ★★★

102 PINE AVE, LONG BEACH; 562/628-8866 Set in one of Pine Avenue's most stunning historic buildings, this elegant 1920s-style supper club offers the grand experience of fine dining in a majestic setting reminiscent of opu-

113

lent ocean liner dining salons. Coffered mahogany walls, gilded ceiling beams, sparkling oversize crystal chandeliers, and enormous two-story windows framed with rich brocade draperies provide the backdrop for service that's deferential without being stuffy, and a menu that delivers fine-quality steaks and seafood. Originally a bank and more recently a private club, the 1890s building has been beautifully restored and features a lavish bar, where on Friday and Saturday nights small bands are brought in for dancing. The Madison serves exceptional dry-aged beef broiled and accompanied by à la carte sides like buttery garlic potatoes, tender asparagus hollandaise, and perfectly seasoned creamed spinach. You'll find some grand old dishes like oysters Rockefeller and beef Wellington on the menu, too. The menu includes lavish preparations of lobster tail and salmon (with mussels and clams), and an outstanding Caesar salad. The drink list details some 15 different martinis and 30 single-malt Scotches, to give you an idea of its depth. *$$$; AE, MC, V; no checks; lunch Mon–Fri, dinner every day; full bar; reservations recommended; www.madisonsteakhouse.com; at 1st St.* &

Shenandoah Café / ★★

4722 E 2ND ST, LONG BEACH; 562/434-3469 In an era when "New American" is the culinary buzzword, here's a place where American food means only one thing— big, filling portions of regional home-style dishes. Located in trendy, upscale Belmont Shore, the restaurant was part of the first wave of new businesses to open on Second Street and has been a popular mainstay since 1987. The high-ceilinged parlor is decorated with hanging quilts, floral wallpaper, and ornate columns; regulars agree it's equal parts New Orleans mansion and Grandma's house. Dinner here is definitely not for vegetarians or light eaters; even fresh fish specialties are given rich and heavy Southern treatments, and meats take up most of the menu. Start by nibbling on the irresistible apple fritters and yeasty dinner rolls brought fresh from the oven, and loosen your belt a notch in anticipation of an enormous meal that also includes soup or salad and filling side dishes. Recommended specialties include Louisiana okra gumbo made with chicken or seafood, Texas-size chicken-fried steak with country gravy, Santa Fe–style baby back ribs glazed with smoky chipotle, Cajun-blackened fresh catch of the day, and Granny's deep-fried chicken. If you're tempted by rich desserts like bananas Foster or Shenandoah's special double fudge brownie with ice cream and two chocolate sauces, one order is enough for the table. *$$; AE, DC, MC, V; no checks; dinner every day, brunch Sun; beer and wine; reservations recommended; at Park Ave.* &

LODGINGS

Hotel Queen Mary / ★

1126 QUEENS HWY, LONG BEACH; 562/435-3511 If you're too young to have made an Atlantic crossing on one of the grand old luxury liners, staying here might be the closest you'll come to reliving the romance of those voyages. A stateroom can be yours for a night on the RMS *Queen Mary*, permanently docked in Long Beach. You'll need a sense of adventure and some imagination, because these once-lavish quarters aren't that exceptional compared to contemporary hotels; few modern amenities have been added lest they destroy the ship's historic authenticity. The idea is to enjoy the novelty of features like original porcelain bathroom fixtures, walls paneled in tropical hardwoods with intricate art deco detailing, and the historic charm that pervades each hallway and well-walked deck. Quarters vary widely; try to splurge on an ocean-view first-class or deluxe stateroom. The *Queen Mary* features a full complement of restaurants and bars. Sunday's champagne brunch, an overwhelming orgy including ice sculptures and a harpist, is served in the ship's Grand Salon, the original ballroom so lovely it's worth the price of admission alone. Don't miss the Observation Bar, a chic art deco cocktail lounge with panoramic views. On site are numerous shops and the ship's own spa, with full spa services. *$$–$$$; AE, DIS, MC, V; no checks; reservations@queenmary.com; www.queenmary.com; from the end of I-710, follow signs to ship.*

Lord Mayor's B&B Inn / ★

435 CEDAR AVE, LONG BEACH; 800/691-5166 This elegant Edwardian home was built in 1904 and belonged to Long Beach's first mayor, Charles H. Windham, who earned his unofficial title of "Lord Mayor" from a group of British beauty contestants visiting the seaside resort. In 1988, after a sensitive restoration that earned a National Trust for Historic Preservation award (and acknowledgment as Long Beach Preservationist of 1999), innkeepers Laura and Reuben Brasser opened the area's best bed-and-breakfast. The main house offers five guest rooms, each with 10-foot ceilings and furnished with carefully chosen antiques, high-quality linens, and heirloom bedspreads and accessories. Each room boasts a private bath cleverly re-created with vintage fixtures. All the rooms are upstairs, and utterly charming; three open onto a wooden deck overlooking the back garden, including the cozy Hawaiian Room, with its ornately carved wedding bed and island memorabilia. A sun porch overlooks the street, and the entire house radiates warmth with original wood floors, a Vermont granite hearth, and vintage clocks whose gentle chiming enhances the historic ambience of the inn. More rooms are available in three less-formal adjacent cottages, also dating from the early 20th century; they offer a private option for families or those seeking seclusion. Rates include expansive homemade breakfasts. *$$; AE, DIS, MC, V; checks OK; innkeepers@lordmayors.com; www.lordmayors.com; 1½ blocks from 6th St.*

Catalina Island

Often compared to Mediterranean jewels like Malta or Capri, this local island—easternmost in the Channel Island chain—offers sun-filled skies, clean sea air, and shimmering azure waters just 22 miles off the California coast. **AVALON,** named after the Arthurian paradise as described in Tennyson's *Idylls of the King,* is the island's only town, occupying barely a square mile; 86 percent of the island is wilderness under the protection of the Catalina Island Conservancy. The Avalon you see today owes its popularity to chewing-gum magnate and baseball fan William Wrigley Jr., who purchased the island around 1918, constructed a Wrigley Field replica here so his Chicago Cubs could come for spring training (1929 to 1959), and channeled his considerable resources into making his beloved island a stylish offshore playground. Today Catalina is a mecca for outdoor enthusiasts, who come to kayak, fish, dive, hike, bike, camp, and much more. It also draws day-trippers eager to stroll the streets of charming bayfront Avalon, live out *Gilligan's Island* fantasies, and absorb the infectious, laid-back island vibe.

The usual way to reach Catalina Island is via **CATALINA EXPRESS** (562/519-1212 or 800/481-3470; www.catalinaexpress.com), which operates up to 22 daily departures from San Pedro and Long Beach. The company's high-speed catamarans are outfitted with airplane-style lounge chairs, a snack bar, rest rooms, and outdoor deck seating. If you're in a rush, or just looking for a thrill, **ISLAND EXPRESS HELICOPTER SERVICE** (1175 Queens Hwy S; 310/510-2525 or 800/2-AVALON; www.islandexpress.com) can fly you to the island in less than 15 minutes, landing at a lovely Spanish-style heliport a short taxi ride from Avalon. Island Express also operates Catalina sightseeing tours, which do not land.

You can't get lost in Avalon. Aptly named Crescent Avenue follows the bay's horseshoe curve from end to end, and nearly everything is on this main street or one of the half-dozen side streets radiating outward from it. At the center is the 1909 **GREEN PLEASURE PIER,** which is still a hub of activity even though visitors now arrive at a high-volume terminal across the bay. The **CATALINA ISLAND CHAMBER OF COMMERCE & VISITORS BUREAU** (310/510-1520; www.catalina.com) operates at the base of the pier, answering questions and distributing tons of helpful brochures and guides. The town is easily explored on foot, and rental cars are nonexistent (most residents motor around in golf carts, and many homes only have cart-size driveways). Other options include **RENTING A BICYCLE** from Brown's Bikes (107 Pebbly Beach Rd, near the passenger terminal; 310/510-0986). Gas-powered **GOLF CARTS** are available for rent on an hourly basis from Cartopia (on Crescent Ave at Pebbly Beach Rd; 310/510-2493).

Avalon's most distinctive landmark is the elegant **CASINO,** an art deco masterpiece housing a theater and a ballroom and featuring spectacular murals, revolutionary engineering, and impeccable design. You can see the theater any night for the price of a movie ticket—the Casino screens first-run films—but the 10th-floor ballroom is accessible only by guided tour or during one of the many special dance events throughout the year. These include June's **SWING CAMP CATALINA** (626/799-5689), **CATALINA JAZZ TRAX FESTIVAL** (888/330-5252; www.jazztrax.com) in October, and the gala **NEW YEAR'S EVE CELEBRATION** (the Visitors Bureau has complete details). On the ground floor of the Casino is the **CATALINA ISLAND MUSEUM** (310/510-2414), featuring exhibits on island history and archaeology, plus a contour relief map of Catalina that's helpful to hikers.

Other landmarks visible from the bay include Wrigley's stately hilltop home, an ornate Georgian Colonial mansion built as a summer home and named for Mrs. Wrigley. It's now been converted to a bed-and-breakfast, the Inn on Mount Ada (see Lodgings, below). Nearby is the distinctive **HOLLY HILL HOUSE,** easily recognized by its Queen Anne frills and prominent striped cupola. Built in 1888–90 by Peter Gano, who used his blind horse Mercury to haul most of the materials uphill, the house was meant as a wedding present for Gano's intended—who then refused to move to the isolated island and ultimately married another. Gano lived alone in

Holly Hill House, never marrying and posting "No Women Allowed" signs at the threshold. The home, listed on the National Register of Historic Places, is privately owned and superbly restored with period antiques.

About 1½ miles from downtown Avalon—a short taxi drive or an invigorating walk—is the imposing **WRIGLEY MEMORIAL AND BOTANICAL GARDEN** (end of Avalon Canyon Rd; 310/510-2288), built from quarried Catalina Island flagstone and glazed tiles from the once-active Catalina Island Pottery. You can walk to the bell tower's observation deck for a panoramic view out to the ocean. Wrigley's widow, Ada, personally supervised the specialized botanical gardens that surround the monument, showcasing plants endemic to California's coastal islands. A few blocks away is William Wrigley's historic **CATALINA ISLAND COUNTRY CLUB,** a Spanish Colonial landmark originally built as a clubhouse for the spring-training Chicago Cubs. There's a nine-hole golf course here (call 310/510-0530 for tee times and club rental information), plus the elegant mission-style Clubhouse Bar & Grille (see Restaurants, below).

Much of the most interesting stuff on Catalina Island—rugged back roads, dramatic shorelines, isolated coves, the Casino Ballroom, Arabian horses at the Wrigley family's El Rancho Escondido—is either restricted or too remote for the casual visitor. Luckily, there are numerous options for **GUIDED EXCURSIONS,** ranging in length from a couple of hours to three-quarters of the day. Santa Catalina Island Company's **DISCOVERY TOURS** (310/510-TOUR or 800/626-7489; www.scico. com) offers the greatest variety: in addition to scenic day and night tram tours of Avalon, glass-bottomed boat cruises, and bus trips into the island's interior, they conduct some unusual outings none of the other operators offer. These include the Undersea Tour of Lover's Cove Marine Preserve in a semi-submerged boat, nighttime boat trips to see Catalina's famed flying fish, and an exclusive tour of the landmark Casino Theater and Ballroom. If you venture into the island's interior, be sure to look out for wild **BUFFALO**—descendants of a long-ago herd brought over for a movie shoot, then abandoned—that meander the hillsides (and sometimes block auto traffic).

Around the point marked by the Casino lies the **DESCANSO BEACH CLUB** (310/510-7410), nestled in its own small cove and looking like a mini–Club Med. Facilities include showers, changing rooms, a restaurant and bar, volleyball nets, and thatched beach umbrellas. Year-round rentals of kayaks, snorkel gear, rafts, and wetsuits are available. If you're interested in a fishing or diving excursion, they depart from the Green Pleasure Pier in the bay; call the Visitors Bureau for details.

When you find yourself in town after dark, it quickly becomes apparent that Avalon's bar scene is the center of **NIGHTLIFE** in this small, virtually car-less (no drunk drivers) hamlet. Like the denizens of some island version of a close-knit Lake Wobegon, residents gather at their favorite watering holes to socialize, recreate, and simply pass some time before the next brilliant sunrise. Nearly every bar on Catalina serves up the potent local invention called "buffalo milk," a frothy mix of vodka, crème de cacao, banana liqueur, milk, and whipped cream. The oldest bar in town is the raucous **MARLIN CLUB** (108 Catalina Ave; 310/510-0044; www.marlinclub. com), whose doorway is capped by a giant wooden—you guessed it—marlin. The fish tales are extra-long here during local tournaments, when the Club serves as de facto headquarters for competing fishermen. Live and DJ music provides the dance-music beat at the **CHI CHI CLUB** (107 Sumner Ave; 310/510-2828), named for Latin bombshell Carlita "Chi Chi" Fazzari, who danced on the island in the 1950s. Sooner or later, though, everyone ends up at **LUAU LARRY'S** (509 Crescent Ave; 310/510-1919), a cozy tropical enclave where fake parrots, puffed-up blowfish, and shell lamps swing from the thatched ceiling. The house drink is a frightening rum-based concoction called the Wicky Wacker, and Larry's burgers and other pub-style food are among the best eats on the island.

RESTAURANTS

The Channel House / ★★☆

205 CRESCENT AVE, AVALON; 310/510-1617 With a secluded outdoor patio that's generally agreed to be the most romantic dining spot in Avalon, this very traditional continental restaurant manages to attract jeans-clad vacationers as well as dressed-to-the-nines islanders. The patio is the way to go (put in a request when making your reservation), festooned with twinkling lights and surrounded by vine-covered trellises that obscure the sidewalk traffic along busy Crescent Avenue. Indoor seating is refreshingly quiet, aided by plush carpeting and a pitched, open-beam ceiling; the Channel House projects an aura of elegance without pretension. Dinner always begins with an enormous platter of crisp, fresh crudités and creamy dip, whose bounty unfortunately dispels any thought of a first course, even the bread-bowl clam chowder or the tableside-prepared Caesar salad. The menu here is enticing, with local seafood offerings like mako shark, fresh Catalina lobster, or grilled island sand dabs. Meat and poultry are invariably served sauced; you'll see plenty of rich touches like goose liver, béarnaise, and butter galore. Surprisingly, the restaurant offers just a couple of perfunctory desserts, hardly the lavish selection of mousses and rich cakes you might expect. *$$; AE, DIS, MC, V; local checks only; lunch every day (July–Oct only), dinner every day (subject to Mon–Tues closure in winter); full bar; reservations recommended; at Sumner Ave.* &

Clubhouse Bar & Grille / ★★

1 COUNTRY CLUB DR, AVALON; 310/510-7404 The most elegant meals in this typically casual town can be found here, at the historic Catalina Country Club. A 1997 renovation upgraded the stunning golf course and tastefully restored this Spanish-Mediterranean clubhouse, built by William Wrigley Jr. during the 1920s and designed by the same team responsible for the stylish casino. It's now got a chic and historic atmosphere, favored by well-heeled golfers with a taste for its California/Pacific Rim cuisine. The menu is peppered with historic anecdotes and photos of the many celebrities who've frequented the club throughout the years. Seating is either outdoors, in an elegant tiled courtyard complete with splashing fountain and Mediterranean earthenware, or in an intimate, clubby dining room filled with dark woods and polished brass fixtures. Much of the menu is served all day, including gourmet pizzas (such as smoked prime rib with sweet peppers, pesto, and caramelized onions), appetizer samplers (seared jerk ahi, Southwest satay, seafood pot stickers, and more), and soups (fisherman's bisque, or French onion with apple, shallots, and Gruyère—try either in a sourdough bowl), plus thick, satisfying sandwiches. Dinner offerings follow a similar fusion-style pattern, such as tender New Zealand lamb sirloin accented with a piquant mango-mint chutney; cioppino with Gulf shrimp, scallops, clams, Alaskan king crab and mahimahi; and pad thai. Sunday brunch is a genteel treat, especially in nice weather on the sun-splashed courtyard. The club is a few blocks uphill, so shuttle service is available from Island Plaza (on Sumner Ave) on weekends. *$$; AE, DIS, MC, V; local checks only; lunch, dinner every day, brunch Sun; full bar; reservations recommended; from the bay, take Sumner Ave to Country Club Dr.* &

El Galleon / ★★☆

411 CRESCENT AVE, AVALON; 310/510-1188 Here at Catalina's answer to Disneyland's "Pirates of the Caribbean," diners step from the busy bayside promenade into a fantastic collage of brass portholes, ship's rigging, ample red-leather booths, and wrought-iron conquistador decor. Owner Jack Tucey consciously preserves El Galleon as a tribute to the restaurants of Avalon's vacation heyday (circa 1959)— places with names such as Tally-Ho, Waikiki, Chi-Chi Club, and the Flying Yachtsman. This setting feels just right for the hearty menu of steaks and seafood, featuring enormous cuts of aged Midwest beef (petite filets and smaller cuts are available) and fresh local and regional fish (Catalina swordfish, Hawaiian mahimahi, Alaskan halibut). The traditional special-occasion splurges are all here; prime rib complete with all the fixings, and Maine or local lobster with ramekins of drawn butter. You can also make a respectable meal—think of it as "grazing"—from the many appetizer selections, each large enough to be a main course. Choose from zesty barbecue pork ribs with a mesquite tang, Cajun crab cakes with Creole rémoulade sauce, or a whole steamed artichoke with Thai peanut or roasted-pepper sauce. The house specialty "sourdough ensemble" is highly recommended—a basket of chewy bread accompanied by warm spinach-artichoke dip, roasted-garlic olive oil, and crumbly Romano cheese. The bar does a brisk business all day long. *$$; AE, DIS, MC, V; no checks; lunch, dinner every day; full bar; reservations recommended; on the bay between Catalina and Claressa Aves.*

Pancake Cottage / ★★☆

118 CATALINA ST, AVALON; 310/510-0726 This island fixture—for over 60 years—is the ultimate coffee shop, where waitresses store pencils behind their ears, balance about 10 plates on each arm, and don't care if they splatter some coffee refilling your cup. You probably won't even notice, as you struggle to choose from a mile-long menu that begins with a dozen kinds of pancakes, including plain, oat bran, buttermilk, buckwheat, banana-filled, strawberry-topped, or chocolate-chip. Piping hot Belgian-style waffles get similar treatments, as do homemade crepes and blintzes. There are meaty breakfast combos (to satisfy your inner longshoreman), huevos rancheros, and omelets of every variety, culminating with the legendary "Chef's Mess" (six eggs wrapped around eight fillings plus potatoes). You shouldn't skip Pancake Cottage's special hash brown potatoes, a crispy-edged heap sautéed with bell peppers, onions, and bacon, then topped with melted cheese. The interior is early-mess-hall, with a long Formica counter (great for impatient or single diners) and a jumble of mismatched dinette sets. The prices would be reasonable anywhere, but seem especially so on Catalina, where isolation brings everything up a notch. The Cottage opens early enough (6:30am) to feed divers, bikers, and anyone needing a hearty start to an active day. *$; No credit cards; checks OK; breakfast, lunch every day; no alcohol; reservations not accepted; ¹/₂ block from Crescent Ave.*

LODGINGS

Hotel Metropole / ★★☆

205 CRESCENT AVE, AVALON; 310/510-1884 OR 800/300-8528 When Avalon was in its infancy, around 1887, a large, elegant hotel was constructed on the crescent-shaped bay. The old Metropole was a destination hotel in the Victorian style, and its distinctive green paint and imposing facade dominated early picture postcards. Today's Metropole, built on the spot formerly occupied by this historic grande dame, is the cornerstone of a shopping plaza that looks like Disneyland's New Orleans Square. Much smaller than its namesake, this modern replacement has 48 rooms and the ambience of a boutique inn. Built in the early 1990s, the hotel is sleek and well appointed, affording nice views from almost every room on its three floors. There's a wind-shielded rooftop deck and whirlpool overlooking the harbor, and rooms have luxurious touches like bathrobes, snack bars, air-conditioning, and in-room phones; some have fireplaces, whirlpool bathtubs, and balconies. Furnishings throughout public areas and guest rooms alike are contemporary with a tropical air, reminiscent of a Florida plantation. Rates include a continental breakfast, and just outside the front door is all of Avalon Bay's activity, starting with the theme-y Metropole Market Place in the ground-floor courtyard. It may look touristy from the outside, but the Metropole shapes up as a classy, comfortable retreat that's equally suitable for romantic interludes or family getaways. *$$–$$$; AE, MC, V; no checks; www.hotel-metropole.com; on Crescent Ave between Metropole and Whitley Aves.* &

The Inn on Mount Ada / ★★★

398 WRIGLEY RD, AVALON; 310/510-2030 OR 800/608-7669 William Wrigley Jr. purchased Catalina Island in 1918, and by 1921 he built this ornate Georgian Colonial mansion on the best hillside property in Avalon, which he promptly named for his wife, Ada. Home to the Wrigley family for 37 years, the house is now an intimate and luxurious bed-and-breakfast that's consistently rated one of the finest small hotels in California. The ground-floor salons include a club room with warm hearth, a plush-seated formal library, and a wicker-filled sunroom where tea, cookies, and fruit are always available. The wrap-around main porch still offers the same spectacular vista of Avalon Bay that inspired Wrigley to build on this spot. Each of the six guest rooms and suites upstairs has breathtaking ocean views and a private bath; the best is the Grand Suite, which boasts a fireplace and a large private patio. The innkeepers' meticulous attention to detail will make you feel like the special guest at the summer home of wealthy friends, especially since you need never leave this hilltop Eden. Rates include a hearty full breakfast, a full lunch menu (or packed picnic for adventurers), and an array of evening hors d'oeuvres accompanied by fine wines. For those who aren't content to merely bask in this pampering solitude, your stay also includes a private golf cart for exploring Avalon. And don't fret about lugging your bags uphill—the inn will arrange to have a car meet you when you arrive on the island. The price of such luxury *can* be rather steep; if you've got champagne taste on a beer budget, try staying midweek between November and May, when rates plummet by $100 or more. *$$$$; MC, V; checks OK; www.catalina.com/mtada; from the harbor, take Claressa Ave to Beacon St, turn right and proceed to Wrigley Rd, then left uphill.*

Snug Harbor Inn / ★★★

108 SUMNER AVE, AVALON; 310/510-8400 This aptly named boutique hotel is an ideal place to drop anchor in Avalon. The owners (who also operate the more affordable European-flavored Vista del Mar around the corner) spared no expense in renovating a dark rooming house (circa 1895) into a skylit, intimate retreat in the heart of the action. Located above shops on a prime bayfront street corner, the six upstairs rooms are light, airy, and impeccably decorated in a relaxing Nantucket theme, with hardwood floors, thick hooked rugs, and the maximum amount of pampering comfort per square inch. Solid new doors and triple-paned windows keep street noise out of your boudoir, leaving you to enjoy your goose-down comforter, cozy gas fireplace, TV, VCR, CD player, whirlpool bathtub, plush terry robe (and slippers!), and the convenience of an in-room phone. The tasteful seashore/nautical decor is worthy of *House Beautiful*—watercolor lighthouses, wooden model sailboats, striped beach umbrellas, and well-chosen colors work together to create a truly soothing environment. The inn provides coffee, tea, juice, fresh-baked muffins and seasonal fruit delivered to your room each morning, along with complimentary wine and cheese served in the cozy study every afternoon. The rooms are all modestly sized—with the exception of the Santa Catalina Room, sporting two bay windows and a panoramic ocean view—and offer either partial or full bay views. If cost is a consideration, opt for a partial view and try to visit between November and April, when off-season and midweek rates offer a substantial discount. *$$$–$$$$; AE, DIS, MC, V; snug@catalinas.net; www.snugharbor-inn.com; on the bay at Crescent and Sumner Aves.*

Zane Grey Pueblo Hotel / ★★

199 CHIMES TOWER RD, AVALON; 310/510-0966 OR 800/3-PUEBLO Author and avid fisherman Zane Grey spent his later years in Avalon and wrote many books here, including *Tales of Swordfish and Tuna,* which recounts his fishing adventures off California's coast. (Avid fans will want to visit the historic Tuna Club on the waterfront, of which Grey was a member.) His home, named the Pueblo, is built on a hilltop with superb bay views and reflects Grey's love of the Arizona desert as well as his frequent South Seas fishing expeditions. Now a hotel, the house is built from teak beams imported from Tahiti, and sports Hopi touches like rough-hewn exposed beams. The Pueblo is one of only two hotels in Avalon with its own swimming pool—and it's even heated! This is a welcoming, unfancy place, with a fireplace, grand piano, and TV in the intact original living room. The 16 simply furnished guest rooms have been updated with private baths and ceiling fans, gaze upon either the bay or the hills, and are named for Grey's various novels. Complimentary coffee, tea, and morning toast is served, and a shower room is conveniently available after checkout. The hotel also offers complimentary shuttle service to and from town for those hesitant to make the aerobic uphill climb. And despite having no in-room phones or TVs, the front office does offer wireless Internet access for your laptop. *$–$$; AE, MC, V; checks OK; www.virtualcities. com; follow Vieudelou Ave up from town.*

THE ORANGE
COUNTY COAST

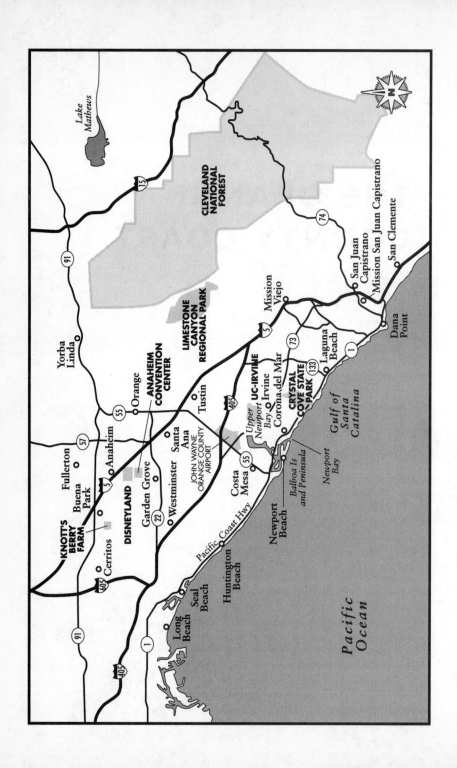

THE ORANGE COUNTY COAST

A string of seaside jewels that have been compared to the French Riviera or the Costa del Sol, the Orange Coast is one of Southern California's best-kept secrets. More than 42 miles of premier shoreline offer pristine stretches of sand dotted with luxury resorts, tidepools teeming with marine life, charming secluded coves and pleasure-boat harbors, quintessential California beach towns, and legendary waves that draw surfers from around the world. If this description doesn't fit with the images usually associated with Orange County—business parks, cookie-cutter suburbs, and strip malls—that's because the county's coast is a world unto itself. From postcard-size Seal Beach at the county's northern tip to Spanish-flavored San Clemente at the southern county line, each sandy community—and each separate beach—has a unique character and appeal that set it apart from its neighbors along the scenic Pacific Coast Highway (PCH).

ACCESS AND INFORMATION

Coastal Orange County stretches from tiny Seal Beach—tucked just below the sprawl of L.A.'s Long Beach—down to the surfing enclave of San Clemente. From Westside communities around LAX—Santa Monica, Venice, Manhattan Beach—Orange County is most easily reached by Interstate 405. From Hollywood and downtown Los Angeles, take Interstate 5 south; from San Diego, take I-5 north.

JOHN WAYNE AIRPORT (949/252-5200; www.ocair.com) has always been more convenient than LAX if your destination is in Orange County, and is even more so following stepped-up security measures. It is centrally located on the borders of Santa Ana, Costa Mesa, and Newort Beach near the 405 Freeway. It's served by many of the major carriers, and most who don't fly into John Wayne have arrangements with air shuttle services. There are major **CAR RENTAL** agencies at the airport, and each community is served by **SUPERSHUTTLE** (714/517-6600; www.supershuttle.com). Orange County has light-rail service by **METROLINK** (714/636-7433; www.octa.net). **AMTRAK** (800/USA-RAIL; www.amtrakwest.com) trains stop in Fullerton, Anaheim, Orange, Santa Ana, Tustin, Irvine, Laguna Niguel, San Juan Capistrano, and San Clemente.

Seal Beach

Thanks to its slightly off-the-beaten-track location, Seal Beach has a reputation as Southern California's last great beach town. What this means to visitors is that the area has retained a lot of its small-town charm and the atmosphere here is more relaxed with less gridlock than in neighboring beach communities.

There are municipal parking lots at Main and Electric Avenue and at Central Avenue and Eighth Street. Both lots are close to one of Seal Beach's prettiest attractions, the **RED CAR MUSEUM** (itself housed within a maintenance car from the old Pacific Electric Railway Commuter Line). Along Main Street, between the museum and a wooden pier—once the heart of an amusement park called Jewel City—are several antique shops, boutiques, ice cream and candy stores, and moderately priced

ORANGE COUNTY COAST THREE-DAY TOUR

DAY 1. In **SAN JUAN CAPISTRANO**, begin with fresh-roasted java and a delicious muffin at **DIEDRICH COFFEE** (31760 Camino Capistrano; 949/488-2150), then spend the morning meandering through the historic **MISSION SAN JUAN CAPISTRANO**. Have lunch at **RAMOS HOUSE CAFÉ**, take the Historic Walking Tour of old San Juan Capistrano, wander along Antique Row, and stop and visit the old Capistrano Depot. Drive south on Camino Capistrano to Pacific Coast Highway and the beach, then head northwest to **LAGUNA BEACH** to check into one of the **MANZANITA COTTAGES,** where Joan Crawford often stayed. Have margaritas and contemporary Mexican seafood on the terrace at **LAS BRISAS** with its sweeping views of Main Beach.

DAY 2. In the morning, enjoy a hearty breakfast in the bungalow setting of either the **COTTAGE RESTAURANT** (949/494-3023) or its next-door neighbor, **MADISON SQUARE AND GARDEN CAFE** (949/494-0137), both on PCH across from your next stop, the **LAGUNA ART MUSEUM**. Then check out the many nearby art galleries. After a light lunch at **CAFÉ ZINC**, spend the afternoon lying on beautiful **1,000 STEPS BEACH**. Enjoy the short drive along the Southern California Riviera to Newport Beach and check in to the **DORYMAN'S INN,** across from the **NEWPORT PIER**. Have dinner downstairs at **21 OCEANFRONT,** then enjoy a nightcap and live music at the **BLUE BEET** (on the Newport Pier; 949/675-2338), right around the corner.

DAY 3. After breakfast across the street at **CHARLIE'S CHILI** (102 McFadden Pl; 949/675-7991), spend time checking out the day's catch at the **DORY FLEET,** the West Coast's oldest continuing operating fishing fleet. Then take the ferry from the Balboa Pavilion to **BALBOA ISLAND** and window-shop along Marine Avenue. Afterward, head back toward the hotel, where just up the street is **TK'S BURGERS** (2119 W Balboa Blvd; 949/673-3438), where you'll have to stand in line to grab one of the best hamburgers in Southern California. In the afternoon rent a bike or roller blades from the kiosk in front of the **BALBOA PIER** and check out the exclusive ocean-facing homes while cruising up the boardwalk. For dinner walk over to the **CRAB COOKER** for fresh swordfish or skewers of barbecued fish. Finish off the evening with drinks and live jazz at the **STUDIO CAFÉ** (100 Main St; 949/675-7760).

restaurants. Walk to the end of the pier for an ice cream shake at **RUBY'S,** a '40s-style diner that rocks along with the pier, to the delight of locals but the consternation of out-of-towners. Listings of special events, like the town's annual sand castle festival in September, can be found at the **SEAL BEACH CHAMBER AND BUSINESS ASSOCIATION** (201 8th St #120, next door to City Hall; 562/799-0179; www.seal beachchamber.org).

RESTAURANTS

Ruby's Diner / ★

END OF SEAL BEACH MUNICIPAL PIER; 562/431-RUBY One of several SoCal seaside branches of this retro burger diner, Ruby's gleams like a red, white, and chrome beacon perched above the waves on the tip of Seal Beach's pedestrian pier. Shoestring fries—smothered in chili, cheese, and green onions—are the perfect accompaniment to one of several burgers, like the green chile–laden Southwestern or the guacamole burger. Then try to decide between a cherry vanilla coke (with extra cherries) or a luscious orange 50/50 shake (remember creamsicles?) that your server—in a white paper hat if it's a guy; red pinstripe dress if it's a gal—brings in a tall glass, complete with a second serving still chilled in the stainless-steel mixer. *$; AE, DC, MC, V; no checks; breakfast, lunch, dinner every day; beer and wine; reservations not accepted; at the end of Main St.* &

Walt's Wharf / ★★

201 MAIN ST, SEAL BEACH; 562/598-4433 Justly revered for fresh seafood expertly grilled over oak embers, this village fixture is a casual favorite with both locals and visitors. Once the wood fire leaves its oaky accent behind, the kitchen adds layers of flavors with creative sauces that complement (not overwhelm) the varied fresh catches. Although the lineup changes daily, good examples include Alaskan halibut with roasted yellow bell pepper cream sauce and orange roughy with papaya–red chile salsa. The house specialty is the oak-grilled artichoke with Lea & Perrins aioli—not to be missed. But not everything gets a grilling. Traditionalists can enjoy the fresh fish and chips (with shoestring fries), the beer-batter jumbo shrimp, or a cream-laden clam chowder. Fresh oysters, crispy pizzas, choice beef, and lively pastas also have their place—the menu seems to stretch on forever. Even the wine list is ample, featuring well-chosen bottles at fair prices. *$$; AE, DC, MC, V; no checks; lunch, dinner every day; full bar; reservations recommended; at Central Ave.* &

LODGINGS

The Seal Beach Inn & Gardens / ★★☆

212 5TH ST, SEAL BEACH; 562/493-2416 OR 800/HIDEAWAY This B&B with bright blue awnings, shuttered windows, wrought-iron grillwork, hanging baskets of geraniums, and old-fashioned lampposts looks as though it belongs in New Orleans's Garden District, although it's only a block from the beach. The check-in desk in the main building shares space with an elaborate gift shop selling reproduction Tiffany-style lamps and expensive toiletries; beyond are a bright, sunny coffee bar, wicker and wingback chairs, and three oak bookcases crammed with reading material. French doors lead out to the kidney-shaped pool surrounded by greenery, lounge chairs, and a fountain, all of which make a prime setting for the full breakfast on warm mornings and tea, wine, and cheese in the evenings. When a chill sets in, the Tea Room's mammoth gas-burning fireplace is the place to get cozy. The inn's 24 rooms, which include 13 suites, are decorated in highly distinctive style. The Primrose Room has a gas-burning fireplace, raspberry flowered wallpaper, a coffered ceiling with a deep purple inset, and a bathroom with a Jacuzzi tub for two. The

Azalea King Suite is larger, with a bright pink floral theme, a canopy bed covered in white flouncy gauze, a kitchen, and a Roman soak tub in the bathroom. Most, but not all, of the rooms and suites have kitchenettes, fireplaces, and whirlpool tubs. If you're a light sleeper, avoid the first-level rooms at the front next to the parking lot. *$$$; AE, DC, DIS, MC, V; checks OK if reserving a month ahead; hideaway@seal beachinn.com; www.sealbeachinn.com; 4 blocks west of Pacific Coast Hwy.* &

Huntington Beach

We're not sure the "two girls for every boy" ratio has any basis in fact here in Surf City, USA. A mile east of Pacific Coast Highway, the community of Huntington Beach could pass for a middle-class suburb in Anywhere, USA, with hundreds of square miles of scarily indistinguishable rabbit-warren housing developments and an excess of strip malls. However, as the Surf City sobriquet implies, the coastal area offers visitors and residents alike the chance to experience quintessential Beach Boys and Jan & Dean beach life.

In summer, parking in Huntington Beach's coastal lots is a nightmare if you arrive after 9am; a better choice for poking around town is to use the large municipal lot just off Main Street. **BOLSA CHICA STATE BEACH** (714/846-3460), which parallels PCH from the town's northern tip to its most southern edge—and the oft-perfect waves that pound it—are all about California dreamin'. The southern end of Bolsa Chica is also the location of the **BOLSA CHICA ECOLOGICAL RESERVE** (714/846-1114), where many species of marine life are protected. Anyone interested in the history of surfing will surely find gratification in the exhibits at the **INTERNATIONAL SURFING MUSEUM** (411 Olive Ave, between Main and 5th Sts; 714/960-3483; www.surfingmuseum.org), where the history of the sexy sport is illustrated. Pictures and biographies of surfing hall-of-famers are displayed in the museum, and not far away, at PCH and Main Street, they're immortalized (à la the Hollywood Walk of Fame) in polished granite stars on the **SURFING WALK OF FAME.** Get info on the **SURF CITY FESTIVAL,** held the first weekend in October, at the **HUNTINGTON BEACH CONFERENCE & VISITORS BUREAU** (417 Main St; 714/969-3492 or 800/SAY-OCEAN; www.hbvisit.com).

Though the city limits extend from the San Diego Freeway in the north to Huntington State Beach in the south, most visitors tend to end up cruising a three-block stretch of Main Street beginning at the foot of the pier. **JACK'S SURF SHOP** (101 Main St; 714/536-4516), one of the oldest surf wear establishments in California, is a required stop. Locals like to grab a late breakfast (after surfing) from one of the many inexpensive sidewalk cafes along here; a popular choice is the **SUGAR SHACK** (213½ Main St; 714/536-0355), where bare-chested dudes scarf down huge plates of eggs and hash browns while their dogs laze in the sun.

SURFING AND THE CALIFORNIA DREAM

Whether the world's first surfers were Hawaiian kings riding wooden boards or (as some anthropologists have recently suggested) Peruvian Indians on reed rafts, no one disputes that the heart and soul—and booming industry—of global surfing is Southern California.

The sport of surfing was first imported in 1910 to L.A.'s Manhattan Beach by Oahu's legendary surfer Duke Kahanamoku. As it gained popularity among SoCal beach boys, wave-riding not only carved itself an identity as a sport and a lifestyle, but also evolved into a $2 billion global industry, shaping the world's perception of surfing, surfers, and California culture through the sale of clothing, music, and accessories.

Surfers now number 750,000 in California, compared to half that number in Hawaii and four times that in surfing's other heartland, Australia. But beyond the devout enthusiasm and sunny climate, the reason Southern California is the true heart of global surf culture is because it's fortunate enough to possess surfing's most essential element: good waves. Along Orange County's coast there are more than 50 prime surf spots, not to mention nearby headquarters of industry giants such as Quicksilver, OP, Gotcha, Rip Curl, and the sport's twin bibles, *Surfing* and *Surfer* magazines.

For the visitor, the best place to watch surfers ripping into Pacific waves is off the legendary pier at Huntington Beach, also known as Surf City, USA. As the longtime host to professional surfing contests such as the U.S. Open of Surfing (held annually in August), the old pier tends to build up sand around its pilings, resulting in consistent and well-shaped waves. The pier is a safe, dry vantage point from which spectators can hear the yells of surfers continually attempting to outmaneuver each other for the best waves, see the spray as riders hit the lip and carve tight cutbacks, and feel the mist and salt as the waves smash against the pilings below. From the pier it's only a few steps across the asphalt to Main Street's Surfing Walk of Fame. Bronze plaques embedded in the sidewalk recognize surfers influential to the sport, from *Endless Summer* filmmaker Bruce Brown to six-time world surfing champion Kelly Slater. And there's a bust of the man who started it all, Duke Kahanamoku.

—Sandow Birk

RESTAURANTS

Red Pearl Kitchen / ★★★

412 WALNUT AVE, HUNTINGTON BEACH; 714/969-0224 For years the most famous place to eat in Huntington Beach was a place serving fish tacos for a couple of bucks each. Then chef extraordinaire Tim Goodell opened Red Pearl in an old brick building in downtown, finally giving diners a real reason to hang around after dark. As the name implies, Red Pearl is primarily Asian cuisine—with a nouvelle California twist. Tangerine peel chicken, instead of the usual orange peel, with bird's-eye chile, for instance. Or pork short ribs seasoned with Chinese five-spice and Thai basil. Equally impressive are pastry chef Shelly Register's deserts like kaffir lime and lemongrass panna cotta. The perfect topper after a long day on the beach. *$$; AE, MC, V; no checks; dinner every day; full bar; reservations not accepted; between Main and 5th Sts.* &

LODGINGS

Hilton Waterfront Beach Resort / ★★

21100 PACIFIC COAST HWY, HUNTINGTON BEACH; 714/960-7873 OR 800/ HILTONS One of the prettiest in the Hilton chain, this large establishment has a special ambience that makes it seem much smaller than its 290 guest rooms and 12 stories would suggest. The reason is obvious: it's directly across from the ocean, at the quieter south end of Huntington Beach. Awash with sunlight reflecting on the water, the hotel's exterior wears a perpetual rosy gold glow. The marble lobby is light, airy, and impressive, with its coffered ceiling and skylight. It's peaceful to rest awhile in the cushy padded wicker armchairs and the overstuffed sofas in conversation-group arrangements. The staff are helpful, and the bellhops seem to whoosh your luggage to your room in record time. All the rooms have private lanais and ocean views, but the corner suites are the best because their wraparound terraces seem to turn the Pacific Ocean into a roommate. The bathrooms are polished travertine, extraordinarily clean and spacious, and the suites have both wet bars and fully stocked minibars. Added perks include an outdoor pool, fitness center, spa, and three restaurants. Casual Surf Hero snack bar will also sell you firewood, hot dogs, and s'mores fixings to take across PCH to the beach's fire rings. On the concierge level, continental breakfast, soft drinks, and afternoon tidbits are gratis. *$$$$; AE, DC, DIS, MC, V; checks OK; www.hilton.com; between Golden West St and Beach Blvd.* &

Newport Beach

With its glittering harbors, seven islands, expensive waterfront homes, thousands of seagoing vessels, miles of gorgeous beach, tanned natives in elegant shabby-chic garb, and most especially its atmosphere of wealth and ease, Newport Beach could easily pass for Newport, Rhode Island. Newport West has one advantage, however: the season here doesn't end with the Labor Day regatta. Plainly put, the lovely seaside jewel is among the best destinations Orange County has to offer and is easily accessible via PCH or Interstate 405 south to the 55 Freeway, which becomes Newport Boulevard. The **NEWPORT BEACH CONFERENCE AND VISITORS BUREAU** (3300 W Coast Hwy; 949/722-1611 or 800/94-COAST; www.newportbeach-cvb. com) offers a 24-Hour Information Center (949/729-4400).

Of the abundant picturesque attractions, a good starting point is **BALBOA PENIN-SULA**, a historic area lined with homes and shops featuring vintage clothing, antiques, curios, and eateries surrounding Newport Boulevard. The waterfront village on **LIDO ISLE** (at Balboa Blvd) and the cobblestoned and leafy **VIA OPORTO** are perfect places to enjoy a latte at one of the outdoor cafes and shop in the charming boutiques and galleries. Southeast on Newport Boulevard is the quaint and historic **CANNERY VIL-LAGE,** home to a commercial fishing fleet, shops, and galleries. Nearby Newport Pier boasts the **DORY FISHING FLEET,** an energetic and resourceful cooperative established in 1889 where you can shop the open-air market for the catch of the day, and a beach that's an extremely popular surfing spot, with a horseshoe-shaped strand lined with fun and funky food concessions and beachwear shops. The roller-skate, blade, and bicycle rental concerns usually do a land-office business because there are miles of smooth boardwalk and bicycle paths. At **BALBOA PIER,** where the harbor meets the jetty, is a body-surfers' and boogie-boarders' heaven called the Wedge. The waves are powerful—and so is the undertow. The **BALBOA PAVILION** (end of Main St, at the intersection of Edgewater St; 949/673-4633) is a wooden, gabled, cupola-topped confection more reminiscent of the other Newport. Constructed in 1905, it's the city's most famous landmark. The pavilion is the departure point for **WHALE-WATCHING** (in season from December through March) and **SPORTFISHING,** both of which are available through Davey's Locker (949/673-1434), as well as **HARBOR CRUISES** and **CATALINA ISLAND JAUNTS** via Catalina Passenger Service (949/673-5245). The kiosk at the pavilion's entrance is full of brochures about all the tours and other available activities. The **BALBOA FUN ZONE** (600 E Bay Ave, at Main St; 949/673-0408; www.thebalboafunzone.com), another Newport institution, boasts a Ferris wheel, carousel, bumper cars, and arcade games.

Across the harbor is **BALBOA ISLAND,** an excellent excursion via the **BALBOA ISLAND FERRY** (ferry landing off Palm St; 949/673-1070). The charming, spic-and-span auto/pedestrian shuttle has been in operation since 1919 and accommodates three vehicles per trip. Drivers are free to leave their vehicles at the craft's gunwales and admire the harbor's blue sparkle. Balboa Island is a tiny community with an East Coast fishing village ambience, its narrow streets lined with a jumble of cottages and garage-top apartments. The island's main drag, Marine Avenue, leads to the tiny village's Shangri-la of unique boutiques and diminutive restaurants.

On the other side of PCH, a few turns in the car lead to one of the entrances to Back Bay, the name residents have given to **UPPER NEWPORT BAY ECOLOGICAL RESERVE AND REGIONAL PARK** (600 Shellmaker Island; 949/640-1751). The 752-acre saltwater marsh is a protected sanctuary for 200 species of birds and encompasses six different habitats. Rowing and kayaking are excellent ways to explore the area. Contact the **NEWPORT AQUATIC CENTER** (1 Whitecliffs Dr, below the reserve and PCH; 949/646-7725) for information on kayak and canoe rental.

The **ORANGE COUNTY MUSEUM OF ART** (850 San Clemente Dr; 949/759-1122; www.ocma.net), formerly the Newport Harbor Art Museum, may seem unprepossessing, but the collection of works inside by California artists is spectacular, from dreamy impressionist-style paintings from the turn of the 20th century to edgier postmodern installations. More attainable visuals are abundant at **FASHION ISLAND** (401 Newport Center Dr, between MacArthur Blvd and Jamboree Rd; 949/721-2000; www.fashionisland-nb.com), Newport Beach's premier outdoor shopping oasis. To sample Newport's tony side, stop in at **THE RITZ** (see Restaurants, below) and let Charles, the bartender, make you one of his special martinis—hold the vermouth.

RESTAURANTS

The Arches / ★★☆

3334 W COAST HWY, NEWPORT BEACH; 949/645-7077 It seems like this venerable restaurant, at the beginning of a stretch of the Coast Highway known as Restaurant Row, has been here forever. It's a throwback to another time, as you'll discover when elegant white-haired maitre'd Jimmy, with a slow sweep of his arm, grandly leads you into a main dining room with red leather banquettes and dark hardwood paneling. Start with a martini; they're almost big enough to split. For dinner you'll want something thick and juicy, like a giant veal steak stuffed with mushrooms and slathered in a rich sauce—the Arches serves the sort of meal you couldn't finish in two days. If Jimmy likes you, he'll come by later and take a Polaroid of you, presenting it in its own sleeve with THE ARCHES embossed in red ink at the bottom, courtesy of the restaurant. The desserts are equally oversize and lush . . . or you could just order another martini. *$$$; AE, DC, MC, V; local checks only; lunch, dinner every day; full bar; reservations recommended; www.the archesrestaurant.com; near Newport Blvd.* &

Aubergine / ★★★☆

508 29TH ST, NEWPORT BEACH; 949/723-4150 The celebrated team of Tim and Liza Goodell began their rise to culinary fame in 1994 when they transformed a tiny florist shop into Aubergine, a dainty California-French charmer. Instant success soon led to broader horizons, and the duo shuttered tiny Aubergine for renovation while they opened Troquet, their wildly triumphant French bistro. Almost 18 months later, Aubergine reopened with an ambitious, all-prix-fixe tasting menu of three, five, or nine courses that's bound to impress the savviest palates. Typical examples: Maine lobster strudel with fresh tarragon and julienned leeks; roasted chestnut soup with crumbled pancetta, crème fraîche, and fresh truffles; confit of veal heart with potatoes, haricots verts, and organic baby greens; and squab breast with roasted sweetbreads and melted savoy cabbage. Pastry chef Shelly Register is acclaimed for her desserts, which include a peerless warm Valrhona chocolate soufflé cake and a daring roasted pineapple–cornmeal cake with vanilla bean ice cream and pink peppercorn infusion. A creative, sometimes quirky wine selection with plenty of boutique choices is enhanced by adept service and proper stemware. The remodeled cottage now includes a roomier dining room and new front and rear patios. Stone floors, antique furnishings, and an embossed zinc-topped bar add to the space's charm. Limoges china, Christofle flatware, and Spigelau crystal add notes of undeniable elegance to what is clearly one of Orange County's most refined dining experiences. *$$$; AE, MC, V; no checks; dinner Tues–Sun; full bar; reservations recommended; off Lido Park Dr.* &

The Crab Cooker / ★★

2200 NEWPORT BLVD, NEWPORT BEACH; 949/673-0100 Bob Roubian, the owner of this Newport institution, is the first to tell you that he's not a cook. He is, however, an accomplished fisherman, one who is against net fishing and in favor of traditional hook-and-line. He's also an expert on all aspects of fish and seafood, which becomes abundantly clear when you first walk into this modest restaurant—housed in a former Bank of America—and watch the cooks fire up choice cuts of broad-billed swordfish, as well as skewers of shrimp and scallops, over a mesquite fire. There's nothing glamorous about the Crab Cooker. Waitresses can be a little cranky at times, but they'll tell you they have a right to be since many of them have been working here for 20 years or more. Food comes on a paper plate, utensils are of the plastic variety, and wine is served in the sort of little clear cups usually reserved for a picnic. But nobody complains. In fact, the biggest downside to a meal here is that there's always a wait to be seated. So put your name in for a table and order a cup of Manhattan clam chowder or a shrimp cocktail to eat seated on the wooden bench fronting the restaurant. Downing what Roubian only half-jokingly calls "the World's Best Chowder," you'll understand why a meal here is worth the wait. *$; AE, DC, MC, V; local checks only; lunch Mon–Sat, dinner every day; beer and wine; reservations not accepted; near 21st St.* &

Pascal / ★★☆

1000 N BRISTOL ST, NEWPORT BEACH; 949/752-0107 Its location—in a strip mall along a busy stretch of highway—may leave something to be desired, but this homespun bistro's country-French cuisine does not. Pascal Olhats's small eatery, with an emphasis on Provençal fare like rack of lamb in a mustard sauce or thyme-crusted sea bass, has been consistently rated one of the best restaurants in all of Southern California since opening in 1988. And for good reason. Unless you come in August (when Pascal and his wife, Mimi, who runs the front of the restaurant, take their annual trip home to France), chef Olhats is almost always there, paying rapt attention to the details of every dish coming out of the kitchen. The wine list, focusing on French vintages, is small but varied and as good a value as the entrees. The adjacent Epicerie is a gourmet jewel box stocked with beautiful cheeses, breads, wines, and other edibles. *$$; AE, DC, MC, V; no checks; lunch Mon–Fri, dinner Tues–Sun; full bar; reservations recommended; www.pascalnewportbeach. com; at Jamboree Blvd.* &

Pavilion / ★★★

690 NEWPORT CENTER DR (IN THE FOUR SEASONS HOTEL), NEWPORT BEACH; 949/760-4920 Commendable for its excellent service and top-notch treatment of Cal-continental cuisine, this lovely low-key dining room—which exudes elegance while remaining tastefully understated—is something of a sleeping beauty, often overshadowed by glitzier competitors in the neighborhood. But those who prefer substance over sizzle will appreciate the splendid room's quiet magic, colossal pillars and oversize floral arrangements. Civilized service is just what you'd expect from a Four Seasons operation, and the food matches that mood. Much of the menu borrows from the Mediterranean, but seasonal changes and daily specials add many California touches. Representative appetizers include a sculptural ahi tartare with wonton spirals and sweet corn soup with smoked shrimp, while entrees might include Canadian salmon en croute with roasted shallots, grilled veal chop with sweet corn polenta in truffle jus, pepper-crusted lamb with port wine reduction, or roasted vegetable ravioli with root-vegetable ribbons and Madeira sauce. Housemade desserts are fabulous and first class. *$$$; AE, DC, DIS, MC, V; no checks;*

breakfast, lunch, dinner every day; full bar; reservations recommended; near Fashion Island center at Santa Cruz Dr. &

Restaurant Abe / ★★

2900 NEWPORT BLVD, NEWPORT BEACH; 949/675-1739 Few Orange County sushi bars stand out enough to be worthy of a drive across the county, but this spot qualifies. Chef/owner Takashi Abe's enticing (if pricey) lineup of hot and cold "platters" is a gourmet effort that will appeal most to seafood connoisseurs. The menu's spare descriptions scarcely do justice to creative offerings that taste (and look) more lovely than expected. Rock shrimp tempura drizzled with truffle oil is a good place to start. Decadent bets from the hot side of the menu include broiled sea bass and foie gras with shiitake mushrooms, crisp soft-shell crab *kara-age* with ponzu and a spicy tomato sauce, or the mixed *kinoko tobanyaki* (three varieties of deftly sautéed mushrooms). Cold-side winners include toro tartare with caviar or salmon *kinuta*, a cylinder of delicate vegetables surrounding the freshest of salmon. Ambience is spare here, the lighting too harsh, and the chefs not overly chatty. The real art is on the plate, not the walls. But for sushi zealots, it's worth the trip. *$$; AE, DC, MC, V; no checks; lunch Mon–Fri, dinner Mon–Sat; beer and wine; reservations recommended; at 28th St.* &

The Ritz / ★★★★

880 NEWPORT CENTER DR, NEWPORT BEACH; 949/720-1800 Dining at the Ritz (no relation to the hotel empire) is a time-honored Orange County treat. The classic continental fare is nearly perfect, and the luxurious, clublike setting is easy to savor. Impeccable service makes everyone feel like royalty—it's no surprise the Ritz consistently gets top ratings for both food and service from critics and publications. Cordial owner Hans Prager and his expert team deftly deliver memorable meals served with panache. Popular dishes include American rack of lamb rotisseried with rosemary and thyme, chateaubriand adorned with diced truffles, and their legendary Harlequin Soufflé, made with Belgian chocolate and Grand Marnier. In addition to the handsome dining room (briefly notorious for its collection of tasteful nude paintings), guests have the option of dining in the beautiful garden room. All this glorious elegance only gets better after dark, when one of two accomplished vocalists performs at the piano on Fridays and Saturdays. Cole Porter, George Gershwin, and Nat King Cole add a nostalgic note just right for the elegant bar. *$$$; AE, DIS, MC, V; no checks; lunch Mon–Fri, dinner every day; full bar; reservations recommended; Newport Fashion Island at Santa Barbara Dr.* &

Roy's / ★★★

453 NEWPORT CENTER DR, NEWPORT BEACH; 949/640-7697 Anyone who's been to Hawaii a few times has probably heard of chef Roy Yamaguchi and his Asian–Pacific Rim fusion cuisine. Though you won't find some of the more popular Hawaiian seafood dishes here, there are plenty of other choices, from blackened ahi tuna to a sesame-crusted ono. There are also some savory dim sum–style appetizers, like lobster pot stickers, that make great starters or a light meal. If fish isn't your thing, try the rack of lamb with a Mongolian chili glaze or chef Roy's signature short ribs of beef covered in a honey-mustard glaze. The dining room, while outfitted in soothing, neutral Asian motifs, is large and noisy, though that somehow seems right for a restaurant re-creating the aloha spirit here on the mainland. Not only does Roy's have an extensive wine list, they also specialize in sake—and the waiters are more than happy to explain why you want a ginger-flavored semi-dry sake with ono but a dry Junman Daiginjo with the ribs. Decadent desserts are faithful to the island original, especially the legendary molten-centered chocolate cake/soufflé—Roy's has always done it better than anyone. *$$$; AE, DC, MC, V; no checks; dinner every day; full bar; reservations recommended; www.roysrestaurant.com; between Jamboree Rd and MacArthur Blvd.* &

LODGINGS

Doryman's Inn Bed & Breakfast / ★★★

2102 W OCEANFRONT, NEWPORT BEACH; 949/675-7300 This splendid little place with only 10 rooms is in sharp contrast to the fun funk of the beachwear and surf shops just up the block. Guests who enter the elegantly etched glass front doors and step into the old elevator to the second-floor wood-paneled lobby are likely to feel as though they are in one of the posh smaller hotels in the Mayfair district of London. Each lovely room is decorated in plush, comfortable (and genuine) Victoriana and luxuriously appointed with marble window seat, sunken marble tub, deep-pile carpeting, and gas-log fireplace. Some rooms have ocean views. Although each room is special in its own way, the master suite, fabled Room 8, with its brocade canopy bed and deep-blue-tiled bathroom, is guaranteed to add a little vacation zing to any relationship. Breakfast, served in the parlor, consists of cereal, fruit, yogurt, pastries, and hard-boiled eggs. In summer the rooftop view overlooking the Newport Pier and surrounding beach is fantastic. The 21 Oceanfront restaurant, just below, provides room service. *$$$; AE, MC, V; cashier's checks only; www.dorymans inn.com; on Balboa Peninsula off Newport Blvd.*

Four Seasons Hotel Newport Beach / ★★★

690 NEWPORT CENTER DR, NEWPORT BEACH; 949/759-0808 OR 800/268-6282 A stay at a Four Seasons hotel in any part of the world is always a treat, and this one is no exception. Perhaps it's the thick, soft carpet underfoot, or maybe it's the bowl of gleaming red crunchy apples placed within easy reach on the check-in desk. Whatever the case, guests are soothed the moment they enter the magnificent lobby, with its coffered ceiling and gorgeous floral arrangements. Within the 19 stories are 285 rooms, including 96 suites. All have terraces with views of the surrounding area and/or the Pacific in the distance. Spacious guest rooms are furnished with cushy modern pieces in neutral tones and have minibars. Large bathrooms sparkle and are well stocked with hair dryer, terrycloth robe, and top-of-the-line toiletries. Additional services include 24-hour room service, twice-daily maid service, complimentary shoe-shine, one-hour pressing, and overnight dry cleaning. As if that isn't enough, the property also boasts an excellent landscaped pool, a state-of-the-art fitness center, and a full spa where facialists and massage therapists are ready to smooth away any tension not already erased by a night spent in this haven. Dining options include the world-class Pavilion (see Restaurants, above) and the more casual Gardens Lounge and Café. *$$$$; AE, DC, MC, V; checks OK; www.fourseasons.com; near Fashion Island center at Santa Cruz Dr.* &

Portofino Beach Hotel / ★★

2306 W OCEANFRONT BLVD, NEWPORT BEACH; 949/673-7030 OR 800/571-8749
You can't miss this two-story oceanfront hotel; it's painted a cheery and pleasing vermilion. The cushy interior, done up in a style something between old-world elegance and new-world glitz, is full of pleasant surprises and charming idiosyncrasies. There are half a dozen charming areas to sit and socialize or have a quiet moment, including an inviting corner with a large gas-burning fireplace. The 15 guest rooms are upstairs along a long, carpeted corridor, which is pleasantly spooky (as the best old buildings are), and are flouncily furnished with a blend of genuine antiques—Edwardian and Victorian, predominantly—and attractive older, but not quite antique, pieces. All have cable TV. Only premier rooms have ocean views, although a few others have ocean "peeks" through side windows; five options have spa tubs and some have gas-log fireplaces. Complimentary continental breakfast, which is served each morning in the Portofino's Bar La Gritta lounge, consists of coffee, tea, fresh fruit, cereal, juice, muffins, and croissants. Wine, tea, and treats are served each afternoon. Patrons may also order room service (for dinner only) from Renato, the Italian restaurant downstairs. A bonus for families: the hotel also rents one- and two-bedroom furnished apartments, which come with full kitchens and daily maid service (for an additional fee). *$$$; AE, DC, DIS, MC, V; checks OK; www.porto finobeachhotel.com; on Balboa Peninsula in Old Newport, near the Newport Pier.*

The Sutton Place Hotel / ★★★☆

4500 MACARTHUR BLVD, NEWPORT BEACH; 949/476-2001 OR 800/243-4141 From the subdued but cushy lobby with its tinkling fountain to the staff that absolutely heaps attention on guests, this 10-story establishment in the Newport Beach business district perfectly captures the cool California ease of the breezy, booming '80s. A small anteroom before the grand main lobby always features a lovely flower arrangement, and the corridor leading to Accents restaurant and the lobby bar is a veritable art gallery displaying stunning glass sculptures. Capacious, comfortable rooms are decorated in comfy modern style and offer amenities such as room service, cable TV with movies and games, robes, hair dryers, Gilchrist & Soames toiletries, and data ports—plus a cheery welcome of limited-edition Sutton teddy bears, tea, and fresh cookies. Each has a view of the surrounding—partially developed—countryside. Added amenities, such as a complimentary continental breakfast, large glass-enclosed pool, excellent fitness center, concierge-arranged massages, and a shuttle service to shopping areas, contribute to the overall sumptuous atmosphere. Business travelers will appreciate the hotel's proximity to John Wayne Airport as well as the Panache Floor with its business center and private concierge. *$$$$; AE, DC, DIS, MC, V; checks OK; info@npb.sut tonplace.com; www.suttonplace.com; at Campus Dr.* &

Corona del Mar

The topography of Orange County beaches begins its dramatic change in Corona del Mar, transitioning from the smooth and broad shoreline at the north to become sculpted and rocky, surrounded by steep bluffs. **LITTLE CORONA BEACH** (below Pacific Coast Hwy and Ocean Ave at Poppy Ave) is a pretty cove with some of the best scuba diving and tide pools going. **BIG CORONA BEACH** (off Marguerite Ave below Ocean Ave) is famous for its snorkeling. Surfboards and boogie boards can be rented at **HOBIE SPORTS LTD** (2831 E Coast Hwy; 949/675-9700). Volleyball courts are available, too, along with picnic tables, fire rings, rest rooms, showers, and a snack bar. Along PCH, Corona del Mar also offers several blocks of galleries, restaurants, and shops where handcrafted jewelry, Southwestern furniture, and antiques are available.

On the land side of the PCH, exquisite homes cling to the terraced hillsides above the highway. The streets of the tiny community are named after plants, trees, and flowers—and appropriately so, since the **SHERMAN LIBRARY AND GARDENS** (2647 E Pacific Coast Hwy, 2 blocks east of MacArthur Blvd; 949/673-2261) is one of Corona del Mar's main attractions. Modestly begun in 1966, it now boasts more than 2,000 plant species in its carefully cultivated two acres. Stroll through the green and cool setting, past fountains, sculptures, and precisely maintained shrubbery, and view the bountiful botanical collection, which includes everything from rare cacti to tropical vegetation. The library includes a historical research center focusing on the Pacific Southwest, a prime lunch spot—**CAFÉ JARDIN** (949/673-0033), which serves Monday through Friday and requires reservations—and a gift shop absolutely crammed with cute garden and kitchen items.

Duffers will truly appreciate the Tom Fazio–designed courses at the **PELICAN HILL GOLF CLUB** (22651 Pelican Hill Rd S; 949/759-5190), just past Corona del Mar. **CRYSTAL COVE STATE PARK/EL MORO CANYON** (south of the Corona del Mar city limits and approximately 2 miles north of Laguna Beach at 8741 Pacific Coast Hwy; 714/771-6731) offers 2,200 acres of backcountry terrain with campgrounds, hiking trails, biking paths, horse trails, and 3.5 miles of unbelievably beautiful beaches. Exact change of $2 is required for parking, and all vehicles are strictly prohibited beyond the parking area. There are rest rooms off the parking lot, but hikers, bikers, and campers must carry in their own water. Fires are prohibited except for backpackers' camp stoves. Across PCH, about a quarter of a mile down, just beyond the entrance to Crystal Cove State Beach, the **CRYSTAL COVE SHAKE SHACK** (7408 Pacific Coast Hwy; 949/497-9666), a Southern California institution, perches on the bluffs overlooking the beach. There's a weathered patio with tables and chairs next to the shack, and it's the perfect spot to enjoy a cool, creamy, surprisingly delicious date shake after a hike in the canyons or a jog along the beach. The **CORONA DEL MAR CHAMBER OF COMMERCE AND VISITORS BUREAU** (2843 E Coast Hwy; 949/673-4050; www.cdmchamber.com) is a helpful source for further information.

RESTAURANTS

Five Crowns / ★★

3801 E COAST HWY, CORONA DEL MAR; 949/760-0331 Merrie Olde England lives again at this long-revered haven for beef lovers and special-occasion celebrants. Roaring fireplaces, low ceilings, dark wood beams, and ivy-draped walls set the stage for costumed servers plying guests with near-perfect platters of prime rib and Yorkshire pudding. But don't think it's just a kitschy theme joint—this Lawry's-owned operation consistently meets high standards for food and service. Though top-notch beef and other hearty continental fare are king, salads, seafood, and chicken choices abound. Of course with all that red meat on the menu, it only makes sense to offer equally mighty wine bottles, and the list here has garnered awards for decades. *$$$; AE, DC, MC, V; no checks; dinner every day, brunch Sun; full bar; reservations recommended; at Poppy Ave.* &

Laguna Beach

For many years visitors zooming along Pacific Coast Highway into Laguna Beach did a double-take when they spotted the cheery old gent standing alongside the road enthusiastically waving them into town. His name was Eiler Larsen, and he was the community's beloved greeter until his death at the age of 89. Larsen's colorful Danish spirit lives on in a bronze reproduction at his former Coast Highway post, and at Eiler's Inn (see Lodgings, below). But even before Larsen took up his perch in 1938, visitors had been flocking to this friendly community, camping on beaches and exploring the tidepools since the late 1800s. Hollywood's golden-age celebrities adored Laguna Beach: filmmakers appreciated the area's photogenic topography, and stars like Bette Davis, Victor Mature, and Judy Garland had vacation homes here.

Attracted by the spectacular ocean vistas, hillsides covered with brightly colored wildflowers, and the intense Mediterranean-esque light, artists flocked here as well. By 1917 Laguna Beach was a recognized artists' colony; California plein air impressionists who worked here include William Wendt, Edgar Payne, Guy Rose, and Anna Hills. In 1932 the artists formed a cooperative and presented the first **FESTIVAL OF ARTS/PAGEANT OF THE MASTERS** (949/494-1145 or 800/487-FEST; www.foapom.com), which became the annual event that put Laguna Beach on the map. Still held every summer on a 6-acre patch of park land just off of Laguna Canyon Road, the festival is a juried exhibition of original works from dozens of local artists; on festival evenings the pageant is presented at the adjacent Irvine Bowl. Visitors are treated to *tableaux vivants*—live, staged re-creations of classical paintings, accompanied by orchestral music and narration. These evenings draw art lovers from all over the country, and tickets must be purchased months in advance. The annual **SAWDUST FESTIVAL** (949/494-3030; www.sawdustartfestival.org), held concurrently with the Festival of Arts and directly across Laguna Canyon Road, provides a venue for local artisans to display and sell their pottery, jewelry, and other crafts amid food booths, entertainment, and hands-on demonstrations. Sharing space with the Sawdust Festival is the annual **ART-A-FAIR** (949/494-4514;

www.art-a-fair.com), where fine arts—predominantly paintings and sculpture created by artists worldwide—are displayed for sale.

For information on these and other area events, contact the **LAGUNA BEACH VISITORS BUREAU** (252 Broadway; 949/497-9229 or 800/877-1115; www.laguna beachinfo.org); they can send you a pocket-size *Visitor Guide,* the latest copy of Orange County's "Local Arts" gallery guide, and brochures about local activities. These materials are also available at their friendly walk-in center, located a block from the beach; or you can pick up the **HERITAGE WALKING COMPANION,** a self-guided walking tour of Laguna's north and south historic residential districts, complete with famous former residents, historical anecdotes, and notable architects. Points of interest along the way include the Bette Davis home, Cope House (built in 1887, it's the oldest structure in downtown Laguna), and the Murphy-Smith Historical Bungalow, which was constructed in 1923 and now displays local photos and artifacts. The **LAGUNA PLAYHOUSE** (606 Laguna Canyon Rd, next to the Irvine Bowl; 949/497-ARTS; www.lagunaplayhouse.com), which opened its doors in 1920, is one of Orange County's most reputable professional theaters. The five-play main season runs from September to June.

Even people who find most museums overwhelming will enjoy the boutique-size **LAGUNA ART MUSEUM** (307 Cliff Dr; 949/494-6531; www.lagunaartmuseum. org), whose contemporary galleries hold a small but interesting permanent collection; visiting and rotating exhibits usually follow a regional theme, highlighting California surf photography or plein air impressionism, for example. Across the street is a section of North Coast Highway (numbered from 300 to 500) that's been officially dubbed **GALLERY ROW** for the numerous art galleries that line each side; the oldest is Quorum Art Gallery (374 N Coast Hwy; 949/494-4422), run by a collective of artists, some of whom have been painting in Laguna for decades. A great way to tour the galleries—and meet many of the artists in person—is the **FIRST THURSDAYS** program, a city-sponsored art walk held the first Thursday evening of each month from 6pm to 9pm. More than 30 different galleries around town participate, staying open in the evening and offering refreshments; even the Laguna Art Museum gets into the act with extended hours and free admission. A free trolley runs from the museum to gallery locations.

Laguna's **MAIN BEACH** (a.k.a. Laguna Beach Municipal Park) is at the center of town, an always-bustling arena of volleyball, basketball, picnic greens, a winding boardwalk, and a scenic ribbon of soft, white sand. There are also smaller cove beaches almost hidden all along the Coast Highway in Laguna: favorites include **VICTORIA BEACH** (along Victoria Dr, off S Coast Hwy), which is one of Laguna's prettiest beaches—and hardest to find. It's broad, uncrowded, and mostly used by savvy locals and folks from the stunning homes that line Victoria Drive above. Another worthwhile trek is down the never-ending staircase of **1,000 STEPS BEACH** (entrance on S Coast Hwy at 9th St). There are really only 225 steps down to this idyllic crescent, and the solitude is worth every one. Look up and you'll see houses clinging to the steep cliffs, many with private staircases or electric funiculars that lead to day-use beach houses on the sand.

RESTAURANTS

Café Zinc / ★☆

350 OCEAN AVE, LAGUNA BEACH; 949/494-6302 All the elements of Laguna Beach village life merge at this bustling Euro-style sidewalk cafe with zinc-topped tables. Its central location is only a minor reason for long lines at the counter; exceedingly tasty and creative morning and midday eats are the major draws (transcending service that is often coldly brusque). Superior baked goods, home-blended granolas, robust frittatas, and inventive sandwiches all share makings of the highest quality— even the coffee drinks meet sublime standards. The few inside tables fill up only when all of the patio spots are taken. Expect to witness a colorful display of locals at leisure—artists and writers noshing beside cyclists and CEOs, with plenty of dogs leashed to chair legs. The adjacent market is a good source for beach-picnic fixings. *$; No credit cards; checks OK; breakfast, lunch every day; beer and wine; reservations not accepted; between Ocean and Forest Aves.* &

Café Zoolu / ★★

860 GLENNEYRE ST, LAGUNA BEACH; 949/494-6825 Artsy, funky, crowded, noisy—this is dining in true Lagunatic style. The work of local artists provides much of the ambience here, and the varied crowd provides the rest. Villagers and inlanders alike flock to this pint-size eatery to dine on Cal-eclectic dishes prepared in the open kitchen only a few steps from the front door. Hearty soups (often encircling a mound of the famous house mashed potatoes), grilled meats, vegetarian fare, and plenty of daily specials make up a small but creative menu that also includes what many consider the best (and biggest) serving of swordfish on the coast. In keeping with the lack of square footage, the wine list is also small, but it's well chosen. Even with reservations, prepare to wait (sans drinks) on the sidewalk as tables turn over slowly. A speedier alternative can be a seat at the counter overlooking the kitchen action, an eye-opening entertainment for anyone who is starry-eyed about the restaurant biz. *$$$; AE, MC, V; no checks; dinner Tues–Sun; beer and wine; reservations recommended; between St. Ann's Dr and Thalia St.* &

Las Brisas / ★★

361 CLIFF DR, LAGUNA BEACH; 949/497-5434 In any other location, this restaurant might go largely unnoticed, but when you're situated on top of a craggy, scenic bluff with some of the most panoramic views of the ocean anywhere in Southern California—well, let's just say it gets your attention. The "young and the restless," in fine linen dresses and sharply pressed shirts, find the outdoor patio bar to be the perfect after-work rendezvous, particularly on Friday nights when it's difficult to even make your way to the bar to order a drink. Inside, the elegant and tasteful dining room is more refined. It's reminiscent of a clifftop restaurant in Acapulco where, at any moment, a dozen well-tanned divers in tiny swim trunks will leap into the surging waters below. No divers here, but the servers are always warm and gracious. As for the food . . . it's good. Not great, but good. But few come here because of the menu; the scene's the thing. *$$$; AE, DC, MC, V; no checks; breakfast, lunch, dinner every day, brunch Sun; full bar; reservations recommended; www. eltorito.com/lasbrisas; at Pacific Coast Hwy, behind the Laguna Art Museum.* &

Five Feet / ★★☆

328 GLENNEYRE ST, LAGUNA BEACH; 949/497-4955 What do we call this food? Contemporary Chinese? Asian eclectic? Nouvelle Pacific Rim? Whatever it's called, chef-owner Michael Kang certainly pioneered it in Orange County, and it has remained popular for over a decade, long outliving the trendy stage. Seafood lovers are very happy here, and few can leave without ordering the signature whole catfish, first marinated in wine, then flash-fried and served with a tomato-peanut-citrus sauce. "Wild Vision" is a typical entree—fresh Hawaiian opakapaka grilled with a soy-balsamic reduction plus tempura soft-shell crab topped with mango-papaya relish and champagne ginger sauce. Prices can edge up here, but portions are hefty and even the wonderful appetizers can make a fantastic feast. The wine list is cleverly chosen. The feel of this place is pure Laguna Beach—small, unusual, and crowded. The joint bustles on weekends, so too much noise is inevitable. It's a rather petite space, boldly decorated with arty industrial flair (Kang, who studied architecture, designed the room). A word of warning: On busy nights, the too-small foyer makes waiting and checking in quite problematic, and parking is tough too. *$$$; AE, DC, DIS, MC, V; no checks; dinner every day; beer and wine; reservations recommended; between Forest Ave and Mermaid St.* &

Picayo / ★★☆

610 N COAST HWY, LAGUNA BEACH; 949/497-5051 This enchanting cafe reflects the European character of Laguna Beach, offering delicious rewards for those who venture beyond downtown. Partners David Rubin and chef Laurent Brazier combine the flavors of the Mediterranean with the spirit of Southern France to create careful, pretty meals served with finesse. After operating for years in a tiny cottage—charming, but difficult to find—Picayo moved in 2001 to a newly built storefront adjacent to Pavilions supermarket. They quickly transformed the space, using wall murals, romantic lighting, Provençal fabrics, and warm wood accents to create two intimate dining rooms that encourage leisurely meals. Tables also line the outdoor patio. The attractive space handles only 20 at a time (dinner is split into two seatings on weekends), but the effect is totally engaging. Seafood often dominates the short dinner menu of select starters and entrees. Don't miss the silky lobster bisque accented with fragrant ribbons of orange zest. A typical entree might be sautéed sea scallops with braised fennel and curried zucchini in lemon chardonnay beurre blanc. Other dishes include pistachio-crusted halibut over mushrooms or charbroiled lamb chops in a beaujolais thyme sauce. The predominantly domestic wine list includes a few gems and a few European imports. Service is courteous and subdued, making this one of Laguna's finest hidden treasures. *$$$; AE, DC, MC, V; no checks; dinner Tues–Sat, brunch Sun; call for summer lunch schedule; full bar; reservations recommended; at the corner of Boat Canyon Rd.* &

Taco Loco / ★

640 S COAST HWY, LAGUNA BEACH; 949/497-1635 For over 12 years, this quirky joint has attracted a steady stream of daring diners eager to feast on an offbeat menu of cheap, tasty Mexican munchies. A roster of nearly 20 tacos is the core of the menu here. You can order the standard beef, chicken, or carnitas versions, but that's almost missing the point. Instead, go for an uncommon taco interpretation such as blackened mushroom (tofu optional, but surprisingly good), blackened salmon, or mahimahi. The blackened lobster taco is the priciest choice, but worth it. Slapped together in the tiniest kitchen imaginable, tacos are drizzled with your choice of hot, hotter, or hottest sauce and are accompanied by a chunky relish of fresh avocados. The warm tortillas are superfresh and may be made of corn, blue corn, or whole wheat, depending on what item you've chosen. After placing your order at the cramped counter, grab a wobbly patio table overlooking busy PCH. Add some sunshine, a cold microbrew, and amusing people-watching, and you have the quintessential Laguna Beach feast. *$; AE, DC, DIS, MC, V; no checks; lunch, dinner every day; beer and wine; reservations not necessary; between Clio and Legion Sts.* &

LODGINGS

The Carriage House / ★

1322 CATALINA ST, LAGUNA BEACH; 949/494-8945 This disarming two-story seaside country B&B is a designated landmark built in the early 1920s in French-Mediterranean style. Located in a pleasant villagelike neighborhood in Laguna's less bustling lower reaches, it's only a mile from the interesting shops, galleries, and eateries of Laguna proper, and the beach is right across PCH, only two blocks away. Guests are welcomed with complimentary California wine, fresh fruit, and other goodies. Six themed suites—some of them with two bedrooms and/or kitchenettes—are built around an open, well-manicured brick courtyard. Each has a sitting room, private bath, and TV, plus a unique personality all its own. Mandalay features an ocean view and Asian tropical decor; in Primrose Lane, which boasts a pretty breakfast nook, the theme is English country cottage; Home Sweet Home is a riot of calico and not unlike sleeping in granny's bedroom; and Mockingbird Hill is a two-bedroom with country-French decor and the feel of a wonderful old apartment. A generous breakfast, served family style in the homey dining room, can also be enjoyed in the courtyard; expect fresh homemade muesli and granola, a delicious egg dish, fresh baked goods, and more. For $10 extra per night pets are welcome, although leaving them in the room unattended is against the rules. One of the best features of the inn is the hosts'—Andy and Lesley Kettley—attention to detail and pride they take in every aspect of their establishment. *$$; AE, MC, V; checks OK; www. carriagehouse. com; from Pacific Coast Hwy (near the Pottery Shack), east onto Cress St, past Glenneyre St, south on Catalina St.*

Casa Laguna / ★★

2510 S COAST HWY, LAGUNA BEACH; 949/494-2996 OR 949/233-0449 Entering the grounds of this romantic terraced inn is like stepping back in time to the halcyon days of Laguna Beach's artists' colony. The establishment is an appealing series of mission-style structures, comprising 21 rooms and suites, all connected by a series of lush and green pathways, stone stairways, and secluded gardens. The entire landscape burgeons with azaleas, hibiscus, bougainvillea, and impatiens, and also with the colorful mosaic of vintage Catalina tile. Some rooms—especially the suites—are downright luxurious, with fireplace, bathrobes, CD/DVD player, and other in-room goodies. But courtyard and garden rooms are more basic and simply furnished, though balcony rooms open onto an upper terrace with a 180-degree view of the Pacific. The most popular accommodation is the charming vintage Cottage, which has a living room, dining room, stained-glass windows, a shower for two, and an ocean-view private deck. Breakfast is part of the deal here, and it's a decent one—nothing fancy, but including fresh fruit and baked goods, cereal, juice, tea, and coffee. Tea and wine, cookies, and hors d'oeuvres are laid out each afternoon in the cozy Craftsman-style living room of the former Mission House, now the reception entry. The swimming pool, surrounded by avocado and banana trees, is heated to 82 degrees year round; a brand-new whirlpool perches on the hillside directly above. *$$$; AE, DIS, MC, V; no checks; www.casalaguna.com; between Laguna Canyon Rd and Crown Valley Pkwy.*

Eiler's Inn / ★

741 S COAST HWY, LAGUNA BEACH; 949/494-3004 Built around a lovely overgrown courtyard with a brick floor, comfy chairs, and a tinkling fountain, this French-Mediterranean-style establishment is located on a section of Coast Highway shaded by magnolia trees. Guests enter the charming brick foyer and get hints of the sweet appointments beyond: a phone booth reminiscent of the old London boxes, a cozy little parlor where tea and wine are available each evening, and a more formal but completely homey parlor with a gas-burning fireplace. Rooms are decorated in individual floral motifs with complementing bedspreads, throw pillows, and curtains. The eclectic mix of furnishings—wicker chairs, predominantly mahogany or cherry dressers, headboards, and side tables—aren't old enough to be classified as rare antiques, but they do give the impression that someone discovered a treasure trove of turn-of-the-century odds and ends in their granny's attic. Some of the ground-floor rooms aren't large, but all are cozy; upstairs rooms offer more privacy. One such gem is the Larsen Suite (named for longtime greeter Eiler Larsen, whose statue stands out front), which has a large, comfortable sitting room with a gas-burning fireplace, full kitchen, bedroom with a king bed, the only TV and VCR in any room, a tremendous ocean view, and easy access to the rooftop patio, which welcomes all guests with umbrella tables, chairs, and chaises. It's worth noting that the inn has no bathtubs or phones, but does offer a fine breakfast of fresh fruit, cereal, baked goods, boiled eggs, juice, coffee, and tea. Live music is often presented on weekends. *$$; AE, DIS, MC, V; no checks; near Cleo St.* ♿

Hotel Laguna / ★☆

425 S COAST HWY, LAGUNA BEACH; 949/494-1151 OR 800/524-2927 Easily recognizable by its landmark bell tower, this lustrous old Spanish-style pearl is right on the water at the south end of Main Beach, where it's been weathering storms and earthquakes since 1888. The cream-colored lobby, with a Saltillo-tile floor and a comfortable sitting area, isn't much to look at, but it leads to a charming rose garden that displays many varieties of fragrant roses and brilliant hibiscus, which are in bloom almost year-round. It's a favored spot for weddings, with its handsome white gingerbread gazebo near the back wall. Just past the garden is the acclaimed restaurant Claes Seafood, Etc., along with the open-air Terrace Café, and Le Bar. Patronizing any of them is like having a picnic right on the beach, with the sun streaming down and waves crashing onto the sand only yards away. Because this little gem harbors the most popular terrace in the city, count on crowds—usually including a high percentage of Europeans—during fair weather. The 65 pastel-decorated rooms are not nearly as impressive; they're on the small side, and the furnishings, although comfortable, are a bit motel-like. Bathrooms are tiny with showers, but only a few have tubs. On the bright side, all the rooms have cable TV and are very clean, and your reservation ensures access to the hotel's private beach club. Even considering the downsides, staying here is a quintessential Southern California experience, best enjoyed by securing an ocean room, where the roar of the waves can actually be heard through a closed window. *$$$; AE, DC, DIS, MC, V; no checks; hotellaguna@ msn.com; www.hotellaguna.com; just south of Main Beach.* &

Manzanita Cottages / ★★

732 MANZANITA DR, LAGUNA BEACH; 949/661-2533 There's a definite Hansel-and-Gretel charm to this secluded inn, which seems appropriate since the original cottages were built in 1927 by Hollywood producer Harry Greene, who wanted a secluded compound, close to the beach, so he could invite friends like Joan Crawford for weekend getaways. Seventy-five years later, the four small cottages and one studio apartment are still serving as a quiet little vacation retreat. Each cottage, with shingled roofs, fireplaces, hardwood floors, and hand-painted tiles, has a private patio just outside French doors in the bedroom. The owners, Debbie and Todd Herzer, who renovated the cottages in 1999, do a great job of landscaping the grounds with fragrant flowers and vines. Main Beach and the center of town are only a 10-minute walk away—but that's if you find a reason to leave your cottage, which many guests don't. *$$; AE, MC, V; checks OK; www. manzanitacottages.com; north of Dana Point, between La Vista Dr and Skyline Dr.* &

Surf and Sand Resort / ★★

1555 S PACIFIC COAST HWY; 949/497-4477 OR 800/524-8621 Beach lovers think they've died and gone to seaside heaven in this place. It's a great environment for kicking back and being lazy. Nothing, except the elevator in the center of this building of 164 rooms and suites, obscures the view of the shimmering Pacific. Upon entering each guest room (all have unobstructed oceanfront balconies directly over the sand), your eyes are immediately drawn past the handsome wooden plantation shutters on the sliding glass doors to the sensational view beyond. The decor throughout is peaches-and-cream, with cushy beds, luxurious modern furnishings, in-room movies, velour robes, hair dryers, a minibar, a spacious marble bath, two-line phones, and a dressing area. VCRs are available through the concierge. Suites have hydro-spa baths and wood-burning fireplaces. But whichever room you choose, at sundown, with the tangerine rays of light beaming through the glass, all the guest rooms and everything in them positively glows. The attached upscale Mediterranean restaurant, Splashes, sits directly on the hotel's 500-foot stretch of beach; there's a lovely, glass-enclosed sea-view pool with a surfside bar; and a new oceanfront spa offers additional pampering. *$$$$; AE, DC, DIS, MC, V; checks OK; www.surfandsandresort.com; near Bluebird Canyon Rd.* &

San Juan Capistrano

Father Junípero Serra and his brown-robed group of Franciscan missionaries were drawn to San Juan Capistrano in the 18th century by the area's abundance of fresh water, its fertile land, and its extensive population of Native American prospective converts. Construction on the **MISSION SAN JUAN CAPISTRANO** (Ortega Hwy at Camino Capistrano; 949/234-1300; www.missionsjc.com), the seventh in the Spanish mission system in California, began in 1776. It was periodically expanded to accommodate the increasing number of "neophytes" enslaved to work the hundreds of acres of surrounding farmland, herd the livestock, and staff the weaving, soap- and candle-making, tanning, and iron-smelting operations the mission's economy depended on, and by 1796 its population had swelled to almost 2,000. The crown jewel of California's mission chain, which has undergone constant restoration, still stands on the original 10-acre plot. The historical site's attractions include the ruins of the original stone church, the cool white Serra Chapel (one of the oldest Spanish structures in California), the museum where the mission's founding documents are on display, the friars' quarters, soldiers' barracks, the ancient olive mill, the cemetery full of broken headstones, and the well-tended gardens that lead to the lovely central courtyard.

For a larger taste of the area's history, try the city-sponsored, do-it-yourself **SAN JUAN CAPISTRANO WALKING TOUR**. The tour includes Rios Adobe house, constructed in 1794, the Los Rios area (California's first residential neighborhood, circa 1870), Garcia Adobe house (circa 1880), and Egan House. Maps may be obtained from the helpful folks at the **CHAMBER OF COMMERCE** (31781 Camino Capistrano, #306, between Forster and Del Obispo Sts; 949/493-4700; www.sanjuan capistrano.com).

Apart from its historical importance, the city itself is as attractive for visitors as it is for the **SWALLOWS** who instinctively return each March and stay through October. The birds may be indifferent to the community's wide array of gift and clothing boutiques, cafes, and numerous antique shops along **ANTIQUE ROW** (at Camino Capistrano between Acjachema and Del Obispo Sts; 949/493-4700), but they're wild about the mission, the power lines, and the eaves of many other town structures. The red-brick **CAPISTRANO DEPOT** (26762 Verdugo St, below Camino Capistrano; 800/USA-RAIL) is noteworthy for its dome as well as historical significance. Constructed in 1894 by the Santa Fe Railroad, the miniature station (still an Amtrak stop) now houses a restaurant and shops too. The **VINTAGE BRICK JAIL**, out of use since the mid-1800s but great for photo ops, is just across the tracks. Both are adjacent to the beautifully landscaped red-brick **CAPISTRANO PLAZA**, one of the prettiest and most pleasant spots in the entire community. For nightlife, try the popular **COACH HOUSE** concert/dinner hall (33157 Camino Capistrano, just north of Stonehill Dr; 949/496-8930; www.thecoachhouse.com).

RESTAURANTS

Ramos House Café / ★★

31752 LOS RIOS ST, SAN JUAN CAPISTRANO; 949/443-1342 Talented and inventive chef/owner John Humphries plays seasonal changes on a small but ever-changing menu of new and regional American daytime meals. But equally beguiling is the old California character of this tiny, virtually hidden historic structure (circa 1881) whose dining room is simply a lush brick patio shaded by mature trees and colorful vines. A hearty spinach, bacon, and caramelized-onion scramble is typical morning fare, joined by sautéed potatoes, spiced applesauce, and one perfect biscuit. Lunch might be an ample crock of garden-inspired soup with cheesy bread twists, a robust warm salad, or a smoked turkey and wild mushroom sandwich. Humphries is a gifted baker as well, so it pays to order any dish involving his oven skills (try warm berry and banana shortcake for dessert). Partner Lisa Waterman oversees the front of the house, ably leading a breezy crew of young locals sporting denim overalls and warm smiles. The city's historic Rios District offers lots of charm, and live entertainment is provided by the rumbling and whistle of the train you can almost touch from your table. *$; AE, DC, DIS, MC, V; no checks; breakfast, lunch Tues–Sun; beer and wine; reservations accepted for large parties only; at Del Obispo St.* ♿

Dana Point

Cape Cod architecture and evocatively named streets are only part of the charm this tiny community holds for residents and visitors. It was named in homage to Richard Henry Dana, who immortalized the area in his much-adored *Two Years Before the Mast,* which he penned after a sail around Cape Horn in 1835 aboard the *Pilgrim.* The author wrote admiringly about the region's windswept headlands, sweeping ocean vistas, and steep bluffs and the violent smash of the sea against them. In the early 19th century, the coves along the beach were a haven for pirates raiding the nearby Catholic mission, San Juan Capistrano. Today you can gaze down from any of the dizzying blufftop vantage points at the replica of the **TALL SHIP** *Pilgrim* anchored in the harbor below, and imagine those bygone days. Under the auspices of the **ORANGE COUNTY MARINE INSTITUTE** (24200 Dana Point Harbor Dr; 949/496-2274), there are activities aboard the *Pilgrim.* The Institute also sponsors marine-mammal-watching expeditions and educational cruises aboard the research vessel Sea Explorer. **DANA COVE PARK,** a popular picnicking spot, is on the left abutting the institute. To the south is the entrance to **DOHENY STATE BEACH** (949/496-3627). Managed by the Department of Parks and Recreation, the beach park is a 62-acre site with tidepools, a mile of sandy beach, some of the best surfing in the county, camping, and picnicking. North of Doheny State Beach at the north end of Dana Point is **STRANDS BEACH,** perhaps Orange County's most beautiful beach. Here, the steep and rocky headlands gently smooth out. Farther south, Capistrano State Beach, followed by Prima Deshecha Canada Beach, are both broad, sandy, and exquisite, with plenty of parking along the way. The Dana Point

Chamber of Commerce's **VISITORS CENTER** (24681 La Plaza; 949/496-1555; www.danapointvisitorcenter.com) has a hotline with tourist information.

RESTAURANTS

Olamendi's / ★★☆

34660 PACIFIC COAST HWY, DANA POINT; 949/661-1005 Ask just about anyone in south county where to go for good Mexican food and they'll say Olamendi's. Jorge and his wife, Maria, opened their first restaurant in 1973, attracting everyone from local surfers to Richard Nixon (you'll see several photos of the ex-prez on the walls), who went into exile not far from here. This is a family operation. On any given day, you'll find Maria bustling about the restaurant, welcoming customers by name, while one or the other of the kids—Raquel, Jorge Jr., Gloria, Oscar, and Esmeralda—is either waiting on tables or helping out in the back. The food is traditional—chiles en nogada, Oaxacan mole, chicken Veracruz—and nicely represents different Mexican cuisines. The place is always busy and the mood casual as the regulars joke with Jorge or beg Maria for just one more *cerveza* before heading back for the beach. *$; AE, MC, V; no checks; lunch, dinner Tues–Sun; full bar; reservations recommended; south of Dana Point at Capistrano Beach.* &

Ritz-Carlton Dining Room / ★★★☆
Ritz-Carlton Club Grill & Bar / ★★★

1 RITZ-CARLTON DR, DANA POINT; 949/240-5008 One of the county's choicest venues for a formal, opulent evening, the Dining Room at the Ritz-Carlton, Laguna Niguel, is favored by traditionalists for its serene setting and first-class approach to service and cuisine. As is the Ritz-Carlton custom, menu choices are many, but all make use of the finest ingredients available. Much of chef Yvon Goetz's seasonal menu borrows from Southern France and the Mediterranean with a welcome touch of his native Alsace added. Entrees include wild mushroom and foie gras–crusted fillet of turbot with champagne and watercress cream, or Colorado lamb medallions with cannellini beans, roasted eggplant, thyme flowers, and red pepper essence. The prix-fixe menu pairing five courses with wines is always noteworthy—and a (relative) value. The hotel's Club Grill & Bar is less ceremonious, slightly more affordable, and somewhat more approachable. Here, guests enjoy more traditional but still outstanding fare like whole roast baby chicken with garlic potatoes and chardonnay jus or ale-marinated rib-eye with crisp zucchini and potato-herb hash. *$$–$$$; AE, DIS; MC, V; no checks; lunch, dinner every day; full bar; reservations recommended; www.ritzcarlton.com/resorts/laguna_niguel; off Pacific Coast Hwy, north of Dana Point.* &

LODGINGS

The Ritz-Carlton, Laguna Niguel / ★★★

1 RITZ-CARLTON DR, DANA POINT; 949/240-2000 OR 949/241-3333 For almost 20 years, the Ritz-Carlton, royally poised on a tranquil blufftop overlooking the sea, had been the only game in town when it came to five-star elegance in Southern California. Then the St. Regis moved in and the Ritz, though still swank as ever, began to look a little down-at-the-heels. Major renovations are under way, but even if you stay here before they're completed, you'll find it still represents what gracious living is all about. "Choice" is the adjective that describes everything here, from the manicured grounds and the two mammoth swimming pools—especially the glittering aquamarine Dana Pool surrounded by towering palms—to the magnificent lobby with its plush carpets, gleaming woodwork, and lavish floral arrangements. The guest rooms—393 of them, including suites and Club Suites—are spacious, yet cozy and hushed. Every possible concession to comfort has been made including plush terry robes, marble tubs, and a well-stocked minibar. Though it's worth paying extra for an ocean view, all rooms have French doors to a charming private terrace. The ultrachic and exclusive Ritz-Carlton Club Floor has a private concierge, open bar, all-day light meals, and a secluded after-dinner lounge. Golfers can take advantage of the challenging 18-hole Links at Monarch Beach, adjoining the property; there are also tennis courts on the hotel property along with a top-of-the-line gym. The gleaming spa offers an array of services to underscore the pampering ambience that surrounds guests the moment they enter the lobby. The use of beach equipment—chairs, towels, umbrellas, and boogie boards—is included in the price of the room; despite the Ritz's poshness, guests still pad barefoot and bathrobe-clad through the lobby and back and forth along the beach path. *$$$$; AE, DC, DIS, MC, V; checks OK; www.ritzcarlton.com/resorts/laguna_niguel; off Pacific Coast Hwy, north of Dana Point.* &

St. Regis Monarch Beach Resort & Spa / ★★★★

1 MONARCH BEACH RESORT, DANA POINT; 949/234-3200 OR 800/722-1543 Built in Tuscan style on 172 acres, this new player along the Southern California Riviera has just about every resort bell-and-whistle you can imagine: huge rooms, almost all with spectacular views of the Pacific; Sony Wega flat-screen TVs; high-speed Internet access; a lagoon family pool; private beach club; and an 18-hole championship golf course designed by Robert Trent Jones. The biggest problem with the St. Regis is that there's no reason to ever leave the resort. In fact, the whole palm-tree-swaying, bougainvillea-blooming elegance of the place is perfectly summed up in a magnificent reproduction of Maxfield Parrish's *Garden of Allah* painting that you'll find in the Lobby Lounge. The Mediterranean mood is complemented by the groves of olive, pine, and cypress trees, all trucked in from other locales and plopped into the lush landscape to look as if they'd been here forever. Eight on-site eateries cover every conceivable need, including a poolside bar for post-swim sushi, an on-the-sand beach clubhouse restricted to resort guests, a Euro-style deli/espresso bar, and a branch of San Francisco's formal seafooder Aqua; there's even a private wine cellar dining room for high-level entertaining. The spa, with 25 luxurious treatment rooms, is the largest in the area. Health freaks will be impressed by a state-of-the-art fitness facility, lap pool, and tennis courts. The whole thing screams decadence. And if you can afford it, what's not to like? *$$$$; AE, DC, DIS, MC, V; checks OK; www.stregismb.com; turn east from Pacific Coast Hwy onto Niguel Rd.* &

San Clemente

This relaxed and uncomplicated little beach town is something of a welcome respite after the frenetic activity in Huntington, Newport, and Laguna Beach. The village, which runs along Avenida del Mar below North El Camino Real, is comfortably down-at-heel and crammed with antique shops and resale clothing shops a bit more downscale than those in Corona del Mar and Newport Beach. The **HERITAGE OF SAN CLEMENTE MUSEUM** (415 N El Camino Real/Pacific Coast Hwy, between Avenida Palizada and Avenida del Mar; 949/369-1299) strives to maintain the uniquely sleepy charming character of the community, modeled on turn-of-the-20th-century developer Ole Hanson's idea of a Spanish village. The museum has several interesting permanent exhibits including "Remembrances of San Clemente: Photos of the 1920s and 1930s," "Legends of Surfing," and "The Western White House: President Nixon's Years in San Clemente." On palm-fringed **SAN CLEMENTE STATE BEACH**, near the historic San Clemente Pier, volleyball playing and watching are favored activities. The pretty 1-mile stretch of beach, abutting headlands with landscaped blufftops, also offers opportunities for scuba and abalone diving (seasonal), swimming, and board- and body surfing. For beach equipment rentals, try **ROCKY'S SURF CITY** (100 S El Camino Real, at the corner of Avenida Del Mar; 949/361-2946). The **CALAFIA PARK** beach area is just south of the state beach. It's wilder and more secluded and has great surfing. The staff of the **SAN CLEMENTE CHAMBER OF COMMERCE** (1100 N El Camino Real; 949/492-1131; www.sc chamber.com) is extremely helpful and friendly.

LODGINGS

Beachcomber Motel / ★☆

533 AVENIDA VICTORIA, SAN CLEMENTE; 949/492-5457 OR 888/492-5457
There's nothing even remotely fancy about this 50-year-old place. Don't expect any frills, any extra services, or even a lot of privacy. But this is one of the few Orange County hostelries that fulfill your primary reason for visiting the region in the first place: it's virtually on the beach. The glistening Pacific is just beyond a green grassy bluff fronting each of the motel's 12 vaguely Spanish-style cottages. Rooms are studios or one-bedrooms, each with cable TV and a kitchenette. The decor is strictly motel (basic and slightly shabby in a friendly, beachy way), and there's not much in the way of added amenities, but the place is exceedingly clean and tidy inside and out. Each cottage has its own porch with a set of comfortable chairs. Barbecue facilities and picnic tables are scattered over the lawn. The motel is also right next to the San Clemente Pier, and an easy walk to San Clemente shops and restaurants. Rates vary wildly according to season, with the highest prices in July and August. Relaxing in a chair on the porch of a Beachcomber cottage and gazing out over the sea, you'll really appreciate San Clemente's city motto: "Where the good life comes in waves." *$$–$$$$; AE, DIS, MC, V; no checks; www.beach combermotel.com; near San Clemente Pier.*

DISNEYLAND AND INLAND ORANGE COUNTY

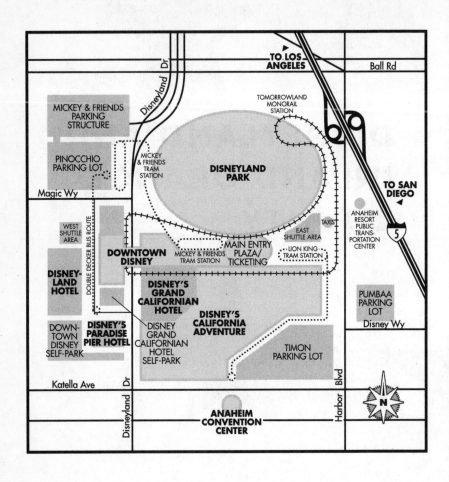

DISNEYLAND AND INLAND ORANGE COUNTY

Orange County defies generalization. Oh, you can try. You can get a glimpse of a freeway-close neighborhood where hundreds of homes are so uninspiringly homogeneous you end up thinking Orange County is conservative, predictable, and very beige. But then you amble around the historic French Park neighborhood of Santa Ana, with its lovely turn-of-the-century Arts and Crafts homes, or see the brightly painted restored Victorians around Old Towne Orange and think, "Well, this can't be Orange County . . . can it?"

It can and it is.

Yes, a lot of the county looks like it was just built yesterday, which it was, but there are also dense woodlands of old oaks, ocher-colored sandstone canyons rich in fossils, some of the most pristine beaches in the world, and quiet country roads where farmers still sell baskets of just-picked strawberries or jars of homemade honey. There are glittering glass cathedrals and a crumbling adobe mission; the world's most famous amusement park and little-known natural waterfalls; astonishing restaurants serving artichoke ragout and sidewalk vendors offering spears of papaya or cups of watermelon.

All this points to one fact: Orange County's greatest strength is its astonishing diversity. It's what both delights and befuddles newcomers, for just when you think you have it figured out, that you know what these 782 square miles are all about, you stumble across a vision of Southern California that is nothing like what you imagined, whether it be the bustling community of Little Saigon, home to the largest concentration of Vietnamese Americans in the United States, or rustic Silverado Canyon, where a stagecoach service ran more than a hundred years ago and where some of the residents still ride a horse to pick up their mail.

People have always come to Orange County because it is a land largely unencumbered by the past. It is a place that tends to look to the future rather than to bygone days. That's what Walt Disney did in 1955 when he saw something other than just orange trees in Anaheim. In fact, even the county's name was visionary: when it was first proposed in the mid-1880s, there were no orange trees here. But county leaders suggested the name because they felt it was evocative and that settlers would be more inclined to move to a land with such promise in its name. And they were right.

The day that Walt Disney cut the ribbon opening up the Magic Kingdom, he noted that the park would "never be completed as long as there is imagination left in the world." The same could be said for the future of Orange County.

ACCESS AND INFORMATION

Anaheim is about 40 miles south of downtown Los Angeles and 90 minutes north of San Diego. Disneyland is conveniently located just off the freeway. Take Interstate 5 until you see signs for Disneyland; recent highway expansion built high-volume off-ramps (for both carpool and regular lanes) that lead directly to the attractions' parking lots and surrounding streets. If you're traveling in from out of town and

Anaheim is your first—or only—destination, you can fly directly into Santa Ana's **JOHN WAYNE AIRPORT** (949/252-5200; www.ocair.com), the largest airport in Orange County. It's about 15 miles from Disneyland. Check to see if your hotel has a free shuttle to and from either airport (some will also pick you up at LAX, 30 minutes away), or call one of the following commercial **SHUTTLE SERVICES**: L.A. Xpress (800/I-ARRIVE), Prime Time (800/262-7433), or SuperShuttle (714/517-6600). **CAR-RENTAL AGENCIES** located at the John Wayne Airport include Budget (800/221-1203) and Hertz (800/654-3131).

The **ANAHEIM/ORANGE COUNTY VISITOR & CONVENTION BUREAU** (800 W Katella Ave; 714/765-8888; www.anaheimoc.org) can offer helpful information on the area and its attractions.

Anaheim

German settlers initially bought the region they named Anaheim (derived from the German word for "home" plus the name of the local river) to establish vineyards—and did so for about $2 an acre. The vineyards thrived, and the region was for many years considered the wine-producing capital of the state. In the late 1880s, the vineyards were decimated by a blight, and the wine industry here collapsed. Within a few years, however, the citrus industry developed, and by World War II Anaheim was considered a prosperous agricultural community. But it was in 1955, when Walt Disney opened the doors to Disneyland, that Anaheim put itself on the global map.

Practically within the shadow of the park's Matterhorn are two other Disney properties (at least, for the time being): the **ARROWHEAD POND** (2695 E Katella Ave, at Douglass Rd; 714/704-2400; www.arrowheadpond.com), home to the NHL **MIGHTY DUCKS** (714/940-2159; www.mightyducks.com) and a popular venue for big-name musical events; and **EDISON INTERNATIONAL FIELD** (2000 Gene Autry Wy, near Katella Ave), home to the American League (and 2002 World Series winners) **ANAHEIM ANGELS** (714/634-2000; www.angelsbaseball.com). The Angels play April through October and the Mighty Ducks' season is September through April, so there's something sporting going on year-round. Sharing one end of the parking lot at Edison Field is **THE GROVE** (714/712-2700; www.thegroveofanaheim.com), a midsize concert hall that brings in some big-name acts: Ray Charles, Dwight Yoakam, Los Lobos, even REO Speedwagon.

For listings of Disney restaurants and lodgings, see the next section, The Disneyland Resort.

RESTAURANTS

Anaheim White House / ★★

887 S ANAHEIM BLVD, ANAHEIM; 714/772-1381 Old-world elegance applied to service, setting, and cuisine is the specialty at this restored 1909 Colonial-style home once surrounded by orange groves. Since 1987 Paris-born Bruno Serato has earned a loyal following by gracefully serving a Northern Italian menu (with a few French items tucked in) to those in search of a fine meal near Disneyland. Diners enjoy a choice of candlelit rooms with Victorian decor,

DISNEYLAND AREA THREE-DAY TOUR

DAY 1. Get revved up for the day with a double espresso to go with one of Nancy Silverton's indulgent pastries at the **LA BREA BAKERY** in Downtown Disney. Buy tickets to **DISNEY'S CALIFORNIA ADVENTURE** an hour before it opens, then head straight for Soarin' Over California for a hang glider's view of the Golden State. After that it's a white-water plunge down Grizzly River Run and loop-de-loops on the California Screamin' coaster. Take a break in Downtown Disney for a casual lunch at **NAPLES RISTORANTE E PIZZERIA.** Reserve the afternoon for some cool adventures beneath ground in the 3-D-enhanced film *It's Tough to Be a Bug.* Spend the night at the **GRAND CALIFORNIAN HOTEL,** with its own entry and exit to Disney's newest theme park, and splurge with dinner at the elegant **NAPA ROSE.**

DAY 2. Put a smile on your face with a Mickey Mouse waffle in the hotel's **STORY-TELLER'S CAFE** before walking over to the monorail station at the eastern end of **DOWNTOWN DISNEY** for the quick elevated ride into **DISNEYLAND.** Head for the galaxies on Star Tours and through meteor showers in Space Mountain. Get tossed and turned on the Indiana Jones Adventure, then relax a bit with ride on the Jungle Cruise. If you've made reservations earlier, grab some chuck-wagon chili at the **GOLDEN HORSE-SHOE STAGE** before the half-hour song-and-dance revue starts. The afternoon would be well spent paddling a canoe around Tom Sawyer's Island or having your photo taken with Mickey and Minnie in Toontown. Have tapas and a glass of California wine at **CATAL** in Downtown Disney, then take your pick of evening entertainment from rock at **HOUSE OF BLUES,** or New Orleans–style jazz at **RALPH BRENNAN'S JAZZ KITCHEN.**

DAY 3. It's a 10-minute drive to **KNOTT'S BERRY FARM** in Buena Park. Get your bearings by taking a ride around the park on the Ghost Town Calico Railroad. If you love coasters, you'll want to ride Montezooma's Revenge, Boomerang, and Xcelerator. For lunch, have fried chicken at **MRS. KNOTT'S CHICKEN DINNER RESTAURANT** (8039 Beach Blvd; 714/220-5080). Be sure and save room for a slice of the boysenberry pie. If you're theme-parked out, why not use the day instead to explore the antique haven of **OLD TOWNE ORANGE**—or treat the family to Santa Ana's **DISCOVERY SCIENCE CENTER,** billed as an "amusement park of the mind"? In the evening, enjoy a relaxed and romantic end to your adventure with dinner at the **ANAHEIM WHITE HOUSE.**

though service seems most attentive downstairs (tables near the fireplace are highly coveted). Steak, veal, lamb, and pasta choices include all the standards we've seen before, but a capable kitchen does justice to every dish. Examples include filet mignon with baked polenta, caramelized shallots, and thyme-scented veal reduction, as well as Italian potato dumplings in a silky Gorgonzola sauce. The widely praised wine list features more than 200 California and European vintages, offering top choices befitting the many special occasions celebrated here. *$$$; AE, MC, V; no checks; lunch Mon–Fri, dinner every day; full bar; reservations recommended; www. anaheimwhitehouse.com; between Ball Rd and Lincoln Ave.* &

Foxfire / ★★

5717 E SANTA ANA CANYON RD, ANAHEIM; 714/974-5400 What used to be a rather ho-hum restaurant is now a strong player in the north county's fine dining scene, thanks to a completely retooled menu that puts the spotlight squarely on prime cuts of meat, game, and poultry. Tea-smoked duck is sided with grilled pears and wild rice pancakes stacked with creamed turnips and dressed with a cherry-port sauce, and pan-roasted lotte (a.k.a. monkfish) medallions are matched by crab-corn-risotto cakes topped with fresh spinach. Foxfire's setting has changed less than its menu: it remains a rambling series of smaller rooms that feel more intimate than the total square footage would suggest. Service varies considerably from server to server. Another warning: Dinner is Foxfire's forte, and lunch often falls short. The lively adjoining lounge attracts mostly baby-boomer singles. *$$$; AE, DC, MC, V; no checks; lunch Mon–Fri, dinner every day, brunch Sun; full bar; reservations recommended; www.foxfirerestaurant.com; at Imperial Hwy.* &

Mr. Stox / ★★

1105 E KATELLA AVE, ANAHEIM; 714/634-2994 Open since 1967, Mr. Stox could well be labeled an old reliable, but that would understate this restaurant's obvious enthusiasm for change and ever-higher levels of excellence. The current menu illustrates how well Mr. Stox blends the fresh with the familiar. Chef Scott Raczek has a gift for taking a basic like certified Angus beef culotte steak and gussying it up with red wine, caramelized onions, and a rosemary potato roll, or for siding mesquite-grilled swordfish with pesto risotto, grilled vegetables, and roasted red chili oil. Also on the menu are lamb, duck, rabbit, and several seafood selections. If you're fond of authentic crab cakes, order them here; the owners, former Marylanders Ron and Debbie Marshall, are justifiably proud of their lump-meat crab cakes, served on a light Dijon sauce with a medley of garden vegetables and peppered potatoes. Entrees are supported by incredible site-baked breads and an exquisite, widely praised wine cellar. Add polished service and tranquil, sumptuous surroundings, and you have an experience worth repeating for another three decades. *$$$; AE, DC, DIS, MC, V; no checks; lunch Mon–Fri, dinner every day; full bar; reservations recommended; www.mrstox.com; between State College Blvd and Levis St.* &

LODGINGS

The Anabella Hotel / ★★

1030 W KATELLA AVE, ANAHEIM; 714/905-1050 OR 800/863-4888 Uniting several formerly independent low-rise hotels across the street from California Adventure, the two-year-old Anabella started from scratch, gutting each building to create carefully planned rooms for park-bound families and business travelers alike. The new complex features a vaguely mission-style facade of white-washed walls and red-tiled roofs, though guest room interiors are strictly contemporary in style and modern in appointments. Bathrooms are generously sized and outfitted in honey-toned granite; most have a tub-shower combo—just a few are shower only. Though parking areas dot the grounds, you'll also find a pleasant garden around the central swimming pool and whirlpool; a separate adult pool hides out next to the streetside fitness room. Business travelers will appreciate the in-room executive desks with high-speed Internet access, while families can take advantage of "kids' suites" complete with bunk beds and separate bedrooms. There's a pleasant indoor-outdoor all-day restaurant, and the hotel is a stop on both the Disney and Convention Center shuttle routes. Note: Rooms and rates vary wildly in terms of room size, layout, and occupancy limits; extra time spent with the reservationist will pay off in the most comfortable room for your needs. *$$–$$$; AE, DC, DIS, MC, V; checks OK; www.anabellahotel.com; east of Disneyland Dr.* &

Anaheim Hilton and Towers / ★★

777 W CONVENTION WY, ANAHEIM; 714/750-4321 OR 949/222-9923 Perhaps because Disneyland is nearby, this branch of the Hilton chain is more garish than the others. As you enter the lobby, you wish they'd turn down the volume of the fountain because the rush of the water is so loud it's hard to hear yourself think. However, in customary Hilton style, management makes everything easy at this city within a city. Arrangements for outings to Disneyland and the region's other attractions are made with a wave of the concierge's hand. The 1,600 rooms and suites—some of them in a pretty, landscaped garden area—are uniformly cozy, designed for maximum efficiency and with plenty of amenities, including a free continental breakfast. They are spacious, decorated in modern style, in shades of mauve, pink, and green, with pale wood furniture. The excellent fitness center includes weight training, aerobics and spinning (stationary bike) classes, and a basketball court. Guests also enjoy the spa, full-service salon, and gargantuan pool, replete with a pool bar and whirlpool spa, the rooftop gardens, and sundecks. The hotel also offers lobby shops, a foreign currency exchange, a post office, and airline and car-rental offices. Dining options include Hastings Grill, Pavia for Italian specialties, and Café Express for quick bites. The Lobby Bar, oozing California cool, is a terrific spot for a drink. The Anaheim Convention Center is next door. *$$$$; AE, DC, DIS, MC, V; checks OK; www.hilton.com; 2 blocks from Disneyland.* &

Anaheim Marriott / ★★

700 W CONVENTION WY, ANAHEIM; 714/750-9100 OR 800/228-9290 For years, this was a flagship Marriott, a place where founder J. W. made a point of providing special amenities, like daily delivery of the paper to your door, and his signature restaurant. It's still largely that way. Not only will you find *USA Today* waiting for you when you get up, but the inviting aroma of freshly brewed lattes will lure you to the Starbucks in the downstairs lounge. Their famed restaurant, known for its continental cuisine and extensive wine list, has been transformed into JW's Steakhouse. The chops are fine as is the rest of the California-cuisine-oriented menu. Down comforters and feather pillows add a nice touch to the rooms, and given the location on the backside of the Convention Center, it's not surprising to find work desk and data ports in every unit. A shuttle will run you over to the Disneyland

Resort, though it's so close you might prefer to walk. *$$$$; AE, DC, DIS, MC, V; checks OK; www.marriott.com; 2 blocks from Disneyland.* &

Candy Cane Inn / ★★☆

1747 S HARBOR BLVD, ANAHEIM; 714/774-5284 OR 949/345-7057 This modest, U-shaped motel used to boast of being only a block from Disneyland, but the park's recent expansion puts it right in the center of the action. The Candy Cane responded with a timely renovation, sprucing up the exterior with cobblestone drives and walkways, old-time street lamps, a Mediterranean fountain, and flowering vines engulfing the balcony railings. It's a bargain hunter's dream, offering stylish and well-located digs for around $100 (most of the time). The 172 guest rooms are comfortably sized and attractively furnished with two queen beds, down comforters, and a separate dressing and vanity area; in-room conveniences include coffeemakers, minifridges, and hair dryers. A large pool is tucked into a neatly landscaped garden courtyard, along with a whirlpool; the children's wading area is almost always splashing with young bathers. Complimentary continental breakfast is served in the courtyard or dining room. Extra amenities such as valet services, free shuttle to the Disneyland/California Adventure main gate, coin-op laundry facilities, a helpful staff, and kid-friendly ambience make this a family favorite. *$–$$; AE, DC, DIS, MC, V; no checks; near Katella Ave.* &

The Disneyland Resort

The sleepy agricultural town of Anaheim first stirred in the public consciousness when a post–World War II housing boom began transforming acres of orchards into geometrical tract neighborhoods. But it was the West's most famous theme park, brainchild of animator Walt Disney, that really put Anaheim on the map.

Disney had been dreaming since the 1930s of an "amusement park" (he himself invented the phrase) where children and parents could enjoy good, clean fun together. In 1955 he blended the noble goal of embodying America's diverse past (in features like the replica 19th-century Main Street, USA, rugged Frontierland, and jazzy New Orleans Square), the ambitious vision of a World of Tomorrow (soon renamed Tomorrowland), fantasy settings from his features *Snow White* and *Sleeping Beauty,* and the astounding creativity and technological feats performed by his "Imagineering" department. Throw in some typical Walt-style optimism in the form of employee "hosts" and "hostesses" who treat every tourist as a "guest" (and refer to each ride as an "adventure"), and the world's greatest family park was born.

As Disneyland rockets toward its 50th anniversary in 2005, the landmark theme park still inspires wonder in children and long-since-grown fans. Though old Walt's original blueprints were abandoned long ago, every new development remains true to his distinctive personal vision, employing the trademark Disney imagination, creativity, and attention to detail that's always set Disneyland apart. In 2001, after several years of hectic construction, Anaheim proudly unveiled some additions to the Disney family: a next-door park celebrating the Golden State called California Adventure; the adjacent Downtown Disney entertainment/dining/shopping district;

and the masterful Grand Californian Hotel. Bound together by a new name—the Disneyland Resort—these attractions have kick-started the surrounding neighborhood as well; civic improvements include much-needed freeway expansion, newly widened tree-lined boulevards, and flower-filled medians and public spaces. Hotels and businesses around the resort have been quick to jump on the bandwagon, too, as new investors and longtime establishments spruce up in the new millennium. Disneyland, and Anaheim, have certainly come a long way.

WHEN TO VISIT

Several factors can influence your decision about when to head to the Disneyland Resort, the most important, obviously, being your own schedule—when you have vacation time, when the kids are on school break, or when Aunt Mildred is visiting from Decatur. If you're flexible enough to plan around Disney seasons, though, here are a few pointers to help out.

Without a doubt the resort is busiest in summer (between Memorial Day and Labor Day), on holidays (Thanksgiving week, Christmas week, Easter week, and Japan's "Golden Week" in early May), and on weekends year-round. All other periods are considered "off-season." You can best avoid the crowds by visiting on a weekday, preferably during November, December, or January (excluding Thanksgiving and Christmas weeks). Remember, though, that fewer shows are scheduled during the off-season and you run the risk of some attractions (though never more than three or four at a time) being closed for maintenance. Here's a tip: If Disneyland and California Adventure are open late (past 10pm), you'll know they're expecting larger crowds—and so should you. On summer weekends, for example, the parks don't close till midnight or 1am. If closing time is early, crowds will probably be light; on off-season weekdays, they rarely stay open past 6 or 7 in the evening.

What about the weather? Despite the fact that Southern California is widely believed to not have weather, there are some factors to keep in mind. On a scorching summer day (July, August, and September are the likeliest months), even a short wait for a ride can feel like an eternity—with everyone crowding into available shady spots, and superlong lines to buy cold drinks. If you visit on a hot day (say, over 85 degrees), plan on plenty of rest time during the midday heat—a good time to check out indoor attractions. You'll be pleasantly surprised after dark, though, because sweltering days are always followed by pleasantly balmy evenings. Worried about rain? Southern California isn't known for precipitation; what we do get usually arrives between January and April, but only a sustained downpour should affect your Disney plans. If showers are in the forecast, plan ahead with a collapsing umbrella and waterproof rain poncho (or you can splurge on the cute Mickey Mouse ponchos that suddenly appear throughout the resort when the first raindrop falls). A light drizzle will have little effect on your fun, and intermittent heavy showers can be managed by heading to indoor attractions or taking a break at Downtown Disney's multiplex movie theater. You may get a little damp, but you'll enjoy the lightest crowds of the year!

VISITOR INFORMATION

When you're planning a Disneyland visit, you can get a wealth of information—on Disneyland and California Adventure parks, Downtown Disney district, and the

Disney hotels—from the **DISNEYLAND INFORMATION LINE** (714/781-4565 for recorded information; 714/781-7290 to consult with a live person between 8am and 7pm every day). You'll be able to find out park hours, current ride closures, and up-to-date show schedules. The same information—plus online ticket sales—is also available at www.disneyland.com.

If you're looking for general area visitor information, the **ANAHEIM/ORANGE COUNTY VISITOR & CONVENTION BUREAU** (800 W Katella Ave; 714/765-8888; www.anaheimoc.org) can fill you in on other local activities, shopping shuttles, and upcoming events. Their Visitor Center is at 1500 S Harbor Boulevard, across the street from the Disneyland Resort; it's open Monday to Friday from 8:30am to 5pm, and Saturday and Sunday from 9:30am to 1pm (later in summer).

ESSENTIALS: DISNEYLAND AND CALIFORNIA ADVENTURE
The Disneyland Resort's enormous **PARKING** structure is difficult to miss; street signs are easy to see, and employees direct traffic to available spaces. Frequent shuttles carry passengers to Disney's main entrance and to the resort hotels. Parking is $7 per car.

Disneyland and California Adventure are open every day of the year, but **OPERATING HOURS** vary; call 714/781-4565 for the schedule on the day you'll be visiting. The same information, including ride closures and show schedules, can also be found online at www.disneyland.com. Generally speaking, the parks are open from 9 or 10am to 6 or 7pm on weekdays, fall to spring; and from 8 or 9am to midnight or 1am on weekends, holidays, and winter, spring, or summer vacation periods. If you're going to spend the night in Anaheim, you might want to consider staying at one of the three official Disneyland Resort hotels—the Disneyland Hotel, Paradise Pier Hotel, or Disney's Grand Californian; their guests get to enter Disneyland early almost every day and enjoy the major rides before the lines form. (There is no early admission at California Adventure.) The head start varies from day to day, but usually you can enter 1½ hours early. Call ahead to check the schedule.

TICKET PRICES for admission to *either* Disneyland or California Adventure, including unlimited rides and all festivities and entertainment, is $45 for adults and children over 11, $41 for seniors 60 and over, $35 for children 3 to 11, and free for children under 3. Multiday Park Hopper tickets are available; they allow you to "hop" between the two parks as often as you like. Prices for adults/children are $117/$93 (3-day) and $145/$115 (4-day). The parks often run seasonal promotions that might feature reduced admission deals, complimentary kids' tickets with adult admissions, discounts for local residents, and the like. Be sure to inquire about any special offers when you make your Disney plans. If you plan on arriving during a busy time (when the gates open in the morning, or between 11am and 2pm), purchase your tickets in advance and get a jump on the crowds at the ticket counters. **ADVANCE TICKETS** may be purchased through Disneyland's Web site (www.disneyland.com), at Disney stores in the United States, or by calling the ticket mail-order line (714/781-4043).

If you have any extra items you don't want to carry around the Disney parks, **LOCKERS** are available for a $3 rental fee. At Disneyland you'll find them next to the newsstand outside the main entrance, on Main Street, USA, and in Fantasyland

IS A DISNEY VACATION PACKAGE FOR YOU?

If you intend to spend two or more nights in Disney territory, it pays to investigate the bevy of packaged vacation options available. Start by contacting your hotel to see whether they have Disneyland admission packages. Many vacation packagers include Disneyland and/or California Adventure (and other attractions) with their inclusive deals; or contact the official Disney agency, **WALT DISNEY TRAVEL COMPANY** (800/225-2024 or 714/520-5050). You can request a glossy catalog by mail, or log on to www.disneyland.com and click "Book Your Vacation" to peruse package details, take a virtual tour of participating hotel properties, and get online price quotes for customized, date-specific packages. Disney Travel's packages are value-packed time-savers with abundant flexibility. Hotel choices range from the official Disney hotels to one of 35 "neighbor hotels" in every price range (economy to superior) and category (from motel to all-suite); a wide range of available extras includes admission to other Southern California attractions and tours (like Universal Studios or a Tijuana shopping spree) and behind-the-scenes Disneyland tours, all in limitless combinations. Rates are always highly competitive, considering that each package includes multiday admission, early park entry, free parking (at the Disney hotels), plus keepsake souvenirs and Southern California coupon books.

—*Stephanie Avnet Yates*

(across from Toontown). At California Adventure lockers are located outside the main entrance and just inside the gates (in the Golden Gateway).

Parents can rent **STROLLERS** for use inside the parks; the daily rental fee is $7. They're available at Disneyland just inside the main entrance and also in Tomorrowland at Star Trader. For California Adventure, rental stations are located inside the main entrance in Golden Gateway, and across from Soarin' Over California at Fly 'n' Buy.

For decades Disneyland regulars had their own personal method of "doing" the park—and like Vegas gamblers with a "system," each was fiercely loyal to his or her tried-and-true way. Mostly it involved strategies for waiting in the shortest possible lines to ride the most popular rides, and each morning eager visitors would run to be first in line at perennial favorites like Space Mountain, Indiana Jones, Splash Mountain, and Star Tours. But in 2000, all that changed with the advent of **FAST-PASS,** an innovative system of pacing riders (almost like freeway on-ramp metering). Here's how it works: say you want to ride Space Mountain, but the wait sign indicates a 75-minute standstill. Automated FastPass ticket dispensers allow you to swipe the magnetic strip of your park entrance ticket, get a FastPass for a time slot later in the day, and head off to enjoy other attractions before you return to use the reduced-wait (usually 5-10 minutes) FastPass entrance. The only catch: you can be holding only one unused FastPass at a time, which you must use (or let expire) before the parkwide system will issue another. About 10 of the best-loved Disneyland rides are equipped with FastPass, with another handful at California Adventure; for a complete list at each park, check your official map/guide when you enter.

EXPLORING DISNEYLAND PARK

Disneyland is divided into several themed "lands," arranged according to Walt Disney's original blueprint around a circular hub. Clockwise, here's what you'll find:

Entry to the park is along **MAIN STREET, USA,** a cinematic version of turn-of-the-20th-century small-town America. Complete with curbs, street lamps, and horse-drawn wagons, Main Street is lined with gift shops, candy stores, and a silent theater that continuously runs early Mickey Mouse films. Because there are no rides, save Main Street for either the middle of the afternoon (when ride lines are longest) or the evening, when you can start buying souvenirs on your way out of the park.

At the end of Main Street is the meticulously landscaped round Plaza, the park's central hub. The Plaza is one of the best viewing spots in the park for both Disney's nightly parade and the fireworks show over Sleeping Beauty Castle. To your left will be **ADVENTURELAND,** inspired by the most exotic regions of Asia, Africa, and the South Pacific. Popular rides include Tarzan's Treehouse, the African-themed Jungle Cruise, and the sedate Enchanted Tiki Room. Adventureland's star ride is the Indiana Jones Adventure, a joltingly realistic ride into the perilous Temple of the Forbidden Eye, complete with bubbling lava pits, whizzing arrows, fire-breathing serpents, collapsing bridges, and the familiar cinematic tumbling boulder.

Beyond Adventureland is **NEW ORLEANS SQUARE,** a faux French Quarter that's home to two Disney oldie-but-goodies: the Haunted Mansion, a ghoulish and creative walk/ride through a decaying and otherworldly setting; and the Pirates of the Caribbean, a boat ride through an enchanting world of swashbuckling, rum-running, and buried treasure. Even in the middle of the afternoon you can dine by the cool moonlight and to the sound of crickets in the Blue Bayou restaurant, situated in the middle of the ride itself.

Tucked away behind New Orleans Square lies the backwoods of **CRITTER COUNTRY,** home to the audio-animatronic musical Country Bear Jamboree show, and popular Splash Mountain, a thrilling—and soaking—water flume ride based on the Disney movie *Song of the South*. Critter Country is connected to **FRONTIER-LAND,** which pays homage to America's 19th-century can-do settlers with Tom Sawyer's Island (reached by raft), an explore-on-your-own play area with balancing rocks, caves, and a rope bridge. The Big Thunder Mountain Railroad roller coaster races through a deserted 1870s gold mine. On Saturdays, Sundays, and holidays, and during vacation periods, Frontierland's Rivers of America is home to the after-dark extravaganza FANTASMIC!, which mixes magic, music, live performers, and sensational special effects in a pyrotechnic crowd pleaser. Much of New Orleans Square is cordoned off for viewers—get there plenty early (as much as 90 minutes) to reserve the best space.

If you reenter the central Plaza from Frontierland, you'll see the stunning Sleeping Beauty castle, beyond which is the storybook-themed **FANTASYLAND,** where many of the rides are inspired by classic Disney animated films *(Dumbo, Peter Pan, Alice in Wonderland, Snow White)* and fairy tales or folktales. The famous (love it or hate it) It's a Small World presides over Fantasyland, as does the thrilling Matterhorn

Bobsleds, a zippy roller coaster through chilled caverns and drifting fog banks. Tucked into a former staging area behind Fantasyland is **MICKEY'S TOONTOWN**, a colorful, whimsical world inspired by the Roger Rabbit films. There are several rides, including Roger Rabbit's CarToonSpin, but they take a back seat to Toontown itself—a trippy, smile-inducing world without a straight line or right angle in sight.

Conceived as an optimistic look at the future, **TOMORROWLAND** has been reinvented over the years, since the "future" keeps arriving. The latest incarnation employs an angular, metallic look popularized by futurists like Jules Verne. Two of Disneyland's don't-miss rides are here: the pitch-black indoor Space Mountain roller coaster and the joint Disney–George Lucas simulator Star Tours, an outer space misadventure with Star Wars' R2-D2 and C-3PO. (Trivia buffs take note: The R2-D2 and C-3PO that appear during the ride's in-line "pre-show" are the actual droids from the film.) The freeway ride Autopia is here, where updated minicars traverse curvy highways in and around Tomorrowland.

EXPLORING CALIFORNIA ADVENTURE

California Adventure is only about 75 percent of the size of Disneyland, with a much smaller crowd capacity—and it also takes less time to experience the lion's share of the park. Very few visitors will want to see California Adventure instead of Disneyland, but most will see the new attraction as part of a multiday Disney experience. Out-of-towners, especially, are the target audience for the park, which celebrates the Golden State with an idealized taste of California's fun, diversity, and lifestyle. Step through the scenic entrance, described by Disney planners as "an idealized postcard of California," and you're staring at a replica of the Golden Gate Bridge—with the monorail zooming overhead. Handmade tiles of across-the-state scenes glimmer on either side, and an enormous gold titanium "sun" shines all day. From this point visitors can head into three distinct themed areas, each containing rides, interactive attractions, live-action shows, and plenty of dining, snacking, and shopping opportunities. A California-themed nightly parade also winds through the park, as does the resurrected Electrical Parade.

First, there's **THE GOLDEN STATE**, representing California's history, heritage, and physical attributes. It may sound dull, but actually, the park's splashiest attractions are here. Part of a tribute to daring aviators, a re-created test pilots' hangar is home to Soarin' Over California, the ride that instantly emerged as the latter-day equivalent of a coveted "E ticket" thriller. It uses cool cutting-edge technology (and the surprise of smell-o-vision) to combine suspended seats with a spectacular IMAX-style surround-movie—so riders "soar" over California's scenic wonders. Nearby, California Adventure's iconic "Grizzly Peak" towers over the Grizzly River Run, a splashy gold-country ride through caverns, mine shafts, and waterslides; it culminates with a wet plunge into a spouting geyser. Kids can cavort nearby on the Redwood Creek Challenge Trail, a forest playground with smoke-jumper cable slides, net climbing, and swaying bridges. Pacific Wharf was inspired by Monterey's Cannery Row and features mouthwatering demonstrations by Boudin Sourdough Bakery, Mission Tortillas, and Lucky Fortune Cookies. If you get hungry, each has a food counter where you can enjoy soup in a sourdough bowl; tacos, burritos, and enchiladas; and teriyaki bowls, egg rolls, and wonton soup. A handful of attractions

BETCHA DIDN'T KNOW: DISNEY TRIVIA

Ever since July 17, 1955, when Walt Disney lowered the drawbridge of Sleeping Beauty Castle to allow the first eager visitors into Fantasyland, Disneyland has garnered a unique legion of followers utterly obsessed with every detail of the "Happiest Place on Earth." There are fan clubs, collectors' books, Disneyana conventions, and countless Internet sites devoted to the subject. For example, did you know that the drawbridge connecting Main Street Plaza to the Fantasyland castle is functional? It wasn't raised and lowered again until Disneyland's 25th anniversary in 1980, when engineers were doubtful the creaky machinery would still work. It did, though—and what a photo op! Here are some other little-known facts from Disneyland's distant (and recent) past:

Disneyland was carved out of orange groves, and the original plans called for carefully chosen individual trees to be left standing and included in the park's landscaping. On ground-breaking day, July 21, 1954, each tree in the orchard was marked with a ribbon—red to be cut and green to be spared. But the bulldozer operator went through and mowed down every tree indiscriminately . . . because no one had known he was color-blind.

Disneyland designers utilized forced perspective in the construction of many of the park's structures to give the illusion of height and dramatic proportions while keeping the park a manageable size. The buildings on Main Street, USA, for example, are actually 90 percent scale on the first floor, 80 percent on the second, and so forth. The stones on Sleeping Beauty Castle are carved in diminishing scale from the bottom to the top, giving it the illusion of towering height. Look carefully and you'll see the same proven technique employed throughout California Adventure, built 45 years after the original park.

geared toward the youngest visitors lies in A Bug's Land, inspired by the Pixar film *A Bug's Life*. There's the interactive adventure film *It's Tough to Be a Bug,* which uses next-generation 3-D technology; characters Flik and Hopper lead the audience on a slaphappy underground romp with bees, termites, grasshoppers, stink bugs, spiders, and a few surprises that keep everyone hopping, ducking, and laughing along. Nearby, Flik's Fun Fair offers several tame, toddler-friendly rides designed to emulate bug-size adventures in a giant-size world.

PARADISE PIER is a flashy corner of the park that pays homage to the glory days of California's beachfront amusement piers. The fantasy boardwalk is home to California Screamin', a classic roller coaster that replicates the whitewashed, wooden white-knucklers of the past—but with state-of-the-art steel construction and a smooth, computerized ride. There's also the Maliboomer, a trio of towers (giant strongman sledgehammer tests) that catapult riders to the tip-top bell, then lets them down bungee-style with dangling feet; the Orange Stinger, a whooshing swing ride

Walt Disney maintained two apartments inside Disneyland. His private quarters above the Town Square Fire Station have been kept just as they were when he lived there. The other, above Pirates of the Caribbean in New Orleans Square, now serves as the Disney Gallery.

It's a Small World was touted at its opening as "mingling the waters of the oceans and seas around the world with Small World's Seven Seaways." This was more than a publicity hoax—records from that time show such charges as $21.86 for a shipment of seawater from the Caribbean.

The peaceful demeanor of Disneyland was broken during the summer of 1970 by a group of radical Vietnam War protesters who invaded the park. They seized Tom Sawyer Island and raised the Vietcong flag over the fort before being expelled by riot specialists.

When Splash Mountain had only 24 hours of operational testing under its belt, Disney CEO Michael Eisner insisted on taking a not-so-dry run. Since engineers hadn't yet adjusted the flume on the ride's signature splash, Eisner donned an unglamorous trash bag—with a hole cut through for his head—to protect him from a drenching, and boarded with several Imagineers. After the ride he asked, "Can we go again?"

Despite Disneyland's teetotal reputation (California Adventure, on the other hand, has two restaurants that serve alcohol), the oft-rumored private Club 33 has stood unobtrusively next to the Blue Bayou restaurant since 1967, when Walt Disney created the dining room/cocktail lounge himself for hosting sponsors, celebrities, and wealthy guests. It's easy to spot the door labeled "33," but harder to sneak a peek; you must be invited by a member, each of whom typically pays at least $10,000 to join.

—*Stephanie Avnet Yates*

inside an enormous orange, complete with orange scent piped in; Mulholland Madness, a wacky wild trip along L.A.'s precarious hilltop street; and the Sun Wheel Carousel, featuring unique zigzagging cars that bring new meaning to the familiar ride. There are all the standard boardwalk games (complete with stuffed prizes), plus guilty-pleasure fast foods like pizza, corn dogs, and burritos.

The **HOLLYWOOD PICTURES BACKLOT** will be familiar to anyone who's visited Disney World in Florida—you'll recognize many elements of this trompe l'oeil recreation of a Hollywood movie studio lot. Pass through a classic studio archway flanked by gigantic golden elephants and you'll find yourself on a surprisingly realistic Hollywood Boulevard. In the Disney Animation building visitors can participate in six different interactive galleries—learn how stories become animated features; watch Robin Williams become an animated character; listen to a Disney illustrator invent Mushu from *Mulan;* and even take a computerized personality test to see which Disney character you resemble most. At the end of the street, the replica movie palace Hyperion Theater presents live-action revues, and the "Get a Grip" stunt presentations showcase the work of stagehands and reveal some of the simple tricks behind movie illusion. For TV fans, the audience participation show Who Wants to Be A Millionaire—Play It! promises fun and prizes (but no cool mil). The Backlot's main attraction is Jim Henson's MuppetVision 3-D, an on-screen blast from the past featuring Kermit, Miss Piggy, Gonzo, Fozzie Bear—and even hecklers Waldorf and Statler. A plethora of dining options is led by the ABC Soap Opera Bistro, where you can enjoy casual diner fare in replicated sets from your favorite soap operas.

DOWNTOWN DISNEY

Based on the success of its predecessor at Walt Disney World in Florida, Downtown Disney is a district filled with **RESTAURANTS, SHOPS, AND ENTERTAINMENT** for all ages. Whether you want to stroll with kids in tow, have an upscale dinner for two, or party into the night, this colorful and sanitized "street scene" fills the bill. The promenade begins at the amusement park gates and stretches toward the Disneyland Hotel; there are nearly 20 shops and boutiques and a dozen-plus restaurants, live music venues, and entertainment options.

If you compare the stores in Downtown Disney to other area shopping, they're dwarfed by über-malls like South Coast Plaza or Fashion Island in Newport Beach. But Disneyland planners have achieved their goal of providing just enough diverse and non-Disney options to keep many tourists from leaving in search of greener shopping pastures—and keeping visitors (and their dollars) close to the fold was the main objective of the entire Disneyland expansion. The number-one shopping highlight is **WORLD OF DISNEY** (800/362-4533), the ultimate Disney shopping experience. The supermarket-size (40,000 square feet) labyrinth of Disney logo items, keepsakes, toys, collectibles, and other souvenirs is an easy place to get lost—and the best place to do your gift shopping for everyone from infants to in-laws. Also worth a visit is the mall's only other Disney-themed store, **MARCELINE'S CONFECTIONERY** (714/300-7922), patterned after the old-style candy emporium in Walt Disney's hometown of Marceline, Missouri. Outside the shop plate-glass windows let you watch the workers making fudge, caramel apples, and cookies in the open candy kitchen. The rest of Downtown Disney's limited selection of stores offers a little something for everyone, including **LEGO IMAGINATION CENTER** (714/991-6512), where small play stations are set up throughout a store filled with all things LEGO; **COMPASS BOOKS & CAFE** (714/635-9801; www.bookinc.net) is a branch of Books, Inc., the respected Northern California independent chain whose socially conscious neighborhood bookstores are thoughtfully tailored to each location; and the ultimate chick-magnet **SEPHORA** (714/758-1700; www.sephora.com), the European beauty and cosmetics superstore.

Even if you're not staying at one of the Disney hotels, Downtown Disney is worth a visit. Locals and day shoppers take advantage of the free entry and validated Downtown Disney parking lots (three hours free; five with restaurant or theater validation). For recorded information on Downtown Disney events and stores, call 714/300-7800.

Downtown Disney fills the after-dark void that's plagued adult Disneygoers for years, with exciting and convenient options on nights when the parks close early (or when you've simply had enough Mickey Mouse for one day). There's a fine choice of **LIVE ENTERTAINMENT**: the Mississippi delta–flavored **HOUSE OF BLUES** (714/778-BLUE; www.hob.com) is a funky, midsize (900 people) venue that features blues, rock-and-roll, and country performers as varied as Merle Haggard, Dogstar, George Thorogood, and Duran Duran. Every night a rowdy jazz ensemble plays at the French Quarter–style **RALPH BRENNAN'S JAZZ KITCHEN** (714/776-5200; www.rbjazzkitchen.com). Sports fans will be happy to see an outpost of the Disney-owned **ESPN ZONE** (1545 Disneyland Dr; 714/300-ESPN; www.espnzone.com), where sporting events are broadcast throughout the dining rooms and indoor-outdoor bar, creating a loud, arena-style atmosphere that's the perfect backdrop for crowd-pleasing American grill food and pub favorites; the interactive "Sports Arena" offers virtual and actual competitive games. Other entertainment options include a state-of-the-art multiplex AMC Theater.

RESTAURANTS INSIDE THE RESORT

Catal Restaurant/Uva Bar / ★★★

1580 DISNEYLAND DR, ANAHEIM; 714/774-4442 L.A.'s high priest of cuisine, Joachim Splichal, branches out to Anaheim (from food temple Patina) with this combo-concept eatery in the heart of Downtown Disney. The main restaurant, Catal, features a series of quiet, intimate second-floor rooms that combine rustic Mediterranean charm with fine-dining style. Complemented by an excellent international wine list, the menu is a collage of flavors from around the Mediterranean Sea: seared sea scallops appear over saffron risotto dotted with baby artichokes, traditional osso buco rests on creamy polenta drizzled with white truffle oil, and Moroccan-spiced grilled lamb is paired with a flaky spinach-feta pie. Downstairs, the Uva Bar (*uva* means "grape" in Spanish) is a casual tapas bar offering 40 different wines by the glass in an outdoor pavilion setting. The affordable menu features the same pan-Mediterranean influence, even offering many items from the Catal menu; standouts include cabernet-braised short ribs atop horseradish mashed potatoes, marinated olives and cured Spanish ham, and Andalusian gazpacho with rock shrimp. *$$–$$$; AE, DC, DIS, MC, V; no checks; lunch, dinner every day; full bar; reservations recommended Sun–Thurs, not accepted Fri–Sat (Catal), reservations not accepted (Uva Bar); www.patinagroup.com; in Downtown Disney.* &

La Brea Bakery Express & Cafe / ★★

1556 DISNEYLAND DR, ANAHEIM; 714/490-0233 Fresh from the ovens of L.A.'s artisan bakery dynasty, this La Brea Bakery duo occupies a coveted position at the beginning of Downtown Disney, right across from the theme parks' ticket kiosks. In the morning bleary-eyed early birds disembark from the parking lot tram and head to La Brea's cafeteria-style Express for a jolt of espresso or a quick energy bite—light breakfast items are served in addition to creator Nancy Silverton's irresistible breads and pastries. Relax for a moment in a comfy woven bistro chair on the outdoor patio before braving the Disney throngs. Throughout the day folks stop in for a lunch of sandwiches, filled brioche, or herb-laden focaccia—the kids' menu offers less-grown-up choices like grilled cheese and PB&J.

Meanwhile, the next-door Cafe is busy serving more thoughtful sit-down meals, complete with wine-by-the-glass selections. Entrees feature the Mediterranean flavors popularized at Silverton's (and husband Mark Peel's) acclaimed Campanile restaurant, and range from lighter fare (seared salmon or ahi) to a hearty lamb-sirloin-sausage stew atop creamy polenta. *$–$$; AE, DIS, MC, V; no checks; breakfast, lunch, dinner every day (Express), lunch, dinner every day (Cafe); beer and wine (Cafe only); reservations recommended (Cafe only); www.labreabakery.com; in Downtown Disney.* &

Napa Rose / ★★★

1600 S DISNEYLAND DR, ANAHEIM; 714/300-7170 Napa Rose is the first really serious restaurant ever to appear at the Disneyland Resort. Situated inside the upscale Grand Californian Hotel, the warm and light dining room mirrors the Arts and Crafts style of the hotel, down to the Frank Lloyd Wright stained-glass windows and Craftsman-inspired seating throughout the restaurant and its relaxing lounge. Executive chef Andrew Sutton hails from the Napa Valley's chic Auberge du Soleil and brings a Wine Country sensibility and passion for fresh, inventive preparations. Sutton personally seeks out California's best ingredients for the Rose's expertly equipped open kitchen; his latest finds are Sierra golden trout, artisan cheeses from Humboldt County and the Gold Country, and Sonoma rabbit for his signature braised mushroom-rabbit tart. The tantalizing Seven Sparkling Sins starter platter (for two) features jewel-like portions of foie gras, caviar, oysters, lobster, and other exotic delicacies; the same attention to detail is evident in seasonally composed main course standouts like grilled yellowtail with tangerine-basil fruit salsa atop savory couscous, or free-range veal osso buco in rich bacon-forest mushroom ragout. Leave room for dessert, or at least share one of pastry chef Jorge Sotello's creative treats—our favorites are Sonoma goat cheese flan with riesling-soaked tropical fruit, and gooey chocolate crepes with house-made caramelized banana ice cream. Napa Rose boasts an impressive and balanced wine list, including 45 by-the-glass choices; outdoor seating is arranged around a rustic fire pit, gazing out across a landscaped arroyo toward California Adventure's distinctive Grizzly Peak. Despite their silly Disney-mandated Mickey Mouse name tags, the staff provides sophisticated and practiced service. *$$$; AE, DC, DIS, JCB, MC, V; no checks; lunch, dinner every day; full bar; reservations recommended; www.patinagroup.com; in Disney's Grand Californian Hotel.* &

Naples Ristorante e Pizzeria / ★★

1550 DISNEYLAND DR, ANAHEIM; 714/776-6200 Step right up to the whimsical entrance of this just-stylish-enough Italian eatery, where a two-story papier-mâché harlequin—wearing an impish expression—wields a pizza peel and invites you to enter. Designed to be sophisticated enough for discerning palates while still wholly appropriate for casual families, Naples features a colorful, high-ceilinged dining room filled with padded loveseats and comfy chairs. One side of the room is dominated by busy chefs working the white-tiled open kitchen's wood-burning oven, while a floor-to-ceiling cherry-wood bar anchors the other. Naples also boasts some of the most scenic outdoor seating in Downtown Disney—be sure to request a patio table when reserving. At dinner you can also opt for the quieter ambience of the upstairs dining room. Piedmontese executive chef Corrado Gionatti is a master of the thin-crust Neapolitan pizza and uses an appropriately light hand saucing the menu's selection of pastas. Salads, antipasti, and calzone round out the menu; everything is very good and—be forewarned—portions are quite large. *$$; AE, DC, DIS, MC, V; no checks; lunch, dinner every day; full bar; reservations recommended; www.patinagroup.com; in Downtown Disney.* &

Rainforest Cafe / ★★☆

1515 S DISNEYLAND DR, ANAHEIM; 714/772-0413 Recently unearthed from an overgrown Central American jungle, this ancient Aztec temple was moved stone by stone to Anaheim. . . . OK, not really—but the deception is entertainingly real at the newest branch of this national favorite. There are cascading waterfalls inside and out, a canopy of lush vegetation, simulated tropical mists, and even a troupe of colorful parrots beckoning shoppers into the adjoining "Retail Village." Ensconced in this fantasy world, diners choose from an amalgam of wildly flavored dishes inspired by Caribbean, Polynesian, Latin, Asian, and Mediterranean cuisines. Fresh fruit smoothies and tropical specialty cocktails are offered, as well as a dessert—best when shared—called Giant Chocolate Volcano. During the inevitable wait for a table, you can browse through logo items, environmentally educational toys and games, stuffed jungle animals and puppets, straw safari hats, and other themed souvenirs in the lobby store—or make reservations by the day before, especially for peak mealtimes. There's a complete children's menu, and the Rainforest Cafe is one of the few Downtown Disney eateries to have full breakfast service (starting at 7am). *$–$$; AE, DC, DIS, MC, V; no checks; breakfast, lunch, dinner every day; full bar; reservations recommended; www.rainforestcafe.com; in Downtown Disney.* &

Ralph Brennan's Jazz Kitchen / ★★★

1590 S DISNEYLAND DR, ANAHEIM; 714/776-5200 If you thought Disneyland's New Orleans Square looked authentic, wait till you get a taste of this concept restaurant at Downtown Disney. Ralph Brennan, of the New Orleans food dynasty responsible for NoLa landmarks like Commander's Palace and a trio of Big Easy hot spots, commissioned a handful of New Orleans artists to create the handcrafted furnishings that give the Jazz Kitchen its believable French Quarter ambience. Lacy wrought-iron grillwork, cascading ferns, and trickling stone fountains enhance three separate dining choices: the upstairs Carnival Club is an elegant dining salon with silk-draped chandeliers and terrace dining that overlooks the "street scene" below; casual Flambeaux is downstairs, where a bead-encrusted grand piano hints at the nightly live jazz that sizzles in this room; and the Creole Cafe is a quick stop for necessities like muffaletta or beignets. Expect traditional Cajun-Creole fare with heavy-handed seasonings and rich, heart-stopping sauces—just like the creamy yet powerful jambalaya, andouille-laced gumbo, and spicy seafood rémoulades one finds in New Orleans. *$$–$$$; AE, DC, DIS, MC, V; no checks; lunch, dinner every day; full bar; reservations recommended; www.rbjazzkitchen.com; in Downtown Disney.* &

Yamabuki / ★★★

1717 S DISNEYLAND DR, ANAHEIM; 714/239-5683 OR 714/956-6755 (RESERVA-TIONS) Yamabuki may just be the sleeper of the Disneyland Resort. Hidden for years in the poor-stepchild Pacific Hotel (now reinvented as Disney's Paradise Pier Hotel), this upscale and quietly traditional Japanese restaurant thrives on a clientele of Asian tourists and businessfolk, plus discerning expense-account suits from throughout Orange County. Step inside and you enter a temple of deep red lacquer, delicate porcelain vases, discreet teak shutters, and translucent rice paper screens that together impart a sense of very un-Disney nobility. The staff is elegantly kimono-clad—even at lunch, when the fare is more affordable with casual bento boxes, lunch specials, and sushi/sashimi selections. At dinner, tradition demands a languorous procession of courses, from refreshing seafood starters and steaming noodle bowls to grilled teriyaki meats or table-cooked specialties like sukiyaki or shabu shabu. The menu, in Japanese and English, rates each dish as "contemporary," "traditional," or "very traditional," presenting the opportunity to try unusual squid, soybean, and pickled root dishes common in the Far East. If you're willing to spend the time—and the money—Yamabuki is a cultural trip across the globe. *$$–$$$; AE, DC, DIS, JCB, MC, V; no checks; lunch Mon–Fri, dinner every day; full bar; reservations recommended at dinner; www.disneyland.com; in Disney's Paradise Pier Hotel.*

LODGINGS INSIDE THE RESORT

The Disneyland Hotel / ★★★
Disney's Paradise Pier Hotel / ★★

1150 MAGIC WY, ANAHEIM; 714/778-6600 OR 714/956-MICKEY (RESERVA-TIONS) / 1717 S DISNEYLAND DR, ANAHEIM; 714/999-0990 OR 714/956-MICKEY (RESERVATIONS) For years the Holy Grail of Disneygoers has been this, the "Official Hotel of the Magic Kingdom." Now that the Disneyland Resort has welcomed the more serenely upscale Grand Californian to the fold, the original Disneyland Hotel has been undergoing a renovation and personality adjustment to define its place in the pecking order. Some perks are the same: a direct monorail connection to Disneyland (and California Adventure) means you'll be able to return to your room anytime, and hotel guests can take advantage of early admission to Disneyland Park. While all the Disney hotels are family-friendly in the extreme, the Disneyland Hotel boasts meandering grounds and on-site amusements that make it an attraction unto itself—and the appearance of characters throughout (Mickey and friends are everywhere!) makes it the best choice for families with small children on whom architecture and high style would just be lost. The rooms have never been fancy, but they're comfortably and attractively furnished, each with its own balcony, minibar, and coffeemaker. Other in-room amenities include movie channels (each resort hotel offers free Disney Channel, natch) and cute-as-a-button Disney-themed toiletries and accessories. Combined, the complex offers more than 10 restaurants, snack bars, and cocktail lounges; every kind of service desk imaginable; a fantasy swimming lagoon with white-sand beach; and a video game center.

The property also includes the adjoining Paradise Pier Hotel, formerly a semi-ignored satellite with a tranquil Asian ambience. A partial remodel has left it with a split personality, as Disney repositions it to reflect the California boardwalk-themed section of California Adventure seen from about half the high-rise's rooms. Public spaces sport colorful and whimsical add-ons, while guest rooms remain more homogenous. But guests enjoy all the same perks, including playtime at the adjacent Disneyland Hotel—with a quiet retreat just when you need it. *$$–$$$; AE, DC, DIS, JCB, MC, V; checks OK; www.disneyland.com; from I-5, take the Disneyland exit and follow hotel signs.* ₫

Disney's Grand Californian Hotel / ★★☆

1600 S DISNEYLAND DR, ANAHEIM; 714/635-2300 OR 714/956-MICKEY (RESERVATIONS) Disney spared no details when constructing this enormous version of an Arts and Crafts–era lodge (think Yosemite's Ahwahnee or Pasadena's Gamble House), hiring craftspeople throughout the state to contribute one-of-a-kind tiles, furniture, sculptures, and artwork. Taking inspiration from California's redwood forests, mission pioneers, and plein air painters, designers managed to create a nostalgic yet state-of-the-art high-rise hotel. Enter through subtle stained-glass sliding panels to the hotel's centerpiece, a six-story "living room" with a William Morris–designed marble "carpet," an angled skylight seen through exposed support beams, display cases of Craftsman treasures, and a three-story walk-in "hearth" whose fire warms Stickley-style rockers and plush leather armchairs. Outside, two beautiful swimming pools (the kids' pool is bear-shaped) are nestled in a landscaped garden surrounded by an extensive health club/spa, game room/video arcade, and three dining choices, including the magnificent Napa Rose.

Guest rooms are spacious and smartly designed, maintaining the Arts and Crafts theme surprisingly well considering the hotel's grand scale. The best ones overlook the park, but you'll pay for that view. In-room comforts reflect the upscale bent, with minibars, bathrobes, hair dryers, irons, and quality bath products standard. Despite the sophisticated, luxurious air of the Grand Californian, this is a hotel that truly caters to families, with a bevy of room configurations including one with a double bed plus bunk beds with trundle. You'll find folding cribs in every room, and the hotel provides sleeping bags (rather than rollaways) for additional kids. *$$$–$$$$; AE, DC, DIS, JCB, MC, V; checks OK; www.disneyland.com; from I-5, take the Disneyland exit and follow hotel signs.* ₫

Buena Park

Buena Park is just 10 miles northwest of Disneyland. Like Walt Disney's former orange groves, Buena Park was rich farming land, and an enterprising berry farmer named Knott would one day be immortalized in the midst of an otherwise bland bedroom community. Today **KNOTT'S BERRY FARM** (8039 Beach Blvd, ½ mile south of Hwy 91; 714/220-5200; www.knotts.com) is the second largest amusement park in California, with an average of five million visitors annually. Down the street, you can also visit **MOVIELAND WAX MUSEUM** (7711 Beach Blvd; 714/522-1155;

KNOTT'S BERRY FARM: SECOND ONLY
TO THE MIGHTY MOUSE

Unlike Walt Disney, farmer Walter Knott never intended to get into the amusement park business. He was best known, if for anything, for taking a new strain of berry, developed by one of his neighbors, Rudolph Boysen, and marketing enough of the superb fruit to literally keep the farm during the Great Depression. Of course, it wasn't easy. Money was tight and 20 acres of boysenberries and rhubarb only went so far. So his wife, Cordelia, came up with the idea of fixing chicken dinners, served on her wedding china, on Sunday afternoons. By 1940, Cordelia's roadside restaurant, right next to Walter's berry stand, was serving as many as 4,000 Sunday dinners. People lined up for blocks waiting for a meal. Which is when Walter figured that maybe he'd build a little Western ghost town behind the restaurant to give people something to do while they waited for a seat. Next thing you know, people were visiting the farm not just for Cordelia's chicken dinners but to spend an afternoon wandering around looking at the old stagecoaches and mining equipment Walter collected.

By the time Disneyland opened in 1955, Knott's Berry Farm was already a huge success. While some worried that the berry farm might wither on the vine once Mickey and friends showed up, Walter Knott never did. In fact, Orange County's two Walts always felt their amusement parks complemented, rather than detracted from, each other. After all, Disneyland was all about the future and fantasy while the Farm, as locals called it, focused on the past and Western heritage. But while Disneyland continued to expand, adding new rides and attractions every year, Knott's stayed pretty much the same up till 1969. Eventually it decided to focus more on coasters than stage coaches, and new owners of the farm have put a heavy emphasis on thrill rides like Xcelerator, a high-octane '50s-themed coaster, and Perilous Plunge, a water ride with a 115-foot drop guaranteed to soak. Each Halloween the park continues a tradition begun in 1972, with a total transformation into the truly hair-raising "Knott's Scary Farm" for the entire month of October.

The Knott's family also includes Soak City, USA, a companion park with 21 water rides, slides, and get-wet adventures; chicken dinners are still being served up by Mrs. Knott's Chicken Dinner Restaurant (and there's still always a line waiting to get in). Not bad for a boysenberry farm.

—David Lansing

www.movielandwaxmuseum.com). Inspired by the equally weird Madame Tussaud's in London, this 30-plus-years Buena Park mainstay receives lots of snickers—but also lots of paid admissions!

Additional information is available at the **BUENA PARK CHAMBER OF COMMERCE** (6601 Beach Blvd; 714/521-0261; http://buenaparkchamber.org), and on the city's Web site at **WWW.BUENAPARK.COM**.

Costa Mesa

Costa Mesa is one of the fastest-growing cultural, retail, and business centers in the United States. It's also the location of **TOWN CENTER**, universally accepted as Orange County's cultural core. At first glance, the Town Center complex resembles just another concrete-and-glass corridor of professional office buildings, a place one passes through on the way to somewhere else. Take a closer look and you'll see that the facade of one of the buildings—Segerstrom Hall—is graced with Richard Lippold's stunning steel-and-aluminum *Fire Bird*. Segerstrom Hall and its companion tower, the more intimate Founders Hall, compose the **ORANGE COUNTY PERFORMING ARTS CENTER (OCPAC)** (600 Town Center Dr; 714/556-ARTS; www.ocpac.org). Segerstrom Hall, with its 3,000-seat capacity, fantastic acoustics, and excellent sight lines, hosts **OPERA PACIFIC**, the **PACIFIC SYMPHONY ORCHESTRA**, **PACIFIC POPS**, and the **PACIFIC CHORALE**, along with engagements by such world-renowned performers as the **AMERICAN BALLET THEATER** and Sir Neville Marriner's **ACADEMY OF ST. MARTIN-IN-THE-FIELDS** orchestra. Founders Hall hosts a wide variety of concerts offering jazz, blues, and other forms of popular music. Tours of both halls are available Monday, Wednesday, and Saturday. Adjacent to OCPAC is the outdoor **NOGUCHI SCULPTURE GARDEN**. It parallels Anton Boulevard (the intersection just east of Town Center Dr) and features Noguchi's visually startling *California Scenario,* which simultaneously captures the essence of the area's Southwestern soul and the terror of the yawning San Andreas fault, all in the tranquil setting of a Japanese rock garden. There are notable works by **HENRY MOORE, JOAN MIRÓ**, and others as well.

Costa Mesa's ascension to the throne as the county's cultural crowned head began more than 35 years ago, when **SOUTH COAST REPERTORY** (655 Town Center Dr; 714/708-5500; www.scr.org) opened its doors. Like L.A.'s Mark Taper Forum, SCR mounts consistently fine productions of wide appeal, often featuring big-name talent. And, like the Taper's, several of SCR's productions have gone on to the Great White Way and have earned Tony awards from there.

Blessed with tinkling fountains, elegant courts, and an ornate and lovely children's carousel, **SOUTH COAST PLAZA** (Bristol St at I-405; 714/435-2000 or 800/782-8888; www.southcoastplaza.com) and its adjacent partners—Crystal Court, South Coast Village, and Metro Square—compose one of the largest shopping megalopolises in the world, where the best major department stores and designer boutiques are only steps apart. Another nice stop to make in this area is the **ROBERT MONDAVI WINE & FOOD CENTER** (1570 Scenic Ave, off S Harbor Blvd; 714/979-4510; www.robertmondavi.com/wfcenter); here, in a building set in a rose garden and a sculpture garden, the Mondavi chefs share their secrets, wine experts offer lectures, and there are various other wine and food events.

In amusing contrast to the ultramodern, ultra-high-hat Town Center and South Coast Plaza, Costa Mesa is also the location of the **ORANGE COUNTY FAIR AND EXPOSITION CENTER** (88 Fair Dr; 714/708-3247; www.ocfair.com). The County Fair runs annually in July, but almost every weekend of the year there's a **SWAP MEET**—the best in the county—and admission is only $2. In addition, there's a **FARMERS MARKET** each Thursday morning in the parking lot, with incredibly fresh and delicious produce. In spring, summer, and fall, enjoy hair-raising motorcycle racing at the **SPEEDWAY,** and tour **CENTENNIAL FARM,** a genuine working farm, any time of the year.

Further information is available from the **COSTA MESA CONFERENCE & VISITOR BUREAU** (714/384-0493 or 800/399-5499; www.costamesa-ca.com).

RESTAURANTS

Diva / ★★★

600 ANTON BLVD, COSTA MESA; 714/754-0600 As any producer will tell you, divas are gorgeous, theatrical, enchanting, and capricious, and this one is no exception. Just a short, pleasant walk from the Orange County Performing Arts Center and the South Coast Repertory, upscale Diva is a natural for pre- or post-theater dining with a dramatic flourish. Seductively lit with a soaring ceiling and lavishly adorned with jewel tones and an imposing gilded mirror, this is clearly a Big Night Out destination. Featuring contemporary creations by Orange County chef/entrepreneur John Sharpe (also of Bistro 201 and Topaz Café), Diva's menu is organized into "small" and "large" plates, such as the house seafood sampler and grilled hearts of romaine with Stilton/port swirl (both small plates) and grilled prawns on spaghetti squash or roast rack of lamb on wilted spinach with crisp fingerling potatoes (large plates). Appearances reign supreme here, from the sky-high food presentations to the spiffily dressed wait staff to the designer-clad diners. Kitchen performance is solid (if slightly uninspired), but service is frustratingly uneven, bouncing from adroit to amateurish. Live jazz on weekends makes the lounge a stylish choice for nightcaps or dessert. *$$$; AE, MC, DC, V; no checks; lunch Mon–Fri, dinner Mon–Sat; full bar; reservations recommended; Divascp@aol.com; lobby level of Plaza Tower building.* &

The Golden Truffle / ★★

1767 NEWPORT BLVD, COSTA MESA; 949/645-9858 Maverick chef/owner Alan Greeley uncharacteristically understates his position when he says, "It's never boring here; we cook on the edge." Indeed, Greeley continues to excite chefs, foodies, and other daring souls with his broadly eclectic cuisine. With a menu that bounces between "utility foods" such as macaroni and cheese with black truffles and weekly specials on regional, ethnic, or ingredient themes, diners should expect the unexpected (duck tacos, veal dumplings). A decidedly unchic location in a quirky strip mall hardly deters fans of this low-key bistro. Insiders call ahead to be sure Greeley is in the kitchen. Also noteworthy is Greeley's adventurous approach to his wine selections, featuring unsung varietals from far-flung locales. *$$$; AE, MC, V; no* *checks; lunch, dinner Tues–Sat; beer and wine; reservations recommended; www.the goldentruffle.com; between 17th St and Industrial Wy.* &

Memphis / ★★☆

2920 BRISTOL ST, COSTA MESA; 714/432-7685 Housed in a former tavern of dubious repute, Memphis preserves a bit of the previous tenant's funkiness while adding a spin all its own. It's pretty much Aunt Lizzie's kitchen meets *Melrose Place* and takes her act to Orange County. The backbone of the compact menu here is Southern cooking, updated with contemporary ingredients and the quirky vision of chef/partner Diego Velasco. Diners here get a lot of talent on their plate for little cash. A grilled center-cut pork chop is accompanied by grits and a balsamic-cherry sauce. Creole shrimp gets its fire from chipotle chile vinaigrette. Roasted chicken breast with mustard greens and grilled corn is set off with a lemon-thyme sauce. The feisty gumbo is also a winner. The scene is pretty basic—a simple room of spare tables, good tunes, and retro touches. The mixed crowd stays jovial even when service fluctuates from positively gracious to perfunctory. *$$; AE, DC, MC, V; no checks; lunch Mon–Fri, dinner every day, brunch Sat–Sun; beer and wine; reservations recommended; between Randolph and Baker Aves.* &

Pinot Provence / ★★★

686 ANTON BLVD, COSTA MESA; 714/444-5900 Orange County foodies were positively giddy in 1998 when celebrity chef Joachim Splichal, longtime darling of the L.A. gourmet scene, opened this addition to his empire. Gastronomes familiar with Splichal's other efforts (Patina in Hollywood, Pinot Bistro in Sherman Oaks, Pinot Blanc in the Napa Valley) will note that this bistro has its own distinct personality—that of a Provençal château complete with village antiques, a mammoth fireplace, and a limestone archway. French-born Florent Marneau (formerly of Aubergine and Pascal) is executive chef here, executing a novel menu divided between Provençal dishes and those from other regions of France. Marneau, who shops local farmers markets for the freshest ingredients, presents somewhat lighter French fare than the bistro menus at other Splichalian haunts. If you're lucky, it will include appetizers such as a mélange of marinated haricots verts, baked tomatoes, sautéed fennel, quail egg-topped brioche, and a pungent olive tapenade; or perhaps a sampling of seasoned olives, chilly raw oysters, or fritters of brandade, a tasty salt-cod purée. Noteworthy entrees include heaven-scented lavender lamb chops, tender rack of pork with cherries, and plats du jour such as a hearty daube of stewed lamb shanks with couscous. Yellow-striped banquettes with pillows provide tasteful seating indoors, and two cozy garden rooms make for lovely patio interludes. Though some grumble the wait staff has not yet hit its professional stride, management is earnest, and the wine service supporting an inviting list can be quite expert. *$$$; AE, DC, DIS, MC, V; no checks; breakfast, lunch, dinner every day; full bar; reservations recommended; www.patinagroup.com; in South Coast Plaza, facing Bristol St.* &

Sidestreet Café / ★

1799 NEWPORT BLVD, COSTA MESA; 714/650-1986 Wedged into an offbeat shopping strip, Sidestreet Café is a tiny operation with a big heart. One glance at the handwritten menu in this homey, cheerful spot and it's clear breakfast is a passion here. Pages of appetizing scrambles, egg sandwiches, omelets, burritos, and "griddle goodies" make decisions difficult, and everything tastes even yummier than it sounds. Typical items include roasted corn cakes, spicy chorizo and eggs (including the essential beans, rice, and tortillas), and diced ham scramble loaded with cheese plus taters and toast. Rightfully billed as "huge and delicious," the cinnamon roll is too big for two—but what a way to indulge. Hearty eaters will appreciate "Soul Food" platters of robust stuff like sirloin tidbits and eggs covered with mushroom-wine sauce. A loyal following creates long waits for only 40 or so seats. To avoid delays, come weekdays, or early (before 8am) or late (after 2pm) on weekends. *$; No credit cards; checks OK; breakfast, lunch every day; no alcohol; reservations not accepted; between 17th St and Industrial Wy.* &

Troquet / ★★★☆

333 BRISTOL ST, COSTA MESA; 714/708-6865 Troquet is a bistro in the finest sense. Neither hectic nor noisy, it's a poised, seductive room where time slows and astute patrons savor the area's best French cuisine. Unlike at some of Orange County's French restaurants, there is no worn-out reverence for all things Gallic; but chef/owner Tim Goodell's considerable talent is evident on every plate. He and wife Liza (also a chef, and the designer of the sensuous setting) have rapidly vaulted to the top of the culinary scene with their newest try. Originally the creators behind Aubergine (the tiny Newport Beach bistro with a big reputation—see review in Chapter 2), the duo temporarily closed their first effort to open this larger spot, awash in amber lighting, vintage French liquor posters, and fine crystal. One can easily build an impressive repast just from the many appetizer offerings, such as a tart of plump escargots and wild mushrooms with a pungent herb salad, or prawns wrapped in prosciutto atop fragrant curried couscous. Main course options are dazzling: from potato-wrapped salmon with baby artichokes to crisp veal sweetbreads with sautéed leeks to an impeccably roasted chicken with perfect pommes frites, each plate is an indulgence. True foodies will fancy Troquet's tasting menu, several small courses that showcase the kitchen's many fortes. This is one of Orange County's few such menus—a special event with great value (you can drive to L.A. and pay more for less). Desserts are mostly divine, and the cheese platter positively seduces. *$$$; AE, DC, MC, V; no checks; lunch, dinner Mon–Sat; full bar; reservations recommended; 3rd floor on the north side of South Coast Plaza near Nordstrom, near Sunflower Ave.* &

Irvine

The original Irvine Ranch, acquired by James Irvine and his partners in 1864, was composed of acreage included in Spanish and Mexican land grants dating back to the 16th and 17th centuries. The 200 square miles of the original ranch represented a full quarter of Orange County's land area. Although the Irvine Company has sold off more than half its holdings for development, it still retains more than 54,000 acres. Today's Irvine is a modern bedroom-and-office-park community, surrounded by 20,000 acres of open cattle pasture and 8,000 cultivated acres producing citrus, avocados, and various other food crops plus flowers, trees, and shrubs for Southern California commercial nurseries. In an emphatic nod to ecological concerns, the Irvine Company has apportioned more than 21,000 acres as a reserve for endangered species of plants and animals, which will become the center of a 36,000-acre Orange County Nature Reserve.

The community of Irvine sprang up around the **UNIVERSITY OF CALIFORNIA'S IRVINE CAMPUS (UCI)** (bounded by University Dr to the north, Culver Dr to the west, Bonita Canyon Dr to the south, and Newport Coast Dr to the east; 949/824-5011; www.uci.edu), constructed on land donated by the Irvine Company. The focus at the cool, quiet, and spartan **IRVINE MUSEUM** (12th floor, 18881 Von Karman Ave, near Campus Dr; 949/476-2565; www.irvinemuseum.org) is California impressionism between 1890 and 1930, a regional offshoot of the American impressionism movement. Though its permanent collection once consisted almost exclusively of the works of Joan Irvine Smith (now exhibited at UCI), in recent years the museum has built a wider collection, and in addition presents a variety of shows that change quarterly.

Built into a hillside, **VERIZON WIRELESS AMPHITHEATER** (formerly Irvine Meadows; 8808 Irvine Center Dr; 949/855-8095; www.verizonwirelessamphitheater. com) is Irvine's answer to the Hollywood Bowl—sort of. It is possible to picnic there on delicacies from your own basket, but only before performances of the Pacific Orchestra. For other large-venue musical events, unimpressive food and drink must be purchased inside the grounds. Still, with 10,000 reserved seats and 4,500 lawn seats, it's one of Irvine's main draws.

For a change of pace, try Irvine's **OLD TOWNE**. It was established in 1887 by James Irvine II as the shipping center for produce from the Irvine Ranch. There are shops and restaurants, and among the historic buildings you may tour are the blacksmith shop, the old garage, a tenant farmhouse, the general store, and La Quinta Inn (see Lodgings, below). The **IRVINE CHAMBER OF COMMERCE** (17755 Sky Park E, Ste 101; 949/660-9112, www.irvinechamber.com) is a useful source of tourist information.

RESTAURANTS

Bistango / ★★

19100 VON KARMAN AVE, IRVINE; 949/752-5222 A happening scene ever since it opened in 1987, stylish Bistango continues to attract the movers and shakers of corporate Irvine. A sprawling art gallery, lively jazz club, and dashing restaurant fused together under one atrium, Bistango hums with energy from lunch to happy hour to dinner to late-night dancing. The cuisine is American-Continental, if there is such a thing, featuring such entrees as melt-in-your-mouth tuna grilled rare on Asian vegetables with subtle sesame vinaigrette and green horseradish, and juicy rack of lamb with mashed potatoes and a rich port wine sauce. Daily specials always include one of the county's best-value prix-fixe dinners. There's a long list of wood-oven pizzas, deservedly favored by many. Weekly wine and champagne tastings are well run and a great value for discriminating palates. And if you feel like something sweet and heady at the same time, sample the dark chocolate martini from the martini bar. *$$$; AE, DC, MC, V; no checks; lunch Mon–Fri, dinner every day; full bar; reservations recommended; Bistango@net999.com; www.Bistango.com; ground floor of Atrium office complex.* &

Prego / ★☆

18420 VON KARMAN AVE, IRVINE; 949/553-1333 Given its mundane location in the maze of corporate Irvine, it's rather amazing that Prego oozes so much undiluted Italian style and spirit. Sleek and chic (think Milan, not Florence), the inflection here is utterly Italian, from the pop songs and magazines in the bar to the dapper waiters to the basket of grissini that begins every meal. All pastas are homemade and of the highest quality; some of the best are spinach gnocchi with Gorgonzola, pumpkin tortelloni with mascarpone sauce, and lobster-filled agnolotti with lemon sauce. Rotisserie meats (duck, rabbit, chicken) are also handled well, and grilled items like veal chops, rack of lamb, and flank steak round out the diverse menu. Crisp white linens, gleaming wood floors, and low-slung banquette seating give the room an air of sophistication. The executive crowd adds its own panache. *$$$; AE, DC, MC, V; no checks, lunch Mon–Fri, dinner every day; full bar; reservations recommended; between Main St and Michelson Dr, entrance faces Michelson Dr.* &

Trilogy / ★★

18201 VON KARMAN AVE, IRVINE; 949/955-0757 Tucked into Irvine's hypercorporate zone, Trilogy succeeds by supplying a warm, handsome gathering place that's short on attitude and long on comfort. Muted acoustics allow easy conversation, even when a jazz combo performs (generally Wednesday through Saturday). The owners label the cuisine Creative American, though it also qualifies as New Continental. Whatever the designation, it could also be dubbed scrumptious. The menu offers a balanced mix of the fantastic and the familiar. Commendable starters include spicy Maryland crab cakes with parsnip slaw and saffron aioli or the rich corn chowder with rock shrimp and the mellow zing of chiles. Entree choices are enticing: Pacific halibut in a golden crust of potato slices with a side of "melted" leeks, crisp Muscovy duck breast with tart cherries in a zinfandel reduction, or seared ahi enhanced with smoked-trout hash and braised baby artichokes. The seasonally changing menu is reinforced by a fitting wine list with some excellent by-the-glass options. Service is adept without being overly mannered. When weather permits, consider the green, serene, bamboo-walled patio—one of the area's better outdoor rooms. *$$$; AE, DC, DIS, MC, V; no checks; lunch Mon–Fri, dinner Mon–Sat; full bar; reservations recommended; between Main St and Michelson Dr on ground floor of Transamerica Bldg.* &

LODGINGS

La Quinta Inn / ★

🐷 **14972 SAND CANYON AVE, IRVINE; 949/551-0909 OR 949/687-6667** A large portion of this establishment, which is listed on the National Registry of Historic Places and is located at the edge of Irvine's Old Towne, once functioned as an Irvine Ranch granary for the storage of several hundred tons of lima beans. The hexagonal granary's 98 honeycomb silos have been converted to comfortable, pleasant, and atmospheric guest rooms, decorated in a sophisticated country style. The newer part of the inn features 50 more straightforward rooms, which have big-screen TVs, cable, in-room movies, video games, and data ports. The inn is very clean, and the staff is accommodating. The continental breakfast is complimentary, and there's a free shuttle to the airport. One of the pluses of staying here is its proximity to the Irvine Spectrum business complex and the Irvine Spectrum Center entertainment complex. *$$; AE, DC, DIS, MC, V; no checks; www.laquinta. com; off the 5 Fwy's Sand Canyon Ave exit.* ☁

Orange

They say Disneyland's Main Street, with its turn-of-the-century shops and circular plaza, was modeled after Walt Disney's boyhood hometown of Marceline, Missouri. Perhaps. But it could just as easily have been designed after Old Towne Orange.

The homey atmosphere rivals that of the fictitious Mayberry of the old *Andy Griffith Show*. Across from Orange's shady plaza, where mothers push strollers down paths lined with rosebushes, is an old-fashioned barbershop where Floyd might just be giving a trim. You could probably catch Andy over at Watson Drugs and Soda Fountain, sipping a cherry coke while Opie slurps a chocolate malt. And Aunt Bea, no doubt, is getting a perm at the beauty academy next to the Masonic Temple and Lodge.

Everything about Old Towne Orange, from its Victorian homes to its laid-back atmosphere, speaks of a time gone by, which may be why this nostalgic village has blossomed into the self-proclaimed **ANTIQUE CAPITAL** of Southern California. The heart and soul of Old Towne is recently renovated Plaza Park, a rather unassuming little circle of green in the middle of town. Ringing the historic plaza, which has been around almost since the city's inception in 1871, are more than 50 antique shops as well as 10 antique malls swallowing up over 500 smaller dealers who specialize in everything from beatnik-era Streamline furniture to hand-stitched samplers from the early 1800s. But the real emphasis here is on nostalgia, not rare finds. Thus you'll find Ricky Nelson's first album as well as the Debbie Reynolds classic "Am I That Easy to Forget?" along with thousands of other vinyl platters at Mr. C's Rare Records (148 N Glassell St; 714/744-7444). Tony's Architectural Salvage (123 N Olive St; 714/538-1900) carries hundreds of old doors, leaded-glass windows, iron gates, and, yes, even the kitchen sink. Tons of them. You'll find an **ANTIQUE SWAP MEET** the fourth Sunday of every month from 8am to 2pm in the parking lot of the Antique Station Mall (178 S Glassell St; 714/633-3934). You can pick up a free brochure of antique shops at most Old Towne businesses or at the **ORANGE CHAMBER OF COMMERCE & VISITOR BUREAU** (439 E Chapman Ave, 4 blocks east of the plaza; 714/538-3581; www.orangechamber.org).

RESTAURANTS

Citrus City Grille / ★★

122 N GLASSELL ST, ORANGE; 714/639-9600 This 1996 addition to Old Towne, the charming historic heart of Orange, was heartily embraced by locals hungry for contemporary cuisine close to home. Almost hip for Old Towne (but in an easygoing way), the stylishly renovated space boasts lofty ceilings, daring colors, and giant reproductions of bright, vintage orange-crate labels; outdoor foyer tables are nicely protected from the street. A strong selection of starters includes dishes like roasted tomato and mushroom napoleon with saffron essence, coconut shrimp tempura with a spicy apricot sauce, and potato and charred leek soup. On the entree side, pastas, fish, and meat dishes dominate. Solid bets include the sea bass in an oyster and lemongrass sauce with couscous and the grilled pork loin chop with fig-balsamic demi-glace, caramelized onions, and garlic mashed potatoes. The lunch menu features pizzas, sandwiches, and lighter entrees like blackened fish tacos with tomatillo salsa and black bean–corn hash. Service can be iffy, and the wine list needs depth, but that doesn't deter a diverse clientele that creates a din during peak hours. *$$; AE, DC, MC, V; no checks; lunch Mon–Sat, dinner Tues–Sun; full bar; reservations recommended; ½ block north of Chapman Ave.* &

Felix Continental Cafe / ★

36 PLAZA SQUARE, ORANGE; 714/633-5842 This sidewalk cafe is the place to be on a nice Sunday afternoon. Pigeons and antique-hunters cruise the brick sidewalk stocked with formica tables and white plastic chairs. You'd never know it from the name, but there's absolutely nothing continental about Felix. It's a mostly Cuban restaurant that also serves some Spanish dishes, such as *tortilla de papa y cebolla*, a heavy, rich omelet from Malaga bursting with potatoes and onions that have been sautéed in olive oil. The food here is simple, plentiful, and incredibly inexpensive. A typical Cuban sandwich, the luscious *media noche* (which combines baked ham, roasted pork, Swiss cheese, and pickles on an egg bun and comes with soup or the salad), costs about $5. Or try the *picadilo criollo*, a typical Cuban dish of seasoned beef and pork cooked in sofrito sauce with raisins and olives and brought to your table by gracious waiters in blue or white guayabera shirts. There's also seating inside, but then you'd miss the sidewalk parade! *$; AE, MC, V; no checks; lunch, dinner every day; no alcohol; reservations recommended; corner of Chapman Ave and Glassell St.* &

Watson Drugs and Soda Fountain / ★

116 E CHAPMAN AVE, ORANGE; 714/633-1050 The best—and oldest—soda fountain in Orange County (established in 1899) might already seem familiar to you. Jimmy Stewart wooed Donna Reed here in Frank Capra's 1946 masterpiece *It's a Wonderful Life,* and it impersonated the '60s in Tom Hanks's *That Thing You Do!* In fact, Hollywood comes knocking quite often, and any employee will proudly recite Watson's screen credits. Fully half the historic store is taken up with dinette tables, and the shelf behind the lunch counter gleams with industrial milk shake mixers. They don't limit the menu to nostalgic specialties from the Fanny Farmer cookbook, though there are plenty of comfortable diner standbys for those who want them. You can get biscuits and gravy for breakfast (and yes, they still call it SOS, as any military man would know), but there's also breaded veal and a chicken Caesar salad. No matter what you order, save room for their spectacular fountain desserts: old-fashioned shakes, malts, floats, or ice cream sodas. *$; AE, DC, MC, V; checks OK; breakfast, lunch, dinner every day; no alcohol; reservations not necessary; 1 block east of Plaza Park.* &

Santa Ana

Once part of Los Angeles County, the city of Santa Ana broke away in 1889, becoming the county seat for the newly created Orange County. It remains the financial and government center for the region. You might not have heard of Santa Ana's **BOWERS MUSEUM** (2002 Main St; 714/567-3600; www.bowers.org), but it's well-known in the art world—and manages to combine its scholarly pedigree with compelling exhibits that celebrate the diversity of the human family by presenting the art of world cultures. The adjacent Kidseum is a hands-on cultural entertainment/learning tool for children. Another place where kids are stimulated to learn while having fun is the **DISCOVERY SCIENCE CENTER** (2500 N Main St; 714/542-CUBE; www.discoverycube.org). You can see the museum's distinctive askew cube sculpture from the freeway; inside the modern building, provocative exhibits are designed to spark children's natural curiosity; there are also live science shows and a 3-D laser theater. To find out more about what to see and do around town, contact the **SANTA ANA CHAMBER OF COMMERCE** (714/541-5353; www.santa anacc.com).

RESTAURANTS

Antonello / ★★☆

1611 SUNFLOWER AVE, SANTA ANA; 714/751-7153 This longtime darling of the power-dining set maintains its lofty perch by consistently supplying premium service and refined Italian cuisine amid lavish surroundings. Gracious owner Antonio Cagnolo adds warmth and style to the proceedings, personally overseeing a highly skilled kitchen that turns out what Cagnolo calls *cucina nostalgica* (though we deem it mostly Northern Italian), handling special requests with aplomb. The broad menu touches on classics old and new such as delicate miniature veal ravioli with bolognese sauce (his mother's recipe) or creamy risotto blessed with shrimp and champagne—hardly the same old take on the dish. A notable wine list is well supported by a wine-savvy wait staff. The meandering layout and faux-palazzo design of the dining room includes many nooks and crannies for privacy or romance. Utterly upscale yet perfectly, endearingly gracious, this top-notch enterprise offers some of Orange County's foremost Italian cuisine in a setting suited to any special occasion. *$$$; AE, DC, MC, V; no checks; lunch Mon–Fri, dinner*

Mon–Sat; full bar; reservations recommended; www.antonello.com; in South Coast Plaza Village. &

Gustaf Anders / ★★★
Back Pocket / ★★★

3851 BEAR ST, SANTA ANA; 714/668-1737 Chef Gustaf Anders has a stellar reputation as a purveyor of superlative Swedish and continental cuisine. Virtually impossible to find by chance, this hidden treasure succeeds with its keen balance of style, civility, and culinary distinction. Partners Wilhelm Gustaf Magnuson and chef Ulf Anders Strandberg turn out meals that are memorable by virtue of both exceptional cooking and a serene setting that is sleek and spare, with muted hues accented by an occasional shock of bold color. Typical dishes include sugar-and-salt-cured salmon with creamed dill potatoes, fillet of beef in Stilton-red wine sauce with creamed morels, and Arctic char roasted on savory vegetables with light tomato and extra-virgin olive oil sauce. Also legendary are many signature breads and a host of herring preparations, all made on the premises. The partners recently fired up a wood-burning oven and rotisserie to anchor their adjacent Back Pocket cafe. In Sweden, *bakficka* (back pocket) refers to a satellite eatery attached to a fine dining establishment. Here they offer similar fine food at popular prices in more casual surroundings. Though a few items are lifted directly from the main room's menu, there are plenty of comfort food dishes like sea bass with tomato broth, honey-glazed pork loin, and a baked gravlax sandwich dressed with Parmesan, fresh dill, and tomato concassée. *$$$; AE, DC, MC, V; no checks; lunch Tues–Sat, dinner Tues–Sun; full bar; reservations recommended; mailgustaf@aol.com; www.gustaf-anders.com; in rear of South Coast Plaza Village.* &

The Gypsy Den / ★

125 N BROADWAY, SANTA ANA; 714/835-8840 Sagging couches, threadbare Oriental rugs, secondhand furniture, dark art—is it an artist's atelier? A student's apartment? A thrift store? None of the above, though it's not easy to label this bohemian cafe with its home-cooked fare that includes everything from cream cheese and olive sandwiches (on homemade bread, of course) to giant squares of carrot cake. Tables and chairs are all mismatched and the curtains screening the traffic from busy Broadway are made from Indian saris. In case you weren't sure, the Den's counter-culture aspirations are made obvious by house specialties like veggie tacos in wheat tortillas and, for breakfast, the "hobo bowl," a big, fat mound of granola topped with fresh fruit and vanilla yogurt. But the food is only half the draw to this homey cafe that's become a central meeting place for anyone visiting, or living in, Santa Ana's Artists Village. There are poetry readings Monday evenings, jazz or blues on Wednesdays, and something called Trainwreck Theatre—sort of a musical smorgasbord produced by local musicians—every third Saturday night. Don't forget to wear your Birkenstocks. *$; MC, V; no checks; breakfast, lunch, dinner every day; no alcohol; reservations not accepted; along the 2nd St mall in the Artists Village.* &

SAN DIEGO AND ENVIRONS

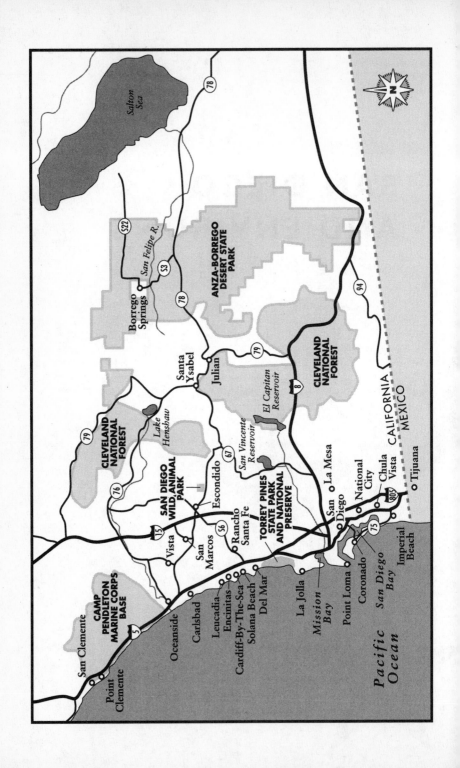

SAN DIEGO AND ENVIRONS

Perhaps the most shocking thing about San Diego County is that almost every single thing publicized about it is true. The climate is divine, the beaches are heavenly, and the healthy (some might say health-nut) inhabitants are laid-back, good looking, perpetually bronzed, and smiley-face friendly.

San Diegans love to play outdoors, and there's plenty of opportunity, with more than 70 miles of beaches and bays, a plethora of world-class golf courses and tennis courts, some real show-off city parks, and semi-isolated forests, mountains, and desert.

When it's time to get down to business, many San Diegans can be found ensconced in one of the high-tech firms or medical research facilities that have set up shop here; others devote their energies to hawking New Age wares and services in markets, offices, and pulpits throughout the county. This business boom, combined with an influx of those who couldn't live through one more icy winter or hellish summer in their own home states, may be economically rewarding, but it has unfortunately transformed many parts of the county into a snarl of condos, strip malls, and traffic jams. Nonetheless, this is the only place in the United States where within the span of one day you can jump ocean waves, frolic on a snowy mountain, hike a forest trail, off-road in the desert, attend a big-city event, and stroll across an international border.

ACCESS AND INFORMATION

Two major north-south routes traverse San Diego County. From Los Angeles, **INTERSTATE 5** (which originates at the Canadian border) more or less follows the coast, passing the Marines' Camp Pendleton base, North County's beach communities, the University of California (UCSD) campus, and the turnoffs to La Jolla, Mission Bay, Old Town, and San Diego proper, before ending at the Mexican border. **INTERSTATE 15,** from Las Vegas, is the inland route—skirting wine country, the city of Escondido, high-tech campuses, and Marine Corps Air Station Miramar (previously Miramar Naval Air Station), ending just south of San Diego, where it meets up with Interstate 5. From Arizona, **INTERSTATE 8** follows the Mexican border, moving northwest as it enters San Diego, and ends at Ocean Beach. From the coast, **HIGHWAYS 76 AND 78** offer varied options for reaching Indian reservations, Mount Palomar, the Cleveland National Forest, the mining and tourist town of Julian (also reached via Hwy 79, from I-8), and the vast Anza-Borrego Desert State Park.

Major domestic and some international carriers serve **SAN DIEGO INTERNATIONAL AIRPORT–LINDBERGH FIELD** (3707 N Harbor Dr, near downtown; 619/231-2100), and rental cars are readily available through all the big-name chains. Taxis are generally readily available, or you can grab a shuttle from **CLOUD NINE** (858/974-8885 or 800/9-SHUTTLE) or **SAN DIEGO EXPRESS AIRPORT** (619/222-5800 or 800/900-RIDE), or catch a **SAN DIEGO TRANSIT BUS** (619/233-3004) for the short ride into the city. **MCCLELLAN PALOMAR AIRPORT** (2198 Palomar Airport Rd; 760/431-4646), in Carlsbad (about 35 miles from San Diego), is served by America West Express for flights to Phoenix with connections around the United States and Mexico, and United Express for flights in and out of Los Angeles. **AMTRAK** (800/USA-RAIL; www.amtrakwest.com) provides daily train service between Los Angeles and **SAN DIEGO'S SANTA FE DEPOT** (at Kettner Blvd and Broadway), with additional stops in Oceanside and Solana Beach. **GREYHOUND** (120 W Broadway; 619/239-3266 or 800/231-2222; www.greyhound.com) runs buses from all major cities to its San Diego station.

The usually perfect temperate weather of San Diego is legendary. Even the dreaded El Niño in the winter of '98–'99 hit San Diego with only a few big storms. Daytime temperatures rarely dip below 55°F in winter or rise above 85°F in summer. Desert areas, however, sizzle well above the 100-degree mark most of the summer. Both deserts and mountains can turn bitterly cold during winter, with occasional frost and snow at higher elevations. June is traditionally foggy in the beach areas.

For more information, contact the **SAN DIEGO INTERNATIONAL VISITORS INFORMATION CENTER** (11 Horton Plaza, on the corner of 1st and F Sts; 619/236-1212), or visit the **SAN DIEGO CONVENTION & VISITORS BUREAU** Web site (www.sandiego.org).

San Diego

California's second-largest city—tagged "America's Finest City" by its Convention & Visitors Bureau—is, if not the finest, certainly one of the prettiest and most low-key big cities in the country, despite the fact that it still has a huge naval presence. Though it lacks the slick sophistication of San Francisco and the lovable gaudiness of Los Angeles, San Diego reigns as both year-round playground and thriving metropolis—all set against a backdrop of shimmering sea, open parklands, rugged cliffs, verdant valleys, and a blend of contemporary and Spanish architecture. One big-city component that visitors will probably not find, though, is attitude. Hyper-active egos are a distinct minority here—anyone getting pushy or aggressive is more apt to be confronted by healing crystals and aromatherapy potions than by angry words or weapons.

Considered the birthplace of California after Juan Rodriguez Cabrillo landed at the tip of Point Loma in 1542, San Diego wasn't actually "put on the map" until 1769, when Franciscan padre Junípero Serra dedicated the Presidio and San Diego de Alcalá—first in the string of California's 21 missions. Nearly 100 years later, San Francisco merchant Alonzo E. Horton moved in and relocated the center of the city from Old Town (now preserved as a historical park) to its current site near the all-important harbor. Horton's "New Town" took on a sleazy ambience during World War I and the Depression, when the area—then known as "the Stingaree"—was packed with brawling sailors, bawdy women, and a variety of sins and vice. That very same district—now called the Gaslamp Quarter—has been restored and revitalized and is rife with swank hotels, chic cafes, funky shops, trendy boutiques, contemporary galleries, and performing arts venues, with the convention center and the Embarcadero nearby. Though the city sprawls for miles in three directions, most of the business and entertainment action is centered in or near the downtown core, giving San Diego yet another rub-their-nose-in-it-edge over its urban competitors: an upmarket and relatively crime-free downtown that attracts rather than repels visitors and residents.

SAN DIEGO COUNTY THREE-DAY TOUR

DAY 1. Begin the day with a waterfront walk, along scenic Harbor Drive past **SEA-PORT VILLAGE** and the Embarcadero. At **SAN DIEGO HARBOR EXCURSIONS,** board the first ferry (9am) to Coronado. At the Ferry Landing you can fuel your energies with a latte and croissant at **IL FORNAIO,** then rent a bike at **BIKES AND BEYOND**—or set out on foot. (If you prefer sightseeing without exercise, board the #94 bus, also known as the **CORONADO SHUTTLE.**) Cruise down Orange Avenue, the most beautiful main drag in San Diego. Trees, gazebos, and lawns decorate **SPRECKELS PARK,** and side streets are rich with impeccably maintained vintage homes. Stop by the **MUSEUM OF HISTORY AND ART** to check out the displays on the island's early days as a seaside resort. For a taste of Hollywood glamour, have lunch at the **HOTEL DEL CORONADO,** then stretch your legs on the beach before returning to catch the ferry back. In the evening, head to the **GASLAMP QUARTER,** and wander around Fifth and Fourth Avenues enjoying the Quarter's distinctive architecture, perhaps browsing the shops at **HORTON PLAZA,** a fantasyland mall. Attractive restaurants line the streets of the Gaslamp Quarter; if you're undecided, try the Spanish flavors at **SEVILLA.** After dinner, hail a horse-drawn **CINDERELLA CARRIAGE** for a romantic ride back to your hotel.

DAY 2. Head to **BALBOA PARK** and spend the first half of the day at the incomparable **SAN DIEGO ZOO.** Go ahead and pose for photos by the zoo's flamingo pond (everyone does). After a quick lunch at one of the zoo's food stands, stroll along the park's **EL PRADO,** home to San Diego's best museums. The best bets are the **MUSEUM OF MAN,** the **SAN DIEGO MUSEUM OF ART,** and the **REUBEN H. FLEET SPACE THEATER AND SCIENCE CENTER.** Linger on the lawn by the **LILY POND** in front of the **BOTANICAL BUILDING,** where tree ferns stretch toward the sky under a lath roof. After such a strenuous day, you deserve to splurge on dinner at **STAR OF THE SEA,** the most elegant seafood restaurant downtown. End the night at the **TOP OF THE HYATT,** sipping a Cognac on the 40th floor of the hotel while gazing at the harbor lights.

DAY 3. Ready for some quality beach time? If you're traveling with the family, submit to your kids' pleas and head out for **SEAWORLD,** where you'll want to spend most of the day. If there's time in the afternoon, pile in the car and cruise around **MISSION BAY PARK,** and consider paddling about in a kayak or canoe—you can rent them at the bay's Santa Clara Point. Later, watch the sun settle into the sea as you dine on fresh fish and burgers at **QWIIGS BAR & GRILL;** arrive early and claim a window table for a view of surfers riding the waves under rosy skies. After dinner, take a walk on the **OCEAN BEACH PIER,** where you can see fireworks explode from SeaWorld every summer night at 9:30pm.

More changes are blowing in the (barely discernible) breeze for this city. A new baseball stadium, scheduled to open circa 2004, is to be located in the warehouse district, an area very close to the Gaslamp Quarter now referred to as the "East Village."

ACCESS AND INFORMATION

San Diego is easily accessed by air via **SAN DIEGO INTERNATIONAL AIRPORT–LINDBERGH FIELD** (3707 N Harbor Dr, near downtown; 619/231-2100). Taxis and door-to-door shuttles are plentiful at San Diego International Airport, and a ride downtown costs around $10–$12. For further information, see San Diego County "Access and Information" above.

Because of the influx of tourists and residents, driving is becoming more and more of an L.A.-esque pain. Visitors can expect freeway congestion throughout the day. Plentiful downtown public parking is available at Westfield Shoppingtown Horton Plaza (bounded by Broadway, G St, and 1st and 4th Aves; 619/239-8180), as well as several inexpensive city-run lots in the Gaslamp Quarter. Street parking is metered in downtown areas and in some uptown locations.

San Diego Metropolitan Transit System runs buses on more than 20 downtown routes, and day-tripper passes allow a full day of unlimited rides. Tickets can be purchased on board, and exact change is required. For passes, maps, and information, contact the **TRANSIT STORE** (102 Broadway, at 1st Ave; 619/234-1060). The bright red **SAN DIEGO TROLLEY** (619/233-3004) whisks visitors south to the Mexican border, north to Old Town, and east to Mission Valley. Purchase tickets at self-service machines at station stops. The **COASTER** (800/COASTER) commuter rail line operates between Oceanside and San Diego, with several stops en route (hooking up with the trolley at Old Town and downtown). **AMTRAK** (800/USA-RAIL; www.amtrakwest.com) trains stop in Solana Beach and Oceanside as they chug up the coast toward Los Angeles.

Like many large cities, San Diego is composed of a downtown hub and neighborhood spokes—though here half those spokes dip into the bay or ocean. **DOWNTOWN** is the designated city center. This is where businesses, retail enterprises, commerce, tourism, transportation depots, and the convention center buzz—the trendy **GASLAMP QUARTER** is downtown, with Balboa Park and the San Diego Zoo on the periphery. North of downtown lies **HILLCREST,** a stylish—and predominantly gay—neighborhood of nicely restored historic homes and sizzling restaurants and nightlife. **OLD TOWN,** the city's Spanish-era historic heart, lies adjacent to **MISSION VALLEY,** a broad flat plain best known for its super-duper shopping malls. The beachy communities of **MISSION BAY, PACIFIC BEACH, POINT LOMA,** and **OCEAN BEACH** cluster between Old Town and San Diego's watery edges. **CORONADO** and **LA JOLLA** are distinct seaside enclaves—notable for wealth, trendy shops, and historic dwellings.

The **SAN DIEGO INTERNATIONAL VISITORS INFORMATION CENTER** (11 Horton Plaza, corner of 1st and F Sts; 619/236-1212), with a multilingual staff, provides maps and brochures. Useful Web sites include www.infosandiego.com and www.sandiego.org.

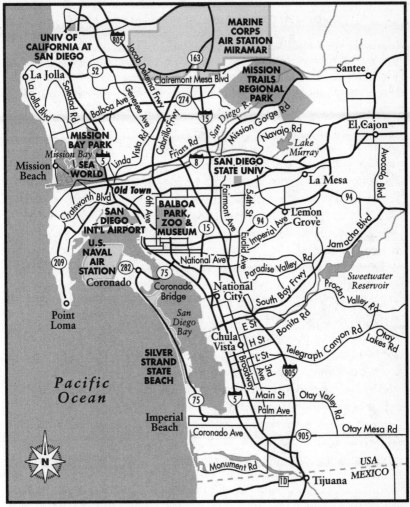

GREATER SAN DIEGO

MAJOR ATTRACTIONS

It's not a walking city like San Francisco, nor does it sprawl endlessly like Los Angeles. San Diego falls somewhere in between, and you can best enjoy its attractions by taking a combination of inner-city walks and short drives. In addition, **OLD TOWN TROLLEY TOURS** (619/298-TOUR) provides convenient minibus service to eight points of interest, including some of the top attractions such as Balboa Park, SeaWorld, and the Gaslamp Quarter—allowing passengers to get on and off at leisure for one fee. Trolley buses make the loop (which takes about two hours) almost every day of the year.

PANDA-PALOOZA: SAN DIEGO FALLS IN LOVE

The San Diego Zoo has no shortage of irresistible attractions. Polar bears on ice, gorillas in a rain forest, shy koalas on eucalyptus branches, even a two-headed snake. But nothing makes the zoo's visitors behave quite so batty as a giant panda baby.

Hua Mei, a darling ball of soft black and white fur, burst onto the scene August 21, 1999. Billboards celebrated her birth; news bulletins flashed when she passed her fourth day of life—a major milestone for pandas born in captivity. Panda info filled the newspapers. San Diegans learned that pandas really are bears, even though they look like raccoons, and studied panda facts and slides of the new baby on the zoo's Web site. People stood in line for hours to get a glimpse of Hua Mei hiding in a pine tree; sometimes, they had to be content watching the parents roll around in their forest enclaves—an exciting sight in itself. There are fewer than a dozen pandas in captivity in North America, and Hua Mei was the first baby born in the Western Hemisphere to survive beyond a few days.

At first, it had seemed unlikely Hua Mei's parents would ever conceive. Bai Yun, the female, was born in captivity. Shi Shi, the male, was rescued in the wild in China's Qionlai Mountains after a villager found him critically wounded. The two pandas were transported to San Diego in 1996 primarily for reproductive research, and scientists and zookeepers tried everything to get the romance flowing. The third time was the charm, and Bai Yun began building her nest.

The baby's birth and subsequent growth spurts were celebrated with extraordinary fanfare in San Diego and China. It's estimated that only about 1,000 pandas live in their natural habitat high in the mountains of Sichuan and neighboring provinces, and increased development makes the panda population vulnerable to extinction. As part of an intensely negotiated program with the Chinese (pioneers in panda conservation), the San Diego Zoo pays $1 million annually to help purchase land in China for nature reserves.

But another provision of the deal caused considerable dismay in 2002: any panda born at the zoo had to return to China in three years. Hua Mei's third birthday on August 21, 2002, was bittersweet. The zoo organized a massive farewell party, including videotapes of visitors saying goodbye to Hua Mei. The toddler's seemingly sad-eyed face peered from billboards and the home page in the zoo's Internet site, where Web browsers could watch the live Panda-Cam. San Diegans had to say goodbye to Hua Mei. But the zoo's panda program will continue at least until 2008, and panda-philes are eagerly awaiting the next birth.

—Maribeth Mellin

One of the city's top draws is the world-famous **SAN DIEGO ZOO** (2920 Zoo Dr, Balboa Park; 619/234-3153; www.sandiegozoo.org), where more than 4,000 animals thrive in conditions that simulate their natural environments and about 6,500 plant species enrich Tiger River, Gorilla Tropics, Sun Bear Forest, Hippo Beach, and Polar Bear Plunge. The reptile house is home to scaly creatures including two-headed Thelma and Louise, while the Children's Zoo lets kids (and kids at heart) view newborn animals in the nursery. **SEAWORLD** (500 Sea World Dr, Mission Bay; 619/226-3901; www.seaworld.com), another famous local attraction, is one of the largest marine-life amusement parks in the world. Shamu, the kissing whale, has gained the most notoriety, while other exhibits include the Forbidden Reef, Wild Arctic, Penguin Encounter, and California Tide Pool. San Diego's other famous zoo, the Wild Animal Park, is located to the northeast in Escondido (see Escondido section).

Wander around the Gaslamp Quarter, the 16-block national historic district bounded by Broadway and Market Streets and Fourth and Fifth Avenues, encompassing Victorian architecture, cool shops, hot restaurants, and the Disneyland-esque Westfield Shoppingtown Horton Plaza retail complex (bounded by Broadway, G St, 1st and 4th Aves; 619/239-8180). Pick up walking maps or take a Saturday tour at **WILLIAM HEATH DAVIS HOUSE** (410 Island Ave, at 4th Ave; 619/233-4692; www.gaslampquarter.org), one of the city's first residences, which was built in 1850 and is now home to the Gaslamp Quarter Historical Foundation. The **CHILDREN'S MUSEUM OF SAN DIEGO** (200 W Island Ave; 619/233-KIDS; www.sdchildrens museum.org) mesmerizes kids with interactive exhibits, art studios, and improvisational theater, as well as a plethora of art supplies, dress-up costumes, and educational displays. **SEAPORT VILLAGE** (Harbor Dr at Kettner Blvd, close to the Gaslamp; 619/235-4013) is a New England–like, touristy waterfront retail development, but the Broadway Flying Horses Carousel is fabulous. The **MARITIME MUSEUM** (1306 N Harbor Dr, on the Embarcadero; 619/234-9153; www.sd maritime.com) provides a close-up exploration of three restored ships: the 1898 ferryboat *Berkeley,* the 1863 windjammer *Star of India,* and the 1904 steam yacht *Medea.* Hop a ferry over to Coronado, via scheduled **SAN DIEGO WATER TAXI** ferry service (Broadway and Harbor Dr; 619/235-8294) for a terrific view of the city and the Coronado Bridge. Explore Coronado's Ferry Landing Marketplace and the town's spectacular gingerbread icon, the 1888 **HOTEL DEL CORONADO** (1500 Orange Ave, Coronado; 935/435-6611; www.hoteldel.com)—film site of *Some Like It Hot* and a longtime hangout for politicians and dignitaries. It's one of the city's (and the country's) most superb pieces of architecture, and still a top-notch people-watching spot.

OLD TOWN STATE HISTORIC PARK (4002 Wallace St; 619/220-5422), north of downtown, affords a glimpse into San Diego's beginnings, though Presidio Hill, which overlooks the park, is the site of the first mission and fort and is where the city actually began. Old Town's six square blocks encompass 20 historic buildings—most surrounding the Old Town Plaza (bounded by San Diego Ave and Wallace, Calhoun, and Mason Sts), along with assorted restaurants, galleries, and come-hither tourist shops. Free daily **GUIDED WALKING TOURS** depart from Park Headquarters (in the Robinson-Rose Bldg, 4002 Wallace St; 619/220-5422). California's first mission,

SAN DIEGO DE ALCALÁ (10818 San Diego Mission Rd, Mission Valley; 619/281-8449; www.missionsandiego.com), is still an active parish, but was moved from the Presidio and later rebuilt near Mission Valley. Back at the coast and a slight jog north, **CABRILLO NATIONAL MONUMENT** (1800 Cabrillo Memorial Dr, Point Loma; 619/557-5450; www.nps.gov.cabr) commemorates Juan Rodriguez Cabrillo's 1542 exploration of California. The visitors center features films and lectures relating to the Portuguese explorer's landing, and both the promontory and the restored lighthouse provide dizzying views of the surrounding area.

The coastal enclave of **LA JOLLA,** with its gorgeous coves and beaches (La Jolla Cove, Windansea Beach, La Jolla Shores), hillside mansions, and resort ambience, is San Diego's Beverly Hills—a tourist attraction in itself. The zip code called home by wealthy professionals and retirees lures locals, visitors, and visiting celebrities with ritzy shops, galleries, and restaurants along Prospect Street and Girard Avenue, and further tempts them with the wonderful **MUSEUM OF CONTEMPORARY ART** (700 Prospect St; 858/454-3541; www.mcasandiego.org) and the impressive **BIRCH AQUARIUM AT SCRIPPS** (2300 Expedition Wy; 858/534-3474; www.aquarium. ucsd.edu). For more information, contact **LA JOLLA TOWN COUNCIL** (7734 Herschel Ave, Ste F; 858/454-1444) or stop by the **LA JOLLA VISITOR CENTER** (7966 Herschel Ave at Prospect St; no phone).

PARKS

San Diego's **BALBOA PARK** (with entrances on 6th Ave at Laurel St, and along Park Blvd at President's Wy and Zoo Pl) is a glorious 1,200-acre showpiece—and one of the largest and loveliest city parks in the country. The park houses the world-famous San Diego Zoo, most of the city's museums, the **GLOBE THEATRES** (1363 Old Globe Wy; 619/239-2255; www.theglobetheatres.org), the **REUBEN H. FLEET SCIENCE CENTER,** with hands-on science exhibits, plus an IMAX theater (1875 El Prado; 619/238-1233; www.rhfleet.org), the awe-inspiring 4,500-pipe Spreckels organ, and a kid-in-a-candy-store slurp of other attractions. The park was the site of the Panama-Pacific Exposition in 1915, and many of the exuberant Moorish and Spanish Renaissance buildings built for that event remain along El Prado, the main boulevard, coexisting beautifully with the **BOTANICAL BUILDING'S** 500 species of tropical and subtropical plants (1550 El Prado; 619/239-0512), the contemplative-style **JAPANESE FRIENDSHIP GARDEN** (2215 Pan American Rd E; 619/232-2721; www.niwa.org), and the regal **ALCAZAR GARDEN,** patterned after the gardens of Spain's Alcazar Castle (off El Prado, across from the Museum of Man). The cultural and educational cornucopia includes the **SAN DIEGO HISTORICAL SOCIETY MUSEUM** (1649 El Prado; 619/232-6203; www.sandiegohistory.org), **MUSEUM OF MAN** (1350 El Prado; 619/239-2001; www.museumofman.org), **NATURAL HISTORY MUSEUM** (1788 El Prado; 619/232-3821; www.sdnhm.org), **HALL OF CHAMPIONS SPORTS MUSEUM** (2131 Pan American Rd; 619/234-2544; www.san diegosports.org), **MODEL RAILROAD MUSEUM** (1649 El Prado; 619/696-0199; www.sdmodelrailroadm.com), and **AEROSPACE MUSEUM** (2001 Pan American Plaza; 619/234-8291; www.aerospacemuseum.org). (For art museums in Balboa Park, see Art Museums, below.) Not surprisingly, the park is jammed with locals as well as visitors (especially in summer and on weekends), and magicians, mimes, musicians, jugglers, and palm readers all vie for the attention—and pocket money— of passersby. Interspersed with all this activity are ice-cream vendors and hot-dog wagons, and the whole shebang is overseen by the 200-foot California Tower, whose 100-bell carillon signals approval every 15 minutes. For information, maps, and schedules for the free trams through the park, stop by the **BALBOA PARK VISITOR CENTER** (in the House of Hospitality, 1549 El Prado; 619/239-0512; www.balboa park.org).

MISSION BAY PARK, north of downtown and Old Town, is the sports-and-water equivalent of Balboa Park. This 4,600-acre aquatic park—once an unsightly marsh and swampland—is a humongous playground, encompassing 17 miles of ocean frontage, 27 miles of bayfront beaches, an artificial island, almost one hundred acres of parklands, and countless coves, bays, and hideaways, as well as plenty of parking spots and boat slips. Sailing, waterskiing, jet skiing, windsurfing, swimming, golf, roller blading, jogging, softball, and kite flying are just some of the hits. Bike and sports-equipment rentals are readily available at **MISSION BEACH CLUB** (704 Ventura Pl; 858/488-5050). Maps and guides are available at **MISSION BAY PARK HEADQUARTERS** (Quivera Basin, at the western edge of the park; 619/221-8901) and at the **VISITOR INFORMATION CENTER** (at the E Mission Bay Dr exit off I-5; 619/276-8200).

BEACHES

With 70 miles of Pacific coast, it would be difficult not to find a pleasing beach. Top bets are wide, sparkly, happy-to-be-alive **CORONADO BEACH,** fronting Ocean Boulevard and the Hotel del Coronado; funky, dog-friendly **OCEAN BEACH,** where experienced surfers challenge the riptides and gather around the pier; and **MISSION BEACH,** farther north on the ocean side of Mission Bay Park, good for surfing and *Baywatch* fantasies, with an L.A./Venice Beach ambience. Farther up the coast is Pacific Beach's **TOURMALINE SURFING PARK** (no swimming, only surfing), off La Jolla Boulevard at the end of Tourmaline Street. North of Pacific Beach, La Jolla is home to **WINDANSEA** (off La Jolla Blvd, at the end of Nautilus St), the famous surfing beach popularized in Tom Wolfe's *Pump House Gang.* **LA JOLLA COVE** (off Coast Blvd) is a clear, calm, heaven-sent stretch for swimming, snorkeling, scuba diving, beginner surfers, and family dips; **LA JOLLA SHORES BEACH** offers a wide, flat expanse where families and beginning board and body surfers gather. **BLACK'S BEACH** (off N Torrey Pines Rd), a steep, dangerous climb from the Glider Port, is the officially illegal unofficial nude beach popular with an active gay crowd. For beach reports, call 619/289-1212.

ART MUSEUMS

SAN DIEGO MUSEUM OF ART (1450 El Prado, Balboa Park; 619/232-7931; www. sdmart.org), with its striking replica Spanish Renaissance facade, exhibits everything from Renaissance and contemporary European and American paintings to Indian miniatures and Southeast Asian collections, along with six major traveling shows each year. The courtyard sculpture garden is a great place to linger with a journal or a sketchbook. For lovers of Russian icons, **TIMKEN MUSEUM OF ART** (1500 El Prado, Balboa Park; 619/239-5548; www.timkenmuseum.org), next door, offers a superb collection, as well as Old Master paintings. The **MUSEUM OF PHOTO-**

GRAPHIC ARTS (1649 El Prado, Balboa Park; 619/238-7559; www.mopa.org), across the way, is a world-class museum devoted to photography. Expect to see thought-provoking, sometimes-controversial works by world-class photographers (Mary Ellen Mark, Edward Weston, and others) as well as la crème of newcomers. The two-story MINGEI INTERNATIONAL MUSEUM OF WORLD FOLK ART (1439 El Prado, Balboa Park; 619/239-0003; www.mingei.org) presents permanent and changing exhibits of crafts, textiles, and wearable art from around the globe. Also in Balboa Park is the SPANISH VILLAGE ART CENTER (1770 Village Pl, Balboa Park; 619/233-9050), with 35 studio galleries where working artisans show off their techniques in ceramics, wood carving, glassblowing, jewelry making, and other artsy-craftsy pursuits. Though small, the downtown annex of the MUSEUM OF CONTEMPORARY ART (the main museum is in La Jolla; 1001 Kettner Blvd, across from the Santa Fe Depot; 619/234-1001; www.mcasandiego.org) features changing exhibitions by renowned contemporary artists. ART WALK (619/232-3101), a weekend event each April, is a self-guided bonanza of gallery receptions and artists' open houses.

SHOPS AND BOOKSTORES

Bright, colorful, multilevel HORTON PLAZA (bounded by Broadway, G St, and 1st and 4th Aves; 619/239-8180; www.hortonplaza.shoppingtown.com) is the Gaslamp Quarter's centerpiece attraction. Architect Jon Jerde's tour de force is a sort of Alice in Wonderland retail paradise, containing 140 specialty shops, chic boutiques, fast-food stands, fine restaurants, book and record stores, high-tech toy and computer outlets, a multiscreen cinema, and three department stores including Nordstrom. Nearby, on the Embarcadero, New Englandesque SEAPORT VILLAGE (849 W Harbor Dr; 619/235-4014) is touristy but has some interesting finds. FERRY LANDING MARKETPLACE (1201 1st St, Coronado; 619/435-8895), across the bay in Coronado, features some unique gift, jewelry, and craft shops, as well as clothing stores and restaurants. Mall rats usually head for MISSION VALLEY CENTER (1640 Camino Del Rio N; 619/296-6375) and FASHION VALLEY (7007 Friars Rd; 619/688-9100) in Mission Valley, where hundreds of shops and retail outlets await, including a branch of Neiman Marcus.

Diehard ANTIQUE HOUNDS go snooping along Newport Avenue, in Ocean Beach, or Adams Avenue in the Normal Heights/Kensington section of town (between Park Blvd and 40th St). BAZAAR DEL MUNDO (2754 Calhoun St, Old Town; 619/296-3161; www.bazaardelmundo.com) is the best place to go for Mexican arts, crafts, clothing, and textiles without making a trip across the border. The most extensive selection of travel guides, maps, and travel-related paraphernalia is at LE TRAVEL STORE (745 4th Ave, across from Horton Plaza; 619/544-0005; www.letravelstore.com). SAN DIEGO HARDWARE is the premier "old-time" hardware store (840 5th Ave; 619/232-7123).

Prowl the streets of the Gaslamp Quarter for hip and TRENDY SHOPS, Pacific Beach's Garnet Avenue for RETRO AND RESALE (and piercing and tattoos), Mission Boulevard and the beach towns for BIKINIS AND SWIMWEAR. La Jolla is the place to cruise for UPSCALE SHOPPING.

Alas, as with many cities, some **INDEPENDENT BOOKSELLERS** have been buried by the superstores. Good shops that still remain are **LIBROS BOOKSTORE** (2754 Calhoun St, Old Town; 619/299-1139), which emphasizes California and Latin American fiction, arts, and history, and **UPSTART CROW AND COMPANY** (835 W Harbor Dr, Seaport Village; 619/232-4855), a bookstore/cafe. **BOOKSTAR** (3150 Rosecrans Pl, Point Loma; 619/225-0465), housed in the refurbished 1945 Loma Theater where best-sellers are heralded on the tail-fin marquee, is one of the more interesting chain establishments.

PERFORMING ARTS

TIMES ARTS TIX (in Horton Plaza at Broadway and Broadway Circle, just steps from the San Diego Repertory Theater; 619/497-5000) sells day-of-performance half-price tickets to many theater, dance, and music events, as well as discounted admissions to various attractions and tours. Payment is cash only. Tickets for Monday performances (when the office is closed) can be purchased on Sunday. Call the above number for recorded information, including which tickets are available. **TICKETMASTER** (locations countywide; 619/220-8497) sells tickets by phone to most performing arts events, with an added service charge and handling fee. For up-to-date information on what's playing in San Diego, log on to www.sandiego performs.com.

MUSIC

THE SAN DIEGO OPERA (at the Civic Theatre, 202 C St; 619/232-7636; www. sdopera.com), thrives under the leadership of artistic director Ian Campbell (whose contract doesn't end until 2011) and presents five operas per season, January through May, performed and conducted by a trove of international superstars. Recent offerings have included *Rigoletto, The Flying Dutchman,* and *The Magic Flute.* The **SAN DIEGO SYMPHONY** (750 B St; 619/235-0804; www.sandiego symphony.com) has made a happy recovery from bankruptcy—and is back at home in its own Symphony Hall, performing a variety of series from blue-jean casual to formal black-tie, October through May, plus a Summer Pops Festival July through September. Other classical groups include the **SAN DIEGO CHAMBER ORCHESTRA** (which plays at various locations; 858/350-0290 or 888/848-7326; www.sdco.org) and the **LA JOLLA CHAMBER MUSIC SOCIETY** (also various locations, 858/459-3728; www.ljcms.org).

In summer, Spreckels Organ Pavilion presents **FREE SUNDAY AFTERNOON CONCERTS** at 2pm on the enormous 4,500-pipe outdoor organ in Balboa Park (2211 Pan American Rd E; 619/702-8138). **ANNUAL MUSIC FESTIVALS** include the Mainly Mozart Festival (various locations; 619/239-0100), and Street Scene (tickets available through Ticketmaster; 619/220-8497), September's three-day music extravaganza in the streets of the Gaslamp Quarter, which draws more than 60 bands—including many big-name international entertainers—to 10 stages.

DANCE

The class-act **CALIFORNIA BALLET COMPANY** (4819 Ronson Rd; 858/560-6741), more than three decades old and under the artistic direction of Maxine Mahon, performs four or five traditional and contemporary productions a year at various venues throughout the county. The company's flagship *Nutcracker* runs from Thanksgiving through Christmas at downtown's Civic Theater. For **MODERN AND CONTEMPORARY WORKS,** seek out Malashock Dance & Company (3103 Falcon St; 619/260-1622), San Diego Dance Theater (619/594-6824), or McCaleb Dance (858/488-5559). The University of California at San Diego Mandeville Auditorium is the scene for the annual Nations of San Diego International Dance Festival (619/220-TIXS), featuring more than 150 dancers and musicians in a multitude of ethnic styles.

THEATER

THE GLOBE THEATRES (1363 Old Globe Wy, Balboa Park; 619/239-2255; www.theglobetheatres.org) is California's oldest professional theater and San Diego's grande dame, staging at least 12 productions—on three stages—from January to October (often with guest actors such as Jon Voight, Marsha Mason, and John Goodman), including classics, contemporary dramas, musicals, experimental works, and the famed summer **SHAKESPEARE FESTIVAL** at the replica Old Globe Theatre. The **LA JOLLA PLAYHOUSE** (2910 La Jolla Village Dr, at Torrey Pines Rd, La Jolla; 858/550-1010; www.lajollaplayhouse.com), winner of a Tony Award for best regional theater, not only draws professional touring groups and big-name talent, but also previewed *Tommy, Big River,* and *How to Succeed in Business Without Really Trying* before the shows ever took a bite out of the Big Apple. Six productions are mounted, May through November, in the Mandell Weiss Theater and the Forum. **SAN DIEGO REPERTORY THEATRE,** the city's premier resident acting company, performs a broad range of classic and contemporary dramas, along with musicals and comedies, at the **LYCEUM THEATER** (79 Horton Plaza; 619/544-1000; www.sandiegorep.com). Its two-week run of *A Christmas Carol*—with a new version each year—is a local favorite.

The roster of small local theaters is burgeoning. **HORTON GRAND THEATRE** (444 4th Ave; 619/234-9583) is home to the long-running *Triple Espresso,* a comedy that's become an institution in several cities; **THEATRE IN OLD TOWN** (4040 Twiggs St; 619/688-2494) is a popular stage for musical revues; **SAN DIEGO JUNIOR THE-ATRE** (Casa del Prado, Balboa Park; 619/239-8355; www.juniortheatre.com) is a hit with youngsters and young-actors-to-be; and **LAMB'S PLAYERS THEATRE** (1142 Orange Ave, Coronado; 619/437-0600; www.lambsplayers.org) offers first-rate productions in an intimate setting. For avant-garde, cutting-edge works, look to **SLEDGEHAMMER THEATRE** (1620 6th Ave; 619/544-1484) or the **FRITZ THEATRE** (420 3rd Ave; 619/233-7505), a cool location for provocative and experimental offerings. **DIVERSIONARY THEATER** (4545 Park Blvd; 619/220-0097) presents gay- and lesbian-friendly works, and **MYSTERY CAFE** (505 Kalmia St, at the Imperial House Restaurant; 619/544-1600) is a mecca for those who like to combine dinner with murder. **SUSHI PERFORMANCE AND VISUAL ART** (320 11th Ave; 619/235-8468), not recommended for prudes, showcases often-controversial performance artists, including top talents from New York, Los Angeles, and San Francisco.

FILM

Though San Diego movie theaters (and the films shown therein) tend to be of the multiplex variety, foreign and art films are shown regularly at the **KEN CINEMA**

(4061 Adams Ave, Kensington; 619/283-5909), **HILLCREST CINEMAS** (3965 5th Ave, Hillcrest; 619/299-2100), and **THE COVE** (7730 Girard Ave, La Jolla; 858/459-5404). UCSD hosts the **SAN DIEGO INTERNATIONAL FILM FESTIVAL** (Price Center Theater, UCSD; 858/534-8497) from February through May, screening premieres of more than 20 international films, as well as short subjects. Animated-film aficionados beeline to the annual **FESTIVAL OF ANIMATION**, held April through May at Museum of Contemporary Art (700 Prospect St, La Jolla; 858/454-3541). The annual **SAN DIEGO LATINO FILM FESTIVAL** (619/230-1938; www.sdlatino film.com) takes place in March at the Mann Hazard Center 7. Check out **MOVIES BEFORE THE MAST** (1306 N Harbor Dr; 619/234-9153), which projects the films onto a "screensail" from April to September aboard the 1863 windjammer *Star of India*; tickets sell out quickly, so get yours in advance. The IMAX screen at the **REUBEN H. FLEET SPACE THEATER AND SCIENCE CENTER** (1875 El Prado, Balboa Park; 619/238-1233; www.rhfleet.org) affords practically-in-the-picture views of everything from Alaska and Mount Everest to outer space and race-car driving.

NIGHTLIFE

BARS: A longtime favorite with San Diego politicians and sophisticates is **DOBSON'S** (956 Broadway Circle, near Broadway, across from Horton Plaza; 619/231-6771). Sports-bar powerhouses include **SEAU'S** (1640 Camino del Rio N, in Mission Valley Center; 619/291-7328), owned by San Diego Charger Junior Seau, and **TROPHY'S** (7510 Hazard Center Dr, Ste 215, Mission Valley; 619/296-9600). Folks in search of a quiet drink try the **TOP OF THE HYATT** (1 Market Pl, in the Hyatt Hotel Downtown; 619/232-1234) with sky-high views of the waterfront, while the pints-and-darts crowd hits the **PRINCESS PUB AND GRILLE** (1665 India St, at Date St; 619/702-3021; www.princesspub.com). College-type ragers favor raunchy **DICK'S LAST RESORT,** so disgustingly rowdy and rude it's almost lovable (345 4th Ave; 619/231-9100). **KARL STRAUS BREWERY & GRILL** (1157 Columbia St; 619/234-2739) continues to win multiple awards for best microbrewery.

    CLUBS: CROCE'S JAZZ BAR (802 5th Ave, at F St; 619/233-4355; www.croces. com), is a top club for traditional jazz, while adjoining **CROCE'S TOP HAT** leans toward the blues; both are run by late musician Jim Croce's widow, and his son A. J. occasionally performs. **PATRICK'S II** (428 F St; 619/233-3077) is another enduring favorite for jazz and blues. The cooler-than-cool crowd frequents **BLUE TATTOO** (835 5th Ave; 619/238-7191) and the **ONYX ROOM** (852 5th Ave; 619/235-6699). Other hopping spots include **JIMMY LOVE'S** (672 5th Ave; 619/595-0123) for the thirtysomething crowd, and **CASBAH** (2501 Kettner Blvd; 619/232-4355; www.casbahmusic.com), the best alternative club in town. **THE FLAME** (3780 Park Blvd; 619/295-4163) caters mainly to lesbians, though guys get a token night; and gay men gravitate to **RICH'S** (1051 University Ave; 619/497-4588). **ON BROADWAY** (615 Broadway; 619/231-0011) is the chic place for dancing.

    In the beach areas, the **CANNIBAL BAR** (3999 Mission Blvd, in the Catamaran Hotel, Mission Beach; 858/539-8650) is a mainstay, featuring local and name entertainment. **HUMPHREY'S BY THE BAY** (2241 Shelter Island Dr; 619/224-3577; www.humphreysconcerts.com) is quite possibly the city's best live music club, hosting a variety of entertainment, including an outdoor series from May through October that features seat-grabbers such as Willie Nelson and Ray Charles. For sheer fun, choose the **COMEDY STORE** (916 Pearl St, La Jolla; 858/454-9176). Big-name hotshots from Los Angeles as well as promising amateurs dish out chuckles at this club.

SPECTATOR SPORTS

Though the **SAN DIEGO PADRES** lost the 1998 World Series, the team still won a baseball stadium. The new venue will be built near the Gaslamp Quarter; until then, the "Pads" can be cheered at **QUALCOMM STADIUM** (9449 Friars Rd, Mission Valley; 619/283-4494). The **SAN DIEGO CHARGERS** also grab cheers at Qualcomm, and the stadium is the site of December's Holiday Bowl, the Western Athletic Conference championship football game.

FESTIVALS

The **SAN DIEGO CREW CLASSIC** is saluted at Mission Bay in April (858/488-0700). As befits its proximity to Mexico, San Diego celebrates **CINCO DE MAYO** throughout the county. On this side of the border, Old Town is one of the best spots to join the festivities. The Blue Angels and other aero-show-offs blast the skies at the **MIRAMAR AIR SHOW,** held in October (45249 Miramar Wy, 858/577-1000). The **U.S. OPEN SANDCASTLE COMPETITION** (619/424-6663), a July event in Imperial Beach, is one of the country's largest, attracting old pros and little kids. Balboa Park's Museum of Man (1350 El Prado, 619/239-2001) is transformed into a fabulously frightening **HOUSE OF HORRORS** at Halloween. The two-day **CHRISTMAS ON EL PRADO** in Balboa Park (619/239-0512) is a festive beginning to the holiday season, with a candlelight procession, entertainment, food stalls, and free evening admission to the park's museums. Another holiday kickoff is El Cajon's **MOTHER GOOSE PARADE** (619/444-8712), held the weekend before Thanksgiving. More than 200 floats are featured in this 50-plus-year-old event. The **SAN DIEGO HARBOR PARADE OF LIGHTS,** on two December weekends, is a dazzling display of decorated boats sailing from Shelter Island to Seaport Village. The **HOLIDAY BOWL** (San Diego State University; 619/283-5808) parade and football game in late December is a traffic- and work-stopper. For more information on annual events contact the **SAN DIEGO CONVENTION & VISITORS BUREAU** (401 B St, Ste 1400, San Diego 92101; 619/232-3101; www.sandiego.org).

RESTAURANTS AND LODGINGS BY NEIGHBORHOOD

Downtown/Gaslamp Quarter

RESTAURANTS

Athens Market Taverna / ★★

109 WEST F ST, GASLAMP QUARTER; 619/234-1955 This Greek restaurant is a favorite with lawyers and other downtown professionals for lunch, dinner, and after-work cocktails; their well-heeled, well-dressed demeanor goes nicely with the under-stated, elegant white linen tablecloths and napkins, tiny candles, and dried flowers gracing each table. Owner Mary Pappas has been cooking up sublime Greek food downtown since 1974, and her devoted clientele followed her from her first location at Fourth Avenue and E Street to the current digs just south of Horton Plaza. Among the most succulent dishes is the fall-off-the-bone baked lemon chicken, served with rice pilaf, roasted potato wedge, vegetable, and soup or salad. The lentil soup is zesty, though the egg-lemon soup is almost too subtle. Still, there's something so chic yet comfortable about Athens Market Taverna that a less-than-inspired batch of soup is instantly forgiven. *$$; AE, DC, DIS, MC, V; no checks; lunch Mon–Fri, dinner Mon–Sat; full bar; reservations recommended; between First and Front Sts.*

Bayou Bar and Grill / ★★

329 MARKET ST, GASLAMP QUARTER; 619/696-8747 Bringing a little bit of Bourbon Street to Market Street—that's what San Diego's best Cajun restaurant is about. Between the Dixieland jazz (including live performances for New Year's Eve and Mardi Gras), the Big Easy posters, and the huge selection of chili sauces for sale, it's easy to imagine yourself in the French Quarter. The Southern cooking delivers authentic punch as well, generating lots of requests for the jambalaya, shrimp po' boy, fiery blackened fish, and soft-shell crab. Save a little room for dessert because the place is famous for a chilled peanut butter mousse pie and a bourbon-spiked bread pudding. In addition to the bar area and dining rooms, there's patio seating on the sidewalk fronting Market Street, a favorite vantage point on busy weekend nights. If you're in town during Mardi Gras season, this is the place to be for hearty partying and hurricanes that go down smooth and cold. *$$; AE, CB, DC, DIS, MC, V; no checks; dinner every day; full bar; reservations recommended; bayoubar@ aol.com; between 3rd and 4th Sts.*

Bella Luna / ★★

748 5TH AVE, GASLAMP QUARTER; 619/239-3222 Downtown's Gaslamp Quarter offers a staggering number of trattorias, but those in the know keep going back to this eye-catching Italian restaurant whose name means "beautiful moon." The dining room is one of the Gaslamp's most striking; the ceiling evokes blue sky and clouds and has dozens of artworks celebrating the moon. There's also seating at the bar and on the sidewalk patio, a prime vantage point for Fifth Avenue people-watching. The tempting menu is strong on appetizers, with assorted carpaccios (we especially like the salmon version) and a particularly nice starter of tiny grilled eggplant wrapped in pine nuts and raisins. Main courses of note include the veal saltimbocca, bow tie pasta with fresh salmon and spinach, spicy penne with eggplant, and risottos that change with the season. Along with a decent wine selection, the restaurant serves six varieties of grappa and a number of fine aged tequilas. Service is skilled (though it can lag when there's a crowd), and the restaurant has a distinctively European cachet that sets it apart from the crowd. *$$; AE, DC, MC, V; no checks; lunch, dinner every day; full bar; reservations recommended; between F and G Sts.*

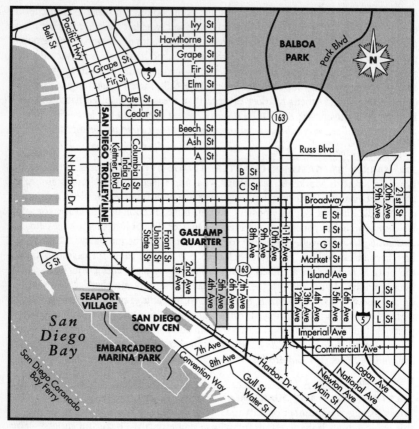

DOWNTOWN SAN DIEGO

Bertrand at Mr. A's / ★★★

2550 5TH AVE, DOWNTOWN; 619/239-1377 Generations of San Diegans have counted on this 12th-floor restaurant to deliver sweeping views, formal service, and "special occasion" atmosphere. Now, the fare is equally notable. Mr. A's, as the place used to be known, was purchased by local restaurateur Bertrand Hug (of Mille Fleurs fame) in spring 2000 and completely refurbished. Gone are the red velvet wallpaper and heavy draperies, as well as the old-fashioned menu. These days, the rooms are dressed in sleek, self-assured neutrals and the kitchen staff turns out modern French and California cuisine. Dishes change often, but be on the lookout for standout versions of cassoulet, duck confit, roasted veal and Maine lobster (the lobster salad with a truffle strudel is to swoon for). The book-size wine list is heavy on fine Bordeaux and Burgundy, as well as California's top reds, and the skilled bartenders make a darn good cosmopolitan. Although the restrictive dress code of days past is no more (jacketless men and women in pants were once frowned upon), this is definitely the place to dress for success. Most tables offer wonderful views of downtown, the harbor or Balboa Park, making this a can't-miss choice for out-of-town guests, business associates, or a special date. Valet parking is available underneath the building with an entrance on Fourth Avenue. *$$$$; AE, DC, DIS, MC, V; no checks; lunch Mon–Fri, dinner every day; full bar; reservations recommended; asrestaurant@aol.com; www.bertrandatmisteras.com; between Maple and Laurel Sts.*

Cafe 222 / ★★

222 ISLAND AVE, DOWNTOWN; 619/236-9902 "The man who gets breakfast in bed is probably in the hospital," reads the menu at this irreverent egg-and-waffle eatery, run by the imaginative Terry Gavre. The cafe is tiny—a corner storefront with a half dozen tables and whimsical chandeliers made of teacups and spoons. The menu is hearty: "big, thick, golden brown waffles" are irresistible—especially the five-grain or pumpkin versions. The kids' pancake is "supposed to look like Mickey Mouse, but often looks like a pig or small dog." Despite the lighthearted prose and the rubber chickens hanging on the wall, the food is great and attracts a waiting line of hungry downtowners. For breakfast, order Joe's special—"a frittata-ish thing with toast." For lunch, choose grilled turkey, goat cheese, and pesto on rosemary focaccia or one of 222's other trendy sandwiches. A smaller breakfast menu is served until closing time. Gavre writes restaurant reviews and is always hip to the local dining scene. *$; Cash only; breakfast, lunch every day; no alcohol; reservations not accepted; www.cafe222.com; at 2nd Ave.*

El Indio Shop / ★★☆

3695 INDIA ST, DOWNTOWN; 619/299-0333 In San Diego, the name El Indio is pretty much synonymous with Mexican food. Just about everyone in town knows this little shop, which has built a reputation on tortilla chips, fresh salsa, beef taquitos, and combo plates. The chili-dusted tortilla chips and freshly prepared corn or flour tortillas are favorite souvenirs—locals regularly mail these as care packages to less-fortunate East Coast dwellers. In a nod to the times, a vegetarian menu was added a few years ago, offering surprisingly tasty items such as mashed potato tacos and vegetarian tamales. Dine inside or across the street on a patio in the shadow of Interstate 5. To order, head for the counter, then wait until your number is called. Be prepared at lunch: some days it seems as though everyone in town is lined up and ready to place their order. Catering is available too—many a local wedding reception has featured El Indio selections—and many items on the menu are available refrigerated or frozen for bulk orders. *$; MC, V; checks OK; breakfast, lunch, dinner every day; beer and wine; reservations not necessary; www. elindio.net; near San Diego Ave.*

Filippi's Pizza Grotto / ★

1747 INDIA ST, DOWNTOWN (AND BRANCHES); 619/232-5094 Mom and Pop are long gone, but seven sisters and brothers run this string of dependable Italian restaurants, situated all over San Diego. The original is in Little Italy and is the only one with a store. (That's how Filippi's began.) To enter, customers file past cases of cheese, sliced meats, a barrel of salted and filleted cod, breads from three bakeries, oils, vinegars, and every kind of pasta imaginable. The fragrance is

BALBOA PARK: JEWEL OF THE CITY

It's a rare city that will devote 1,200 acres of prime downtown real estate to an urban park. But San Diego's forefathers had a prescient vision, and did just that in the early 1900s. They hired Kate Sessions (the horticulturalist responsible for many of the city's oldest gardens and parks) to oversee the planting of trees on hills overlooking San Diego Bay. Then they decided San Diego needed a major exposition to show off the city's marketable charms. Architects Bertram Goodhue and Carleton Winslow designed a series of Spanish-Moorish-Colonial-Baroque palaces to house exhibits for the 1915–16 Panama-California Exposition celebrating the opening of the Panama Canal. Balboa Park was born.

Secretary of the Navy Franklin D. Roosevelt opened the exposition after riding across the cantilevered bridge that now straddles Highway 163. The carillon in the architects' elaborate 200-foot-high California Tower still chimes on the quarter hour. The California Building, originally designed by minimalist architect Irving Gill and later embellished by Goodhue and Winslow, was the welcoming entrance to the fair. It later housed artifacts left from various international exhibits, and is now home to the Museum of Man. Animals left behind were assembled in a small menagerie above a remote canyon; in 1941, the Zoological Society of San Diego was granted 200 acres in the park for a permanent zoo—now one of the most famous zoos in the world.

The exposition was such a success that the city leaders planned a second fair, the 1935–36 California Exposition. Architect Richard Requa designed the Globe Theatre, where actors presented 40-minute condensations of Shakespeare's most famous plays. A generally permissive air prevailed, and the exhibits included midgets, nudists, and a midway with games and rides. Several significant structures housed more educational exhibits. William Templeton Johnson designed the decorative façade for a building to house natural history exhibits; it's now been dramatically remodeled for the San Diego Natural History Museum.

overwhelmingly Parmesan. The restaurant itself is large, with an open kitchen and pizza oven, grotto-dark and busy-noisy. Tables are covered with red checkered cloths; Chianti bottles (hundreds, maybe thousands) hang from the rafters. The same theme prevails in other Filippi's locations in Pacific Beach and outlying neighborhoods. Specialties are lasagne, pizza, ravioli, spaghetti, hot sausage (made on the premises), and a variety of sandwiches on freshly crisp buns. Servings are ample; most diners leave with leftovers. Customers are clearly regulars, addressed by name by waitresses who seem to have been there forever. *$; AE, DC, DIS, MC, V; no checks; lunch, dinner every day; beer and wine; reservations not accepted; between Date and Fir Sts.* &

The military took over the park during World War II. The grand lily pond from 1915 became a therapy pool for wounded soldiers and sailors; the pepper grove, planted in 1910, became an outdoor USO dance hall. The House of Hospitality, one of Winslow and Goodhue's 1915 masterpieces, became a dorm. The war effort greatly taxed Balboa Park's buildings, and it seemed as though many would be demolished. But San Diegans couldn't bear to see their park destroyed. The Committee of 100 was formed in 1967 to protect the park's treasured buildings; dilapidated stonework was removed, and castings made of the buildings' elaborate facades to facilitate faithful reconstruction. Perhaps the most cherished of all the park's structures, the Spreckels Organ Pavilion, is still used much as it was in 1915. Sugar magnates John D. and Adolph B. Spreckels donated the enormous pipe organ to the city for the first exposition; today's visitors still enjoy free organ concerts every Sunday afternoon.

—Maribeth Mellin

Fish Market Restaurant / ★★
Top of the Market / ★★

750 N HARBOR DR, DOWNTOWN; 619/232-3474 The panoramic views of San Diego Bay are as much an attraction as the huge menu of fresh catches at the Fish Market Restaurant and its upstairs, upscale sister, Top of the Market. Downstairs you'll find a full-service cocktail bar, a busy oyster bar, and the friendly, casual Fish Market Restaurant. Seating overlooks the bay; the best tables are the ones on the outdoor patio, directly over the water. The menu features a huge selection of fresh-caught seafood grilled, Cajun style, or fried, served with a side of rice or au gratin potatoes (a sinfully delicious choice) and steaming hot sourdough bread. For the money and bustling ambience, the downstairs restaurant is the better bet. Upstairs, the more formal Top of the Market serves imported fresh seafood with more refined presentations and service and price tags to match. The list of offerings is astounding; you can tour the seven seas with Norwegian salmon, Alaskan halibut, New Zealand mussels, and Mississippi catfish, all flown in daily. The linen and candlelight setting is soothing; window tables present a romantic view of twinkling lights on boats floating in the bay. The wine list is excellent; servers will assist in matching grape and sea flavors. *$$ (Fish Market), $$$ (Top of the Market); AE, CB, DC, DIS, MC, V; no checks; lunch, dinner every day; full bar; reservations recommended for large groups; www.thefishmarket.com; at Broadway and the end of Pacific Coast Hwy.* &

The Grant Grill / ★★★

326 BROADWAY (U. S. GRANT HOTEL), DOWNTOWN; 619/232-3121 With its dark-paneled walls, quaint hunting prints, and formally clad waiters, the Grant Grill resembles an old-fashioned gentlemen's club. Indeed, this hotel dining room, opened in 1910, once barred females from entering before 3pm. That all changed in 1969, when a group of San Diego women demanded a table for lunch. Since then, the restaurant has alternately thrived and languished as executive chefs have arrived and departed. These days, the Grant is on an upswing again, serving breakfast, lunch, and dinner items that are both generous and appealing. French toast made with banana bread; a delicious Monte Cristo sandwich served with a tangy berry sauce; a perfect Caesar salad; buttery seared foie gras with apples; and grilled wild salmon are just a few of the recommendable successes. The service remains consistently good, with an old-fashioned, courtly feel. The spacious booths are generally filled with businesspeople at lunch and theatergoers at night, so dress up a bit. An adjacent bar is every bit as handsome as the dining room, though it's modern enough to sport a wide-screen TV. The bar also offers a selection of sandwiches, pizzas, and salads for under $10. *$$$; AE, CB, DC, DIS, MC, V; checks OK; breakfast, lunch, dinner every day; full bar; reservations recommended; between 3rd and 4th Aves.* &

Indigo Grill / ★★★

1536 INDIA ST, DOWNTOWN; 619/234-6802 Chef Deborah Scott—the talent behind the fiery, multicultural cuisine at Kemo Sabe (see Hillcrest neighborhood reviews)—has created another stunningly designed restaurant. Conceived as a salute to the indigenous cultures of the Americas, from Oaxaca to the Pacific Nothwest, Indigo Grill offers a dazzling experience for the palate as well as the eye. The strongest influence is Mexican—the chile is used in countless dishes here. Scott uses poblanos, serranos, and jalapeños to add complexity of flavor or a shimmer of heat, rather than all-out fire. You won't need a flame-proof palate to enjoy beef enchiladas, delicate trout, slow-roasted pork ribs, or superb roasted baby chicken seasoned with sage and mole. Smooth-as-satin corn pudding, an offbeat Caesar salad fashioned with grilled romaine, and a rich portobello mushroom fettuccine are other signature dishes. The decor is as artistic as the fare, with Oaxacan animal masks, Inuit carvings, and totem poles surveying the eclectic group of diners. In addition to several high-quality tequilas and mescals, there's an adequate wine list and some imaginative cocktail creations. *$$–$$$; AE, DC, DIS, MC, V; no checks; lunch Mon–Fri, dinner every day; full bar; reservations recommended; www.cohn restaurants.com; between Cedar and Beech Sts.* &

Laurel Restaurant & Bar / ★★★

505 LAUREL ST, DOWNTOWN; 619/239-2222 Laurel is so sophisticated you might think you're in some chic spot in San Francisco or New York. While it's true that many come to Laurel simply for the panache of pricey furnishings, flattering light, and exquisite martinis, many more are drawn by the memorable fare. Founding chef Doug Organ has left the restaurant, but his influence continues in the mix of Mediterranean, North African, Provençal, and classic French cuisine. Longtime Laurel fans still enjoy the Provençal chicken stewed in a pot with fragrant herbs, and a masterful duck confit with silken meat and crackly skin. Long-simmered osso buco and an appetizer tart flavored with Roquefort and caramelized onions are also still present. An outstanding wine list offers many unfamiliar bottles from various regions of France, although the list by the glass is lacking. Service is generally quite good, but it's the genial bartenders who really set the standard for Laurel's staff. Maybe that's why so many regulars drop by for a quick bite at the bar. *$$$; AE, DC,*

DIS, MC, V; no checks; dinner every day; full bar; reservations recommended; www. laurelrestaurant.com; at 5th Ave.

Le Fontainebleau / ★★★

1055 2ND AVE (WESTGATE HOTEL), DOWNTOWN; 619/557-3655 Ever since stellar French chef Christophe Vessaire took command in 2001, this Versailles-inspired dining room has become a destination for serious foodies. The much-awarded Vessaire (whose credits include Michelin-starred restaurants in France and Switzerland) seamlessly blends classic French and updated California cuisine in one of the most elegant settings in town. The windowless room is opulent and appealing, with extravagant chandeliers, a grand piano, and immaculately dressed tables. And the fare is divine, from the duck foie gras served with braised fennel and feathery fennel salad to the splendid seared halibut paired with fava beans and olives. Other tempting choices: artichoke soup infused with black truffles; butter-poached scallops with tender baby pea shoots; Sonoma duck breast complemented with an apricot compote; and escargot sautéed in fragrant Pernod. The chef takes special pride in his tasting menu featuring multiple courses of foie gras, but also offers more populist fare with a Friday night seafood buffet and a Sunday champagne brunch. The service is formal and correct; the ambience definitely special occasion. *$$$–$$$$; AE, CB, DC, DIS, MC, V; checks OK; lunch Mon–Fri, dinner Mon–Sat, brunch Sun; full bar; reservations recommended; www.westgatehotel. com; between Broadway and C St.*

Morton's of Chicago / ★★★

285 J ST (HARBOR CLUB), DOWNTOWN; 619/696-3369 Welcome to the land of expense-account dinners, prime Midwestern beef, expertly shaken martinis, and baked potatoes almost the size of footballs. Morton's offers steak-house dining at its best, which means all the wood-paneled ambience and waiterly ceremony you can handle. The crowd is much less formal, however; this national chain draws a mix of Hawaiian-shirted tourists, name-tagged conventioneers, and others dressed in Gap and Gucci. Steaks, vegetables, and other items (including outsized live lobsters) are presented for your approval at the table before being turned into top-notch all-American fare. Black bean soup and Caesar salad are the appetizers of choice; then it's a toss-up between the New York strip, the double-thick lamb chops, or the lightly breaded Veal Sicilian. Portions are enormous, but you'll still want to indulge in one of the fabulous dessert soufflés or the Godiva chocolate truffle cake that takes the rage for warm, gooey, melted-center desserts to new heights. A pricey but well-chosen wine list offers top California cabernets and double magnums of premium champagnes. Be ready to spend some money, and prepare for a splendid evening of excess. *$$$–$$$$; AE, CB, DC, DIS, MC, V; no checks; dinner every day; full bar; reservations recommended; www.mortons.com; between 2nd and 3rd Aves.* &

Prado Restaurant at Balboa Park / ★★

1549 EL PRADO (IN THE HOUSE OF HOSPITALITY), DOWNTOWN; 619/557-9441 For too many years, this prime piece of real estate in Balboa Park housed a mediocre eatery and rather dusty bar. Then the Cohn family— proprietors of the Blue Point (Gaslamp Quarter) and Kemo Sabe (Hillcrest) eateries, among others—took over, and one of San Diego's most appealing dining destinations was born. Set off a lush courtyard in the House of Hospitality, the Prado has a spacious, multilevel dining room, separate bar, and a garden view patio, all done up in Modern Hacienda decor. Start out with a trendy mojito or pisco sour to set the Latin tone, then choose just about anything on the ambitious Mexican- and Cal-cuisine-influenced menu; the chef is remarkably consistent. A few of the standouts: chicken-tortilla soup, pork prime rib, and a clever combo of lemon-thyme grilled swordfish with butternut squash (prepared two different ways) and red beet–truffle purée. With its charming location, fun ambience and dependably good food and drink, the Prado is great for a leisurely lunch, a relaxed dinner date, or for pre-theater dining before heading across the plaza to a performance at the Globe. The restaurant also offers catering and is the site for numerous indoor and outdoor weddings. *$$; AE, DC, DIS, MC, V; no checks; lunch, dinner every day; full bar; reservations recommended; www.cohnrestaurants.com; in Balboa Park.*

Royale Brasserie / ★★

224 5TH AVE, DOWNTOWN; 619/237-4900 Although the cheeky Parisian decor seems more authentic than the cuisine, this popular downtown bistro is a fun stop for diners in search of onion soup, escargot, and ambience. The interior is sheer déjà vu for anyone who's visited Montparnasse, with a series of dining rooms done up with mosaic floors, banquette seating, gleaming paneling, and painted ceilings. On the menu, decent versions of bouillabaisse, coq au vin, and cassoulet share space with grilled yellowfin or swordfish and a New York strip steak. Steamed mussels (cooked in white wine, beer, or fresh tomatoes) are a specialty of the house and come with the requisite pommes frites. Shellfish fans with deep pockets can share an oversize platter of fresh oysters, clams, shrimp, and crab for about $100, but we're perfectly happy with the excellent duck and pork pâté that's under $10. Service ranges from skilled to spacey; if you're in a hurry, it's generally best to duck into the bar for a beer and a quick bite. *$$; AE, DC, MC, V; no checks; dinner every day; full bar; reservations recommended; www.royalebrasserie.com; between K and L Sts.* &

Saffron Noodles and Saté / ★★★

3737 INDIA ST, DOWNTOWN; 619/574-7737 Nobody has done more to introduce San Diegans to the pleasures of Thai cuisine than owner/chef Su-Mei Yu, who founded the tiny original Saffron next door (still a favorite takeout joint). Today, she's expanded her original rotisserie chicken shop into a full-scale noodle house, with dozens of choices that explore a range of styles from mild to incendiary. Classic noodle dishes such as pad thai and spicy noodles are done well, but it's the exotic daily specials flavored with pickled vegetables or fried shallots and the silken curries that are the true stars of this aromatic show. New specials are always popping up: each time Su-Mei travels to Thailand, she brings back additional regional recipes to tempt us. In addition to the artful food, the restaurant features works by glass sculptor Dale Chihuly and painter Italo Scanga. The place is a feast for the eyes as well as the palate, and the low prices make it an affordable treat. *$; MC, V; no checks; lunch, dinner every day; beer and wine; reservations not accepted; at Washington St.*

Sevilla / ★★

555 4TH AVE, GASLAMP QUARTER; 619/233-5979 / 3050 PIO PICO RD, CARLSBAD; 760/730-7558 Downtown office workers unwind at this Spanish tapas bar in the Gaslamp; empty bar stools are rare after 5pm. Bullfight posters and oil paintings of Andalusian beauties surround the mirrored bar, where slow-moving bartenders and waitresses dispense plates of Spanish olives stuffed with anchovy paste and glasses of Spanish and domestic wine. You can make a dinner of such tapas as tortilla española, fried calamari, or mushrooms in white wine garlic sauce at the bar. Or head to the dining room, El Patio Andaluz, which is dressed up like a courtyard from southern Spain. The most popular dish is traditional paella valenciana—seafood, sausage, and chicken in saffron rice; seafood and vegetarian versions are also superb. Some of the desserts shine, like the sinful crema catalana, a chocolate espresso crème brûlée with whipped cream. In the downstairs Club Sevilla, there's a different brand of live Latino music nightly, with samba lessons, Spanish rock, salsa, and, on Fridays and Saturdays, a dinner show (tango or flamenco) for $40. The Carlsbad restaurant has a more formal feeling, with several dark and cozy dining rooms and an upstairs bar. You must make advance reservations for the dinner shows there. *$$; AE, DC, DIS, MC, V; no checks; dinner every day; full bar; reservations recommended; www.cafesevilla.com; between Market and Island Sts (downtown); off Carlsbad Village Dr (Carlsbad).* &

Star of the Sea / ★★★

1360 HARBOR DR, DOWNTOWN; 619/232-7408 Since opening in 1966, this wharfside restaurant has always been busy. But the cuisine and decor took a quantum leap forward in 1999, when the building was redesigned with floor-to-ceiling windows overlooking the bay, lots of artistic flourishes (a jewelry designer created the silverware), and a dramatic over-the-water entryway. The restaurant is in skilled hands with Brian Johnson, whose local cooking credits include the well-regarded El Bizcocho in Rancho Bernardo. At the Star, Johnson whips up dazzling lobster with basil gnocchi, Norwegian salmon garnished with feta cheese and saffron sauce, and succulent scallops arranged on a bed of truffle risotto. Order the puffy Belgian chocolate soufflé garnished with three sauces at least 20 minutes before you'd like to dig in. The wide-ranging wine list offers lots of fish-friendly sauvignon blancs and chardonnays, along with a dozen lesser-seen whites and reds from California, Australia, France, Italy, and the Pacific Northwest. Not up for a full dinner? Grab a seat in the bar or the over-the-water patio and graze on appetizers. *$$$-$$$$; AE, DC, DIS, MC, V; no checks; dinner every day; full bar; reservations recommended; www.starofthesea.com; off Ash St.* &

LODGINGS

Courtyard by Marriott / ★★☆

530 BROADWAY, DOWNTOWN; 619/530-4000 OR 800/321-2211 The grand marble lobby of one of downtown's finest old bank buildings now serves as the entryway to a charming hotel. The painted coffer ceilings, brass teller's cages, and turnstile doors have all been restored to the grandeur they presented bank customers in the 1930s. The Italian Romanesque Revival building was designed by architect William Templeton Johnson when Broadway was in its heyday, and it stood vacant for many years when the focus of redevelopment turned to Horton Plaza and the Gaslamp. The hotel's designers managed to turn offices into 246 guest rooms and suites that suit the building's design, and guests feel as though they're staying in a venerable downtown inn. Check out the original vault in the basement, which now holds a meeting room. *$$$; AE, DC, MC, V; checks OK; www.courtyard.com; between 5th and 6th Sts.* &

Hilton San Diego Gaslamp Quarter / ★★★

401 K ST, GASLAMP QUARTER; 619/231-4040 OR 800/774-1500 You might expect a hotel located right across the street from the convention center to be enormous and frantically busy. Instead, this 275-room gem has the ambience of a boutique hotel. In the Enclave section, the rooms are designed much like artists' lofts with high windows letting in streams of natural light that illuminates velvety couches and cushy beds draped with Frette linens. The brick and steel Bridgeworks building, which houses the hotel and other businesses, has a contemporary feel that's enhanced by the use of original glass objets d'art placed around a blazing fireplace in the lobby. Guests unwind after business meetings at the soothing Artesia spa or work off their tensions in the fitness center, then stroll to excellent restaurants in the building or the Gaslamp Quarter. *$$$; AE, DC, DIS, MC, V; checks OK; www.hilton.com; between 4th and 5th Sts.* &

Horton Grand Hotel / ★★

311 ISLAND AVE, GASLAMP QUARTER; 619/544-1886 OR 800/542-1886 The Horton Grand Hotel offers a touch of Victorian-era gentility in the heart of the historic Gaslamp Quarter. Composed of two historic Victorian hotels, the Horton Grand has quite a colorful history. Wyatt Earp slept here when he lived in San Diego, and the restaurant, Ida Bailey's, is named in honor of Ida Bailey, a notorious turn-of-the-20th-century madam whose bordello once occupied this site. All 132 rooms are decorated with period antiques, lace curtains, and working gas fireplaces. But we'll bet Wyatt Earp never had a microwave or a hair dryer. For more space, request one of the 600-square-foot minisuites. While the hotel has plenty of its own quirky charm, its location is the real bonus. You can live it up at the Gaslamp's many clubs and bars, then stroll or catch a pedicab back to the hotel. *$$$; AE, DC, DIS, MC, V; checks OK; horton@connectnet.com; www.hortongrand.com; at 4th Ave.* &

La Pensione Hotel / ★

1700 INDIA ST, DOWNTOWN; 619/236-8000 OR 800/232-4683 This modern, architecturally innovative hotel is a boon for budget travelers. Most of the 80 rooms have kitchen facilities and large tables or desks; some have views of San Diego Bay; all have windows opening to sea breezes and sunlight, along with high ceilings that add a sense of space. Laundry facilities, a tiled courtyard, a marble fireplace in the lobby, and two adjacent restaurants are added perks, as is the colorful cast of multilingual travelers. The hotel is in the midst of the redevelopment activity in Little Italy. The neighborhood has good Italian restaurants and bakeries, and the trolley runs nearby. *$; AE, DC, DIS, MC, V; no checks; la-pensione@travel base.com; www.lapensionehotel.com; corner of Date and India Sts.* &

Wyndham U. S. Grant Hotel / ★★★

326 BROADWAY, DOWNTOWN; 619/232-3121 OR 877/999-3223 Ulysses S. Grant Jr. thought of San Diego as a grand spot for a monument to his more famous dad, and he commissioned Harrison Albright to design an Italian Renaissance palace in the heart of downtown. The hotel opened in 1910 amid much fanfare; after all, how many urban inns could boast a saltwater swimming pool and ladies' billiard hall amid marble pillars? Fortunes rose and fell in this hotel over the decades. It seems anyone who purchased the property felt like the poor offspring of a British duke saddled with the family mansion. The 285 rooms and 60 suites are visions of far nobler times, with two-poster beds, Victorian chairs, and fireplaces (in some suites). The lobby and bar are popular gathering spots for San Diegans, and the restaurant is a treasured landmark (see review). *$$$; AE, DC, MC, V; www.wyndham.com/USGrant; between 3rd and 4th Aves.* ᴦ

Hillcrest

RESTAURANTS

Bombay / ★★

3975 5TH AVE, HILLCREST; 619/298-3155 This Indian restaurant is a pleasing place to pass the time over lunch or dinner, especially if you sit near the trickling indoor fountain or on the sheltered outdoor patio. It's a peaceful refuge from bustling Fifth Avenue, with unobtrusive service and calming earth-toned decor. The wide-ranging menu is designed to please just about everyone. Top selections for carnivores are the excellent lamb stews (the red-hot vindaloo with ginger is a standout) and the moist tandoori-style chicken prepared in a real tandoor oven. Vegetarians will be delighted with a choice of more than 20 meat-free dishes, especially the curries and the delicious purée of fresh spinach. And everyone should love the breads, especially a garlicky naan that's just right for sopping up any last bits of sauce. Prices have gone up in the past year or so, but the best deal here is still a luncheon buffet for around $9; it's all-you-can-eat and includes basmati rice, various stews and curries, condiments, soups, and that terrific tandoori chicken. *$$; AE, DIS, MC, V; no checks; lunch, dinner every day; beer and wine; reservations recommended; www.bombayrestaurant.com; between University Ave and Washington St.*

Cafe W / ★★★

3680 6TH AVE, HILLCREST; 619/291-0200 This snazzy new restaurant is a dream come true, both for foodies and chef/owner Chris Walsh, who spent over a decade as the executive chef at California Cuisine before opening Cafe W in late 2001 to immediate acclaim. Created as a reflection of the way he himself likes to dine—grazing on a variety of little items—Walsh's dining room features about 40 "small plates," or appetizer servings. Just about everything on the menu is appealing, but our current faves are the rare, marinated steak served over citrus-dressed greens; grilled sweetbreads accompanied by mushroom duxelles and truffle oil; crab cakes (blended with scallops) served with a curry-garlic coleslaw; and mussels steamed in coconut milk. Most of the beautifully presented dishes are priced well under $10. The setting oozes style, from the well-spaced tables and shiny steel fireplace to the servers dressed in fitted T-shirts and camouflage pants. The wine list is short, but long on unusual choices such as New Zealand pinot noir and Rueda, a Spanish white; for beer drinkers, there's Guinness on tap. In addition to the main dining room, front and back patios offer alfresco dining. *$$; AE, MC, V; no checks; dinner Wed–Mon; beer and wine; reservations recommended; near Pennsylvania Ave.*

Chilango's Mexico City Grill / ★★

142 UNIVERSITY AVE, HILLCREST; 619/294-8646 Some of the most interesting and authentic Mexican fare in San Diego is served here in the heart of Hillcrest. The restaurant is small and so are the prices, but the flavors are big, bold, and irresistible. Bring an asbestos palate for the superspicy chicken-tortilla soup, a particular favorite here (for something milder, choose the black bean porridge). Move on to entrees such as roasted chicken, distinctively flavored with citrus juice and achiote paste; *huaraches* (thick corn tortillas topped with pork, salsa, and Mexican cheese); and *chilaquiles,* the comfort-food casserole fashioned from tortillas, chicken, onion, and cilantro. Need a palate quencher? Sample the fresh fruit salad laced with lime juice and cilantro, and you'll never touch fruit cocktail again. *$; DIS, MC, V; no checks; lunch, dinner Tues–Sun; no alcohol; reservations not accepted; at 3rd St.*

Hash House a Go Go / ★★★

3628 5TH AVE, HILLCREST; 619/298-4646 "Exuberant" pretty much sums up the cooking style at this Hillcrest hot spot, known for hulking portions and imaginative presentations of updated diner cuisine. Yes, there's classic fried chicken—but here, it's served on a stack of bacon-flavored waffles, drizzled with a maple glaze, and skewered with a rosemary spear for good measure. Other fun variations: a basic Caesar is gussied up with polenta croutons; fresh grilled fish arrives on vast beds of flavored mashed potatoes; meat loaf is served sandwich-style topped with mozzarella cheese. Even dessert gets an unusual spin: the signature bread pudding comes flavored with peanut butter and chocolate one night, Snickers candy bars the next. The dining room has a comfy, urban-meets-the-family-farm feeling, complete with an ancient wood-burning stove, trendy faux-finished walls, and old tools serving as wall decor. During warm weather, the back patio offers a nice alternative to the bustling dining room, which tends to be noisy. Tip: Unless you have the appetite of a sumo wrestler, spend the extra few dollars to split one of the massive entrees. *$$; AE, DC, DIS, MC, V; no checks; breakfast, lunch, dinner every day; beer and wine; reservations recommended; between Brookes and Pennsylvania Aves.*

Jimmy Carter's Cafe / ★★

3172 5TH AVE, HILLCREST; 619/295-2070 Jimmy Carter's (named for its owner, not the former prez) is the kind of homey but hip cafe we'd love to see in every neighborhood. It's worth a trip to Hillcrest and a wait for a table to sample a meal here. The restaurant serves plenty of homey comfort food—corned beef hash, fluffy omelets, assorted flapjacks, terrific hamburgers and grilled cheese sandwiches—but you can also walk on the wilder side with dishes from the international portions of the menu. The savory *dhosas* (Indian crepes) filled with spicy vegetables are a signature dish; other ethnic fare here includes *huevos rancheros, chilaquiles* (a yummy tortilla casserole), even Mongolian barbecue. A lively, mixed crowd (families, singles, gay, straight, old, young) frequents the cafe, known for its fast service and low prices. Sit in the homey main dining room or in the slightly more spacious area, which includes a smallish bar. Parking around here can be tight; check the side streets off Fifth Avenue for nonmetered spots. *$; AE, MC, V; no checks; breakfast, lunch, dinner every day; beer and wine; reservations not accepted; between Spruce and Redwood Sts.* &

Kemo Sabe / ★★☆

3958 5TH AVE, HILLCREST; 619/220-6802 Forget any references to the Lone Ranger. In this part of town, Kemo Sabe simply means Wow, referring equally to this eatery's spicy fusion fare and the chic, confident decor. From the metal-inlaid tables to the intricate ironworks inspired by primitive Native American art, the look is smashing. The faint of palate need not drop by; chef Deborah Scott's cuisine is fashioned from the fiery personalities of Thailand, Mexico, and the American Southwest. Typical dishes include a grilled fish napoleon layered with pesto, goat cheese, and grilled vegetables; Asian-style dim sum served as a platter for two; and a grilled skirt steak that ought to be served with a fire extinguisher. A good selection of food-friendly wines and bold microbrew beers accompanies the food, and service is hip and accommodating. The location in a happening part of Hillcrest keeps Kemo Sabe hopping; make reservations on weekends. *$$; AE, DIS, MC, V; no checks; dinner every day; full bar; reservations recommended; www.cohnrestaurants.com; between University Ave and Washington St.* &

MiXX / ★★☆

3671 5TH AVE, HILLCREST; 619/299-6499 Consistently one of San Diego's most exciting eateries, trendy MiXX is a place where innumerable culinary influences and ingredients blossom into a nightly kaleidoscope of flavors. The kitchen's goal, as stated on the menu, is "cuisine with no ethnic boundaries." That would explain executive chef Deborah Helm's bold mix of Southwestern, Pacific Rim, traditional French, Vietnamese, and fusion cooking. Daily specials featuring lamb, pork tenderloin, or fish are always worth a try, but don't ignore the regular lineup: a French burnt walnut salad, peppered seared ahi, and duck ravioli helped make MiXX an instant hit on the local dining scene. The two-level restaurant offers a trio of seating options: the piano bar downstairs, a very see-and-be-seen dining room on the second level (with banquette seating and a fairly high noise quotient), and a plant-filled patio offering more privacy at the back. MiXX is known as a showcase for contemporary art—much of it available for sale. *$$; AE, CB, DC, DIS, MC, V; no checks; dinner every day; full bar; reservations recommended; at Pennsylvania Ave.*

Old Town/Mission Valley

RESTAURANTS

Adam's Steak & Eggs / ★★

1201 HOTEL CIRCLE S, MISSION VALLEY; 619/291-1103 Go on a weekday at 10am and you might not have to wait for a table at what may be the best breakfast hangout in town. Yes, you can get a plump, perfect steak and eggs here, with fresh, crispy fried potatoes, but regulars who stop by for a quick meal or full family celebration have more discerning tastes. They order the down-home corn fritters with honey butter, the homemade sausage patty, the enormous Spanish omelet smothered in spicy sauce and sour cream, or the meal-size cinnamon bun. Kids love the fruit smoothies and pancakes. Check out the daily specials, including the Philly steak and eggs covered with sautéed onions—order it with melted cheese on top. The wood tables are tightly packed, and strangers end up sharing sugar, cream, and local tidbits. Adam's is only open till 11:30am (1pm on Saturday and Sunday), but some of the breakfast items are served throughout the day at Albie's, the adjacent steak house. *$; AE, DC, DIS, MC, V; no checks; breakfast every day; full bar; reservations not accepted; frontage road south of I-8.*

Dave & Buster's / ★★

2931 CAMINO DEL RIO N, MISSION VALLEY; 619/280-7115 Fun's the name of the game at this popular restaurant-bar-game arcade, part of a large nationwide chain. Although the dozens of video games, sports simulators, and classic pastimes like Skee-ball attract lots of families, D&B's actually caters to the over-21 crowd. The food and service both tend to be excellent, with a welcoming staff and an ambitious menu that runs from nibbles to full-scale noshes. A few of our favorite plates: crisp bacon-topped potato skins, a shiitake mushroom–avocado quesadilla, falling-off-the-bone pork ribs, halibut-stuffed fish tacos, and a generous cut of ribeye steak. Other excellent choices: the unusual cobb salad topped with spicy, batterfried chicken fingers; the Philly cheese steak sandwich; and the moist grilled mahimahi. For dessert, both the Key lime pie and the chilled bananas Foster are worthwhile. In addition to a small wine list, D&B has several dozen beers and scores of fancy cocktails. Food service is available in the spacious main dining room as well as at the booths and tables scattered throughout the game room. Minors (anyone under 21) must be accompanied by an adult at all times, and the entire place is off-limits to minors after 10pm (11pm during the summer). *$–$$; AE, DC, DISC, MC, V; no checks; lunch, dinner every day; full bar; reservations not accepted; www.dave andbusters.com; near Qualcomm Wy off I-8.*

El Agave / ★★★

2304 SAN DIEGO AVE, OLD TOWN; 619/220-0692 Notorious for its incredible selection of fine tequilas, El Agave is also considered the city's top destination for regional Mexican cuisine. It's a welcome change from most of the other eateries in Old Town, where gringo-style chimichangas and gooey enchiladas reign. This is the place to savor real mole sauce ladled over chicken or pork (the dark, smoky mole poblano here is a standout), rarely seen Mexican soups (the squash soup shouldn't be missed); and other artful dishes, including quesadillas stuffed with vegetables, Mexican cheeses, or shredded seasoned poultry. Another menu favorite is the plump marinated shrimp tossed with beans, cactus strips, and orange. For dessert, authentic versions of flan, a custardlike dish, showcase the sweeter side of Latin cuisine. Now, about that tequila: the restaurant offers more than 100 varieties by the shot, ranging in price from around $4 for familiar brands to well over $100 for rare aged tequilas smoother than old sippin' whiskey. *$$; AE, MC, V; no checks; lunch, dinner every day; full bar; reservations recommended; www.elagaverestaurant.com; corner of San Diego Ave and Old Town Ave.*

King's Fish House / ★★☆

825 CAMINO DE LA REINA, MISSION VALLEY; 619/574-1230 Although this restaurant is part of a chain, it has its own vibrant personality. Servers are smart and friendly; the decor is imaginative (with enormous mounted fish on the walls and Christmas lights in the bar); and the menu is lengthy and appealing. Brilliantly fresh seafood is the star of the show. New Orleans–style barbecued shrimp, deep-fried calamari, and spicy seafood chowder are the best ways to start out. Move on to Parmesan-crusted soft-shell crabs, plank-roasted salmon, pearly white halibut paired with tomato pesto, or simply grilled mahimahi. Two side dishes are included with meals, as are soup or a salad. Oh, and don't forget the refreshing Key lime pie for dessert. The warehouse-like main dining room is a popular choice for families (kids love looking at the stuffed fish, as well as the tanks of live lobsters) though it's certainly comfortable for grown-ups as well. The noisier bar area, where you can dine or simply have a drink, offers live rhythm and blues on the weekends. *$$; AE, DC, DIS, MC, V; no checks; lunch, dinner every day; full bar; reservations recommended; www.kingsfishhouse.com; off Mission Center Rd.* &

Old Town Mexican Cafe / ★★

2489 SAN DIEGO AVE, OLD TOWN; 619/297-4330 For more than 20 years, this local institution has been packing 'em in with a combination of hefty margaritas, festive atmosphere, and filling, well-prepared Mexican food. Invariably crowded and frequently deafening, it's a favorite of both tourists and locals in search of good-size portions, party ambience, and reasonable prices. The cafe is known for its tasty carnitas and carne asada; other worthy choices include sizzling fajitas made with chicken, vegetables, or beef, heaping combo plates served with rice and beans, and chicken enchiladas topped with salsa verde. The original restaurant has expanded to include several dining rooms, but there's still a lengthy wait for a table on most weekend nights. Watch the hardworking "tortilla ladies" plying their craft in the front window while you wait, or angle for a seat at the bar, which serves dozens of high-quality tequilas by the shot. The atmosphere is ultracasual, making this a popular spot for families with children, and the servers and bartenders are unfailingly pleasant. *$–$$; AE, DC, DIS, MC, V; breakfast, lunch, dinner every day; full bar; reservations accepted for 10 or more; www.oldtownmexcafe.com; at Harney St.*

LODGINGS

Comfort Inn and Suites / ★☆

2201 HOTEL CIRCLE S, MISSION VALLEY; 619/291-2711 OR 800/772-6318 Mission Valley has many chain motels for budget travelers who care more about price than luxury. This small inn is one of the nicest, since it is set back a bit from Interstate 8. Don't be thrown by the name; this used to be called the Hotel Circle Inn, and many of the longtime staff members are still around. The inn's 220 rooms were renovated in 2001 and are surprisingly comfortable; those at the far back are the quietest. All rooms have satellite TV with movie channels; rooms with kitchenettes are nearly twice as expensive as those without. There's a wading pool for kids and a laundry room for guests. We think this is one of the best family-oriented bargains in town, and it's also good for business travelers who prefer friendliness to anonymity. Make reservations way in advance of your stay, since the prices rise as room supply diminishes. *$$; AE, CB, DC, DIS, MC, V; checks OK if mailed in advance; www.hotelcircleinn.com; on the south side of I-8.* &

Heritage Park Inn / ★★★

2470 HERITAGE PARK ROW, OLD TOWN; 619/299-6832 OR 800/995-2470 Nestled in a cluster of restored Victorian homes overlooking Old Town, Heritage Park Inn is true to its elegant, old-time roots. Twelve rooms are contained in two historic homes—the circa 1889 Christian House and the Italianate Bushyhead House. With a formal Victorian parlor, period antiques, and stained-glass windows throughout, the ambience is sure to slow your pace. We recommend the romantic Turret Room overlooking the gardens, or the Garret, with its own secret staircase. For more luxury, reserve one of the three rooms in Bushyhead House, with whirlpool tubs for two. Rates include a gourmet breakfast plus a filling afternoon tea of finger sandwiches and sweets. The location is a short stroll from Old Town's shops and restaurants and the trolley stop. *$$–$$$; AE, DC, DIS, MC, V; checks OK; innkeeper@heritageparkinn.com; www.heritageparkinn.com; at the corner of Juan and Harney Sts.*

Mission Beach/Pacific Beach

RESTAURANTS

Cafe Athena / ★

1846 GARNET AVE, PACIFIC BEACH; 858/274-1140 Service has always been the Achilles heel of this comfy, casual Greek eatery in one of Pacific Beach's wood-shingled strip malls, but the food makes up for it. Locals in casual clothes amble in to eat and converse, not to see and be seen. The restaurant's interior, although architecturally uninspired, is gladdened by oil paintings of the Greek Isles crowding the walls. In addition to satisfying dishes such as lemon chicken soup (a bit chunky, with lots of rice) and cinnamon-laced moussaka with a side of rice pilaf, there are some memorable house specialties. Try the Shrimp Scorpio: shrimp grilled and then baked in a spicy sauce of garlic, olive oil, parsley, and tomatoes. Spinach pastitsio is another house specialty; it's a creamy casserole of penne pasta, spinach, and béchamel sauce. For an appetizer, split an order of four delicately flavored bourekia, fried rolls of phyllo stuffed with flavorful ground lamb, onion, and pine nuts. The hummus, tzatziki, and taramasalata are all inspired. There's a brisk business in takeout and a catering service, too. *$; AE, CB, DC, DIS, MC, V; no checks; lunch, dinner every day; beer and wine; reservations recommended for 6 or more; at Lamont in Pacific Plaza II.* &

Cass Street Bar & Grill / ★★

 4612 CASS ST, PACIFIC BEACH; 858/270-1320 No fussy yuppie bar this. Cass Street Bar & Grill caters to locals, who drop by for the camaraderie, the pool tables, the connoisseur's beer selection, and the best bar fare at the beach. Burgers are a customer favorite, and those in the know choose a topping of sautéed onions and melted cheese. The chicken sandwich decorated with avocado and served on a baguette is pretty impressive, and there's a reason that huge marlin is hanging on the wall: the fish is great. Get a fish taco platter with grilled or fried fish, or the fresh fish of the day served with two side dishes, and you'll have plenty to cheer about besides the low prices, microbrews, and congenial crowd. Lose the tie and the high heels before you drop by; this is a shorts and T-shirt kind of a place. *$; Cash only; breakfast, lunch, dinner every day; beer and wine; reservations not accepted; at Felspar St.* &

Ichiban / ★★

1441 GARNET AVE, PACIFIC BEACH; 858/270-5755 / 1499 UNIVERSITY AVE, HILLCREST; 619/299-7203 A ceramic Korean good-luck cat beckons from the window—heed his call and enter. Order at the counter before slipping into one of the comfortable C-shaped black Naugahyde booths. Everything at Ichiban (which means "number one" in Japanese) is delicious and authentic. The teriyaki chicken is an intense trio of chicken, fresh mushrooms, and zucchini in a thick, powerful teriyaki. It's accompanied by perfect sticky rice, a small seafood salad, marinated bean sprouts, and green salad with ginger dressing. The Fried Seafood Mixed has the same side dishes and arrives piping hot. Every day brings four new lunch and dinner specials, usually including a noodle dish and a sushi or sashimi combo. The original Ichiban, in Hillcrest, serves equally delicious food in a more cramped setting, although now with an outdoor patio on busy Washington Street. *$; Cash only (Pacific Beach); MC, V (Hillcrest); no checks (PB & H); lunch Mon–Sat, dinner every day (PB); lunch, dinner every day (H); beer and wine (PB); no alcohol (H); reservations not accepted (PB & H); between Gresham and Haines (PB); near Normal St (H).*

The Mission / ★

3795 MISSION BLVD, MISSION BEACH; 858/488-9060 Longtime fans of this admittedly funky cafe don't mind the faded decor, the thrift-shop furnishings, or the tough parking situation during summer. They're interested in one thing: good food, and lots of it. The menu at this beachy eatery (just a block from the Mission Beach boardwalk) makes a big deal of breakfast—well worth a long, calorie-burning stroll afterwards. Pancakes, waffles, smoothies, breakfast burritos, and other morning foods shine; standouts include banana-blackberry pancakes, rosemary roasted potatoes, thick French toast, and low-fat fruit smoothies. Best off all, breakfast items are served until 3pm for you sleepyheads. Be prepared to wait quite a while on the weekends for a table, and don't dress up: sandals, tanks, and shorts fit this place to a tee. *$; AE, MC, V; no checks; breakfast, lunch every day; beer and wine; reservations not accepted; off W Mission Bay Dr.*

Nick's at the Beach / ★★

809 THOMAS ST, PACIFIC BEACH; 858/270-1730 Nick's is really two restaurants in one, both of them fun. On the first floor, a small bar area and spacious dining room offer a wide variety of well-priced, well-prepared meals ranging from meat loaf to Cajun gumbo. We're certain that the mussels steamed with tomatillos and lime juice take top honors here, but the competition is stiff from Nick's Caesar salad, the quesadilla stuffed with garlic mashed potatoes, the well-seasoned crab cakes, and the fresh fish specials. Upstairs, a young crowd parties with a CD jukebox, four pool tables, lots of TVs, and a terrific late-night menu served daily till 1am. A recent remodel added an ocean-view patio upstairs, while creating a needed bit of sound-proofing and intimacy in the main dining room below. In addition to a stellar collection of beers on tap, the wine list offers lots of selections by both glass and bottle at user-friendly prices. No one under 21 is allowed upstairs. *$–$$; AE, DIS, MC, V; no checks; lunch, dinner every day (bar menu until 1am); full bar; reservations recommended; www.nicksatthebeach.com; at Mission Blvd.* &

Rubio's / ★★

4504 MISSION BAY DR, PACIFIC BEACH (AND BRANCHES); 858/272-2801 What a success story: local boy visits Baja, falls in love with the fish tacos there, opens a tiny restaurant in Pacific Beach selling same, and gains fortune and fame. Millions of battered-and-fried fish tacos later, founder Ralph Rubio has extended the menu at this thriving chain of restaurants, which numbers more than two dozen in San Diego County alone and is rapidly spreading through the West. These days, you'll find fresh, flavorful takes on Mexican cuisine: everything from grilled mahimahi tacos and shrimp burritos to Baja Bowls (a beans-and-rice spin on the ubiquitous Asian rice bowl). A special HealthMex menu offers entrees with less than 22 percent of their calories from fat. But it's the original fish taco, made with a plump white fillet, a flurry of shredded cabbage, and a ranchlike dressing folded into a corn tortilla, that keeps Rubio's ardent fans coming back for takeout or a quick bite in the informal, sparkling-clean dining rooms. *$; AE, DC, DIS, MC, V; no checks; lunch, dinner every day; beer and wine; reservations not necessary; www.rubios.com; between Grand and Garnet Aves.* &

LODGINGS

Crystal Pier Hotel & Cottages / ★★★

4500 OCEAN BLVD, PACIFIC BEACH; 858/483-6983 OR 800/748-5894 Drive your car across the boardwalk and onto the pier. Park in front of a blue-and-white country cottage with flowers abloom beneath shuttered windows. Open the front door; gaze across the living room and kitchen to your back porch perched over the sea. The 26 Crystal Pier cottages are claimed months in advance by families who set out barbecue grills, fill the fridge, and hang their beach towels over lounge chairs and wood railings. The scene is more peaceful during the off-seasons, when couples and singles claim the cottages as private escapes. Winter nights are particularly exciting when the surf is high and the air has a salty chill. One longs for a fireplace to complete the ambience; sadly, there aren't any. The boardwalk scene is just a few steps away if you want to grab a great meal, rent a bike or boogie board, or mingle with humanity. Advance reservations are absolutely essential in summer. *$$$; AE, MC, V; no checks; www.crystalpier.com; at Garnet Ave.* &

Dana Inn / ★★

1710 W MISSION BAY DR, MISSION BAY; 619/222-6440 OR 800/445-3339
Among the expensive resorts at Mission Bay, this simple hotel stands as family-friendly and affordable. The 196 rooms are spread about the property in two-story wood buildings. Sensible rather than picturesque, the rooms all have small refrigerators, coffeemakers, and single or double beds; the wood-veneer and plastic furniture withstands sandy bodies and wet towels. Family members stay entertained with shuffleboard and tennis courts; two pools; bike, skate, and water-sports rentals; and all the parks and playgrounds on the bay. SeaWorld sits just across the water (there's a shuttle from the hotel), providing free entertainment with the nighttime fireworks exploding overhead. The coffee shop does a decent job with home-style meals. Rooms book quickly in summer and get more expensive as supply diminishes. *$$; AE, DC, DIS, JCB, MC, V; checks OK if mailed in advance; at Dana Landing Rd.*

Hilton San Diego Resort / ★★★

1775 E MISSION BAY DR, MISSION BAY; 619/276-4010 OR 800/221-2424 Craving action and adventure with spa treatments on the side? You belong at this swath of beach, bike paths, lawns, and terraces beside Mission Bay. Facilities include several swimming pools, tennis courts, fitness center, and equipment rentals for nearly every water or land sport you can imagine. The 357 tropical-style rooms and suites, with tables and chairs for group snacks and games (or laptops if you must), are scattered through Mediterranean-style low-rise buildings (complete with terraces and balconies) beside the bay and one eight-story building facing Interstate 5. Rollerbladers whiz by from dawn to dusk, following trails for miles along the bay. Kites of every shape float in the sky. Multigenerational families celebrate weddings, birthdays, and sunny Sundays with elaborate picnics all around the hotel, and visitors are completely immersed in the SoCal scene. *$$$; AE, DC, MC, V; checks OK; between Clairemont and Sea World Drs.* &

Paradise Point Resort / ★★★

1404 W VACATION RD, MISSION BAY; 858/274-4630 OR 800/344-2626 Originally opened by a Hollywood producer in the 1960s as Vacation Village South Seas Paradise, this sprawling 44-acre resort has gone through several transformations. The 462 rooms and suites are housed in single-level buildings and have private patios, refrigerators, and coffeemakers. Most have dark patterned carpeting (to hide the marks of sandy feet), red, white, and blue linens, and marble baths. Guests are kept ultrabusy with four swimming pools, an 18-hole putting course, tennis courts, and volleyball nets on the sand. The marina offers water-sport rentals; the activity center provides bikes. The luxurious spa is a major plus—you can always sneak away for a Balinese massage while the kids are playing. Restaurants include the ever-popular Barefoot Bar on the sand along with the upscale Baleen dining room. *$$$; AE, DC, DIS, MC, V; checks OK if mailed in advance; www.paradisepoint.com; at Ingraham St.* &

Ocean Beach/Point Loma

RESTAURANTS

Point Loma Seafoods / ★★

2805 EMERSON ST, POINT LOMA; 619/223-1109 Generations of San Diegans have lined up at the counter of this seafood market, purchasing fresh fish or ordering takeout. The place is almost always jammed, and with good reason: year after year, the quality of the goods and service here are superior to that of any other fish market in San Diego. Fish and seafood (including live clams, crabs, and lobsters) are expensive, but always divinely fresh. The shop is also known for moist, just-smoked fish (which makes terrific picnic fixings), appealing seafood salads, sourdough bread, and a decent wine selection. Top takeout foods (which you can eat on the harborside patio) are the excellent clam chowder, seafood ceviche, fresh tuna sandwich, and shrimp or crab cocktails. Service is knowledgeable and cheerful, even during rush hours. The location adjacent to the busy sportfishing docks can make parking a pain, but one bite of this restaurant's smoked swordfish or fried calamari and you'll be glad you dropped by. *$; No credit cards; local checks only; lunch, dinner every day (until 7pm); beer and wine; reservations not necessary; off Scott St.* &

Qwiigs Bar & Grill / ★★

5083 SANTA MONICA AVE, OCEAN BEACH; 619/222-1101 Snag a window table at sunset for the ultimate Ocean Beach dining experience right across from the water. Qwiigs offers spectacular views of surfers, joggers, seagulls, and the O.B. Pier. Locals gather for steamed artichokes, bountiful house salads, fried calamari, and gourmet pizzas in the upper-level cocktail lounge or hover around the busy little sushi bar. The dining room features cozy ocean-view tables with prized window seats and raised U-shaped booths that also face the outdoor spectacle. The place is packed at sunset, naturally. Enormous fresh cobb salads (we prefer the chicken version over the seafood salad) and thick burgers are good bets at lunch. Dinner specials might include rack of lamb or penne pesto with Japanese breaded chicken breast along with the fresh fish and blackened prime rib. A sit-down Sunday brunch includes average-to-good breakfast fare. The ambience and service are fairly low-key; while some people show up in ties and work suits at lunch, this is definitely one of those come-as-you-are neighborhood haunts. Use the underground parking lot if possible; spots on the street can be tough to find. *$$; AE, DC, DIS, MC, V; no checks; lunch Mon–Fri, dinner every day, brunch Sun; full bar; reservations recommended; off Abbott St.*

Thee Bungalow / ★★★

4996 W POINT LOMA BLVD, OCEAN BEACH; 619/224-2884 For 30 years, this family-run restaurant in a converted bungalow home has kept a faithful clientele while attracting new fans. Some diners stick with the classics: roast duck garnished with green peppercorns, sea bass in a luscious seafood sauce, and rack of lamb. Others are attracted by chef/owner Ed Moore's newer creations, including superb steamed mussels, black-pepper-crusted salmon, and grilled halibut.

Since you get soup or salad with your entree (we adore the smoked tomato soup and the tarragon-dressed house salad), you don't need to order a starter. But if you're extra ravenous, do start with the simple cream-sauced tortellini. Wrap up the evening with a crackle-topped crème brûlée, a Bungalow specialty. The lengthy wine list earns praise for both depth of selection and excellent prices, and the restaurant regularly hosts reasonably priced, heavily attended wine dinners. Although the service and menu are a tad on the formal side, the setting is casual and comfy. Show up in jeans or in jewels—the good people of Thee Bungalow will welcome you just the same. *$$; AE, DC, DIS, MC, V; no checks; dinner every day; full bar; reservations recommended; bungalow@adnc.com; www.theebungalow.com; at Bacon St.* ♿

Coronado

RESTAURANTS

Azzura Point / ★★★

4000 CORONADO BAY RD (LOEWS CORONADO BAY RESORT), CORONADO; 619/424-4477 A perennial contender for most scenic restaurant in San Diego, this dining room at the Loews Coronado Bay Resort is a star. A multimillion-dollar renovation turned the harbor-view restaurant into a vision of safari chic that perfectly reflects the resort atmosphere. Service is polished and knowledgeable, the wine list extensive (and expensive). Despite a few chef changes over recent years, the kitchen still turns out fantastic dishes incorporating Pacific Rim, classic French, and Mediterranean flavors. Pristinely fresh fish and shellfish imported from around the world always sparkle; particular standouts are the oysters splashed with sake vinaigrette, the lobster risotto, and France's rare loup de mer. Hearty red meat dishes like beef tenderloin complemented with a heavenly blue cheese tart are also nicely done. Nightly prix-fixe dinners offer multicourse tasting menus that are a signature of this dining room and a fine way to sample the cuisine. A lighter menu of small plates and appetizers is available in the adjacent bar. *$$$–$$$$; AE, MC, V; no checks; dinner Tues–Sun; full bar; reservations recommended; www.loewshotels.com; off Silver Strand Hwy.* ♿

Chez Loma / ★★☆

1132 LOMA AVE, CORONADO; 619/435-0661 Before you even enter this restaurant, you'll be charmed by the handsome Victorian house and old-money elegance of the Coronado neighborhood. Inside, chef Ken Irvine's graceful mix of classic and updated French cuisine is sure to impress. The small menu emphasizes seasonal seafood and usually includes stellar preparations of duck, salmon, and filet mignon (including a signature steak in a heady blue cheese sauce). The servers here are particularly well trained—always available when needed, but never intrusive. Add a carefully chosen wine list, romantic enclosed patio, and very fair prices for the quality, and you've got one of Coronado's most delightful eateries. It's an especially good choice for couples celebrating anniversaries. Although children are welcome, this is one of the more grown-up-feeling establishments in town. *$$–$$$; AE, DC, DIS, MC, V; no checks; dinner every day, brunch Sun; full bar; reservations recommended; www.chezloma.com; at Orange Ave.* ♿

The Prince of Wales / ★★☆

1500 ORANGE AVE (HOTEL DEL CORONADO), CORONADO; 619/522-8819 All the glamour of the Hotel del Coronado's past comes to life in its elegant dining room, where strains of live jazz piano accompany leisurely meals. You can dine under the stars on the candlelit terrace, or view the sea from the long windows in the serene champagne and gold dining room. Reserve a booth for privacy, and order slowly. Start with a flute of imported bubbly with the osetra caviar parfait or oysters with sweet sake sorbet while you study the entrees and consider whether you want to experiment with the wild boar tenderloin or the yellowfin tuna with sautéed foie gras and truffle coulis. While a tie isn't mandatory, it certainly isn't out of place and makes for a nice change of pace in laid-back San Diego. This is the place to come for the special celebration—or just to revel in the good life for an evening. A wonderful wine selection complements the menu and impeccable service. *$$$$; AE, CB, DC, DIS, MC, V; no checks; dinner every day; full bar; reservations recommended; www.hoteldel.com; at Glorietta Blvd.* &

LODGINGS

Glorietta Bay Inn / ★★☆

1630 GLORIETTA BLVD, CORONADO; 619/435-3101 OR 800/283-9383 John Spreckels, the sugar baron fond of all things grand and glorious for his vision of Coronado, hired architect Harrison Albright to design his family mansion on a sloping lawn facing the bay in 1908. The mansion now houses 11 of the hotel's rooms; the rest are in less glamorous (and less expensive) buildings with balconies and gardens above the bay. The original house is a wonder of polished wood, brass, glass, swooping marble stairways, and eye-boggling antiques. The rooms are the perfect beginning for a tour through Coronado's history. The hotel attracts an amiable clientele, and guests tend to linger in the Music Room exchanging vacation tips while eating the complimentary continental breakfast. The staff has justifiably garnered several awards for service—guests tend to feel quite at home here. *$$$; AE, DC, DIS, MC, V; checks OK (2 weeks in advance); www.gloriettabayinn.com; at Orange Ave.* &

Hotel del Coronado / ★★★☆

☀ **1500 ORANGE AVE, CORONADO; 619/435-6611 OR 800/HOTEL DEL** Opened in 1888, this sprawling, white-frame Victorian confection of red-roofed turrets, stained glass, and crown-shaped chandeliers is a National Historic Landmark that has hosted 14 U.S. presidents. It also played a starring role—alongside Marilyn Monroe, Jack Lemmon, and Tony Curtis—in *Some Like It Hot*. If you like the bustling activity of a full-service resort, with its scheduled activities, shopping arcade, and such, the Del should fit the bill. Many of the rooms in the original building overlook the lovely Windsor Lawn and the beach. Eight beachfront cottages set right above the sand command high nightly rates, though their decor is rather motel-like. The more peaceful Ocean Tower's spacious, comfortable rooms overlook the Pacific or the bay, and are decorated like country cottages in shades of blue and green; the tower has its own pool and a nice stretch of beach. Several dining choices are led by the upscale Prince of Wales, where a fine seasonal menu is served in an indoor-outdoor beachfront setting (see review). The Babcock & Story Bar is a great spot for sunset cocktails. Locals and tourists mob the Crown Room for Sunday brunch—make advance reservations. *$$$; AE, DC, DIS, MC, V; checks OK; www.hoteldel.com; on Coronado Island.* &

Loews Coronado Bay Resort / ★★★

4000 CORONADO BAY RD, CORONADO; 619/424-4000 OR 800/235-6397 This self-contained compound sprawls beside San Diego Bay at the southern end of Coronado. The 438 rooms and suites all have water views and balconies; the best sit at the tip of the resort facing the 80-slip marina. Kids get rubber ducks and bubbles in the giant bathtubs—although first they have to kick out the grown-ups. Chairs, couches, and beds are all comfy; it's hard to leave them for the padded pool chairs—though the idea of Häagen-Dazs bars sold poolside is enticing. Energized souls sign up at Action Sports for sailboats, paddleboats, and bikes; lovers drift under the setting sun in gondolas. The hotel's spa should be completed by the time you read this, so there will be yet another reason to stay put. If you must go out, shuttles run regularly to Coronado's shopping area and downtown's Horton Plaza. Consider splurging on the hotel's picturesque Azzura Point restaurant, one of San Diego's very finest (see review). *$$$$; AE, DC, MC, V; checks OK; www.loews hotels.com; off Silver Strand Hwy.* &

La Jolla

RESTAURANTS

Azul La Jolla / ★★☆

1250 PROSPECT ST, LA JOLLA; 858/454-9616 Since opening in 1999, this striking eatery owned by the Brigantine Restaurant Corporation has become a destination for both tourists and locals lured by the wide-ranging menu and the terrific locale. Azul (Spanish for "blue") is anchored on the hill above La Jolla Cove with a see-forever view of the Pacific. An extensive renovation turned this site of many a failed restaurant into a gorgeous grotto-like room, dramatically lit and decorated. The best tables are along the windows, of course, but the two-level dining room assures an ocean view from many of the booths farther back. The menu, which changes often, is heavy on Mediterranean-influenced dishes, including seafood paella, a marinated calamari salad, and assorted tapas served as a buffet. As befits the seaside locale, fish is a specialty—do try the salmon on a bed of ratatouille and the John Dory offered as a nightly special. Service is unfailingly pleasant, and there's a special menu just for kids. Along with the dining room, there's seating in a more intimate bar area and a patio warmed by a fire. *$$; AE, CB, DC, MC, V; no checks; lunch Tues–Sat, dinner every day, brunch Sun; full bar; reservations recommended; www.azul-lajolla.com; between Ivanhoe Ave and Cave St.*

Cafe Japengo / ★★

8960 UNIVERSITY CENTER LN, LA JOLLA; 858/450-3355 Owned by the adjacent Hyatt Regency La Jolla, Cafe Japengo is one of the most stylish and sophisticated restaurants in San Diego County, catering to the unabashedly trendy who relish attitude along with their order. (On weekend nights in particular, the young professional crowd pours in for drinks, sushi, and a serious singles scene.) The decor is a marvelous combination of industrial chic, Asian design, and California cliché—exposed-duct ceilings, Japanese-pebble flooring, Chinese paper lanterns, bamboo and bird-of-paradise, an exhibition kitchen, and a showpiece sushi bar. The menu is well coordinated with the environment—an eclectic blend of Asian inspiration and North and South American influences. Dinners include an excellent green tea–smoked salmon paired with pearly Israeli couscous, slow-roasted duck served moo-shu style with plum sauce and tortillas, glistening pot stickers to be dipped in cilantro pesto, and 10-ingredient wok-fried rice. For dessert, exotic gelatos in flavors like red bean or green tea make refreshing palate cleansers. *$$$; AE, DC, DIS, MC, V; no checks; lunch Mon–Fri, dinner every day; full bar; reservations recommended; www.cafe japengo.com; at La Jolla Village Dr.*

George's at the Cove / ★★☆

 1250 PROSPECT ST, LA JOLLA; 858/454-4244 Without a doubt, the three-level property has one of the finest views in the city—a panorama of La Jolla Cove and miles of Pacific coast. But unlike many a view restaurant in town, George's offers some terrific eating as well. The formal downstairs dining room is best for inventive fresh fish dishes that incorporate the flavors of France and the Pacific Rim. The must-have starter is a smoked chicken and broccoli soup (yes, they'll share the recipe). Follow that with the likes of crab cakes with shiitake "hash browns," diver-harvested scallops partnered with lobster risotto, or duck breast paired with buttery foie gras. Upstairs, in the bar (a top destination for singles) and on the rooftop terrace, the menu is a lower-priced affair featuring excellent seafood salads, a gourmet meat loaf sandwich, very good focaccia, and splendid desserts. Two more reasons to drop by: the ever-changing collection of contemporary art in the main dining rooms, and owner George Hauer's thoughtfully chosen wine list. Reservations aren't accepted on the upstairs terrace, which is open daily for lunch and dinner, but the open-air setting and throngs of swell-looking diners make it worth the wait. *$$–$$$; AE, DC, DIS, MC, V; no checks; lunch, dinner every day; full bar; reservations recommended downstairs; www. georgesatthecove.com; at Torrey Pines Rd.*

Karl Strauss Brewery & Grill / ★★

9675 SCRANTON RD, SORRENTO VALLEY (AND BRANCHES); 858/587-2739 Part of a locally founded chain that's become wildly popular over the last decade, this casual brewery-restaurant is set in a deceptively elegant Japanese garden. Half the fun of visiting here is winding along the paths and through the greenery to the koi pond and inviting deck; the other is knocking back well-made ales (along with an impressive selection of wines by the glass) and chowing down on filling traditional bar fare. Specialties of the house include plump, spicy sausages, well-made burgers, sandwiches from Philly-style steak to portobello mushroom, filet mignon, and grilled salmon. Given the sizable business crowd that populates Sorrento Valley and the nearby Golden Triangle area, this can be heaven for yuppie singles, especially during happy hour. Keep in mind that the restaurant is closed on Saturdays, when it's often booked for wedding receptions and corporate parties. Also located in the downtown business district (1157 Columbia St; 619/234-2739) and in La Jolla's village (1044 Wall St; 858/551-2739). *$; AE, MC, V; no checks; lunch, dinner Sun–Fri (closed Sat for private parties); beer and wine; reservations recommended; www.karl strauss.com; at Mira Mesa Blvd.*

The Marine Room / ★★★⯪

2000 SPINDRIFT DR, LA JOLLA; 858/459-7222 Between the unparalleled oceanfront location, the special-occasion ambience, and the talents of executive chef Bernard Guillas, the Marine Room is a true original. The dining rooms offer unrestricted views of the coastline; the central bar has the cozy buzz of locals gossiping over gin and tonics. Light-colored decor and crisp white linens create an airy, open feel. The French native chef infuses his brand of Mediterranean–Pacific Rim–California fare with imaginative flavors, from sambuca and fresh lavender to candied shallots and crunchy greens from the sea. Halibut, foie gras, ahi, and sweetbreads are some of the standouts on the menu, which changes according to the season and the chef's whims. Recent highlights include halibut poached in pinot noir, dry-aged strip steak with truffle-based potatoes, and the goose liver paired with preserved cherries and Cognac. Check out the restaurant's dramatic High Tide Breakfasts during winter, complete with a luxurious buffet and waves misting the windows. Since the dining room is connected to the La Jolla Beach and Tennis Club, you'll see some casually clad folks here, along with plenty who are dressed to complement the formal cuisine. *$$$; AE, CB, DC, DIS, MC, V; no checks; lunch Tues–Sun, dinner every day, brunch Sun; full bar; reservations recommended; www.marineroom.com; at Torrey Pines Rd.*

Roppongi / ★★⯪

875 PROSPECT ST, LA JOLLA; 858/551-5252 Local restaurateur Sami Ladeki, founder of the hugely popular, family-friendly Sammy's Woodfired Pizza chain (see review), has gone upmarket with this flashy La Jolla endeavor. It's a sight to behold, from the expensive bric-a-brac to the spectacular aquarium with Day-Glo tropical fish. And the requisitely trendy menu, colored with influences from cutting-edge Pacific Rim to classic Americana, dazzles as well—as long as you stick to the appetizers and skip the so-so entrees. The key to dining at Roppongi is to graze, tapas style, through the list of superb starters. A multilayered crab napoleon; skewered scallops, plump and pretty as South Pacific pearls; fiery kung pao calamari; pot stickers filled with shrimp; and more—each is an exquisite, if expensive, little treat. The open dining room includes booth and table seating. Out front, a raised fire pit keeps diners comfortable on the coolest evenings. Service ranges from adept to iffy, and the wine list is overpriced, but those top-notch tapas keep us coming back. *$$$; AE, DIS, MC, V; no checks; lunch, dinner every day; full bar; reservations recommended; www.roppongiusa.com; at Fay St.* ♿

Sammy's California Woodfired Pizza / ★★

565 PEARL ST, LA JOLLA (AND BRANCHES); 858/456-5222 San Diego has never been the same since Sami Ladeki brought wood-fired pizza to town. Savor varieties such as Jamaican Jerk Shrimp (with cilantro and carrots), Artichokes (with tomato sauce, mozzarella, and Gorgonzola cheese), or Smoked Duck Sausage (with spinach, Roma tomatoes, garlic, and smoked Gouda). Other mouthwatering offerings include Norwegian salmon fillet, grilled chicken salad, and some exquisite pasta dishes (the Four Cheese Ravioli in cream sauce with wild mushrooms and spinach is an artery-clogging trip to heaven). The open kitchen lets you keep a close eye on your order. A full takeout menu is offered. Over a dozen San Diego County branches include Horton Plaza downtown (770 4th Ave; 619/230-8888), Mission Valley (1620 Camino de la Reina; 619/298-8222), and Del Mar (12925 El Camino Real; 858/259-6600). *$; AE, DC, MC, V; no checks; lunch, dinner every day; full bar; reservations not accepted; www.sammyspizza.com; at Del Mar Heights.* &

The Sky Room / ★★★⯪

1132 PROSPECT ST (LA VALENCIA HOTEL), LA JOLLA; 858/454-0771
Saying La Valencia's the Sky Room is romantic is like calling Placido Domingo a pretty good singer. This ocean-view dining room atop La Jolla's venerable pink hotel is the place to treat yourself to an evening of elegance and pomp. Gorgeous flower arrangements, tuxedo-clad servers, Wedgwood china, and long-stemmed roses for the ladies provide a feeling of old-world elegance and a lovely showcase for California and French cuisine. Selections range from contemporary (free-range chicken with morels; fine Kobe beef imported from Japan) to classic (delicate smoked salmon paired with julienned cucumber; cream of mushroom soup; velvety foie gras). If they're offering the filet mignon finished with a merlot demi-glace, it's a must-have. So is the dessert plate, a selection of sweets that generally includes tidbits of tiramisu, cookies, and sublime chocolate truffles. An extensive wine list is particularly strong in California cabernet and chardonnay; high rollers find plenty of premium French labels, including vintage champagnes. The courtly waiters and helpful sommelier, along with the rarefied ambience, leave you feeling like royalty. Stop by the piano bar in the lobby after dinner for a nightcap of good music in one of La Jolla's loveliest rooms. *$$$–$$$$; AE, CB, DC, DIS, MC, V; no checks; dinner every day; full bar; reservations required; www.lavalencia.com; at Herschel St.* &

Top o' the Cove / ★★★

1216 PROSPECT ST, LA JOLLA; 858/454-7779 With its lushly planted courtyard entrance, piano bar, and several tables overlooking the Pacific, Top o' the Cove is a romantic's dream, as well as a choice spot for upscale business dining. (Table 6 is considered the top spot for couples in love.) The kitchen's blend of classic French, Pacific Rim, and Mediterranean flavors is as impressive as the view. Over the past two years, the restaurant has undergone a couple of chef shuffles, but the kitchen manages to remain consistent. An appetizer of risotto and white truffles is exquisite (and should be, for the price). Entree-wise, grilled swordfish or salmon, often sauced with a cabernet sauvignon reduction that's perfect for these full-flavored fish, are our first choices. A rare-roasted Muscovy duck breast is another standout. The restaurant's wine list is breathtaking in both depth and price; you can easily drop $100 or more on a bottle. Note that reservations are confirmed with a credit card; for parties of six or larger, you'll be charged unless you cancel 48 hours

TIDEPOOL TANGO

The small animals that inhabit coastal tidepools are some of the most adaptive and tenacious on the planet. Living in an environment that undergoes tidal changes four times a day, these little creatures are the commandants of compromise. At low tide their watery sanctuary disappears, exposing them to the broiling sun, increased salinity, and hungry predators. To survive, mussels collect seawater inside their bodies, then slowly release it to cool by evaporation. Sea anemones fold inward, trapping tiny drops of water to sustain themselves until the flow of water returns. At high tide, they are once again flooded, with rough swirls of seawater threatening to evict them from their homes. Barnacles hold on to rocks for dear life or risk being hurled up on the beach or out to sea. Sea urchins stay put by burrowing their spines deep into the rocks on which they live. There is also a constant threat of being eaten by a neighbor. Clams, scallops, and oysters are the favored dinner of the carnivorous sea star, which in turn makes a fitting snack for a gull or a crow. If this wet, miniature-scale drama sounds interesting, San Diego has several prime spots for front-row viewing. Put on your rubber-soled tennis shoes and head for **BIRD ROCK**, the **COVE** in La Jolla, or the tidepools located on the western side of **POINT LOMA**, near Cabrillo Monument. **BIRCH AQUARIUM AT SCRIPPS** offers classes on tidepooling and can provide information on the best times for viewing. Call 858/534-7336 for more information.

—Susan Humphrey

in advance. $$$–$$$$; AE, CB, DC, MC, V; no checks; lunch, dinner every day, brunch Sun; full bar; reservations recommended; www.topofthecove.com; between Ivanhoe Ave and Cave St. &

Trattoria Acqua / ★★☆

1298 PROSPECT ST, LA JOLLA; 858/454-0709 This indoor-outdoor restaurant is nestled into a La Jolla Cove hillside with ocean views that won't quit. But pretty views are a nickel a dozen in this seaside town; Acqua stands apart for delivering high-quality food and service too. The Mediterranean-influenced menu roams gracefully from Tuscany to Provence to Tangiers, with stops for excellent designer pizzas, a variety of antipasti and salads, about a dozen pastas, and lots of grilled fish and meats. Start your meal with the complimentary spicy hummus dip while you peruse the lengthy wine list, where notable names from California and Italy are sold at reasonable prices. Must-have dishes are the grilled portobello mushroom or bruschetta for starters; among the pastas, the lobster ravioli, penne Piedmontese, or rigatoni with eggplant; and for main dishes, the veal shank or herb-crusted halibut. Prime seating is on the patio or at one of the inside tables with a view of the water (reserve these well in advance). Validated parking is available in the garage under the building. $$; AE, MC, V; no checks; lunch, dinner every day; full bar; reservations recommended; www.trattoriacqua.com; at Torrey Pines Rd. &

LODGINGS

The Bed & Breakfast Inn of La Jolla / ★★☆

7753 DRAPER AVE, LA JOLLA; 858/456-2066 OR 800/582-2466 It's easy to miss the ivy-covered entrance to this pleasant hideaway just a few blocks from busy Prospect Street. Designed by architect Irving Gill in 1913 as a private home, it's a historic treasure once occupied by John Philip Sousa in the '20s. Kate Sessions, San Diego's grande dame of horticulture, designed the original gardens. Today, the 16 rooms offer a taste of genteel living. You'll find plenty of nice touches—fresh flowers, sherry, and fruit in the rooms, antiques and original artworks that lend the air of a private home. The Holiday Room is a romantic retreat with a four-poster bed and working fireplace. If you want a view of the water, reserve the Irving Gill Penthouse Suite, which has a private deck. The upstairs Peacock Room has a private balcony for sunbathing—you'll feel like you're at an elegant Côte d'Azur pension. Breakfast is served on Royal Albert bone china in the dining room or by the fountain on the patio. *$$$; AE, MC, V; no checks; bed+breakfast@innlajolla.com; www.innlajolla. com; off Prospect St.*

Hotel Parisi / ★★★

1111 PROSPECT ST, LA JOLLA; 858/454-1511 OR 877/4PARISI More urban and hip than what you'd normally expect in San Diego, the Parisi is a 20-room boutique property in the heart of La Jolla. The spare, contemporary high-design concept seems to float above the hubbub of Prospect Street. Indeed, the hotel occupies the top floor of a mixed-use retail building. Guests are greeted by a calming lobby with a natural stone fountain and a fireplace, in keeping with the elements of feng shui that were incorporated in the design. The rooms are restful cocoons in shades of sand and taupe, outfitted with simple custom-made furnishings and beds dressed in inviting white-linen duvets. Flame-cut steel and wood nightstands are offset by cozy, slipcovered chairs; the overall effect is serenely uncluttered without being cold. Rooms overlooking Prospect Street have a view of La Valencia Hotel just across the street, as well as a partial ocean view. *$$$$; AE, DIS, JCB, MC, V; no checks; www. hotelparisi.com; corner of Herschel and Prospect Sts.* &

La Valencia Hotel / ★★★★☆

1132 PROSPECT ST, LA JOLLA; 858/454-0771 OR 800/451-0772 To many residents and visitors, La Valencia Hotel is La Jolla. The Mediterranean-style "Pink Lady" has reigned over Prospect Street since 1926, and it's always been a hub of activity for well-heeled guests and local bigwigs. The hotel's 117 rooms, suites, and villas are individually decorated. Some have a green floral motif; others boast a beachy blue-and-white seashell theme. Naturally, rooms with million-dollar views of La Jolla Cove are the most desirable, though guests with ample discretionary cash opt for the 17 smashing villas (where rates start at $550 per night). Private butlers stock the villas' fridges with the guests' favorite treats—a sampler of pâtés and cheeses, perhaps, or just the right bubbly. The butlers also unpack your luggage, draw your bath, take your shoes to be shined, and do whatever you desire (within reason). The hotel's public spaces have a pleasant hum of activity. Every afternoon, the Mediterranean Room patio is filled with ladies who lunch, and the

Whaling Bar is a favorite local hangout. At sunset, head to La Sala Lounge, sink into a sofa, and enjoy the view. Be sure to check out the hand-painted ceiling overhead. *$$$$; AE, DC, DIS, MC, V; checks OK; www.lavalencia.com; at Herschel St.* &

The Lodge at Torrey Pines / ★★★★

11480 N TORREY PINES RD, LA JOLLA; 858/453-4420 OR 800/656-0087 Combining understated elegance with authentic Arts and Crafts style, this new resort, whose peaceful grounds line the oceanfront Torrey Pines Golf Course, is an homage to the Craftsman aesthetic. Guest rooms and public spaces all meticulously recreate the rich woods, sensuous stained glass, low-slung architecture, and organic motifs that characterize classic Arts and Crafts style of the early 20th century—many elements are faithfully reproduced from iconic designs by Frank Lloyd Wright, Gustav Stickley, and others. Modestly sized yet fully equipped, the lodge feels like a warm Craftsman mansion, but boasts essential modern amenities and comforts for today's upscale traveler. Guests receive preferred tee times at the hard-to-book Torrey Pines Golf Course, the longtime home of PGA's Buick Invitational and site of the 2008 US Open. The full-service spa features authentic Charles Rennie MacIntosh designs, and offers a sleek, chic respite from the cares of the day. Just the tranquil relaxation lounges (snuggly chaises for the ladies, wide-screen TV for men) stocked with tea and snacks are lure enough, but don't miss the signature Coastal Sage Scrub, a three-part ritual featuring intoxicating custom-blended lemongrass-sage products. For a memorable meal, make reservations for A.R. Valentien, named for the early California artist whose collectible works grace the restaurant. Impeccably prepared fresh regional fare draws foodies from across San Diego county to this well-regarded dining room. *$$$$; AE, DC, DIS, MC, V; checks OK; www.lodgeattorreypines.com; adjacent to Torrey Pines Golf Course.* &

Scripps Inn / ★★

555 COAST BLVD S, LA JOLLA; 858/454-3391 Guests check in to this tiny hotel for weeks, setting up housekeeping just steps from the coastline and stately Ellen Browning Scripps Park. Two buildings face each other in a narrow lot; some privacy is lost, but the location and reasonable room rate are worth the close quarters. Most of the 14 rooms have views of the sea; the best have working fireplaces and ocean-view balconies. Rooms and suites (some with two bedrooms) have refrigerators, sitting areas, and fold-out sofas; white walls, pale tan furnishings, and French doors give a breezy, relaxed feel. A complimentary breakfast of pastries and coffee is served on the lobby terrace. There's no pool—but who needs one when the best snorkeling spot on the coast is just a few steps away? Book a room at this little gem way in advance of your trip, and consider splurging on rooms 6 or 12, both with fireplaces and full views. *$$$; AE, DIS, MC, V; checks OK; www.scrippsinn.com; at Cuvier St.*

Sea Lodge / ★★★

8110 CAMINO DEL ORO, LA JOLLA; 858/459-8271 OR 800/237-5211 Lucky are those who happen upon this hidden beachfront hotel, tucked down a side street at La Jolla Shores Beach. Low-rise tiled roof buildings frame a central courtyard and pool; Mexican painted tiles and terra-cotta fountains add a Spanish feel to the 128-room complex. Floral plants and light rattan furnishings lighten up the rooms facing the courtyard; those with a view of the sea are filled with sunlight. The restaurant has a full ocean view, and a sidewalk just outside the door leads to a playground area and the beach. The staff is like family to the many returning guests, who don't mind a bit of sand in their carpets and a casual ambience. The courtyard pool is a cool retreat from the beach, and underground parking protects cars from the salt air. The hotel's restaurant is overseen by Bernard Guillas, the star chef at the nearby Marine Room. There's a five-night minimum stay during the summer. $$$; AE, DC, DIS, MC, V; no checks; www.sealodge.com; at Avenida de la Playa. &

Del Mar

Del Mar has always attracted those who love sojourning at the beach. Its 2½-mile-long stretch of sand from Torrey Pines State Reserve north to the mouth of the San Dieguito River (near the Del Mar Fairgrounds) is one of the best public strands in Southern California for walking, swimming, surfing, or simply lazing under an umbrella. Most beachgoers access it from the neighborhood between 18th and 29th Streets. **SEAGROVE PARK** (5th St and Ocean Ave) overlooking the beach at the foot of 15th Street is perfect for picnicking and sunset watching; small summer concerts and other events are held here.

Del Mar's compact town center lies at the intersection of Camino Del Mar and 15th Street. Walk southward along Camino Del Mar to 12th Street to window-shop at the town's eclectic stores. Notable among the independents are **EARTH SONG BOOKSTORE** (858/755-4254) and **OCEAN SONG MUSIC OF DEL MAR** (858/755-7664), sharing the same space at 1438–1440 Camino Del Mar. The first is an excellent neighborhood bookseller with an emphasis on spirituality and self-help, the other an art, gift, and music shop with a Latin American flair.

DEL MAR PLAZA (1555 Camino Del Mar; 858/792-1555), designed to resemble an Italian hill town, shouldn't be missed. Among its upscale shops and restaurants, you'll have to hunt for **ESMERALDA BOOKS & COFFEE** (858/755-2707), but this small shop is a real gem, with an impressive book selection, a coffee bar serving pastries and light meals, and indoor and outdoor seating. The Plaza's grandest feature is its huge terrace overlooking the ocean. You can sit in this public space as long as you please in comfortable Adirondack chairs and feel as though you are on Del Mar's front porch. The Plaza's paid parking lot is a blessing in this congested area.

The **DEL MAR FAIRGROUNDS** (I-5 at Via de la Valle, main entrance on Jimmy Durante Blvd; 858/792-4252, 858/793-5555 for 24-hour event hotline; www.del marfair.com) hosts one of California's best fairs during the last two weeks of June through July 4th weekend. The **DEL MAR THOROUGHBRED CLUB** hosts a racing season every summer, late July through early September, that's legendary not only for its founder, Bing Crosby, but also for a grand slogan: Where the Turf Meets the Surf.

If you crave hiking, clamber through the Del Mar side of **TORREY PINES STATE RESERVE**. Park with the surfers at the south end of Camino del Mar. If you'd rather stroll along the sand while admiring multimillion-dollar mansions, walk north along the beach from the foot of Seagrove Park to the San Dieguito River. Look east, away from the sea, if you're walking in late afternoon. You may see hot air balloons drifting above canyons and neighborhoods. For further information, call or visit the **DEL MAR REGIONAL CHAMBER OF COMMERCE** (1104 Camino Del Mar; 858/755-4844; www.delmarchamber.org).

RESTAURANTS

Americana / ★★½

1454 CAMINO DEL MAR, DEL MAR; 858/794-6838 Chef/owner Randy Gruber has a hit on his hands with this versatile dining room. During the morning hours, the place feels like a bright and cozy coffee shop, complete with just-baked muffins, challah bread French toast, omelets, and pancakes with granola or chocolate chips. Lunch brings an equally homey lineup: egg salad sandwiches, a classic BLT, turkey burgers, and attractive salads. At dinnertime, however, Americana takes on a much more sophisticated aura, with candlelight, white tablecloths, and artful gourmet cuisine. Don't miss the quickly seared scallops with red lentils, the silken sliced duck breast paired with perfect green beans and pearly couscous, or the salmon perched on a clever succotash of beans and vegetables. For dessert, there's lemon tart brûlée or an unusual banana tarte Tatin. The wine list, while short on by-the-glass selections, offers a decent lineup of food-friendly varietals. *$$; AE, DC, DIS, MC, V; no checks; breakfast, lunch every day, dinner Tues–Sat; beer and wine; reservations recommended; between 14th and 15th Sts.* &

Bully's / ★★½

1404 CAMINO DEL MAR, DEL MAR; 858/755-1660 / 4401 CAMINO DEL RIO S, MISSION VALLEY; 619/291-2665 Though the atmosphere is not quite the same since California's no-smoking law went into effect (some places are just meant to have clouds), Bully's still exudes plenty of character (and characters). At the Del Mar location, locals and the summer racetrack crowd have been patronizing the dark and clubby restaurant with its deep red booths since the 1960s—making it their preferred haunt for a meat fix. In Mission Valley, the crowd has a definite fondness for sports. The restaurant is near Qualcomm Stadium, and local heroes have been known to fuel up here after games. Another nice touch at this location is the table for singles at the end of the bar; you needn't eat alone if you don't want to. The full- or half-cut prime rib, filet mignon, New York, porterhouse, and prime top-sirloin steaks are renowned among local meat lovers (the prime rib is hand-selected USDA Choice, prime-grade Midwestern, corn-fed aged beef). Other favorites include the steadfast Bully Burger, French dip, New York steak sandwich, and baby back ribs. Non–bovine eaters can select from various seafood or chicken dishes or daily specials that might include fresh sea bass or halibut. The bars are local institutions, particularly during summer. *$$; AE, DC, MC, V; local checks only; breakfast, lunch, dinner every day (Del Mar); breakfast Sat–Sun, lunch, dinner every day (Mission Valley); full bar; reservations not accepted; between 14th and 15th Sts (MV); at Texas St (DM).* &

Epazote / ★★

1555 CAMINO DEL MAR, DEL MAR; 858/259-9966 An enduring favorite of the North County see-and-be-seen crowd, Epazote features Southwestern decor and cuisine with an ocean view. The dining room is bright, light, and chic, though most diners clamor for seats on the patio-with-a-view. The vast assortment of tapas grabs top honors, and the wait staff doesn't sniff at those who make a meal out of green corn tamales with lime cream, Dungeness crab corn cakes with chipotle aioli and tropical fruit salsa, shrimp pot stickers, or Navajo flatbread pizza. Favorite entrees include enchiladas suizas topped with tomatillo sauce, an unusual shrimp and scallop enchilada, and the soft taco platter starring your choice of grilled fish, smoked or grilled chicken, or carne asada. Frosty margaritas are the beverage of choice, followed closely by so-called Power Cocktails made with Red Bull and vodka. Service can be leisurely to a fault, but the bar is a happening spot at sunset, and live jazz is featured every Wednesday night. *$$; AE, DC, MC, V; no checks; lunch, dinner every day, brunch Sun; full bar; reservations recommended; www. epazote.com; off 15th St.* &

Il Fornaio / ★★☆

1555 CAMINO DEL MAR, DEL MAR; 858/755-8876 This ever-growing chain dazzles fans with stunning decor and interesting takes on gourmet pasta, pizza, and bread. The elegantly designed dining rooms are an instant transport to Italy with plenty of Carrara marble, terra-cotta flooring, vaulted ceilings, hand-painted trompe l'oeil friezes, and an open oven where meats and signature breads are baked to perfection (breads, pastries, and all food items are available for takeout). At times, the food doesn't live up to the ambience and prices. Most of the pasta dishes are good (*ravioli di verdura al funghi* is filled with Swiss chard, pine nuts, basil, Parmesan, and mixed mushrooms, and topped with fresh tomatoes and artichokes), and the pizzas are nearly perfect (try pizza capricciosa with prosciutto cotto, kalamata olives, artichokes, and mushrooms). Other specialties include well-executed renditions of veal, steaks, chicken, and lamb. For dessert, the tiramisu is a must. Regulars choose outdoor tables with a view and order cappuccino and almond and anisette biscotti or wine and bread. *$$; AE, DIS, DC, MC, V; no checks; lunch, dinner every day, brunch Sun; full bar; reservations recommended; www.ilfornaio.com; at 15th St.* &

Pacifica Del Mar / ★★

1555 CAMINO DEL MAR, DEL MAR; 858/792-0476 "Pacific Rim" may be a term that's getting a little tired, but the concept remains fresh and exciting at this ocean-view restaurant in Del Mar. Given the proximity to the sea, it's only fitting that seafood dominates the extensive menu. A clever "takoshimi" appetizer starring seared peppered ahi is one of the top dishes here. But don't rule out the likes of wok-seared catfish, ginger-marinated salmon, seafood pastas, a mixed seafood grill, and imaginative sandwiches, as well as some truly inspired Sunday brunch dishes. The dining room is pretty, but the real treat here is a seat on the patio. Don't just drop by for the food; the list of martinis and wines by the glass here is impressive, and the singles scene in the eye-catching bar is legendary. Troll here on a Friday night and you might end up with the catch of the day. And no, we don't mean catfish. *$$; AE, CB, DC, DIS, MC, V; no checks; lunch, dinner every day, brunch Sun; full bar; reservations recommended; www.pacificadelmar.com; at 15th St.* &

Spices Thai Cafe / ★★★

3810 VALLEY CENTRE DR, DEL MAR; 858/259-0889 / 16441 BERNARDO CENTER DR, RANCHO BERNARDO; 858/674-4665 Locals tried valiantly to keep the original Spices in Del Mar an unofficial secret, but word spread rapidly and now the place is almost always packed. Nonetheless, the soothing dining room—decked out in pastel paint, black lacquer, and fresh flowers—still feels like a calm oasis. Starters range from Thai spring rolls to dumplings, calamari, and tempura. The list of entrees is long and thought-provoking, including myriad curries, vegetables, noodle and rice dishes (prepared with or without meat and fish), and seafood. House specialties include sizzling lemon grass chicken, roast duck in curry, and pineapple stuffed with chicken, shrimp, and cashew nuts in delicious special sauce. All dishes are individually prepared, MSG is a no-no, and you can regulate the spiciness by using the restaurant's 1-to-10 scale (10 is for fire-breathing dragons). The lunch specials are a terrific value, with soup of the day, green salad, steamed rice, spring roll, fried wonton, and choice of entree thrown into one very inexpensive package. *$$; AE, DC, DIS, MC, V; no checks; lunch, dinner every day; beer and wine; reservations accepted for 7 or more; at El Camino Real.* &

LODGINGS

L'Auberge Del Mar / ★★★★

1540 CAMINO DEL MAR, DEL MAR; 858/259-1515 OR 800/505-9043 This deluxe 120-room resort may be right on Del Mar's main drag, but you'll find ample privacy for any rendezvous. Small and wonderful, L'Auberge has all the elements of a great getaway. Rooms are decorated in an upscale Provençal coastal cottage theme, and all have a private balcony or patio. Bring your swimsuit, because the inn has two pools—one for lounging, another for lap swimming—and the beach is a short stroll away. There are also tennis courts, a small but well-equipped fitness room, and a terrific little spa where you'll want to indulge in a treatment or two. L'Auberge's central location means you can explore Del Mar's shops and restaurants on foot—but you'll likely eat at the inn's J. Taylor's restaurant frequently. For the most privacy, request a top-floor corner room from which you can gaze at the treetops and get a glimpse of the Pacific. *$$$; AE, DC, DIS, MC, V; checks OK; www.lauberge delmar.com; at 15th St.*

Les Artistes / ★★

944 CAMINO DEL MAR, DEL MAR; 858/755-4646 This rambling adobe inn just south of Del Mar's village center is a favorite of those who like quirky, personable lodgings. Behind the magenta bougainvillea, purple wisteria, and gurgling fountains out front, the 12 rooms boast creative tile work and prints, objets d'art, and original paintings to various themes. Seven "designer" rooms are larger than standard accommodations, and each is decorated to commemorate a different artist. The Diego Rivera room is a large upstairs unit with an ocean view and cozy, rustic Mexican decor. Similarly, with its wood beams and white stucco walls, the spacious Georgia O'Keeffe room befits its namesake. The hotel is walking distance from Del Mar's hopping restaurants and shops. If you like your accommodations on the bohemian side, you'll appreciate Les Artistes' offbeat charm. *$$–$$$; AE, DIS, MC, V; no checks; www.lesartistesinn.com; at 10th St.*

Solana Beach/Cardiff-by-the-Sea

Funky yet trendy **SOLANA BEACH** is home to the **CEDROS DESIGN DISTRICT,** the offspring of a neighborhood association of merchants who breathed new life into a quarter-mile section of South Cedros Avenue. The district's gateway (signaled by arching signs over the roadway) lies at Lomas Santa Fe Drive, one block east of the main coast route, Highway 101. Artists, furniture and antique dealers, importers, and high-end gift retailers have now completely taken over the neighborhood. Allow yourself at least two hours to visit some of the district's highlights, including **KERN & CO.** (858/792-7722) for Indonesian-made furniture and other designer finds and **BIRDCAGE** (858/793-6262) for casual-chic gifts and decor (both located in the neighborhood's longest building at 142 S Cedros Ave). **TRIOS GALLERY** (130 S Cedros Ave; 858/793-6040) is one of the county's best showcases for fine arts and crafts and jewelry. Although not much larger than a large closet, nearby **MISTRAL LA COMPAGNIE DE PROVENCE** (146 S Cedros Ave; 858/755-3613) packs every inch of its shop with soaps, oils, and other bathing paraphernalia, all imported from southern France. The **ANTIQUE WAREHOUSE** (212 S Cedros Ave; 858/755-5156) packs dozens of small dealers' booths into a tidy mall of collectibles, while **SOLO** (307 S Cedros Ave; 858/794-9016) features multiple independent importers of new crafts and furnishings from Mexico, Africa, Indonesia, and Europe. Anchoring it all is the **BELLY UP TAVERN** (143 S Cedros Ave; 858/481-9022; www.bellyup.com), which has brought headliner bands into town since 1975 when they pioneered the district's makeover.

One of the north coast's most intimate beach parks is at the foot of the west side of Lomas Santa Fe Drive. **FLETCHER COVE BEACH PARK** (858/755-1569), bounded by tall cliffs, is a gem for safe swimming and beach walking. At low tide, you can walk a mile or more in either direction beneath wind- and wave-sculpted cliffs. Freshwater and tidewater meet at **SAN ELIJO LAGOON,** alive with fish, insect life, and wading birds like herons and curlews. The county's best lagoonside hiking trail skirts San Elijo's southern edge to eroded sandstone cliffs behind a eucalyptus grove.

CARDIFF-BY-THE-SEA borrowed its name from Wales; the developer also gave most of the streets British Isles place names. Cardiff's main attraction, **SAN ELIJO STATE BEACH** (S Hwy 101 at Chesterfield Dr; 760/753-5091), offers excellent camping, swimming, and tidepooling along a wide beach beneath crumbling bluffs. A parking lot at the north end of the camping area is available for day use only. Prowl around the little town by taking Chesterfield Drive east one block from San Elijo State Beach. **SEASIDE MARKET** (2087 San Elijo Ave; 760/753-5445) is a real find for premade beach picnic necessities like salads, sandwiches, and cold cuts.

RESTAURANTS

Cafe Zinc / ★★

132 S CEDROS AVE, SOLANA BEACH; 858/793-5436 The first eatery to set up shop in the Cedros Design District was destined to be a hit just by virtue of location. The fact that the food is terrific is a happy bonus. Dining is mainly alfresco on the people-watching front patio, the sunny side area, or the reclusive rear yard (where tables teeter precariously atop gravel). Feel free to bring well-mannered dogs; there's almost always a laid-back Lab or bright-eyed terrier accompanying a doting owner here. Breakfast items run from simple bagels and muffins to oatmeal with sour cherry and nut topping and frittata with cucumber salsa; ever-comforting fruit crisp or bread pudding are available on weekends. Lunch entrees, salad samplers, and specialty soups change daily, and all creations are meatless. Good bets are the vegetarian Zinc burger and the colorful mixed vegetable sandwich (pain rustique filled with thinly sliced fennel, aioli, red and green bell peppers, radish, celery, arugula, hard-boiled egg, olive tapenade, and vinaigrette). Personal pizzas are nouvelle hard-liners with pesto, Mexican, or Southwestern toppings. *$; No credit cards; checks OK; breakfast, lunch every day; no alcohol; reservations not accepted; at Lomas Santa Fe Ave.* &

Fidel's / ★

607 VALLEY AVE, SOLANA BEACH; 858/755-5292 / 3003 CARLSBAD BLVD, CARLSBAD; 760/729-0903 Fidel's has a touristy feel and real appeal to anyone who wants Mexican-party ambience without crossing the border. The sprawl of dining rooms, bars, and patios, combined with Mexican tile, dangling piñatas, and Norteño music, all contribute to the atmosphere. Accordingly, the place is a frenzied melange of first dates, celebratory groups, families, and fair and racetrack goers, not counting the buoyant students and surfers who show up for happy hour and the cheap taco bar. Standard Mexican favorites top the menu and nachos remain the appetizer of choice. Specialties include various renditions of chiles rellenos, carne and chicken asada, tortas, and tostadas. For something different, try nopales (nopal cactus in a spicy tomato and serrano chile sauce, topped with Monterey Jack cheese), or pescado ranchero (grilled dorado, topped with semispicy ranchero sauce). Burgers and fries are at the ready for kids, and logo T-shirts and baseball caps are for sale. At the newer Fidel's Norte in Carlsbad, prime dining is on the sunny patio. *$-$$; MC, V; no checks; breakfast, lunch, dinner every day; full bar; reservations recommended for 8 or more; at Genevieve St (Solana Beach); at Carlsbad Village Dr (Carlsbad).*

Ki's / ★

2591 S COAST HWY 101, CARDIFF; 760/436-5236 Years ago, Ki's was just another hole-in-the-wall health food cafe, where local surfers and the organic crowd congregated for smoothies, wheat grass juice, and Ki burgers. After moving to a prime ocean-view location just across from Cardiff Beach, Ki's has managed to up the ambience and the menu considerably, while holding prices way down. Both indoor and patio seating are plentiful, though the best seats in the house are at the long upstairs bar facing the ocean. Place your order at the counter, then find a seat and await your meal. Organic fruits, veggies, and grains are incorporated into the mostly low-fat dishes, though cholesterol-laden eggs, avocados, and nuts are visible on the menu. The sizable chicken or salmon salads combine baby greens, roasted red bell peppers, tomatoes, and cucumbers, topped with either a grilled chicken breast or salmon fillet and orange-basil vinaigrette. Veggie lasagne remains a perennial favorite, and Mexican standbys such as burritos, tostadas, and fish tacos have been improved with whole wheat tortillas, organic rice, and lard-free beans. The fruit smoothies are filling, delicious, and healthy. *$; AE, MC, V; checks OK; breakfast, lunch, dinner every day; beer and wine; reservations recommended for dinner; at Chesterfield Ave.* &

Pamplemousse Grille / ★★☆

514 VIA DE LA VALLE, SOLANA BEACH; 858/792-9090 High rollers, socialites, businessfolk, and trophy spouses abound at this stylish bistro across from the Del Mar racetrack. While many are no doubt drawn by the ambience—a chic, sophisticated take on country French—others come for the imaginative fare. The food isn't always Triple Crown material, but the kitchen delivers artfully garnished, creatively conceived variations on nouvelle American and classic French cuisine. The foie gras is always outstanding, as are the grilled fish specials prepared with your choice of a half-dozen sauces. Lamb stew, a very tender pork prime rib, and a roasted tomato–fennel soup are also perennial favorites. Salads and side dishes make fine use of the vegetables from Chino's produce farm (favored by chefs from L.A. and S.F.) just down the road, and desserts—especially the semibaked, melting chocolate truffle cake or the trio of crème brûlées—are worth an extra hour on the StairMaster. Pamplemousse is busy during the racing season (linger in the bar and you might get a hot tip), but the prosperous mood and society gossip stay in the air year-round. *$$$; AE, CB, DC, DIS, MC, V; checks OK; lunch Wed–Fri, dinner every day, brunch Sun; full bar; reservations recommended; www.pgrille.com; at Jimmy Durante Blvd.* &

Tony's Jacal / ★☆

621 VALLEY AVE, SOLANA BEACH; 858/755-2274 Family-owned and -operated since 1946, Tony's Jacal obviously does everything right. Even if you overlook the autographed photos of celebrity diners, you can't miss the long lines—up to an hour on weekends and during Del Mar's racing season. Hang out at the bar with a margarita while listening for your name to be sung out over the loudspeaker. A waitress in blue ruffles will show you to an aqua-upholstered booth in a cavernous room with wood paneling, open beams, Mexican knickknacks, and half-moon-shaped stained-glass windows, or to a table on the outdoor patio with small pond, gurgly waterfall, and flowering plants. Customary Mexican combination plates fill a big chunk of the menu, featuring pork and turkey along with the ubiquitous chicken. Special entrees include chili con carne, steak ranchero, and chicken mole, and the platillos speciales include various enchiladas, carnitas, tortas, quesadillas, and carne asada. *$–$$; AE, MC, V; no checks; lunch Mon, Wed–Sat (closed Tues), dinner Wed–Mon; full bar; reservations recommended for 10 or more; at Genevieve St.* &

Rancho Santa Fe

Hardly anyone even knew Rancho Santa Fe existed—let alone that it's one of the country's wealthiest enclaves—until 1997, when the Heaven's Gate cult members chose it as the spot for their mass suicide. In fact, this eucalyptus-shrouded, super-exclusive community has, since the 1920s, been the coveted home to a crowd of celebrities, politicians, and tycoons.

"The Ranch," as it's known to its denizens, had an illustrious beginning and easily grew into its tight-as-a-fresh-face-lift skin. Designed by esteemed architect Lillian Rice, who used Spanish villages as her inspiration, the community evolved into a genteel grouping of Spanish Colonial Revival buildings surrounded by huge estates (many with fruit groves and horse paddocks), golf courses, and riding trails. Once you've driven around the winding roads, ogling the mansions and taking in the countrified atmosphere, return to "town" and park your wheels—this tiny village is best explored on foot. The village hub is dominated by realtor offices, though there is an array of chic boutiques, jewelers, and art and antique dealers in and around Paseo Delicias, the main drag. Wise shoppers stop by the **COUNTRY FRIENDS SHOP** (Avenida de Acacias at El Tordo; 858/756-1192) packed with donated or consigned furniture, crystal, silver, paintings, and all matter of objets d' art.

Even if you can't afford to eat at any of the enclave's pricey restaurants, you can buy the same exotic produce, baby veggies, and gourmet herbs as many of the top chefs at **CHINO'S VEGETABLE SHOP** (6123 Calzada del Bosque, at Via de Santa Fe; 858/756-3184). Though it might look like just another roadside stand (don't be deceived by the simple Vegetable Shop signs), many of California's culinary artists (including Alice Waters, who started the whole California cuisine commotion) wouldn't dream of handpicking their ingredients anywhere else when they're in town.

RESTAURANTS

Delicias / ★★★

6106 PASEO DELICIAS, RANCHO SANTA FE; 858/756-8000 Delicias is drop-dead gorgeous. Spectacular flower arrangements punctuate the bar and adjacent dining room, which is bedecked with intricate tapestries. The place even has miniature footstools for ladies' purses, so that Vuitton bag never has to be slung over a chair. The visibly affluent, well-groomed clientele comes as much for the scene as for the cuisine, and you'd better not walk in unless you're dressed to impress. The cooking tends to be a well-balanced mix of new California and classic French. The kitchen has a winning way with fish, and regulars know you can never go wrong with any of the seafood specials. Swordfish, salmon, escolar, and ahi make regular appearances, generally grilled and served with anything from tropical fruit salsa to polenta to garlic- or truffle-mashed potatoes. Hearty risottos are another specialty, and if they're serving the oversize veal chop, go for it. Desserts are simpler than the rest of the menu, with homey selections like apple bread pudding or chocolate "baby cakes." Prime seating is at the bar near the entrance, at the edges of the grand dining room, or in the flower-filled patio near the wood-burning fireplace. Definitely a place for those with Dom Perignon tastes and titanium credit cards, this gorgeous restaurant is a delicious find indeed. *$$$; AE, CB, DC, DIS, MC, V; no checks; dinner every day; full bar; reservations recommended; at La Granada.* &

Mille Fleurs / ★★★★

6009 PASEO DELICIAS, RANCHO SANTA FE; 858/756-3085 Possibly the most rarefied and romantic of all San Diego restaurants, Mille Fleurs manages to combine a fabulously lush atmosphere with spectacular cuisine. Tucked into a quiet courtyard, Mille Fleurs attracts with a seductive whisper rather than a flashy wink. Much of its allure is due to the team of Bertrand Hug, the legendary host/proprietor who never seems to forget a face, and Martin Woesle, the stunningly talented chef who's a stickler for using only the very finest ingredients. The cuisine leans toward updated French, with typical dishes including truffle-oil-dressed salads made from a variety of organic greens, sautéed sweetbreads, artful duck creations, and game specials such as venison and quail. Start with delicate cream of parsley soup, fragrant as a patch of herbs, followed by sautéed soft-shell crab nestled on a salsa of local white corn and tiny tomatoes. Woesle's best creations include venison medallions punched up with a juniper berry marinade, stuffed quail sauced with red currants, and monkfish flown in from France. For dessert, there's a selection of imported cheese—surprisingly hard to find as a finale in this area—as well as pastries and sorbets often based on the season's best local fruit. Wine selections are limited only by your pocketbook, as Mille Fleurs offers one of the most impressive lists in town. The sophisticated service, understated Mediterranean decor, and welcoming piano bar all serve to show that gastronomically speaking, at least, money can buy happiness. *$$$$; AE, CB, DC, MC, V; no checks; lunch Mon–Fri, dinner every day; full bar; reservations recommended; milfleurs@aol.com; www. millefleurs.com; on the corner of Avenida Acacias.*

Rancho Valencia Resort Restaurant / ★★★

5921 VALENCIA CIRCLE, RANCHO SANTA FE; 858/756-1123 Rancho Valencia, in the new-money enclave of Rancho Santa Fe known as Fairbanks Ranch, is far enough off the usual restaurant rows to feel like a secret destination. The dining room is at once rustic and upscale, spacious and intimate. Glowing fireplaces, artful flower arrangements, high-beamed ceilings, and highly polished service all complement the meals. A number of notable chefs have passed through the kitchen here, each leaving a trademark dish or two. Steven Sumner, the personable executive chef at this writing, is especially fond of Asian dishes. His Hawaiian sashimi crisp is an irresistible artful creation of finely diced ahi topped with a papaya mango salsa all wrapped in a spring roll taco. The quickly sautéed foie gras could hold its own in a French kitchen; other highlights are spicy sautéed crab cakes and veal with chanterelles. For dessert, choose the perfectly caramelized tarte Tatin. After dinner, take a stroll through the bougainvillea-bedecked courtyards. *$$$–$$$$; AE, DC, MC, V; no checks; breakfast, lunch, dinner every day; full bar; reservations recommended; www.ranchovalencia.com; at Rancho Valencia Rd.* &

LODGINGS

The Inn at Rancho Santa Fe / ★★

5951 LINEA DEL CIELO, RANCHO SANTA FE; 858/756-1131 OR 800/654-2928 OR 800/843-4661 In the heart of Rancho Santa Fe's tony but low-key village, the Inn at Rancho Santa Fe is an unassuming charmer that doesn't rush to embrace every trend. Eighty-seven rooms are spread throughout a cluster of cream-colored adobe buildings and cottages, surrounded by carefully manicured grounds. The inn's cool, wood-beamed main building was designed in 1923 by Lillian Rice, the architect responsible for Rancho Santa Fe's genteel Spanish Colonial look. All rooms are individually decorated with gingham couches and Windsor chairs in a retro-1940s take on American Colonial. For extra privacy, request one of the garden cottages with a private patio. Still, you'll want to hang out on a chaise longue by the pool or borrow equipment for a rousing round of croquet on the front lawn. Boutiques and more fine restaurants are a short stroll away. If you want to put in some time at the beach, the inn maintains a private day cottage on the sand in nearby Del Mar. *$$–$$$; AE, DC, MC, V; no checks; www.theinnatranchosantafe.com; from I-5, take Via de la Valle or Lomas Santa Fe east to the center of town.* &

Rancho Valencia Resort / ★★★★

5921 VALENCIA CIRCLE, RANCHO SANTA FE; 858/756-1123 OR 800/548-3664 You never know whom you might see at this deluxe hideaway—maybe Regis Philbin, Gene Wilder, or an oil tycoon on an extended vacation. They're among the well-heeled regulars who come for the resort's first-rate pampering and bucolic setting. City lights don't obstruct the clear night skies; pollution doesn't mar the view of hot air balloons drifting by at sunset. The fragrance of citrus blossoms is a nearly constant perfume. Naturally, days begin with a tray with fresh-squeezed orange juice and morning newspaper left just outside your door. The 43 suites here are no bargain, but the setting is utterly lovely. The smaller Del Mar suites are each a roomy 850 square feet of airy, Mediterranean elegance—terra-cotta floors, gas fireplaces, high-beamed ceilings, custom-made furnishings, and spacious private patios. The one-bedroom Rancho Santa Fe suites offer even more room to relax. New casitas have private hot tubs, rain-forest showerheads (fixtures that simulate rainfall in the shower), and televisions in the bathrooms. Rancho Valencia began as a tennis resort, and it constantly ranks in *Tennis* magazine's top lists. There's no spa, but you can have excellent massages and facials in your suite. *$$$$; AE, CB, DC, MC, V; checks OK; www.ranchovalencia.com; from I-5, exit at Via de la Valle east, right on El Camino Real, left on San Dieguito Rd, and look for signs to the resort.*

Encinitas

At the south edge of **ENCINITAS,** the **SELF-REALIZATION FELLOWSHIP** (939 2nd St; 760/436-7220) shimmers like an Eastern mystic's vision with its lotus-blossom-shaped towers and mysterious inner gardens. Visitors are welcome—the gardens are quite peaceful. Surfers gave a park on a coastal point just south of the Fellowship

NOT JUST SKIN DEEP: SPA RESORTS
AND WELLNESS RETREATS

Pampering is as popular as surfing in San Diego, home to some of the nation's most prestigious spas. The **GOLDEN DOOR** (777 Deer Springs Rd, San Marcos; 760/744-5777 or 800/424-0777; www.goldendoor.com) has catered to spa aficionados since 1958. It sets the standard for privacy, mind-body awareness, and physical challenges, and is favored by the elusive elite. Located 40 miles northeast of downtown San Diego, the spa looks like a rambling Japanese garden and exudes a privileged ambience. Women reign at the Golden Door most of the year. Men are only allowed stay here five days a year; couples are allowed entry four weeks each year. Located in the same part of San Diego's backcountry, **CAL-A-VIE** (2249 Somerset Rd, Vista; 760/945-2055 or 866/772-4283; www.cal-a-vie.com) also caters to a well-heeled clientele. Capacity is limited to 48 guests per week, and the emphasis is on yoga, healthy nutrition, fitness, and weight loss. Guests relax in cottages tucked beside citrus trees and hiking trails, ramble through the 220-acre property (which includes a golf course), and indulge in wraps and massages after vigorous workouts. A computerized fitness evaluation sets the tone for the week; diet and exercise plans are designed to optimize fitness and weight management.

Professional tennis and golf players frequent the courts and courses at **LA COSTA RESORT & SPA** (Costa del Mar Rd, Carlsbad; 760/438-9111 or 800/854-5000). Recent renovations have updated rooms and facilities at this venerable 400-acre prop-

grounds the somewhat irreverent, but now accepted, local name of **SWAMI'S** (Hwy 101, one block south of K St; 760/633-2750). Downtown Encinitas hasn't changed much since the 1930s. Cars park at an angle by the classic theater, the **LA PALOMA** (471 S Hwy 101; 760/436-5774), which hosts everything from movies and surf film festivals to folksingers.

RESTAURANTS

Vigilucci's / ★★☆

505 S HWY 101, ENCINITAS; 760/942-7332 When Roberto Vigilucci opened his Italian restaurant in 1993, he not only brought his delectable hometown Milano recipes to North County, but also managed to turn one corner of an innocuous intersection into an elegant and intimate haven. Most afternoons and evenings the place is swamped with the well-heeled looking to be well fed. Tables swathed in crisp linen and topped with fresh flowers are laden with gnocchi al Gorgonzola e nocchi (potato dumplings with Gorgonzola cheese sauce and walnuts), pollo alla florentina (chicken breast stuffed with spinach and ricotta cheese in a creamy white sauce), and saltimbocca alla romana (veal scaloppini topped with prosciutto, sage, and mozzarella in white wine sauce). Portions are large, and all entrees erty, where guests have long enjoyed diet and exercise programs, spa treatments, and plenty of sporting options. The resort is now home to the **CHOPRA CENTER** (www. chopra.com), headed by San Diego's famed wellness guru Deepak Chopra. Medical programs are combined with techniques for spiritual, physical, and emotional health, and the center offers both a day spa and longer workshops.

Day spas and beauty salons combine pampering with the usual maintenance treatments; most offer day packages that leave you with a satisfied glow. At the **ARTESIA DAY SPA AND SALON** (240 5th Ave, downtown; 619/338-8111), office workers indulge in lunchtime pedicures and massages. The spa is located in the same complex as the **HILTON SAN DIEGO GASLAMP QUARTER,** just across the street from the Convention Center. Set amid La Jolla's chic boutiques and cafes, the **GAIA DAY SPA** (1299 Prospect St, La Jolla; 858/456-8797; www.gaiadayspa.com) sets the mood with private suites containing saunas, showers, and soaking tubs. Feng shui principles are used in the spa's design, and treatments include thalassotherapy, Vichy salt glows and showers, and herbal wraps. **BEAUTY KLINIEK DAY SPA AND WELLNESS CENTER** (3268 Governor Dr, Golden Triangle; 858/457-0191; www.beautykliniek.com) has been one of San Diego's most popular day spas for more than 18 years. The 5,000-square-foot spa's specialty is aromatherapy, but there are tons of specialized treatments, including massage and pedicures for couples. At the front of the spa, French bath and body care products are sold; most are based on botanicals.

—Maribeth Mellin

come with fresh vegetables and spaghetti aglio e olio. Lunch specials are quite reasonable, and the wine list is extraordinary, with generally reasonable prices and an outstanding selection of Italian reds and whites. The charming all-Italian staff remains much the same, offering unpretentious and welcoming service. *$$; AE, DIS, MC, V; no checks; lunch Mon–Fri, dinner every day; beer and wine; reservations accepted for 4 or more; www.vigiluccis.com; at D St.* &

When in Rome / ★★★

1108 1ST ST, ENCINITAS; 760/944-1771 Restaurateurs Joe and Rosemary Ragone run this fine Italian restaurant the old-fashioned way, doing just about everything themselves. They grow many of their own herbs, do much of the cooking, choose produce and meats with finicky precision, and even prepare their own breads and desserts. The results show in the perfect tomato and basil salad, the falling-off-the-bone osso buco (sometimes made with veal, sometimes with lamb), a velveteen fusilli with vodka, and the nightly fish specials. Particular treats include the swordfish Livornese dressed with capers and black olives and the buttery sea bass matched with a saffron sauce. Desserts rate an equal rave, especially Rosemary's tiramisu, crème brûlée, and fluffy fresh-fruit mousses. The spacious restaurant offers an especially cozy dining room with a fireplace, as well as a covered patio complete with bar and piano. A visit to When in Rome means spending the evening in the company of very talented, very gracious people who make you want to return. *$$$; AE, MC, V; no checks; dinner every day; full bar; reservations recommended; at J St.* &

Carlsbad

Situated along the coast, about 35 miles north of San Diego, this low-key coastal community was originally named for its mineral water said to be like that of a 19th-century spa in Bohemia (now the Czech Republic). Today's **CARLSBAD MINERAL WATER SPA** (2802 Carlsbad Blvd; 760/434-1887; www.carlsbadmineralspa.com) is housed in the **ALT KARLSBAD HAUS,** site of the original well discovered by retired sea captain John Frazier as he was drilling away on his homestead in the 1880s. Frazier is also credited with naming the town (quite benevolently, since it had been previously known as "Frazier Station") and inspiring its Bavarian styling. German immigrant Gerhard Schutte took over the well and opened a seaside sanatorium in the late 1800s. It wasn't long before Carlsbad became a favorite stopover for the ailing public who came to "take the waters." Today, guests luxuriate in carbonated mineral-water baths said to soothe all sorts of ailments and smooth the skin. The water is also bottled and sold in local convenience stores and delivered to local homes.

Carlsbad's "village" area—just a few blocks from the beach along U.S. Highway 101—is filled with shops, cafes, and restaurants. **STATE STREET** is a popular prowl for antique hunters. The nearby 1887 Santa Fe Depot is now home to the **CARLSBAD CONVENTION & VISITORS BUREAU** (400 Carlsbad Village Dr; 760/434-6093; www.carlsbadca.org), the perfect place to pick up maps and other tourist information. History and architecture buffs should visit **ST. MICHAEL'S EPISCOPAL CHURCH** (1896), **HERITAGE HALL** (1926), and **MAGEE HOUSE** (1887), all located near Garfield Street, between Beech and Cypress Avenues. The seawall near the village is a great spot for watching the ocean's ebb and flow, while three lagoons afford plenty of bird-watching, fishing, and nature-walk opportunities. **SNUG HARBOR MARINA** (Agua Hedionda Lagoon; 760/434-3089), on an inlet waterway, offers waterskiing, Jet Skis, kayak and canoe rentals, Waverunners, and water bikes, as well as a pro shop, equipment rentals, and instructions.

Serious shoppers won't want to miss **CARLSBAD COMPANY STORES** (on Paseo del Norte, off I-5 between Palomar Airport and Cannon Rds; 760/804-9000). Although this complex seems like an innocent Mediterranean village from afar, it actually houses a credit-card-defying complex of outlet stores (including Donna Karan, Jones New York, Crate and Barrel, Gap, Oshkosh B'Gosh, and Royal Doulton), along with fine dining, art galleries, fast food outlets, and—naturally—Starbucks.

If you visit anytime from mid-March to early May, you'll be in sync with the blooms of the famous **FLOWER FIELDS AT CARLSBAD RANCH** (Paseo del Norte, off I-5 at Palomar Rd; 760/431-0352; www.theflowerfields.com), one of California's major commercial flower-growing centers. In March and April, you'll be knocked out by the thousands of vibrantly colored ranunculus covering more than 50 acres of hillsides. For a fabulous overview of the flowers and the coastline zoom above the scene with **AVIATION ADVENTURES** (2160 Palomar Airport Rd; 760/438-7680; www.barnstorming.com). During the December holiday season, Paul Ecke Ranch in nearby Encinitas sparks spirits with a virtual blaze of scarlet poinsettias arranged in the shape of a 166-foot star. Stock up on flowers (like Carlsbad's official flower—the bird-of-paradise—first developed commercially here), bulbs, plants, and other unique products at the gift shop by the flower fields. Carlsbad is also home to **LEGOLAND** (1 Lego Dr, off I-5 at Cannon Rd; 760/918-5346; www.legolandca.com), a colorful, kid-pleasing amusement park almost literally built from the well-loved interlocking blocks.

RESTAURANTS

Bellefleur Winery & Restaurant / ★★☆

5610 PASEO DEL NORTE, CARLSBAD; 760/603-1919 Looking somewhat like a beautiful fish out of water, this upscale restaurant/bar anchors one end of an outlet store mall (the Carlsbad Company Stores). It's a welcome presence among the fast food joints, discount shoe stores, and displays of last year's fashions. Inside the villa-esque building, soaring ceilings and graceful architecture provide a chic showcase for an international lineup of foods. The restaurant has recently undergone restructuring, with new management creating an ambitious menu influenced by Pacific Rim, Italian, French, and classic American styles. Fancy wood-fired pizzas and Tuscan white bean soup rub elbows with cheeseburgers, grilled lamb loin, and steamed local mussels in a yellow curry sauce; on the bar menu, you'll find smoked salmon, sushi style, alongside French onion soup. At lunch, the place has a casual feeling; a dressier, older crowd shows up at night. Some customers may enjoy the wines sold under the Bellefleur label, but discerning drinkers will shell out more for the better-known California brands on the extensive list. *$$$; AE, DIS, DC, MC, V; no checks; lunch, dinner every day; full bar; reservations recommended; www.belle fleur.com; at Car Country Dr.* &

LODGINGS

Carlsbad Inn Beach Resort / ★★

3075 CARLSBAD BLVD, CARLSBAD; 760/434-7020 OR 800/235-3939 This gem right in the heart of Carlsbad is just across the street from the beach, yet it feels like an urbane European inn. The Tudor-style facade gives way to a peaceful carpeted lobby, with curved stairways leading to upper-floor rooms (there's also an elevator). Peaked, shingled roofs and wooden balconies continue the European theme in buildings framing the pool and a broad lawn. The 62 rooms in the main building are cozy and reminiscent of the inn's origins as a 1920s mansion. Those in the wing buildings have varying shapes and sizes; some are used as time-share units (sometimes available as hotel rooms) and have kitchenettes or kitchens and separate bedrooms. Hotel guests can participate in activities designed for the time-share owners—day trips to San Diego attractions are sometimes offered, as are wine and cheese parties and live music on the lawn. The hotel has a beach club just across the street. *$$$; AE, DC, MC, V; checks OK in advance of stay; www.carlsbadinn.com; on the corner of Carlsbad Village Dr.*

Four Seasons Resort–Aviara / ★★★★

7100 FOUR SEASONS PT, CARLSBAD; 760/603-6800 OR 800/332-7100 Yes, the Four Seasons is sleek, swank, and serene. But we love it best for its beds, which feel like fluffy clouds. Soft green walls, understated furnishings, and marble baths with soaking tubs make it hard to leave the room, though it is nice to settle on the private balcony's cushioned deck chairs for sunset cocktails. There are plenty of other diversions in this 329-room hotel overlooking Batiquitos Lagoon. The spa offers such sensory delights as citrus sugar scrubs and avocado wraps. The Jose Eber Salon is the perfect place to primp for dinner at Vivace. A to-die-for brunch (with a separate serving table overflowing with kids' treats) is displayed at the California Bistro, which also hosts a Friday night seafood buffet. Afternoon tea is graciously presented in the flower-filled Lobby Lounge. Golfers rave about the Arnold Palmer–designed Aviara Golf Course. Tennis buffs head for the six lighted courses; swimmers delight in a seemingly endless pool. Though the hotel is lush and luxurious, children aren't ignored. The Kids for All Seasons program is excellent, and there are PlayStations in all rooms. Special programs include a jazz series on summer nights. *$$$–$$$$; AE, DC, DIS, JCB, MC, V; checks OK; www.fourseasons.com; at Aviara Pkwy.* ⅅ

Escondido

The English translation of Escondido is "hidden valley," though this burgeoning city is anything but hidden these days. Situated about 30 miles northeast of downtown, the once-sleepy little community has become firmly entrenched in nouveau San Diego's space-sucking urban sprawl.

The biggest draw in this north San Diego area is the **SAN DIEGO WILD ANIMAL PARK** (15500 San Pasqual Valley Rd; 760/747-8702; www.sandiegozoo.org), which allows visitors to ogle more than 3,000 animals, including elephants, tigers, rhinos, and several endangered species. The animals roam (at least semifreely) through their natural habitat. Monorails take visitors on 50-minute rides, hovering over areas that mimic Asia and Africa, and animal shows are scheduled daily.

One of the things that makes this minimetropolis a cultural standout is the prominent **CALIFORNIA CENTER FOR THE ARTS, ESCONDIDO** (340 N Escondido Blvd; 760/839-4100 or 800/988-4253), which showcases plays, dance performances, and concerts. Though bandleader Lawrence Welk has flown off to that big champagne bubble in the sky, his 1000-acre-plus, circa-1960s **WELK RESORT CENTER** (8860 Lawrence Welk Dr; 760/749-3000; www.welkresort.com) still flourishes. Aside from the plethora of hotel amenities and recreation options (including three golf courses), the resort boasts a museum laden with Welk memorabilia and a 339-seat dinner theater that presents first-rate musicals and variety shows. The resort's attractions are open to nonguests.

RESTAURANTS

150 Grand Cafe / ★★☆

150 W GRAND AVE, ESCONDIDO; 760/738-6868 This casual yet classy cafe is overseen by boyish-looking chef Carlton Greenawalt, who has a special way with what he calls new American cuisine. International recipes and ingredients are combined to create healthful recipes familiar to American palates. Dressed like New Age security guards in black trousers and Nehru shirts of subdued colors, attentive servers deliver crusty bread from the Upper Crust bakery in Mission Valley. Move on to appetizers (try the excellent carpaccio) and a variety of yummy entrees with complex sauces and impressive presentation. Dessert here should be a priority, not an afterthought: the cinnamon chocolate cake glazed in orange ganache and topped with caramel mascarpone mousse is worth every calorie. Reservations for even one person are certainly in order before a performance at the nearby California Center for the Arts and on weekend evenings. *$$; AE, MC, V; no checks; lunch, dinner Mon–Sat; full bar; reservations recommended; www.150grand.com; between Broadway and Maple St.* &

Rancho Bernardo

RESTAURANTS

El Bizcocho / ★★★

17550 BERNARDO OAKS DR (RANCHO BERNARDO INN), RANCHO BERNARDO; 858/675-8500 One of the most consistent dining rooms in the county, El Bizcocho charms diners with artful service, gifted chefs, and understated elegance. The spacious room evokes an upmarket country inn, with fireplace, well-spaced tables, and a view of the golf course. Updated French cuisine is a signature here, with classics like escargot topped with puff pastry and quickly seared foie gras. More innovative creations include fingertip-size scallops arranged on ravioli and drizzled with vanilla, or a napoleon of lobster and caviar amid layers of phyllo. Don't miss the roasted monkfish (garnished with black truffles and wild mushrooms) or sautéed John Dory paired with fennel and tiny potatoes. Roasted free-range chicken and braised duckling paired with fresh fruit are other standouts. Order the dessert soufflés at the beginning of a meal and they'll arrive just as you're ready for espresso. Waiters are personable yet professional and the wine list is superb, with several hundred topnotch brands from California and France. Sunday brunch is an elegant affair, worth a night's stay at the hotel so you can take a proper siesta afterward. *$$$; AE, CB, DC, DIS, MC, V; checks OK; dinner every day, brunch Sun; full bar; reservations recommended; www.ranchobernardoinn.com; off I-15/Rancho Bernardo Rd.* &

LODGINGS

Rancho Bernardo Inn / ★★★

17550 BERNARDO OAKS DR, RANCHO BERNARDO; 858/675-8400 OR 800/770-7482 Gourmands, golfers, business bigwigs, and vacationing families all feel at home in this hacienda-style inn set amid rolling fairways and clear valley air. Sculptures, fountains, and flowers mark the entrance to the lobby, where hand-painted tiles, hardwood beams, and blazing fireplaces evoke early California style at its most gracious. The best of the 288 rooms and suites have living room fireplaces, bedroom whirlpool tubs, and patios the size of an urban backyard. The rest are comfortable, though it's best to ask for a view of the grounds or distant mountain peaks. Guests in the know make time for at least one dinner and Sunday brunch at El Bizcocho, one of the county's finest restaurants (see above). They can always work off the calories at the inn's championship golf course (along with four others in the neighborhood), 12 tennis courts, and fitness center, or vegetate beside the two pools, both so ensconced in flowering bushes and trees they feel like country lakes. *$$$–$$$$; AE, CB, DC, DIS, MC, V; checks OK; www.ranchobernardoinn. com; off I-15/Rancho Bernardo Rd.* &

Julian

Still rustic after all these years, this 1880s mining town is a favorite day-trip destination for San Diegans. The best time of year is fall, when visitors devour apple pies at the local bakeries that line the highway from Julian to Santa Ysabel, or take the chill off with hot cider. Fewer people come in spring, when exquisite wildflowers take over the hillsides and meadows, and in winter months, which often bring snow. Interesting explorations include the **EAGLE MINING COMPANY,** an authentic gold mine (end of C St; 760/765-0036); the Pioneer Cemetery, with miners' graves (off A St); and the antique and collectible shops on and around Main Street. Don't leave town without sipping a soda at the fountain in the old-fashioned **JULIAN DRUG STORE** (2134 Main St; 760/765-0332). Another mandatory stop near Julian is **DUDLEY'S BAKERY** (30218 Hwy 78, Santa Ysabel; 760/765-0488), where people have been lining up for decades to buy 20 or so varieties of freshly baked bread. The hike up the **VOLCAN MOUNTAIN WILDERNESS PRESERVE** (off Farmers Rd; no phone) is steep but short; views overlooking town, the surrounding meadows, and the Cuyamaca Mountains are ample reward. You can also explore Volcan Mountain on a trail ride with **JULIAN STABLES** (760/765-1598). Drop-in visits are discouraged; call ahead for reservations. If driving is your preferred mode of touring, head south on Highway 79 through the Cuyamaca Mountains and stretch your legs on any of the many marked trails (Green Valley Falls is especially nice). Then end the day with samples of locally made chardonnay and sauvignon blanc at Julian's **MENGHINI WINERY** (open Mon–Thurs; 1150 Julian Orchards Dr; 760/765-2072;). Once you begin exploring, you may want to spend the night in pine-scented air. The **JULIAN BED & BREAKFAST GUILD** (760/765-1555; www.julianbnbguild.com) has over a dozen member B&Bs that offer comfortable mountain lodgings. For more information, contact the **JULIAN CHAMBER OF COMMERCE** (2133 Main St; 760/765-1857; www.julianca.com).

LODGINGS

The Artists' Loft / ★★☆

4811 PINE RIDGE AVE, JULIAN; 760/765-0765 Owner/artists Nanessence and Chuck Kimball's serene 11-acre oasis outside the town of Julian is just the place to kick back and listen to the wind rustle through the manzanita trees. Two rooms in the main house are decorated with rustic antiques, Persian rugs, and the Kimballs' own artwork. The Cabin at Strawberry Hill boasts an inviting couch, a wood-burning stove, a king-size bed, and a fully equipped kitchen. The 70-year-old Big Cat Cabin is named for a mountain lion that hides nearby. They've lavishly remodeled this one-bedroom gem, which features a massive stone fireplace, fully equipped kitchen with countertops made of local oak, and a bathroom with a wood-paneled shower and a vintage cast-iron tub. You'll drift to sleep in an antique Balinese wedding bed, and the bedroom's screened study area is the ideal spot to curl up with a book. *$$; MC, V; checks OK; mail@artistsloft.com; www.artistsloft.com; at Pine Ridge Wy.*

Anza-Borrego Desert State Park/Borrego Springs

Tiny Borrego Springs is best known for **ANZA-BORREGO DESERT STATE PARK**, whose 600,000 acres (1,000 square miles) surround the town on all sides and stretch as far as the Mexican border. The park is a wild wonderland where roadrunners dash across the asphalt, dodging cars and trucks; golden eagles soar in the sky; kit foxes, mule deer, and bighorn sheep hide in isolated habitats; and desert iguanas and four species of rattlesnake slither about the desert floor. Blooming cacti and wildflowers bring visitors by the thousands from January through March, while 110-degree-plus temperatures during summer discourage all but the most stoic "desert rats." One easy way to explore the region during any season is with **SAN DIEGO OUTBACK TOURS** (619/980-3332 or 888/BY-JEEPS; www.desertjeeptours.com), whose wild—but air-conditioned—four-wheel-drive excursions cover both the desert and the mountains, always with a well-versed guide.

Begin your desert experience at the park's **VISITORS CENTER** (200 Palm Canyon Dr; 760/767-5311; www.anzaborrego.statepark.org) in Borrego Springs, where signs lead to the easy 1½-mile **PALM CANYON TRAIL**. Additional displays and guidebooks can be found at the **DESERT NATURAL HISTORY ASSOCIATION** (682 Palm Canyon Dr; 760/767-3098; www.abdnha.org), while information on dining, lodging, and golf is available from the **BORREGO SPRINGS CHAMBER OF COMMERCE** (786 Palm Canyon Dr; 760/767-5555 or 800/559-5524; www.borrego springs.org).

LODGINGS

La Casa del Zorro / ★★

3845 YAQUI PASS RD, BORREGO SPRINGS; 760/767-5323 OR 800/824-1884
There's no need to suffer and sweat in the desert. Instead, book a room or casita at this lush oasis buried in date palms set against a mountain backdrop. The casitas, with one to four bedrooms, are spread about in clusters throughout the 42-acre property. Some have fireplaces and private pools; all have kitchen facilities and living and dining rooms. Two-story white buildings with tiled roofs house the large guest rooms, most with fireplaces (the desert gets mighty chilly on winter nights). Several pools, one reserved for adult use only, are scattered about the gardens, and a river flows over boulders between the buildings. Prices are high in the restaurant, but you can get lots of touring tips from the staff. Tours of the desert are available, in jeeps or on foot. Rates here drop considerably in summer. *$$$; AE, DC, DIS, MC, V; no checks; www.lacasadelzorro.com; at State Rd 3 (S3).* &

CALIFORNIA'S CENTRAL COAST

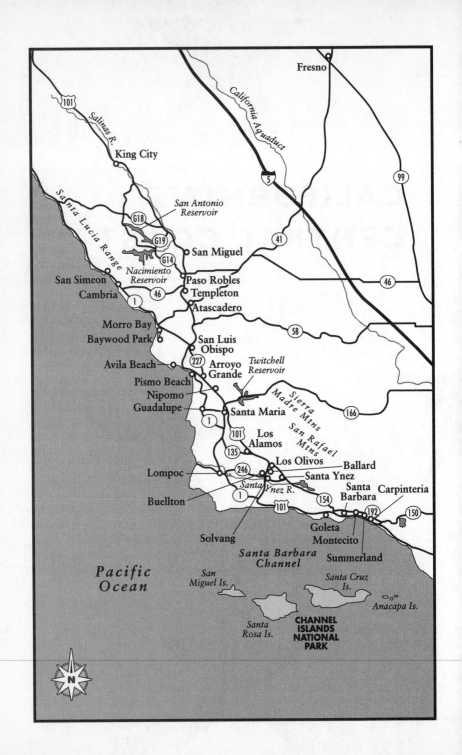

CALIFORNIA'S CENTRAL COAST

The dramatic scenery of California's Central Coast unfolds like an accordion of picture postcards: pristine beaches, windswept cliffs, cow-studded pastures, historic mission towns, tree-shaded country roads. The area's diversity is part of its continued appeal. You can bask in sunshine at ocean's edge, bicycle through lush vineyards, ride horses along rural backroads, and shop a boulevard of chic boutiques—whatever your pleasure may be.

Glorious vacation destinations are sprinkled throughout the beachfront towns. The coastline itself has a distinct personality: sunny white-sand beaches segue into rocky, cliff-lined shores, then give way to calm, picturesque bays. Quintessential California beach towns reflect the influence of the Native American tribes who first lived here, and residents of upscale suburbs retain something of the frontier flair of pioneer ranchers.

Though the name "Central Coast" refers primarily to the coastline between Cambria in the north and Ventura County to the south, and though the region is best known for attractions such as the opulent tourist mecca Hearst Castle and the wealthy beach city of Santa Barbara, some equally intriguing destinations are tucked into the inland mountains and valleys, where citrus orchards and vineyards beckon to the discerning traveler. Agriculture is the economic mainstay of both Santa Barbara and San Luis Obispo Counties. Everywhere you drive you'll see roadside stands peddling fresh-from-the-fields strawberries, apples, oranges, avocados, corn, tomatoes, cucumbers, and more. The weekly farmers market is a Central Coast tradition in San Luis Obispo and many neighboring towns.

Central Coast residents are as diverse as the region itself. Well-heeled urban escapees coexist with lifelong farmers who still work the land; bohemian artists inspired by their surroundings are juxtaposed with college students whose presence brings up-to-date trends. Yet all share an appreciation of this laid-back collection of old-fashioned communities, close to, yet a world apart from, the bustling metropolis of Los Angeles.

ACCESS AND INFORMATION

The Central Coast stretches from San Luis Obispo County in the north down to Ventura County, almost nudging the Los Angeles city limits. **U.S. HIGHWAY 101,** a major four-lane freeway, nicely bisects the region, complemented by scenic **HIGHWAY 1 (PACIFIC COAST HIGHWAY, OR PCH).** (In spots, notably from San Luis Obispo to Grover Beach and from Gaviota to Oxnard, the two highways share the same roadbed.) Smaller scenic highways, such as Highways 33, 46, 150, 154, and 246, provide access to inland destinations. **CAR RENTALS** and major travelers' services are available primarily in Santa Barbara and San Luis Obispo. **AIRPORTS** in Santa Barbara and San Luis Obispo are served by Skywest Airlines and American Eagle; Santa Barbara is also served by United Express and US Airways Express; flights are frequent from Los Angeles, less frequent from San Francisco.

CENTRAL COAST THREE-DAY TOUR

DAY 1. Get an early start at San Simeon's **HEARST CASTLE** to avoid midday crowds. After touring this landmark, enjoy lunch on the dramatic cliffs at **RAGGED POINT INN,** followed by a leisurely afternoon strolling the antique stores and boutiques of **CAMBRIA'S MAIN STREET.** Have dinner by the welcoming fireplace at the **SOW'S EAR CAFE,** then bed down in one of Cambria's charming B&Bs, such as the **OLALLIEBERRY INN.**

DAY 2. After breakfast, head down scenic Highway 1 toward **SAN LUIS OBISPO,** where you can explore the historic mission and see the downtown sights. Take a lunch break at the eclectic and colorful **BIG SKY CAFE** in the heart of town. When you're ready, continue to funky Pismo Beach and check into an oceanfront room at luxurious **SEAVENTURE RESORT.** If the weather's nice, take a predinner stroll on the pier, perhaps stopping for a bowl of clam chowder. Or proceed directly to dinner at popular **GIUSEPPE'S CUCINA ITALIANA.**

DAY 3. Leave the beach behind for a day of wine touring in the idyllic **SANTA YNEZ VALLEY.** Stop first in tiny **LOS OLIVOS** for lunch provisions, then ramble leisurely from winery to winery. When you get hungry, buy a bottle of wine and enjoy the **PICNIC GROUNDS AT A VINEYARD** such as Gainey, Sunstone, or Zaca Mesa. Later on (perhaps after an afternoon nap), make your way to the Danish storybook town of Solvang for a relaxed dinner at the intimate **CABERNET BISTRO.** Spend the night at the luxe new **SANTA YNEZ INN** before heading to Santa Barbara for a few days (see Santa Barbara Three-Day Tour, page 266, for complete details).

Oxnard

LODGINGS

Embassy Suites Mandalay Beach Resort / ★★★☆

2101 MANDALAY BEACH RD, OXNARD; 805/984-2500 OR 800/EMBASSY Oxnard is a rather unlikely home for this decidedly impressive getaway, which is run by the equally unlikely Embassy Suites chain. Feeling more like a privately owned retreat, the hotel would be as at home on Hawaiian shores as it is on these pristine sands (which are enjoyed mainly by residents of chic surrounding condos). In sharp contrast to nearby marshes where the Chumash Indians once hunted, the posh Spanish Colonial complex sports a red-tile roof, tall palm trees and lush tropical plants, a sparkling blue swimming pool, and a variety of luxurious one- and two-bedroom suites with garden or ocean views. Guest rooms are tastefully decorated with neutral furniture, Mexican tile, marble flooring, and two of everything: telephones, TVs, even two full bathrooms. Room rates include full sit-down breakfast plus afternoon snacks and free well drinks. A recreation shack rents bikes and skates on weekends—bicycles are complimentary for midweek guests.

The restaurant, Capistrano's, serves three meals daily as well as a Sunday brunch and features decent California-Mediterranean fare in a pleasant indoor-outdoor patio setting. There's a tropical-themed indoor cocktail lounge and a poolside bar. If the beach, pool, or tennis courts lose their appeal, Channel Islands Harbor is a short drive or a healthy walk away. Much smaller and less commercial than Ventura Harbor up the coast, it's a pretty enclave of marina homes with private docks and a small shopping and restaurant complex, and it's a jumping-off point for harbor cruises, whale-watching excursions, and fishing charters. *$$$–$$$$; AE, DC, DIS, MC, V; checks OK; www.embassysuites.com; at Costa de Oro, west of Harbor Blvd.* ♿

Ventura

Nestled between gently rolling foothills and the sparkling blue Pacific, Ventura is endowed with the picturesque setting and clean sea breezes typical of the California coast. Since most of the city's development has taken place inland and to the south, there's a charming small-town character to the historic district, known nostalgically by its Spanish mission name, San Buenaventura. To learn more, make the **VENTURA VISITORS AND CONVENTION BUREAU** (89-C S California St; 805/648-2075 or 800/333-2989; www.ventura-usa.com) your first stop, since their office is in the heart of old downtown.

The town grew up around **MISSION SAN BUENAVENTURA** (225 E Main St; 805/643-4318; www.anacapa.net/~mission), which was founded in 1782 as part of the California mission chain. Still in use for daily services, the current buildings date from 1815 and have been restored to depict the everyday mission life of the 19th century. Touring the interior garden, you'll see the antique water pump and olive press once essential to survival, and get a look at the whitewash-and-red-tile architecture whose influence can be seen throughout town. Across the street is the **VENTURA COUNTY MUSEUM OF HISTORY AND ART** (100 E Main St; 805/653-0323; www.vcmha.org), worth a visit for its rich Native American Room, filled with Chumash treasures, and its enormous archive of historical photos depicting Ventura County from its origin to the present time. Don't miss the majestic **SAN BUENAVENTURA CITY HALL** (501 Poli St; 805/658-4726), which presides over town from a hillside at the end of California Street. Built in 1912 to serve as the county courthouse, this neoclassical landmark is filled with architectural detail inside and out—look for the carved heads of Franciscan friars whimsically adorning the facade. In the summertime, City Hall can be fully explored by escorted tour.

Antique hounds have been flocking here for many years, and even casual browsers can spend the better part of a day shopping for collectible treasures along Main Street. Start with one of the mall-style places, where dozens of different sellers present a mind-boggling selection that ranges from Hawaiian aloha shirts to antique armoires, from fine china to art deco lithographs, or even *Star Wars* lunch boxes and Nancy Drew first editions. Our favorites are **HEIRLOOMS ANTIQUES** (327 E Main

St; 805/648-4833); **TIMES REMEMBERED** (467 E Main St; 805/643-3137); **NICHOLBY ANTIQUES** (404 E Main St; 805/653-1195); and **PORTOBELLO ANTIQUES** (494 E Main St; 805/641-1890), an antique furniture warehouse.

If the weather's nice—and it usually is—take a stroll along the **VENTURA PROM-ENADE,** a paved oceanside pathway wide enough to accommodate bicyclists and in-line skaters. On the weekends, **BICYCLES** and **CANOPIED SURREYS** are available for rent in front of the Holiday Inn (450 E Harbor Blvd, at California St; 805/648-7731) at the boardwalk.

A short drive south of old San Buenaventura lies picturesque **VENTURA HARBOR,** headquarters of Channel Islands National Park (see Channel Islands section later in this chapter). Nearby is **VENTURA HARBOR VILLAGE** (on Spinnaker Dr off Harbor Blvd; 805/642-8538; www.venturaharborvillage.com), a vaguely Mediterranean shopping/entertainment complex spread along the length of the marina. In addition to waterfront restaurants, gift shops, and paddleboat rentals, there's a small carousel for kids and a fresh fish market. Sportfishing and dive charters operate nearby, and a narrated **HARBOR CRUISE** departs from the village aboard the *Bay Queen* (805/642-7753). If you're here during the annual gray whale migration season—from late December through March—consider taking a **WHALE-WATCHING CRUISE** to observe the graceful leviathans up close. **ISLAND PACKERS** (1867 Spinnaker Dr; 805/642-1393; www.islandpackers.com) offers half- and full-day excursions. Inland from the harbor lies the historic **OLIVAS ADOBE** (4200 Olivas Park Dr; 805/644-4346). Built in 1847 as the showplace of prosperous Rancho Miguel, the restored two-story house is filled with antiques and surrounded by tranquil, century-old gardens; one grape arbor dates to the 1840s. The grounds are open daily, but the adobe is open only on weekends.

RESTAURANTS

Eric Ericsson's on the Pier / ★

668 HARBOR BLVD, VENTURA; 805/643-4783 When the coveted restaurant space on Ventura's pleasure pier became vacant, this local crowd-pleaser wasted no time moving from its landlocked former spot. Perched atop the beach, an airy, multisto-ried building echoes the simple wood construction of the pier itself, with huge windows lining the walls to exploit a terrific view (and let in ocean breezes). The crowd here is varied: scruffy beachgoers mingle with suited businessfolk at lunch, sports fans and twentysomethings scarf down shellfish and deep-fried appetizers at cocktail hour, families come early for generously sized dinners, and dating couples linger at window tables past sunset. The staggering array of seafood includes clams, oysters, mussels, shrimp, scallops, cod, halibut, lobster, and calamari. Add specialties like Mexican cioppino or traditional clambake, plus a handful of nonfish entrees, and it's hard to imagine anyone being disappointed by this menu. No one expects subtlety from this kitchen, just gobs and gobs of food. The service is equally unpolished, but that doesn't stop Eric Ericsson's from packing 'em in. *$$; AE, MC, V; no checks; lunch, dinner every day; full bar; reservations recommended; where the pier meets Harbor Blvd, south of California St.* &

JUNÍPERO SERRA AND THE BIRTH
OF THE CALIFORNIA MISSIONS

Throughout California you'll find highways, canyons, schools, and monuments bearing the name of Junípero Serra (pronounced who-NEE-per-oh SARE-uh). Who was this Spaniard and why is he held in such high esteem?

Junípero Serra, born on Mallorca in 1713, was a Franciscan friar who was sent to the New World to administer the church's missions in Baja ("lower") California (in present-day Mexico). He was later sent north to found missions in the ports of San Diego and Monterey in the little-explored Alta ("upper") California, a Spanish territory populated with "heathen" natives and threatened by Russian imperialism. Though small of stature and quiet of nature, Father Serra led his expedition on a six-week march north to San Diego in May 1769. Discouraged by the failure of previous expeditions and facing dwindling supplies and escalating illness, the group survived on the strength of the determined friar's faith and will. They finally staggered into San Diego in July, raised a wooden cross, and conducted Mass before a crowd of curious Native Americans.

On reaching Monterey Bay, Serra and his men found that a cross erected by an earlier expedition had been surrounded by offerings—arrows and feathers stuck in the ground, a string of sardines, pieces of meat and fish—placed there by wary natives to appease the unfamiliar gods. A few days later Father Serra conducted, with great pageantry, the services that finally symbolized the definitive presence of the Spanish in Alta California.

Constantly challenged by insufficient supplies, resistant natives, and Spanish bureaucratic red tape, Serra ultimately went on to found a total of nine thriving missions before his death in 1784. The mission chain eventually totaled 21, situated a day's travel apart (on horseback) along El Camino Real ("the royal road"), which stretched up through present-day California from Mexico. U.S. Highway 101 runs along this historic route for most of its concrete path, and intact portions of the original road can be seen at several mission sites. Recognized for the role he played in spreading the Christian faith and establishing a strong Spanish legacy in California, Father Junípero Serra was beatified by the Vatican in 1988.

—*Stephanie Avnet Yates*

Deco / ★★☆

394 E MAIN ST, VENTURA; 805/667-2120 Anyone looking for evidence of downtown Ventura's slow-but-steady improvement, need only step into this stylish new restaurant in the heart of pedestrian-friendly Main Street. Opened in 2002 by successful Santa Barbara restaurateur Norbert Furnée (visionary behind S.B.'s sublime Sage and Onion, see review), Deco offers a sophisticated yet accessible menu that raises the bar for Ventura's chefs—the seamless blending of fresh regional ingredients, Mediterranean and Asian accents, and thoughtful presentation often referred to as "wine country cuisine"—as well as a waitstaff often unaccustomed to wine pairings and *amuse bouches*. Deco's historic storefront has been reclaimed as a gallery-like space, where fine paintings and diners are equally well-lit by flattering indirect light and flickering votives—the balance is warm and cozy, yet modern and chic. From the seasonally composed menu, you may expect dishes like Asian-style Dungeness crab cakes sweetened by vanilla-wasabi cream; pork tenderloin glazed with Kahlua and served with aromatic green tea–jasmine rice; pinot noir braised lamb shank atop a roasted garlic risotto cake; and desserts that highlight market-fresh fruit and premium chocolate. The handsome bar attracts its own wine-tasting clientele each evening. *$$$; MC, V; no checks; lunch Mon–Fri, dinner every day; wine only; reservations recommended; www.decorestaurant.com; near the corner of Oak St.*

Rosarito Beach Cafe / ★★☆

692 E MAIN ST, VENTURA; 805/653-7343 Got a hankering for traditional Baja-style and regional Mexican cooking, spiked with tangy elements borrowed from the West Indies? Here's where you'll find a culinary sophistication that's rare in modest Ventura. The staid appearance of this 1938 Aztec Revival Moderne building (the historical marker out front reveals that it was originally a bank) is deceiving. Inside, bright Pacific colors and intoxicating aromas pervade the dining room and wide, enclosed patio. If you're lucky, the resident tortilla maker will be in plain view, patiently patting discs of flour and corn masa for the cafe's trademark fresh tortillas. Resist the temptation to fill up on these warm treats, though, to save room for truly superb specialties like pork *adobado* (rubbed with ancho chiles and mesquite-grilled), chicken in savory dark mole sauce, crab and white cheddar chile relleno, or lobster-spinach lasagne made with chile-spiked pasta. In true Baja style, seafood is the main attraction here: a daily selection of fresh fish or shrimp can be prepared in one of five regional ways ("Veracruz" is poached with capers, olives, onions, and tomatoes; "Yucatan" is marinated with achiote and citrus, then mesquite-grilled), and you can always fall back on a platter of fish tacos served with crema, cabbage, and lime. *$$; AE, DIS, MC, V; no checks; lunch Tues–Sat, dinner Tues–Sun; full bar; reservations recommended; corner of Fir St.* &

71 Palm Restaurant / ★

71 N PALM ST, VENTURA; 805/653-7222 Inside a charmingly restored 1910 Craftsman home just a block off Main Street, this ambitious restaurant is still working out some details. Quality of service can be uneven, and the well-composed country-French menu sometimes promises better than the kitchen can deliver. Still, the delightful setting helps make 71 Palm a pleasant change of pace in a town of limited dining options. The two-story house was once a showplace home, and you can still see the ocean from the airy upstairs dining room. Downstairs, simple bistro tables are arranged around the original tile fireplace, which crackles pleasantly during nearly every meal. The decor features the warm woods and rich muted colors associated with the Arts and Crafts period, and the home's original moldings and built-in features have been expertly preserved. As a rule, dinner is more thoughtfully prepared than lunch, and you won't go wrong sticking with bistro basics like steak au poivre with crispy pommes frites, Provençal lamb stew, or roasted Chilean sea bass with horseradish-Dijon crust. Authentic French appetizers shine at both lunch and dinner; coarse country pâté is served with crusty bread and tangy cornichons, the charcuterie sampler is sized for two, and the onion soup *gratinée* is rich and cheesy—just the way it should be. Be sure to visit the antique-filled original rest rooms upstairs. *$$; AE, DC, DIS, MC, V; no checks; lunch Mon–Fri, dinner Mon–Sat; full bar; reservations recommended; www.71palm.com; between Main and Poli Sts.* &

LODGINGS

Bella Maggiore Inn / ★★☆

67 S CALIFORNIA ST, VENTURA; 805/652-0277 OR 800/523-8479 Looking as if it just jumped out of a European art film into Ventura's historic downtown, this intimate Italian-style hotel scores points for affordability, character, location, and hospitality. From the sidewalk, step through Bella Maggiore's Romanesque entrance into a lobby filled with classic antiques, sparkling chandeliers, a cozy fireplace, and a grand piano. Up a shapely marble staircase are 24 simply furnished rooms, each overlooking either the romantic courtyard or the roof garden. Each Mediterranean-casual room is unique; some have extras like fireplace, balcony, bay-window seat, air-conditioning, or kitchenette, and all have shutters, ceiling fans, and fresh flowers. A full breakfast is included in the room rate, as are complimentary beverages and appetizers each afternoon. A central courtyard is the inn's focal point, with fountains and flowering trees. Adding to its European-plaza ambience is Nona's Courtyard Cafe, the hotel's charming restaurant—a favorite with locals, who stop in to dine in the small dining room or on the pleasant canopied patio. The menu offers bistro basics with a Mediterranean flair. *$–$$; AE, DC, DIS, MC, V; no checks; www.bellamaggioreinn.com; between Main and Santa Clara Sts.*

La Mer Bed & Breakfast / ★★

411 POLI ST, VENTURA; 805/643-3600 Visit La Mer and you'll soon discover the European ambiance behind this 1890 Cape Cod-style house, whose perch near Ventura's imposing neoclassical City Hall is within convenient walking distance of San Buenaventura's historic district and the beach. Former proprietor Gisela Baida originally created a cozy German hideaway here, but new owners have freshened the inn in recent months. In addition to luxurious pillowtop beds and DVD players (an extensive borrowing library is downstairs), they renamed the five guest rooms after the Channel Islands offshore, and tempered their Old World furnishings with some neutral touches. Whether you choose the Santa Barbara suite with its wood-burning stove, the Anacapa hideaway with its sunken bathtub, the San Miguel room with its nautical theme, or one of the others, you'll enjoy a private entrance, a private bath, and complimentary wine in your room. There's a spectacular coastal view from two of the five guest rooms as well as the parlor. The rest of the cottage is small and cluttered with antiques (definitely not a place for kids), including a cozy parlor where breakfast is served. Gisela's distinctive

CALIFORNIA'S CENTRAL COAST

Bavarian-style breakfast remains the standard, featuring tradiutional foods like muesli and Black Forest ham in addition to cakes, breads, cheeses, fresh fruits, and plenty of strong coffee. The innkeepers are happy to arrange for cruises to Anacapa Island, country carriage rides, or therapeutic massages to enhance your stay. *$$–$$$; AE, DIS, MC, V; no checks; www.lamerbnb.com; at Oak St.*

Pierpont Inn / ★

550 SANJON RD, VENTURA; 805/643-6144 OR 800/285-4667 One of those places you see from the freeway but never learn about, the Pierpont is a landmark property well worth further investigation. Inside the main building—a 1908 California Craftsman—the Arts and Crafts style reigns, and photos from the inn's rich and colorful past adorn the warm wood-paneled walls. When it was built, the hotel enjoyed unobstructed views of and access to the beach, but US 101 rudely intruded in 1962. Today clever landscaping manages to obscure the highway without hiding the Pacific, but some automobile noise is inevitable. Though the property is no longer luxurious, it doesn't take long to appreciate the sense of history, style, and dedication to hospitality that pervade here. The newly renovated guest rooms are spacious but otherwise unremarkable. Many have terrific (freeway notwithstanding) ocean views, and the best also have fireplaces to cozy up the evenings. Two utterly darling cottages—displaced from their original spot on the old beach path—are available as well; they're a short stroll from the main hotel but are happily insulated from the freeway. There's a classic kidney-shaped swimming pool, and massage and spa services on the premises.

Room rates include a full breakfast in the Pierpont's dining room, the ocean-view Austen's restaurant. Open to the public for lunch and dinner, this relaxing spot is best appreciated by sitting at a window table so you can gaze over the large, sunny lawn dotted with Adirondack chairs to the sea beyond. Informal but dignified, Austen's offers the same reasonably priced menu throughout the day, featuring an amalgam of California cuisine, European specialties, and American classics. Recommended dishes are soup (gazpacho, clam chowder, and French onion are always on the menu), fresh and crisp main-course salads, seafood "shepherd's pie," and traditional bouillabaisse. *$$; AE, DC, DIS, MC, V; checks OK; info@pierpontinn.com; www.pierpontinn.com; near Harbor Blvd.* &

The Victorian Rose / ★

896 E MAIN ST, VENTURA; 805/641-1888 Owners Richard and Nona Bogatch have taken a 19th-century church—complete with soaring steeple— and created a truly unique five-room bed-and-breakfast that nearly defies conventional description. Indulging their passions for religious paraphernalia, antique clocks, Victorian knickknacks, and sundry other collectibles, the Bogatches have filled literally every corner of their theatrical creation with so many items it's often precarious just navigating from the formal breakfast table—elevated on the former altar—through the large chapel (now filled with velvet settees and antique armchairs) to the guest rooms. The rooms are also dramatically decorated, though are thankfully less busy than the public areas, with each adhering to a chosen theme—the Chinese Emperor's Suite is a bordello-esque room popular with honeymooners. Paneling and other features from the church's remodel were also saved and used in crafting private bathrooms for each room, and welcoming comforts include turndown chocolates, plus fireplaces and balconies in select rooms. If you love poking through vintage collections, appreciate ecclesiastical artifacts, and don't mind a little clutter, the Victorian Rose is for you. It's well located, too, just a few blocks from the heart of old downtown, in a stretch increasingly filled with art galleries. *$$–$$$; AE, DIS, MC, V; checks OK; victrose@pacbell.net; www.victorian-rose. com; at Kalorama St.*

Mussel Shoals

LODGINGS

The Cliff House Inn / ★★

6602 W PACIFIC COAST HWY, MUSSEL SHOALS; 805/652-1381 OR 800/892-5433
This small hotel perched cliffside is often booked solid by intrepid guests seeking a dramatic vantage point for watching winter storms—though it has plenty of appeal during the calm warmer months as well. Located between Ventura and Santa Barbara where US 101 snakes right alongside the rocky beach, the Cliff House punctuates an isolated strip of beach houses overlooking an artificial reef. The inn makes the most of its dramatic surroundings; every room has a spectacular ocean view, as does the impressive swimming pool, which is surrounded by deck lounges and graced by an enormous Chilean wine palm with seductively rustling fronds. Guest rooms are just large enough to hold a few basic pieces of white wicker furniture with cheerful floral upholstery, and bathrooms are equally utilitarian. The location, though untouristy, is a good one: decent beaches and surfing are close by, as are Santa Barbara's restaurants and attractions, and even Ojai is only a short jaunt inland.

The hotel's own Shoals restaurant boasts the same stunning ocean view—they even serve poolside in pleasant weather. The dining room is simple and sparsely adorned, but the restaurant does a good job of creating a mood with subdued lighting and polished service. Not surprisingly, seafood figures prominently on a seasonally composed menu that highlights fresh local ingredients and familiar California cuisine. A very nice lunch menu features lighter adaptations of dinner entrees. *$$; DC, DIS, MC, V; local checks only; info@cliffhouseinn.com; www.cliffhouse inn.com; Mussel Shoals exit from US 101.* &

Ojai

Ojai sits in a secluded crescent-shaped valley, a spot whose natural beauty has inspired Hollywood filmmakers, artists, and free spirits for decades. Still blanketed with citrus groves stretching toward wild, rocky foothills, the Ojai Valley can trace its popularity back to the 1870s, when journalist Charles Nordhoff praised its ideal climate, natural mineral baths, and spectacular setting. The farmers who began settling the area named the new town in Nordhoff's honor, but anti-German senti-ment during World War I led to its being renamed in 1917. *Ojai* is a Chumash word that can mean either "nest" or "moon." Bohemian artisans, well-heeled equestrians, camera-shy celebs, and New Age gurus have all embraced idyllic Ojai and left their mark on the valley. This area still radiates the magic that captivated movie producer-director Frank Capra who, when scouting locations for *Lost Horizon* in 1936, selected sleepy little Ojai to stand in for legendary utopia Shangri-la. To see the **SPECTACULAR VISTA** admired by Ronald Colman in the movie, drive east on Ojai Avenue, continuing uphill until you reach the gravel turnout near the top; a stone bench provides the perfect spot for contemplation. Another mystical phenomenon praised by residents and visitors alike is the so-called **PINK MOMENT,** when the bril-liant sunset over the nearby Pacific is reflected onto the Topa Topa Mountains, cre-ating an eerie and beautiful pink glow. Although you can catch a glimpse from town, the effect is amplified when you ride uphill with **PINK MOMENT JEEP TOURS** (805/ 653-1321; www.ojaijeep.com), whose four-wheel-drive excursions position you at the valley's perfect vantage point just in time for sunset.

Ojai's downtown is both charmingly rustic and pleasantly sophisticated, thanks to the influence of urban émigrés from Los Angeles and Santa Barbara. Shops, gal-leries, and cafes are concentrated in the **ARCADE,** whose Mission Revival arches shade pedestrians from the midday sun. Across the street is **LIBBEY PARK,** center-piece of the community and home to open-air Libbey Bowl, where musical notes enhance many summer evenings. Classical music fans throughout the state look for-ward to June's **OJAI MUSIC FESTIVAL** (for schedule information and tickets, call 805/646-2094; www.ojaifestival.org), which has been drawing world-class per-formers since 1947. Past appearances by Igor Stravinsky, Aaron Copland, the Juil-liard String Quartet, and others of their caliber ensure sold-out crowds—and sold-out lodgings—each year. While strolling downtown, pick up a free *Visitors Guide* at the **OJAI VALLEY CHAMBER OF COMMERCE** (150 W Ojai Ave; 805/646-8126; www.the-ojai.org).

There's no understating the powerful influence of the visual arts on Ojai. The town is home to more than 35 well-regarded artists working in a variety of mediums. Most have home studios and are represented in one of Ojai's many galleries. Every October visitors get a chance to enter the private studios of many area painters, sculptors, potters, and wood carvers during the two-day **OJAI STUDIO ARTISTS TOUR** (for tickets and information, call the chamber of commerce at 805/646-8126, or log on to www.ojaistudioartists.com). This unique event includes an evening reception and benefit art auction, and it's also a great way to bring home an original piece without paying the gallery markup.

You can't visit Ojai without hearing about local legend **BEATRICE WOOD,** an internationally acclaimed ceramic artist responsible for putting Ojai on the art world's map. Wood, who was declared a California Living Treasure, worked up until her death in 1998 at 104 years of age. Her luminous lusterware pottery and whimsical sculpture are occasionally displayed in local galleries but are more commonly found at museums such as New York's Whitney or San Francisco's Craft & Folk Art. You can learn more about Wood and her Ojai studio online at www.beatricewood.com.

Numerous galleries represent other Ojai artists, including **HUMANARTS** (310 E Ojai Ave; 805/646-1525; www.humanartsgallery.com), specializing in jewelry and smaller pieces (they have a home accessories annex several doors away); **GRAND DAMES GALLERY** (1211 Maricopa Hwy; 805/640-1252), showcasing the work of Ojai's female painters and sculptors along with a token male artist now and then; and **PRIMAVERA** (214 E Ojai Ave; 805/646-7133), featuring an eclectic collection of glass, jewelry, wood, ceramics, and paintings.

Any bibliophile who's been to Ojai knows about used-book purveyor **BART'S BOOKS** (302 W Matilija St; 805/646-3755), a quirky local institution whose books are displayed in every nook and cranny of a converted cottage, including the patio, garden shed, and even along the sidewalk outside the entrance gate. After hours these sidewalk racks are on the honor system, and patrons drop money into a little payment box. If browsing bookshelves isn't active enough for your tastes, rent a bicycle from **BICYCLES OF OJAI** (108 Canada St; 805/646-7736) or a horse (the Ojai Valley Inn offers guided horseback rides; 805/646-5511) and hit the **OJAI VALLEY BIKE & EQUESTRIAN TRAIL**, which winds scenically for 8.8 miles, most of it parallel to Ojai Avenue. Even more recreational activities are available at sparkling **LAKE CASITAS** (follow Hwy 150 northwest from Ojai until signs direct you to Lake Casitas; 805/649-2233), hidden just minutes uphill from the valley floor. Site of the 1984 Olympic rowing events, the lake boasts a shoreline full of coves and inlets. Swimming is not allowed because the lake serves as a domestic water supply, but you can rent rowboats and small motorboats from the boathouse (805/649-2043).

The serenity of this valley was first recognized by its Native American inhabitants, but it wasn't long before Ojai began to draw outsiders seeking to cultivate inner peace and enlightenment. Long before "New Age" was a national buzzword, Ojai was home to several esoteric sects with various metaphysical and philosophical beliefs. One of the oldest is the **KROTONA INSTITUTE OF THEOSOPHY** (46 Krotona Hill, off Hermosa Rd; 805/646-2653; www.theosophical.org/centers/krotona/index.html), which moved here from Hollywood in 1924. The center is notable for its natural beauty, important metaphysical research library, bookshop, adult education school, and the architecture of its buildings. The noted philosopher Jiddu Krishnamurti stayed at Krotona before the founding of the **KRISHNAMURTI FOUNDATION** (1070 McAndrew Rd, off Reeves Rd; 805/646-2726; www.kfa.org), named for the theosophist who first visited in 1922. Though he traveled the world speaking on his philosophy, Krishnamurti always returned to Ojai, the place he called a "vessel of comprehension, intelligence, and truth." The foundation includes a research library, historical archives, and a retreat center. If Ojai inspires you to seek a little enlightenment of your own, head to **MEDITATION MOUNT** (805/646-5508; www.meditation.com), several bucolic acres located at the east end of the valley on Reeves Road (about 2½ miles off Ojai Ave). This nonprofit organization encourages and facilitates meditation on the laws and principles of humanity and nonsectarian spirituality, in the belief that doing so will serve humanity by spreading light and energy between souls. They invite visitors to use their meditation room, which is open daily from 10am till sunset.

RESTAURANTS

Boccali's / ★★

3277 SANTA PAULA–OJAI RD, OJAI; 805/646-6116 You'll find this small wood-frame restaurant set among citrus groves, in a nostalgic pastoral setting that hasn't changed for decades. Sit outdoors at one of the picnic tables shaded by umbrellas and twisted oak trees, or inside where the tables are covered with red-and-white-checked oilcloth. Like an old-style roadhouse, Boccali's has a complete lack of pretension, coupled with excellent homestyle Sicilian grub, including a lasagne that could win a statewide taste test hands down. An equally delicious meatless version is available, with spinach filling and marinara sauce. The pizzas run a close second, even though they can be topped with suspiciously trendy ingredients like crab, whole garlic cloves, shrimp, and chicken. Fresh lemonade, squeezed from fruit plucked off local trees, is the usual drink of choice. Come hungry, and plan on sharing. *$; No credit cards; local checks only; lunch Wed–Sun, dinner every day; beer and wine; reservations recommended; on Hwy 150 at Reeves Rd.* &

L'Auberge / ★★

314 EL PASEO, OJAI; 805/646-2288 Often touted as the most romantic restaurant in Ojai, L'Auberge is a swank holdover from the days when classic French cuisine was the epitome of fancy dining. Housed in a 1910 mansion with fireplace and ornate chandeliers, a short, pleasant walk from downtown, the restaurant has a charming terrace with a marvelous view of Ojai's "pink moment" at sunset. The French-Belgian menu is unswervingly traditional, and L'Auberge is known for its exceptional escargots and sweetbreads. Among the other selections are scampi, frogs' legs, poached sole, tournedos of beef, and duckling à l'orange. The weekend brunch menu offers a selection of perfectly prepared crepes. This kind of place has gone seriously out of style, so if you love classic French you'd do well to take advantage of this still-excellent grande dame. *$$; AE, MC, V; no checks; dinner every day, brunch Sat–Sun; full bar; reservations recommended; corner of Rincon St.* &

The Ranch House / ★★★

S LOMITA AVE, OJAI; 805/646-2360 If you're going to have only one meal in Ojai, have it here. The name may suggest steaks 'n' spuds, but the reality of this Ojai Valley gem couldn't be more different. Originally conceived in 1949 by Alan and Helen Hooker—two Krishnamurti followers drawn to Ojai's natural beauty—the restaurant began life as a vegetarian boardinghouse. The Hookers were hippies before hippie was hip, and it wasn't long before they turned their "ranch house" into a full-fledged restaurant, adding meat dishes and exceptional wines to a menu that continues to emphasize the freshest vegetables, fruits, and herbs in what is now ubiquitously known as California cuisine. Freshly snipped sprigs from the lush herb garden will aromatically transform your simple meat, fish, or game dish into a work of art, and diners are encouraged to stroll through this splendid kitchen garden during their visit. From an appetizer of Cognac-laced liver pâté served with its own chewy rye bread to leave-room-for desserts like fresh raspberries with sweet Chambord cream, the ingredients always shine through. With guests driving in from as far as Los Angeles just for a Ranch House meal, everything has to be perfect, and this peaceful and friendly retreat never disappoints. Equally impressive are the polished yet friendly service and magical setting, with alfresco dining year-round on a wooden porch facing the scenic valley, as well as in the romantic garden amid twinkling lights and stone fountains. $$$; AE, DC, DIS, MC, V; checks OK; dinner Wed–Sun, brunch Sun; beer and wine; reservations recommended; www.theranch house.com; south of El Roblar Dr off Hwy 33. &

Suzanne's Cuisine / ★★★

502 W OJAI AVE, OJAI; 805/640-1961 Ojai's roster of exceptional restaurants includes this understated charmer a few blocks from the center of town where every little detail bespeaks a preoccupation with quality. Each ingredient is as fresh and natural as it can be, and these menu offerings—a blending of California cuisine with Italian recipes from chef/owner Suzanne Roll's family—show them off to advantage. Every meal begins with a basket of home-baked rolls served with butter squares, each accented by a single pressed cilantro leaf. Vegetables are al dente, and even the occasional cream sauce tastes light and healthy. A highlight of the lunch menu is the Southwest salad: wild, brown, and jasmine rice tossed with smoked turkey, feta cheese, veggies, and green chiles. At dinner, pepper-and-sesame-crusted ahi is served either sautéed or seared (your choice). Suzanne's covered outdoor patio should be your first seating choice. Its marble bistro tables are shaded in summer by lush greenery and warmed in winter by a fireplace and strategically placed heat lamps. When it rains, a plastic cover unfurls to keep water out while maintaining an airy garden feel. This is the kind of restaurant that makes you long for three-hour lunches and decadently unhurried dinners; so sit back, enjoy, and—by all means—don't skip dessert! $$; DC, DIS, MC, V; local checks only; lunch, dinner Wed–Mon; full bar; reservations recommended; www.suzannescuisine.com; east of Bristol Rd. &

LODGINGS

The Moon's Nest Inn / ★★

210 E MATILIJA ST, OJAI; 805/646-6635 Ojai's oldest building—a former schoolhouse (circa 1872)—has been reborn as a bed-and-breakfast that stays charmingly historic while offering every modern comfort. This old-fashioned clapboard building, located within easy walking distance of downtown shopping, dining, and attractions, was fully renovated in 1998 by innkeepers Rich and Joan Assenberg, who carefully preserved, replaced, or complemented the inn's historic details. Five of the seven guest rooms now boast private bathrooms, and several also enjoy private balconies. In addition to being greeted by an afternoon wine reception, you'll find bottled water and chocolates in each room. Throughout the house, from the cozy fireplace parlor to the sunny breakfast room, architectural features like crown molding are highlighted by dramatically painted walls, and the entire inn is furnished with a mix of carefully chosen antiques and quality contemporary pieces. A once-neglected side lawn has been transformed into a restful tree-shaded garden retreat, complete with a rock-lined pond and a large trellised veranda where breakfast is served on pleasant days. A cottage on the grounds houses a friendly beauty-and-massage salon (in-room massage is available), and guests enjoy full day-use privileges at the Ojai Valley Athletic Club for a nominal fee. *$$; AE, MC, V; checks OK; info@ moonsnestinn.com; www.moonsnestinn.com; 1 block north of Ojai Ave between Signal and Montgomery Sts.* &

The Oaks at Ojai Health Spa / ★★

122 E OJAI AVE, OJAI; 805/646-5573 OR 800/753-6257 Physical fitness guru Sheila Cluff opened this low-key, affordable spa in the heart of downtown in 1977, and it remains one of Ojai's most enduring draws. Leave your designer sweatsuits at home; the Oaks capitalizes on its spectacular natural setting and Ojai's laid-back personality to encourage people—mostly women, but men aren't uncommon—to focus on personal renewal and stress reduction. Rates here include full board, with a 1,000-calorie-a-day diet consisting of three meals plus snacks. The spa cuisine is surprisingly good, incorporating a variety of flavorful accents and ethnic influences to help compensate for the minimal fat and salt. (Guests are free to go snacking off the grounds, but don't tell them we said so.) The spa specializes in providing a custom-tailored experience: you can plan a day of fitness classes and activities (morning hikes, step aerobics, yoga, body sculpting, and so on), or simply float from one pampering spa treatment to another (choose from massage, facial, body wraps, reflexology, salon treatments, and more). There's a swimming pool that's often filled with aquarobicizers, plus saunas and whirlpools—and all of Ojai is outside the front door. Rates are per person, per day, and vary depending on your accommodation choice. The spa offers private or shared rooms in detached cottages or the main lodge; all are comfortably appointed but otherwise unremarkable. The Oaks also offers day-spa packages that include lunch and use of the entire facility. *$$; DIS, MC, V; checks OK; www.oaksspa.com; at Signal St.* &

Ojai Valley Inn & Spa / ★★★

905 COUNTRY CLUB RD, OJAI; 805/646-5511 OR 800/422-OJAI Chic travelers have been sojourning at this genteel resort since 1923, when Hollywood architect Wallace Neff designed the clubhouse that's now the focal point of the quintessentially Californian, Spanish Colonial–style complex. Guest accommodations on the sprawling ranch can be individual cottages, low-rise buildings, or modern condos. Many of the unusually spacious rooms have fireplaces; most have sofas, writing desks, and secluded terraces or balconies that open onto picturesque views of the valley and mountains. A beautiful oak-studded Senior PGA Tour golf course ambles throughout the property, offering moderately challenging play in a stunning setting. Gracious elegance pervades the property, along with a "something for everyone" philosophy. "Camp Ojai" offers kids' programs during peak holiday periods; a pampering "Pet Package" includes a sleeping mat, food bowl, and poop-pick-up kit; tennis courts, complimentary bicycles, horseback riding, and two swimming pools provide active recreation. Next to the golf course, the jewel of the resort is pampering Spa Ojai, where stylish spa treatments—many modeled on Native American traditions—are administered inside a beautifully designed and exquisitely tiled Spanish-Moorish complex. Mind/body fitness classes, art classes, nifty workout machines, and a sparkling outdoor pool complete the relaxation choices; it's easy to spend an entire splendid day at this rejuvenating spot.

The inn's formal dining room is Maravilla, whose excellent and intriguing California-Mediterranean menu can derail even the most frugal intentions. Yes, it's *very* expensive, but if you're looking for a supremely gourmet splurge, this is the place. Mere mortals might opt for the more affordable Oak Cafe & Terrace, whose scenic golf-course views are a nice backdrop for a menu that's also in the Mediterranean family and uses plenty of fresh local ingredients. *$$$$; AE, DC, DIS, MC, V; checks OK; www.ojairesort.com; turn off Ojai Ave at the west end of town.* &

Theodore Woolsey House / ★

1484 E OJAI AVE, OJAI; 805/646-9779 Built in 1887 by Theodore S. Woolsey, attorney and Yale University dean, this grand American Colonial stone and clapboard home was converted into a bed-and-breakfast exactly 100 years later by innkeeper Ana Cross. Don't expect a perfectly restored "museum" of a house, though. The Woolsey-Cross home displays many idiosyncrasies, ranging from an incongruous (but refreshing) 1950s kidney-shaped swimming pool to a curious mix of antique furniture and modern tchotchkes throughout. A veritable backyard playground also includes a fish pond, putting green, horseshoe pit, volleyball court, and croquet lawn, all scattered among seven acres of countryside near Ojai's citrus orchards. The five guest rooms are decorated in an old-fashioned lace-and-floral fashion, each with equally frilly private bath (although some baths aren't en suite). Be sure to get all the specifics when booking, since there are rooms offering fireplace, claw-footed tub, or other extras. A one-bedroom country cottage with kitchenette is available as well. What the inn lacks in polish, it makes up for in character, with a virtually unchanged living room and plenty of corners for some discreet snooping. *$$; No credit cards; checks OK; www.theodorewoolseyhouse.com; on Hwy 150 east of Gridley Rd.* &

The Channel Islands

Channel Islands National Park consists of five unspoiled islands a mere 25 to 40 miles offshore from Ventura and Santa Barbara. Remote and wild, the islands are said to closely resemble what Southern California's landscape looked like hundreds of years ago when Native Americans were the only inhabitants—here *and* on the mainland. Facilities are few—just primitive campgrounds and ranger stations—so visitors are usually hikers, divers, kayakers, and wildlife watchers. Relative isolation has led to the development of distinct species like the island fox. The rocky shorelines are home to sea lions and seals and provide nesting areas for dozens of species of seabirds. The many coves make for colorful scuba diving and snorkeling. During the annual gray-whale migration in winter and early spring, pods of the graceful mammals pass close to the islands with their newly born young in tow. The unpredictable climate on the islands adds to the wildness; though breezy, clear days with strong, hot sun are the norm, thick fog banks or howling windstorms can often descend suddenly.

Each island has a distinct personality. **ANACAPA** is the most commonly visited, being the closest to shore. Ninety minutes is all it takes to reach this tiny (1.1 square miles) isle, whose principal appeal is a network of easy hiking trails that lead to scenic overlooks. **SANTA CRUZ** is the largest in the chain—nearly 100 square miles—and the most diverse, with huge canyons, beaches, cliffs, Chumash village sites, and a copious variety of flora and fauna. Nine-tenths of the island is protected by the Nature Conservancy. The remaining tenth was, for many decades, a privately held sheep ranch; when the National Park Service took over that property in 1997, it eliminated the Channel Islands' only noncamping accommodations, lodges that are being converted to interpretive centers. Windy **SANTA ROSA** also has a strong ranching past, one that ended in 1998 in a storm of controversy that pitted the Park Service against both environmental groups and the 97-year-old Vail & Vickers cattle ranch. The cows are all gone now, taking with them a slice of history and leaving uncertainty that nature's balance can ever be restored on Santa Rosa. Ranger-led tours explore the island's canyons, beaches, and unique endangered plant species. **SAN MIGUEL**, the farthest west in the chain, is also the wildest, a collection of contradictory images: picture-postcard lagoons belie dangerous waters, and constant howling winds can't drown out the barking from crowded seal and sea lion breeding grounds. Explorer Juan Cabrillo is rumored to be buried here; a simple memorial cross stands in his honor. Grass-blanketed **SANTA BARBARA** sits alone to the southeast, an isolated isle out of visual range of the other islands, and often of the mainland as well. Other than the landing cove, the island has no boat access, since it is rimmed with rocky cliffs inhabited by elephant seals, sea lions, and abundant seabirds.

Visiting the Channel Islands requires some advance planning. Your first step should be to contact the **CHANNEL ISLANDS NATIONAL PARK VISITORS CENTER** (1901 Spinnaker Dr; 805/658-5700; www.nps.gov/chis) in Ventura Harbor, where you can get maps, weather reports, and individual guidance. The park's official concessionaire for boat transportation is **ISLAND PACKERS** (1867 Spinnaker Dr; 805/642-7688; www.islandpackers.com), next door to the visitors center. Regularly scheduled boat excursions range from 3 1/2-hour nonlanding tours to full-day naturalist-led trips. If you just want a quick overflight and maybe a picnic stop with a short hike, **HELI-TOURS, INC.** (805/964-0684 at the Santa Barbara Municipal Airport), offers three- to four-hour excursions to Santa Cruz Island. **CAMPING** is permitted on all the park-owned islands, but is limited to a certain number of campers per night, depending on the island. You must bring everything you'll need; there are no supplies on any of the islands. To reserve free camping permits for any of the islands, call 800/365-CAMP or log onto http://reservations.nps.gov.

The visitors center has information on scuba, kayak, and whale-watching tours.

Santa Barbara

It's often called "America's Riviera," and with good reason. Nestled in a picturesque curve of the Southern California coastline, Santa Barbara is fringed with palm-lined, white-sand beaches, while the green sloping foothills of the Santa Ynez Mountains form a scenic backdrop. The city's distinctive Mediterranean architecture—a Spanish/Moorish/ Mission Revival mosaic of whitewashed stucco, red-tile roofs, and oak-shaded courtyards—is its most memorable feature. Santa Barbara grew up around the Spanish presidio (military fortress) at the heart of today's downtown. When a 1925 earthquake and resulting fire destroyed much of "modern" Santa Barbara, city planners mandated that all new construction would mimic the historic style; those regulations are still in place, resulting in a charmingly consistent citywide "look." Whether you come to bask on the area's sun-kissed beaches, prowl the shops and galleries that line its tree-shaded streets, or enjoy a meal at one of many top-notch restaurants and cafes, Santa Barbara is equally ideal for an indulgent afternoon or an entire weekend.

ACCESS AND INFORMATION

Santa Barbara is 92 miles from Los Angeles and 332 miles from San Francisco, on U.S. Highway 101. Highway 154, through the San Marcos Pass, joins 101 from the Santa Ynez Valley to the north. United Airlines offers the most flights daily, but American also flies from L.A. into the **SANTA BARBARA MUNICIPAL AIRPORT,** located in Goleta (15 minutes north of downtown Santa Barbara; 805/967-7111). Most major **CAR RENTAL COMPANIES** are conveniently located at the airport, and the Superride (805/683-9636) **SHUTTLE SERVICE** provides passengers with advance-reservation rides to and from the airport. The **AIRBUS COACH** (800/733-6354) arrives daily from Los Angeles. **AMTRAK** (800/872-7245; www.amtrak.com) makes several stops daily at State and Yanonaly Streets. State Street is Santa Barbara's **MAIN COMMERCIAL THOROUGHFARE,** an always-crowded tree-shaded avenue of shops and cafes; it runs perpendicular to the waterfront. A 25-cent **ELECTRIC SHUTTLE** runs regularly along Cabrillo Boulevard and up and down State Street; it's a convenient way to traverse the most popular part of town without having to hunt for parking. The **SANTA BARBARA TROLLEY CO.** (805/965-0353) offers a round-town continuous tour from 10am to 4pm that stops at all major sites. For more information on events and activities in town, contact the **SANTA BARBARA VISITORS BUREAU** (1 Santa Barbara St, Santa Barbara, CA 93101; 805/966-9222 or 800/927-4688; www.santabarbaraca.com).

MAJOR ATTRACTIONS

Santa Barbara's most distinctive—and most visited—landmark is the elegant **SANTA BARBARA MISSION** (at Laguna and Los Olivos Sts; 805/682-4149; www.sbmission. org), a 1786 masterpiece known as the "Queen of the Missions" for its Greco-Roman Revival grandeur and stunning hillside setting with commanding ocean views. You can tour the old padres' quarters (now a small museum), the eerily beautiful cemetery, the fragrantly landscaped inner courtyard, and the still-active parish church—the only one of the mission chain with twin bell towers. A short drive uphill from the mission is the 65-acre **SANTA BARBARA BOTANIC GARDEN** (1212 Mission Cyn Rd; 805/682-4726; www.sbbg.org), where more than 5 miles of paths meander through a landscape of indigenous California plants arranged in representational habitats (redwood forests, canyon woodlands, meadows, deserts, and the like).

The paintings, photographs, furniture, clothing, and artifacts at the museum of the **SANTA BARBARA HISTORICAL SOCIETY** (136 E De la Guerra St; 805/966-1601; www.santabarbaramuseum.com) portray town life from the 1780s to the

SANTA BARBARA THREE-DAY TOUR

DAY 1. Start your day with a rousingly good breakfast at **TUPELO JUNCTION CAFE,** then take the **RED TILE WALKING TOUR** of historic downtown; don't miss the stunning **COUNTY COURTHOUSE,** whose magnificent 360-degree view is post-card-perfect. Then hop on the shuttle bus and head over to the harbor for some clam chowder at **BROPHY BROS.** Spend part of the afternoon enjoying the **BEACH** and views of the Channel Islands, and then take the shuttle bus as far as the **ZOOLOGICAL GARDENS.** Or, if you are feeling energetic, **RENT A BIKE** and follow the **COASTAL PATH** from Stearns Wharf to Montecito. Have afternoon tea at the **FOUR SEASONS BILTMORE,** then cycle back, ending the day back on State Street to browse some shops and dine at the **WINE CASK** before bedding down in the boutique hideaway **INN OF THE SPANISH GARDEN.**

DAY 2. Take scenic **CLIFF DRIVE,** starting at Cabrillo Drive near the harbor, and following the signs all the way to the **BROWN PELICAN** in the Arroyo Burro Nature Preserve for a beachfront breakfast. Continue on the scenic drive past Hope Ranch. Drive up Las Palmas Drive back onto State Street to the **SANTA BARBARA MISSION,** situated off Los Olivos. Walk through the nearby **BOTANICAL GARDENS** before heading into the hills for an amazing view and lunch on the terrace of **EL ENCANTO,** high up in the wealthy Riviera section of town. After lunch, drive along Alameda Padre Serra through the scenic area and continue on Alston Road to Montecito. Visit **LOTUSLAND** (by appointment only) or shop on **COAST VILLAGE ROAD** in the charming village. Dine at the San Ysidro Ranch's **STONEHOUSE** restaurant, or its intimate little sister, the **PLOW & ANGEL BISTRO.**

DAY 3. Depending on the day and time of year, go **WHALE-WATCHING, SAILING,** or just spend the morning kicking back at any of the area's pristine beaches. In the afternoon look for **ANTIQUES** on State Street or Brinkerhoff Avenue, then drive through Los Padres National Forest over the San Marcos Pass for a hearty lunch at **COLD SPRING TAVERN.** Head back to Santa Barbara to the **SANTA BARBARA MUSEUM OF ART** or the **SANTA BARBARA MUSEUM OF NATURAL HISTORY.** Cap off your trip with a romantic dinner at charming **EMILIO'S.**

1920s, with scenarios depicting the lives of the Spanish, Mexican, Chumash, Chinese, and American pioneers. The diverse collection of objects includes a magnificent Chinese altar, an original Pony Express saddle, an unusual Victorian hair wreath, and the beautiful 17th-century oil *Coronation of the Virgin* by Miguel Cabrera. Across the courtyard is the Gledhill Library, a researcher's paradise where newspapers and periodicals dating back over a hundred years are bound in huge leather volumes and available for your perusal.

Other highlights include the **SANTA BARBARA MUSEUM OF ART** (1130 State St; 805/963-4364; www.sbmuseart.org), a jewel of a small museum beloved by this tight-knit, affluent community. Its permanent collection excels in 20th-century western American paintings and 19th- and 20th-century Asian art and artifacts; they also attract some esoteric visiting exhibits. The **SANTA BARBARA MUSEUM OF NATURAL HISTORY** (2559 Puesta del Sol Rd; 805/682-4711; www.sbnature.org) is a favorite with kids, who can enjoy a planetarium, lizard lounge, insect arena, and exhibits of everything from a 72-foot whale skeleton to a space lab and outstanding Native American artifacts. At the base of State Street lies **STEARNS WHARF,** California's oldest working wharf. Though the days of freight and passenger shipping are over, you can still see local fishing boats unload their daily catch, and stroll the souvenir shops and snack stands of the boardwalk. The **SEA CENTER** (211 Stearns Wharf; 805/962-0885) on the wharf is run in cooperation with the Natural History Museum, and tells the story of local marine life illustrated by models and by a touch tank filled with starfish, sea anemones, crabs, urchins, and other tactile treats. About a half mile away off Cabrillo Boulevard at the Waterfront Center, you'll find the brand-new **SANTA BARBARA MARITIME MUSEUM** (113 Harbor Wy; 805/962-8404; www.sbmm.org), an interactive and hands-on look at the area's maritime history, from the seafaring Chumash tribe to state-of-the-art diving technology. The museum isn't afraid to cast a critical eye on local oil drilling, and also explores ways to preserve the dwindling marine environment. A visit to Santa Barbara would hardly be complete without seeing the extraordinary **MORETON BAY FIG TREE** (on Montecito St, near Chapala, south of US 101), an Australian native that's related to both the fig and rubber trees—though it produces neither. Legend has it the seed was presented in 1874 by a visiting sailor to a local girl, who planted it in her yard; the tree is now the largest of its kind in the country, with an impressive 160-foot branch spread that would cover half a football field and shade 1,000 people at high noon.

If you're visiting on Sunday, don't miss one of Santa Barbara's favorite traditions, the weekly **WATERFRONT ARTS & CRAFTS SHOW** (805/962-8956) along Cabrillo Boulevard between Stearns Wharf and the Fess Parker/DoubleTree Resort. Locals and visitors alike—with dogs and baby strollers in tow—linger at the hundreds of booths selling unique arts and crafts by local artists. Wares featured include pottery, oil and watercolor paintings, handmade jewelry, ethnic weavings, carvings and sculpture, and more.

ARCHITECTURE

Downtown Santa Barbara is rich in the Spanish/Moorish–inspired style that incorporates distinctive arched arcades, trailing bougainvillea adorning creamy stucco walls, black wrought-iron accents, and thick red-tile roofs. An excellent example is **EL PASEO** (800 block of State St), a unique, Spanish-style shopping arcade established in the 1920s; it's one of California's first shopping centers. At the center of El Paseo is the historic adobe **CASA DE LA GUERRA** (15 E De la Guerra St), a coveted remnant of Santa Barbara's Spanish-Mexican heritage. The classic U-shaped adobe dates back to 1827; during the 20th century, it became a traditional gathering place for cultural celebrations. Now a museum, Casa de la Guerra is home to the annual **OLD SPANISH DAYS FIESTA** in August. Santa Barbara's earliest days are reflected at **EL PRESIDIO DE SANTA BARBARA STATE HISTORIC PARK** (123 E Canon Perdido St; 805/966-9719), founded in 1782 as the military and political center of an area that stretched from southern San Luis Obispo County to the then-tiny pueblo of Los Angeles. The park is a terrific example of original Spanish Colonial architecture and of life in early California; restoration and reconstruction of significant buildings continues at this work in progress (donations from visitors are gratefully accepted). Already complete are the 1788 chapel and a row of former private quarters, furnished in authentically reproduced period furniture. If you'd like more information on Casa de la Guerra and El Presidio, contact the Santa Barbara Trust for Historic Preservation (805/965-0093; www.sbthp.org). For a larger sampling of downtown's historic flavor, take the appropriately named **RED TILE WALKING TOUR,** a self-guided walking tour of the city's historic core (maps are available at the visitors center; allow one to three hours to complete). Encompassing 12 blocks, the tour begins at the lovely **SANTA BARBARA COUNTY COURTHOUSE** (1100 Anacapa St; 805/962-6464), a grandiose 1929 example of flamboyant Spanish Colonial Revival architecture. If you have time for only one activity in town, take the elevator up the four-story clock tower, where you can see from the mountains to the bay, and helpful signs help you identify the buildings and gardens you're eyeing. The courthouse's sunken gardens are well worth a stroll, as are its ornate hallways, where carvings and exotic woods replicate the ambiance of a European castle. The Architectural Foundation of Santa Barbara (805/965-6307; www.afsb.org) also offers informative **GUIDED WALKING TOURS** of the city.

ACTIVE EXCURSIONS

For activity of a more participatory kind, **HIKING** and **BIKING TRAIL MAPS** are available at the visitors center main office (on the corner of State St and Cabrillo Blvd at the ocean; 805/965-3021) or in downtown Santa Barbara (504 State St; 805/568-1811); or at the Chamber of Commerce Visitor Center (1 Garden St; 805/965-3021 www.sbchamber.org). **BIKES** and **IN-LINE SKATES** are available for rent at Beach Rentals (22 State St; 805/966-6733). If you'd rather travel by four-legged friend, call the people at **CIRCLE B STABLES** (1800 Refugio Rd; 805/968-3901), who arrange all kinds of rides, including sunset and sunrise, English- or Western-style excursions. You can rent a **SAILBOAT, JET-SKI-STYLE PWC,** or **SPEEDBOAT** from the Sailing Center of Santa Barbara (at the breakwater, enter from Shoreline Dr; 800/350-9090; www.sbsail.com), or let someone else steer your craft with Sunset Kidd Sailing Charters (at the breakwater; 805/962-8222), which offers **DAY TOURS,** seasonal **WHALE WATCHES,** and **SUNSET CRUISES** on a 41-foot Morgan. The *Condor* (board at Sea Landing at the harbor; 805/882-0088 or 888/77-WHALE), operated through the Natural History Museum, is an 88-foot boat that offers educational trips with knowledgeable volunteers (during February, March, and April only). For the more adventurous, Truth Aquatics (Sea Landing at the harbor; 805/962-1127) offers **CHANNEL ISLANDS TRIPS** including kayaking, snorkeling, scuba diving, and hiking.

SHOPPING

Santa Barbara's shopping is excellent. There are specialty stores and boutiques in historic **EL PASEO** (State St, above De la Guerra St) and **LA ARCADA** (State St, above

Figueroa St) and the beautiful modern mall **PASEO NUEVO** (State St at De la Guerra St) with Spanish Colonial facades and faux balconies, which holds anchor stores Macy's and Nordstrom, boutiques, and a cinema. While State Street is the main shopping area and the prime destination for antiques and vintage clothing, some of the best shops are on side streets. For bibliophiles, the **BOOK DEN** (11 E Anapamu St; 805/962-3321) has been the place to go for used books since 1979; **SULLIVAN GOSS BOOKS** (7 E Anapamu St; 805/730-1460) stocks art books and California art, old and new prints, photographs, and paintings such as those of revered local wine-label painter James Paul Brown. **A WALK IN THE WOODS** (15 E Anapamu St; 805/966-1331) has refinished and reproduction English furniture from the 1920s and 1930s. Browsing **TIENDA HO** (1105 State St; 805/962-3643) is like walking through a bazaar in a tropical rain forest: sarongs, masks, primitive wall hangings, and tribal rugs compete for space with flowing exotic women's clothes from Indonesia, India, and China. The **ITALIAN POTTERY OUTLET** down near the beach (19 Helena St; 877/496-5599; www.italianpottery.com) has a huge selection of Italian serving dishes, plates, vases, and bowls for a third less than elsewhere. For shopping with a truly antique flavor, head to **BRINKERHOFF AVENUE** (1½ blocks west of State St between Cota and Haley Sts). Several of the well-preserved Victorian homes on this single historic block have opened their doors as antique shops, rare booksellers, and collectibles stores.

BEACHES

The broad stretch of beach hugging the ocean from Stearns Wharf to Montecito is **EAST BEACH**, the city's most popular beach; along it are places to fish, swim, and play volleyball, plus some grassy areas for sitting and a children's playground. Rest rooms, showers, a playground, and volleyball courts are scattered in the area, and the **CABRILLO PAVILION BATHHOUSE** (1118 Cabrillo Blvd; 805/965-0509) provides lockers and use of its weight room for a minimal fee. **WEST BEACH**, on the other side of Stearns Wharf, includes the Santa Monica Harbor, and offers a gentle-wave lagoon that's perfect for toddlers and nonswimmers. **LEADBETTER BEACH**, between West Beach and Shoreline, is sheltered by a high cliff and is good for swimming and beginning surfers. At **SHORELINE PARK** (Shoreline Dr, north of the harbor), take the steps down to the secluded white-sand beach to escape the crowds, or for an even more remote spot head to **MESA LANE BEACH** (north, at Mesa Ln, off Cliff Dr), a very private strip of sand hidden by bluffs, which is also a good surf spot. Also off Cliff Drive is the beach locals refer to as **HENDRY'S BEACH**, with good picnic areas, snack bars (such as the Brown Pelican), and excellent swimming, fishing, and surfing. (Its official name is **ARROYO BURRO NATURE RESERVE**; 2981 Cliff Dr; 805/687-3714.)

NIGHTLIFE

Beautiful people, many of them famous, drift up to Santa Barbara from L.A. for long weekends, and they come out at night in Santa Barbara to socialize, dine, and hear music. Most of the nightlife scene is centered in Old Town Santa Barbara, particularly on State Street. **Q'S SUSHI A-GO-GO** (409 State St; 805/966-9177) and **ZELO** (630 State St; 805/966-5792) are great for dancing to the latest sounds. Q's serves sushi and other dinners until midnight, and offers dancing nightly (or billiards if you don't dance) and action on three levels. The sound at **SOHO** (1221 State St; 805/962-7776) changes nightly, from jazz, blues, dance, funk, and reggae to Eastern European traditional folk. Also on State, in Paseo Nuevo, is the popular **ROCKS** (801 State St; 805/884-1190), where the food has an Asian twist, and lemon-drop martinis and cigars are practically mandatory. The nightclub upstairs has live jazz or R&B and the easygoing crowd is a mix of all ages, from 20s to 70s. A more sophisticated and consistently older set is drawn to the bar scene and upstairs lounge at **BLUE AGAVE** (20 E Cota St; 805/899-4694), which serves a great margarita and has a porch for smoking cigars. It's not unusual to see celebrities at this cozy two-story restaurant/lounge. During warmer months the **SANTA BARBARA BOWL** (805/962-7411; www.sbbowl.com), an outdoor arena set into the Santa Ynez foothills, attracts all the major concert tours.

RESTAURANTS

Aficionado European Bakery / ★★

10 E CARRILLO ST, SANTA BARBARA; 805/963-8404 No ordinary bakery, this. Here you'll find breadsticks in flavors like chocolate-walnut and lemon-vanilla, plus Mediterranean flatbreads in pecan, lemon-pepper, or ginger-almond flavors. They make special breads and rolls served at Santa Barbara's finer tables (Simpson House, the Four Seasons Biltmore, bouchon, and Wine Cask, just to name a few). But, happily, there's plenty left over for all the folks who come here the rest of the week. Regional bread specials are featured and include herbed *fougasse, levain boules* (sourdough), onion focaccia, sweetly perfumed olive rolls, simple flatbreads, and Tuscan breadsticks. At lunchtime the breads become sandwiches: tuna with sesame-ginger mayonnaise, rosemary-marinated chicken, or roasted vegetable with crumbly feta. Start the day on a sweet note with a fruit-filled pastry or a lemon-blueberry muffin and a foamy cappuccino, and savor it outside at a cafe table or perched on a stool inside. *$$; AE, DC, MC, V; checks OK; breakfast, lunch Mon–Sat; no alcohol; reservations not accepted; on Carrillo St, just east of State St.* &

Arigato Sushi Bar / ★★

1225 STATE ST, SANTA BARBARA; 805/965-6074 After frustrating loyal patrons with a formerly cramped space and long waits, Santa Barbara's most inventive Japanese restaurant has finally moved to this cavernous, brick-walled storefront around the corner from Victoria Street's hot restaurant "row" (where bouchon, Olio e Limone, and Epiphany stand side-by-side). With a couple dozen small tables and another dozen stools at the sushi bar, Arigato can accommodate more people, but reservations are still a must, and the place buzzes with activity every night. There's something for everyone here; cleanly executed nigiri sushi for the purist, Arigato's two-page menu of wacky signature rolls for the adventurous (imagine a zesty confab of blackened ahi, albacore, asparagus, avocado, daikon sprouts, red onion, and Dijon mustard), and traditional cooked selections (including a Matsuhisa-inspired miso-glazed black cod) for more conservative palates. It's hot, it's hip, and it's really yummy—plus casual enough for beachy walk-ins. Nothing's perfect, though, and we'd be less than honest not to warn you about the oversteamed edamame (a priced appetizer, no freebies). The beverage menu includes a nice selection of premium sakes (about 16), Japanese beers, and—of course—plenty of Santa Barbara County wines. *$$; AE, MC, V; no checks; dinner every day; beer and wine; reservations recommended; between Victoria and Anapamu Sts.* &

bouchon / ★★☆

9 W VICTORIA ST, SANTA BARBARA; 805/730-1160 Although the name is French for "wine cork," almost all of the corks are coming out of local bottles at this newcomer serving wine country cuisine. Owner Mitchell Sjerven and chef Charles Fredericks worked at many of the town's finer eating establishments before teaming up in 1998. The list of local wines by the glass is impressive, as is the wine list in general, including such selections as an excellent sangiovese from the Cambria region and a viognier from Santa Ynez. The well-informed staff love to help with menu selections; seasonal dishes they might recommend include pan-roasted bluefin tuna with roasted tomato tapenade and lemon confit with Santa Barbara olives; lime-seared sea scallops with sweet corn risotto; or rosemary and garlic–marinated lamb loin with sweet potato gnocchi. Don't miss the Meyer lemon pudding cake or the warm chocolate cake with homemade banana ice cream. The simple dining room is adorned with paintings by Paul Brown (a respected local painter of wine labels), the kitchen is in view beyond beautiful etched glass panels, and the garden patio is heated. If you just want to drop in for the ambience and a glass of fine local wine, an adjoining wine bar is open on weekends. *$$$; AE, DC, MC, V; checks OK; dinner every day; beer and wine; reservations recommended; www.bouchonsantabarbara.com; between State and Chapala Sts.* &

Brophy Bros. Clam Bar & Restaurant / ★★★

119 HARBOR WY, SANTA BARBARA; 805/966-4418 Unrivaled harbor views and famous clam chowder—leading contender for best in SoCal—are the main draws at this cheerful, lively restaurant. However, there are plenty more treasures from the sea served amid the ocean breezes: cioppino; the cold combo platter of shrimp, crab, oysters, clams, and ceviche; or its hot counterpart with steamed clams, oysters Rockefeller, and beer-boiled shrimp. The fresh fish menu changes daily; you may find Hawaiian ahi breaded with roasted cashews, served with tarragon mustard cream sauce; local thresher shark marinated in olive oil, citrus, garlic, cilantro, and red onion; traditional lobster; fresh mahimahi; or succulent swordfish steak grilled and topped with tarragon-crab cream sauce. Meat eaters, however, needn't be disappointed: the burgers here aren't bad either. Lunch outside on the balcony and absorb the sights and sounds (and sometimes smells) of the fisherman's world around you, or in the evening join regulars at the inside bar as they trade tales of the sea over draft beer and steamers. Expect a wait, as this in one of Santa Barbara's well-known treasures. *$$; AE, MC, V; no checks; lunch, dinner every day; full bar; reservations recommended; enter the harbor off Cabrillo Blvd.*

The Brown Pelican / ★★

2981½ CLIFF DR, SANTA BARBARA; 805/687-4550 Come as you are to the Brown Pelican, a lone restaurant tucked perfectly into a cove on Hendry's Beach in the Arroyo Burro Nature Reserve—you can sit on the patio and watch waves roll in just a few yards away. It's possible the ocean view and scenic surrounding cliffs make the food taste better than it actually is. However, the fare is actually quite good if you stick to the fresh fish specials: fish-and-chips in an ale batter, light but hearty seafood linguine, crab cakes, or steamed local mussels. The ahi tuna on focaccia and the grilled chicken sandwich are simple and tasty, and there's a children's menu with the usual requests—grilled cheese, pasta, burger and fries. Breakfast is especially satisfying, with delectable offerings such as fluffy French toast, buttermilk pancakes, and ocean hash (poached eggs, crab cake, and a potato sauté). An even sweeter temptation is the heavenly chocolate chip pancakes. Don't worry: afterward you can just step down onto the picture-perfect 2-mile stretch of beach to walk it off, along with a multitude of dogs and their owners. *$; AE, MC, V; no checks; breakfast, lunch, dinner every day; full bar; reservations accepted for dinner only; Cabrillo Blvd W, turn right on Loma Alta, left on Cliff Rd about 3 miles.*

Downey's / ★★★

1305 STATE ST, SANTA BARBARA; 805/966-5006 A Santa Barbara classic, Downey's has become synonymous with great California food during its lengthy tenure on State Street, although its unassuming appearance inside and out offers no hint of its reputation. Inside the small dining tables are double-hung with champagne-and-white linens, and the walls hold just a few oil paintings of California scenes. Chef John Downey, who honed his talents on that most royal of cruise liners, the QE2, has perfected the art of taste-bud-awakening with his simply prepared but unerringly conceived creations. The menu changes daily, but everything is guaranteed to be fresh and delicious. Expect magical offerings like melt-in-your-mouth smoked pheasant with ginger-infused pear, Sonoma foie gras with buttery potato and Madeira-soaked raisins, and tenderloin of lamb floating in a veal stock reduction with roasted eggplant. Indulge in the special house dessert—a rhapsody of white chocolate cream and raspberries sandwiched between two layers of buttery, sweet flaky pastry. *$$$; AE, DIS, MC, V; local checks OK; lunch, dinner Tues–Sun, brunch Sat–Sun; full bar; reservations recommended; www.downeyssb.com; between Sola and Victoria Sts.*

El Encanto / ★★☆

1900 LASUEN RD, SANTA BARBARA; 805/687-5000 It's set in an area of Santa Barbara known locally as "the Riviera," and the mountain-to-ocean views from this restaurant's rambling perch are second to none. Whether you're enjoying lunch on a sunny afternoon or dinner under the stars, the food just makes the view seem even grander. Chef Mark Kropczynski offers a fairly consistent menu that may include appetizers such as carrot cream soup or imported caviar served with buckwheat blinis; main courses include paella brimming with local black mussels, Manila clams, chorizo, rock shrimp, chicken, and cilantro. A grilled veal chop arrives with braised endive and red wine–cranberry sauce; rack of lamb is redolent of Provençal herbs;

beef tenderloin is enriched by shallot-morel sauce; and vegetarian entrees like grilled asparagus risotto cakes are frequently offered. Superb desserts—such as classic floating island—are served as the stars compete with the harbor lights. *$$$; AE, DC, MC, V; checks OK; lunch, dinner every day, brunch Sun; full bar; reservations recommended; www.placestostay.com; past the mission, left onto Laguna, right onto Los Olivos, right on Alameda Padre Serra to Lasuen Rd.*

Emilio's Ristorante and Bar / ★★★

324 W CABRILLO BLVD, SANTA BARBARA; 805/966-4426 At this romantic Italian restaurant, arched windows open to Pacific breezes on warm nights and candles provide the only light as evening sets in. As if that weren't enchanting enough, add whitewashed walls, exposed wood beams, soft jazz, and clinking wineglasses and you've got yourself one amorous dining room. Soulful dishes include oak-grilled salmon and the signature "Oscar's paella," created by longtime staff member Oscar Garcia and overflowing with mussels, clams, and spicy sausage. As you feast, enjoy the ever-changing display of works by local artists. Chef Max Hernandez also offers great vegetarian selections like a truffle-laced portobello spring roll with sweet pea purée and whipped curry potatoes, house-made sundried tomato–goat cheese raviolis topped with braised spinach, or butternut squash tortellini bathed in sage butter and walnuts. Whatever your choice, arrive with a good appetite; the beautiful painted Italian plates bear hefty portions. *$$; AE, MC, V; no checks; dinner every day; full bar; reservations recommended; emailios@ msn.com; www.sbweb.com/emilios; near Castillo St.*

Epiphany / ★★

21 W VICTORIA ST, SANTA BARBARA; 805/564-7100 Kevin Costner is one of the partners (with husband-wife team Alberto and Michelle Mastrangelo) in this spare and elegant new restaurant just off State Street, but there's no Hollywood attitude here. Located in the former 1892 home and office of the first female doctor in Santa Barbara, it has a homey feel, with hardwood floors, and banquettes and couches in striped silk with lots of brushed silk pillows. There are some surprises on the menu, particularly the signature raw bar, made possible because all the fish is sushi-grade. Raw bar appetizers include crusted tuna, ceviche, and opa (moonfish) tartare. Main courses include vodka-cured salmon, cured in house and served with Yukon gold potatoes; Atlantic salmon served with morels, braised leeks, and sauce foie gras; and amberjack (in the tuna family) with fingerling potatoes and heirloom tomatoes. Chef Michael Goodman also offers a roasted beet salad with citrus vinaigrette, quail egg, and brioche toast. The decor throughout is what Michelle Mastrangelo calls "urban elegance," with the walls in the bar painted Ralph Lauren red behind the mahogany and marble counter, and the restaurant's walls in a khaki color. The welcoming foyer has a Victorian brick fireplace crowned with a stained glass window, and candles glow from every corner. *$$$; AE, DIS, MC, V; no checks; dinner every day; full bar; reservations recommended; www. epiphanysb.com; 1/2 block west of State St.* &

La Super-Rica / ★★

622 N MILPAS ST, SANTA BARBARA; 805/963-4940 This out-of-the-way Mexican place is one of those finds you usually learn about from friends who live here, although its reputation has been burnished by the enthusiasm of local resident and fan Julia Child. The turquoise-trimmed white shack with its blackboard menu offers authentic and entirely unfussy south-of-the-border fare. Bite into your first soft taco filled with steak, pork, or chile and cheese—all with soft buttery onions—and you'll be a believer. Try the *sopes* (corn tortillas filled with spicy chicken, avocado, and cheese), or the chilaquiles (eggs, cheese, and tortilla strips with a spicy tomato sauce), the quesadillas, or the special corn tamales (served only on Friday and Saturday)—and don't forget to check the daily specials board. And if somehow you still have room, try the hot *atole* (a delicious milk drink laced with vanilla and cinnamon). Though most menu items cost less than $5, you're likely to end up spending more than you anticipated because the selections are too delicious to pass up and because they generally come in rather small portions. *$; Cash only; lunch, dinner Mon–Sat; beer only; reservations not accepted; between Cota and Ortega Sts.* ⅙

The Palace Grill / ★★★

8 E COTA ST, SANTA BARBARA; 805/966-3133 Fun is a complimentary side order at this lively Cajun-style eatery where spicy temptation starts with the cocktails (the Cajun martini is served in a mason jar). They serve up New Orleans–style fare, from jambalaya to crawfish étouffée. Every meal begins with a basket of muffins in flavors like blackstrap molasses with raisins or buttermilk-rosemary. Then it's a matter of choosing among blackened prime rib, Louisiana soft-shell crabs, veal Acadiana in oyster-sherry cream sauce, or Creole crab cakes. However, the food is only half the reason lines form out the door; entertainment includes zydeco music or Friday's magic show. The award-winning staff also deserves credit, because several times a night they lead a rowdy sing-along, always including that perennial Louis Armstrong favorite "What a Wonderful World." There are lots of good places to eat in Santa Barbara, but for pure fun, this place is number one. Incidentally, the bread pudding soufflé with warm—and potent—whiskey cream sauce should not be missed. *$$–$$$; AE, MC, V; no checks; lunch, dinner every day; full bar; reservations required; www.palacegrill.com; just off State St.*

Paradise Cafe / ★★

702 ANACAPA ST, SANTA BARBARA; 805/962-4416 The Paradise's secluded patio, shaded with market umbrellas and palm fronds, has been a local alfresco lunch favorite for more than 15 years. People who come for a simple burger often end up ordering a bottle of hard-to-find boutique wine and spending the whole afternoon. Equally appealing is the vintage diner-style interior, with chrome bar stools and a retro mural of a Native American and his maiden behind a bar stocked with an array of exotic tequilas. A small but creative wine list pairs well with the menu, which ranges from tasty local mussels, oak-grilled swordfish or fresh ahi steak, and New York steak to the legendary burgers (teriyaki, bacon, chili, turkey, garden, or Paradise), Greek salad, rock shrimp–spinach salad, or penne pasta with peppery sausage and onions. *$$; AE, MC, V; no checks; lunch, dinner every day, brunch Sun; full bar; reservations accepted for large groups only; on the corner of Anacapa and Ortega Sts.*

Sage and Onion / ★★★

34 E ORTEGA ST, SANTA BARBARA; 805/963-1012 A consistent favorite since opening in 2000 (and culinary spawning ground for chefs who've since moved on to other prestigious kitchens), Sage and Onion is located in a beautifully renovated downtown Spanish storefront. The simple, understated room is as stylish and comfortable as a favorite tweed sweater, with high ceiling, elegant wood bar, and chic white table settings. It's an effect Martha Stewart might call classic, aided by a Mediterranean undertone that perfectly suits the "California Riviera." Chef Steven Giles fuses his English heritage, French training, and passion for American food into a contemporary cuisine that's creative without being ostentatious. The kitchen "brigade" (Giles gets high marks for crediting his cooks on the menu) delivers impeccably groomed platters, served by an equally dedicated waitstaff. Giles is a farmers market devotée, always utilizing the region's best and freshest ingredients; menu standouts include quail ravioli in a tangy gooseberry reduction, Hawaiian ono atop coconut-infused jasmine rice; sea bass bathed in saffron-mussel cream; and the Sage and Onion pot pie, a British-inspired crust filled with braised rabbit, sweet onion, and slow roasted root vegetables. Dessert lovers won't want to miss the perfect version of a liquid center chocolate cake, served here with house-made roasted banana ice cream. For a nostalgic flavor, try the butterscotch pudding, all dressed up with toffee and chantilly cream. *$$$; AE, MC, V; no checks; dinner every day; full bar; reservations recommended; www.sageandonion.com; corner of Anacapa St.*

Stella Mare's / ★★⯪

50 LOS PATOS WY, SANTA BARBARA; 805/969-6705 If you're looking for a romantic restaurant with rustic European flair, this is it. The house now known as Stella Mare's was built by a sea captain in 1872 and moved a hundred years later from its original site in town to a charming and tranquil spot overlooking a bird-haven pond. The friendly personalities of owners Eva Ein and Philippe and Kym Rousseau pervade this inviting country farmhouse with painted pine chairs, distressed fireplace mantels, and hand-painted Italian plates on the walls. The crowning glory is a restored greenhouse with a bar and cozy fire-front sitting area, where each Wednesday night a jazz trio performs. All entrees from the wood-fired grill (chicken, salmon, New York steak) are excellent, but the specialties are just that: special, including the bacon-wrapped boneless quail stuffed with morels and served with a rustic blue cheese–potato tart. Lunch favorites include croque monsieur (the classic French grilled ham and cheese sandwich) and a steak sandwich topped with caramelized onions. For dessert, try the crème brûlée of the day. *$$; AE, MC, V; no checks; lunch, dinner Tues–Sun, brunch Sun; full bar; reservations recommended; www.stellamares.com; off Channel Rd.*

Tupelo Junction Cafe / ★⯪

739 CHAPALA ST, SANTA BARBARA; 805/899-3100 Tupelo Junction wins the prize as having the most creative menu in town. Order a tall iced tea and prepare to wait for your meal, as everything is made absolutely from scratch here and worth the delay. This cheerful Southern-style cafe has red linoleum floors, orange crate label art, light cafe tables, and a view of the traffic on Chapala Street. The breakfast menu offers buttermilk biscuits with chocolate gravy, vanilla-dipped French toast with homemade berry syrup, and a hash good enough to make you weep, full of chicken, andouille sausage, sweet corn, and potatoes, all of it supporting a couple of poached eggs and smothered in homemade barbecue sauce. Lunch offers homemade potato chips with caramelized shallot dip for starters, and for seconds, a salad tossed with caramelized pears, blue cheese, and candied pecans. Another outstanding salad is the fried chicken salad with cornbread and dried cranberries, pumpkin seeds, and herb buttermilk dressing. Like everything else on the menu, the BLT is made with a twist: it contains fried green tomatoes and avocado. Southern desserts rule here, including homemade praline pecan ice cream pie with sweet peach compote and chocolate beignets with white chocolate sauce. *$–$$; MC, V; no checks; breakfast, lunch, dinner Tues–Sat, brunch Sun; beer and wine; reservations recommended; on Chapala St across from the Paseo Nuevo shopping arcade entrance.*

Wine Cask / ★★★☆

813 ANACAPA ST, SANTA BARBARA; 805/966-9463 Informal elegance in the tradition of great European restaurants has been captured within these stucco walls, which are accented by a stunning hand-stenciled ceiling and a grand stone fireplace. Owner Doug Margerum, who also has a small adjoining wine shop, presides over a vast cellar of more than 2,000 labels and ensures they will beautifully complement the restaurant's cuisine, a sophisticated repertoire of dream-worthy dishes such as delicate, tangy duck spring rolls; grilled foie gras with apple risotto and blackberry sauce; porcini-crusted salmon; lamb sirloin with mint-infused cabernet sauce; or filet mignon on a bed of truffle-laced potatoes. The best dessert choice is warm caramel bread pudding—with a vintage port or Madeira accompaniment. We also recommend the Sunday or Monday prix-fixe tasting, which includes six courses and five wine pairings. An outdoor patio offers a charming alternative to the main room, especially on warmer nights. *$$$; AE, D, MC, V; no checks; lunch, dinner every day, brunch Sat–Sun; full bar; reservations recommended; www.winecask.com; between Canon Perdido and De la Guerra Sts.*

LODGINGS

El Encanto Hotel and Garden Villas / ★★☆

1900 LASUEN RD, SANTA BARBARA; 805/687-5000 OR 800/346-7039 For those who want to revel in the old Santa Barbara resort style, this famous romantic retreat's 84 cottages are perched on 10 lushly landscaped acres high above town. Some were built as early as 1912 in the popular Craftsman style, and others have a Spanish Colonial sensibility, but all are set among tropical foliage, waterfalls, arbors, a Japanese garden, and lawns rolling down to views of the ocean beyond. By the 1920s El Encanto had opened as a resort hotel, when railway lines brought East Coast families to spend an entire season here. Many of the cottages have wood-burning fireplaces, porches, and French doors; some are ideal for families, with multiple bedrooms and baths. The intimate main building houses an airy lounge, bar, and the acclaimed El Encanto restaurant (see review), whose million-dollar views hardly detract from a rather dated decor. For many years the local buzz has been about this grande dame's much-needed renovation, planned for "next year" since Clinton was in office. In 2002, El Encanto recruited general manager Kerman Beriker, who previously oversaw a massive—and massively publicized—renovation of the landmark Beverly Hills Hotel. With his guidance, it looks like the improvements may finally happen—and when the furnishings, amenities, and service here finally live up to historic charm of these cottages and gardens, El Encanto will be a world-class retreat for an exclusive, upscale clientele. Until that time, take advantage of their pre-rehab rates to enjoy one of the most exquisite settings in Southern California. $$$; AE, DC, MC, V; checks OK; www.placestogo. com; from Mission St, left on Laguna St, right on Los Olivos St, right on Alameda Padre Serra, left on Lasuen Rd.

Hotel Oceana / ★★★

202 W CABRILLO BLVD, SANTA BARBARA; 805/965-4577 OR 800/965-9776 This is a sister property to Santa Monica's Oceana, a sophisticated and upscale boutique hotel. Here they've kicked it down a notch, eschewing ultraservice and amenity-laden suites for a lighter, more beach-friendly feel that still offers a more upscale experience than the surrounding budget motels . . . but without the four-star price tag. The Oceana "compound"—low-rise amalgam of four formerly independent motel properties—deftly maintains its vintage-era architecture and charm (including splendid original tile work) while injecting contemporary comforts and a breezy, colorful coastal style. Chic Italian linens, in-room CD players, and designer furniture unify the diverse layouts of all completely remodeled rooms, and provide a serene counterpoint to the bustle of Cabrillo Boulevard and East Beach outside the front door. (You'll also be walking distance from State Street, Stearns Wharf, and the harbor.) Ocean-view rooms come at a premium, but many guests prefer the quieter garden- or poolside rooms. With swimming pools, the beach, a minispa, and the original Sambo's coffee shop next door, Oceana is equally well suited for family vacations and romantic weekends. $$$–$$$$; AE, DIS, MC, V; checks OK; www. hoteloceana.com; between State and Castillo Sts. &

Inn of the Spanish Garden / ★★★

915 GARDEN ST, SANTA BARBARA; 805/564-4700 OR 866/564-4700 Because Santa Barbara is a conservative, low-growth city, frequent visitors were delighted to welcome, in 2002, the rare appearance of a brand-new boutique hotel in the heart of the city's historic center. Newly constructed to blend seamlessly with the surrounding low-rise Spanish Colonial offices—all white stucco, with graceful arches, and distinctive red-tiled roofs—this 23-room inn is imbued with creative spirit from the colony of artists' studios that once stood on this site. Frette linens, fireplaces and French press coffeemakers are the hallmarks of sophisticated service that includes a bed-and-breakfast style encyclopedia of local menus, complimentary gourmet continental breakfast and espresso bar, top-of-the-line imported bath products, and the overall sensation of staying at a wealthy friend's villa. The ambiance is pure Santa Barbara, with meandering gardens and gurgling fountains; interiors blend

Mediterranean style (golden sponge-painted walls, terra-cotta floor tiles) with authentic Spanish Colonial flavor (rustic wooden doors, colorful woven rugs) and Asian accents (raw silk upholstery and Chinese vases). No detail is overlooked; there's a well-equipped exercise nook, quiet lap pool surrounded by gardens, and a path to the historic artist cottages, some converted to unique meeting spaces. Check with the hotel for workshop packages featuring noted Central Coast artists. *$$$$; AE, DC, DIS, MC, V; no checks; www.spanishgardeninn.com; between Carillo and Canon Perdido Sts.* &

Simpson House Inn / ★★★☆

121 E ARRELLAGA ST, SANTA BARBARA; 805/963-7067 If you were rich and had a very good *majordomo,* life would be like this. The Simpson House is the only B&B in North America that's been given AAA's five-diamond rating, and it's well deserved. This imposing Victorian estate is an elegant world of its own, despite being near the heart of downtown. Guest rooms in the main house feature period detailing on the ceilings, color-coordinated with Oriental rugs and plush upholstery, and complemented with brass beds, European goose-down duvets, and fine antiques. In back, beyond the stone patio and lawn (the domain of Bella, the most petted black Lab in town), guests enjoy more privacy in old barn suites and two-story cottages with private courtyards and stone fountains, tucked between tall oaks and magnolias. Each is stylishly modern country-cottage in decor, with open-beam ceiling, river-rock fireplace, whirlpool tub, and wet bar. Service is pampering, practiced, and discreet, and includes a complete gourmet breakfast—with china and silver—delivered to your room or secluded patio. Wine and a lavish array of hors d'oeuvres are served nightly in the sitting area or can be enjoyed on the main house's wisteria-draped porch. A facial or a massage can be arranged, and a game of croquet on the lawn is most civilized entertainment. Bicycles and beach equipment are also offered, along with an extensive collection of videos. *$$$; AE, DIS, MC, V; checks OK; www.simpsonhouseinn.com; between Anacapa and Santa Barbara Sts.* &

The Upham Hotel and Country House / ★★

1404 DE LA VINA ST, SANTA BARBARA; 805/962-0058 OR 800/727-0876 The Upham, oldest continually operating hotel in Southern California, combines the intimacy of a bed-and-breakfast with the service of a small hotel. It was built in 1871, and contains 50 rooms in the main building and garden cottages. Still, feather duvets, botanical prints, plush settees, louvered wood shutters, and grand armoires make this feel more like a vintage country house. A walkway with trellised arches and a gazebo weaves its way around the pretty garden and into the main building, where continental breakfast, afternoon cheese and wine, and evening milk and cookies are served. The Upham also boasts its own highly regarded bistro-style eatery, Louie's, which serves lunch and dinner daily. It fills up with more than just hotel guests, so be sure to make a reservation. The hotel also owns the former Tiffany Inn down the street, a restored seven-bedroom Victorian offering the classic B&B experience, with loads of antique details and a full-service breakfast. *$$$–$$$$; AE, DIS, MC, V; checks OK; www.uphamhotel.com; on the corner of Sola St, 2 blocks west of State St.*

Montecito

The name means "little mountain" in Spanish; this lushly wooded little mountain is characterized by gentry horse farms, mansions, tennis courts, and money. Begun as a resort for the wealthy—scions with household names such as Armstrong, Du Pont, Fleischman, Pillsbury, and Stetson built Montecito mansions in the early part of the 20th century—Monetecito continues today as an exclusive enclave, where celebrities and personalities with a taste for country living hide behind opulent, camera-monitored gates.

Shopping is the primary pastime in Montecito. It's centered around several well-heeled blocks of **COAST VILLAGE ROAD**, where upscale but affordable boutiques share the sidewalk with all-day cafes and wonderful dinner spots, all caressed by clean sea breezes. If you continue west from here on East Valley Road to where it meets Hot Springs Road, you will stumble onto the beautiful adobe **MOUNT CARMEL CHURCH**, with its primitive painted interior complete with Mexican silver chandeliers, set in a cactus garden typical of the area. Continue west and follow Sycamore Canyon Road to Cold Springs Road and you will behold **LOTUSLAND** (by appointment only; 695 Ashley Rd; 805/969-9990; www.lotusland.org), a spectacular Montecito estate that combines whimsy and artistry, showcasing succulents, cacti, and tropicals. Rare specimens include the last living examples of some prehistoric varieties, plus vast, romantic pools of lotus flowers. Call well ahead for reservations to experience the beauty of this 37-acre property, the loving creation of Madame Ganna Walska, a European-born opera singer and eccentric plant lover who hired the era's most prestigious gardeners to create this lush oasis.

RESTAURANTS

Little Alex's / ★★☆

1024A COAST VILLAGE RD, MONTECITO; 805/969-2297 Tucked away in a bustling local shopping center that houses everything from a barber to a gas station, you'll find a small but very busy Mexican eatery that makes up for in taste what it lacks in charm. Whatever your choice from the variety of enchiladas, burritos, tacos, or chimichangas, know that the portions are huge (even the ones that are purportedly small)—so come here with an appetite. From the popular *primo* burrito, chile verde, and chile relleno to the house-special arroz con pollo (chicken breast simmered in ranchera sauce), you won't be disappointed. Phone ahead for orders to take to the beach. The perfect picnic item is "burrito-on-the-run," a hand-held burrito available in large or small sizes and chock-full of beans, rice, cheese, salsa, and your choice of *carnitas,* chile colorado, veggies, or more. *$; No credit cards; checks OK; breakfast, lunch, dinner every day; beer and wine; reservations not accepted; at the junction of Coast Village Rd and Hot Springs Rd in the Vons Shopping Center.*

Lucky's / ★★

1279 COAST VILLAGE RD, MONTECITO; 805/565-7540 One of the newest restaurants in town is this hip retro steak house, part of the Santa Barbara-and-beyond empire created by Lucky Jeans founder Gene Montensano, whose other area eateries include Ca'Dario, Bucatini, and Primo. Already popular with local movers-and-shakers, not to mention sports figures and celebrities from nearby L.A., this is one spot vegetarians should avoid, as they would be aghast at the 22-ounce porterhouse or the enormous rack of lamb for one. The New York pepper steak with Cognac gets raves, as does the New York strip steak with Roquefort. Seafood is not neglected: you'll find a salmon fillet, grilled or poached; a Maine lobster, steamed or grilled; and daily fish specials. Other old-fashioned dishes include creamed spinach, jumbo shrimp cocktails, and wilted spinach salad. The sauces alone are more reminiscent of 1960s France than America in the new millennium: rich béarnaise, hollandaise, and a buttery red wine–shallot concoction. Chef James Sly seems to know what diners want; it is often packed here and can be hard to get a reservation, especially on weekends. You can always sit at the bar, where they serve the full menu. Decor is restrained, with plush seating. This revolving-door restaurant location next to the Montecito Inn is said by some to be jinxed; guess Montensano's hoping the name delivers on its promise. *$$; AE, DIS, MC, V; no checks; dinner every day, brunch Sat–Sun; full bar; reservations recommended; luckys@west.net; south end of Coast Village Rd, next to the Montecito Inn.*

Pane e Vino / ★★☆

1482 E VALLEY RD, MONTECITO; 805/969-9274 Good luck finding this terrific but nearly hidden restaurant with a red-tiled roof and ivy-covered patio, tucked into the corner of a quiet shopping center. However, at this popular Italian trattoria (part of a San Francisco chain), it's the patrons who are truly lucky. The authentic country fare attracts quiet power brokers, well-heeled locals, and many fellow restaurateurs, who rave about the fresh pasta (Thursday-night gnocchi is legendary), risotto, simple grilled fish, *bistecca alla fiorentina* (steak with spinach), *bresaola con rucola* (dried cured beef with arugula, sweet onions, and vinaigrette), and juicy veal chops. Daily specials—which sometimes outnumber the regular menu—include seasonal items such as local mussels in garlic sauce or spaghetti with rock shrimp and radicchio. The wine list is largely Italian; desserts include classically good tiramisu, crème caramel, and an assortment of gelati. The outdoor patio, which is especially appealing on balmy summer nights, provides the largest seating area, but the more intimate interior, which evokes old-world charm and comfort, is equally coveted and replete with its shelf of assorted plates, bowls—and children's soccer trophies. *$$–$$$; AE, MC, V; no checks; lunch Mon–Sat, dinner every day; beer and wine; reservations recommended; San Ysidro Rd to Montecito Village.* &

Pierre Lafond Deli / ★★☆

516 SAN YSIDRO RD, MONTECITO (AND BRANCHES); 805/565-1502 Early risers need only follow the aroma of freshly brewed coffee to this gourmet deli, which offers a large selection of delicious pastries and bagels to be savored on a vine-covered patio. Long after the deli's crack-of-dawn opening hour, they begin filling breakfast burritos with eggs and cheese. When lunchtime rolls around it's a treat to sample the rolls filled with crab cake or duck sausage, Caesar chicken wrap, black bean burger, individual quiche, or salad bar. You might want to pair a cappuccino or chai tea with one of their famous farm cakes—a dense and decadent chocolate muffin swirled with cream cheese and chocolate chips. Late lunch/early dinner items include heartier grilled sandwiches till 6pm. Additional branches are located in downtown Santa Barbara (516 State St; 805/962-1455) and in the Paseo Nuevo shopping mall (805/966-5290). *$–$$; AE, MC, V; local checks only; breakfast, lunch, dinner every day; no alcohol; reservations not accepted; www.pierrelafond.com; northeast corner of E Valley Rd.*

Stonehouse Restaurant / ★★★⯪
Plow & Angel Bistro / ★★★

900 SAN YSIDRO LN, MONTECITO; 805/969-4100 Though regarded by many as Santa Barbara County's finest gourmet dining, the Stonehouse restaurant at the exclusive San Ysidro Ranch has a low-key, welcoming atmosphere. The romance starts along a winding tree-lined road in the Montecito foothills, and continues when you behold the bucolic setting—the restaurant is housed in the Ranch's 1889 stone-walled citrus packing house, where a warren of small dining spaces lends an intimate feel. Downstairs, the more casual Plow & Angel Bistro occupies the former wine cellar, now warmed with broad fireplace. Executive chef Jamie West, trained at the Culinary Institute of America, heads one kitchen for both eateries, capitalizing on local seafood and premium meats—as well as produce from the Ranch's own organic garden—to craft his award-winning menu of American regional cuisine. Tempting starters include phyllo-wrapped baked brie surrounded by sweet-tart honey-fig-balsamic syrup, or Hudson Valley foie gras perfectly accented with peppery and fruity flavors. Main courses range from citrus-braised local lobster accompanied by corn-crab risotto and enhanced with musky truffles to fruit- and fontina-stuffed chicken breast, and include vegetarian, Atkins, and Zone diet selections. At the Plow & Angel, West concentrates on hearty bistro fare like saffron steamed mussels in Pernod broth, Asian-style pan-seared salmon, expertly grilled steaks and chops, and a prosciutto-laced mac 'n' cheese that's out of this world. In addition, anything from the Stonehouse menu can be served downstairs, allowing you to mix and match flavors (and prices!). The wine list is superb, and desserts are worth saving room for. *$$$ (Bistro), $$$$ (Stonehouse); AE, MC, V; checks OK; www.sanysidroranch.com; take San Ysidro exit from the US 101, drive north to San Ysidro Ln, turn right.* &

LODGINGS

Four Seasons Biltmore / ★★★★

1260 CHANNEL DR, MONTECITO; 805/969-2261 OR 800/332-3442 This elegant 236-room property, loaded with the luxury associated with the Four Seasons chain, is one of the state's most beautiful old-world-style hotels. The regal main Spanish Revival building, built in 1927, stands amid towering palms overlooking the Pacific. Magnificent wrought-iron gates lead into a pale-hued lobby with hand-decorated archways, bowls of orchids, and polished antiques resting on waxed terra-cotta tiles. Rooms are tastefully furnished in soft tones with beds of the utmost comfort, plantation shutters, botanical prints, and marble bathrooms with big fluffy towels and robes. Heat lamps, hair dryers, book lights, and bowls of candy are some of the extra amenities, and at the touch of a button, earplugs, hot water bottles, nonallergenic soap, and even that toothbrush you forgot will magically appear. For more privacy book one of the green-trimmed California bungalows, many of which have fireplaces and patios. In addition to the pool and tennis courts, the expansive lawn area behind the main building is home to croquet, shuffleboard, and an 18-hole putting green. The gym is fully equipped and bikes are at the ready along with a map of local bike paths. Complimentary day passes to the exclusive Coral Casino Beach and Cabana Club across the street are available for guests who want to swim in an Olympic-size pool or try some surfing. The Patio restaurant, with its retractable glass roof, offers casual fare and also hosts a famous Sunday brunch where chefs staff a multitude of food stations serving everything from roast beef to custom omelets. In the La Sala lounge, afternoon tea by the fire gives way to live jazz nightly, with dancing on Friday and Saturday. *$$$$; AE, DIS, MC, V; www.fshr.com/santabarbara; Olive Mill Rd exit from US 101 to Channel Dr.* よ

Montecito Inn / ★★

1295 COAST VILLAGE RD, MONTECITO; 805/969-7854 This Mediterranean-style red-tiled stucco hotel was once owned by actors Fatty Arbuckle and Charlie Chaplin (whose image is everywhere, from the etched glass doors to the vintage movie posters lining the hallways). In their day, only the train tracks stood between the inn and the beach, while today U.S. Highway 101 runs directly alongside; double-paned windows help mute the hum. The hotel is as popular now as when it opened in 1928 and hosted Hollywood royalty from Norma Shearer to Marion Davies. Its popularity is due in part to a prime location in Montecito Village, within walking distance of a beautiful beach shared with the nearby Biltmore. The 61 rooms with their colorful Provençal prints and wooden shutters are reminiscent of Southern France. Seven one-bedroom luxury suites have hand-painted designs, whirlpool tubs set in marble, fireplaces, French doors, and arched windows. The original 1927 Otis elevator still brings guests up handily, and an abbreviated continental breakfast is laid out each morning in the lobby. The central sitting area leads to a modest heated pool, where piped-in music mutes the traffic noise from the freeway below; there is an attached gym. A video library that includes all of Chaplin's work is available to guests, and the hotel's casual cafe serves California cuisine throughout the day. *$$$; AE, DC, DIS, JCB, MC, V; checks OK; info@montecitoinn.com; www.monte citoinn.com; Olive Mill Rd exit from US 101.* よ

San Ysidro Ranch / ★★★★

 900 SAN YSIDRO LN, MONTECITO; 805/969-5046 OR 800/368-6788 Imagine a summer camp for the wealthy, with quaint winding trails overgrown with flowers and trees, and peaceful rolling hills beyond. Here, quiet seclusion has been elevated to an art form. Upon arrival, guests are escorted to a private cottage already bearing their name, impeccably outfitted in country luxury, with wood-burning stove or fireplace, outdoor terrace, goose-down comforter, cozy Frette robes, fresh flowers, and dozens of other luxuries to pamper every aspect of their being. Folks have been replenishing themselves here for years, including Laurence Olivier and Vivien Leigh—who were married here—and honeymooners John and Jackie Kennedy. The hotel's verdant 540 acres have been compared to the city's Botanic Garden for their diversity. Guests have the run of the ranch, including tennis courts, swimming pool, bocce ball court, driving range, and wilderness hiking trails. The Stonehouse restaurant, with rustic but pricey regional American cuisine, is considered by some the best in the county (see review). Dogs are welcome, too, and are greeted on check-in with biscuits and a doggie bed. For those who can afford the best money can buy, the Ranch is a slice of heaven on earth. *$$$$; AE, MC, V; checks OK; www.sanysidroranch.com; take the San Ysidro exit from US 101, drive north to San Ysidro Ln, turn right.* &

Summerland

This tiny coastal suburb of Santa Barbara has an intriguingly colorful past and a countrified present, though the boundaries it shares with upscale Montecito are growing fuzzier by the moment. Founded in 1883 by an eccentric rancher and spiritualist named Henry L. Williams, Summerland was originally conceived as a secluded community where mediums would congregate each summer to swim, sunbathe, and conduct séances. But when a few intrepid settlers digging water wells struck oil, it triggered a full-scale oil boom instead. Williams built an ornate Victorian home for himself (now the **BIG YELLOW HOUSE** restaurant; 108 Pierpont St; 805/969-4140).

After the wells went dry in the 1950s, bikers, surfers, and hippies moved in and erected shanties that earned Summerland the epithet of "Where the Debris Meets the Sea." As land values soared in the 1980s, yuppies took over, building quaint hillside cottages and restoring decrepit Victorian houses. Today the town is a great place for strolling around antique shops and boutiques along Lillie Avenue, having a seaside lunch, and even spending a night or two. Summerland's tiny beach is secluded **LOOKOUT COUNTY PARK** (take Evans St under the freeway to the small parking lot), where you have the option of hanging out on the wooded bluffs or playing on the white sand below.

RESTAURANTS

Stacky's Seaside / ★★☆

2315 LILLIE AVE, SUMMERLAND; 805/969-9908 Looking as if it has stepped from the Technicolor frames of a classic beach-party flick, this ivy-covered shack is filled with fish nets, surfboards, and local memorabilia. The menu of sandwiches is enormous, just like most of the pita pockets, hoagies, and club sandwiches that emerge from a deceptively small kitchen. A sign proudly proclaims "Half of Any Sandwich, Half Price, No Problem"—and Stacky's has made plenty of friends with that policy. Eat inside or out on the shaded wooden deck, or join the legions of beachgoers, picnickers, and road-trippers picking up lunch to go. Sandwiches include the Santa Barbaran (roasted tri-tip and melted Jack cheese on sourdough with lettuce, salsa, and mayonnaise); the Rincon pita (Jack and cheddar, green chiles, onions, lettuce, tomato, and ranch dressing); and the hot pastrami hoagie (with Swiss, mustard, and onions). The menu also lists burgers, fish 'n' chips, and hearty soups, and there's Dreyer's ice cream for dessert. Stacky's serves fantastic breakfast items; most have a south-of-the-border flair, such as the fat breakfast burritos with your choice of bacon, sausage, chili, or roast beef, but the classic scrambled-egg sandwich is all-American goodness that goes perfectly with thick-cut French fries. *$; Cash only; breakfast, lunch, dinner every day; beer and wine; reservations not necessary; Summerland exit from US 101.* &

Summerland Beach Cafe / ★

2294 LILLIE AVE, SUMMERLAND; 805/969-1019 Set in a gray Victorian beach cottage in the heart of town, this funky and casual cafe is the trendiest eatery in the vicinity, yet it's still a place where comfortable workout clothes and flip-flops are appropriate. Most seating is on the wraparound porch to take advantage of sea breezes and sunshine, though tables inside get pressed into use during inclement weather. Serving only breakfast and lunch, the Summerland specializes in omelets (from plain-Jane to everything-but-the-kitchen-sink), waffles, French toast, and egg dishes such as huevos rancheros or eggs Benedict. All items have cutesy names like Belgian Wonder Wa-Fulls, Singin' the Bleus, and Indian Summerland, but the food is fresh, hearty, and always satisfying. If you opt for a burger or sandwich (Cobb salad pita, tuna-filled croissant, grilled veggie, or club), get a side of the thick, beer-battered onion rings—you'll be glad you did. *$; AE, DIS, MC, V; no checks; breakfast, lunch every day; beer and wine; reservations not accepted; Summerland exit from US 101.* &

LODGINGS

Inn on Summer Hill / ★★☆

2520 LILLIE AVE, SUMMERLAND; 805/969-9998 OR 800/845-5566 This beige Craftsman-style inn may look as vintage as the town of Summerland, but inside it's brand-spanking new, with all the modern amenities. If you simply can't live without a fireplace, VCR, and whirlpool bathtub, this luxury bed-and-breakfast is for you. Each of the 16 guest rooms also has a balcony or patio. Decor is heavy-handed English country (think layers and layers of fabric prints and frills, romantic canopy beds, fluffy down comforters). If you'd like an ocean-view room, ask when you book, but remember that you'll have to look across U.S. Highway 101, which zooms the length of Summerland like an inescapable concrete-and-steel river. Inside the inn, however, pampering is taken to the highest level: rooms have instant hot water taps for coffee or tea, small refrigerators, and even bathroom phone extensions. A video library is available for those who want to cocoon in their room. Rates include a lavish gourmet breakfast each morning, as well as hors d'oeuvres and wine in the afternoon. Before bedtime, the dining room is sweetened with complimentary desserts. A variety of celebration packages, custom gift baskets, and a breakfast-in-bed option make this B&B a popular anniversary getaway. *$$$$; AE, DIS, MC, V; no checks; innkeeper@innonsummerhill.com; www.innonsummerhill.com; Summerland exit from US 101.* &

Carpinteria

This low-key beach town just a few minutes south of Santa Barbara got its name from Spanish explorers, who watched the native Chumash shaping redwood planks into canoes and dubbed the spot *la carpinteria,* or the carpenter's shop. Still exuding the aura of a true small town, Carpinteria is centered around historic Linden Avenue, where vintage **THE PALMS** restaurant (701 Linden Ave; 805/684-3811) has been luring grill-your-own steak and seafood fans since 1905. Each year during the **CALIFORNIA AVOCADO FESTIVAL** (first weekend in October; 805/684-0038; www. avofest.com), a stretch of Linden Avenue is cordoned off for revelry celebrating the town's agricultural mainstay. You can enjoy live music on an outdoor stage, get rowdy in a carnival-like atmosphere, or simply stroll and sample the avocado-based food offerings, from avocado ice cream to superfresh guacamole stirred up by volunteers from the local high school, who annually mix more than 3,000 pounds of the green stuff. Carpinteria is also known for orchid growers; at **GALLUP & STRIBLING** (3450 Via Real; 805/684-1998; www.gallup-stribling.com), visitors are welcome to browse some of the 1.5 million square feet of greenhouse space, where hybrids of this enchanting, delicate flower are continually being developed. A wide variety of samples in various sizes are for sale and come with detailed instructions on care and feeding.

But to most visitors, Carpinteria is—first and foremost—about the beach. Within walking distance of downtown, you'll find **CARPINTERIA CITY BEACH** (at the end of Linden Ave), a wide stretch of welcoming, though occasionally tarry, sand with Channel Island views and legendary gentle waves for sea bathers. To the east is **CARPINTERIA STATE BEACH PARK,** whose scenic, hilly dunes fill with RVs and campers every weekend. To the west, you'll find the **SALT MARSH NATURE PARK** (also known as the Estuary), where an easy, 1-mile trail leads into bird-rich wetlands next to the sand. For more information, contact the **CARPINTERIA VALLEY CHAMBER OF COMMERCE** (5285 Carpinteria Ave; 805/684-5479; www.carp chamber.org).

LODGINGS

Prufrock's Garden Inn / ★

600 LINDEN AVE, CARPINTERIA; 805/566-9696 OR 877/837-6257 Aptly named for the lovingly tended gardens that surround the house on all sides, this circa-1904 bungalow in the historic part of town was a single-family home until 1995, when innkeepers Judy and Jim Halvorson decided to create a folksy bed-and-breakfast, perfectly located a short walk from the beach. Carpinteria's old-fashioned small-town attitude reminded them of their Iowa roots, so Prufrock's feels like a casual grandma's house, complete with warm cookies and lemonade each afternoon, hand-lettered signs, and a mismatched decor combining antiques, family bric-a-brac, and modern updates. Rooms are outfitted with simple amenities, though some have whirlpool tubs, private balconies, or other features; two separate garden cottages offer the most private quarters. Frequent specials offer free nights or midweek discounts (call or check online), and the house is conveniently (though noisily) situated in the middle of the annual Avocado Festival each fall. *$$$–$$$$; DIS, MC, V; checks for advance payment only; www.prufrocks.com; corner of 6th St.*

Goleta

Historically the site of agricultural concerns from burgeoning Santa Barbara nearby, Goleta has streets still bearing the names of ranchers and farmers who ruled the vast 19th-century ranches around here: Hollister, Winchester, Sexton. During World War II, Navy and Marine bases obliterated what was left of native Chumash villages; that military land later became the **UNIVERSITY OF CALIFORNIA, SANTA BARBARA** campus and **SANTA BARBARA MUNICIPAL AIRPORT**. Today the community of Goleta, a mere 15 minutes north of its more glamorous neighbor Santa Barbara—but with unsung beaches and mountain views that rival S.B.'s—is known as an urban bedroom community and high-tech research enclave; at press time it was vying for incorporation as a city on its own. For additional information, contact the **GOLETA VALLEY CHAMBER OF COMMERCE** (5582 Calle Real, Ste A; 805/967-4618; www.goletavalley.com).

RESTAURANTS

Beachside Bar Cafe / ★★☆

5905 SANDSPIT RD, GOLETA; 805/964-7881 Goleta Beach Park is a picture postcard of the quintessential California beach scene: grassy bluffs behind a white-sand crescent-shaped cove, palm trees waving in the breeze, a friendly wooden fishing pier, and the promise of glorious sunsets at day's end. In the middle of it all sits Beachside Bar Cafe, a come-as-you-are crowd pleaser, where sandy-toed surfers, book-toting students, lunch-hour professionals, and early-dining retirees commingle over an all-day menu of chowders, salads, sandwiches (including a zesty ahi "burger"), as well as an extensive raw shellfish bar and cocktail-hour noshes. Come sunset, it's standing room only, and everything from oysters and ceviche to Yucatan seafood skewers or outstanding crab cakes—as well as tropical cocktails that enhance the island vibe—sports happy hour prices. You'll enjoy an ocean view from nearly every indoor seat, as well as from the wind-shielded covered patio (with heat lamps in case of chill). The restaurant is done up in a beachy blend of gray clapboard, island rattan, and nautical paraphernalia. The food here is good and satisfying, served up by a youthful waitstaff who occasionally point out a pelican offshore diving for *its* lunch. *$–$$; AE, MC, V; checks OK with guarantee card; lunch, dinner every day; full bar; reservations not necessary; from Hwy 217 (Ward Memorial Blvd), follow signs for Goleta Beach County Park.*

LODGINGS

Bacara Resort / ★★★☆

8301 HOLLISTER AVE, SANTA BARBARA; 805/968-0100 OR 877/422-4245 The newest resort around Santa Barbara for the sleek and chic is Bacara Resort & Spa, with more than 350 luxurious guest rooms and suites, all with stunning views from private patios or balconies, high-speed Internet access, 24-hour in-room dining, minibars, multiline telephones, and nightly rates starting at roughly $400 and soaring to $2,500. The resort was obviously built to appeal to the movie star and mogul crowd from L.A.—witness the 225-person screening room so no one will miss seeing the rushes of their latest film project. The lodgings are in one-, three-, and four-story Mediterranean villas, each graced with Frette linens, plush robes, and Spanish dark wood furniture with blue and white fabrics. Located 20 freeway minutes from downtown Santa Barbara, it is suspended between the Pacific Ocean and the Santa Ynez Mountains and has a 2-mile white-sand beach. The resort is designed with a nod to Spanish Colonial and mission architecture in a villagelike setting, with tile roofs, splashing fountains, covered archways, and wooden trellises. Adjacent is the resort's own 1,000-acre Ranch of Bacara, a lemon and avocado ranch, where you can hike and ride mountain bikes or have a picnic. The three-level spa offers a full menu of treatments, including a citrus avocado body scrub, Thai massage, and an ultimate body blitz (if you have to ask, you don't need one). Three zero-edge swimming pools with cabanas keep you from being bored paddling in circles. There are also three restaurants: Miro, a fine dining restaurant on the bluff over the ocean; the Bistro, a relaxed cafe with Mediterranean food; and the informal Spa Cafe. *$$$$; AE, MC, V; checks OK, www.bacararesort.com; Winchester Canyon/Hollister Ave exit off US 101.* &

San Marcos Pass

California Highway 154 is a beautiful drive, and one we highly recommend as a scenic alternative to U.S. Highway 101 as it traverses the Santa Ynez Mountains on its way to Santa Barbara. After passing Cachuma Lake, the San Marcos Pass climbs to around 2,200 feet amid thickly chaparral-covered hillsides, brightened each spring with blooming wildflowers. Whatever the time of year, a stellar ocean view comes into sight just as you reach the summit. This mountain pass has been used by people for centuries, including Colonel John C. Frémont, who sneaked through to surprise a band of Mexican soldiers during the American conquest of California in 1846. Stagecoach Road traces the original pathway through the pass, and until a bridge was built in 1963 this winding and rugged road served as the only way across 400-foot-deep Cold Spring Canyon near the top of the pass. Unfortunately, most drivers never appreciate the marvelous **COLD SPRING ARCH BRIDGE**, since its graceful, swooping arc (supporting the roadway in a single 700-foot span) cannot be seen as you cross it. For a glorious view of the bridge, turn off the main highway at Stagecoach Road.

The earliest evidence of inhabitants in the pass can be seen at **CHUMASH PAINTED CAVE HISTORIC PARK**, a worthwhile 10-minute detour from Highway 154. Turn off onto Painted Cave Road; after 2 miles, look for the small sign and parking turnout. On foot, follow the rocky path a few yards to the cave. It's dark inside, but not too dark to distinguish the vivid drawings, probably made by Chumash shamans, which include geometric and swirling designs, horned animals, human figures, and a sun drawing believed to represent a 17th-century eclipse.

RESTAURANTS

Cold Spring Tavern / ★★☆

5995 STAGECOACH RD, SANTA BARBARA; 805/967-0066 These days, more car tires than horse hooves kick up dust along the road, but little else has changed about this former stagecoach stop. House in a charming moss-covered shingled cabin with gingham-draped windows and cozy fireplace nooks, nestled among the trees next to a babbling brook, the restaurant and bar have dark interiors furnished with mounted animal trophies, rusty oil lanterns, and memorabilia from the tavern's 100-plus years of service. The lunch menu is simple and hearty, featuring burgers of buffalo, ostrich, or beef, plus sandwiches, salads, and Cold Spring's renowned chili. Dinner is more elegant than you might expect; excellent-quality cuts of meat and fresh vegetables abound. Look for stuffed chicken with sherry–sour cream sauce, barbecued baby back ribs, or rack of lamb with champagne-mint glaze. Venison sausage–stuffed mushrooms in garlic butter is the house appetizer, a tasty but rich artery-clogger best shared. Weekends and nights, especially during summer, the saloon-style bar next door is packed with revelers singing along to Wurlitzer classics or dancing to local bands. In addition to visiting the rustic restaurant and bar, you can roam around the remaining outbuildings and namesake artesian springs that made this spot an ideal watering stop. Don't miss the resident 19 cats, all named George. It'll take you 20 minutes to drive here from downtown, but the incredible coastline views along the way make the trip worthwhile. *$$; AE, MC, V; no checks; breakfast Sat–Sun, lunch, dinner every day; full bar; reservations recommended; cst@silcom.com; from Hwy 154, turn west on Stagecoach Rd.*

Lompoc

Nicknamed "Valley of the Flowers," the fertile, flat Lompoc Valley is indeed probably best known for its vast **FLOWER FIELDS**, which supply more than half the world's seeds. Since the early 1900s, flower farmers—beginning with W. Atlee Burpee, whose name would eventually grace seed packets in potting sheds throughout the world—have been cultivating flowers for seed here, and today nearly 2,000 acres of the valley floor are planted with more than 30 different kinds of blossoming plants. In peak blooming season, between May and September, colorful and fragrant sweet peas, larkspur, petunias, asters, marigolds, zinnias, and others create a splendid rainbow as majestic as New England's fall foliage display. The **LOMPOC CHAMBER OF COMMERCE** (111 South I St; 805/736-4567 or 800/240-0999; www.lompoc.com) publishes a map to guide you along country roads to the various fields and to a designated Observation Point in town that offers a panoramic look at the patchwork valley floor. In June the annual **LOMPOC VALLEY FLOWER FESTIVAL** (805/735-8511; www.flowerfestival.org) begins with a colorful downtown parade and continues with many bus tours through acres of brilliant blooms. (You can also follow a self-guided tour.) Festivities continue with a carnival, flower show, arts and crafts fair, and more.

While you're in Lompoc it's worth admiring the results of the **LOMPOC MURALS PROJECT,** an ongoing effort in which enormous murals depicting Lompoc's heritage and natural history are being executed on building extensions scattered through downtown. Often painted by nationally renowned muralists, these public works of art currently number around 40. For a map and guide to each mural's subject matter, contact the chamber of commerce (see above).

Anyone who grew up in California learned all about the Spanish mission chain in grade school, and Lompoc's **MISSION LA PURISIMA** (2295 Purisima Rd; 805/733-3713; www.lapurisimamission.org) is widely accepted as the best preserved and most educational surviving example of these 18th-century colonial outposts. Founded in 1787 along El Camino Real, the original Spanish road from Mexico, La Purisima has been completely reconstructed in its still-rural setting, and its intricate water-supply system of elaborately tiled aqueducts and fountains is still relatively intact. As a California State Historic Park, La Purisima is constantly visited by busloads of schoolchildren taking their turn to learn this chapter in early California history, especially during **MISSION LIFE DAYS,** once a month from spring through autumn, when costumed docents provide a living history lesson in tortilla-baking, candle-dipping, soap-making, and other once-essential chores.

Buellton

RESTAURANTS

Hitching Post / ★☆

406 E HWY 246, BUELLTON; 805/688-0676 Would you believe the *New York Times* and *Gourmet* magazine have blessed this steak house in the middle of nowhere, calling it one of the best in the country? Looking for all the world like an ordinary roadhouse, it offers oak-fired barbecue steaks, lamb, pork, turkey, seafood, and smoked duck, not to mention grilled artichokes with smoked tomato mayonnaise. These robust meals are served with the restaurant's own label of pinot noir, made and bottled at Au Bon Climat/Qupe wineries. The bar also functions as a tasting room for house-produced wines. The restaurant is dark and rustic, a real man's kind of place, with photographs of real and would-be cowboys on a trail ride in the 1940s. Owner Frank Ostini's family has been in the business of serving up Santa Maria–style grilled meats since they bought the original Hitching Post in Casmalia, a small community one hour north of Santa Maria, the year he was born—50 years ago. His brothers now run that one. Frank has had the Buellton version, which he thinks of as "Hitching Post 2," for 15 years. If you get hooked on the steaks you can later order and have them sent to you, seasoned and already grilled, on two days' notice. The staff cooks them rare, packs them up, and ships them overnight, with instructions for reheating. *$$; AE, MC, V; checks OK; dinner every day; full bar; reservations recommended; www.hitchingpostwines.com; on Hwy 246, east of Buellton.* &

Pea Soup Andersen's

376 AVE OF THE FLAGS, BUELLTON; 805/688-5581 Nearly everyone puzzles over the unconventional syntax of the name of this highway mainstay whose familiar billboards—and far-flung franchises—dot Southern California. Shouldn't it be "Andersen's Pea Soup"? Opened in 1924 by Anton and Juliette Andersen as a little roadside cafe, the original restaurant was called Andersen's Electrical Cafe in honor of its newfangled electric range, but it was soon renamed for Juliette's specialty, which was gaining statewide popularity. And what about those trademark pea-splitters? The cartoon pair of workmen wielding hammer and chisel were originally drawn for a magazine feature depicting "little-known occupations," but were licensed to Andersen's in 1946, who then held a contest to name them. The winning names: Hap-Pea and Pea-Wee. You can pose outside the chain's original restaurant with your face filling a cutout of one of the two (kids love this). Except for what could be in the running for the world's largest restaurant gift shop, Andersen's itself is simply a familiar coffee-shop kind of place where split-pea soup is always on the menu. Because surrounding Buellton offers little else, Andersen's makes a welcome highway stop; Solvang and the Los Olivos wine country are a five-minute drive away. *$; AE, MC, V; no checks; breakfast, lunch, dinner every day; full bar; reservations not necessary; www.peasoupandersens.net; at Hwy 246.* &

Solvang

One of the state's most popular tourist stops, nestled in the Santa Ynez Valley, the town of Solvang would look out-of-place cutesy if everyone weren't so accustomed to it by now. Here everything that *can* be Danish is Danish: you've never seen so many windmills, cobblestone streets, and wooden shoes and so much gingerbread trim—even the sidewalk trash cans look like little Danish farmhouses with pitched-roof lids. At night, though, the village truly does radiate a storybook charm, as twinkling lights in the trees illuminate sidewalks free of the midday throngs. Solvang (whose name means "sunny field") gets a lot of flak for being a Disneyfied version of its founders' vision, but it does possess a genuine old-world lineage, which you can learn about with a quick visit to the small **ELVERHØJ MUSEUM** (1624 Elverhoy Wy; 805/686-1211). Set in a traditional handcrafted Scandinavian-style home, the museum consists of fully furnished typical Danish rooms and artifacts from Solvang's early days. Most intriguing are promotional pamphlets distributed in Nebraska and Iowa nearly 100 years ago to lure more Danes to sunny California.

Solvang can be easily explored on foot, but you might like to pedal your way around town in a fringe-top surrey from **SURREY CYCLES** (at Mission Dr and First St, on the park; 805/688-0091), which also offers 18-speed bikes suitable for exploring the surrounding hills and wine country. In the center of town, upstairs from the Book Loft and Kaffe Hus, you'll find the **HANS CHRISTIAN ANDERSEN MUSEUM** (1680 Mission Dr; 805/688-2052), which is more interesting than it sounds. The gallery is filled with memorabilia pertaining to Andersen, father of the modern fairy tale and Danish national hero. In addition to rare and first editions of his works, displays include manuscripts, letters, photographs, and a replica Gutenberg printing press. But most folks come to Solvang to enjoy groaning Danish **SMOR-GASBORDS**; sample delectable old-world pastries, such as those found at the best storefront, **OLSEN'S BAKERY** (1529 Mission Dr; 805/688-6314); and shop in town for gifts and souvenirs—or for bargains at Solvang Designer Outlets. You can get more information by picking up a glossy *Destination Guide* at the **SOLVANG VISITOR BUREAU** (1511 Mission Dr; 805/688-6144 or 800/GO-SOLVANG; www.solvangca.com). The Bureau also has details about Danish Days, a three-day festival of old-world customs and pageantry held during September. There's a parade, demonstrations of traditional Danish arts, dancing by the Solvang Dancers, and a raffle to win a trip to Denmark. Of course, plenty of *aebleskiver* (Danish apple fritters) are served up along with the fun. February's **FLYING LEAP STORYTELLING FESTIVAL** (805/688-9533) grows in popularity each year, with events ranging from nationally renowned storytellers to local folks swapping impromptu tales in the park or ghost stories in the school barn.

On the edge of town is a historic building *without* windmills, roof storks, or other Scandinavian embellishment—the **SPANISH MISSION SANTA INES** (1760 Mission Dr; 805/688-4815; www.missionsantaines.org), built of adobe by Native Americans in 1804, destroyed by the earthquake of 1812, partially rebuilt, and then burned in 1824 in a violent Native American revolt. Santa Ines never regained its initial prosperity or its harmonious existence. Today little of the original mission remains, but the structures you see painstakingly replicate the originals. The chapel, still in use for daily services, features the ornate painting and tile work typical of Spanish missions. The grounds also include the well-restored and well-maintained monks' garden.

RESTAURANTS

Bit O' Denmark

473 ALISAL RD, SOLVANG; 805/688-5426 It's nearly impossible to visit Solvang without sampling the Danish fare that traditionally fills the groaning smorgasbord table, and Bit O' Denmark has the freshest and highest-quality offering around. It's not only the oldest restaurant in town, it's also housed in Solvang's oldest building. Constructed in 1911, the two-story wood-frame structure served first as a college and later as a church before it welcomed its first diners in 1929. Inside, pleasant farmhouse tables are scattered throughout, and collections of blue-and-white china adorn every wall. The traditional all-you-can-eat smorgasbord (offered at both lunch and dinner) consists of a variety of hot and cold dishes, many pickled according to Scandinavian custom, and includes sauerbraten, roast pork, mashed potatoes, Danish salami, gravlax, marinated herring, pumpernickel, deviled eggs, salads, Jell-O molds, and more. The regular menu includes Scandinavian fare such as roast beef with red cabbage and applesauce and *frikadeller* (Danish meatballs), sautéed golden and drenched in brown gravy. At breakfast you'll enjoy Solvang's famous *aebleskiver*, deep-fried apple dumplings served with powdered sugar and raspberry jam. Casual and convenient, Bit O' Denmark is sometimes *too* popular—in other words, expect crowds when tour buses are parked outside the front door. *$$; AE, DIS, MC, V; no checks; breakfast, lunch, dinner every day; full bar; reservations recommended; between Copenhagen and Mission Drs.* &

Cabernet Bistro / ★★

478 4TH PL, SOLVANG; 805/693-1152 This little pocket of France will delight gourmets. Chef/owner Jacques Toulet comes from a family of restaurateurs in the Pyrenees. He developed a fine reputation in Los Angeles when he and his brother opened their own restaurant, Les Pyrenees, in Santa Monica in the 1970s. A few years ago Jacques and his wife, Diana, moved to the Santa Ynez Valley and opened Cabernet Bistro. Open beams, antiques, and light pink tablecloths make the dining room elegant but relaxed. The menu offers veal Escoffier with morel mushrooms, T-bone steak, and fresh swordfish, as well as quail and rack of lamb. The signature dish is duck; you can order duck à l'orange, duck amaretto, duck with peppercorn sauce, duck with cherries, and duck cassis, and those aren't the only duck options. In fact, they sell 2,000 orders of duck a year, even in this town known for Danish pancakes. For dessert order the creamy almond praline cake, invented by Jacques for Diana on their wedding anniversary. *$$–$$$; AE, DIS, MC, V; no checks; dinner Thurs–Tues; beer and wine; reservations recommended; www.cabernetbistro.com; at Copenhagen Dr.* &

Paula's Pancake House / ★

1531 MISSION DR, SOLVANG; 805/688-2867 There's something for everyone on Paula's menu, which begins with three full pages of *just breakfast*. Wafer-thin Danish pancakes are served plain and simple, sweet and fruity, or with sausage and eggs. Buttermilk and whole wheat–honey pancakes can be topped with fresh fruit or chopped pecans. Paula's French toast is made with dense sourdough bread. There's every omelet you can imagine, plus egg dishes served with country or Danish sausage. Farmhouse breakfasts like pork chops and eggs share menu space with more timid Egg Beaters and granola. Paula's, friendly and casual, is right on Solvang's busiest street, so you can eat on the patio and watch the world go by as the seasoned staff makes sure your coffee is always hot. Breakfast is served all day, and there's also a lunch menu with burgers, sandwiches, homemade soups, and Santa Maria–style chili with ham, all of which go down smoothly with an ice-cold beer. Champagne is also available to turn any breakfast into a mind-tingling mimosa morning. *$; AE, DIS, MC, V; local checks only; breakfast every day, lunch Mon–Sat; beer and wine; reservations not accepted; at Fourth Pl.* &

LODGINGS

Alisal Guest Ranch & Resort / ★★

1054 ALISAL RD, SOLVANG; 805/688-6411 OR 800/4-ALISAL Part of a working cattle ranch, this rustic yet quietly posh retreat is ideal for anyone who wants an Old West vacation. But you certainly won't be asked to pitch hay or groom horses—it might interfere with your golf game, guided horseback ride, or poolside lounging. *Alisal* is Spanish for "alder grove," and the ranch is nestled in a vast, tree-shaded canyon, offering 73 guest cottages equipped with wood-burning fireplaces, refrigerators, and covered brick porches ideal for sitting and soaking up the scenery. There aren't any TVs or phones to spoil the serenity, but restless visitors will never tire of the resort activities, which include hiking trails, tennis, croquet, bicycling, and fishing in the Alisal's private lake, where sailboats, pedal boats, and canoes sit ready for use. Wildlife abounds on the ranch's 10,000 acres, so don't be surprised to see eagles, hawks, deer, coyotes, and mountain lions. Golf here is top-notch, with two championship 18-hole courses, both of which offer impeccably maintained fairways accented by mature oak, sycamore, and eucalyptus trees. The River Course, which is also open to the public, winds along the Santa Ynez River and offers spectacular mountain vistas. Resident PGA and LPGA pros are on hand for instruction. As if a visit here weren't sybaritic enough, breakfast and dinner, featuring fresh local ingredients and a wide range of choices, are included, and during the day a poolside snack bar and a golf-course grill make it entirely possible to never leave this peaceful getaway. In the evening the upscale ranch-style Oak Room lounge features live entertainment in a comfortable setting. *$$$$; AE, MC, V; checks OK; info@alisal.com; www.alisal.com; 3 miles south of Mission Dr.* &

Inn at Petersen Village / ★

1576 MISSION DR, SOLVANG; 805/688-3121 OR 800/321-8985 Anchoring a small plaza of shops, cafes, and cobblestone paths, this boutique inn eschews ubiquitous Danish kitsch in favor of a more elegant old-world style. Mahogany lines the lobby and hallways, rich carpeting muffles the passing of tour groups, and strategically placed antiques lend a touch of class. Each of the 39 rooms is different, but all are decorated in a subdued country motif with print wallpaper, canopy beds, and high-quality antique reproductions. Some overlook the bustling courtyard, while others face the scenic hills. The smaller rooms have private balconies, and the more spacious ones have noisier outlooks. But it's the impressive little touches that set this hotel apart: dimmable bathroom lights, lighted magnifying mirrors, and free coffee/tea service in your room. Complimentary wine and hors d'oeuvres each evening in the piano lounge and desserts served while a pianist tickles the ivories are included in the cost of laying your head. The reasonable rates here even include a generous breakfast buffet with sit-down coffee and juice service, and two decent cafes are right outside in the plaza. *$$; AE, MC, V; no checks; www.petersen inn.com; just east of 4th Pl.* &

Royal Scandinavian Inn

400 ALISAL RD, SOLVANG; 805/688-8000 OR 800/624-5572 Solvang's largest hostelry is this full-service hotel neatly tucked away from the town's congested main drag. Attractive and comfortable, the Royal Scandinavian is also popular with convention and tour groups (and, as a result, it can be fully booked at unexpected times). Guest rooms are furnished in vaguely Danish country decor, and the hotel does a good job with maintenance by replacing soft goods before they show wear, and keeping bathrooms sparklingly up to date. There's a recently added fitness center. Most rooms look out onto the lovely Santa Ynez Valley; some have private balconies overlooking the courtyard, where a heated swimming pool and whirlpool provide welcome refreshment in the summertime. There's an all-day restaurant and a cocktail lounge. The hotel is within easy walking distance of village attractions, and it offers some terrific golf and breakfast packages featuring play at the nearby pristine Alisal River Course. *$$; AE, DC, DIS, JCB, MC, V; checks OK; sroyal@silcom.com; www.solvangrsi.com; between Mission Dr and Oak St.* &

Santa Ynez

The center of cattle ranching in this valley since the 1880s, Santa Ynez remains a farm town whose centerpiece is the historic Santa Ynez Feed & Mill, which still supplies hay, grain, and tack to valley ranchers and cowboys. Spanning just two blocks, downtown Santa Ynez sports false-front Old West facades and down-home hospitality—notably illustrated by the local service station, which cheerfully offers full service at the self-serve price. For a look at conveyances of yesteryear, stop into the **PARKS-JANEWAY CARRIAGE HOUSE** (corner of Sagunto and Faraday Sts; 805/688-7889), operated by the Santa Ynez Valley Historical Society. This small but exceptional museum comprises the largest collection of horse-drawn vehicles west of the Mississippi, featuring rare examples of stagecoaches, covered wagons, a horse-drawn hearse, personal surreys, and more. Tour-bus groups are common in the valley, drawn to nearby Solvang and to Santa Ynez's **CHUMASH CASINO** (on Hwy 246 in Santa Ynez; 805/686-0855 or 800/728-9997; www.chumashcasino.com), where high-stakes bingo, Las Vegas–style video gaming, and spirited card games entertain 24 hours a day (on certain days) while adhering to state guidelines that permit gaming on Native American lands.

Follow Highway 154 south from here and you'll soon see picturesque **CACHUMA LAKE** (805/686-5054). The reservoir, created in 1953 by damming the Santa Ynez River, is the primary water source for Santa Barbara County and the centerpiece of a 6,600-acre county park with a flourishing wildlife population and well-developed recreational facilities. Migratory birds—including **BALD EAGLES**, rarely sighted in these parts—abound during the winter months, and full-time residents include blue herons, osprey, red-tailed hawks, golden eagles, deer, bobcats, and mountain lions. The best way to appreciate all this bounty is by taking a naturalist-led **EAGLE CRUISE** or **WILDLIFE CRUISE**, offered year-round on the lake; call 805/686-5050 for reservations. Camping, boating, and fishing are all popular activities centered around a small marina.

Nearby is the new 18-hole **RANCHO SAN MARCOS GOLF COURSE** (on Hwy 154 south of the lake; 805/683-6334), designed by Robert Trent Jones Jr. to wind scenically along the Santa Ynez River next to the Los Padres National Forest.

RESTAURANTS

Trattoria Grappolo / ★

3687-C SAGUNTO ST, SANTA YNEZ; 805/688-6899 Almost hidden at the eastern end of this Old West town, Grappolo is no secret to valley residents hungry for the flavor of an authentic Italian trattoria. Incongruously set in a frontier-style storefront, complete with boardwalk and wooden porch, the restaurant's interior features tight rows of rustic stone mosaic tables and wooden schoolhouse chairs. A wraparound mural of the surrounding hills covers all four walls; old-fashioned sconces cast a subdued light. Throngs of locals crowd in every evening, and the ever-increasing decibel level seems to suit the food, a stylishly composed but heartily prepared (more heavy handed with sauce and seasoning than most contemporary Italian) menu complemented by plenty of local wines. Glance into the open kitchen, and you'll see the tile-framed wood-burning brick oven that churns out delicious gourmet pizzas; the menu also includes delicious house-made pastas and hearty meat dishes (there's a different veal scallopine preparation daily). *$$; MC, V; no checks; dinner every day; beer and wine; reservations recommended; in a mini-mall between Edison St and Meadowvale Rd.*

The Vineyard House

3631 SAGUNTO ST, SANTA YNEZ; 805/688-2886 Until the 1980s, this lavish Victorian on Santa Ynez's main drag was a private residence. Now it serves as a welcome addition to the valley's interesting, but limited, dining scene. Though the food served here—a pleasant mix of American standards and lighter California-style dishes—isn't always competitive with some other gourmet hot spots, the Vineyard House's utterly charming setting is a winner. Diners who choose a table on the wide front deck enjoy a bucolic view that has changed little since the house was built over a century ago. Diners inside are treated to the same picturesque vista through a giant picture window. Standout dishes include a souplike venison chili verde made with tomatillos and served with avocado salsa, a main-course salad topped with beer-battered fried chicken and creamy Gorgonzola cheese, and some inventive pastas. Other choices include rack of lamb, filet mignon, and salmon in an aromatic fennel sauce with spinach. The menu is complemented by a reasonably priced list of fine Central Coast wines and a worthy dessert list. *$$; AE, MC, V; local checks only; lunch, dinner Wed–Mon, brunch Sun; beer and wine; reservations recommended; 3 blocks from Hwy 246 via Edison St.* 占

LODGINGS

Santa Ynez Inn / ★★☆

3627 SAGUNTO ST, SANTA YNEZ; 805/688-5588 OR 800/643-5774 Oenophiles now have a luxurious new hotel to bed down in after a day of "swill-and-chill." Set in the Western-rich outpost of Santa Ynez, this 14-room Victorian-style inn features Frette linens, DVD/CD systems, beautiful extensive gardens, an on-site minispa, and personalized white-glove treatment. Each guest room sports a richly dramatic decor—some have balconies with valley and vineyard views—and it's all done up in a bygone style of elegance and opulence hand-orchestrated by owners Douglas and Christine Ziegler, whose attention to detail is astounding. Though the inn is newly built, the Zieglers were determined to replicate everything about the style prevalent 100 years ago when Santa Ynez was a major overnight coach stop: they painstakingly sought reproduction antique fixtures with modern technology, including Victorian-style lamps with dimmers, remote-control gas hearths behind grand mantels, and authentic looking door handles with microchip security. The all-marble bathrooms are royal in size and scope, featuring dual steam showers, oversize vanities, addictive apricot bath products, and the innovative Ultra Tub whirlpool, which uses powerful air jets, thus eliminating hygiene

SANTA YNEZ VALLEY WINERIES

You might think of Santa Barbara County as a "new" wine region, but winemaking here is a 200-year-old tradition, first practiced by Franciscan friars at the area's missions. In the past 20 to 30 years, area vintners have been gaining recognition, and today wine grapes are one of the top crops in the county. To understand their success, you need only look at geography. Like most renowned wine regions, the Santa Ynez and Santa Maria Valleys are bounded by transverse (west-to-east) mountain ranges, which allow ocean breezes to flow in and keep the climate temperate. Variations in temperature and humidity within the valleys create numerous microclimates, in which vintners have learned how to cultivate nearly all the classic grapes. White grapes flourish here, so everyone makes a chardonnay, but several reds are also well regarded, including cabernet sauvignon, syrah, and viognier, a Rhône varietal that's gaining in popularity. A good way to familiarize yourself with the local wine country is by contacting the **SANTA BARBARA COUNTY VINTNERS' ASSOCIATION** (3669 Sagunto St, Unit 101, Santa Ynez; 805/688-0881 or 800/218-0881; www.sbcountywines.com). Be sure to pick up a copy of the *Winery Touring Map*, which is also available at hotels and the wineries themselves. If you'd like to sample wines without driving around, head to **LOS OLIVOS TASTING ROOM & WINE SHOP** (2905 Grand Ave; 805/688-7406), located in the heart of town, or **LOS OLIVOS WINE & SPIRITS EMPORIUM** (2531 Grand Ave; 805/688-4409; www.sbwines.com), a friendly barn in a field half a mile away. Both offer a wide selection, including wines from vintners—like Au Bon Climat and Qupé—who don't have their own tasting rooms.

FESS PARKER WINERY & VINEYARD: Part of a Santa Barbara dynasty that also includes an oceanside resort, cattle ranches, and a chic B&B (see review in this chapter), this grandiose operation turns out some critically acclaimed syrahs and chardonnays. Lest you think Parker has forgotten his Hollywood past (he played Davy Crockett and Daniel Boone), the winery's gift shop even peddles coonskin caps. Located at 6200 Foxen Canyon Road, Los Olivos; 805/688-1545; www.FessParker.com.

FIRESTONE VINEYARD: Started by Brooks Firestone of tire-manufacturing fame, this winery is one of the county's largest producers and now includes two "second" labels, one of which specializes in Chilean-grown grapes. The tasting room and gift shop are a three-ring circus of merchandise, but Firestone offers a quick, worthwhile tour. Located at 5017 Zaca Station Road, Los Olivos; 805/688-3940; www.firestone wine.com.

THE GAINEY VINEYARD: This visitor-oriented winery has a large terra-cotta-tiled tasting room, plenty of logo merchandise, and a deli case for impromptu lunches at their garden tables. Gainey draws huge crowds thanks to a prime location on Highway 246 and the in-depth tours it offers seven days a week. Located at 3950 East Highway 246, Santa Ynez; 805/688-0558; www.gaineyvineyard.com.

LAFOND WINERY & VINEYARDS: Pierre Lafond is something of a local legend, with his minichain of upscale bakery cafes, his wife's fashionable boutiques, and this high-profile winery in the newly approved Santa Rita Hills appellation. Lafond's vineyard-designated pinot noir and syrah, however, are seriously crafted and well worth the rambling country drive from U.S. Highway 101. Located at 6855 Santa Rosa Road, Buellton; 805/688-7921; www.lafondwinery.com.

SUNSTONE VINEYARDS & WINERY: This classy winery's wisteria-wrapped stone tasting room and lavender-fringed picnic courtyard lie nestled in an oak grove overlooking the river. Don't be misled by the rambling dirt entrance road—Sunstone boasts a superior merlot (its flagship varietal) and features a sophisticated gift shop with gourmet foods, cigars, and souvenirs. Located at 125 North Refugio Road, Santa Ynez; 805/688-WINE or 800/313-WINE; www.sunstonewinery.com.

ZACA MESA WINERY: Situated on a serene plateau and named "the restful place" in Spanish, Zaca Mesa offers the usual syrahs and chardonnays plus Rhône varietals such as grenache, roussanne, and viognier. Subtle hippie/New Age mumbo jumbo reinforces the organic atmosphere. Located at 6905 Foxen Canyon Road, Los Olivos; 805/688-9339 or 800/350-7972; www.zacamesa.com.

—*Stephanie Avnet Yates*

concerns about recirculated water. Breakfast each morning is a multicourse treat served in the formal dining room, and the inn offers enough daylong munching that guests need never leave: afternoon tea and snacks, evening wine and hot hors d'oeuvres, and a scrumptious dessert hour before bedtime. Room service is also available from the Vineyard House next door (see review). *$$$$; AE, DIS, MC, V; checks accepted 30 days prior to arrival; info@santaynezinn.com; www.santaynezinn.com; on Sagunto St at Edison St.* &

Ballard

Occupying just a few square blocks, Ballard is the Santa Ynez Valley's smallest community, but it still lays claim to a popular gourmet restaurant and to the valley's most charming bed-and-breakfast. Situated midway between Los Olivos and Solvang, Ballard is surrounded by **APPLE ORCHARDS** and **HORSE FARMS** kept with as much care as any Kentucky breeding farm. **SHETLAND PONIES** abound along Alamo Pintado Road near town—drive through slowly (especially if you're with children) to see these darlings frolicking in their pastures. In Ballard itself, stroll past the **BALLARD SCHOOL** (School St, between Cottonwood and Lewis Sts), an archetypal "little red schoolhouse" with a wooden steeple accented by white gingerbread trim.

Built in 1883, it's been in continuous use as an elementary school; Ballard youngsters spill out the front door, *Little House on the Prairie*–style, at morning recess.

RESTAURANTS

The Ballard Store / ★★

2449 BASELINE AVE, BALLARD; 805/688-5319 The facade may look like a country general store, but this is hardly the place to come for a sack of flour. Built in 1939, the former market/gas station was purchased in 1971 by the Elliott family, who began serving French-continental cuisine to a farming community unaccustomed to such gentility. These days it seems more at home, a natural complement to the many local wineries and the upscale Ballard Inn across the street, and folks from throughout the region come here for chef Dennis Everett's regional and European fine cuisine, including bouillabaisse, rack of lamb, and fresh seafood. Baked artichoke hearts or oysters Rockefeller are elegant starters, followed by main courses like New York steak, macadamia-crusted halibut, veal marsala, and other rich culinary classics. They're eager to flambé just about anything tableside, including spinach–sea scallop flambé and bananas Foster. The roving martini cart is famous; it rolls to your table and your martini is prepared to order as you watch. The adjacent Cottage Caffe coffeehouse serves coffee drinks and breakfast bakery treats, along with the famous Ballard Store homemade soups, salads, and sandwiches at lunchtime. Families will love the enclosed play area for children. *$$–$$$; AE, MC, V; local checks only; dinner Tues–Sun, brunch Sun; full bar; reservations recommended; just east of Alamo Pintado Rd.* &

LODGINGS

The Ballard Inn / ★★★

 2436 BASELINE AVE, BALLARD; 805/688-7770 OR 800/638-2466 Built to look like it's been standing proud for 100 years, this two-story gray-and-white inn is actually of modern construction, offering contemporary comforts to gentleman farmers and city-weary celebs alike. Charming country details abound, from the wicker rocking chairs that decorate the inn's wraparound porch to the carefully tended rosebushes and white picket fence. Step inside, and the first thing you'll notice is a fire warming the giant hearth that serves both the lobby and the inn's restaurant. The downstairs public rooms, including an enormous, sunny parlor, are tastefully furnished with a comfortable mix of hand-hooked rugs, bent-twig furniture, and vintage accessories. Upstairs, each guest room is decorated according to a theme from the valley's history or geography. Some have fireplaces and/or private balconies. All have well-stocked bathrooms, and many feature an antique washbasin in the room as well. The best (and most expensive) is the Mountain Room, a minisuite decorated in rich forest green, with a fireplace and a private balcony. Other favorites are the hardwood-floored Vineyard Room, with a grapevine motif and a large bay window, and Davy Brown's Room, whose tall stone fireplace, wood paneling, and hand-stitched quilt lend a log-cabin appeal. Included in the rate are a gracious wine-and-hors-d'oeuvres reception each afternoon, evening coffee and tea, and a delicious full breakfast each morning; be forewarned, however, that a 10 percent service charge for the staff is added to your bill.

Cafe Chardonnay is the inn's own restaurant, tucked into a cozy room downstairs by a crackling fire. The short, often inspired (though occasionally uneven) menu can include grilled meats, seafood pastas, and catch-of-the-day specials. Inn guests and nonguests alike need to reserve in advance, since Cafe Chardonnay's few tables are always in demand. *$$$–$$$$; AE, MC, V; checks OK; innkeeper@ ballardinn.com; www.ballardinn.com; just east of Alamo Pintado Rd.* &

Los Olivos

This former stagecoach stop, which looks exactly like the movie set for a small town, has a giant flagpole instead of a traffic light to mark its main intersection. Along the town's three-block business district, a wooden boardwalk contributes to the Wild West atmosphere. But although this tiny dot on the map has starred as a backward Southern hamlet in such TV shows as *Return to Mayberry,* Los Olivos sits squarely at the heart of the **WINE COUNTRY**—and it boasts all the upscale sophistication you'd expect from a place that attracts big-city transplants and cosmopolitan tourists. Next to wine touring and dining, the favorite pastime here is shopping, and Los Olivos has more than its share of art galleries and antique shops. **GALLERY LOS OLIVOS** (2920 Grand Ave; 805/688-7517) is for serious collectors of regional artists; **JUDITH HALE GALLERY** (2890 Grand Ave; 805/688-1222) showcases paintings and Navajo-crafted silver jewelry; and **PERSNICKITY** (2900 Grand Ave; 805/686-8955) is a darling niche filled with antique linens and laces.

RESTAURANTS

Brothers Restaurant at Mattei's Tavern / ★★★

2350 RAILWAY AVE, LOS OLIVOS; 805/688-4820 Brothers Jeff and Matt Nichols are two creative chefs who came to the valley in 1996 (by way of L.A.'s revered Spago and Ocean Avenue Seafood), quickly winning over the hearts of smorgasbord-weary Solvang-ites in their first tiny venue. After a sorely mourned hiatus of a couple years, they reemerged in 2002, setting up shop in a landmark rambling white Victorian, submerged in wisteria and history. Italian-Swiss immigrant Felix Mattei built this roadside tavern in 1886 to accommodate stagecoach travelers preparing for the mountainous journey to Santa Barbara; although the tavern stopped accepting overnight guests in the 1960s, Mattei's has always been known throughout the county for fun and good food. You might find yourself seated in one of several downstairs dining rooms: in the Mattei family's formal dining room, on the white-wicker-enclosed sun porch, or inside the former water tower, looking up through the skylight at nesting owls on top. The brothers' seasonal California-international menu will be familiar to their loyal fans, emphasizing the bounty of the fertile surrounding valley, and composed to pair well with the abundant local wines offered. There are always numerous selections from the grill, such as Scottish salmon on vegetable rice, accented with roasted bell pepper salsa. A tender rack of lamb is fanned over mashed potatoes studded with tangy black olives on a rich rosemary sauce. Dessert selections, often as numerous as main course choices, include a fudge brownie with house-made roasted banana ice cream, warm chocolate truffle cake, and fresh sorbets served with "Mom's" oatmeal cookies. *$$$; MC, V; local checks only; dinner every day; full bar; reservations recommended; Railway Ave runs beside Hwy 154, Mattei's is just west of Grand Ave.* &

Los Olivos Cafe / ★

2879 GRAND AVE, LOS OLIVOS; 805/688-7265 This local favorite is always filled with folks waving to friends from tables on the trellis-shaded wooden porch and enjoying uncomplicated but thoughtfully prepared Mediterranean meals. Inside, the simple cafe resembles an Italian country kitchen. Lunch consists mainly of sandwiches prepared in the gourmet deli (also a great place for buying a picnic lunch), including the favored smoked turkey on a baguette with oven-dried tomatoes, radicchio, and creamy aioli and a roasted-vegetable sandwich with a smoky undertone that calls out for a glass of wine. At dinner the short menu consists of chicken (marsala, piccata, cacciatore, or parmigiana), several light and savory pastas, and specialty pizzas. You can't go wrong by starting with the roasted-vegetable appetizer served with smoked mozzarella and olive tapenade. Always packed at lunch, Los Olivos Cafe is also a pleasantly casual dinner alternative to the ritzy Vintage Room across the street (see Fess Parker's Wine Country Inn & Spa, below). *$; DIS, MC, V; local checks only; lunch, dinner every day; beer and wine; reservations recommended; south of Alamo Pintado Ave.* &

Panino / ★★

2900 GRAND AVE, LOS OLIVOS; 805/688-9304 For the best gourmet sandwiches in the wine country, head to this charming little cafe just a stone's throw from the flagpole that marks the center of Los Olivos. You can dine at simple bistro tables on the garden patio (cooled by a fine mist during the hotter months) or pack an upscale picnic lunch for a day of wine touring, bicycling, or boating. Choose from 31 sandwiches—all served on fresh-baked Italian-style breads—including grilled chicken with sun-dried tomatoes, fresh basil, and provolone; Genoa salami with kalamata-olive tapenade, basil, and roasted red peppers; smoked salmon with Caprino goat cheese, capers, and olive oil; or English Stilton with Asian pear on fresh walnut bread. Several Mediterranean salads are also available, and the shop is great at arranging easy-to-carry box lunches complete with all the necessary utensils. There's also a small branch in downtown Solvang (475 1st St; 805/688-0608). *$; No credit cards; checks OK; lunch every day; beer and wine; reservations not accepted; at Alamo Pintado Ave.* &

LODGINGS

Fess Parker's Wine Country Inn & Spa / ★★

2860 GRAND AVE, LOS OLIVOS; 805/688-7788 OR 800/446-2455 With an elegance (and a price) that comes dangerously close to being out of place in this unpretentious town, the newest holding in the wine-country dynasty of Fess Parker prides itself on state-of-the-art pampering. The first thing Parker did after taking over the former

Los Olivos Grand Hotel was to inaugurate a deluxe spa featuring French sea spa treatments that use ocean products such as seaweed, algae, and mud in a variety of exfoliating and soothing therapies. Each of the spacious guest rooms is luxuriously appointed, with a fireplace, oversize bathroom (some have whirlpool tubs), wet bar, and cozy down comforter. A turndown fairy leaves Godiva chocolates on your pillow. The inn's decor conjures up the tasteful French country home of a Parisian dignitary. Staying in the main building makes you feel more like a country-house guest, but the annex across the street has easier access to the heated outdoor swimming pool and whirlpool. A warm lobby/sitting room woos guests with its fire roaring in the main hearth; there's also a quiet cocktail lounge and a pretty back garden often used for weddings or small luncheons.

Parker brought in some culinary heavy hitters for the inn's restaurant, the Vintage Room, a polished spot that wouldn't be out of place in one of L.A.'s or San Francisco's choicer hotels. Breakfast and lunch are both a notch above average, but chef Kurt Alldredge pulls out the stops with dinner entrees like pan-seared venison medallions atop a couscous flan accented with Asian pear-molasses chutney, or herb-crusted halibut alongside Dungeness crab dumplings bathed in tamari-ginger jus. Starters can be even more intriguing, with choices like pan-seared scallops glazed with pinot noir served atop potatoes whipped purple with beets; grilled quail with spinach–goat cheese stuffing drizzled with aged balsamic; or venison carpaccio layered with fennel and arugula and topped with dried-cherry aioli. *$$$$; AE, DC, DIS, MC, V; checks OK; www.FessParker.com; south of Alamo Pintado Ave.* &

Los Alamos

Founded in 1876, Los Alamos became a Wells Fargo stagecoach stop in 1880 with the inauguration of the old Union Hotel. Though the original structure burned to the ground and was rebuilt in 1915, Los Alamos continued to be a traveler's stop and local gathering place well after the demise of the stagecoach route. When the streamlined U.S. Highway 101 was completed in the 1960s, though, it circumvented little Los Alamos, and now you can't even see the town from the freeway. Not content to slide quietly into ghost-town status, the hamlet reinvented itself as an authentic Old West attraction, complete with wooden boardwalks, a historic hotel and bed-and-breakfast (the restored **UNION HOTEL & VICTORIAN MANSION**), and the Old Days festival and barbecue each September. The growth of the surrounding wine country has also helped, since many **VINEYARDS** are within easy driving distance of town. Several **ANTIQUE STORES** have sprung up along the main drag, including the enormous Los Alamos Depot Mall (in the old Pacific Coast railroad station at the south end of town; 805/344-3315), a 17,000-square-foot warehouse with a surprisingly good selection of antiques and collectibles, especially furniture. Don't be surprised to find yourself asking that all-important question, "Will it fit in the trunk?"

LODGINGS

Union Hotel & Victorian Mansion / ★

☀ **362 BELL ST, LOS ALAMOS; 805/344-2744 OR 800/230-2744** This lodging duo, a fantastic time-travel fantasy set in a sleepy historic town, must be seen to be believed. Like the original 1880 building, the Union Hotel, once a stagecoach stop, has boardinghouse-style rooms upstairs and a dining room and saloon below. In 1972 the late Dick Langdon began painstakingly restoring the hotel to 19th-century authenticity, using old photographs to ensure an exact re-creation. Walk through the front door and it's like entering the *Wild Wild West* TV series' soundstage. Overstuffed velvet wing chairs adorn the front parlor, gilded wrought-iron grating frames the bell desk, and swinging saloon doors lead into the adjacent barroom. Upstairs, where fading carpet runners and creaky hardware reinforce the illusion, most of the rooms share a common bath (although they're equipped with in-room sinks). A single shower room is the hotel's only concession to modernity; the few rooms with private bath have only a tub—claw-footed, of course. Even though the double beds overwhelm the simple, tiny bedrooms, the charm of this place is truly infectious. Breakfast—a generous family-style feast—is included, and diversions like billiards, shuffleboard, and card tables provide entertainment. The hotel's dining room also serves dinner on weekends, offering steaks, seafood, and a nightly family special.

As if the Union Hotel weren't enough, next door stands the Victorian Mansion, an ornate Queen Anne built around 1890 in nearby Nipomo. Langdon moved it here, then spent nine years creating over-the-top B&B theme rooms. Each has a fireplace, a hot tub, a chilled bottle of champagne upon guest arrival, and a secret door through which breakfast appears each morning. Sleep in the '50s Room and you'll bed down in a vintage Cadillac at a drive-in movie, watching *Rebel Without a Cause*. The Pirate Room is a schooner's stateroom where lanterns sway gently and the sound of seagulls provides the backdrop for the 1938 film *The Buccaneer*. The Egyptian Room, a tapestry-laden sheik's tent, boasts a hieroglyphic-papered bathroom entered through a mummy's sarcophagus while *Cleopatra* plays onscreen—you get the idea. *$$ (Union Hotel), $$$$ (Victorian Mansion); AE, DIS, MC, V; no checks; Hwy 166 at Centennial St.* ⅃

Santa Maria/Guadalupe

The largest city in the region, Santa Maria is a bustling community of aerospace and farm employees, drawn by both nearby **VANDENBERG AIR FORCE BASE** and the wealth of profitable agriculture throughout the Central Coast valleys. Although tourism has never been a great draw, one local gastronomic tradition has taken on such legendary proportions that word of it has traveled far beyond the city limits. We're talking about Santa Maria–style barbecue, the featured grub at all festive occasions, both public and private. In the early days of huge ranchos, the *rancheros,* the *vaqueros* (cowboys), and their families and friends would gather midday under the towering oaks to enjoy Spanish barbecues. The recipe is deceptively simple: sirloin tri-tip steak is seasoned with salt, pepper, and garlic (and sometimes parsley, depending on whom you ask) and then cooked over the hot coals of a red-oak fire. The red oak is important; unlike Southern-style barbecue, which hides underneath tangy glazes, the Santa Maria variety is all about simple seasoning and the freshness of the meat, which must be served immediately after cooking. Customary accompaniments are sweet-and-spicy barbecue piquinto beans, garlic toast, salsa, and green salad. On weekends throughout Santa Maria, the tangy aroma of barbecue floats on the air from streetside vendors and local restaurants (although the Far Western Tavern in neighbor Guadalupe usually wins the Santa Maria–Style Barbecue Cook-Off).

RESTAURANTS

Far Western Tavern

899 GUADALUPE ST, GUADALUPE; 805/343-2211 It may be out of the way, but this hearty eatery has been praised in *Gourmet* magazine and on the Discovery channel, and it's a frequent winner of the Santa Maria–Style Barbecue Cook-Off. Operating in a reclaimed Old West theater (whose entire lobby is now a raucous barroom), the restaurant packs 'em in for every variety of steak and chop, each given the traditional barbecue treatment and each presented in a cowboy-size portion. They've got it down to a science, seasoning sirloin tri-tip, rib-eye, or New York with a dry rub of salt, pepper, garlic, and parsley, then throwing the meat on a sizzling oak fire until it's perfectly done. The menu also includes Alaskan king crab, scampi, lobster, pasta primavera for the faint of heart, and a "Little Wrangler" menu for the kids. Appetizers run the gamut from nachos to crisp mountain oysters. Breakfast here invariably involves meat, served with the classic Santa Maria sides—barbecue beans, salsa, and potatoes. The dining room is a decorator's nightmare, a 19th-century Western saloon ambience celebrated with red velvet wallpaper, fuzzy cowhide draperies, enormous mounted steer heads, and plenty of cowboy hats—oh, wait, those are on the patrons. If you've got a hankering to sample the legendary Santa Maria–style barbecue, this place is a real hoot. *$$; AE, DIS, MC, V; local checks only; lunch Mon–Sat, dinner every day, brunch Sun; full bar; reservations recommended; on Hwy 1 at 9th St.* &

LODGINGS

Santa Maria Inn

801 S BROADWAY, SANTA MARIA; 805/928-7777 OR 800/462-4276 The best hotel in Santa Maria is happily the one with the most character, even if it does have a split personality. Originally opened in 1917, the Santa Maria Inn boasts a charming historic side: one entire wing of rooms occupies the original building, as does the hotel's Garden Room restaurant, a reasonably good place completely upstaged by its vintage decor. What was formerly an outdoor promenade is now a relaxing enclosed porch, and there's also a cozy taproom. To the other side is a newer six-story tower whose oversize guest rooms sport bay window seats and decorative crown molding, tasteful decor uncommon in this price range, and modern conveniences including refrigerators, VCRs, hair dryers, and coffeemakers. The original wing offers very small rooms (with large closets), and unfortunately all the original bathroom tile here was demolished in a careless renovation. Perhaps retaining more original detail would've been enough to make up for small space and no air-conditioning, but most guests do prefer the tower. A secluded stone patio with trickling fountain is a nice place for strolling or relaxation, and beyond the garden lie a swimming pool and heated spa. *$$; AE, DC, DIS, MC, V; checks OK; north of Stowell Rd.* &

Nipomo

RESTAURANTS

Jocko's Steakhouse / ★★

125 N THOMPSON AVE, NIPOMO; 805/929-3565 Don't be surprised if you've never heard of Nipomo, a bucolic, blue-collar farm town north of Santa Maria. But it might be a surprise to hear that Nipomo has been a cherished stopping place along U.S. Highway 101 for more than a century. Jocko's is the reason; they've been serving up some of the best—and best priced (some might say ridiculously priced)—Santa Maria–style barbecue since Emery Knotts first built a rancher tavern here in 1886. The Knotts family still owns Jocko's; in 1964 they finally built a permanent structure that houses a series of dining rooms and large bar, whose wood paneling sports the singed brands of local ranches. If cinder-block walls, tired brown dinette sets, paper place mats, and mounted deer trophy heads doesn't sound like loyalty-inspiring atmosphere, the enormous steaks grilled outside over a 3-foot flame along with the indomitable spirit of decades-long regulars—everyone from urban golfers winding down from a day on the local links to spur-clad cowboys who spent their day riding the herd—combine to make this simple street-corner joint a place that's easy to love. Even when the rest of town seems deader than a doornail, there's *always* a wait at Jocko's, often up to an hour; reservations are imperative on Friday and Saturday. If you can't wait for a table, try a platter of bite-size steak morsels from the bar menu. Once seated, it's all about enormous and perfectly prepared steaks, chops, ribs, and other meaty selections, with sweetbreads and spaghetti rounding out the menu. All dinners come with enough food—crudités, salad, garlic bread, beans, salsa, and even dessert—to feed an average eater for two days. *$; AE, MC, V; local checks only; dinner every day; full bar; reservations recommended; corner of W Tefft St.*

Arroyo Grande

Although Arroyo Grande is now more or less a suburb of San Luis Obispo, residents work hard to maintain the small-town atmosphere and Old West heritage of their "village." The main interest of visitors seems to be shopping the many **ANTIQUE STORES** that line Branch Street, the village's main drag, but an ice-cream stop at **BURNARDO'Z** (114 W Branch St; 805/481-4021), an antique ice-cream parlor with plank floors, marble-topped tables, and vintage soda-fountain equipment, is practi-

ARROYO GRANDE WINERIES

Often overshadowed by the Central Coast wine regions in Paso Robles and the Santa Ynez Valley, the wineries around Arroyo Grande are slowly but surely coming into their own. Growing conditions have long been ideal, as ancient volcanoes created soil rich in granite and tufa, which, combined with cooling ocean breezes, makes for a long, fruitful growing season. The **SAN LUIS OBISPO VINTNERS & GROWERS ASSOCIATION** (5828 Orcutt Rd; 805/541-5868; www.sanluisobispowines.com), which used to be headquartered at Corbett Canyon Vintners, has since moved into San Luis Obispo proper and is an excellent source for wine country information. A helpful map of the wine region is available from their office or at many participating wineries. (**CORBETT CANYON VINTNERS,** the best-known area winery, is sadly not open to the public.)

CLAIBORNE & CHURCHILL WINERY: Specializing in the dry Alsatian riesling and gewürztraminer varietals, Clay Thompson's boutique winery might be best known for its unusual straw-bale construction. Though the foot-thick walls have been stuccoed over for looks, you can peek through a "truth window" and see the naturally insulating walls beneath. Located at 2649 Carpenter Canyon Road (Hwy 227), San Luis Obispo; 805/544-4066; www.claibornechurchill.com.

EDNA VALLEY VINEYARD: Edna Valley's beautiful tasting room also has an impressive selection of Provençal pottery and wine-country gifts; stand at the wine bar to get the best panoramic view of the valley below. Outside is our favorite feature— demonstration vines that illustrate the art of grape growing. Located at 2585 Biddle Ranch Road, San Luis Obispo; 805/544-5855; www.EdnaValley.com.

LAETITIA VINEYARD & WINERY: The former Maison Deutz still boasts superior sparkling wines, along with a selection of Burgundy-style whites. Stylish gourmet oils and specialty foods bear the Laetitia label as well. Located at 453 Deutz Drive, Arroyo Grande; 805/481-1772; www.laetitiawine.com.

TALLEY VINEYARDS: An 1860 two-story adobe house stands atop a quiet, peaceful hill amid the grapevines of this out-of-the-way winery—it's one of the area's more unusual tasting rooms. Talley's pinot noir grapes are hand-tended and aged only in French oak, resulting in a locally respected wine whose small production always sells out quickly. Located at 3031 Lopez Drive, Arroyo Grande; 805/489-0446; www.talley vineyards.com.

—Stephanie Avnet Yates

cally mandatory. The annual gathering that began in 1983 as a small-town ice-cream social has grown into Memorial Day weekend's **STRAWBERRY FESTIVAL,** which draws a quarter of a million people to locations around town for game and craft booths, music, and entertainment, plus every strawberry treat imaginable. For more information on this and other happenings around town, contact the **ARROYO GRANDE VILLAGE IMPROVEMENT ASSOCIATION** (805/473-2250; www.arroyo grande.com), which also offers a self-guided walking tour of historic sites that includes the **SWINGING BRIDGE** across Arroyo Grande Creek and the 1895 Victorian **HERITAGE HOUSE AND MUSEUM** (126 S Mason St; 805/481-4126), which displays photographs and artifacts from Arroyo Grande's history as farmland, railroad route, and occasional outlaw hideout.

Pismo Beach/Shell Beach

The native Chumash, who lived here as far back as 9,000 years ago, named Pismo Beach for the abundance of *pismu*, or tar, found in the sand. In the 1900s, with saloons, brothels, and a dance hall established, the town had become a tourist getaway for wild times, and that reputation was furthered during the Depression when Pismo Beach became a well-known source for illicit booze. Currently, it's merely a time-warp shrine to days when California beach towns were unpretentious places meant for just goofing off. Surfers roam the sands year-round, drawn by the timeless song of that siren, the perfect wave—and upscale weekenders come to let it all hang out (even though the new beachfront resorts are the height of luxury).

Here is where you'll find the acclaimed Pismo clam, which reached near-extinction in the mid-1980s due to overzealous harvesting. If you'd like to get your feet wet digging for bivalves, you'll need to obtain a license and follow strict guidelines. Or come for the annual **CLAM FESTIVAL**. Held at the pier each October since 1946, the weekend celebration features a chowder cook-off, sand-sculpture contest, Miss Pismo Beach pageant, and competitive clam dig. For more information on this and other local attractions and events, visit the **PISMO BEACH CHAMBER OF COMMERCE** (581 Dolliver St; 805/773-4382 or 800/443-7778; www. classiccalifornia. com or www.pismochamber.com). If you're around between October and March, don't miss the **MONARCH BUTTERFLY** preserve on Pacific Coast Highway in nearby Grover Beach. The brilliantly colored monarchs nest in a grove of eucalyptus and Monterey pine, where an information board tells you about their unique habits. During cold weather (below 40°F), they remain densely clustered on tree branches, but on warm days you'll see their stately orange-and-black wings fluttering throughout the area as they search for flower nectar.

Near Pismo Beach—and claimed by Oceano, Grover Beach, and even inland Nipomo—lies a stretch of extraordinary **SAND DUNES**. Walk along the shifting sands at Pismo State Beach, or, alternatively, visit the livery stable in Oceano; they'll outfit you with a horse to match your riding ability and send you (alone or with a guide) along their private trail to the dunes, where you can gallop along the surf's edge or just mosey around. The Pismo dunes are also the only place in California where it's legal to drive on the beach—in the specially designated **OCEANO DUNES STATE VEHICULAR RECREATION AREA** (805/473-7230), accessed via a ramp from Pier Avenue in Oceano. A 5½-mile "sand highway" at the ocean's edge parallels the mountainous dunes; you can take the family car onto the sand, but the dunes are off-limits to all but 4WDs and ATVs.

RESTAURANTS

F. McLintocks Saloon & Dining House / ★

750 MATTIE RD, SHELL BEACH; 805/773-1892 If you've got a hankerin' for stick-to-your-ribs ranch-style meals in a corny Old West setting, then mosey up to the table at McLintocks. Set in a 100-year-old former farmhouse (later the local speakeasy), this headquarters of the McLintocks chain offers ocean views and abundant meals. Best known for oak-pit-barbecued steaks and ribs, they also feature fresh local shellfish and a few oddball selections like chicken cordon bleu and liver and onions. Stick with the basics, though, and you won't be disappointed by either the quality of beef or the gargantuan portions. Every dinner starts with onion rings and salsa, then salad, and includes sides of barbecue beans, garlic bread, and fried potatoes, plus ice cream or an after-dinner liqueur. Parents are relieved to know there is a kids' menu. The staff is spirited and helpful—all part of that "genuine Western hospitality," we reckon, which means you can't help but roll up your sleeves and enjoy yourself—unless, that is, you had a romantic evening in mind. *$$; DIS, MC, V; local checks only; breakfast, lunch Sun, dinner every day; full bar; reservations accepted Sun–Thurs only; www.mclintocks.com; at US 101 (Shell Beach exit).* &

Giuseppe's Cucina Italiana / ★★

891 PRICE ST, PISMO BEACH; 805/773-2870 The enticing aroma wafting from this always-crowded standout on Pismo Beach's Italian restaurant row is enough to lure you inside. Known countywide for consistently good home-style food, generous portions, and a friendly, casual ambience, Giuseppe's can get a little boisterous, but it retains a classy touch just a notch above the usual family-style pizza joint. Paso Robles vintner Gary Eberle even chose to have one of his famed Winemaker Dinners in Giuseppe's private rear cottage—a 40-minute drive from the winery itself. White linen rather than red-checked tablecloths sets the stage for a menu that offers both traditional Southern Italian–style fare (pizza, lasagne, veal parmigiana), and trattoria-influenced California cuisine such as peppercorn-seared ahi tuna, grilled portobello mushrooms in an arugula-tomato salad, and individual gourmet pizzas. Dinners come with soup or salad; try the highly recommended "alternate" salad, butter lettuce with creamy Gorgonzola. Appropriately, given its seaside location, Giuseppe's menu includes plenty of ocean fare—favorites include an appetizer of clams stuffed with shrimp, scallops, and lox, baked in the wood-fired oven and served with aioli. *$$; AE, DIS, MC, V; local checks only; lunch, dinner every day; full bar; reservations not accepted; www.guiseppesrestaurant.com; at Pismo Ave.* &

Splash Cafe / ★

197 POMEROY AVE, PISMO BEACH; 805/773-4653 You might expect Pismo Beach restaurants to sell a lot of clam chowder, and you'd be right—although the bivalves are actually imported, since Pismo's famous clams aren't sold commercially. But that doesn't stop Splash from serving up a darn good bowl of the stuff. Although Splash is a beachy burger stand with a short menu and just a few tables, locals agree its creamy, New England–style chowder is the best in town, which explains why the place makes 10,000 gallons annually. If you like, you can order it in a sourdough bread bowl. If that's not enough of a meal, the menu also includes fish-and-chips, hamburgers, hot dogs, and other sandwiches. Come as you are: sandy feet and damp swimsuits are the most common attire here. *$; No credit cards; local checks only; lunch, dinner every day; beer and wine; reservations not accepted; www.splashcafe. com; between Dolliver St and the pier.* &

LODGINGS

The Cliffs at Shell Beach / ★★

2757 SHELL BEACH RD, SHELL BEACH; 805/773-5000 OR 800/826-7827 What it lacks in personality, this efficiently luxurious clifftop resort hotel makes up for in comfort. Guest rooms are light and airy, stylishly furnished with antique reproductions, and outfitted with extras like hair dryers, irons, and private balconies. Poolside beverages and snack service give more reason to recline by the heated swimming pool and whirlpool, which are shielded from the wind and situated to capitalize on the bay views. The Cliffs has its own spa, so a massage or facial is a convenient reward after a workout at the on-site fitness center. However, a more leisurely treat is accessible via the private staircase, which zigzags down to a prime, albeit small, strip of sandy beach. (However, be forewarned that high tide comes nearly to the base of the cliffs.)

The adjacent Sea Cliffs Restaurant features an eclectic menu of grilled meats and fish accented by international flavors (a little Caribbean here, a little Pacific Rim there) and is more formal than it ought to be considering the area. However, it does have a terrific wine list featuring Central Coast labels reasonably priced and available by the glass. The only Sunday brunch more extensive and formal than the one served here is down the coast at Santa Barbara's Four Seasons. *$$$–$$$$; AE, DC, DIS, MC, V; no checks; www.cliffsresorts.com; north of Spyglass Dr.* &

Kon Tiki Inn / ★★☆

1621 PRICE ST, PISMO BEACH; 805/773-4833 OR 888/KON-TIKI The over-the-top Polynesian architecture of this three-story gem is easy to spot from the freeway—and once you're inside it fulfills that kitschy promise, with decor reminiscent of Waikiki hotels of the 1960s. Rooms are modest, small, and simply furnished with faux bamboo and island prints, yet each has an oceanfront balcony or patio, refrigerator, TV with free HBO, convenient in-room vanity separate from the bathroom sink, and groovy retro-style stationery on the bureau. If the weather turns raw once the sun sets, individual heaters quickly and quietly toast your room. Outside, vast lawns slope gently toward the cliffs, broken only by the wind-shielded, kidney-shaped heated swimming pool flanked by twin whirlpools. This humble hotel—which is privately owned and does no advertising—has several advantages over most along these Pismo cliffs, including a sandy beach with stairway access, lack of highway noise, and ground cover that discourages gatherings of pesky seagulls. The adjacent Steamers oyster bar and seafood grill, part of the F. McLintocks's management family, offers lunch and dinner; the Kon Tiki's continental breakfast is served in its Admiral's Room. *$; AE, DIS, MC, V; checks OK; info@kon tikiinn. com; www.kontikiinn.com; 8 blocks north of the pier.* &

SeaVenture Resort / ★★☆

100 OCEAN VIEW AVE, PISMO BEACH; 805/773-4994 OR 800/662-5545
Guests are pleasantly surprised to find that this heavenly beachfront resort offers exceptional pampering without a trace of pretentiousness. Each room is decorated in a soothing blend of deep greens, with thick carpeting, white plantation-style furnishings, and a gas-burning fireplace. With the beach directly below, private balconies or decks are welcoming enough, but in addition almost all rooms have irresistible private hot tubs with soft leatherette rims. Whether the night is foggy or clear, slide into the spa tub, and the invigorating yet ethereal experience is worth the entire cost of the room. It's almost as enticing to release your cares without leaving your feather bed as you loll in a terry-cloth robe, splurge on refreshments from the excellently stocked wet bar, or slip into mindlessness with a rental movie from the hotel's video library. Morning wake-up is both melodic and flavorful, thanks to the CD alarm clock and the continental breakfast basket delivered to your door. If you're still having problems relaxing, SeaVenture has an on-site therapeutic massage center, and the restaurant offers dinner room service and a lovely brunch. Additional amenities include free use of cruiser bikes and beach pedal-surreys. *$$–$$$$; AE, DC, DIS, MC, V; checks OK; seaventure@fix.net; www.seaventure. com; from Price or Dolliver Sts, follow Ocean View to the beach.* &

Avila Beach

Half the fun of Avila Beach might be getting here; from San Luis Obispo, scenic San Luis Bay Road leads toward the ocean. During the late summer and fall harvest seasons, take a detour into woodsy, sun-dappled **SEE CANYON**, where makeshift roadside fruit stands and U-Pick signs mark this apple-producing region. Continuing on, you'll come to **SYCAMORE MINERAL SPRINGS**, a 100-year-old therapeutic hot springs that's also popular as a day spa. **SAN LUIS OBISPO BAY** is as lovely as ever, with its azure, crescent-shaped natural harbor filled with bobbing sailboats. Follow its natural curve to the **OLD SAN LUIS PIER** for a day's sportfishing or a hearty fresh-caught meal. Avila Beach is a little bit like Rip Van Winkle, just waking from a period when it was effectively asleep for several years. Thanks to an environmental tragedy from the seepage of underground crude oil, the waterfront was essentially leveled to allow for complete cleanup. At press time, the still-bare town was starting to flourish with attractive bayfront seating and landscaping and the resurgence of local businesses—like the casual **CUSTOM HOUSE PUB** (402 Front St; 805/595-7555) overlooking the bay; plans call for Avila Beach to spring back to the sunny and popular resort it once was, though a little less funky.

No amount of soil contamination could destroy the charm of Avila's picture-perfect cove, surrounded by mountains and dramatic ocean cliffs. One enduring pleasure is the **PECHO COAST TRAIL**, a 3½-mile hike leading to the Point San Luis Lighthouse. The landmark lighthouse, built in 1889 in the Prairie Victorian style, is the only remaining example of its type on the West Coast. Organized by the Land Conservancy, docent-led hikes ascend steep cliffs to attain stunning views. The entire hike takes about half a day, departing about 9am. For schedule and reservations, call

805/541-8735. If you're interested in less strenuous recreations, the **AVILA BEACH GOLF RESORT** (805/595-4000; www.avilabeachresort.com) offers a regulation course nestled in the foothills overlooking the bay. There's a full-service restaurant and bar on site, and the tranquil setting and breathtaking views will make you forget your high handicap.

RESTAURANTS

Olde Port Inn / ★☆

PORT SAN LUIS, AVILA BEACH; 805/595-2515 You can drive all the way out onto the pier, but if the handful of parking spaces are filled you'll have to park on shore and stroll out past sportfishing outfitters and snack stands to reach this unique seafood restaurant. In the mornings, the wooden platform bustles with commercial fishermen unloading their daily catch of rock cod, halibut, crab, and the like, while pelicans and seagulls vie with sea lions for undersize fish. You can count on the family-run Olde Port Inn to serve the absolute freshest seafood, from the hearty fresh-catch cioppino (a house specialty) to the morning's fresh scallops and shrimp tossed in pasta. (There are also filet mignon and chicken piccata for any landlubbers tagging along.) They make clam chowder, of course, and also offer fish-and-chips, scallops-and-chips, and shrimp-and-chips. Dinners, sized for hungry dockworkers, include soup or salad, potatoes, vegetables, and plenty of warm sourdough bread. Though the upstairs dining room has a nice bay view through picture windows, request one of the glass-topped tables downstairs if you want a straight-down view of the churning waters below through a mirror-lined cutout. Gooey, decadent desserts include a homemade peach cobbler that's well worth the extra calories. *$$; AE, MC, V; no checks; lunch, dinner every day; full bar; reservations recommended; www.oldeportinn.com; 4 miles west of US 101 via Avila Beach Dr.* ⅙

LODGINGS

Sycamore Mineral Springs Resort / ★★

1215 AVILA BEACH DR, SAN LUIS OBISPO; 805/595-7302 OR 800/234-5831 First discovered in 1886 by prospectors drilling for oil, these natural bubbling mineral springs provide relaxation and rejuvenation in an idyllic natural setting. Until the mid-1970s, the spa facility was a therapeutic center staffed by doctors and nurses. Today no one feels obliged to plead medical necessity in order to enjoy the sensuousness of Sycamore Springs. There are close to 75 private mineral baths on the property—one on each room's private deck or balcony, with two dozen more tucked away on the wooded hillside above the spa. Hot-tub rentals for nonguests are available 24 hours a day, and a half-hour soak is included with massage and facial services. The spacious guest rooms, many of which have fireplaces, are in contemporary condo-style two-story buildings. During the monarch butterfly nesting season (October to March) you can spot hundreds of the splendid orange-and-black-winged creatures around the property's dense sycamore trees.

The resort's Gardens of Avila restaurant isn't much to look at, but its outdoor setting shines and its casually elegant, if slightly expensive, California eclectic menu is often hailed as one of the Central Coast's finest. Seafood is prepared especially well, so you can't go wrong with one of the fresh-catch specials. Other offerings include red curry–coconut chicken pot stickers, tiger shrimp in a Mediterranean ragout, and an excellent prime rib. All overnight guests receive a breakfast credit for the restaurant. *$$$–$$$$; AE, DIS, MC, V; local checks only; info@smsr.com; www.sycamoresprings.com; 1 mile from US 101.* &

San Luis Obispo

Pretty San Luis Obispo can't be seen from U.S. Highway 101 and, as a result, many motorists think the garish pink, roadside Madonna Inn (see review in Lodgings, below) is all there is to the place. But nothing could be further from the truth—just ask some of the big-city transplants flocking to live in this relaxed yet vital college town. With its beautiful surrounding countryside, charming neighborhoods of historic cottages, and developing wine region nearby, SLO—as the locals call it—has been growing by leaps and bounds. Recently, the town's population topped 40,000, a magic number for corporate marketing gurus, which explains why big-name businesses like the Gap, Barnes & Noble, Victoria's Secret, and Starbucks have been popping up all over the place. But even with the influx of new residents and commerce, SLO's downtown is wonderfully compact and perfect for exploring on foot, while the sparkling coastline is only minutes away.

Like several other charming Central Coast towns, this one began life as a Spanish mission outpost. Founding friar Junípero Serra chose this valley in 1772, based on reports of friendly natives and bountiful food, and established **MISSION SAN LUIS OBISPO DE TOLOSA** (782 Monterey St; 805/781-8220; www.oldmissionslo.org). The hospitality of the local Chumash Indians had been greatly exaggerated, though—the mission became the first to use the now-traditional red-tile roof after its original thatched roofs repeatedly fell to burning arrows. The well-restored mission church, padres' quarters, and colonnade are in the heart of town, fronted by the pedestrian-friendly **MISSION PLAZA**, a pretty park that serves as SLO's town square for festivals and other events. Around the corner the **SAN LUIS OBISPO CHAMBER OF COMMERCE** (1039 Chorro St; 805/781-2777; www.visitslo.com) offers a colorful, comprehensive *Visitors Guide* and the self-guided *Mission Plaza Walking Tour*. One of the town's most enduring landmarks is the circa-1874 **AH LOUIS STORE** (800 Palm St; 805/543-4332), once the anchor of a thriving Chinatown. This small storefront is packed with exquisite Asian imports, remnants of the store's once-flourishing herb business, and personal mementos from the lifetime Chinese immigrant Wong On (later known as Ah Louis) spent during the Central Coast's formative years. At press time, Ah Louis's son Howard Louis, well into his 90s, opened the place to visitors only by prior arrangement; he's a gentle but spirited man, and we encourage those interested to call for an appointment. On Thursday nights everyone comes out for the **FARMERS MARKET** (6:30 to 9pm, rain or shine; Higuera St, between Osos and Nipomo Sts), a beloved local tradition. Emptied of auto traffic, Higuera Street fills with a colorful and festive assemblage of vendors and entertainers. Shoppers stroll through, clutching bags of luscious fruits and vegetables, fresh flowers, locally made arts and crafts, and warm baked goods. The sounds of Peruvian street musicians, old-fashioned brass bands, or lively dance troupes fill the air as the tantalizing aroma of oak barbecue wafts from sidewalk grills. Come hungry and graze your way through a classic SLO evening.

Another favorite attraction for kids and parents is the **SAN LUIS OBISPO CHIL-DREN'S MUSEUM** (1010 Nipomo St; 805/544-KIDS; www.slonet.org/~slokids), which helps youngsters learn about the past with an authentic reproduction Chumash cave dwelling, and inspires their imaginations with a music room, computer corner, pint-size bank and post office, and more. This area is also a terrific region for **BICYCLING,** with scenic terrain for riders of all levels. Pick up the *San Luis Obispo County Bike Map,* a color-coded guide that includes mileage, terrain descriptions, and a list of local bike shops, which is available at the chamber of commerce (see above for address and phone). **ALAMO BICYCLE TOURING COMPANY** (805/781-3830 or 800/540-BIKE) offers bicycle rentals and to-your-door delivery, as well as guided specialty bike tours that range from three hours to three days.

RESTAURANTS

Big Sky Cafe / ★★☆

1121 BROAD ST, SAN LUIS OBISPO; 805/545-5401 Anyone who's familiar with L.A.'s Farmers Market knows funky Kokomo Cafe and its cousin, the Gumbo Pot, and will recognize some signature recipes on the menu of this eclectic, imaginative restaurant opened by a former Kokomo chef. At breakfast they serve the same red-flannel turkey hash, a beet-fortified ragout topped with basil-Parmesan glazed eggs, and the Cajun-Creole influence spices up the menu at almost every turn. In fact, Big Sky might be the only place on the Central Coast to find decent jambalaya, gumbo, or authentically airy beignets. The menu is self-classified "modern food," a category that here means a dizzying international selection including Caribbean shrimp tacos with chipotle-lime yogurt, Thai curry pasta tossed with sautéed tiger shrimp, Moroccan pasta with spicy tomato-cumin-peanut sauce, and Mediterranean broiled chicken infused with garlic, rosemary, and olive oil. The setting is comfy casual; creative paint treatments and weathered furniture create a vaguely Southwestern ambience accented by local art and a blue, star-studded ceiling. Big plush booths and small wooden tables coexist happily and complement the long counter/bar. Big Sky is well known and well liked, as evidenced by the benches thoughtfully placed outside for customers who encounter a wait. *$; AE, MC, V; local checks only; breakfast, lunch, dinner every day; beer and wine; reservations not accepted; www.bigskycafe.com; between Higuera and Marsh Sts.* ⅼ

Buona Tavola / ★★★☆

1037 MONTEREY ST, SAN LUIS OBISPO; 805/545-8000 Situated next to the art deco masterpiece Fremont Theater, this upscale dining room and its charming outdoor patio offer well-prepared Northern Italian cuisine in a setting that's fancy enough for special occasions but welcoming enough for the casually dressed. Checkerboard floors and original artwork adorn the warm, intimate interior, while lush magnolias, ficuses, and grapevines lend a garden atmosphere to terrace seating out back. Begin by choosing one of the traditional cold salads on the antipasti list, then proceed to a main course menu that highlights delicious homemade pastas. Favorites include *agnolotti di scampi allo zafferano,* half-moon purses pinched around a scampi filling, then smothered in saffron-cream sauce, and *spaghettini scoglio d'oro,* a rich pasta dish overflowing with lobster, sea scallops, clams, mussels, shrimp, diced tomatoes, and saffron sauce. The balance of the menu can be equally tongue-twisting, filled with rich, intense sauces and satisfying meat dishes. The wine list is a winner, with traditional Italian offerings complemented by stellar choices from the surrounding wine region. A second location just opened in nearby Paso Robles (943 Spring St; 805/237-0600). *$$; AE, DIS, MC, V; local checks only; lunch Mon–Fri, dinner every day; beer and wine; reservations recommended; between Osos and Santa Rosa Sts.* &

SLO Brewing Company

1119 GARDEN ST, SAN LUIS OBISPO; 805/543-1843 Hang out with the area's collegiate population at this local-brewpub-makes-good success story. The homemade beers—Pale Ale, Amber Ale, and Porter—have created such a buzz (no pun intended) that they're now nationally distributed. Located downtown in a historic 100-year-old brick commercial building, the Company offers a bar (all beer, all the time) downstairs and a cavernous dining room upstairs. Illuminated by industrial skylights and filled with hardy wooden tables and chairs, the restaurant is comfortable, although it can get loud. The menu—burgers, deep-fried appetizers, and other pub basics—is far from gourmet, but quite satisfying with a tall, cold one. All in all, this is a great place to meet friends, celebrate a sports victory, or grab a premovie bargain bite. *$; AE, DIS, MC, V; local checks only; lunch, dinner every day; beer and wine; reservations not accepted; www.slobrew.com; between Higuera and Marsh Sts.* &

LODGINGS

Apple Farm Inn / ★★

2015 MONTEREY ST, SAN LUIS OBISPO; 805/544-2040 OR 800/255-2040 Even though it's adjacent to busy U.S. Highway 101, this ultrapopular frilly getaway is remarkably quiet and always booked well in advance. The entire complex—which includes a restaurant, gift shop, and working cider mill—exhibits an over-the-top Victorian-style cuteness, with floral wallpaper, fresh flowers, and sugar-sweet touches. No two guest rooms are alike, although each has a gas fireplace, large bathroom with plush terry robes, canopy or brass bed, and lavish country decor. Some bedrooms open onto cozy turreted sitting areas with romantic window seats, while others have wide bay windows overlooking the creek that rambles through the property. Morning coffee and tea are delivered to your room, or you can opt for breakfast in bed at an additional cost. Rooms in the motel-style Trellis Court building have virtually the same amenities as those in the main inn (including fireplaces and cozy decor), but cost less and include a discount voucher for breakfast at the restaurant. The hotel's also got a heated outdoor swimming pool and whirlpool, and there's unlimited hot apple cider on hand in the lobby. *$$ (Trellis Court), $$$ (Main Inn); AE, DIS, MC, V; checks OK; www.applefarm.com; just south of US 101.* &

Garden Street Inn / ★★

1212 GARDEN ST, SAN LUIS OBISPO; 805/545-9802 The prettiest accommodations in town are to be found in this gracious Italianate/Queen Anne bed-and-breakfast near downtown. Built in 1887 and fully restored in 1990, the house is a monument to Victorian gentility and to the good taste of owners Dan and Kathy Smith. Each bedroom and suite is decorated with well-chosen antique armoires, opulent fabric or paper wall coverings, and vintage memorabilia. Choose one with a claw-footed tub, fireplace, whirlpool bath, or private deck—whatever suits your fancy. Breakfast is served in the morning room as the sun filters through original stained-glass windows, and each evening wine and cheese are laid out. The well-stocked library is always available to guests. *$$$; AE, MC, V; checks OK; innkeeper@gardenstreetinn.com; www.gardenstreetinn.com; between Marsh and Pacific Sts.* &

Madonna Inn / ★

100 MADONNA RD, SAN LUIS OBISPO; 805/543-3000 OR 800/543-9666 Conjured from the fertile imaginations of owners Alex and Phyllis Madonna, this eccentric hotel is a wild fantasy world where faux-rock waterfalls, velvet-flecked wallpaper, marbled mirrors, and deep shag carpeting are just the beginning. The only consistent element of the decor is Phyllis Madonna's favorite color, a ubiquitous pink that pops up even on the specially printed bottles of Neutrogena bath products. The 109 rooms are individually decorated in themes so unusual the Madonna Inn sells 109 different postcards—just in case your friends can't believe you slept in digs reminiscent of *The Flintstones*. Everybody's favorites include the all-rock Caveman rooms, featuring waterfall showers and giant animal-print rugs. Other over-the-top options include Swiss Chalet and English Manor, which look like they sound. Many guests of this Disneyland for adults request their favorite rooms annually, celebrating anniversaries or New Year's Eve, and the Madonnas host hundreds of honeymooners each year. Although it's best known for its outlandish features, the inn pays attention to guests' comfort—after all, it takes more than kitsch to keep 'em coming back. The rooms are spacious and very comfortable; if the loud decor doesn't keep you up, there's a very good night's sleep to be had. A surprisingly good coffee shop adjoins a delectable European bakery. Don't miss the formal Gold Rush dining room, an eyeful beyond description that's flaming with fuchsia carpet, pink leather booths, and gold cherub chandeliers. Even those checking out early are treated to coffee and tea in the registration office. *$$–$$$; AE, MC, V; checks OK; www.madonnainn.com; Madonna Rd exit off US 101.* &

Baywood Park

LODGINGS

Baywood Inn Bed & Breakfast / ★★☆

1370 2ND ST, BAYWOOD PARK; 805/528-8888 Nestled in one of the southernmost inlets of vast Morro Bay, the tranquil little community of Baywood Park is popular with folks who like to explore nearby Montana de Oro State Park or quietly launch their kayaks from the small wooden landing right across the street from this romantic bed-and-breakfast. At first glance, the two-story gray inn facing out onto Morro's "back" bay looks like a garden-style office building. Though the building was indeed constructed in the 1970s for business tenants, its spacious interiors lent themselves perfectly to a remodel into B&B suites, each furnished in a distinctive theme. From the knickknacks and ruffles of Granny's Attic to the pale pastels of California Beach or the rough cedar beams and stone fireplace of Appalachian, there's a room for every preference and taste. Our favorite is Quimper, a country-French room with a tiled hearth and vaulted ceiling illuminated by a clerestory window. Every room has a separate entrance, fireplace, microwave oven, coffeemaker, and refrigerator stocked with complimentary snacks and nonalcoholic beverages; many have bay views. Included in your stay are a full breakfast each morning and a late-afternoon wine and cheese reception highlighted by a tour of many of the rooms. If you're looking for solitude, the Baywood Inn fits the bill; and there are a couple of decent restaurants on the block, so you never really have to wander far. *$$; MC, V; checks OK; innkeeper@baywoodinn.com; www.baywood inn.com; 2 blocks south of Santa Ysabel Ave.* &

Morro Bay

Vast and filled with birds and sea mammals, scenic Morro Bay is named for the peculiarly shaped **MORRO ROCK** anchoring the mouth of the waterway. This ancient towering landmark, whose name comes from the Spanish word for a Moorish turban, is a volcanic remnant inhabited by the endangered peregrine falcon and other migratory birds. Across from the rock, a monstrous oceanfront electrical plant mars the visual appeal of the otherwise pristine bay.

Morro Bay Boulevard is the main route into town from the freeway; it will drop you at the harborfront Embarcadero, site of a **GIANT CHESSBOARD,** inspired by open-air boards in Germany, with 3-foot-tall redwood pieces. Farther down the Embarcadero is the **MORRO BAY AQUARIUM** (595 Embarcadero; 805/772-7647). This modest operation with its tanks displayed in a dank and grim basementlike room won't be putting SeaWorld out of business any time soon, but it is officially sanctioned to rehabilitate injured and abandoned sea otters, seals, and sea lions. During their stay, all the animals learn to perform tricks for a morsel of fishy food (50 cents a bag). If you're new to town, stop in at the **MORRO BAY CHAMBER OF COMMERCE** (880 Main St; 805/772-4467 or 800/231-0592; www.morrobay.com) for helpful information.

Water recreation is a mainstay in the bustling marina, and you can venture out on a **KAYAK TOUR** from Kayak Horizons (551 Embarcadero; 805/772-6444). If you've always yearned for **SAILING LESSONS**, call ahead to the Sailing Center of Morro Bay (551 Embarcadero; 805/772-6446). They're next to the Morro Bay Yacht Club and offer everything from one-day intro classes to weeklong series and scheduled sunset sails. Just south of Morro Bay is the 8,400-acre **MONTANA DE ORO STATE PARK** (805/528-0513), encompassing sand dunes, jagged cliffs, coves, caves, and reefs. Named "mountain of gold" by the Spanish for the golden poppies that carpet the hillsides each spring, the park contains trails for hiking, biking, and horseback riding as well as rest rooms and picnic facilities.

RESTAURANTS

Hofbrau / ★

901 EMBARCADERO, MORRO BAY; 805/772-2411 When you're hungry for casual food in Morro Bay and want something other than the ubiquitous wharfside fish-and-chips, Hofbrau is the place for you. Situated on the bay, with a delightful deck and warm inside tables, this German-tinged cafeteria has been an Embarcadero favorite for years, recently moving from a cramped location a few doors down. Although they do offer the standard wharfside fare, the star here is the roast beef French dip, served from a gleaming carving station. Those in the know order the mini sandwich, which is a dollar less and just an inch shorter. As the name would suggest, they have a nice selection of imported and domestic beers, as well as a kids' menu that makes this a great value for families. *$; AE, DIS, MC, V; no checks; lunch, dinner every day; beer only; reservations not necessary; at the end of Harbor St.* ও

Windows on the Water / ★★★

699 EMBARCADERO, MORRO BAY; 805/772-0677 If you're looking for a special meal in Morro Bay, you'll find it at this respected restaurant overlooking the waterfront and distinctive Morro Rock. An airy, high-ceilinged, multilevel space that takes full advantage of bay views, the bistro has Tuscan golden-ocher walls nicely complemented by dark wood accents. But chef Pandee Pearson's cuisine—a California/French/pan-Asian hybrid incorporating local fresh seafood and produce—is the main attraction, and it's presented with a welcome level of sophistication. On any given evening, the menu might boast local abalone served with tangy Japanese cucumber salad; cedar-planked salmon with cilantro pesto and citrus-scented rice; crustacean-rich Pacific bouillabaisse; or oak-fired steaks with garlicky jus. The wine list is composed of the choicest Central Coast vintages and selected French wines. All in all, Windows is one class act. *$$–$$$; AE, DC, DIS, MC, V; local checks only; dinner every day, brunch Sun; full bar; reservations recommended; www.windows onthewater.net; at the end of Pacific St, upstairs.* ও

LODGINGS

The Inn at Morro Bay / ★★

60 STATE PARK RD, MORRO BAY; 805/772-5651 OR 800/321-9566 Though its sleek brochure hints at a snooty, ultraglamorous resort, you'll be pleasantly surprised by this exceedingly comfortable and affordable place that's smart enough to let its splendid natural surroundings be the focus of attention. Two-story Nantucket-style buildings have contemporary interiors tempered by blond-wood cabinetry, polished brass beds, and reproduction 19th-century European furnishings. Rates vary wildly according to the view; the best rooms enjoy unobstructed views of Morro Rock plus convenient access to a bayfront sundeck, while those in back face the swimming pool, gardens, and eucalyptus-forested golf course at Morro Bay State Park. Guests receive a discount on pampering treatments at the on-site Therapeutic Massage Center, and the hotel has a romantic bayside lounge and dining room, which serves California-Mediterranean cuisine and three meals daily. *$$–$$$$; AE, DC, DIS, MC, V; checks OK; www.innatmorrobay.com; take Main St south past park entrance.* ♿

Marina Street Inn / ★

305 MARINA ST, MORRO BAY; 805/772-4016 OR 888/683-9389 This warm and pleasant inn in a yellow old-fashioned captain's-style house is run by former teachers Vern and Claudia Foster. There are great views from its bay windows, and the inn has four rooms decorated differently, all special. Our favorite is the Dockside Room, which has a four-poster bed, a matching bureau, nautical antiques, and an attached patio. In case you forget you're near the water, you can hear the foghorns from here. From the window you can see a bit of the ocean and bay, plus a fantastic view of Morro Rock. Another favorite, the Rambling Rose Room, is decorated in warm red and green colors, with Battenburg lace curtains and bedspread. A four-poster bed, armoire, and English writing desk add to the charm, and the attached patio looks out over the garden. The Garden Room has a romantic four-poster made of willow. Each morning a full gourmet breakfast is served in the dining room. *$–$$; AE, MC, V; checks OK; vfoster105@aol.com; www.marina streetinn.com; corner of Main and Marina St.* ♿

Cayucos

Roughly 5 miles north of Morro Bay and just 15 miles south of Cambria lies Cayucos, a small town that has retained its Old West feel and remains an authentic California beach town. A boardwalk and old-style storefronts give it a look of a Ponderosa on the Pacific. People come here for the beach, night fishing on the pier, or to eat at renowned **HOPPE'S GARDEN BISTRO**. The 940-foot **CAYUCOS PIER** was built in 1875, and the Pacific Steamship Company's ships stopped here to pick up dairy products. Later, abalone and sea lettuce were shipped from the pier. It's a great place for a walk, or to sit on one of the benches to gaze at the Pacific. There's picnicking in a wind-protected area next to the pier. **CAYUCOS BEACH** is reached by nine different stairways placed along Pacific Avenue between First Street and 22nd Street. **CAYUCOS STATE BEACH**, at Ocean Drive and Cayucos Road, is great for surfing and boogie boarding. It has a third of a mile of sandy beach, excellent for swimming, wading, sunning, and surfing. At noon on New Year's Day every year, on the south side of the pier, 3,000 to 5,000 people take part in the **CAYUCOS**

POLAR BEAR DIP. Some dippers go in and immediately retreat, but others even swim around the pier. The water is very cold, and maybe that's why people dress in costume to, er, bear it. The gentleman who leads the charge into the water always comes dressed in top hat and tails, teenage boys have come dressed as hula dancers, and families have appeared as a bunch of crabs or a pack of polar bears. Restaurants are open, there is live music, and certificates are given at the end to all those who are wet and not wearing a wetsuit to keep warm. Call the chamber of commerce for more information at 805/995-1200. If you'd rather celebrate when it's warmer, the town has a **FOURTH OF JULY CELEBRATION** that draws 10,000 to 15,000 people and includes an old-time parade open to all, a street fair, and fireworks from the pier.

RESTAURANTS

Hoppe's Garden Bistro / ★★☆

78 N OCEAN AVE, CAYUCOS; 805/995-1006 Chef Wilhelm Hoppe, already well-known for exceptional Central Coast dining—most recently a duo of acclaimed eateries in Morro Bay—brought his CIA (Culinary Institute of America) training and well-developed, Europe-honed style to tiny Cayucos in late 2000. His culinary originality shows in unexpected touches, like the garlicky house-made hummus that accompanies each basket of focaccia, croissants, and baguettes, or the surprising herbal sweetness of "Mediterranean" lemonade. Set in a vintage downtown building—once the turn-of-the-20th-century Cottage Hotel, a coastal landmark—Hoppe's offers seating in the simple, airy dining room or tucked outside among decades-old gardens, where some bricks date to the original hotel oven, and morning glories climb across romantic trellises. The menu begins with a shellfish bar, daily selection of artisan cheeses, and impressive list of reasonably priced local wines (Hoppe's adjoining wine shop has a similar selection of hard-to-find boutique wines). The lunch menu offers such dishes as a goat cheese and red pepper omelet with chives, a warm salmon terrine with garlic aioli, or apple-wood-roasted brisket with horseradish sauce. At dinner, choose from the likes of seared king salmon glazed with honey and sesame, fresh local swordfish with a mussel-curry broth with Dungeness crab, or the signature dish, sautéed Cayucos red abalone in hazelnut-mango butter. After the meal, exotically flavored house-made sorbets and ice cream accompany luscious desserts composed of local products, and a short-but-sweet list tempts with ports and dessert wines. *$$; AE, DIS, DC, MC, V; checks OK; lunch, dinner Wed–Sun, brunch Sun; beer and wine; reservations recommended; www. hoppesbistro.com; between D and E Sts.* &

Atascadero

Located along U.S. Highway 101 about midway between San Luis Obispo and Paso Robles, the growing community of Atascadero has centuries-old ranching roots. In 1913, an East Coast visionary bought the land to establish a utopian colony; one celebrated landmark from that period is the Italian Renaissance–style City Hall and Historical Society Museum, built with bricks made from local clay, and now a designated California Historical Landmark. Atascadero was incorporated in 1979, and still maintains the rural feel envisioned a century ago.

One of the city's main attractions is the **CHARLES PADDOCK ZOO** (9305 Pismo Ave, Atascadero; 805/461-5080), jointly administered by the Zoological Society of San Luis Obispo and located next to scenic Atascadero Lake Park. Atascadero's old-fashioned downtown is eagerly anticipating the reopening of the historic **CARLTON HOTEL** (6005 El Camino Real, Atascadero; 805/461-5100; www.the-carlton.com), a 1928 landmark being restored to (more than) its early splendor by the team responsible for Paso Robles's luxurious Villa Toscana. Set to debut in late 2003, the 52-room Carlton will feature sophisticated decor, upscale amenities, and fine dining, all within an architectural treasure.

Each June the town celebrates the surrounding wine country with the **ATAS-CADERO WINE FESTIVAL** (www.atascaderowinefest.org) in the park, a weekend-long party that includes winemaker dinners, wine tasting, art exhibits, a golf tournament, and admission to the zoo, which benefits from the proceeds. For more information on this and other local happenings, contact the **ATASCADERO CHAMBER OF COMMERCE** (6550 El Camino Real; 805/466-2044; www.atascaderochamber.org).

Templeton

Situated just a few minutes south of Paso Robles, Templeton has an almost cartoonlike Old West flavor, with wooden boardwalks and antique-style signage. But this agrarian frontier town is the genuine article, continuing to flourish ever since its founding during the Civil War era. The grain elevator of Templeton Feed & Grain is still the centerpiece of downtown business; across the street, period storefronts house modern establishments.

RESTAURANTS

McPhee's Grill / ★★☆

416 MAIN ST, TEMPLETON; 805/434-3204 Inside what used to be Templeton's general mercantile store (circa 1860), chef/restaurateur Ian McPhee has created an eatery that manages to perfectly balance the town's rural Americana with the big-city culinary eclecticism he honed so successfully at Cambria's much-missed Ian's. An old-fashioned pressed-tin ceiling complements sponge-painted walls adorned with English livestock prints and stenciled barnyard animals. Through the open kitchen chefs can be seen busily garnishing McPhee's most popular plates: chewy ancho chile strips adorn the Mexican tortilla soup, and baby orange wedges frame the rustic bread salad—country bread draped with warm Duberki cheese and topped with vinaigrette-tossed mesclun. Main courses range from lighter fare, like shiitake-mushroom ravioli in macadamia-nut butter dotted with sun-dried tomatoes, to hearty peppered filet mignon in cabernet-olive reduction over tangy blue cheese potatoes. Fresh fish specials always reflect McPhee's innovative style, and wife June presents delectable desserts. An impressive list of Central Coast wines, many available by the glass, ensures a perfect match for your meal. *$$; MC, V; checks OK;*

lunch Mon–Sat, dinner every day, brunch Sun; beer and wine; reservations recommended; between 4th and 5th Sts. &

San Miguel

Eight miles up the road from Paso Robles lies San Miguel, site of **MISSION SAN MIGUEL ARCHANGEL** (on old US 101; 805/467-3256), founded in 1797 and still run by the Franciscan order. It's not uncommon to see brown-robed friars going about their daily business on the grounds. Less extensively restored than many others in the state, San Miguel's modest exterior hides a breathtakingly elaborate and well-preserved church, which was painted and decorated by area Native Americans under the supervision of Spanish designer Estevan Munras. The walls and woodwork glow with luminous colors untouched since their application in 1820. Behind the altar, with its statue of San Miguel (St. Michael), is splendid tile work featuring a radiant Eye of God.

Paso Robles

Although its Spanish name means "pass of oak trees," Paso Robles is today better known for the grapevines that blanket the rolling hills of this inland region. Part of the up-and-coming Central Coast wine country, Paso Robles currently boasts almost 40 wineries (see Wineries, below). The town is also proud of its faintly checkered past: it was established in 1870 by Drury James, uncle of outlaw Jesse James (who reportedly hid out in these parts). In 1913, pianist Ignace Paderewski came to live in Paso Robles, where he planted zinfandel vines on his ranch and often played in the Paso Robles Inn (which today maintains a small exhibit in his honor).

Paso Robles is blessed with a well-preserved turn-of-the-20th-century downtown that could have leapt from the play *The Music Man*. At the center of town is **CITY PARK** (at Spring and 12th Sts), a green gathering place—complete with festival bandstand—anchored by the 1907 **CARNEGIE HISTORICAL LIBRARY** (805/238-4996), a Classical Revival brick masterpiece that today houses an exhibit of area maps, early photographs, and historical documents. Several downtown side streets are lined with splendid historic Victorian, Craftsman, and Queen Anne homes, all shaded by grand trees. Drive along Vine Street between 10th and 19th Streets for a superb peek into the past, including the **CALL-BOOTH HOUSE** (1315 Vine St; 805/238-5473), a carefully restored Victorian on the National Register of Historic Places, which is now an art gallery featuring local painters and artisans. The **PASO ROBLES PIONEER MUSEUM** (2010 Riverside Ave, near 21st St across the railroad tracks; 805/239-4556) is worth a visit for insight into the heritage of a working frontier town. The small museum is filled with donated artifacts presented as a series of life-size dioramas illustrating the town's history, ranging from Native American settlements and vintage ranching equipment to a primitive turn-of-the-20th-century medical-surgical office.

Antique hounds have been flocking to Paso Robles since long before the wine-country explosion, and downtown still proves fertile hunting ground for treasure-seekers. The best are the giant mall-style stores representing dozens of dealers each; you can easily spend hours in just one building. Two reliable choices are **ANTIQUE EMPORIUM MALL** (1307 Park St; 805/238-1078) and **GREAT AMERICAN ANTIQUES MALL** (1305 Spring St; 805/239-1203). For more information, contact the **PASO ROBLES CHAMBER OF COMMERCE** (1225 Park St; 805/238-0506 or 800/406-4040; www.pasorobleschamber.com).

RESTAURANTS

Alloro / ★★

1215 SPRING ST, PASO ROBLES; 805/238-9091 Newly arrived in constantly improving historic downtown Paso, Alloro is the brainchild of chef/owner Fabrizio Iannucci, who offers a taste of Southern Italy and specialties of his native Sardinia. Already a recipient of *Wine Spectator*'s Award of Excellence, this unassuming eatery knows how to showcase area wines along with their cuisine, and is a popular local favorite. Set in a renovated storefront across the street from the park, Alloro's sunny interior is simply furnished with colorful paintings and solid bistro seating, and attracts as big a crowd for their affordable lunch specials as for relaxed and romantic dinners. Fresh Mediterranean flavors star on an authentic menu that includes the whimsically named *strozzapreti* (priest stranglers), spinach-ricotta dumplings with grilled sausage in tomato sauce; mushroom-filled *agnolotti* sautéed in proscuitto-mushroom cream sauce; macadamia-crusted salmon in a *picatta* sauce; and the surprising addition of Bubble & Squeak, the English cabbage-potato mash. *$$; AE, DC, MC, V; no checks; lunch Tues–Fri, dinner Tues–Sun; full bar; reservations recommended; near the corner of 12th St.* ⅙

Bistro Laurent / ★★

1202 PINE ST, PASO ROBLES; 805/226-8191 Although it was inevitable that fine dining would follow on the heels of fine wine, chef Laurent Grangien nevertheless created quite a stir when he opened this cozy yet sophisticated bistro in a town unaccustomed to innovations like a chef's tasting menu. With his extensive French cooking background and his Los Angeles restaurant experience, Grangien offers a California-tinged style of French cuisine while maintaining an unpretentious atmosphere that locals have come to love. Banquette-lined walls make virtually every table in the historic brick building a cozy private booth, and there's alfresco dining on a romantic patio. While you peruse Bistro Laurent's impressive list of Central Coast wines, you'll enjoy a complimentary hors d'oeuvre (goat cheese toasts, perhaps). Menu highlights include traditional bistro fare such as roasted rosemary garlic chicken, pork loin bathed in peppercorn sauce, or ahi tuna in red-wine reduction. If you're daring, choose the four-course tasting menu, which changes nightly to reflect the chef's current favorite ingredients or preparations. During lunchtime, the shady patio magically becomes its own separate restaurant, dubbed Petite Marcel, and serves a simple, weekly changing Provençal menu. *$$; MC, V; no checks; lunch Mon–Sat (spring–fall only), dinner Mon–Sat; beer and wine; reservations recommended; at the corner of 12th St.* ⅙

PASO ROBLES WINERIES

Although vines have been tended in Paso Robles's fertile foothills for 200 years, the area has until recently been overlooked by wine aficionados—even though it was granted its own appellation in 1983. But sometime around 1992 wine grapes surpassed lettuce as San Luis Obispo County's primary cash crop, and now the whole character of the area has shifted into wine country mode—albeit without the pretension and stifling crowds of California's more established Napa Valley. Wine touring in Paso Robles is reminiscent of another, unhurried time; here it's all about enjoying a relaxed rural atmosphere and driving leisurely along country roads from winery to winery. The region's friendly ambience and small crowds make it easy to learn all about the winemaking process as you go along—often from the winemakers themselves. The **PASO ROBLES WINE FESTIVAL** each May started out in 1983 as a small, neighborly gathering but has grown into the largest outdoor wine tasting in California. Nearly a dozen events make up the three-day weekend, including winemaker dinners with guest chefs, a golf tourney, a 5K run, a 10K bike ride, concerts, winery open houses and tastings, plus the carnival-like festival itself in City Park. For more information on seasonal events and area wineries, contact the **PASO ROBLES VINTNERS & GROWERS** (805/239-8463 or 800/549-WINE; www.pasowine.com). Meanwhile, any time of year is fine for dropping by the following wineries.

EBERLE WINERY: Winemaker Gary Eberle is sometimes called the "grandfather of Paso Robles's wine country" by the local vintners who honed their craft under his tutelage. A visit to Eberle includes a look at its underground caves, where hundreds of aging barrels share space with the Wild Boar Room, site of Eberle's monthly winemaker dinners. Located on Highway 46 East (3½ miles east of US 101); 805/238-9607; www.eberlewinery.com.

EOS ESTATE WINERY AT ARCIERO VINEYARDS: Follow the checkered flag to the 800 acres of wine grapes owned by former race-car driver Frank Arciero, who specializes in Italian varietals like nebbiolo and sangiovese. The facility includes a self-guided tour, race-car collection, spectacular rose garden, and a picnic area. Located on Highway 46 East (6 miles east of US 101); 805/239-2562 or 800/249-WINE; www.eosvintage.com.

JUSTIN VINEYARDS & WINERY: At the end of a scenic country road lies the boutique winery of ex-Angelenos Justin and Deborah Baldwin, whose best wine is Isosceles, a sophisticated Bordeaux-style blend with splendid aging potential. Since 1987 the Baldwins have commissioned a different artist each year to interpret their gorgeous Tuscan-style property for the label, and the results are on display throughout the complex.

Located at 11680 Chimney Rock Road (15 miles west of US 101); 805/237-4150; www.justinwine.com.

MERIDIAN VINEYARDS: Meridian is the largest local producer, the Central Coast's best-known label, and where you'll get the most polished, Napa-like tasting experience. The grounds are beautiful, featuring a man-made lake surrounding by rolling hills. Located on Highway 46 East (7 miles east of US 101); 805/237-6000; www.meridian vineyards.com.

TOBIN JAMES CELLARS: With a Wild West theme based on the unpredictable personality of colorful winemaker "Toby" James (who claims a dubious lineage from the James Gang), this winery is fun and unpretentious. Don't think he's not serious about his craft, though—Tobin James's zinfandel and late-harvest zinfandel are both award winners. Located at 8950 Union Road (at Hwy 46 E, 8 miles east of US 101); 805/239-2204; www.tobinjames.com.

YORK MOUNTAIN WINERY: The first winery to be established in Paso Robles, York Mountain stands on land originally deeded by Ulysses S. Grant. Inside the 100-year-old stone tasting room, look for a dry chardonnay with complex spice overtones, and reserve cabernets made from hand-selected grapes. Located at 7505 York Mountain Road (off Hwy 46 W, 7 miles west of US 101); 805/238-3925.

—Stephanie Avnet Yates

Trumpet Vine Wine & Tapas / ★★

836 11TH ST, PASO ROBLES; 805/238-9692 Frequent visitors to Paso Robles will be delighted to learn that Trumpet Vine, the wine-and-tapas bar that's the toast of local winemakers and chefs, was expanding at press time to feature outdoor patio seating and a full main course menu in addition to the authentic Spanish "small bites" they're best known for. Trumpet Vine is the brainchild of Jill Ogorsolka—formerly at Santa Barbara's venerable Wine Cask—who started small, with a catering kitchen and casual wine tasting. It felt logical to offer some nourishment along with the wine selection, and traditional Spanish tapas seemed an inspired choice. Since then, Trumpet Vine has developed a reputation for a provocative selection of local and imported wine, as well as fine European foodstuffs (don't skip the Spanish cheese plate) and a convivial atmosphere. Favorites from the tapas menu include crispy marinated quail, calamari in tomatoes and beer, Catalan spinach with raisins and pine nuts, and dry Spanish chorizo sausage; the wine list circles the globe, often with themed tasting "flights" to showcase the latest arrivals. Located downtown, on the park, Trumpet Vine is the perfect ending to a day in the wine country. *$$–$$$; AE, MC, V; no checks; dinner Mon–Sat; beer and wine; reservations recommended; at Pine St.* &

LODGINGS

Adelaide Inn / ★

1215 YSABEL AVE, PASO ROBLES; 805/238-2770 OR 800/549-PASO
Though its neighbors are gas stations and coffee shops, this freeway-friendly motel is nicely isolated from its bustling surroundings. Lush, manicured gardens are screened from the street by foliage, a relaxing outdoor hot tub is secluded inside a redwood gazebo, and there's even a miniature golf course/putting green. The result is a surprisingly quiet, comfortable property tended with a loving care that's rare among lower-priced accommodations—and this place is truly a bargain. The rooms are clean and comfortable, with an extra warmth that's a cut above standard motels; unexpected amenities include refrigerators, coffeemakers, hair dryers, and complimentary newspaper, plus work desks and dataports designed specifically for the business traveler. An outdoor heated pool is in the center of the complex, and morning fruit and muffins are provided in the lobby. *$; AE, DC, DIS, MC, V; no checks; www.adelaideinn.com; at 24th St just west of US 101.* &

Paso Robles Inn / ★

1103 SPRING ST, PASO ROBLES; 805/238-2660 If you're attracted to the retro 1940s look of this sprawling downtown inn, you'll enjoy learning about the *first* El Paso de Robles Hotel, a grand landmark favorably compared to the finest hotels in San Francisco. Designed by famed architect Stanford White and built in 1891, the "absolutely fireproof" structure burned to the ground in 1940, leaving only the ballroom wing that sits, boarded up and off limits, behind the hotel. Many photographs and relics of the old hotel are on display in the lobby, whose Spanish-style architecture and tile reflect the passion for Mission Revival that was in full swing when this replacement was built. A stroll through tranquil and lovely grounds leads guests to a footbridge over the creek meandering through this oak-shaded property and to the original two-story hotel units with convenient carports. Well shielded from street noise, these rooms are simple but boast creature comforts (shiny new bathrooms, gas fireplaces, and microwaves in many rooms) added in a massive 2000 update that, unfortunately, removed much of their nostalgic charm. Insider tip: Avoid room numbers beginning with 1 or 2—they're in a less desirable building near the street. The best rooms here are worth the extra bucks: newly built "Spa Rooms" with fireplaces and privacy-shielded outdoor whirlpools supplied by the property's mineral springs. A large heated pool near the creek makes for great afternoon dips, and the dining room (with cocktail lounge) serves three diner-style meals daily. *$$–$$$; AE, DC, DIS, MC, V; no checks; www.pasoroblesinn.com; between 10th and 12th Sts.* &

The Summerwood Inn / ★★

2130 ARBOR RD, PASO ROBLES; 805/227-1111 Across from Summerwood Winery about a five-minute drive from the center of town, this elegant bed-and-breakfast is a favorite with honeymooners because of its splendid setting and luxurious hospitality. Though the main building—a white clapboard cross between Queen Anne and Southern plantation style—looks old, it was actually built in 1994. This means that guest rooms are extra-spacious and bathrooms ultra-modern, though the entire inn is furnished with formal English country antique reproductions. Summerwood's vine-planted acres are just steps from the inn's back patio and visible from every room's private balcony. Each of the nine rooms is named for a wine (Syrah, Bordeaux, Chardonnay, etc.) and has a gas fireplace, color TV, telephone, terry bathrobes, and bedside bottled water. Luxury is achieved through small, thoughtful touches; you'll find fresh flowers accompanying everything from the chocolate on your pillow with turndown service to the morning coffee tray left discreetly outside your door. The room rate includes full breakfast, afternoon wine and hors d'oeuvres, and late-night cookies. If you're looking for a romantic splurge, the Moscato Allegro room features an in-room whirlpool-for-two, and the top-floor Cabernet Suite is as rich and decadent as an aged wine, with sumptuous furnishings, a seven-headed shower, and an ultraprivate patio with a view. *$$$–$$$$; MC, V; checks OK; www.summerwoodwine.com; at Hwy 46 W, 1 mile west of US 101.* &

Villa Toscana / ★★★

4230 BUENA VISTA DR, PASO ROBLES; 805/238-5600 Martin & Weyrich Winery has raised the bar for wine country bed-and-breakfasts with this eight-room sanctuary at its winery just ten minutes from downtown Paso Robles. Just as their tasting room—nearby along Highway 46—reflects a passion for all things Tuscan, this spacious inn could hardly do more to recreate Italy's sun-drenched countryside in the rolling hills of Central California. Italian music wafts through the courtyard and Bistro, where a daily hors d'ouevres spread features Italian nibbles like *bufalo* mozzarella, marinated green beans, imported cheese, warm asparagus sprinkled with tuna and fresh herbs, and a selection of Martin & Weyrich wines served in Speigelau stemware. The entire compound is done up in rich shades of sunflower gold, terra cotta, and elegant jewel tones, and every corner makes the most of a never-ending view across vineyards and the oak-dotted plains beyond. No detail was spared in the guest rooms, whose size and appointments replicate an affluent Italian palazzo rather than an earthy Tuscan villa; each is high-tech and ultraluxe, with deliciously cozy Italian bedlinens, spa-style bathrobes, state-of-the-art satellite TV/VCR/DVD hidden in a remote-controlled cabinet, environmentally sensitive bath products, warm fireplace, private stone balcony, plus a discreet and superbly stocked minikitchen. Gourmet breakfast is served each morning in the Bistro, and at press time Villa Toscana was adding a swimming pool whose infinity edge will frame the adjacent vineyard. *$$$$; AE, DIS, MC, V; checks OK; www.my villatoscana.com; 2 miles from Hwy 46.* &

Harmony

Along Highway 1 just a few minutes south of Cambria lies a town whose big reputation belies its tiny size. The sign says "Harmony, California, Population 18," and this hamlet is truly not much larger than a postage stamp. Highway 1 used to pass right through the center of town along what's now known as Old Creamery Road. It's named for the once-vital dairy operation that provided milk, cream, and butter throughout the county; William Randolph Hearst even used to stop in to stock the weekend larder on his way up to San Simeon. The **OLD CREAMERY BUILDING** now houses a few gift shops and a U.S. postal station.

Far from languishing as a 19th-century ghost town, Harmony has an enduring appeal among folks from all over. You can take home a souvenir Harmony snow-dome, or even get married in the town's tiny wedding chapel. Like its neighbor Cambria, Harmony also has an **ARTS AND CRAFTS** movement, and most visitors stop off here to shop at one of three serious galleries, all on the same street. Inside the barnlike **PHOENIX STUDIOS** (10 Main St; 805/927-0724) you can watch the resident glassblowers create superbly designed vases, lamps, and bowls. Their organic patterns and smooth, iridescent colors have a sophisticated art nouveau style. Next door is **BACKROADS** (2180 Old Creamery Rd; 805/927-2919), a gallery displaying mainly small items like jewelry, glassware, and handmade paper goods by regional artists. Across the street, the cavernous **HARMONY POTTERY STUDIO/GALLERY** (Old Creamery Rd; 805/927-4293) displays ceramic artwork ranging from inexpensive painted bathroom accessories to elegant glazed platters and vases, with hundreds of pieces in between.

Cambria

Many vacationers discover Cambria only when they visit Hearst Castle for the first time, but after that they're hooked on the sophisticated little village that combines the best elements of both Northern and Southern California. The town's name reportedly compares the natural beauty of the area to the lush, rolling countryside of Wales, whose ancient name was Cambria. This place truly has a split personality. The main part of town is known as the **VILLAGE**, a charming enclave of restored Victorians, art galleries, antique stores, boutiques, and exceptional restaurants nestled among pine-blanketed hills. Across the highway, however, **MOONSTONE BEACH** (named for the translucent stones that wash ashore) is lined with inns offering an opportunity to sleep alongside the breaking surf and stroll windswept beaches populated by seals and sea lions. For an introduction to the area, stop by the **CAMBRIA CHAMBER OF COMMERCE** (767 Main St; 805/927-3624; www. cambriachamber.org). For more information about Cambria on the Web, check out www.cambria-online.com.

Shopping is a major pastime in the village; boutique owners are hyper-savvy about keeping their merchandise current—and priced just a hair lower than in L.A. or San Francisco. This close-knit community has always attracted artists and artisans of the highest quality, so listen when you hear phrases like "important piece" and "museum quality" bandied about. The finest handcrafted glass artworks, from affordable jewelry to investment-scale sculpture, can be found at **SEEKERS COLLECTION & GALLERY** (4090 Burton Dr; 805/927-4352; www.seekersglass.com). Nearby, at **MOONSTONES GALLERY** (4070 Burton Dr; 805/927-3447; www.moonstones.com), you'll find a selection of works ranging from woven crafts to jewelry and an exceptional selection of wood carvings and other crafts. If a visit to the nearby Paso Robles wine country has inspired you, **FERMENTATIONS** (4056 Burton Dr; 805/927-7141) has wines, wine accessories and gifts, plus wine country gourmet goodies open for tasting. Across the street, **HEART'S EASE** (4101 Burton Dr; 800/ 266-4372 or 805/927-5224; www.hearts-ease.com) is located inside a quaint historic cottage and is packed with an abundance of garden delights, apothecary herbs, and custom-blended potpourris. Women who appreciate casual style and ease of care mustn't miss **LESLIE MARK** (801 Main St; 805/927-2234; www.lesliemark. com) and her deceptively simple line of versatile cotton and rayon separates.

About 10 minutes east of town, on a rambling country road, sits **LINN'S FRUIT BIN** (east of town on Santa Rosa Creek Rd; 805/927-8134; www.linnsfruitbin.com), a family farm known statewide for freshly baked pies and other goodies. The Linns' cash crop is the olallieberry, a tart blackberry hybrid used in pies, preserves, salsas, teas, mustards, candies, and anything else they dream up. Their most popular pies are apple-olallieberry and rhubarb, which are even sold frozen for easy transport home. Their goods are also available in town at **LINN'S MAIN BIN** (2277 Main St; 805/927-0371; see review, below).

RESTAURANTS

Bistro Sole / ★★☆

1980 MAIN ST, CAMBRIA; 805/927-0887 Nestled against the creek that runs through Cambria's east village, this unassuming bistro is a consistent winner with locals and visitors alike. Occupying a restored cottage, the simply furnished and relaxing cream-hued dining room is joined by a lighter enclosed patio overlooking the garden, where—on pleasant evenings—tables are set next to heat lamps for pleasant alfresco dining. The menu showcases seasonally fresh ingredients in casual wine country Cal-Med fare, ranging from pasta (the house specialty is penne with chicken-apple sausage and spinach in a creamy marsala sauce) and bistro-style steaks to Asian-tinged seafood specials like sesame-encrusted salmon glazed with citrus or blackened catfish with ginger-orange salsa. A vast and well-priced selection of Central Coast wines includes many fine vintages available by the glass. *$$; AE, MC, V; local checks only; dinner every day, brunch Sun; wine only; reservations recommended; 300 yards west of Burton Dr.*

The Brambles Dinner House / ★

4005 BURTON DR, CAMBRIA; 805/927-4716 Looking at the exterior of this Old English cottage–style lodge, it's easy to predict the menu: prime rib, of course, and continental-American specialties reminiscent of the 1950s, when the Brambles first opened. But the Greek influence of owner Nick Kaperonis is everywhere, as *dolmades* and *saganaki* share billing with oysters Rockefeller, chicken cordon bleu, and rack of lamb. Since the dining room's romantic retro atmosphere alone isn't enough to compete with the culinary excellence elsewhere in town, Brambles stays on the top with the freshest fish and beef, expert preparation, and fair prices; they've also augmented the menu with some lighter Mediterranean fare. To do it right, however, forget the diet for a night and order sour cream for your baked potato, extra butter for your lobster, and one of the restaurant's tempting chocolatey desserts. Locals grouse that the place is too popular with busloads of tourists, whose package deals often include the restaurant's early-bird dinner, so it's wise to dine later. *$$; AE, DIS,*

MC, V; checks OK; dinner every day, brunch Sun; full bar; reservations recommended; www.bramblesdinnerhouse.com; 2 blocks south of Main St. &

Linn's Main Bin / ★★

2277 MAIN ST, CAMBRIA; 805/927-0371 The in-town outlet for popular Linn's Fruit Bin (see the Cambria introduction, above), this casual all-day restaurant also carries decorative housewares, gifts, and a selection of Linn's food products. You can't go wrong with a steaming hot chicken or beef potpie, which seems natural, since Linn's most famous products are their superlative berry pies. Other winners are homemade daily soups, hearty sandwiches, and fresh-from-the-farm salads; at breakfast, sweet treats like berry-covered waffles and pancakes prevail. Every town should have a place like this, where a reliably good meal doesn't have to be an event and where you'll feel equally welcome stopping in for just a slice of warm pie and a glass of ice-cold milk. *$; AE, DIS, MC, V; checks OK; breakfast, lunch, dinner every day; beer and wine; reservations not accepted; www.linnsfruit bin.com; 1 block east of Burton Dr.* &

Robin's / ★★

4095 BURTON DR, CAMBRIA; 805/927-5007 "Home Cooking from Around the World" is the slogan at this adventuresome and eclectic cafe that's been a local favorite for many years. Located on the east side of Cambria's still-expanding village, Robin's has a cozy, casual, almost hippie ambience, and a menu that runs the gamut from exotic Mexican-, Thai-, or Indian-tinged recipes to simple vegetarian salads, pastas, and sandwiches. The robust flavors of extremely fresh ingredients shine through in every dish, and the food manages to taste well composed yet distinctly homemade. Best bets include the soup of the day; the "black bean surprise," a tortilla dip appetizer of beans, cheese, guacamole, salsa, and sour cream; salmon fettuccine in cream sauce with fresh dill sprigs; and *roghan josh,* a North Indian lamb dish in a richly spiced nutty yogurt sauce accompanied by sweet-tangy chutneys. Much of the menu is somewhat health oriented, giving many diners the justification to indulge in one of Robin's to-die-for desserts, like vanilla custard bread pudding in Grand Marnier sauce. *$$; MC, V; local checks only; lunch, dinner every day; beer and wine; reservations recommended; www.robinsrestaurant.com; 1 block south of Main St.* &

Sea Chest Oyster Bar & Seafood Restaurant / ★★

6216 MOONSTONE BEACH DR, CAMBRIA; 805/927-4514 No nautical items were spared in decorating this gray clapboard cottage festooned with brass portholes, anchors, fishing nets, buoys, and virtually anything else to accentuate the seaside atmosphere. Warm and welcoming, the Sea Chest also has a game-filled lounge complete with cribbage, checkers, and chess to keep you amused while waiting for your table. Once you're seated—either gazing out at the waves rolling ashore or next to a cozy potbellied stove—choose from an extensive menu of very fresh seafood from local and worldwide waters. Oysters are the main attraction: oysters on the half shell, oyster stew, oysters Casino, oysters Rockefeller, or devils on horseback (oysters sautéed in wine and garlic, then topped with bacon and served on toast). The menu also features steamed New Zealand green-lipped mussels, steamed clams and other clam preparations, halibut, salmon, lobster, and scampi, plus whatever looked good from off the boats that morning. There's a respectable list of microbrews and imported beers, along with a selection of Central Coast wines. *$$; No credit cards; checks OK; dinner Wed–Mon (open Tues May–Sept only); beer and wine; reservations not accepted; west of Hwy 1 at Windsor.* &

The Sow's Ear Cafe / ★★☆

2248 MAIN ST, CAMBRIA; 805/927-4865 If it were in Los Angeles or San Francisco, dinner at the Sow's Ear would cost twice as much and you'd never get a reservation—it's that good. One of Cambria's tiny old cottages has been transformed into a warm, romantic hideaway right on Main Street, where the best tables are in the fireside front room, lit just enough to highlight its rustic wood-and-brick decor. Pigs appear in oil paintings, small ceramic or cast-iron models adorning the shelves, and the Americana woodcut sow logo. Though the menu features plenty of contemporary California cuisine, the most popular dishes are American country favorites given a contemporary lift; these include a warmly satisfying chicken-fried steak with outstanding gravy, chicken and dumplings any grandmother would be proud of, and zesty baby pork ribs. Other standouts are salmon prepared in parchment and grilled pork loin glazed with chunky olallieberry chutney. Although dinners come complete with soup or salad, do share one of the outstanding appetizers—the calamari is melt-in-your-mouth, and marinated goat cheese perfectly accompanies the restaurant's signature marbled bread baked in terra-cotta flowerpots. The wine list is among the area's best, featuring outstanding Central Coast vintages with a large number available by the glass. If you have only one nice dinner in town, make this the place. *$$; AE, DIS, MC, V; local checks only; dinner every day; beer and wine; reservations recommended; www.thesowsear.com;* ½ *block east of Burton Dr.* &

LODGINGS

Beach House Bed & Breakfast / ★★

6360 MOONSTONE BEACH DR, CAMBRIA; 805/927-3136 If you've ever been jealous of friends with vacation homes and wished for your own casual, comfy cabin or beachfront cottage, this is the place for you. Reconfigured as a B&B, this three-story, A-frame wood house still has the vibe of a 1950s vacation retreat, happily sporting unchic decorative touches and a communal kitchen and living room. Guests gather around the main fireplace or on the seaside deck for wine and appetizers each afternoon and take full advantage of the telescopes and binoculars provided for bird-, dolphin-, seal-, and whale-watching. All six quirkily individual rooms have either a full or a partial ocean view, private bath, and cable TV. Consider splurging on one of the best ocean-view rooms (worth every penny), which have private fireplaces to chase the evening chill away. Hosts Penny and Tom Hitch also own the Moonstone Beach Bar & Grill a few doors down, where full breakfast is provided each morning. The restaurant is also a great place to end a sunset stroll or enjoy a nightcap. *$$–$$$; MC, V; no checks; west of Hwy 1 at Windsor.* &

Cambria Pines Lodge

2905 BURTON DR, CAMBRIA; 805/927-4200 OR 800/445-6868 Nestled as it is in 25 acres of wild Monterey pine woods, it's hard to believe this old-style enclave is just minutes from the crashing surf and only a few blocks from the center of town. Equal parts vacation lodge and summer camp, the lodge is composed of 31 different buildings, from rustic, secluded cabins to two-bedroom hotel-style units. At the heart is the main lodge, built in the early 1990s around the great stone hearth of the original 1927 building (which was destroyed by fire). It all has a welcoming, communal feel. Nearly all the rooms have fireplaces; a 1999 upgrade replaced worn furnishings with contemporary (though plain) pieces and added amenities like coffeemakers and cable TV. The only swimming pool on the village side of town is on these grounds, a gorgeous indoor Olympic-size one heated for year-round use. At press time, the circa-1950s pool complex, which includes a separate whirlpool, sauna, and massage room, was slated for a complete refurbishing. Inside the main lodge, there's a moderately priced restaurant and large fireside lounge with occasional live music. A full breakfast buffet is included in the rate. *$–$$; AE, DIS, MC, V; checks OK; www.cambriapineslodge.com; take Burton Dr uphill from the center of town.* &

FogCatcher Inn / ★

6400 MOONSTONE BEACH DR, CAMBRIA; 805/927-1400 OR 800/425-4121 This contemporary hotel's faux English style—featuring thatched-look roofing and rough-hewn stone exteriors—fits right into the architectural mishmash along funky Moonstone Beach, even though the hotel is one of the newest properties here. Its 60 rooms are contained in a U-shaped building situated so that many have unencumbered views of the crashing surf across the street, while some gaze oceanward over a sea of parked cars, and others are hopelessly landlocked. Rates vary wildly according to the quality of view, but all rooms have identical amenities. Inside you'll find a surprising attention to comfort, especially considering the FogCatcher's prices, which can drop dramatically midweek and off-season. Rooms are immaculately maintained and furnished in a comfy cottage style with oversize pine furniture, floral accents, and stylish fixtures. Each is made cozier by a gas fireplace and also boasts a microwave oven, coffeemaker, and stocked refrigerator; the rate also includes a continental breakfast buffet. Unlike many comparably priced Moonstone Beach lodgings, the FogCatcher also has a heated swimming pool and whirlpool. *$$; AE, DIS, MC, V; checks OK; www.fogcatcherinn.com; west of Hwy 1 at Windsor.* &

J. Patrick House / ★★

2990 BURTON DR, CAMBRIA; 805/927-3812 OR 800/341-5258 Hidden in a pine-filled residential neighborhood overlooking Cambria's East Village, this picture-perfect B&B is cozy, elegant, and welcoming. The main house is an authentic two-story log cabin, where each afternoon innkeepers John and Ann offer wine and hors d'oeuvres next to the living room fireplace, and each morning serve breakfast by windows overlooking a garden filled with hummingbirds, Chinese magnolias, fuchsias, white and pink Japanese anemones, flowering Jerusalem sage, primrose, and bromeliads. The eight guest rooms, most of which are in the adjacent carriage house, are named for Irish counties. Each features a private bath, woodburning fireplace, feather duvets, and bedtime milk and cookies. John creates gourmet breakfasts each morning. *$$; DIS, MC, V; checks OK; jph@jpatrickhouse. com; www. jpatrickhouse.com; take Burton Dr uphill from the center of town.* &

McCall Farm Bed & Breakfast / ★

6250 SANTA ROSA CREEK RD, CAMBRIA; 805/927-3140 Most Cambria bed-and-breakfasts are situated either in the village (near shopping and dining) or on Moonstone Beach, with the ocean just across the street—but McCall Farm offers neither of those conveniences. That doesn't mean you should cross it off your list, though, for the bucolic pleasures of this restored farmhouse and the surrounding Santa Rosa Creek valley are worth the 15-minute drive to town or the beach. You can't get any more country than the original 1885 clapboard home and 20-acre working farm the McCall family has called home for two generations. In between harvesting their bountiful fruit orchards and vegetable plots for local farmers markets and tending the flowers and herbs that fringe the gracious porch, the McCalls manage to welcome weekend guests to two upstairs rooms they remodeled after their kids left the nest. The romantic Rose Room features namesake pink hues, Victorian lace, and an en suite bathroom; the cheerful Yellow Bird Room is furnished with simple period pieces and has a private bath (the home's charmingly remodeled original) at the end of the hallway. It's the perfect escape for city-weary folk, who can enjoy a hearty gourmet breakfast each morning and spend a lazy day exploring the grounds, strolling to nearby Linn's farm for their legendary pies and preserves, or simply napping away the hours until wine and hors d'oeuvres appear downstairs at sunset. *$$$; MC, V; checks OK; mccallfarm@earthlink.net; www.mccallfarmbandb.20m.com; 5 miles from Main St.*

Olallieberry Inn / ★★★

 2476 MAIN ST, CAMBRIA; 805/927-3222 OR 888/927-3222 Cambria's bed-and-breakfasts are standard-setters for aspiring innkeepers, and this charming nine-room B&B is one of the best in town. The lovingly maintained 1873 Greek Revival house—a convenient two-block stroll from the heart of Cambria's east end of the village—has recently received a face-lift from new owners, who made the downstairs public rooms more spacious, expanded on the berry theme throughout with artisan-made stained-glass windows and berry-dotted lace drapes, and honed their skills with the legendary breakfast and hors d'oeuvres recipes that were the legacy of the previous innkeepers. Like the home's entry hall and breakfast room, guest quarters are a tasteful blend of antiques and contemporary touches, with fresh carpeting and less lace than before. Six are in the main house; though all have private baths, three of the baths are across the hall rather than en suite. The nicely renovated carriage house has three spacious rooms overlooking the creek or surrounding hillside; one is a suite for up to four people. Seven rooms have fireplaces. The most charming room is Room at the Top, a sunny nook where you can relax fireside or soak in the antique claw-footed tub. Ask about off-season packages with local restaurants. *$$–$$$; AE, MC, V; checks OK; www.olallie berry.com; from Hwy 1, turn east on Main St.* &

Pelican Suites / ★★

6316 MOONSTONE BEACH DR, CAMBRIA; 805/927-1500 OR 800/222-9160 There are simply so many inns and motels on Moonstone Beach—how are you supposed to choose? Price, availability, and previous experience are the usual criteria, but you can stack the deck by picking from among the six hotels managed by Moonstone Hotels, whose properties are all carefully chosen and thoughtfully maintained. Each is unique in appearance and price; their finest is the boutique-style Pelican Suites, a contemporary Cape Cod clapboard with a small swimming pool tucked behind the natural riparian preserve that anchors the property. Of 25 rooms, 16 are fully ocean-facing; the rest offer a sea view from their balconies. All are minisuites, with dark and elegant European-style furnishings, richly colored fabrics, romantic fireplaces, and royal bathrooms. Special pampering touches include luxurious bathrobes in each room and a cheesecake buffet every evening in the book-lined common lounge. Prices here vary wildly by season and day of week, so always ask about applicable packages or discounts (AAA members get preferred rates). *$$–$$$$; AE, DIS, MC, V; checks OK; www.pelicansuites.com; west of Hwy 1 at Windsor.*

San Simeon

Though it started out as a Portuguese whaling port, today the town of San Simeon is synonymous with **HEARST CASTLE** (750 Hearst Castle Rd; 800/444-4445 for tour schedules, prices, and advance ticket purchases; 805/927-2020 for general information; www.hearstcastle.org) and the stretch of highway-side motels catering to the million-plus tourists who flock here annually. The lavish palace that publishing magnate William Randolph Hearst always referred to as "the ranch" sits high above the coastline. It's opulently and almost haphazardly furnished with museum-quality treasures purchased by Hearst, a collector with indiscriminate taste and inexhaustible funds who spent years traveling to Europe buying up complete interiors and art from ancestral collections. Touring the house (advance tickets highly recommended), you'll see carved ceilings from Italian monasteries, fragments of Roman temples, lavish doors from royal castles, and a breathtaking collection of Greek pottery carelessly displayed among equally priceless volumes in the library. The estate boasts two swimming pools—one indoor, one outdoor—whose grandiose opulence must be seen to be believed. Besides viewing the palatial grounds and interiors, visitors learn about Hearst's Hollywood connection and the countless celebrities who were weekend guests. Now operated as a State Historic Monument by the Department of Parks and Recreation, the landmark Hearst Castle can be seen only by guided tour; four separate itineraries cover different areas of the estate.

If you've got a few minutes left over and want to see the other side of San Simeon's history, cross Highway 1 to the sheltering bay where W. R. Hearst's father in the 1880s built a wharf, pier, and mission-style warehouses for the operation of what was then a massive cattle ranch. His son would later use the port to bring in the voluminous building materials and furnishings for the castle, including crates of exotic animals for his private zoo (the zebras you see grazing with cattle alongside the highway are remnants of that short-lived endeavor). Near the end of San Simeon Point, stop into **SEBASTIAN'S GENERAL STORE** (442 San Luis Obispo–San Simeon Rd; 805/927-4217; www.sebastians.com); the rustic country store, which has been in operation since 1852, dispenses basic groceries and souvenirs and operates a small snack bar.

One of the most spectacular natural attractions along this stretch of rugged coast is its abundance of marine mammals. Seals and sea lions are often spotted along Cambria's Moonstone Beach, but the area most popular with **ELEPHANT SEALS** is the rocky shoreline below **PIEDRAS BLANCAS LIGHTHOUSE**, about 12 miles north of Cambria. These enormous creatures are practically year-round residents, allowing visitors the opportunity to eavesdrop on their always intriguing—and frequently noisy—society. The most active time is mating season in December, when females who have just given birth to the pups conceived the previous year almost immediately conceive again. Mothers and pups hang out on shore for several months. Meanwhile, other seals return for molting, and younger seals are nearly always present, as they need to reach maturity before they're able to spend long periods out at sea.

RESTAURANTS

Ragged Point Inn / ★★

 19019 HWY 1, SAN SIMEON; 805/927-5708 Ragged Point shares with its adjacent motel (see review) a million-dollar view and a dramatic clifftop location. The dining room is classic California-redwood architecture with plenty of view-enhancing windows, and there's a partially enclosed patio for alfresco dining when the weather allows. The menu is California cuisine, with hearty American favorites and gourmet European touches. Recommended choices include herb cheese–stuffed mushrooms, baby back ribs in ginger-barbecue sauce, and homemade ravioli in orange-sage sauce. At lunchtime there's a variety of gourmet sandwiches. You'll want to be here during daylight to enjoy the scenery, so plan on lunch or a reasonably early dinner (the dining room serves lunch until 4pm, with dinner starting at 5pm) and make a point of strolling the well-landscaped, Japanese-inspired gardens. Ragged Point also serves up a hearty and satisfying breakfast. *$$; AE, DIS, MC, V; local checks only; breakfast, lunch, dinner every day; beer and wine; reservations recommended; www.raggedpointinn.net; 15 miles north of Hearst Castle.* &

LODGINGS

Best Western Cavalier Oceanfront Resort / ★

 9415 HEARST DR, SAN SIMEON; 805/927-4688 OR 800/826-8168 Of the dozen or more budget and midrange hotels and motels clustered along Highway 1 just south of Hearst Castle, this surprisingly nice Best Western is the only one that's actually an oceanfront property. Composed of a handful of buildings sprawled across a gentle slope, the hotel offers a wide range of accommodations. Every room—whether you choose a basic double or opt for extras such as a fireplace, ocean view, wet bar, or oceanfront terrace—features a stocked minibar, hair dryer, computer jack, and cable TV with VCR (rentals are next door). Two outdoor pools are shielded from the wind—but not from the exceptional view—thanks to glass walls, and guests are invited to huddle around cliffside bonfires each evening. There are several casual dining options within walking distance, plus an exercise room, coin laundry, and telescopes set up for whale- or porpoise-watching. Though travelers focusing on Hearst Castle are probably the only ones who'll choose to stay along this motel-heavy stretch, the Cavalier is top-notch in its class. *$$; AE, DC, DIS, MC, V; checks OK; on Hwy 1, 3 miles south of Hearst Castle.* &

California Seacoast Lodge

9215 HEARST DR, SAN SIMEON; 805/927-3878 If you're looking for a bed-and-breakfast ambience superclose to Hearst Castle, this innlike property really stands out from its motel neighbors. Although most of the rooms have no ocean view, and although the small swimming pool is good for a quick dip but not pretty enough to lounge by, the Seacoast Lodge's loyal followers are drawn by the plush comfort of homey country-French rooms featuring canopy beds and plenty of flowered prints and flounces. You'll never awaken thinking you're in an impersonal chain hotel here. Some rooms have fireplaces or whirlpool tubs to add a romantic mood, and a complimentary continental breakfast is served each morning in the sunny parlor. If the mediocre dining options nearby don't interest you, Cambria is a mere 10-minute drive away. Between September and May, low-season rates offer substantial bargains. *$$; AE, DIS, MC, V; no checks; on Hwy 1, 3 miles south of Hearst Castle.* &

Ragged Point Inn & Resort

 19019 HWY 1, SAN SIMEON; 805/927-4502 The number-one reason to stay here—make that the only reason—is the breathtakingly dramatic setting. Perched on a grassy cliff high above the ocean, this little 20-room motel offers views as spectacular as any farther north in pricey Big Sur. Part of an upscale rest stop complex that includes a gas station, minimart, gift shop, snack bar, and the Ragged Point Inn restaurant (see review), the motel itself is folksy and basic—reminiscent of Alan Alda's and Ellen Burstyn's secluded oceanside tryst in *Same Time, Next Year.* Each spacious room features an oceanfront balcony or patio, along with separate heating controls for getting cozy on blustery nights. The furnishings are contemporary and comfortable; bathrooms are small but serviceable; and the motel is set back a ways from the other roadside facilities, so you can count on silence and seclusion. Foxes and raccoons are often spotted scurrying around the grounds. San Simeon and Cambria are a 25-minute drive south, but the restaurant is good enough to eat all your meals here if you want. Ask for an upstairs room to get the best view—and the most privacy. *$$; AE, DIS, MC, V; checks OK; www.raggedpointinn.net; 15 miles north of Hearst Castle.* &

INLAND EMPIRE AND MOUNTAIN REGION

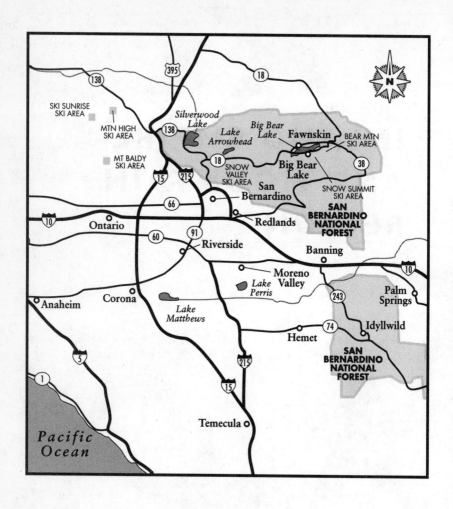

INLAND EMPIRE
AND MOUNTAIN REGION

For a generation or two, it *was* an empire. Groves covered the land with golden-fruited trees that yielded equally golden bank accounts for growers. The orange-growing boom, centered around Riverside and Redlands, brought a prosperity that briefly made Riverside the highest per-capita-income city in the United States. Cross-country rail lines joined San Bernardino and Riverside Counties with the East Coast, and refrigeration technology brought California oranges to eastern seaboard tables in a matter of days.

Today Riverside and Redlands are known for their glorious civic and private architecture from the turn of the 20th century, but the orange boom has been replaced by new housing sprawl. And after generations of terrible smog, the Inland Empire—as it came to be known from those glory years—is finally emerging from a long, hazy bad dream of being all but forgotten except by those who live here. Years of stringent automobile pollution control measures have reduced smog dramatically—although it takes only one drive into the mountains and a view of the inversion layer to realize that the haze is still a fact of life most days. If you want the great views of snowcapped mountains above orange groves that inspired the early crate-label artists, come in winter or spring right after a storm.

Consisting of the western areas of Riverside and San Bernardino Counties (as well as part of eastern Los Angeles County), the Inland Empire embraces 28,000 square miles in the heart of Southern California. The area's population in the year 2005 is expected to range between 3.6 and 4.0 million. Its charm lies in the traveler's discovery of grand residential streets, old restaurants, classic hotels and train stations, and the surrounding mountain ranges—the San Bernardinos and the San Jacintos—that separate the Inland Empire from the desert. Incredibly to people not familiar with Southern California, the region's two highest peaks, San Gorgonio (11,499 feet) and San Jacinto (10,804 feet), are true alpine giants that would not be out of place in the Sierra Nevada or Rocky Mountains.

ACCESS AND INFORMATION

ONTARIO INTERNATIONAL AIRPORT (south of I-10 between Haven and Vineyard Aves; 909/937-2700) is served by numerous commercial airlines connecting to every major U.S. city via nonstop or continuing service. **CAR RENTALS** at the airport include Alamo, Avis, Budget, Dollar, Hertz, and National, while Enterprise and Thrifty are nearby. Amtrak's (800/872-7245; www.amtrakwest.com) **TRAIN SERVICE** linking Chicago to Southern California stops in San Bernardino at 1170 West Third Street. Metrolink's (800/COMMUTE or www.mta.net) **MASS TRANSIT RAIL SERVICE** links the Inland Empire to surrounding metro regions. Riverside's **GREYHOUND BUS** station (800/231-2222) is at 3911 University Avenue. Redlands also has a depot (802 W Colton Ave).

From Los Angeles, motorists take Interstate 10 east to **SAN BERNARDINO COUNTY**. From San Diego, travelers enter **RIVERSIDE COUNTY** via Interstate 15 as it passes northward through Temecula's burgeoning wine region. Interstate 15 skirts

INLAND EMPIRE THREE-DAY TOUR

DAY 1. Drive to **RIVERSIDE** for a morning of antique shopping in the downtown mall area on Mission Inn Avenue, or a little poking around the old Craftsman-house-dominated neighborhoods at the base of Mount Rubidoux and Little Rubidoux. Check in to the **MISSION INN** and get an immediate feel for this architectural fantasyland by taking a guided tour. Spend the afternoon relaxing by the pool before dining that evening at the inn, either in the more casual courtyard bistros, **MISSION INN RESTAURANT** or the new **LAS CAMPAÑAS** Mexican restaurant, or inside in the swankier **DUANE'S PRIME STEAK & SEAFOOD.**

DAY 2. Rise with the sun for a brisk hike up **MOUNT RUBIDOUX.** Return to the inn for breakfast in the courtyard, then take Interstate 215 north to Interstate 10 and go east to the **SAN BERNARDINO COUNTY MUSEUM.** After a tour, drive farther east on Interstate 10 to Yucaipa Boulevard. Go east to the Oak Glen Road loop through **APPLE COUNTRY,** stopping for a piece of fresh apple pie at any of the apple stands and gift shops. Return to Riverside for dinner at **TABLE FOR TWO,** or **GAY AND LARRY'S** if you feel like Mexican food, before a nightcap back at the inn and a soak in the courtyard spa before bed.

DAY 3. A long day awaits. Start off with breakfast at the inn, then check out and drive southwest on Highway 91 to the **CALIFORNIA CITRUS STATE HISTORIC PARK** for a brief tour. Return to Highway 91, continue southwest to Interstate 15, and drive south to **TEMECULA.** Spend the day touring wineries, stopping for lunch at **CAFE CHAMPAGNE,** before checking into the **TEMECULA CREEK INN** for the night and dining at **TEMET GRILL.**

the western edge of San Bernardino County, bypassing the cities of Riverside and San Bernardino.

Motorists reach the **IDYLLWILD** resort area by going east from Interstate 15 on Highway 74 through Hemet to Highway 243 and the final tortuously curved climb into the pines (total distance about 40 miles). Idyllwild has no ski resorts, so you don't have to worry about ski traffic. You can also reach Idyllwild from Interstate 10: at Banning, take Highway 243 south about 25 miles into the heart of the mountains.

Highway 18 leads into the **BIG BEAR** and **LAKE ARROWHEAD** mountain resort region. To reach Big Bear Lake from Interstate 10, take Highway 30 and Highway 330 into the mountains, where it connects with Highway 18 in Running Springs. To reach Lake Arrowhead, bypass Highway 330; Highway 30 also connects with Highway 18 about 25 minutes south of Lake Arrowhead, providing a more direct route. If you're heading east on Interstate 10, Interstate 215 is a shortcut to Highway 30 (for either lake).

For information about Inland Empire tourist destinations, contact the **INLAND EMPIRE TOURISM COUNCIL** (909/890-1090; www.ieep.com/tourism/index.htm).

Idyllwild

Gateway to San Jacinto State Park, this small resort town fills up each weekend with flatlanders who want a breath of crisp alpine air, a whiff of pines, a stay in a homey bed-and-breakfast inn, and perhaps a challenging day hike or overnight backpacking trip into the wilderness. In town, you'll find numerous small curio and gift shops oriented to the tourist trade, as well as several fine galleries that have experienced a real resurgence in recent years. Call the **ART ALLIANCE** (909/659-1948) for a list of art exhibits and events such as Sunday Morning Art Cafe, when each gallery takes a turn at hosting a Sunday morning coffee open house. If you enjoy **PICNICKING,** head up to Humber Park at the northeastern end of Fern Valley Road. **HIKERS** use densely forested Humber Park as their jump-off point for either a day hike up Devil's Slide Trail (great views) or longer expeditions toward the summit of Mount San Jacinto (elevation 10,804 feet), Tahquitz Peak (Southern California's premier rock-climbing site for long-pitch climbs on vertical granite faces), and the beautiful backpacker campsites in Tahquitz Meadow. Don't miss the **IDYLLWILD PARK NATURE CENTER** (909/659-3850; www.idyllwildnaturecenter.org), located about a half mile north of town on Highway 243. The center is the place to learn about the history of the area, watch for birds and other wildlife, hike a trail, or obtain an Adventure Pass for use of some areas of the forest.

The **IDYLLWILD CHAMBER OF COMMERCE** (54295 Village Center Dr, downstairs from the *Idyllwild Town Crier*; 888/659-3259; www.idyllwild. org) can help with trip planning. For backcountry permits and information, stop in at the **IDYLLWILD RANGER STATION** (corner of Hwy 243 and Upper Pine Crest in the village; 909/659-2117). For **ROCK CLIMBING** gear rentals—or just referrals on climbing instruction and guide services—drop by Nomad Ventures (54415 N Circle Dr; 909/659-4853).

RESTAURANTS

Gastrognome / ★★

54381 RIDGEVIEW DR, IDYLLWILD; 909/659-5055 Locals and regulars call this place "the Gnome," and it's cozy enough for any forest creature. Gastrognome combines hearty fare and fine dining to suit mountain appetites quickened by a day on the trails high above town. Set in the pine forest that swathes most of Idyllwild, the restaurant has a rustic-chic vibe, from the floor-to-ceiling wine rack made of stacked clay pipe to the polished copper panels and brick and wood walls. Come in on a chilly night and you'll find a roaring blaze in the fireplace beneath a spectacular landscape painting. Dinner features tasty skewered shrimp brushed with mustard sauce and broiled to pink perfection. Other seafood choices include equally simple versions of broiled salmon, halibut, and lobster. Meat eaters choose rack of lamb or tournedos of beef capped with mushrooms and béarnaise. Lunch takes an informal tack (the Gnome offers one of the better hamburgers in town) and can be enjoyed on either of two decks outside. *$$; AE, DC, DIS, MC, V; no checks, lunch Mon–Sat, dinner every day, brunch Sun; full bar; reservations recommended; www.thegnome.com; turn off Hwy 243 at Texaco and go 1 block.* ♿

Mozart Haus / ★★

264345 HWY 243, IDYLLWILD; 909/659-5500 The interiors of this modest tree-framed cottage are bathed in warm, welcoming natural wood and an abundance of Bavarian knickknacks and decor, right down to the flower-painted toilet bowls and dirndl-clad staff (well, the women). Mozart Haus's cozy dining rooms are ideal for snowy winter dinners of hearty bratwurst, knackwurst, or bockwurst, all served up with ample portions of authentic German potato salad, spaetzle, sauerkraut, or traditional cucumber salad. On warmer days, lighter fare and vegetarian specialties taste especially fine in the enchanting beer garden, a prime spot for enjoying steins of traditional German, Austrian, and Czech beers, most notably Wetenburger Dark, a favorite from Germany's oldest brewery (since 1040). In true Bavarian fashion, the restaurant excels at diet-blasting desserts, including classic crepes Salzburg—wrapped around vanilla ice cream and surrounded by warm chocolate sauce—and a "Black Forest" strudel, filled with chocolate, cherries, and cream cheese. Mozart Haus recently began serving a light breakfast fare that segues from German (with a few strudels) to organic (Incan porridge and organic coffees). During the last week of September, they kick off the harvest season with Oktoberfest revelry. *$–$$; AE, DC, DIS, MC, V; checks OK; lunch, dinner Thurs–Mon; beer and wine; reservations recommended; turn off Hwy 243 at Texaco.*

LODGINGS

Atipahato Lodge / ★

25525 HWY 243, IDYLLWILD; 888/400-0071 Just past the village, perched on a hillside overlooking the San Jacinto State Forest, this lodge has been recently renovated by its current owner, a former hotel executive. Each guest room features a knotty pine interior with vaulted open-beamed ceilings and comes with a complete kitchenette and private balcony with forest views. All accommodations are equipped with coffeemakers and television. The lodge backs up to the 10,000-acre Nature Center, but a seasonal stream and waterfall flow through the lodge's own 5 acres of nature, making a stroll or hike an ideal way to begin or end the day. *$-$$; AE, DIS, MC, V; no checks; www.atipahato.com; from Hwy 243 travel ½ mile north of village.*

Idyllwild Inn / ★

54300 VILLAGE CENTER DR, IDYLLWILD; 909/659-2552 OR 888/659-2552 Idyllwild Inn, family owned since 1909, scatters its 15 cabins through an open pine forest like a gracious little Tyrolean village. Families love it here, and although the inn doesn't have a pool, the tots' playground is a good substitute. Cabins are neat, with a simple mountain decor; each has a wood-burning fireplace, kitchen, and deck. Some were built as early as 1910, others in the 1930s and 1950s, newer duplexes in the 1980s, and some funky theme rooms opened in Christmas 1990—although it's obvious all have been constantly maintained and upgraded. The bustle of Idyllwild is literally outside the front gate, but once you're inside this compound you really feel you're in a mountain town. At some point, asphalt paths were put in so you can drive right to your cabin, and unfortunately they tend to dominate the setting a bit; when you reserve, ask to be on the side farthest from the entrance. *$–$$; DIS, MC, V; checks OK; www.idyllwildinn.com; from Hwy 243, turn at Texaco station onto Ridgeview Rd and go 2 blocks to Village Center.* &

Strawberry Creek Inn / ★★

26370 HWY 243, IDYLLWILD; 909/659-3202 OR 800/262-8969 One of the first bed-and-breakfast inns in the region and long one of the best, Strawberry Creek has a location just far enough outside town (about a quarter mile) to grant it the peace and quiet mountain visitors seek. Yes, there is a Strawberry Creek, and a walking path leads along it all the way into town. The inn was fashioned by owners Diana Dugan and Jim Goff from a large, shingled cabin built in 1941. Five rooms in the main cabin put you closest to the large living room/recreation room/library downstairs—the true heart of the house and a great place to gather around a fire on chilly days. Four rooms out back on the "courtyard" are newer but feel a bit less cozy, and there's a small single cabin close to the creek. Decor elements include a range of window seats, antique bed frames, wood-burning fireplaces, and skylights; all rooms have private baths. A full breakfast is served out on a big glassed-in porch. Smoking is prohibited. *$–$$; DIS, MC, V; checks OK; www. strawberrycreekinn.com; ¼ mile south of the village.* &

Redlands

A treasure trove of Southern California's architectural heritage, this orange-growing town remains one of the best stops in California for anyone with an interest in **EARLY 20TH CENTURY BUILDINGS**, especially Mission Revival style. In fact, Redlands may be one of the few towns in California that can honestly boast more than 1,500 remaining period homes and structures. From the moment you enter town on Orange Street heading south from Interstate 10, you sense the city's grandeur. An open-loggia train station on Orange just south of Pearl is a pillared temple to rail travel. Downtown Redlands has been tastefully redone with brick-pattern streets and circular intersections, and has enjoyed a mild renaissance. To get the most out of your vintage viewing, pick up the *Historic Redlands Driving Tour* booklet from the **REDLANDS CHAMBER OF COMMERCE** (1 E Redlands Blvd; 909/793-2546; www.redlandschamber.org). Outstanding examples in the residential neighborhoods include **HOLT HOUSE** (405 W Olive Ave), **BURRAGE HOUSE** (1205 Crescent Ave), which has the area's only glassed-in swimming pool, and **MOREY HOUSE** (140 Terracina Blvd), perhaps the most photographed Victorian in Southern California. For a peek inside an outstanding local mansion, take a tour of the **KIMBERLY CREST HOUSE & GARDENS** (1325 Prospect Dr; 909/792-2111; www.kimberlycrest.org), an 1897 fairy-tale confection built to resemble a château in the Loire Valley of France. The **A. K. SMILEY PUBLIC LIBRARY** (125 W Vine St; 909/798-7565; www.akspl.org) is a stunning 1984 Moorish landmark with rich interiors, plus a terrific resource to learn more about historic Redlands. Across the interstate is the

SAN BERNARDINO COUNTY MUSEUM (2024 Orange Tree Lane; 909/307-2669 or 888/BIRDEGG; www.co.san-bernardino.ca.us/museum), which depicts the region's heritage and natural history with three floors of exhibits on anthropology, archaeology, history, birds, mammals, reptiles, fossils, and fine arts.

RESTAURANTS

Joe Greensleeves / ★★☆

220 N ORANGE ST, REDLANDS; 909/792-6969 Gourmets in any city would love to have Joe Greensleeves just around the corner, so finding it in out-of-the-way Redlands makes it all the more special. Chef Umberto Orlando fashions a changing menu that intrigues the culinary adventurer who wants to try ostrich, bison, elk, boar, venison, or any of several other farm-raised game dishes. At the same time, anyone who loves osso buco, or pasta, or simply a good steak will find plenty of options. Orlando grills meats over an orangewood fire, and portions are generously sized. Those interested in a vegetarian meal need only ask—the chef will concoct a meatless alternative on request. Few diners have room for dessert, but the cart creaks to your table with tortes, cheesecake, and other temptations. Decor in this narrow historic building includes a classic wooden sailboat hull; a ceiling composed of thousands of wine corks references the numerous *Wine Spectator* awards Joe Greensleeves has won. The crowd is spirited and obviously enjoying themselves, making this a "romantic" place in a celebratory rather than a muted, wine-and-candles way. You'll clink glasses and enjoy the show not only from watching the open kitchen but simply by being part of the happy buzz. *$$$; AE, MC, V; no checks; lunch Mon–Fri, dinner every day; full bar; reservations recommended; from I-10 E, exit Orange St and go right, or from I-10 W exit 6th St and go south to Redlands Blvd, then right on Orange St.* &

Big Bear

Benjamin D. Wilson, onetime mayor of Los Angeles and namesake of Mount Wilson, led a hunting party into the San Bernardino Mountains in 1845, reporting back the "place was alive with bear." These days, you'll stumble across more "bear" in the heart of Big Bear Village, which is blessed with a dizzyingly cute array of business names like Bear Paw Bar, Boo Bear's Den, Grizzly Manor, Teddy Bear's Pantry, and too many other "beary" clever ones to mention. Words like *chalet, alpine,* and *nordic* also turn up frequently; coupled with a preponderance of architectural tricks—pointy pitched roofs, gingerbread cutout trim, and ornate old-world lettering—they do a pretty good job of evoking villages in Bavaria, Austria, and Switzerland. Rough-hewn log cabins and rugged lodges are just as common, though, and hearken back to the real history of the area—one shaped by miners, loggers, and dam builders. When Bear Valley was dammed in 1884, the resulting lake was the largest man-made lake in the world, and tourism began almost immediately. But the majestic grizzly bear, which gave Big Bear Valley and Little Bear Valley (now Lake Arrowhead) their names, has disappeared from the area entirely: if you're lucky enough to spot a rare bear, you'll be seeing the California black bear.

The south shore of Big Bear Lake was the first to be developed and remains the most densely populated. **HIGHWAY 18** passes first through the city of Big Bear Lake and its downtown village; then, as Big Bear Boulevard, it continues east to Big Bear City, which is more residential and suburban. **HIGHWAY 38** traverses the north shore, home to pristine national forest and great hiking trails, plus a couple of small marinas and the cozy community of Fawnskin. In recent years, the Big Bear area has been given a much-needed face-lift: Big Bear Boulevard was substantially widened to handle high-season traffic, and downtown Big Bear Lake (the "Village") was spiffed up without losing its woodsy charm.

For a picture-postcard look at the pine-studded mountains, climb aboard the **BIG BEAR QUEEN** (909/866-3218; www.bigbearmarina.com), a midget Mississippi-style paddle wheeler that cruises the lake on 90-minute tours daily from late April through November. Landlubbers can check out **BIG BEAR JEEP TOURS** (909/878-JEEP; www.bigbearjeeptours.com), which offers thrill-a-minute journeys into Big Bear Lake's backcountry, including historic Holcomb Valley—relic of the Gold Rush—plus the panoramic viewpoint Butler Peak. The **BIG BEAR DISCOVERY CENTER** (a quarter mile west of Big Bear Ranger Station on Hwy 38; 909/866-3437; www.bigbeardiscoverycenter.org), on the lake's north shore, offers free **HIKING TRAIL MAPS**. It's also the western terminus of a bike trail along the lake edge back toward Big Bear City. This is also a good place to pick up an Adventure Pass, which must be displayed on any car parked at a national forest trailhead. For **WINTER ROAD CONDITIONS** in the mountains, call CalTrans (800/427-ROAD; www.dot.ca.gov).

For more information on Big Bear's seasonal activities, including the ski resorts, contact the **BIG BEAR LAKE RESORT ASSOCIATION** (630 Bartlett Rd; 909/866-7000 or 800/4-BIG-BEAR; www.bigbearinfo.com) for its nice, glossy *Visitor's Guide*.

RESTAURANTS

Fred and Mary's / ★★☆

607 PINE KNOT AVE, BIG BEAR LAKE; 909/866-2434 From the just-folks sound of its name, you might expect Fred and Mary's to be a homey little comfort food joint. You'd be wrong. Though the interior is unremarkable—a vaguely Tuscan motif of sponge-painted walls and majolica fruits, with curiously contrasting Western-style wood chairs—it's the impressive California cuisine emerging from talented chef Colin Colville's surprisingly small kitchen that you'll really remember. In typical Big Bear fashion, there's been a minor local backlash from old-time mountain residents who don't know quite what to make of the inventive Alice Waters–esque menu where current ingredient darlings like bluefin tuna, pork tenderloin, and duck confit meet the fresh accents of oven-roasted leeks, spicy fennel, and chipotle chiles. Detractors claim Fred and Mary's is overpriced, but experienced gourmets find the bill modest compared to similar meals in L.A.—and the portions are abundant. The service is unpredictable: attentive one minute, forgetful the next—quite the opposite of the delicate and practiced cuisine that's made Fred and Mary's a favorite of discerning visitors and residents. *$$; AE, DC, DIS, MC, V; no checks; dinner Thurs–Mon; beer and wine; reservations recommended; just below Village Dr.* ♿

Madlon's / ★★☆

829 W BIG BEAR BLVD, BIG BEAR CITY; 909/585-3762 This fairy-tale country cottage just across the Big Bear City line is the undisputed number-one recommendation from local innkeepers. Effusive matriarch Madlon and her friendly staff are as good at composing appealing menus as they are at charming all the locals and regulars who swear by the place. Madlon—who'll probably stop by your table to introduce herself—has been at it since 1987, showing a flair for creating dishes that are upscale enough to intrigue the visiting city folk, but continental enough to maintain a sense of familiarity. Just settle into a deep comfy booth in this whitewashed garden cottage fringed with lace curtains, and order one of Madlon's perennial favorites: chardonnay-poached salmon, ahi Florentine, braised lamb shanks in white bean stew, goat cheese–stuffed chicken, or a traditional filet mignon. The appetizer of choice is her unique jalapeño cream soup, a rich concoction featuring enough cream (read: a lot) to calm the peppers' trademark heat to a mere warmth. Madlon's isn't breaking any new ground here, but she's achieved just the right balance to keep 'em coming back. *$$; DC, DIS, MC, V; no checks; dinner Tues–Sun, brunch Sat–Sun; beer and wine; reservations recommended; at Holcomb View Dr.*

Sushi Ichiban / ★

42151 BIG BEAR BLVD, BIG BEAR LAKE; 909/866-6413 Sushi Ichiban is the best sushi bar on the mountain. Wait a minute, it might actually be the *only* sushi bar on the mountain! If rustic Big Bear seems an odd place to find decent—let alone recommendable—sushi, no one was more surprised than we were. But here it is, courtesy of L.A.-transplant and sushi master Abe-san, who set up shop in a highly visible corner in the midst of Big Bear's resident shopping corridor (it's across the street from K-Mart) and has been winning folks over ever since. Abe-san heads "down the mountain" three days a week to fetch the freshest fish, which he serves up at his tiny (half-dozen seat) sushi bar and the few simple dinette tables along the window. He's mainly a purist, though a few "designer" rolls, like California or spider, show up on the hand-lettered special board. The restaurant also offers cooked dishes, like teriyaki, sukiyaki, and katsu, in addition to some really nice udon noodle bowls (great for a nontraditional post-ski warm-up). *$; AE, MC, V; no checks; lunch, dinner Thurs–Tues; beer and wine; reservations not accepted; corner of Fox Farm Rd.*

LODGINGS

Alpenhorn Bed & Breakfast / ★★★

601 KNIGHT AVE, BIG BEAR LAKE; 909/866-5700 OR 888/829-6600 Owner/innkeepers Chuck and Robbie Slemaker saw a need in Big Bear for the kind of five-star comfort and service found in luxurious wine country B&Bs, and they set out to raise the bar for the rest of the pack. With the eight-room Alpenhorn, whose exterior screams "Adirondack cabin" while the interior whispers "country manor house," they have gloriously achieved their goal. An apron-clad staff sees to your every need—from gourmet evening hors d'oeuvres to an elegant hotel-style turndown—

but doesn't blink if you stumble in wearing snowy mukluks or sandy thongs. Surrounded by beautifully landscaped gardens with a stream rambling just beyond the back deck, these rooms are meticulously outfitted with a semiformal blend of antiques, rich fabrics, luxurious hypoallergenic feather beds, romantic fireplaces, sleek modern bathrooms, and plenty of thoughtful extras. Breakfast alone is worth a visit; it's a multicourse affair of miniportions, featuring sweet grapefruit "brûlée," the creamiest banana-laced oatmeal, custom-coddled eggs or savory cheese strata, and homemade granola with yogurt—all presented on fine Villeroy & Boch china with gleaming Oneida flatware. *$$$; AE, DC, DIS, MC, V; checks OK; www.alpen horn.com;* ½ block south of Big Bear Blvd. &

Gold Mountain Manor / ★★

1117 ANITA AVE, BIG BEAR CITY; 909/585-6997 To call it a log mansion might be an understatement, but this big 1928 log house has good bones and a strong architectural pedigree. Contractor Guy Maltby was known for his rustic structures throughout the famed Peter Pan neighborhood (streets are named for Peter, John, Wendy, Nana, etc.) a Roaring '20s development in north Big Bear City, beyond the lake. The expansive Adirondack-style porch is a shady retreat looking across a front lawn set with pines, providing a dramatic entry to the home owner/innkeepers Trish and Jim Gordon have lovingly restored to its historic grandeur—minus several generations of clutter, and plus some modern-style amenities. The living room with its hulking stone fireplace feels right on a snowy night. The rooms range from the very large Ted Ducey Suite, with a wood stove next to a private whirlpool tub, mission tile, glassed-in-porch-turned-bedroom, and pioneer/Indian motif, to the Lucky Baldwin, a red-and-black-flannel-themed retreat. All seven rooms have private baths. A gourmet full breakfast—reflecting Jim Gordon's professional culinary training—is presented downstairs each morning, and beverages and hors d'oeuvres appear in the afternoon. One drawback is Gold Mountain's location: although it's on the quieter north side of the lake in a pine forest, the historic lodge has been surrounded by neighboring cabins of far more pedestrian scale. Secluded it's not. Still, this is your chance to experience log house living at its grandest. *$$; AE, DC, MC, V; no checks; www.goldmountainmanor.com;* ½ block above N Shore Dr and 2 blocks west of Greenway St.

Windy Point Inn / ★★★½

39015 N SHORE DR, FAWNSKIN; 909/866-2746 No inn in the San Bernardino Mountains has a better view than Windy Point. This contemporary architectural showpiece B&B has such a spectacular setting you'll be tempted to stay in your room all day—luxuriating in front of a fire, soaking in the two-person tub (most guest bathrooms have them), or sliding open a door to the breezes and just gazing over the sparkling 300-degree view of open water and distant peaks. Decor is modern but not stark, thanks to the owners' varied collection of art and sculpture. Furnishings are equally eclectic, but without any sense of hodgepodge: this is an inn with a bit of Zen to it. The welcoming "great room" features a casual sunken fireplace nook with floor-to-ceiling windows overlooking the lake, a telescope for stargazing, a baby grand piano, and menus for every local eatery. Decks off many of the rooms almost hang over the water, and stairs lead directly from the inn to their private dock and beach. Friendly innkeepers Val and Kent Kessler know how to please guests, especially when it comes to breakfast, a custom gourmet treat served in your room or on the tree-fringed lakefront deck. *$$$; AE, DIS, MC, V; checks OK with credit-card guarantee; www.windypointinn.com; off Hwy 330.*

Lake Arrowhead

It seems only natural that early movie stars and filmmakers, in their zeal for both leisure time and cinematic settings, would make the mountains only 90 minutes from Hollywood their favorite year-round weekend playground. Dam construction in Little Bear Valley—as this area was originally known—began in 1893, privately financed by businessmen who intended the reservoir to generate power and divert mountain water to southern ranchlands. But by 1912, when the dam was nearing completion and the lake almost filled, the state of California ruled in favor of irate northern farmers, who protested the diversion of their natural source of irrigation. Presto! Little Bear Lake became a giant money pit. A Los Angeles syndicate stepped in and purchased the lake and surrounding land, renaming it for a nearby arrowhead-shaped rock rooted in Native American legend. Between 1921 and 1923, Arrowhead's Norman-style village—complete with hotels, theater, beach and bath houses, dance pavilion, and golf course—sprouted up, and subdivisions for lakefront estates were sold off. Hollywood flocked to the new recreational lake, lending a celebrity cachet to the area that continues today. Sometimes current star residents—including Eriq LaSalle, Pam Dawber, Arnold Schwarzenegger, Dick Clark, Frankie Avalon, and longtime Arrowhead grande dame Gloria Loring—can be spotted shopping at Jensen's market, or sipping a milk shake at the Cedar Glen Malt Shop.

Arrowhead has always been perceived as an exclusive retreat—especially compared to neighboring Big Bear's down-to-earth, family-friendly ambience—and is characterized by the affluence of its surrounding homes, many of which are gated estates rather than rustic mountain cabins. The center of the Lake Arrowhead community is **LAKE ARROWHEAD VILLAGE,** located on the south shore at the end of Highway 173. The 1920s cluster of faux-Swiss structures, which stood in for European villages in many old Hollywood films, has sadly been lost (the decaying buildings were burned in a 1979 fire department learning exercise). Although the new village was built in the same architectural style, it just feels like another themed shopping mall. The old spire-topped dance pavilion still stands, though; beneath eaves where Glenn Miller and Tommy Dorsey once played, shoppers can now peruse a variety of boutiques. Attached to the village is the sprawling **LAKE ARROWHEAD RESORT** (27984 Hwy 189; 909/336-1511 or 800/800-6792; www.lakearrowhead resort.com), a former Hilton property whose most outstanding feature is a prime lakefront perch.

Since the picturesque lake itself is restricted to use by residents, the only way for visitors to experience this alpine jewel is by embarking on a **LAKE CRUISE** with the

Arrowhead Queen, sister ship to Big Bear's paddle wheeler; 50-minute tours depart hourly from Lake Arrowhead Village. You can also choose the zippier tour aboard the smaller *Lake Arrowhead Princess,* an aerodynamic Hackercraft wood runabout. Purchase tickets for the "Queens" at **LEROY'S SPORTS** (dockside at Lake Arrowhead Village; 909/336-6992). During the summer, water-ski lessons are offered on the lake by **MACKENZIE WATER SKI SCHOOL** (dockside in Lake Arrowhead Village; 909/337-3814), famous for teaching the sport to Kirk Douglas, George Hamilton, and other Hollywood stars.

Most visitors stay in one of Arrowhead's dozens of bed-and-breakfast lodgings tucked away in the woodsy hillsides surrounding the lake. A street map is essential if you venture off the lakefront by car into these neighborhood streets that are as "tangled as angleworms in a bait can," as mystery writer Raymond Chandler might have put it (he featured Lake Arrowhead in his novel *Lady of the Lake*). You can pick up a free detailed map at the **LAKE ARROWHEAD COMMUNITIES CHAMBER OF COMMERCE** (in Lake Arrowhead Village, lower level; 909/337-3715 or 800/337-3716; www.lakearrowhead.net), which also has information on area activities and events, plus real estate listings for those who covet the privileged mountain resort lifestyle.

RESTAURANTS

Avanti's Cucina Italiana / ★★

28575 HWY 18, SKY FOREST; 909/336-7790 Ask any local where to find the best Italian food in these parts, and some will direct you to this relaxing cabin on the aptly named Rim of the World Drive (Hwy 18). As for the others, they'd probably agree, but stay mum just to keep the crowding down at this über-popular newcomer where reservations are a must during the prime dinner hour. With a pleasant mix of robust red-checked-tablecloth standards (rich lasagne, chicken cacciatore, and a killer meatball sandwich) and nouvelle touches (the balsamic salad is adorned with pesto and gorgonzola, the veal delicate as a pillow), Avanti's flourishes in all seasons with two cozy dining rooms and a wraparound porch framed by tall pines. A sound track of vintage classic crooners wafts softly throughout. The restaurant offers a moderately priced selection of wine equally divided between California and Italian varietals, including its very reasonable "house pours" by the glass. *$$; AE, MC, V; local checks only; lunch, dinner every day; beer and wine; reservations recommended; 1 mile east of Hwy 173.*

Belgian Waffle Works / ★☆

DOCKSIDE AT LAKE ARROWHEAD VILLAGE; 909/337-5222 Even the wait here is pleasant. Crowds of hungry diners line the benches overlooking Lake Arrowhead, watching the classic motor launches come and go from neighboring docks. Once inside, you can dig in to one of 15 different styles of waffles, from the classic thick Belgian sugar-dusted favorite to exotica such as a Brussels Belgian stuffed with ham, Swiss cheese, and turkey and fried Monte Cristo style. Many of these variations are a complete sugar rush: piles of strawberries, bananas, spiced apples, peach melba, and whipped cream conspire to turn the most innocent breakfast into dessert. Owners Bob and Mary Baker pride themselves on the crispiness of

347

their waffles, and for a long time, they've been tinkering with the batter recipe in search of ever-lighter confections. Your only disappointment might be the thin and rather tasteless maple syrup. Eggs, bacon, and omelets are also available. Lunch fare includes a wide variety of sandwiches, fish-and-chips (called a "Belgian Basket" here), and a strong selection of heart-healthy salads (to prepare you for a waffle dessert, no doubt). Waffles are served all day, so feel free to segue from breakfast to lunch without missing a caloric beat. A seat on the large outdoor patio is worth the extra wait on a sunny day, unless the wind's kicked up across the lake. *$; MC, V; checks OK; breakfast, lunch every day; beer and wine; reservations accepted for 6 or more; thebww@aol.com; on the waterfront promenade opposite the tour boat docks.* &

Casual Elegance / ★★☆

26848 STATE HWY 189, AGUA FRIA; 909/337-8932 Challengers may come and go, but for years there's been no serious threat to self-taught chef and all-around-great-gal Jan Morrison's unofficial title of Arrowhead's favorite restaurant. She started Casual Elegance in 1991, expanding on a successful catering business by importing her already-signature dishes to this dinner-only haven a five-minute drive from the Arrowhead village. Diners flock to the barely-altered 1939 cottage whose eclectic mountain-rustic rooms feature just a few tables each; in the kitchen, Morrison is hard at work each night, cooking with gusto—but always taking time to work the room, greeting regulars and introducing herself to new friends. Service is warmly personal, but can also be quite relaxed, though no one ever seems to mind the leisurely pace. And as uninspired as the restaurant's name is (sorry, Jan!), that's how creative the menu can be, with specialties that include Maryland-style crab cakes atop papaya-ginger-cream sauce; New Zealand rack of lamb crusted with either honey-hazelnut or roasted garlic; pork medallions with tart Montmorency cherries; perfectly flame-broiled rib-eye and New York steaks; and a duo of luscious ice cream pies (one fudgy, one butterscotchy) for dessert. Jan's daughter Jackie takes pride in assembling a connoisseur's wine list of lesser-known and boutique California labels, each enhanced by crème de la crème Riedel crystal stemware. *$$$; AE, DC, DIS, MC, V; no checks; dinner Wed–Sun; beer and wine; reservations required; ¹/₂ mile south of North Bay Rd.*

LODGINGS

Chateau Du Lac Bed and Breakfast / ★

911 HOSPITAL RD, LAKE ARROWHEAD; 909/337-6488 OR 800/601-8722 You won't find a more spectacular overlook of Lake Arrowhead than the one from this inn's huge downstairs common rooms—or from the ultimate fireplace/whirlpool suite, the Lakeview, at the very top of the house. Almost the equal of the Lakeview Suite, the Loft Suite lets you sleep under a steeply peaked and dormer-windowed ceiling; its bathroom with whirlpool tub is particularly spacious. The house's modern architectural style frames views with tall expanses of glass, but wood-paneled interiors help it feel warm (exterior upkeep is not immaculate here, but the interiors are neat and beautifully furnished). Like many inns, Du Lac has been invaded by teddy bears and dolls, but the house is big enough to keep the cuteness in check (translation: husbands won't be put off). Innkeepers Jody and Oscar Wilson serve not only a good breakfast (eggs or quiche, muffins, croissants, fruit, and so on) but an afternoon tea as well. When the sun cooperates, they serve breakfast on a deck just off the kitchen, part of which extends into a hillside gazebo. *$$–$$$$; AE, DC, DIS, MC, V; checks OK; www.chateau-du-lac.com; from Lake Arrowhead Village, go 3 miles on Hwy 173 to Hospital Rd and turn right.*

Rose Gables Victorian Bed & Breakfast / ★★

29024 MAMMOTH DR, LAKE ARROWHEAD; 909/336-9892 Leave it to the English to give us the most pristine Victorian-themed inn in Lake Arrowhead. In their "retirement," owners Meryl and Don Jacks have fashioned a three-room inn from a former single-family house high on a hilltop with catch-your-breath views over the mountains and the desert beyond. Only half of this duo—Meryl—is truly English, and Don is quick to give her all the credit for Rose Gables's extraordinary decor of English antiques, wallpaper, and plenty of creative touches that have guests asking, "How'd you do that?" Don is an expert craftsman, responsible for all the wood floors, stone fireplaces, and perfectly laid tile throughout the house. Outside, a fairy-tale front garden flowers virtually all year round; downstairs, a cozy den features a fireplace, dartboard, and even a private sauna/steam chamber. The top room here is Pearls and Lace, with a step-up king bed, fireplace in both bedroom and bathroom, big tub, and forest view. All rooms come with his-and-hers cotton robes. Meryl's cooking is first-rate, and her hors d'oeuvres are generous enough to make some guests decide to skip dinner in town. Breakfast centers around her delicious waffles with fresh fruit, or omelets, or fresh-baked quiche. Menu requests are welcome. *$$; MC, V; checks OK; www.rosegables.com; from Hwy 173 on northeast edge of the lake, turn right on Yosemite Dr, right on Yellowstone Dr, right on Banff Dr, and right on Mammoth Dr.*

Willow Creek Inn / ★★

1176 N STATE HWY 173, LAKE ARROWHEAD; 909/336-4582 OR 877/MNTN-AIR Unlike the rustic historic cabins you might associate with a casual mountain resort, the trend around Lake Arrowhead is to build supersize (5,000-plus-square-foot) contemporary homes, usually on generous acreage that makes the most of the surrounding forest terrain. A surprising number of bed-and-breakfasts operate out of these developer showcase homes, and one of the most stunning and meticulous is this gray-and-white Cape Cod–style estate on the northern side of the lake (about a 15-minute drive from the village). Willow Creek Inn is a class act all the way, from the manicured front lawn that slowly climbs toward the entry porch to the river-rock fireplace in the sunken living room, flanked by extra-large windows framing the wooded rear of the house (especially breathtaking after a snowfall). Innkeeper Letty Cummings balances her gracious nature with her inner perfectionist, keeping a watchful eye on every detail and always making each guest feel like an honored family friend. The four guest rooms are upstairs, each carefully decorated with designer florals that never cross the line to frilly; classic crown moldings and chair rails add character to this almost-new house. Each room has a thoughtfully outfitted private bath, the most spectacular of which is in the enormous Celebration Suite and boasts a bay-window spa-tub-for-two. Clean, crisp, and professional, Willow Creek Inn is in a class by itself—and did we mention the scent of Letty's legendary cinnamon rolls at breakfast time? *$$–$$$; AE, DIS, MC, V; checks OK; www.arrow headBandB.com; 3 houses west of Golden Rule Ln.*

Riverside

Entrepreneurs planted the first Washington navel orange trees here in 1875, and Riverside basked in agricultural prosperity for the next 80 years. But smog, sprawling housing, and commercial land development after World War II whittled Riverside's appeal to a nubbin of its former grandeur, and by the '60s and '70s even its crowning glory, the Mission Inn, had fallen into disrepair. Today both the town and the inn are showing signs of a full recovery.

A guided tour of the **MISSION INN** (3696 Main St; 909/781-8241 or 909/784-0300, ext. 5035; www.missioninn.com) is essential to the Riverside experience. Tours last about 1¼ hours and ramble through most of the public areas and up to the topmost parapets. Before you sign up, be sure to task whether you'll be able to see the inside of the chapel. It's often closed on weekends for private weddings, and you'll be disappointed at missing the gilded Mexican altar, Tiffany stained-glass windows, and intricate mosaic work—high points of the tour.

To get the best feel for what life was like here during the glory days, walk to the top of boulder-studded **MOUNT RUBIDOUX** (1,339 feet) via a pedestrians-only road-and-trails system that begins at Ninth Street and Mount Rubidoux Drive. On the way up you'll pass a romantic stone watchtower financed by Mission Inn developer Frank Miller. Standing beneath the Father Serra Cross at the summit, you look almost straight down at the Santa Ana River to the west side, and downtown to the east. **LITTLE RUBIDOUX,** the hill opposite Mount Rubidoux just to the north side of Buena Vista Drive, is a fascinating neighborhood of Craftsman houses; follow the stone wall around it via Indian Hill Road to view several classic mansions.

Downtown Riverside surrounding the Mission Inn has been revamped with a pedestrian-only mall along Main Street. One of the best photography museums in the country, **UCR/CALIFORNIA MUSEUM OF PHOTOGRAPHY** (3824 Main St; 909/784-FOTO; www.cmp.ucr.edu) houses contemporary photography exhibits as well as a permanent collection of equipment and prints that will delight any photo buff. Farther down Main St, don't miss the **RIVERSIDE COUNTY COURT HOUSE** (4050 Main St; 909/955-5536), a beautifully restored temple of justice with a vaulted main hall that copied the Petit Palais of the 1900 Paris Exposition; this is one of the finest beaux-arts buildings in America. For more information, visit the **RIVERSIDE VISITORS CENTER** (3660 Mission Inn Ave; 909/684-4636). Not far from downtown, **CALIFORNIA CITRUS STATE HISTORIC PARK** (Van Buren Blvd at Dufferin Ave; 909/780-6222) preserves some old navel orange groves and a historic irrigation canal, recalling Riverside's early days, when even Queen Victoria was known to have peeled its famous fruit.

RESTAURANTS

Duane's Prime Steak & Seafood / ★★

3649 MISSION INN AVE, RIVERSIDE; 909/341-6767 Steps from the Mission Inn's courtyard restaurant (see review), its other restaurant, Duane's, is a completely indoor experience. Big chairs, big tables, big paintings, and big portions are the theme here. Arched windows and Rapunzel balconies flank the room, and a wonderful Old West painting of a cavalry skirmish dominates the end wall (look closely, and read the plaque, for the artwork tells a fascinating tale). A classic steak-and-prime-rib eatery, Duane's has become the best place in town to come for a no-holds-barred, let's-start-with-a-Scotch-on-the-rocks kind of meal. Duane's lives on the excellent reputation of its beef, and it doesn't disappoint. Steaks are flash-cooked, leaving the insides tender, rare, and juicy. The wine list is extensive, and the inn's swankiest eating establishment succeeds in its harmonious marriage of historic decor and attentive cooking. *$$$; AE, DC, DIS, MC, V; no checks; lunch Mon–Fri, dinner every day; full bar; reservations recommended; www.missioninn.com; exit Mission Inn Ave off Hwy 91 and go west.* &

Gay and Larry's / ★★☆

5556 MISSION BLVD, RIVERSIDE; 909/684-0645 Angelenos escaping to Palm Springs via Highway 60 first fell in love with the Mexican food at Gay and Larry's nearly 60 years ago. The place has a classic roadhouse feel, complete with surrounding tire repair shops and run-down squalid houses. Here the "combination plate" is a steaming, heart-stopping heap of enchiladas, chiles rellenos, tacos, or burritos, with refried beans and rice, all swimming in a pond of brick-red sauce on an oven-heated pewter canoe. Oddly, Gay and Larry's charges for chips—but they're brought with ceremony on a thick crockery plate in your waitress's oven-mitted paw. A chilly pitcher of draft beer costs $6.50. *$; No credit cards; local checks only; lunch, dinner every day; beer only; reservations not accepted; from Hwy 60, exit Rubidoux Blvd and go south to Mission Blvd, then left;* &

Las Campañas / ★★

3649 MISSION INN AVE, RIVERSIDE; 909/341-6767 Las Campañas (the bells), the Mission Inn's newest dining offering, is a perfect alternative for those seeking more casual dining with the same great early mission-style ambience. Lush, colorful foliage makes the terra-cotta tiled patio a true garden setting, and a central fountain adds to the serenity, giving the impression that Las Campañas has been a part of the Mission Inn from the beginning. The totally alfresco restaurant offers authentic Mexican fare made with the freshest of ingredients—house-made salsa and guacamole are prepared daily—and some seasonal offerings; try the Veracruz snapper, chicken Vallarta in a smoky-sweet apricot chipotle sauce, or the popular mahimahi tacos. Most selections are accompanied by black beans and rice, and signature margaritas in refreshing flavors like papaya and kiwi help complete the meal. On chilly days or brisk evenings, effective outdoor heaters keep you as cozy as the melon liqueur in your Midori margarita. *$–$$; AE, DC, DIS, MC, V; no checks; lunch, dinner Mon–Sat; full bar; reservations recommended; www.missioninn.com; exit Mission Inn Ave off Hwy 91 and go west.* &

Mission Inn Restaurant / ★★★☆

3649 MISSION INN AVE, RIVERSIDE; 909/341-6767 Old-timers in Riverside still call this "the Spanish Dining Room," and they're a little ticked off at the Mission Inn's latest owner for changing the name to something as generic as "Restaurant." But, blessedly, everything else remains the same. Step into the courtyard and you enter a Moroccan desert keep. Giant lanterns of cast concrete top—believe it or not—flying buttresses above you. Tier upon tier of windows rise on every side, most arched, many with the inn's famed "rain cross" bell-symbol motif in leaded glass. In the center, a massive tile fountain guarded by three Mayan-motif mutant-frog sculptures splashes happily, while the lighted dome of a miniature Vatican seems to float in the gathering darkness at dinnertime. Caesar salad is a perfectly tart and salty start to a hearty meal of lamb shank, osso buco style (it arrives steaming in the night air, with spears of asparagus propped about like green soldiers). A double pork chop with excellent garlic mashed potatoes is almost too much to eat. Prime rib or fillet of beef are delicious and tender, while lighter choices such as spinach fettuccine with grilled shrimp, Maui onions, and thyme, or seared salmon with red-wine pasta or opal-basil (purple-basil) pasta are equally satisfying. Service is attentive, and the birds flying overhead and bursting blooms all around add extra ambience. *$$; AE, DC, DIS, MC, V; no checks; breakfast, lunch, dinner every day; full bar; reservations recommended; www.missioninn.com; exit Mission Inn Ave off Hwy 91 and go west.* &

Table for Two / ★★

3600 CENTRAL AVE, STE 1, RIVERSIDE; 909/683-3648 This small, sophisticated, and quite immaculate restaurant is located in the kind of building you'd expect to find occupied by an insurance office. Once inside, though, you're surprised by modern, arty decor and the wonderful spicy smells of a Thai kitchen at its best. Dishes are presented with an artful eye for color here, with sprays of thinly sliced vegetables piled high like pick-up sticks. Big white bistro-style plates turn the food into art, and bookshelves filled with wine bottles line the walls. This brilliant feast for the eye is matched by equally vibrant flavors. An unusual ground chicken and shrimp salad with grilled Japanese eggplant, onion, and green onion is bathed in a light vinegar dressing. Salads are reminiscent of flower arrangements. Entrees include stir-fry standards like cashew chicken, but this version is made with a roasted curry paste. Coconut shows up frequently, particularly in the soups and curries that dominate the menu. The neighborhood crowd here includes families, young couples, and retired professors from the nearby university—all loyal devotees of Table for Two's artful creativity. *$; MC, V; no checks; lunch, dinner every day; beer and wine; reservations not necessary; exit Central Ave off Hwy 91 and go west.* &

LODGINGS

The Mission Inn / ★★★

3649 MISSION INN AVE, RIVERSIDE; 909/784-0300 OR 800/843-7755 A National Historic Landmark built in stages between 1902 and 1931 by hotelier Frank Miller, the Mission Inn began life as a two-story adobe home and gradually evolved into one of the West's grandest resort hotels. Architect Arthur B. Benton played off Miller's love of the dramatic, and the Mission Inn developed into a fantastical conglomeration of architectural themes—all handcrafted by an army of artisans who made the Inn part church, part castle, part mission-style. The finest of the 238 guest rooms are located high up along "Spanish Row" or flanking an upper patio (numbers 420 through 431). If cost is no object, this "suites" region of the huge structure is the place to stay. Each room is different, and some have extraordinary architectural elements such as 13-foot-tall arched leaded windows, coffered ceilings, and window seats, plus balconies, patios, views, and fine furnishings and fabrics. Even the more modest rooms have a sense of drama, beginning with the hallways themselves—which were built wide enough to handle the enormous steamer trunks of guests arriving to spend much of the winter. Bonuses include a good-size pool as well as a hydro-spa, set in a spectacular courtyard beside the front entry walk and gardens. The Mission Inn Restaurant, Las Campañas, and Duane's Prime Steak & Seafood (see reviews) are located within the hotel. In all, this is the kind of classic monument hotel that should be experienced at least once in one's traveling life. $$–$$$$; AE, DC, DIS, MC, V; checks OK; www.missioninn.com; exit Mission Inn Ave off Hwy 91 and go west. &

Temecula

Located where Riverside and San Diego Counties meet, the fertile Temecula Valley has attracted settlers for at least a thousand years, from the native Luiseño tribe to today's winemakers and suburbanites. Rainbow Gap, a pass in the coastal mountains to the west, lets a cooling breeze from the Pacific Ocean sneak in each afternoon, blowing away smog and helping offset hot temperatures. These maritime breezes often bring coastal fog to the edge of the valley—hence its name, a Luiseño word meaning "sun shining through fine mist." The climate is ideal for growing grapes, and commercial growers began planting grapes in earnest here in the 1960s. Unfortunately, the fine weather has also attracted developers who seem determined to crust the land with housing subdivisions and chain stores. Today you drive east on Rancho California Road for about 4 miles through new communities before you reach the pleasant, open wine-growing countryside.

A brief drive west from the freeway on the same road brings you to the rapidly growing town's Front Street. Here Old West–style false storefronts and a few historic buildings provide a notion of the good old days. **OLD TOWN TEMECULA** was originally a stop along the Butterfield Overland Stage route in the 1850s. Shop here for **ANTIQUES,** indulge in a burger or some Mexican specialties; if you are in Old Town on a Saturday morning, be sure to wander the Farmers Market—a great place to harvest fragrant bouquets of flowers, fresh-from-the-farm produce and some homemade crafts. Old Town features many well-preserved **ORIGINAL BUILDINGS,** like the Temecula Mercantile, built from local bricks in 1891, or the 1882 Welty Hotel on Main Street. A major multimillion-dollar streetscape improvement project recently added more charm to the six-block area with new boardwalks, lantern-style streetlights, landscaping, a sound system, and ornate metal arches with Old West images. Copies of Bob and Bea Taylor's *Old Town Walking Tour Map* can be found at most local businesses. For more in-depth exploration of the area's history, visit the compact **TEMECULA VALLEY MUSEUM** at Sam Hicks Memorial Park (28214 Mercedes St; 909/676-0021).

If you prefer to leave the planning to someone else, jump aboard one of Destination Temecula's (909/695-1232 or 800/584-8162; www.destem.com) daily tours of Old Town and the wine country. For an airborne adventure, take in the Temecula sunrise from a **HOT-AIR BALLOON** flown by Sunrise Balloons (800/548-9912; www.sunriseballoons.com) or A Grape Escape Balloon Adventure (800/965-2122; www.agrapeescape.com). Nothing beats a sunrise champagne balloon excursion over the Temecula vine country. For visitors' guides and maps, stop by **TEMECULA VALLEY CHAMBER OF COMMERCE** (27450 Ynez Rd, Ste 104, in Town Center Plaza; 909/676-5090; www.temecula.org).

RESTAURANTS

Allie's at Callaway / ★★

32720 RANCHO CALIFORNIA RD, TEMECULA; 909/694-0560 Nestled within and overlooking the vineyards of Callaway Vineyard & Winery, this outdoor bistro's otherwise humble terraced patio features sweeping views of grapevines set against a mountain backdrop—perfect for alfresco sunset dining after a day of wine tasting. Owner Steve Hamlin, formerly executive chef at the nearby Pala Mesa Resort, offers a tasty and creative Cal-Med menu; samples include pan-seared and roasted rosemary rack of lamb with citrus polenta, or spicy serrano chile wraps accompanied by crispy fried leeks. Pair any of the dishes with a fine Callaway vintage or wines from other regions of California, and save room for excellent desserts like a cream puff stuffed with oozing hot chocolate. The popular Sunday champagne brunch is a gourmand's extravaganza; eggs Benedict choices range from the classic to a tenderloin Benedict with seared shaved filet or a create-your-own invention from a list of options. Brunch also features freshly baked pastries, seasonal fruit, and escalloped Yukon gold potatoes. Desserts at Allie's are a must. *$$; MC, V; no checks; lunch Mon–Sat, dinner Thurs–Sat, brunch Sun; beer and wine; reservations recommended; www.alliesatcallaway.com; behind winery about 5 miles east of I-15.*

Baily's / ★★★☆

27644 YNEZ RD, TEMECULA; 909/676-9567 Even though it's in a mall next to a supermarket, not out among vineyards with its namesake winery (see Temecula Wineries sidebar), Baily's fine local vintages, tasteful lighting, gracious service, and excellent California wine-country cuisine make it easy to forget you've left the wineries behind. Phil and Carol Baily (who also own Carol's at Baily Vineyard & Winery) created this upscale but casual restaurant with the intention of providing visitors with an affordable fine dining experience to complement their vintages. Oenophiles will appreciate the cafe's wine list, which features the largest selection of Temecula wines in the world (100). Chef David Wells's fare is excellent, whether you choose the freshly made crab cakes, the chicken schnitzel in lemon-caper wine sauce, the grilled filet mignon topped with sauce bordelaise, or the blackened scallop and shrimp pasta. If you're on your way to the wineries around midday, make a luncheon reservation at Carol's at Baily Winery for the same wonderful cuisine (see review).

$$; AE, DC, DIS, MC, V; no checks; lunch Fri, dinner every day; beer and wine; reservations recommended; www.baily.com; Exit I-15 at Rancho California Rd and go east to Ynez Rd. &

Cafe Champagne / ★★★

32575 RANCHO CALIFORNIA RD, TEMECULA; 909/699-0088 You can't miss the herb garden as you walk into Thornton Winery's Cafe Champagne perched on a north-facing terrace. It's located within steps of the open-plan kitchen so that snips of rosemary, thyme, oregano, and other herbs can immediately make their way into the chef's Mediterranean-inspired infusions, rubs, and marinades. Diners seated in the courtyard watch line cooks chopping vigorously, preparing executive chef Steve Pickell's wine-complementary menu. Calamari sautéed in garlic, lemon, shallots, dill, and Thornton brut arrives for a simple, fragrant beginning to the meal. It's followed, perhaps, by a Cafe Champagne Salad composed of fresh greens, spiced pecans, golden raisins, Gorgonzola, and champagne vinaigrette. Entrees such as pistachio-crusted Colorado rack of lamb, Pacific prawns or sea scallops in black fettuccine, and grilled pheasant breast roll out of ovens, off rotisseries, or off the wood-fired grill. Service by a young collegiate waitstaff is friendly, and the setting, especially on a warm afternoon or summer evening, is conducive to hours of relaxed dining. In summer, jazz concerts further enhance the experience. *$$$; AE, DC, DIS, MC, V; no checks; lunch every day, dinner Tues–Sun, brunch Sun; wine only; reservations recommended; 4 miles east of I-15 from Rancho California Rd exit.* &

Carol's Restaurant at Baily Winery / ★★½

33340 LA SERENA WY, TEMECULA; 909/676-9243 This lunch-only bistro, located right at the winery overlooking the vines, beats its sister cafe (see Baily's above) in ambience while offering the same great cuisine. The restaurant—attached to the tasting room—sports a medieval castle flair. Seating inside the palatial Bacchus Hall is impressive; gargoyles, flags, chandeliers, Oriental carpets and even a great room fireplace bespeak of nobles feasting on pheasant and king-size turkey legs. However, Carol's menu is anything but old world. The very civilized and imaginative offerings are paired beautifully with local wines and often incorporate produce direct from the bistro's gardens. Carol's specialties include a grilled chicken salad with Mediterranean herbs served on baby greens and farfalle pasta. Notable entrees range from a duet of raviolis to a charbroiled salmon filet. Indoor seating may be regal, but on a balmy Temecula day, it's difficult to pass up the alfresco dining offered on the terrace, with idyllic views overlooking the cabernet sauvignon vines. Carol's is just perfect for lunch on a lazy wine-tasting afternoon. *$$; AE, DC, DIS, MC, V; no checks; lunch Tues–Sun; wine and beer; reservations recommended; www.baily.com; corner of La Serena and Rancho California Rd.* &

Temet Grill / ★★

44501 RAINBOW CANYON RD, TEMECULA; 909/587-1465 Set just a short walk from its companion hotel, the Temecula Creek Inn (see Lodgings, below), the Temet Grill glows at night like a small lantern in the woods. Inside, a snapping oak fire often blazes in the stone fireplace in the bar/lounge just

TEMECULA WINERIES

Temecula boasts 15 wineries, some of them competitive with the best in California. Most grow their own grapes; all have tasting rooms open to the public. Take Rancho California Road east from Interstate 15 for only 4 miles to where the strip malls and housing sprawl abruptly give way to rolling hills dressed in mustard flowers, vineyards, and citrus orchards; most of the wineries are clustered along the next few miles. For more information, call the Temecula Valley Vintners Association (909/699-2353 or 800/801-WINE; www.temeculawines.org).

BAILY VINEYARD & WINERY: Phil and Carol Baily opened their winery in 1986. They are best known for their white wines, especially the gold-medal rieslings. The Bailys have two popular bistros, Carol's at the winery and Baily's in town. Tastings daily 10am to 5pm. Located at 33440 La Serena (corner of Rancho California Rd); 909/676-9463; www.baily.com.

CALLAWAY VINEYARD & WINERY: Temecula's largest, oldest, and best-known winery produces a very good chardonnay. Public tours daily. Allie's at Callaway, the separately run restaurant on the grounds, affords sweeping views from its outdoor patio, serving lunch Monday through Saturday, Sunday brunch, and dinner Thursday through Saturday. Tastings daily 10:30am to 5pm. Located at 32720 Rancho California Road; 909/676-4001 or 800/472-2377; www.callawaywine.com.

CILURZO VINYARD & WINERY: Vincenzo Cilurzo planted Temecula's first commercial vineyard in 1968 when he moved to the valley with his wife, Audrey. Their estate-grown petite syrah has been a consistent award winner, and their merlots are also excellent. Don't miss this friendly, family-run winery with its tame peacocks and hand-painted signs. Tastings daily 10am to 5pm. Located at 41220 Calle Contento; 909/676-5250; www.cilurzowine.com.

FALKNER WINERY: Picnics and special events are popular in this winery setting with stately trees and lawn. Stop by to sample some of the award-winning wines daily from

off the main dining room. Decor in the cathedral-ceilinged dining room follows a Native American motif: framed arrows, baskets, and other traditional craft objects hang on the walls, while huge iron chandeliers float like blazing campfires overhead. An entire wall of windows overlooks the golf course and valley—there isn't a bad seat in the house. The menu is equally inspired, featuring chef Tim Stewart's herb-crusted Norwegian salmon with saffron risotto and tomato-basil beurre blanc; excellent beef, such as a New York cut in green peppercorn sauce; and a rich veal scaloppine with marsala and porcini risotto. Vegetarians will love the delicate, smoky flavor of roasted-vegetable ravioli served in a basil pesto cream sauce along with sautéed spinach. For breakfast, try the burrito of avocado, green chile, scram-

10am to 5pm. The winery is located at 40620 Calle Contento; 909/676-8231; www.falknerwinery.com.

HART WINERY: Truly a collector's find is tiny Hart Winery, which frequently out-classes many of California's biggest players at major wine competitions. Former school-teacher Joe Hart specializes in dry, full-bodied reds and premium Mediterranean-style varietals. The tasting room in this cute little barnlike structure is open daily 9am to 4:30pm. Located at 41300 Avenida Biona; 909/676-6300.

MAURICE CAR'RIE WINERY: Maurice and Budd Van Roekel opened this giant, neo-Victorian California ranch manor and antique barn in 1986. The visitor-oriented establishment sells souvenirs and offers tastings of its wines, which include some of the sweeter varietals and are available daily 10am to 5pm. Located at 34225 Rancho California Road; 909/676-1711.

MIRAMONTE WINERY: One of the newest wineries in Temecula, Miramonte has already made a name for itself with premium handcrafted wines. It is a friendly, family operation with valley views and pretty gardens. Open daily from 10am to 4:45pm. The winery is located at 33410 Rancho California Road; 909/506-5500; www.miramonte winery.com.

MOUNT PALOMAR WINERY: With its hilltop views, sunny orchards, soft grass, and shaded tables, Mount Palomar provides the ideal spot for a picnic. One of the valley's three original operations, it made its mark with riesling, exceptional dessert wines, and some lesser-known Italian varietals such as cortese and sangiovese. Tastings daily 10am to 5pm. Located at 33820 Rancho California Road; 909/676-5047 or 800/854-5177; www.mountpalomar.com.

THORNTON WINERY: Although this faux château feels more like a grandly financed marketing concept than a winery, its sparkling wines, formerly bottled under the Culbertson label, have won many awards. Try them at the tasting room, open daily. Located at 32575 Rancho California Road; 909/699-0099; www.thorntonwine.com.

—Kathy Strong

bled eggs, salsa, and black beans. Lunches are strong on salads, especially Asian chicken salad with ginger and plum vinaigrette. *$$; AE, DIS, MC, V; no checks; breakfast, lunch, dinner every day; full bar; reservations recommended; www. temeculacreekinn.com; east on Pala Rd from Hwy 79 exit on I-15.* &

LODGINGS

Inn at Churon Winery / ★★☆

33233 RANCHO CALIFORNIA RD, TEMECULA; 909/694-9070 The 22-room luxury inn at Churon Winery is the area's newest, and by far finest, bed-and-breakfast offering. Set perfectly within the winery's vineyard, each tastefully decorated and spacious one- and two-bedroom suite in the French-style château features a fireplace and a whirlpool. A gourmet breakfast is served in the pleasant dining room of the inn or on your private balcony overlooking the gardens and vines. A late afternoon reception in the winery tasting room downstairs is held exclusively for inn guests. Temecula has long been in need of a romantic overnight destination befitting its growing wine-country charm. This is it! *$$$; AE, DIS, MC, V; no checks; www.innatchuronwinery.com; 4.5 miles east of I-15.* &

Temecula Creek Inn / ★★

44501 RAINBOW CANYON RD, TEMECULA; 909/694-1000 OR 800/962-7335
Draped like a green velvet blanket across a mountainside of oaks, boulders, and streams, Temecula Creek Inn and its golf resort rest above the Temecula Valley like a golfer's vision of paradise. Few courses and settings in Southern California are this naturally beautiful—the oaks and the soaring red-tailed hawks will remind you of Ojai or Northern California. The Inn itself is a series of two-story, tree-shaded, shingled wings set along a knoll above the course's opening holes. Operated by JC Resorts, which also owns the Surf and Sand in Laguna Beach and the Rancho Bernardo Inn (about 45 minutes' drive to the south), Temecula Creek has 130 rooms that feature oversize furniture, Southwest-motif fabrics, and large, firm beds. Even though the pool is a bit small and the outdoor corridors leading to the rooms are showing some age, the inn is still an upscale yet informal country resort for golfing couples and weekend vacationers, without the pomp or the stratospheric prices. It's like a good sports car without a walnut-veneer dashboard. *$$–$$$; AE, DC, DIS, MC, V; no checks; www.temeculacreekinn.com; east on Pala Rd from the Hwy 79 exit off I-15.* &

THE
CALIFORNIA DESERT

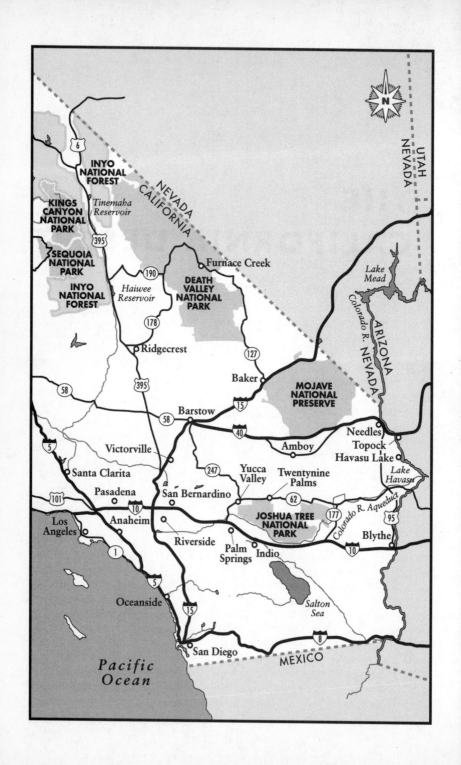

THE CALIFORNIA DESERT

With its searing summer temperatures, purple-tinged mountains, otherworldly rock formations, weird landscapes, and unexpected lakes almost 230 feet below sea level, the California desert remains a place of baffling, exciting incongruities. Despite man's frequent attempts to tame the elements, nature continues to hold the winning hand here and to do what she pleases. Flash floods roar off the mountain flanks and tumble through washes that otherwise might stay bone-dry for years. Dead-calm mornings turn into afternoons riven by moaning winds, often powerful enough to knock a bejeweled Palm Desert matron right out of her stiletto heels.

In the low desert, the Coachella Valley stretches from the San Gorgonio Pass, gateway to Palm Springs (where fields of towering, wind-driven turbines herald your arrival), to the Salton Sea. Movement along the San Andreas Fault over the millennia lowered this area, and also lifted the adjacent mountains to 10,000 feet or more. Snowcapped in winter, these ranges, the San Jacinto and San Gorgonio, loom over the region like Alps on Mars, framing Palm Springs and its neighbor resort communities. Although runaway development of the flat valley floor has created a patchwork of emerald golf courses, gleaming luxury communities, and vast stretches of auto-friendly pavement, there is plenty of wild terrain for exploring, and the telltale perfume of smoky mesquite and fragrant creosote reminds anyone who steps outdoors that this is truly a different environment.

Travel to the north, and you'll begin seeing the burly Joshua tree, so named because its outstretched branches seemed to early Mormon settlers to resemble the hirsute prophet Joshua beckoning them westward. Early pioneers (and many ignorant modern campers) tried to chop down the "trees"—really a member of the succulent yucca family—for firewood, only to discover that their "trunks" were just toughened stalks that won't burn. Joshua Tree National Park is named for its abundant fields of this unusual plant, and is the lowermost boundary of the vast Mojave Desert, which makes up the majority of southeastern California. The range of Joshua trees encompasses much of the Mojave Desert, from the upthrust hills and plateaus protected by Joshua Tree National Park (in dramatic contrast with the nearby glittering carpet of lights better known as Palm Springs) to the Mojave National Preserve situated in the fork between Interstate 15 and Interstate 40 east of Barstow. The region, like the Joshua tree, embodies characteristics of improbable hardiness and range. Visitors willing to log some long, hard miles on interstates and backroads will discover—through the windshield, on a day hike, or especially from the rim of a slumbering desert volcano—that the high desert is a celebration of immensity, of emptiness, of quiet so intense you can hear your heart beating.

Once you enter the apparently forsaken emptiness of Death Valley, though, most recognizable plant life disappears, and your senses must quickly adapt to seeing the natural beauty of one of the earth's most challenging environments. Summertime temperatures often exceed 120 degrees, but life stubbornly persists in this enormous valley. Even so, hard-core adventurers cross paths with lazy sunseekers; throughout the entire California desert, destinations range from gloriously untouched national parks to luxuriously contrived vacation resorts—and it's a rare day when the sun doesn't shine out here.

ACCESS AND INFORMATION

PALM SPRINGS INTERNATIONAL AIRPORT (3400 E Tahquitz Canyon Wy; 760/323-8161) is served from major cities around the United States by Alaska, American, American Eagle, United, United Express, America West Express, and U.S. Airways Express. **CAR RENTALS** (Avis, Budget, Dollar, Hertz, National) are available in Palm Springs at the airport or directly through the Coachella Valley resorts.

Most travelers touring the **LOW DESERT** approach via car on Interstate 10 from the Riverside/San Bernardino area. Immediately after the San Gorgonio Pass, Highway 111 splits off southward from the interstate, enters typical desert scenery of sand, rock, and scrub, and soon becomes a multilane boulevard (with traffic lights) that strings along from one desert resort community to the next—Palm Springs, Cathedral City, Rancho Mirage, Palm Desert, Indian Wells, and Indio. At Indio, a traveler can continue south to see the immense Salton Sea and its bird life, or rejoin Interstate 10 toward the southern entrance of Joshua Tree National Park (Cottonwood Springs Rd). Interstate 10 continues east to enter Arizona at Blythe and is the primary route to Phoenix.

If you're headed to the **YUCCA VALLEY** and **TWENTYNINE PALMS**, the main gateway to Joshua Tree National Park, the Highway 62 exit from Interstate 10 appears just east of the San Gorgonio Pass; from here it's about an hour to Twentynine Palms.

Interstate 15 is the primary route to the **HIGH DESERT** destinations, including Barstow, Mojave National Preserve, Baker, and Death Valley (though many Vegas-bound travelers simply blow straight through on Interstate 15 to the Nevada border). In Barstow, Interstate 40 branches off toward the southern parts of the Mojave Preserve, including Providence Mountains Recreation Area. Interstate 15 skirts the northern boundary of the preserve; the main gateway here is Baker, which is also where Death Valley–bound drivers turn off onto Highway 127; the main entrance to Death Valley National Park—via Highway 190 from Death Valley Junction—is about 90 minutes north.

Keep abreast of the area's highway conditions by calling the California Highway Patrol at 909/849-5646. High winds often kick up sand in open areas outside of cities, causing poor visibility, dangerous conditions for big rigs and recreational vehicles, and, at the very least, damaged auto finishes.

All automobile travel in desert regions can be potentially challenging and sometimes dangerous. Cars should be newly serviced (pay special attention to radiator hoses and fan belts) and in reliable condition. While the Palm Springs resort communities have all the conveniences of your home neighborhood, you won't find any gas stations inside Joshua Tree National Park or the Mojave National Preserve (Death Valley has several), so fill your tank before you leave the interstates, and keep an eye on the gauge and road map. If you're heading away from developed areas, carry an ample supply of drinking water, since the desert's arid conditions cause dehydration even in the cooler winter months. The same goes for sun protection; sunscreen is always a good idea any time of year. Best times to travel are in the shoulder seasons—late fall and spring, when temperatures are generally below 80°F. Winter weather means cool, usually clear days and freezing nights, and when a storm blows through there can even be snow flurries. Spring means great weather and wild-flowers, making it the most popular time to visit the high desert.

General information on high-desert parks and destinations can be obtained from the **MOJAVE DESERT INFORMATION CENTER** in Baker (72157 Baker Blvd; 760/733-4040), the **NEEDLES INFORMATION CENTER** (707 W Broadway; 760/326-6322), or the **CALIFORNIA DESERT INFORMATION CENTER** in Barstow (831 Barstow Rd; 760/255-8760).

Palm Springs

In a letter to a friend in 1914, the widow of famed author Robert Louis Stevenson wrote, "There is a climate of extraordinary purity and dryness, and almost no rain or wind. Wonderful cures have taken place here . . . if I had only known of Palm Springs in my Louis's time!" In those early days, weak-lunged patients gathered in tents amid the palm groves, and there was no notion that the city of today—a place of glamorous golf resorts, sparkling swimming pools, and steak-and-martini restau-rants—might ever exist.

The first big boom hit in the 1920s. Bungalow courts and small motels sprang up, and Hollywood's golden-age celebrities swept in to vacation in the glorious, dry winter sunshine, arriving in automobiles that could now negotiate the improved roads linking Los Angeles to the formerly remote desert. Some of these old lodgings remain, as do others from subsequent booms in the 1950s and '60s, when Frank Sinatra, Bob Hope, President Eisenhower, Liz Taylor, and a host of other big names kept Palm Springs in the limelight. But by the 1980s Palm Springs was dying, its rep-utation tarnished by too many wild spring breaks that drove merchants and resi-dents from the old downtown to newer resort communities like Palm Desert and Rancho Mirage.

Today Palm Springs is in the midst of an unprecedented revival that has it gracing the covers of style and leisure magazines around the world. Hollywood celebrities are back in droves, a stylish gay community has embraced the town, and hipster baby boomers have discovered Palm Springs as an enclave of classic midcentury architecture, much of it by internationally acclaimed Southern California design masters like Richard Neutra, Rudolph Schindler, and Palm Springs's most defining architect, Le Corbusier disciple Albert Frey.

But before golf courses and Cadillacs, before movie stars and socialites, there was the Agua Caliente band of **CAHUILLA INDIANS**. The tribe settled here over 1,000 years ago, living a simple life amid the beauty and spirituality of the open desert. Today, the Cahuilla still own half the land on which Palm Springs is built, and actively work to preserve Native American heritage in the area. Four miles south of Palm Springs is the entrance to their reservation and three spectacular palm canyons open to hikers (S Palm Canyon Dr; 760/325-5673; www.indian-canyons.com). **ANDREAS, MURRAY,** and **PALM CANYONS** contain huge granite formations, water-polished rock, rushing streams and quiet pools, and surprisingly dense groves of

363

PALM SPRINGS AREA THREE-DAY TOUR

DAY 1. Spend the morning browsing the **SHOPS AND GALLERIES** along South Palm Canyon Drive in downtown Palm Springs. Don't miss the **VILLAGE GREEN HERITAGE CENTER** (221 S Palm Cyn Dr; 760/323-8297), where you'll get a sense of the city's early history. Duck in for burgers at **TYLER'S,** then drive a few blocks into the old "Tennis Club district" to check into your room at the **ORBIT IN.** After a swim and a nap, drive 6 miles northwest of Palm Springs to catch the **PALM SPRINGS AERIAL TRAMWAY,** on which you'll ascend almost 6,000 feet up the mountainside to Mountain Station. Stay long enough to enjoy the view and have a light snack on the aerie-like terrace. Return to your room for a freshen-up, then walk to dinner at nearby **JOHANNES.**

DAY 2. Rise early, take your time with coffee and continental breakfast poolside, then drive about a half hour "down valley" on Highway 111 to Palm Desert. Breakfast fans might want to stop at **KEEDY'S FOUNTAIN & GRILL** for huevos rancheros. Next learn which plants and critters call the desert home with a visit in the cool of midmorning to nearby **LIVING DESERT WILDLIFE AND BOTANICAL PARK** (closed in summer). Backtrack to downtown Palm Desert for some colorful Caribbean fare at **TOMMY BAHAMA'S TROPICAL CAFE,** then spend a few hours poking into all the elegant **SHOPS AND GALLERIES** along El Paseo. Head back for an afternoon swim at the hotel; aviation fans might rather visit the **PALM SPRINGS AIR MUSEUM** instead. Venture out in the evening on foot for drinks and dinner at **KAISER GRILLE,** followed by a live performance at either the Annenberg Theater in the Palm Springs Desert Museum or the historic **PLAZA THEATRE.**

DAY 3. Spend the morning playing golf on one of the Coachella Valley's nearly 100 golf courses, then return to your lodgings for one last swim and checkout. If you've worked up an appetite, try a platter of authentic Mexican specialties at **EL MIRASOL** in Palm Springs, then stroll through the spiny world of **MOORTEN BOTANICAL GARDENS.** You'll also have time in the afternoon for a visit to **PALM SPRINGS DESERT MUSEUM,** where art and natural history cohabitate in a splendid building against the mountainside. If a special milestone (especially a romantic one) needs celebrating, wind up the day with a champagne toast at **LE VALLAURIS,** followed by a candlelit dinner on the patio.

indigenous *Washingtonia* palms—they survive on snowmelt and underground water supplies. In 2001, hikers and desert rats thrilled to the reopening of the Agua Caliente–owned **TAHQUITZ CANYON** (500 W Mesquite Ave; 760/416-7044; www. tahquitzcanyon.com), a sacred place filled with Native American legend and stunning natural scenery. Tahquitz's famous waterfall was featured in Frank Capra's 1936 film *Lost Horizon,* but the canyon later became a refuge for hippies, transients, and squatters, who vandalized the natural environment and left mounds of trash behind. In 1969 the tribe closed the canyon to outsiders. Today, there's a modern new visitors center, and two-hour ranger-led tours take hikers as far as the waterfall.

As you drive into town on Highway 111, you'll want to stop in at the **PALM SPRINGS VISITOR INFORMATION CENTER** (2781 N Palm Canyon Dr; 760/778-8416 or 800/34-SPRINGS; www.palm-springs.org), which offers maps, brochures, advice, souvenirs, and a free hotel-reservation service. Pick up a copy of *Palm Springs Life* magazine's monthly *Desert Guide,* a somewhat biased but extremely helpful resource packed with phone numbers, maps, and advertisements. The **PALM SPRINGS DESERT RESORTS CONVENTION & VISITORS BUREAU** (69-930 Hwy 111, Rancho Mirage; 760/770-9000 or 800/41-RELAX; www.PalmSpringsUSA. com) is a terrific source of information on Palm Springs and the entire Coachella Valley. After hours you can even get information and events listings on its 24-hour recorded hotline (760/770-1992).

Downtown Palm Springs is centered around **PALM CANYON DRIVE,** a wide, one-way boulevard that's designed—with tree-shaded benches, brick-paved sidewalks, and hidden courtyards—to be pedestrian friendly. Each Thursday night, in fact, the street is closed to vehicular traffic between Amado and Baristo Roads for the pedestrian-only **VILLAGEFEST.** This popular street fair draws much of Palm Springs out to stroll and schmooze; craft vendors and tempting food booths compete for your attention with wacky street performers and even wackier locals shopping at the mouthwatering fresh produce stalls. Though present-day Palm Canyon is lined with scores of art galleries, antique stores, souvenir shops, restaurants, and hotels, the street has managed to retain a nostalgic, small-town charm reminiscent of 1930s Palm Springs. You can't miss the **PLAZA,** one of the town's original shopping arcades. Open between Palm Canyon Drive and the parallel, other-direction Indian Canyon Drive, the Plaza sports the low-rise Spanish-style—stucco archways, red-tile roofs, bougainvillea-draped railings—that characterizes much of old Palm Springs. Local fixture **DESMOND'S** (160 S Palm Canyon Dr; 760/325-1178) has occupied a prime Plaza space since 1936, long enough for its once-stodgy "mature resort wear" to gain new popularity among today's hipsters, who now shop alongside Palm Springs retirees for brightly patterned sport shirts, polyester golf duds, and pastel trousers. The historic **PLAZA THEATRE** (128 S Palm Canyon Dr; 760/327-0225; www.psfollies.com) hosts the long-running *Fabulous Palm Springs Follies,* a vaudeville-style show filled with lively production numbers—the entire cast are "retired" showgirls, singers, dancers, and comedians who range in age from 50-something to 85-plus. Their energy is an inspiration, though the old-fashioned revue is mostly popular with an older crowd.

Toward the mountains, the **HERITAGE DISTRICT** (known locally as the "Tennis Club district" after the celeb-frequented hotel that used to anchor the neighborhood) features a concentration of historic homes and hotels. It's a time capsule of the '30s, '40s, and '50s, and many vintage motels and inns have been swept up in the current madness for midcentury style and reincarnated as nostalgic versions of their own past. It seems that Palm Springs, once the town that progress forgot, is now a treasure trove of midcentury relics; they continue to emerge from 1950s-era vacation homes and often find their way to the desert's established vintage stores:

MODERN WAY (1426 N Palm Canyon Dr; 760/320-5455; www.psmodernway.com) deals in 1950s and '60s furniture, lighting, accessories, rugs, and art; and **PALM SPRINGS CONSIGNMENT CO.** (1117 N Palm Canyon Dr ; 760/416-8820) is another outlet for groovy period pieces.

To gain a bird's-eye perspective on the entire Coachella Valley, take the **PALM SPRINGS AERIAL TRAMWAY** (Tramway Rd off Hwy 111; 760/325-1391 or 888/515-TRAM; www.pstramway.com); the 2½-mile ascent up Mount San Jacinto takes only 14 minutes, but deposits you in a different world—literally. At 8,500 feet, temperatures are usually around 40 degrees cooler than on the desert floor, and the mountain is blanketed with snow in winter. New rotating cars allow every passenger a panoramic view on the way up; at the top is **MOUNT SAN JACINTO STATE PARK** (909/659-2607; www.sanjac.statepark.org), which features trails for hiking, cross-country skiing, or snowshoeing. You can rent equipment at the Nordic Ski Center in the tramway's upper station. In town, paintings, sculpture, and Native American artifacts as well as the natural sciences are showcased at the big-city-sophisticated **PALM SPRINGS DESERT MUSEUM** (101 Museum Dr, at Tahquitz Canyon Wy; 760/325-7186; www.psmuseum.org), which rests in a deep well of landscaped sculpture gardens set up against the mountainside. The Annenberg Theater on the museum's ground floor hosts concerts, drama, film, and dance. Near the airport, the **PALM SPRINGS AIR MUSEUM** (745 N Gene Autry Trail; 760/778-6262; www.air-museum.org) takes advantage of the dry desert air to preserve some of the world's last examples of still-operable World War II aircraft, including the famous *Flying Fortress* with its ball turret nose.

The main outdoor pursuit around here is golf, golf, and more golf. At this writing, the Coachella Valley boasted more than 100 golf courses, their lush fairways and velvety greens carved incongruously from the arid desert scruff. A majority of the courses are semiprivate, or attached to the Marriott, Hyatt, Westin, Renaissance, La Quinta, and other big-name destination resorts east of Palm Springs. Two excellent public courses right in town are the 36-hole **TAHQUITZ CREEK GOLF RESORT** (1885 Golf Club Dr; 760/328-1005) and the **PALM SPRINGS COUNTRY CLUB** (2500 Whitewater Club Dr; 760/323-8625), the oldest public-access course in the city. Other outdoor activities let you learn about the desert in its natural state, like the four-wheel-drive eco-tours offered by **DESERT ADVENTURES** (760/324-JEEP or 888/440-JEEP; www.red-jeep.com). Experienced naturalist guides helm the company's fleet of red Jeeps, taking visitors into the rugged Santa Rosa Mountains and through untouched desert to learn about native wildlife, or through picturesque ravines that hug the San Andreas Fault. When California had its much-publicized recent energy crisis, renewed interest was generated (no pun intended!) in the wind-powered turbines that line the Coachella Valley. You can learn about this alternate energy source and get a rare up-close look at the behemoths with **WINDMILL TOURS** (Indian Ave exit from I-10; 760/251-1997 or 877/449-WIND; www.windmilltours.com). For an educational and eye-opening trip through the many desert habitats of the Southwest, visit the **LIVING DESERT WILDLIFE AND BOTANICAL PARK** (47900 Portola Ave; 760/346-5694; www/livingdesert.org) in Palm Desert. Anyone who thinks the desert is a barren, lifeless place will be pleasantly surprised by the dizzying array of plants, insects, and animals—including bighorn sheep, mountain lions, rattlesnakes, lizards, owls, golden eagles, roadrunners, and more—that are all around, "hiding" in plain sight.

RESTAURANTS

El Mirasol / ★★☆

140 E PALM CANYON DR, PALM SPRINGS; 760/323-0721 Forget most of the style-over-substance "cantina"-style Mexican restaurants around town: when the taste's the thing, local Latinos and gringos alike know to head for this simple—and simply delicious—mainstay south of downtown. Despite recently doubling its size and extending the front patio, El Mirasol remains inconspicuous along a fast-moving curve of a wide boulevard. Insider's tip: Look for the green awning just before the street begins to curve. Inside, the open double dining rooms feature terra-cotta floors, rustic but comfy hand-stitched leather chairs, and plain tables large enough to spread baskets of warm chips, bowls of fresh salsa (various "heat" levels are available), and platters of El Mirasol's recipes-from-home specialties. We never skip the *chile verde,* a thick stew of tender pork in long-simmered tomatillo sauce, or the signature *pollo mole poblano,* an authentically earthy version of the classic cocoa/pumpkin seed/chile–bathed chicken. A serious selection of meatless dishes includes outstanding spinach enchiladas and a burrito filled with a garden's worth of veggies. If margarita pitchers and sizzling fajitas are your thing, they do that too, always with the attentive service and friendly smiles that make even first-timers instant regulars. *$; AE, DIS, MC, V; no checks; lunch, dinner every day; full bar; reservations not accepted; just south of Avenida Olancha.* &

Johannes / ★★★

196 S INDIAN CANYON DR, PALM SPRINGS; 760/778-0017 After holding St. James at the Vineyard in the P.S. foodie spotlight, talented chef Johannes Bacher left to open this eponymous restaurant that's been flavor of the month for local diners— since 2000! Located in a plain low storefront steps away from Palm Canyon Drive, Johannes is the number-one restaurant recommendation of the many hip and stylish inns downtown. Step inside, and the place oozes casual sophistication: two boxy rooms—one with tangerine walls, a quieter one avocado-green—have spare furnishings, colorful accessories, and an open, industrial flavor, while the open kitchen hums behind a pale birch counter stacked with gleaming white plates at the ready. Bacher melds a Spago-esque California cuisine with European flair and international accents—even including dishes from his Austrian youth (à la Spago's Wolfgang Puck). Some examples from the eclectic menu: roasted beets paired with grapefruit and goat cheese in a tasty salad; meatballs braised in a Malayan blend of yellow curry and kaffir lime; seared scallops bathed in an anchovy-sage-balsamic sauce; crispy duck in a fruity peach-plum sauce; and always Wiener schnitzel with traditional parsleyed potatoes or spaetzle. A selection of multicourse tasting menus is always available (in summer it's a $29.99 bargain!). Johannes perennially wins *Wine Spectator* accolades for an encyclopedic wine list, an achievement extending to an enticing selection of after-dinner spirits, dessert wines, and inventive elixirs that also mirror the outstanding premeal cocktail and martini menus. *$$$; AE, DIS, MC, V;*

no checks; dinner Tues–Sun; full bar; reservations recommended; www.johannes restaurant.com; corner of Arenas Rd. ♿

Kaiser Grille / ★★

205 S PALM CANYON DR, PALM SPRINGS; 760/323-1003 / 74225 HWY 111, PALM DESERT; 760/779-1988 You won't find Wiener schnitzel at Kaiser Grille. Named for owner Kaiser Morcus, the restaurant exemplifies a new energy and spirit in the Coachella Valley that makes some of the more haute valley restaurants seem stuffy. Here the clientele is a little more bare-shouldered, the collars a little more open, and the laughter a little louder than in the clubbier valley restaurants where geriatric decorum rules the evening. At the downtown Palm Springs location, two open-air dining terraces jut into the sidewalk like the prows of twin ships. During blast-furnace summer months, micromisters up in the metal-finned roofline cool diners with their wispy fog. At night, diners see (and are seen by) a constant parade of passersby, but the food commands center stage. Prime rib arrives in a thick fork-tender slab (it can also be ordered blackened, Cajun style). Fish lovers have the unusual option of a "mixed grill" showcasing three different fillets. Sauces are rich, often based on a classic beurre blanc flavored with either mango or local citrus juices. Grilled steak is a specialty, served with heaps of fresh steamed vegetables and mashed potatoes. The only thing better than sitting outside is sitting inside, where you can see the activity in the huge open kitchen. There is a second location in Palm Desert, with a bland exterior but the same vibrant character inside. *$$; AE, DC, DIS, MC, V; no checks; dinner every day; full bar; reservations recommended; www.kaisergrille. com; corner of Arenas Rd, between Deep Canyon Rd and Portola Ave.* ♿

La Provence / ★★★

254 N PALM CANYON DR, PALM SPRINGS; 760/416-4418 Hiding in plain sight—on the town's main drag across the street from the Hyatt hotel—sits this intimate European charmer, a restaurant that's consistently recommended by nearby B&Bs. Once you find the stairway to the second-floor bistro (look along a sideways shopping arcade), you'll enter a world that's utterly French and utterly romantic. A cozy bar and warmly welcoming dining room lead to an even lovelier terrace, festooned with tiny lights, overlooking the street. When reserving, request the terrace in advance; it's delightful on balmy evenings, and heated for winter's chill. Chef Didier Tsirony eschews heavy traditional French cream sauces in favor of carefully combined herbs and spices, offering a pleasant mix of classic French (country pâté with aspic, Marseilles bouillabaisse, sautéed calf's liver, steak au poivre) as well as Mediterranean flair: escargot and mushroom caps are baked in flaky phyllo, couscous and tabbouleh both appear on the menu, and ravioli à la "Grandmère Marie" is filled with roasted duck and bathed in sherry sauce. The wine list offers a nice blend of French and California bottles, with a fine selection of champagne for a truly stylish evening. *$$$; AE, DC, DIS, MC, V; no checks; dinner every day (subject to midweek closure in summer); full bar; reservations recommended; between Amado Rd and Tahquitz Canyon Wy.*

THOSE WONDERFUL "MOP TOPS"

Stand on the floor of the Coachella Valley with your feet firmly planted on a sidewalk in Palm Springs. Look south toward the San Jacinto Mountains. Forbidding, no? A massive pile of crushed rock, barely able to sustain life? True, and not so true, for no plant symbolizes the opportune nature of desert flora more than the noble native fan palm (*Washingtonia filifera*) found in the many folded canyons of the San Jacinto and Santa Rosa Mountains. Here, usually hidden from view to everyone but hikers, the palms send down their thirsty roots toward subterranean year-round springs.

In winter these same canyons come to life with roaring freshets. And out on the desert floor, a few oases such as Thousand Palms also sustain these rustling 50-foot-tall trees. As you walk among them, look closely for the many inhabitants of and visitors to these wildlife "condominiums"—especially tree frogs, and birds such as hooded orioles. Some palms wear "skirts" of dead fronds down much of their trunk length. If a palm is naked, it was probably the victim of sparks from a campfire or vandalism.

To experience a few classic palm groves, consider a hike to Murray Canyon on the Agua Caliente Indian Reservation. To get there, go south on Highway 111 from downtown Palm Springs, following signs to Indian Canyons. Pay a small fee at the reservation's entry station, and continue on to Andreas Canyon, where you can park and hike less than a mile into Murray Canyon. Within the reservation, you can also visit Palm Canyon, where about 3,000 palms line a 7-mile stretch of canyon.

—*Peter Jensen*

Las Casuelas Terraza / ★

222 S PALM CANYON DR, PALM SPRINGS (AND BRANCHES); 760/325-2794
Started in 1958 by Florencio and Mary Delgado, Las Casuelas has been a downtown Palm Springs institution virtually from the beginning. President Dwight Eisenhower was a regular customer, fueling up on Mary's tamales after his golf rounds. Liz Taylor, George Montgomery, Bob Hope, and Dinah Shore all plunked down for big combination plates of enchiladas, tacos, and burritos. The liveliest of the three locations, Las Casuelas Terraza draws its energy from the heavy foot traffic of Palm Canyon Drive. A big palapa-fringed bar and patio opens to the street, and live music pumps out from here as strongly as the straight shots of aged tequilas. If you love black beans Oaxacan style you'll enjoy the black bean "pizza" (really a tostada) with chicken. Unfortunately, Las Casuelas in general seems to have succumbed to too many tourist requests for mildness and offers few dishes that capture a sense of authenticity or innovation. (One of the burrito styles is a rather odd bland packet loaded with diced potatoes and celery.) So why come here? For the Spanish Colonial decor, the crowd, the indoor-outdoor feel, the music, and the great location. Additional locations at Las Casuelas the Original (368 N Palm Canyon Dr, Palm Springs; 760/325-3213), and Las Casuelas Nuevas (70-050 Hwy 111, Rancho

Mirage; 760/328-8844). *$$; AE, DC, DIS, MC, V; no checks; lunch, dinner every day; full bar; reservations recommended; www.lascasuelas.com; at Arenas Rd.* &

Le Vallauris / ★★★

385 W TAHQUITZ CANYON WY, PALM SPRINGS; 760/325-5059 OR 888/525-5852 Named for the small town in the south of France where Picasso took to making pottery later in life, Le Vallauris successfully combines uncompromising elegance with the informality of dining alfresco. The restaurant occupies a historic ranch-style house not far from the hubbub of Palm Canyon Drive (but seemingly a world apart), its ficus-shaded exterior seeming almost too understated—except for the covey of valet-parked Rollses and Mercedeses. Step through the door, however, and you're in a magical setting of indoor and outdoor spaces. Outdoor tables are set with linens and fine china—and with stars overhead, cool night air, and candles aglow, you sense that this is indeed a special dining space. Interior rooms are equally pleasing, with draped alcoves and fine paintings. Belgian-born owner Paul Bruggeman earned his stars operating St. Germain on Melrose Avenue in Los Angeles (the site now occupied by equally famed Patina), and the menu, overseen by executive chef Jean-Paul Lair, reflects Bruggeman's love of what he calls contemporary French-Mediterranean cuisine. The menu is an extravagant journey. One can start with beluga caviar, or terrine of foie gras, or light, crisp crab cakes with whole-grain mustard sauce. Lamb lovers will yield willingly to a perfectly roasted rack, classically seasoned with garlic and thyme, or, at lunch, to the more adventuresome marinated grilled lamb loin with sesame sauce. The veal chop with pommes soufflés is one of Southern California's best. The fish here, either seared or sautéed, accompanied by inventive sauces such as a citrus dressing or red chili sauce, is so buttery and fresh it seems the ocean must be nearly next door. *$$$; AE, DC, DIS, MC, V; checks OK; lunch, dinner every day, brunch Sun; full bar; reservations recommended; vallauris@aol. com; www.levallauris.com; from Palm Canyon Dr go 3 blocks toward the mountains on W Tahquitz Canyon Wy.* &

St. James at the Vineyard / ★★★

265 S PALM CANYON DR, PALM SPRINGS; 760/320-8041 Palm Springs's most interesting dinner menu fuses Pacific Rim, French, Indian Ocean, and American steak house cuisines in a unique style born of owner James Offord's love of travel. Since Offord left the kitchen, a series of pedigreed chefs have taken the reins—including, for a while, talented Johannes Bacher, now of Johannes restaurant (see review). As a result, some regular patrons complain of uneven experiences, but still agree on St. James as one of P.S.'s best. Appetizers change often, but we hope to see more of the coconut-milk steamed mussels and assorted satays with green papaya salad. As for entrees, St. James remains rightfully famous for its curries—lamb, chicken, shrimp, or vegetable—served with traditional condiments and basmati rice. Other standouts include a stir-fried lobster tail over couscous (very pricey), a grilled lamb rack with vanilla-infused reduction, or a fabulous Bouillabaisse Burmese that immerses a bounty of seafood in a sauce enlivened with ginger, pineapple, lime juice, and cardamom. Service is attentive but unhurried; feel free to enjoy a meal that will last several hours. The bar, featuring almost a hundred folk art masks on the walls, is downtown's most sophisticated watering hole, and the restaurant's wine list boasts a *Wine Spectator* Award of Excellence. *$$$; AE, DC, DIS, MC, V; no checks; dinner every day (subject to midweek closure in summer); full bar; reservations recommended; in the rear of the Vineyard shopping center.* &

Tyler's / ★★

149 S INDIAN CANYON DR, PALM SPRINGS; 760/325-2990 There's a perpetual line at the end of the historic Plaza shopping arcade for this humble but universally well-regarded burger joint, a mission-style landmark that began as a '30s-era service station before becoming the local Greyhound depot and later an A&W drive-in. Tyler's was catapulted to local fame when public television personality Huell Howser, a regular customer, took viewers here on his folksy series *California's Gold.* Most folks vie for a shaded outdoor table, where servers ferry basket after basket of burger-and-fry combos—usually their trademark "sliders," succulent miniburgers draped with cheese and grilled onions. The menu is actually pretty extensive, including other California comfort foods such as chili dogs, clam chowder (on Fridays only), egg salad sandwiches, homemade potato salad, fresh lemonade, root beer floats, slurpable milk shakes, and even wine and beer. If you sit inside at the counter, you'll have a front-row view of the bustling fry stations, and a prime spot to eavesdrop on the banter between feisty regulars and the cheerfully brusque staff. *$; Cash only; lunch Mon–Sat; beer and wine; reservations not accepted; on the Plaza, between Tahquitz Canyon Wy and Arenas Rd;* &

LODGINGS

Andalusian Court / ★★★☆

458 W ARENAS RD, PALM SPRINGS; 760/323-9980 OR 888/94-ROOMS The newly-built Andalusian Court blends perfectly with its fashionable neighbors, here in the vintage Tennis Club neighborhood just a few blocks from Palm Canyon Drive's shopping and fine restaurants. Everything is premium quality at this beautiful Spanish-themed cluster of eight lavish minivillas, each boasting private whirlpool, fully equipped kitchen, and over-the-top comforts for guests accustomed to the very best. Landscaped pathways, secluded gardens, tile-framed fountains, and a sparkling pool provide a magical setting that suits privacy-minded celebs, romance-seeking honeymooners, stressed-out sophisticates, and even businessfolk who appreciate a unique setting for intimate, low-profile wheeling and dealing. Discreet, almost telepathic service is the special gift of head innkeeper Jorge Kates, who arranges for everything from in-room massages or post-swim alfresco hors d'oeuvres to activities throughout the valley—for those able to tear themselves away from all this pampering. In the morning, freshly prepared breakfast is brought to each villa, laid out where you desire: in the kitchen, on the patio, or even on breakfast-in-bed trays. The sky's the limit when it comes to special requests: a poolside professional outdoor kitchen is available, as is an on-call chef to throw some shrimp on the barbie—or whip up a gourmet meal in the privacy of your suite's professional kitchen. *$$$$; AE, DIS, MC, V; no checks; subject to midweek closure in Aug; www. andalusiancourt.com; 4 blocks west of Palm Canyon Dr.* &

Ballantines Original / ★★★
Ballantines Movie Colony / ★★★

 1420 N INDIAN CANYON DR, PALM SPRINGS; 760/320-2449 OR 800/780-3464 / 726 N INDIAN CANYON DR, PALM SPRINGS; 760/320-1178 OR 800/780-3464 Given Palm Springs's affinity for all things 1950s, it's easy to see why this offbeat hotel devoted to the decade has made such a splash. Newly renovated with an unerring eye for classic kitsch, Ballantines has made headlines in publications from *Condé Nast Traveler* to *Vogue* as the Next Big Thing in Palm Springs accommodations. Located in a quiet residential neighborhood half a mile from the Palm Canyon "scene," discreet Ballantines Original is small—just 14 rooms and suites—but big on personality, from made-to-look-old rotary dial telephones and blue AstroTurf sunning deck around the pool to fun atomic-age furniture from Eames and Bertoia. This vintage single-story motel is built around the swimming pool, so all rooms are within steps of the water—plus the groovy outdoor bar and adjacent fire pit. Interiors are decorated with a wink and a nod to various celebs—Marilyn Monroe, Douglas Fairbanks Jr., and Audrey Hepburn are among those honored—or in campy themes like French Artist (*sacre bleu,* what a gaudy bedspread!). We especially like the Women of the Movies room, adorned with photos of actresses and a pink television. Even the TVs are tuned in to the '50s, with the in-house movie channel offering classic films of the decade as well as brilliantly bad B movies.

Most of the same amenities (fire pit, retro phones), including an evening poolside cocktail and morning breakfast, can also be found at the equally fabulous Ballantines Movie Colony, a classic 1930s hotel designed by prolific and renowned area architect Albert Frey. After a meticulous remodel that added a warehouse's worth of barely used midcentury furnishings and an explosion of tantalizing colors—brilliant lime edges the pool and the Sinatra Room is boldly orange (Frank's favorite color)—this 18-unit accommodation offers the same quietly hip, highly personalized experience as the Original. *$$$; AE, MC, V; no checks; www.ballantineshotels.com; corner of Stevens Rd (Original), corner of Tamarisk Rd (Movie Colony).* ♿

Korakia Pensione / ★★★

257 S PATENCIO RD, PALM SPRINGS; 760/864-6411 Located on a quiet side street within walking distance of downtown, Korakia immediately transports a visitor to a Moroccan oasis. Scottish artist Gordon Coutts built the white-walled, wedding-cake-like house in 1924 as a retreat and salon for his many artistic and intellectual friends. Today it's a darling of the super-chic fashion/entertainment world, equal parts rustic and luxurious. The absence of alarm clocks and TVs encourage guests to venture outside, reviving the art compound ambience of old. A Mediterranean villa directly across the street with cocoa-brown walls, tile roof, and palm-fringed eaves has also joined the Korakia ensemble; the grounds boast a garden massage hut draped with gauzy sheers, and several secluded cottages fresh from the patented Korakia makeover. Owner Doug Smith virtually invented the term "restorative designer" and has a knack for balancing vintage character (well-worn wood floors, stucco arches, '40s bathroom tile) with modern features like Chinese slate showers and discreetly mounted air conditioners. The decor reflects his frequent worldwide jaunts, and may include giant hand-carved four-poster beds draped in mosquito netting, safari furniture, and African and Balinese influences. Numerous fireplaces lend a magical warmth on cold winter nights. Continental breakfast is served in the walled entry patio to the full-throated accompaniment of 15 lovebirds and parakeets. In season, kitchenettes for light cooking are stocked with Häagen-Dazs ice cream, baguettes, and brie. *$$$–$$$$; No credit cards; checks OK; subject to midweek closure in Aug; www.korakia.com; from Palm Canyon Dr (Hwy 111) take Arenas Rd 4 blocks west to S Patencio Rd, then go left.* &

Orbit In / ★★★

562 W ARENAS RD, PALM SPRINGS; 760/323-3585 OR 877/99-ORBIT From the bones of a classic 1950s motel—all boxy lines and streamlined simplicity—rose this cozy homage to midcentury motifs, cocktails-by-the-pool Rat Pack lifestyle, and the individual architects, photographers, and designers responsible for Palm Springs's reign as a mecca of vintage modernism. It's ultra-groovy in a sophisticated way . . . imagine the chic 1956 living room of your parents' swinging, childless friends, and you won't be far off. Savvy connoisseurs of collectibles will dig the museum-quality furnishings in each carefully themed room (Martini Room, Bertoia's Den, Atomic Paradise, and so on), while the rest of us enjoy tripping down memory lane with amoeba-shaped coffee tables, glowing rocket-ship lamps, Eames recliners, kitschy Melmac dishware, and strappy vintage chaises on every room's private patio. Requisite modern comforts range from super-luxe bedding, Internet access, and lounge-music CDs for your in-room listening pleasure to a fleet of complimentary Schwinn cruiser bikes, secluded whirlpool, and poolside misters to cool even the worst summer scorcher. Restored fixtures, original built-ins, and pristine tile grace kitchenettes and bathrooms. Guests gather at the poolside Boomerang bar; a central "movies, books, and games" closet encourages old-fashioned camaraderie amid this chic atmosphere. At press time, the Orbit In had just expanded to include the Hideaway, another architectural gem just a block away that's been given the same impeccable face-lift. *$$$–$$$$; AE, DIS, MC, V; no checks; subject to midweek closure in Aug; www.orbitin.com; 5 blocks west of Palm Canyon Dr.* &

The Willows Historic Palm Springs Inn / ★★★☆

412 W TAHQUITZ CANYON WY, PALM SPRINGS; 760/320-0771 Everything glorious about Palm Springs's past—its history as a glamorous getaway, intellectual haven, nature sanctuary, and rejuvenative spa—lives on at the Willows. The eight-room inn was built in 1927 as a private estate. New York attorney and multimillionaire Samuel Untermyer bought it soon thereafter and massaged it into elegant perfection. Today the house steps up a hillside above old Palm Springs, its Tuscan-yellow walls, red-tile roofs, and multiple terraces tangoing in and out of a grove of tall palms, fringed willows, and the stone mountainside itself. Owners Tracy Conrad and Paul Marut, both emergency-room doctors with a penchant for architectural triage, purchased the house in 1994.

IT'S ONLY NATURAL: HEALING SPAS OF THE DESERT

Southern California's Native Americans have always lived in harmony with nature, looking to the gifts of the desert for healing and sustenance. The natural hot springs that abound here played a big part in their well-being; earlier desert dwellers soaked in the mineral-laden water, applied mud from the spring beds, and burned sage to clear the air of bad spirits and negative thoughts. These actions enabled physical and spiritual rejuvenation as part of their rituals. Palm Springs grew up around a spring that was the focal point for the Agua Caliente band of Cahuilla Indians. Their name for the area was "Se-Khi" (boiling water), and the Spanish later called it "Agua Caliente" (hot water). Today, the **SPA HOTEL & CASINO** (100 N Indian Canyon Dr, Palm Springs; 760/325-1461; www.sparesortcasino) is built around that original spring and guests soak in pools fed with the same therapeutic water. A native legend about the water's healing powers is illuminated in the sculpture *Cahuilla Women* in front of the spa. Today spas abound in the desert because contemporary philosophy recognizes the native wisdom in the wonders of the waters and herbs—translating it into the latest trends of special signature hydrotherapies and body treatments. The **SPA LA QUINTA** offers Desert Healing Water therapies; if you don't want to submerge in a spring, you can have your own private multiple-head Celestial Shower in an open-air rock-lined grotto. There's a Cahuilla Sage Body Wrap too. At **TWO BUNCH PALMS** you can soak in a natural spring grotto surrounded by palm trees; at dusk you might catch a glimpse of the white owls that played a part in Indian lore. The resort also offers rustic mud baths and a Native American–inspired massage ritual that starts with burning sage. **MARRIOTT'S RANCHO LAS PALMAS SPA** provides a Purification Ritual service based on medicinal mud, mineral waters, massage therapy, and sage-mineral moisturizing cream. Spa and hotel accommodations in the area range from spartan to funky to five star; many allow day stays. Visiting the desert is a harmonious tonic for the mind, body, and spirit—you can enhance it with a soak in natural mineral springs or a modern interpretation at a spa.

—Judith Lazarus

According to Conrad, it was but a forlorn husk of its days when Albert Einstein spent weeks visiting Untermyer, when Clark Gable and Carole Lombard hid away here, and when in the 1950s, Marion Davies, mistress of William Randolph Hearst, owned it and converted the only kitchen to a bar. Today every surface and every furnishing has been restored, from door hinges to flagstones. Rooms are large and tastefully furnished with fine antiques. Each terrace reveals a view of gardens and the ragged curtain of mountains beyond. A 50-foot waterfall burbles down the mountainside into the breakfast patio. The inn's full-time staff serves a glorious breakfast (the bread pudding with walnut and berry sauce is heaven, accompanied by scrambled eggs with chèvre and chives) and keeps the service intuitively unintrusive without being stuffy. No visitors roam the grounds (although many ask); grounds are limited to registered guests only. At twilight, as the desert cools, guests gather in an open veranda room beneath a Moroccan-arched ceiling to sip wine and enjoy hors d'oeuvres. At bedtime (after a day of swimming and reading), crisp cotton sheets welcome your tanned skin, and open terrace doors admit the hushed twitters of birds settling in for a night in the palms. As are you. *$$$$; AE, DC, DIS, MC, V; checks OK; subject to closure during Aug; www.thewillowspalmsprings.com; 2 blocks toward mountains off Palm Canyon Dr (Hwy 111), across from Le Vallauris.*

Desert Hot Springs

No mystery surrounds the naming of this town, which lies north of Palm Springs off Highway 10. It's home to about 40 **HOT-SPRINGS SPAS**, which devotees swear have medicinal properties. Most commonly touted as a remedy for arthritis and rheumatism, the steaming mineral water bubbles up at an average of 140° to 150°F, perfect for filling the various pools, soaking tubs, and private bathtubs offered at the local motels and resorts. Most of these offer day rates for those who just want to drop in for a few hours, as well as treatments such as massage, facials, body wraps, and aromatherapy. Interestingly enough, the Desert Hot Springs cold water provides its own magic: delectably pure, it's won a number of drinking water competitions.

Most people know Desert Hot Springs only as home to **TWO BUNCH PALMS**, a luxurious retreat that played a prominent part in the Robert Altman film *The Player* (Tim Robbins and Greta Scacchi fled L.A. to lounge in one of the resort's mud baths). But the town is also home to about 15,000 people, and while there isn't much to do here, that's just the point. This desert hamlet nestled at the foot of the Little San Bernardino Mountains is a place to slow down, take the waters, and, if you're feeling ambitious, read a good book.

LODGINGS

Two Bunch Palms / ★★★

67-425 TWO BUNCH PALMS TRAIL, DESERT HOT SPRINGS; 760/329-8791 Hollywood glitterati weren't the first to discover how great it feels to soak in the desert's hot springs; native Cahuilla Indians gathered here hundreds of years before Chicago mobster Al Capone allegedly hid out in the '30s-era stone buildings that form the core of today's resort. Two Bunch Palms is annually voted one of the world's "Top Ten" by *Travel & Leisure* and *Condé Nast Traveler* magazines, drawing stressed-out masses seeking relaxation, rejuvenation, and the pure sigh-inducing pleasure only a health spa can deliver. Despite being a celeb magnet, it's still a friendly and informal haven offering renowned spa services, quiet bungalows nestled on lush grounds, and trademark lagoons of steaming mineral water. Service is famously—and excellently—discreet, and the outstanding spa treatments (10 varieties of massage, mud baths, body wraps, facials, salt rubs, and more) fulfill their pampering promise. Two Bunch is a summer camp for grown-ups, where the rich and famous pad about in bathrobes, forbidden by gentle but insistent signs from using cell phones or speaking above a whisper. Lodgings range from guest rooms equipped with minifridges and cable TV (some with private patio) to spacious suites and villas with separate dining areas, minikitchens, and whirlpool spas. Furnishings tend toward a relaxed, Southwest style left over from a slightly stale redecoration, and room amenities are just a hair below standard hotels in the same price range, but no one seems to be complaining. Room rates all include an exceptional buffet breakfast in the Casino Dining Room, which is also open for lunch and dinner, serving a slightly "lite" cuisine (translation: there's no cream in the soup, but you can still get rack of lamb and a glass of wine). *$$$–$$$$; AE, MC, V; no checks; www.twobunchpalms.com; from the Palm Dr exit off I-10, head north 5 miles to Two Bunch Palms Trail.*

Cathedral City

Often overlooked by visitors "just driving through" from Palm Springs, Cathedral City is bordered by Highway 111 to the west and south and Interstate 10 to the north. Currently expanding thanks to some major redevelopment projects, the town is home to a growing number of families and has a year-round population of about 36,000. It's also the site of the **COLLEGE OF THE DESERT,** a community college known not only for education but also for its open-air market each weekend. Many visitors head to **DESERT MEMORIAL PARK** (69-920 E Ramon Rd) to pay their respects to prominent entertainers, including Frank Sinatra—whose headstone reads "The Best Is Yet to Come"—and former Palm Springs mayor, congressman, and singer Sonny Bono.

You won't see any grandiose cathedrals, however. According to the chamber of commerce, the region got its name in 1850, when a member of the U.S. Army Corps of Engineers decided the local canyons resembled the cavernous interiors of grand churches. Hence the name Cathedral Canyon, followed in the 1920s by developers who dubbed a subdivision Cathedral City.

At the heart of the city's redevelopment is the new complex along Highway 111 that holds the city's civic center, police department, Mary Pickford Theater (a movie theater and restaurant complex), and a **3-D IMAX THEATER** (68-510 E Palm Canyon Dr; 760/324-7333 or 888/340-2460). For more information about the community, contact the **CATHEDRAL CITY CHAMBER OF COMMERCE** (760/328-1213; www.cathedralcitycc.com).

Indian Wells

Welcome to one of the valley's upper-crust neighborhoods, indeed, to one of the richest cities in the state of California. This quiet refuge for the super-rich has a median household income of about $110,000, and it's estimated that 75 percent of Indian Wells's residents dwell behind guarded gates. Home owners here include Bill

Gates, John Elway, and Lee Iacocca. Indian Wells is also the site of the über-exclusive Vintage Club, a golf resort where, according to a recent article in *Forbes* magazine, the initiation fee alone is $300,000. However, no one's going to check your net worth if you're just coming to visit, and the area—a short drive from dining and shopping in Palm Springs or Palm Desert—is home to several deluxe resorts that cater to golfers and vacationing families.

LODGINGS

Renaissance Esmeralda Resort and Spa / ★★☆

44-400 INDIAN WELLS LN, INDIAN WELLS; 760/773-4444 OR 800/552-4386 Fresh from a massive 2002 renovation, the Esmeralda Resort attempts to raise the hospitality bar for the rest of the Marriott-owned Renaissance properties by offering five-star boutique personal service and luxury that defy the corporate feel in many corners of the hotel. This much is certain: vacationing families have embraced the Renaissance for its kid-friendly water recreation, which includes waterfalls, wading pools, and a real sandy beach. Many other guests are here for championship golf at the attached Indian Wells Golf Resort, offering 36 Ted Robinson–designed holes and packages with the Renaissance and its nearest neighbor, the Hyatt Grand Champions. Despite the impressive leisure opportunities—which also include some serious pampering at the hotel's discreetly serene on-site full-service spa—the hotel's sheer size and abundant convention-style meeting spaces still scream "business." Almost 600 rooms are spread among several interconnected towers; all have terraces with mountain and/or pool views, elegant new marble bathrooms, and the in-room high-tech advantages working travelers have come to expect. Flexible family suites, outstanding seasonal rates, and numerous thoughtful touches distinguish the hotel from the average chain offering. Several dining options include two fine restaurants and a great Starbucks-style coffee joint in the lobby (don't you wish all hotels had that option!). *$$$$; AE, DC, DIS, JCB, MC, V; no checks; www.renaissanceesmeralda. com; located off Hwy 111.* &

Rancho Mirage

Eleven miles from Palm Springs, quiet Rancho Mirage is perhaps best known to outsiders as the home of the Betty Ford Center (39-000 Bob Hope Dr), as well as **FORMER PRESIDENTS** Gerald Ford and Dwight Eisenhower. But this wealthy, low-profile town is also the site of several high-profile professional golf tournaments, and perhaps some celebrity bodily remains. Rumor has it that after Harpo Marx was cremated, his ashes were scattered into a sand trap at the seventh hole of the Rancho Mirage golf course.

For more information about the community, contact the **RANCHO MIRAGE CHAMBER OF COMMERCE** (42-464 Rancho Mirage Ln; 760/568-9351; www. ranchomirage.org).

LODGINGS

The Lodge at Rancho Mirage / ★★★☆

68-900 FRANK SINATRA DR, RANCHO MIRAGE; 760/321-8282 OR 866/518-6870 The only major resort hotel in the Coachella Valley region that's actually on the mountainside, the ultra-luxurious Lodge is perched high above Highway 111. In contrast to the towering mountains, the hotel's architecture is linear, modern, and horizontal—a broad U open to the view. A bronze statue of a bighorn sheep greets you in the porte cochere, but inside all evidence of the desert's natural world vanishes; you're in a French country palace with gleaming marble floors, French antiques, baroque paintings, and long halls. The elegant guest rooms (240 of them, arranged in three-story wings) all have private balconies with views of the pool, mountains, or valley—or all three. Accommodations are spacious, with elegant stone finishes, fabrics, and crisp linens. A "club" floor offers added amenities: a private lounge, personal concierge, and complimentary food and beverage services during the day. The Lodge's cabana-fringed swimming pool and outdoor hydro-spa have an outstanding view; perched on the rim of the property, they gaze across the entire valley. Tennis players are well provided for here, with 10 courts (one clay) to choose from. Croquet is also available on a permanent grass court on the east side. The first-class Avanyu Spa offers a tantalizing menu of healing and beauty treatments. After Rockresorts bought this former Ritz-Carlton, many expected the corporation to exchange the Ritz's formal European style for a more desert-friendly ambience, similar to the way their other properties (including the cozy alpine Lodge at Vail and the rustic forested Rosario Resort in Washington's San Juan Islands) offer a distinct sense of place. As of press time, we're still waiting. *$$$$; AE, DC, DIS, MC, V; checks OK; www.lodgeatranchomirage.com; from I-10, take Date Palm Dr south to Hwy 111, go left to Frank Sinatra Dr, then right.* &

Marriott's Rancho Las Palmas Resort & Spa / ★★★☆

41000 BOB HOPE DR, RANCHO MIRAGE; 760/568-2727 OR 800/I-LUV-SUN Desert resorts often weave golf holes close to their wings of rooms, but few do it as boldly as Rancho Las Palmas. Here two of the 27 Ted Robinson–designed holes plunge right into the very center of the resort compound, water hazards and all, their greens almost at the feet of diners or sunbathers. Rancho Las Palmas's main lobby, restaurant, and conference buildings, as well as its 450 low-rise rooms and 22 suites, are comfortably spaced across a wide area. Nothing feels crowded here. Appealing tile roofs give everything a hacienda feeling, and hundreds of lanky palm trees dot the grounds. A 25-court tennis club completes the sporting scene, as well as several pools and Tortuga Island, a 6,000-square-foot water playground with slide and pop jets for family fun. More languid luxury is offered at the 20,000-square-foot European-style health spa, which features 26 treatment rooms, saunas, steam, hydrotherapy, two fitness centers, and an outdoor pool with underwater music. While activity is generally geared toward the out-of-doors, the recently remodeled and refurbished rooms, with French doors opening onto private balconies, television armoires, and mission-style furnishings, provide a serene setting for moments of rest. Mediterranean-style fine dining is featured each evening at

Madeira, while Pablo's Restaurant and Tapas Bar is open all day, serving American food as well as Spanish specialties. Alas, like several other large resorts built out on the flat desert plain in the Coachella Valley, Rancho Las Palmas turns inward and doesn't offer a great sense of place: it's just not close enough to the mountains. But it creates its own self-contained world, and families can stay here for days without feeling the need to go anywhere else. *$$$–$$$$; AE, DC, DIS, MC, V; checks OK; www.rancholaspalmas.com; near corner of Hwy 111 and Bob Hope Dr.* &

The Westin Mission Hills Resort / ★★★

71-333 DINAH SHORE DR, RANCHO MIRAGE; 760/328-5955 OR 800/937-8461 Of the valley's many resorts built in the 1980s and 1990s in the flat desert neighborhoods north of Highway 111, the Westin ranks at the top for artful elegance without glitz. Its architecture has a vaguely Moroccan theme, which fits the desert clime perfectly. Rooms are arranged around the grounds in a series of two-story buildings, with accommodations that range from basic to palatial. All have terraces and come with an array of creature comforts befitting this price range—including the Westin trademark "Heavenly Bed," an ultracomfy white confection so popular many guests order one for home. Sounds of splashing children draw you toward an oasislike pool where a 60-foot water slide springs from a mini-mountain (two other pools indulge adults only). The Westin is intertwined with the Mission Hills Country Club courses, one designed by Pete Dye and the other by Gary Player, and two restaurants celebrate indoor-outdoor dining during the high season when cooler winter temperatures prevail. Though the Westin has the business demeanor of a practiced group-and-meeting hotel, it offers a multitude of recreation options for leisure travelers, gamblers attracted to the nearby Agua Caliente Casino, or professionals after the day's business is concluded. In addition to golf, you'll find a running track, bike trails, lawn games, and the freshly expanded Spa at Mission Hills, a stylishly boutique-like oasis whose treatments range from sports massage to pampering Hawaiian body treatments. *$$$$; AE, DC, DIS, MC, V; no checks; ranch@westin.com; www.westin.com; at Bob Hope Dr.* &

Palm Desert

Shoppers, take heart: you've found the equivalent of Beverly Hills's Rodeo Drive transplanted to the desert. Palm Desert's **EL PASEO** boasts almost a hundred boutiques, gift and antique shops, and galleries and restaurants of the highest quality. Simply to walk up one side of the divided street and down the other gives you about a mile of nonstop window-shopping and browsing. **MCCALLUM THEATRE FOR THE PERFORMING ARTS** (in the Bob Hope Cultural Center on the campus of College of the Desert, 73-000 Fred Waring Dr; 760/346-6505) hosts touring big-name entertainers and Broadway shows. The best attraction in town, without question, is the zoo and botanical garden named **THE LIVING DESERT** (about 4 miles south of Hwy 111 at 47-900 Portola Ave; 760/346-5694; www.livingdesert.org). Look for directional signs in town and along Highway 74 (the Pines-to-Palms Hwy leading into the mountains). Budget two or three hours to tour this fascinating collection of gardens

DESERT CASINOS

Look out, Las Vegas. The Indian-owned casinos in the Coachella Valley are hoping to give you a run for your money.

When voters legalized Nevada-style gaming on California's Native American tribal lands, they opened the door for a major boom in casino gambling. The new laws meant that, among other changes, the casinos could replace video-style games that rewarded winners with a receipt that had to be exchanged for cash with real coin-dispensing slot machines. Tribes in the Palm Springs region are both expanding existing casinos and building new ones.

Like most topics in the valley, with a community that includes the young, the old, the conservative, the liberal, the extremely wealthy, and the working poor, the subject of Indian gaming and local casinos is a hot one. Supporters welcome the recreational aspects of the casinos, as well as the job opportunities and enormous revenues they generate. Critics point to the possibility of increased traffic and crowds, gaudy neon signs and bright lights, and the social problems of gambling addiction.

For the visitor, especially seasoned gamblers, the lure can be compelling: in addition to video poker and slot machines, casinos offer card games such as poker and blackjack as well as bingo and other games—24 hours a day. As competition increases, they become virtual Vegas clones, striving for the same level of excitement—and, hopefully, the same stakes!

and more than 130 animal species, including bighorn sheep gamboling over their own mountainside and a mountain lion in a realistic stone grotto.

As befits a community where a household's second car is often a golf cart, the annual parade starring the carts moonlighting as Rose Parade floats is a big deal. Started in 1964 as a bit of a joke, the November **GOLF CART PARADE** (760/346-6111; www.golfcartparade.com) has grown to a well-publicized event attracting an estimated 25,000 spectators and more than 100 whimsically transformed carts. Past parades have seen giant slot machines, outsize golf bags, a spectacular Noah's Ark, and a champagne bottle all motoring majestically up one side of El Paseo and down the other. For more information about the community, contact the **PALM DESERT VISITOR INFORMATION CENTER** (72-990 Hwy 111, at the corner of Hwy 111 and Monterey Ave; 760/568-1441 or 800/873-2428; www.palm-desert.org).

RESTAURANTS

Cuistot / ★★★☆

73-111 EL PASEO, PALM DESERT; 760/340-1000 Cuistot is, simply put, the valley's consistent choice for fine French dining. Since 1987, chef/owner Bernard Dervieux—trained by acclaimed chefs Paul Bocuse and Roger Vergé—has introduced well-heeled local foodies to creative, often healthier French-

Casinos in the Palm Springs area include:

AGUA CALIENTE CASINO, 32-250 Bob Hope Drive, Rancho Mirage (at Dinah Shore Dr); 760/321-2000; www.hotwatercasino.com. Brilliant neon fireballs lead to this glitzy new complex around the corner from the Westin Mission Hills. It already boasts a full house of dining options plus musical entertainers and prestigious boxing matches, and will also eventually include an on-site hotel.

CASINO MORONGO, 49-750 Seminole Drive, Cabazon (off I-10 west of Palm Springs); 800/252-4499; www.casinomorongo.com. Located near the Desert Hills factory outlet stores, this older casino offers valet parking and a gift shop.

FANTASY SPRINGS CASINO, 84-245 Indio Springs Road, Indio (off I-10 at Golf Center Pkwy); 760/342-5695 or 800/827-2946; fantasyspringsresort.com. This casino has a bowling alley, books a number of big-name concert acts, and offers Spanish-language video gaming.

SPA CASINO, 140 N Indian Canyon Drive, Palm Springs (at Tahquitz Canyon Wy); 760/323-5865 or 800/258-2WIN; www.sparesortcasino.com. It used to be an afterthought to the attached hotel, but now this joint is jumping 24 hours a day. Just think: if you lose money, you can always go book a soothing massage at the spa next door.

TRUMP 29 CASINO, 46-200 Harrison Place, Coachella (at Dillon Rd and I-10); 866/TRUMP-29; www.trump29.com. Yes, *that* Donald Trump. The land may be tribal owned, but this sophisticated complex is Vegas all the way, from the big-name shows and a high-roller players club to 24-hour fine dining and even one of those all-you-can-eat prime rib buffets.

—*Robin Kleven Dishon*

California cuisine that displays his unique and masterful flair. In 2003, the restaurant closed its original location—an oddly hidden spot it outgrew two remodels ago—so Dervieux could focus on the construction of a new, elegant Cuistot nearby, designed to dominate its ultra-choice real estate parcel on the corner of El Paseo and Highway 111. The new restaurant plan began with Dervieux's sketch of his dream stove, where we hope he'll continue to prepare the standout dishes that built his reputation: skillet-roasted veal chop with mushrooms, roasted garlic, and fragrant thyme; beef chop with bordelaise sauce and bone marrow, served with green peppercorn beurre; Chinese-style duck in mango-Madeira-ginger sauce; and quail stuffed with sweetbreads over black rice in a chablis sauce. Cuistot is scheduled to open in the fall of 2003. *$$$–$$$$; AE, MC, V; no checks; lunch Tues–Sat, dinner Tues–Sun (closed late July to early Sept); full bar; reservations recommended; near Ocotillo Dr.*

Jillian's / ★★★

74-155 EL PASEO, PALM DESERT; 760/776-8242 Beauty without pretension makes Jillian's a real find amid desert resort bistros that cater to the well-heeled crowd. The decor here is elegantly rustic, with cottagey dining rooms, doors, windows, and porches that open up to a magical center court where palms lit with twinkle lights seem like pillars holding up the night sky. Proprietors Jay and June Trubee are well known in the desert for starting Cunard's in La Quinta (now the La Quinta Grill) in 1986 for the Cunard family. They moved on to open Jillian's in 1994, and to this day Jay does the honors in the kitchen. He trained at the Culinary Institute in Hyde Park, and his style is robust Americana, but with a strong emphasis on homemade pastas. All are made fresh daily and include such favorites as cannelloni—delicate tubes filled with four imported cheeses and served with a tomato-tinted cream sauce. Rack of lamb is another tour de force: a Colorado rack crusted with seasoned bread crumbs and served with a demi-glace scented with home-grown rosemary. Whitefish dijonnaise arrives on a bed of mashed potatoes beneath a Pommery-mustard hollandaise. Desserts are made on the premises (as are all breads). Jay's Hawaiian cheesecake has been featured in *Gourmet* magazine; its macadamia nut crust provides a little crunch beneath a creamy filling, pineapple topping, and fresh raspberry sauce. *$$$; AE, DC, MC, V; local checks only; dinner every day in season (closed June to early Oct); full bar; reservations recommended; jillians@local.net; near Larrea St.* &

Jovanna's / ★★½

74063 HWY 111, PALM DESERT; 760/568-1315 Jovanna Cruz is everywhere: in the kitchen, at the front door, on the outdoor dining porch, in the back room. In her small, narrow restaurant—very much like a New York Italian eatery, where space is so tight the waitstaff brush past each other back to back—Jovanna fills the space like the outgoing, hearty Philadelphian she is. She earned her chef's stripes at her parents' 1,800-meal-a-night restaurant in Acapulco, often putting in 18-hour days. Her pasta dishes are delicious, generous mountains of flavor, especially a chicken edifice of sautéed chicken tenders in a creamy basil sauce topped with bay shrimp and served over a bed of pasta. Osso buco is always on the menu, and her lamb in marsala sauce served over risotto or pasta merits mopping the plate with more bread to get every last rich drop. Cap your meal with one of her seasonal crème brûlées: eggnog during the holidays, orange liqueur in spring, toasted coconut in summer, pumpkin in fall. At press time she is changing her menu to give more emphasis to California-Italian bistro cuisine, but she promises to keep many of the old favorites. *$$; AE, MC, V; no checks; dinner Wed–Sun (Wed–Sat in Aug); full bar; reservations recommended; near Portola Ave on the south side of Hwy 111.* &

Keedy's Fountain & Grill / ★

73633 HWY 111, PALM DESERT; 760/346-6492 Also known as "Keedy's Fix," this classic cafe and its burgers haven't changed an iota since Bob Keedy established the joint in 1957. When he threatened to close the place in 1987 and retire, locals Bob and Patty Downs stepped in, bought it, and kept almost everything the same. They haven't even replaced the Formica on the counter, where 40-plus years of plates being slid in front of customers has all but worn the color off. You know the menu: classic American breakfast and lunch standards like omelets, BLTs, burgers, and patty melts. But a little bit of Mexico sneaks in. Try a menudo and tortillas special, spicy carne asada, or any of the classic enchilada-taco combos. Breakfast boasts more than a bit of Mex, too, with huevos rancheros, chorizo and eggs, and machaca (shredded beef and eggs). The heart-attack classic is still great: a triple-decker burger with bacon, along with a milk shake from the fountain. On your way out, take some time to look over the magazine photo collages on the wall. Americana—you gotta love it. $; AE, DIS, MC, V; no checks; breakfast, lunch every day; no alcohol; reservations not accepted; on the south side of Hwy 111, at San Pablo Ave. &

Tommy Bahama's Tropical Cafe / ★★☆

73-595 EL PASEO, PALM DESERT; 760/836-0188 Carefree attitudes and Caribbean latitudes are inspired by this breezy restaurant in the Gardens at El Paseo mall. Strategically located on the second floor, with a spacious balcony overlooking the street, Tommy Bahama's has a fun "let's party!" ambience that's hard to resist. The dining room and bar have a plantation-house theme, with ceiling fans, potted palms, wood tables, and servers dressed in casual island style. Outside, the patio overlooking El Paseo is sheltered by cafe umbrellas, additional greenery, and cooling misters for those days when the temperatures are equatorial. Tropical drinks are the beverage of choice, although bartenders are just as happy to whip up a martini as a mai tai, and service is swift and pleasant. As for the food, it's as appealing as the lighthearted setting: mango shrimp salad with sweet Bermuda onions; Caribbean plantain combo (conch fritters, grilled chicken skewers, coconut-crusted shrimp); grilled salmon, as a main course or in a sandwich; fish of the day blackened on a fluffy white roll. For dessert, it's got to be chocolate banana bread pudding, a combo that's wickedly good. If the decor and food get you in the mood for a little piece of the Bahamas to take home, just head downstairs to the attached Tommy Bahama's retail store, purveyor of apparel, accessories, and other Tommy Bahamian accoutrements. $; AE, MC, V; no checks; lunch, dinner every day; full bar; reservations recommended for dinner; www.tommybahama.com; corner of Larkspur Ave.

LODGINGS

Mojave / ★★★☆

73-721 SHADOW MOUNTAIN DR, PALM DESERT; 760/346-6121 OR 800/391-1104 Used to be there weren't many lodging options in Palm Desert; visitors either rented private condos or settled in at the self-contained playground-for-all-ages Marriott Desert Springs. Then the savvy boutique hotel group bought this low-slung vintage motel—perfectly situated on a residential street just one block from stylish El Paseo—and transformed it into the retro-chic Mojave. Combining three things Palm Desert's known for (chic decor, lazy relaxation, and top-notch amenities) with three it definitely isn't (nostalgia, seclusion, and reasonable prices) really works here. Each of the 24 rooms, arranged around a sparkling pool and Grecian-draped whirlpool, exudes 1940s glamour in shades of persimmon, saffron, and the grapefruits that grow along meandering pathways outside. Filled with reproductions of iconic period furniture and accented with vintage black-and-white photos of desertscapes, the rooms are all surprisingly unique; some feature kitchenettes, some fireplaces, some deluxe bathtubs—and room 15 is everyone's favorite, a studio-style gem with old-fashioned dressing area and nubby sisal flooring. Despite rates that can plunge as low as $89 in summer, Mojave doesn't skimp on the details: poolside chaises upholstered in the hotel's signature orange sit ready with neatly rolled towels; creamsicle-fringed umbrellas shade tables perfect for alfresco enjoyment of the simple continental breakfast each morning; bathrooms feature imported bath potions in spa-style pump jars; and the in-room honor bar tempts with '40s treats like grape Nehi and Necco wafers. *$$–$$$; AE, DC, DIS, MC, V; no checks; www.hotelmojave.com; corner of San Luis Rey.* &

La Quinta

Here's a glimpse of the old days in the Coachella Valley, but it's disappearing fast under a tide of new houses and golf courses. Still not much more than a village, La Quinta nestles in a "cove" (local parlance for a flat area of desert surrounded by mountains). Nights are dark here: local ordinances forbid bright lights so that residents can better enjoy the stars and the sense of living in the country. Home of historic La Quinta Resort, the village also hosts the annual outdoor **LA QUINTA ARTS FESTIVAL** (760/564-1244) each March, a four-day gatherings of artists selling their latest works.

RESTAURANTS

Adobe Grill / ★★

49-499 EISENHOWER DR (IN LA QUINTA RESORT), LA QUINTA; 760/564-5725
Located upstairs above the hotel's famed fountain, Adobe Grill's dining patio seems almost to press against the velvet night sky. But seating accommodations aside, the menu here has long been a wonderful alternative to the steak-steak-steak mantra of other desert chefs. Adobe Grill has an elegant, inventive, and also quite traditional touch with Mexican cuisine. Sure, you can order a combination plate (wonderful tamales, enchiladas, tacos, etc.), but it's in the mysterious mole sauce that the Aztecan authenticity really shines. Seafood is a highlight, especially the halibut in a maple pecan crust with orange butter sauce. What's Mexican about it? It arrives with *fideo*, a Mexican pasta like angel hair or vermicelli; the thin strands are deep fried for about a minute before being doused with chicken stock, tomatoes, and herbs, then simmered until tender. *Caldo de marisco,* the bouillabaisse with a Southwest flavor, and *ceviche de mariscos marinara* also showcase Mexico's love of seafood. Don't miss the margaritas here; the largest comes in a huge handblown glass filled with 1800 tequila, orange liqueur, and fresh lime and lemon juice. As you sip, wondering how you'll ever walk out across the tile floor, your eyes will wander to the open-beam ceiling, Guadalajara-made glass art, and the passing dessert tray filled with orange custard flan, sopaipillas dripping with honey, and lemon tarts with prickly pear sorbet. You're not in Kansas anymore, Toto. *$$; AE, DIS, MC, V; no checks; lunch, dinner every day; full bar; reservations recommended; www.laquinta resort.com; from Hwy 111 take Washington St south.* &

Azur by Le Bernadin / ★★★½

49-499 EISENHOWER DR, LA QUINTA; 760/777-4835 New York's acclaimed Le Bernadin seafood restaurant is one of the finest dining experiences in that city; executive chef Eric Ripert is said to have revolutionized seafood cookery in America, with skills honed during his years training and cooking at some of France's finest eateries. So it's no surprise the much-touted arrival of the Le Bernardin venture, Azur, has greatly enhanced chic La Quinta Resort, already known for quality on-site restaurants that consistently surpass the conventional idea of hotel dining rooms. Chef de cuisine Jasper Schneider spent time in Ripert's kitchen learning to offer the same high Le Bernardin standards in a casual resort atmosphere, and even has fresh seafood flown in daily from the same suppliers used by Le Bernadin. The restaurant sports an understated Mediterranean ambiance, the perfect backdrop for stunning signature dishes like marinated fluke in lime, ginger, and ponzu; bouillabaisse that features aioli crab cake melting into a rich saffron lobster broth; and poached skate wing with lemon brown butter and toasted hazelnuts. Azur offers an encyclopedic selection of California and international wines, and—despite being downscale compared to its Gotham counterpart—is one of the fancier dining rooms in the desert. *$$$$; AE, DIS, MC, V; no checks; dinner Tues–Sat (subject to closure during Aug); full bar; reservations recommended; www.laquinta resort.com; from Hwy 111 take Washington St south.* &

La Quinta Grill / ★★

78045 CALLE CADIZ, LA QUINTA; 760/564-4443 Arriving at La Quinta Grill will test your faith—but only from the outside. The parking lot is sand, and the building has all the architectural profile of a Texas roadhouse. But beyond the front door, you enter a big-city environment, newly remodeled and expanded. After closing for about four months recently, the bar area has been redone, and one of the dining rooms nearly doubled in size. Elegant surroundings, including crisp white tablecloths and gilt-framed paintings, belie the simple exterior. So popular in winter you may wait two hours unless you have a reservation, La Quinta Grill (once known as Cunard's) draws a clientele hungry for its wonderful chicken marsala or its popular scampi in a parsley-butter and white wine–lemon sauce. Pasta dishes, like the grilled Italian sausage tossed with generous chunks of fresh tomato, fresh basil, white wine, and shaved Parmesan, are redolent of garlic and big enough for two. Service is friendly and efficient. La Quinta Grill offers big portions and a nice atmosphere for prices about 25 percent less than if they were located "up canyon" (closer to Palm Springs). *$$; AE, DC, DIS, MC, V; no checks; dinner every day; full bar; reservations recommended; from Hwy 111 go south on Washington St to 52nd Ave, right to Avenidas Bermudas, right to Calle Cadiz.* &

LODGINGS

La Quinta Resort & Club / ★★★

49-499 EISENHOWER DR, LA QUINTA; 760/564-4111 OR 800/598-3828 The valley's second-oldest resort (it dates back to 1926) is the very definition of the classic Palm Springs experience. Set against a towering mountain backdrop, it boasts rambling oasislike grounds and subdued elegance, with a Hollywood golden-era feel (Mary Pickford was a frequent guest). To this day, no other resort in the desert approaches its grand sense of place coupled with understated charm. Originally a cluster of 56 tile-roofed guest casitas widely spaced on lawns, the resort has grown into a large town-size complex of golf courses, tennis club, new rooms, bungalows, ballrooms, and spa—yet without losing intimacy. From the moment you drive down the long entry road between towering columnar cypresses, you feel as though you're entering a Spanish village. The casitas are almost severe in their white-walled simplicity, with thick walls, small windows, and simple furnishings, but color abounds outside, where billows of bougainvillea spill over the rooftops. Almost all have a porch for sitting in the deep shade and listening to the mariachi music float over from an evening meal at Adobe Grill. Three fine restaurants make it possible never to leave the grounds: Azur (superluxe French seafood), Morgans (steak house), and Adobe Grill (regional Mexican cuisine with muchas margaritas). Named one of *Tennis* magazine's Top 10 U.S. Resorts, La Quinta offers one of the most beautiful settings in the country, along with 23 courts. Add plenty of programs for the kids (Camp La Quinta), championship tournament golf courses, and a heavenly 23,000-square-foot spa that includes a large fitness center—with yoga and other activities and spa treatments ranging from the golfer's massage to open-air showers, warm-stone therapy, and an outdoor aromatherapy tub—and you've got a gracefully aging Eden that continues to attract entire families generation after generation. *$$$; AE, DC, DIS, MC, V; checks OK; www.laquintaresort. com; from Hwy 111, take Washington St south and turn right on Eisenhower Dr.* &

Indio

More of a blue-collar community than its resort brethren just up-valley, this city supports a thriving **DATE PALM INDUSTRY** that goes back to the early 1900s. As the story goes, the president of the railroad, C. P. Huntington, carried back some date shoots from a vacation to Algeria during the 1880s. Sensing a great opportunity, the U.S. Department of Agriculture got into the act; date palms were planted throughout the area, and by 1914 growers had formed the Coachella Valley Date Growers Association. Like a big county fair, the **NATIONAL DATE FESTIVAL** takes over Desert ExpoCentre (46-350 Arabia St; 760/863-8247; www.datefest.org) every February for 10 days. Concerts and classic carney rides are joined by exhibit halls crammed with fruits, vegetables, art exhibits, industrial arts, fossilized blue-ribbon pies—you know, all that great fair bric-a-brac.

The largest community in the Coachella Valley, with approximately 45,000 year-round residents, Indio is still known for acres of date farms and shops selling the ever-popular date shake; the most popular is **SHIELDS DATE GARDEN** (80-225 Hwy 111; 760/347-0996 or 800/414-2555). But it's also earned a place on the map as the host of the crowd-pleasing Skins Game golf tournament, where four pros compete for big money on each hole, and offers big attractions for horse lovers: a major annual equestrian event, and two polo clubs. For more information, contact the **INDIO CHAMBER OF COMMERCE** (82-503 Hwy 111; 760/347-0676 or 800/44-INDIO; www.indiochamber.org).

The Salton Sea

In satellite photos, Salton Sea is a glistening, 35-mile-long-by-15-mile-wide ocean-blue mirror right in the middle of southeastern California's Colorado Desert. As large as it is, this "sea" didn't exist until a monumental engineering accident occurred. In 1905 the levee of an irrigation canal that channeled water from the Colorado River to Imperial Valley fields broke, and for 16 months the river gushed into the Salton Sink—a geographical bathtub with no drain. Today the sea is a refuge for migrating wildfowl and seabirds. Salton Sea is also popular with thousands of trailer- and tent-camping vacationers who flock to the region in winter to bask in 75-degree weather, spot birds through binoculars, catch scads of fish, and count shooting stars in skies of black velvet. The **SONNY BONO SALTON SEA NATIONAL WILDLIFE REFUGE** (760/348-5278) was officially named after the late congressman in 1998 in honor of his efforts to preserve the lake. It is composed of more than 36,500 acres at the southern end of the sea, much of it underwater. A narrow corridor borders the sea, filled with farmed crops and native marsh to provide a habitat for wintering waterfowl. To reach the refuge from Highway 111, turn west on Sinclair Road (about 70 miles south of Indio, between Niland and Calipatria), then continue 6 miles to refuge headquarters. The **INTERNATIONAL BIRD FESTIVAL** (760/344-5FLY) here takes place annually over a weekend in mid-February. For birding updates, call 760/348-5278.

Joshua Tree National Park

Joshua Tree first gained protection in 1936 as a national monument. The region had remained fairly pristine, well protected by its remote location and harsh climate. Miners and homesteaders had been nibbling at the region's acreage for over 50 years without much impact on the natural scenery. A few hardy souls settled amid the jumbled rocks, able to survive by finding natural dams or building their own tiny reservoirs. Others clustered, as Native Americans did before them, around the region's handful of oases, especially **OASIS OF MARA** at what is now the park's northeastern entrance point. Fortunately for "J.T." (as rock climbers and other frequent visitors now call it), the desert was too rugged, too dry, too spiny, and too rocky to attract much interest beyond that shown by adventuresome sightseers. Drawn to the beauty of its balding rocks, awkward-looking trees, and fascinating mix of flora from both low desert (the Colorado, below 3,000 feet) and the high desert (the Mojave), they wandered here then for the same reasons that now draw visitors from around the world.

Recently the park has seen increased visitor interest. J.T. gained the added cachet of national park status in 1994 with the passage of the Desert Protection Act, and the popularity of **ROCK CLIMBING** here has caused its legions of winter visitors to soar to the point that it can be difficult to find a campsite during the cooler season, November through May.

The Protection Act brought more to Joshua Tree than a new name. Wilderness acreage expanded to 630,000 acres, bringing the total park acreage to 794,000, or

HIGH DESERT THREE-DAY TOUR

DAY 1. (Note: This itinerary and its activities are geared for late fall or spring, which is when we recommend you visit the region.) After picking up **PICNIC SUPPLIES** in Joshua Tree, head south on Park Boulevard, which becomes the 35-mile loop road through Joshua Tree National Park. Stop at **HIDDEN VALLEY CAMPGROUND** to watch rock-climbing activity. Don't miss the ranger-led tours of **DESERT QUEEN RANCH.** Two miles northeast of Hidden Valley, be sure to stretch your legs on the **BARKER DAM TRAIL**—the rocks in this region are especially spectacular. Stop for the night at **ROUGHLEY MANOR BED & BREAKFAST INN** just outside the park in Twentynine Palms and sleep in—but not until after you've ventured out for a big dinner at **TWENTYNINE PALMS INN.**

DAY 2. Rise early, fill the ice chest with cold drinks and lunch items at a grocery store or deli in Twentynine Palms, then drive north on Amboy Road over Sheep Hole Pass and down into **AMBOY,** a remnant of the days when Route 66 passed right through here. Pull on your hiking boots and climb to the top of **AMBOY CRATER** before 10am for a view of its long-inactive lava flows. Continue north on Kelbaker Road, leaving pavement to continue on a well-graded road just after you enter **MOJAVE NATIONAL PRESERVE** near Interstate 40. Stop at the **KELSO DUNES** for a picnic lunch (there are no restaurants or stores anywhere in the preserve) and a brief hike before driving to Nipton for a night's lodging at the unique **HOTEL NIPTON.** Backtrack to Baker for dinner at **THE MAD GREEK;** returning to Nipton, gaze at the neon glow of Primm, Nevada, on the nearby state line.

DAY 3. From tiny Nipton drive east on Interstate 15 to Cima Road, then south to reenter **MOJAVE NATIONAL PRESERVE.** Turn east on Cedar Canyon Road (unpaved), then south on Black Canyon Road for a visit to famed **HOLE-IN-THE-WALL'S LAVA FLOWS,** as well as a stop at **PROVIDENCE MOUNTAINS STATE RECREATION AREA** and **MITCHELL CAVERNS,** where you descend into a limestone cave. Leave the preserve via Essex Road and hit Interstate 40 for the long drive back to Barstow . . . and civilization. Or if you have extra days, you may want to drive toward **DEATH VALLEY** this morning instead, making the scenic **FURNACE CREEK INN** your base for exploring compelling extremes of that national park's terrain.

about 1,237 square miles (about the same size as Yosemite National Park). Despite its vastness, the park has a road system so simple and limited (about 100 paved miles connecting three main entry points) that you can drive it in a single day or less. Unfortunately, virtually all park visitors are on or near these few roads, especially in spring (March and April), when the wildflowers bloom.

Don't get the idea that Joshua Tree is a queue of cars, however. Its remote location and harsh weather extremes will always assure some elbow room, even along

Park Boulevard where it skirts Wonderland of Rocks. Visitors must pay $10 per vehicle admission at one of three entry points: West Entrance Station near the town of Joshua Tree, North Entrance Station on Utah Trail near Twentynine Palms, and the Cottonwood Spring entry 22 miles east of Indio.

A one-day drive will take you past miles of interesting **ROCK FORMATIONS**, many swarming with rock climbers. Hikers enjoy the **BARKER DAM TRAIL** near **HIDDEN VALLEY CAMPGROUND**, an easy path through boulders that leads to a rockbound pool built at the turn of the century. The **DESERT QUEEN RANCH** (760/367-5555) offers ranger-led tours for a small fee. Make plans to join one by inquiring at park entrance stations or calling the above number. The Ranch is now a fascinating ghost-town-like ruin that showcases the incredible ingenuity and resourcefulness of homesteader Bill Keys as he raised his family here in the early 1900s.

CAMPING has become so popular at Joshua Tree, because of all the winter rock climbing activity, that getting a site can take some doing. Be sure to contact **JOSHUA TREE NATIONAL PARK** (74485 National Park Dr, Twentynine Palms, CA 92277 by mail, or phone 800/365-2267 or 760/367-5500; www.nps.gov/jotr) in advance for park information. Most camping in the park is first come, first served, but you may reserve a spot at Indian Cove, Black Rock, and Cottonwood. There are no accommodations inside the park, nor can you buy food, gasoline, or any other supplies.

Twentynine Palms

The last town on Highway 62 before the road plunges eastward across empty desert, Twentynine Palms—named for the number of trees at the Oasis of Mara—is best known as the easternmost gateway to Joshua Tree National Park. It's here that you'll find the park's **OASIS VISITORS CENTER** (74485 National Park Dr, corner of Utah Trail before you enter the park; 760/367-5500), which received all-new interpretive exhibits in late 1999. Because Joshua Tree is often the first national park many visitors see as they begin a trip through the Southwest from Los Angeles, Oasis Visitors Center now has a "gateway" **INTERACTIVE EXHIBIT** that introduces Grand Canyon, Bryce Canyon, Zion, and other Southwest parks. While in Twentynine Palms, keep an eye out for the town's 13-and-growing wall-scale outdoor **MURALS**, each featuring a historic moment from the area's past. Lovers of desert paintings should stop at the **TWENTYNINE PALMS ARTISTS GUILD ART GALLERY** (74055 Cottonwood Dr; 760/367-7819), located next door to Twentynine Palms Inn. For more information on the community, contact the **TWENTYNINE PALMS CHAMBER OF COMMERCE** (6455-A Mesquite Ave; 760/367-3445; www.29chamber.com).

LODGINGS

Roughley Manor Bed & Breakfast Inn / ★★☆

74744 JOE DAVIS RD, TWENTYNINE PALMS; 760/367-3238 In 1924 desert pioneers Elizabeth and Bill Campbell turned a once-primitive campsite into an elegant two-story, stone-walled mansion. Today, a rustling oasis of mature fan palms, rose gardens, and trickling fountains surrounds

CITY SLICKER'S RETREAT: RIMROCK RANCH

Beyond the vintage Wild West storefronts of Pioneertown, a two-lane road undulates for miles through desolately beautiful high-desert landscapes. Tucked into the wilderness is a quiet refuge that's especially popular with writers and other artists: Rim-Rock Ranch Cabins.

Built sometime in the 1940s as a homestead, RimRock Ranch is a hidden treasure whose location appears on few maps. It was purchased in the 1990s by Szu Wang and her husband, Dusty Wakeman, as a weekend escape from the Los Angeles area. For several years, they loaned the extra cabins on the property to friends or relatives, then decided the place would make a perfect inn. Far from the main roads, with four individual cabins that feature kitchens and private courtyards, the secluded ranch has become a haven for creative types seeking peace or channeling the muse.

"We've carved out a little niche here," says Wang, a professional set decorator who has furnished each cabin with antiques, found items, and imagination. "We get writers who come up and never leave the ranch for a couple of weeks." Wang says screenwriters, authors, and composers are among the guests who relish the hiking trails (the ranch is adjacent to the Pipes Canyon Wilderness Preserve), the still nights, and the breathtaking sunrises. And their dogs can do the same: the ranch allows neutered, well-socialized canines to accompany their owners for a small extra fee.

After indulging several outdoorsy acquaintances who begged to hold their nuptials at RimRock, Wang has also begun hosting weddings here; the usual request is day's end, when the waning sunset casts a warm glow over all of Yucca Valley, easily visible from the ranch's new wooden observation tower—or the refreshing plunge tank at the top of the property. Some folks cater the entire party at the ranch, while others adjourn to Pappy & Harriet's Pioneer Palace, a legendary local tavern and barbecue joint.

Since it's far from grocery stores and restaurants (aside from the Pioneer Palace a few miles away), visitors generally bring plenty of supplies and cook all their meals. There's a two-night minimum stay, and all rooms are designated nonsmoking. Rates start at $105 for the smaller cottages; higher for the cabin known as J. D.'s House, which will house up to four and includes a fireplace. For information and directions, contact Rim-Rock Ranch Cabins (PO Box 313, Pioneertown, CA 92268; 760/228-1297; www.rimrockranchcabins.com).

—*Robin Kleven Dishon*

the product of their years of toil. Located near the northeast edge of Joshua Tree National Park, Roughley Manor has aged well, and dedicated innkeepers Jan and Gary Peters share the original owners' attributes of industriousness and imagination. The two-story main house has a wood-paneled and relaxing "great room" downstairs—upstairs are two grand suites, each with fireplace and four-poster or canopy bed, and deep-set windows that look out into the treetops and surrounding desert landscape. Other rooms (all are air-conditioned) include a cozy cottage, charming farmhouse, and two rooms in the Campbells' former archeology laboratory, a stone building next to the property's original 1930s reservoir. By the time you visit, the inn will have grown to include three spacious new rooms in the converted barn, with sunset-facing porches and brand-new everything. Gary even has plans to convert the reservoir into a guest-friendly swimming pool. Jan Peters's interior designs are tasteful, classical New England, and the place is immaculate right down to the well-watered lawns and comfortable, upholstered outdoor furniture set in the shade. Guests get a hearty gourmet breakfast, evening desserts, coffee, and tea—plus a stunning skyful of stars to inspire pleasant dreams. *$–$$; MC, V; checks OK; www.roughleymanor.com; off Hwy 111 off of Utah Trail (yellow blinking light at east end of town).*

Twentynine Palms Inn / ★★

73950 INN AVE, TWENTYNINE PALMS; 760/367-3505 Rustic, sparsely landscaped, with dirt roads between the bungalows, this inn captures the essence of an old-time California desert stay. The historic cluster of cottages, which sprawls over 35 acres, has been operated by the same family since 1928. It's the quintessential hideaway for stressed-out film industry types, European travelers, lizard-skinned desert oldsters, and just about everyone else. Built beside the Oasis of Mara, a rare natural source of open water in the high desert, the inn offers bungalow rooms in the 1929 "old Adobe" section with sun patios (great for nude sunbathing) and fireplaces. Wood-frame cottages Gold Park and Faultline were moved here in 1928. Larger lodgings include several houses and cabins; well-known local painter Irene Charlton occupied one, La Querencia, for many years, and her artworks now decorate the walls. Interiors are rustic yet comfortable, with swamp coolers (rather than colder, but more humid, air conditioners) keeping them reasonably comfortable in summer. Bird-watching, swimming, and tours of the inn's large organic vegetable garden are the major activities here. Many guests visit nearby Joshua Tree National Park (no lodging is located closer to the park), or just hunker down in the 100-plus heat if they come in summer. Adjacent to the pool, the restaurant serves the best meals in the area. All seasonal vegetables come from the inn's year-round garden. The menu favors a hearty continental approach to grilled steaks, seafood, and chicken, and the bar blends up some of the best margaritas this side of Palm Springs. *$–$$; AE, DC, DIS, MC, V (and all European cards); checks OK; info@29palmsinn.com; www.29 palmsinn.com; off National Park Dr, about 1/4 mile to Inn Ave.* &

Mojave National Preserve

Mojave National Preserve lies between Interstate 15 on the north (the route to Las Vegas) and Interstate 40 on the south. Look at a map and you'll see why its nickname, "the Lonely Triangle," is catching on (the triangle's eastern boundary is north-south Highway 95). Within the preserve, only one primary north-south route,

Kelbaker Road, splits the region between the interstates. Many roads in the preserve are unpaved, but most routes between major attractions such as Cima Dome, Kelso, and Hole-in-the-Wall are well graded and passable by passenger cars. Inquire locally regarding road conditions if you're visiting immediately after a major winter storm. General information on this and other desert destinations can be obtained from the National Park Service's **MOJAVE DESERT INFORMATION CENTER,** with branches in Baker (760/733-4040) and Needles (760/326-6322), or the **CALIFORNIA DESERT INFORMATION CENTER** in Barstow (831 Barstow Rd; 760/255-8760). You can visit the preserve online at **WWW.NPS.GOV/MOJA.**

Most travelers enter the preserve from Interstate 40 via Kelbaker Road and head straight north on the road to Kelso. Suitable for passenger cars, the wide graded road cuts through the Granite Mountains and descends into a wide valley on the west side of the Providence scarp (in winter, the Providences are occasionally snowcapped). Virtually a secret 20 years ago, the **KELSO DUNES** are now the eastern Mojave's main attraction (if getting a few dozen visitors a day warrants being called a "main" anything). A hikers' paradise, the area has long been protected from motorized vehicles.

These dunes "sing," but don't expect an aria. On a still day, sand dislodged by your footsteps slips like a great tongue of molasses down the dune face, and a chant-like hum can be heard. Nearby **KELSO DEPOT** was once a busy Union Pacific Railroad way point, with a Spanish Revival station grand enough for any major city; you could still get a lemonade and a slice of pie here in the early 1970s. The ghosts of 1920s passengers still haunt the handsome brick platform, now undergoing restoration, and lined with Victorian lampposts. From Kelso, you have a decision to make: Kelbaker Road to the northwest passes through incredible **LAVA FLOWS** and **CINDER CONES.** Kelso-Cima Road heads northeast through the world's largest **JOSHUA TREE FOREST,** which covers Cima Dome, a gently rounded igneous formation called a batholith. The Cima region's 75-square-mile bubble of once-molten rock is so big that humans here seem more like ants exploring the top of the Houston Astrodome. Don't expect to see anything like the granite domes of Yosemite. Mojave travelers commonly drive through and say "Where is it?" for about 20 miles—and never find it because they're actually on it.

Cima Dome has an overstory of Joshua trees in such abundance that if the desert can be said to have a forest, this is it. From the Cima area, return to Interstate 40 via Mid-Hills Campground, Hole-in-the-Wall, and Mitchell Caverns. From the Kelso-Cima Road, take Cedar Canyon Road east to Black Canyon Road, then go south on Black Canyon to Mid-Hills and Hole-in-the-Wall. The two developed campgrounds within the preserve are at **MID-HILLS** (30 miles northwest of I-40 via Essex and Black Canyon Rds) and **HOLE-IN-THE-WALL** (20 miles northwest of I-40 via same roads). Neither has a street address or a phone. Hole-in-the-Wall does have a visitors center (760/928-2572), which is staffed on weekends only and not at all during summer. Mid-Hills is a high area, prone to occasional snowfalls as winter storms sweep over the Providence Range. Always travel in this area with plenty of water, warm clothing in winter, and a close eye on the weather. Travelers have been known to spend the night in a blizzard (these happen once or twice a year), only to hike the following day in a T-shirt at Kelso Dunes. If time is short, save most of it

GET YOUR KICKS . . .

. . . on Route 66! So the famed song goes, and today thousands of travelers still venture into Southern California intent on driving at least part of the original "Mother Road" immortalized by author John Steinbeck in *The Grapes of Wrath*. Many are Europeans, and one wonders what they think of America as they stop at roadside cafes to savor a greasy burger and fries as if these were foods of the gods. In truth, the transcontinental icon known as Route 66 (it actually runs from Chicago to Santa Monica) has been mostly swallowed by the interstate highway system. Significant stretches remain across Southern California between the Pacific Ocean and Needles on the California-Arizona border, but you'll need a guidebook to trace its path: state and county maps are of little help, since they usually don't show the number 66 at all. The best guide is *Route 66 Traveler's Guide and Roadside Companion* (New York: St. Martin's Griffin, 1995, 2nd ed.) by Tom Snyder, founder of the nonprofit US Route 66 Association (PO Drawer 5323, Oxnard, CA 93031). A $20 one-time fee gets you a certificate and an embroidered patch, and helps support the group's efforts to raise traveler awareness and preserve the route's history and important sights.

—Peter Jensen

for Hole-in-the-Wall, a good jumping-off point for an overnight backpacking trip or a day hike into the open desert of the **WILD HORSE CANYON** area and some scrambling among the cave-pocked **LAVA FLOWS** and staunchly upright **RHYOLITE MONOLITHS** nearby. One memorable experience is the short climb down a narrow slot canyon via several iron rings bolted into the rock. Farther south off Essex Road, **PROVIDENCE MOUNTAINS STATE RECREATION AREA** (760/928-2586) offers a mountainside campground and **MITCHELL CAVERNS** (760/928-2586), a must-stop for anyone with an interest in underground mysteries (and cool cave temperatures in summer). Ninety-minute ranger-led cavern tours focus not only on the caves' geological origins, but also the site's long use by Chimehuevi tribesmen—as well as a few Pleistocene epoch critters. Reservations are a must.

LODGINGS

Hotel Nipton / ★★

72 NIPTON RD, NIPTON; 760/856-2335 If you choose to enter the preserve from Interstate 15, you can make the 1885-founded gold mining town of Nipton home base for exploring. The whistle-stop of a town, population 70 (give or take a few), is just a few miles from the Nevada state line. What makes it unique—besides its colorful history of visiting outlaws that hid in the nearby mountain backcountry—are its owners, husband-and-wife team Gerald Freeman and Roxanne Lange. In 1984 the two Santa Monica, California, transplants purchased the whole town with the intent to resume mining. Opened in 1986, their Hotel Nipton bed-and-breakfast includes heated whirlpools alongside the railroad tracks under some of the brightest, starriest skies in the desert—but still feels like you are overnighting on an Old West movie set. The small frontier-style building with wrap-around wooden porch offers four small, but well decorated, period rooms; an inviting parlor features a collector's case of old bottles and memorabilia unearthed during the restoration of the mining town, as well as scrapbooks and decanters of sherry. Guests share two bathrooms at the end of the hall (but you are often liable to be the only guests). You may choose to stay in the Clara Bow room, so named for the "It Girl" who had a ranch nearby with cowboy husband Rex Bell. *$$; DIS, MC, V; checks OK; www.nipton.com; Nipton Rd turnoff from I-15.*

Death Valley

Something perversely fascinating about being in one of the hottest places on earth—not to mention its sinister name—has drawn tourists here since 1927, when the Furnace Creek Inn first opened. There's more to Death Valley than the thermometer's bulb-busting acrobatics, however. Stretching for about 110 miles along the California-Nevada border, Death Valley's boundaries (which expanded sizably in 1994 with the passage of the California Desert Protection Act) contain 11,000-foot peaks, alkali flats, piñon woodlands, rocky, narrow slot canyons, sand dunes, and an 8,000-foot-thick deposit of sediment forming the valley floor. The sediments arrived here via streams and rivers from much of the east side of the Sierra Nevada as well as western Nevada. Some have been exposed by erosion to resemble the folds and crevices of a massive multicolored mushroom.

Death Valley lay beneath a lake 600 feet deep during the Ice Age (the Pleistocene epoch). Today the only water here sneaks in via hot springs working their way up through the baking crust. Some small ponds host the rare desert pupfish, an evolutionary marvel descended from a diminutive species trapped as the giant lake dried up. Pupfish have adapted to supersalty water and temperatures as high as 111°F. In other areas, a strong flow is enough to irrigate a golf course and the grounds of the famed Furnace Creek Inn and nearby Furnace Creek Ranch.

A national monument from 1933 to 1994 and now a national park, Death Valley slowly saw the profile of its human visitors "evolve" as well—from pioneers and miners, who saw the area as nothing more than a source of borax, copper, gold, and other plunder-worthy metals, to a gradually increasing stream of tourists from around the world. Most arrive in winter, when glorious temperatures in the 60s and 70s are conducive to exploring the park's many natural attractions. The park does get visitors in summer, despite midday readings in the 120-plus range. At those temperatures, however, you can only stand outside your air-conditioned automobile or hotel room for a few minutes and gasp—like a pupfish out of water.

Plan to spend at least two days seeing the park. Start with detailed information regarding routes and safety precautions from **DEATH VALLEY NATIONAL PARK VISITOR CENTER** (on Hwy 190, 15 miles inside the park boundary; 760/786-2331; www.nps.gov/deva). Note that without reservations, campsites and lodgings can be very difficult to procure during winter. The Death Valley area does have a small store (at Furnace Creek Ranch) and four service stations (at Furnace Creek Ranch, Stovepipe Wells, Scotty's Castle, and Beatty, Nevada).

Many of Death Valley's attractions are of the scenic-vista sort. **SCOTTY'S CASTLE**, built in 1924 by Chicago tycoon Albert Johnson at a cost of $2.5 million and now administered by Grapevine Ranger Station (760/786-2313), is a must-see. This Moorish mansion with its four towers opens daily for tours of its rooms (the grounds are open for self-guided touring); the stories of the unlikely friendship between Johnson and con man Walter Scott (Scotty)—who both pursued a secret gold mine—are as tasty as the opulent interiors of the mansion. Some of the valley's famed **SAND DUNES** are 8 miles east of Stovepipe Wells via Highway 190. **DARWIN FALLS**, just west of Panamint Springs off the 190, is reached via a creekside trail leading to the striking, 30-foot-high falls. The 2-mile trip is a refreshing departure from the scrub and sand and offers a rare wetlands experience in the midst of the untamed desert landscape. The oddest spot may well be **RACETRACK VALLEY**, a mudflat 29 miles from the last paved road via a graded dirt road. Pushed by howling winds, rocks (some too large for a man to lift) move across the surface when it's been made slick by rain or ice, leaving long, mysterious tracks. Then the surface bakes dry again, and visitors arrive to scratch their heads and wonder. Other Death Valley attractions that will keep you immersed in the area's wealth of history include the **BORAX MUSEUM** (760/786-2345) and **HARMONY BORAX WORKS** ruins—complete with the original 20-mule-team wagons on display—and the one-of-a-kind **AMARGOSA OPERA HOUSE** (760/852-4441) at Death Valley Junction.

An extended Death Valley visit should definitely also include a stop at the **SHOSHONE MUSEUM** (760/852-4414), located off Interstate 15 on Highway 127. The first thing you will discover at the museum is that no Shoshone Indians ever resided in this former mining town area, but visitors to the area can still walk through the hillside caves where the first residents made their homes. A few years ago, university scientists uncovered the skeleton of an entire prehistoric mammoth here. The museum actually constructed a special wing to accommodate the exciting discovery, on display today. Nearby, in Tecopa, are some fabled **HOT SPRINGS** that reach the not-so-refreshing temperature of 109 degrees; the Tecopa Hot Springs, down Hot Water Road, is open 24 hours a day and is free of charge. A hidden desert gem is in close proximity to the springs, **CHINA RANCH DATE FARM** (8 China Ranch Rd; 760/852-4415), a sort of geological wonder. The China Ranch formation marks one of the oldest conglomerates on the planet; geologic students and professors come from all over the world to study it. The canyon hosts old gypsum mines and opens up to a totally unexpected oasis with towering cottonwoods and willows beside a stream that is home to ancient date palms and wildlife. A store at the ranch features dates as the main staple in many creations and crafts fashioned from material found on the ranch.

STAR WATCHING: THE AGELESS DESERT PASTIME

Desert travelers, especially in the remote Mojave Desert region where "light pollution" from cities is virtually nonexistent, often forget to bring one simple item that makes any desert trip more enjoyable: a star chart. Out here you'll see stars as you may never have seen them before—so many that you may have trouble recognizing even familiar, simple constellations as they swim through a truly milky Milky Way.

Many charts show horizon latitude; this can vary in North America, from latitude 30° at St. Augustine, Florida, for example, to latitude 50° for Medicine Hat, Alberta, Canada. For the Mojave, you'll want to reference latitude 35°. Otherwise you'll be looking for stars, especially in the southernmost and northernmost regions of the sky, that may be below your horizon. Most of the sky, however, is the same.

Some experienced desert travelers bring a folding chaise longue or lightweight cot so they can lie on their backs and watch the show. Look for planets traveling through the zodiac constellations along a line known as the ecliptic (shown on star charts). But note that you won't find planets themselves on any star charts because they wander. Five are usually visible to the naked eye: Venus (the brightest, on the western horizon at sunset or the eastern horizon at sunrise), Jupiter, Mars, Saturn, and Mercury.

Although summer heat is intense, some star watchers enjoy the desert night sky most in the month of August, the time of the Perseid meteors—so named because they occur in the region of sky occupied by the constellation Perseus (near Cassiopeia) after midnight. These showers can get intense, with little zips of light crossing the velvet blackness so frequently you'll soon quit exclaiming, "Look, there's a shooting star!" Set your alarm clock and enjoy the show.

—Peter Jensen

LODGINGS

Furnace Creek Inn / ★★☆

ON HWY 190, 1 MILE SOUTH OF VISITORS CENTER, DEATH VALLEY; 760/786-2345 OR 800/236-7916 Seen against the violet-hued backdrop of Death Valley's surrounding mountain ranges, the Mediterranean/Arabian–style Furnace Creek Inn rises three to four stories up a slight hillside. Few resorts seem so suited to their location: the inn's tile-roofed wings sprawl horizontally, linked by arched loggias built of hand-laid desert stone and shaded a bit by scattered towering palms. Opened in 1927 (after a first life as quarters for borax miners), the inn has seen several remodelings over the years. Significant upgrades were made in the 1990s to the dining room—and to its prices, which now hover in the very expensive range. The 66 rooms range from small to quite large, and many, but not all, have been redecorated. Even a trip to your room is a memorable experience: the natural hillside forms one side of some of the corridors. Although the inn has lost a bit of its

Art Deco feel, this venerable hotel still offers the historic ambience you might expect from a grand national park lodge. Remember, it can be too hot here in summer even to brave a trip to the pool. In winter, the inn is so popular with foreign travelers that it can be booked solid weeks in advance. *$$$$ winter, $$$ summer; AE, DIS, MC, V; California checks only; www.furnacecreekresort.com; Hwy 127 to Shoshone, to Death Valley Junction, then left on Hwy 190 into the park.* &

Furnace Creek Ranch / ★

ON HWY 190, 1 MILE SOUTH OF VISITORS CENTER, DEATH VALLEY; 760/786-2345 OR 800/236-7916 Operated by the same owners as Furnace Creek Inn, the Ranch offers a low-cost alternative to the inn's outright luxury. Once a working alfalfa ranch that harvested as many as nine crops a year to feed the borax-mine livestock (those 20-mule teams got hungry!), the spread now hosts 224 two-story motel-like units with indoor and outdoor corridors, 27 cabins, a spring-fed swimming pool, a golf course, a museum of mining history, a small grocery and camping goods store, horseback riding, and even an airstrip if you care to fly here in your own plane. A coffee shop and cafeteria/restaurant stay open all day, making this a low-cost home base for a few days spent exploring the park. The swimming pool is the most attractive feature: a steady supply from underground hot springs keeps it topped up with 85-degree water. Locals call this their "cold water supply"— there's no way to get anything cooler. In the early morning, look for fresh animal tracks in the dunes outside your door. *$$; AE, DIS, MC, V; California checks only; www.furnacecreekresort.com; Hwy 127 to Shoshone, to Death Valley Junction, then left on Hwy 190 into the park.*

Amboy

Once a bustling stop on famed Route 66 for overheated cars and travelers braving the Mojave, Amboy suffered "bypass surgery" back in the 1970s when Interstate 40 pushed through. Located about 17 miles south of the interstate (as the crow flies), Amboy still attracts Route 66 (now known as National Trails Highway) aficionados, many of them European tourists eager to see creaky desert towns like this one. How creaky? Think of the movie *Bagdad Cafe*. The film was actually shot farther west on Route 66, in Newberry Springs, but no matter: the desert sun bleaches and the wind out here batters anything erected by human hands until buildings crumple into anonymous—but starkly appealing—relics that all look identical.

AMBOY CRATER rises 285 feet from the desert's frying-pan flats like a burnt soufflé. After the first eruption about 6,000 years ago, subsequent eruptions up until 500 years ago spewed lava in a south-southwest fan that covers 24 square miles. You can hike to the top via a trail that leads from the south side of National Trails Highway 2 miles west of Amboy. Wear sturdy boots for the steep trail, and allow a few hours: you'll probably linger at the top enjoying the view.

Baker

Smack in the middle of the East Mojave, 60 miles east of Barstow and 150 miles west of Las Vegas, little Baker sustains itself on hungry and sleepy drivers from Interstate 15. Most travelers know the town as the southern gateway to Death Valley via Highway 127 and the location of the **MOJAVE DESERT INFORMATION CENTER** (72157 Baker Blvd, beneath the tall thermometer; 760/733-4040). Its sharp staff help thousands plan their forays into surrounding desert lands.

RESTAURANTS

The Mad Greek / ★

72112 BAKER BLVD, BAKER; 760/733-4354 Its exterior plastered with signs like "Something for Everybody," "Special Bone-In Ham," and "Parking for Greeks Only," the Mad Greek may be the desert's most eclectic restaurant. The signs, of course, hope to pull in auto travelers headed for the more familiar menu at a nearby Denny's. Unless you have your heart set on a Grand Slam, however, you'll enjoy the Greek's food: sizzling shish kebab, eggplant salads, hummus, baklava, and their most popular item, gyros (spicy thin slices of lamb or beef tucked into pita bread with tzatziki sauce). They also have American hamburgers and sandwiches. The Mad Greek is justifiably well known for its milk shakes made with fresh strawberries. They'll even mix you up a margarita if you want one. *$; AE, DIS, MC, V; no checks; breakfast, lunch, dinner every day; full bar; reservations not necessary; Kelbaker Road exit at Baker Blvd.* &

LODGINGS

Bun Boy Motel

72155 BAKER BLVD, BAKER; 760/733-4363 Popular with European travelers on their way to Death Valley as well as gamblers heading for Vegas (or returning, in victory or in defeat), Bun Boy is one of those classic little American motels (20 rooms, one story) from the days before the nationwide chains. Rooms are clean, inexpensive, and plain. There's no pool, but you can go across the street to swim at Wills Fargo, which belongs to the same owners. The name Bun Boy comes from the affiliated 24-hour cafe next door. *$; AE, DIS, MC, V; no checks; Baker Blvd exit from I-15 north.*

Wills Fargo Motel

72252 BAKER BLVD, BAKER; 760/733-4477 Talk to Bakerites and they'll tell you this is the "new" motel in town. It has a small wing that was added back in the early '90s, bringing the total number of rooms to 30. Rates differ slightly between the two sections, primarily because the older wing has queen beds and showers only, while the new has king beds and tubs/showers. (You're livin' now!) But it's essential to know about this basic, clean place to stay, for Baker's motels fill up fast on weekends. Most important, Wills Fargo (named for an owner named Will) has—drum roll, please—a 10-foot-deep pool. Baker gets hot, hot, hot every summer, and this little oasis can be a godsend. *$; AE, DC, DIS, MC, V; no checks; Baker Blvd exit from I-15.* &

Needles

Needles is a welcome sight. The cool, willow-lined Colorado River flows through this fried but friendly little town, whispering under the bridge on Harbor Avenue. To the southeast on the Arizona side, the Needles, a ragged mountain range cresting at 2,353-foot Powell Peak, pokes at hard blue sky.

Founded in 1883, Needles owes its existence to the railroad, highway travelers, and a nearby farming community to the north along the Arizona side. As the easternmost end of Southern California desert exploration, it offers a decidedly undesert attraction: **CANOEING** through nearby Topock Gorge for a day. The gorge, part of **HAVASU NATIONAL WILDLIFE REFUGE**, begins at Interstate 40. Canoeists meet outfitters on the river at **MOABI REGIONAL PARK** (locals call it Park Moabi; 11 miles southeast of Needles; 760/326-3831), then paddle downriver beneath a steel-strut bridge into a wild region of reddish cliffs, hidden coves, rush-lined backwaters, and a pictograph rock or two. The pickup point is on the Arizona side off Highway 95 at Castle Rock, north of Lake Havasu City (home of London Bridge and English Village). Contact **JERKWATER CANOE AND KAYAK COMPANY** (800/421-7803; www. jerkwater.com) for rental and guided-trip information.

The fictional Joad family camped for a while in Needles on their way west along "the Mother Road"—Route 66—in Steinbeck's *The Grapes of Wrath*. Here they debated how to get across the desert in their overloaded jalopies. "'Gonna go 'crost her at night,' says Ruthie, '. . . we get the livin' Jesus burned outa us if we go in daylight.'" We hope your car is in better shape than theirs.

MOJAVE DESERT INFORMATION CENTER (National Park Service; 707 W Broadway; 760/326-6322) can help with local information, as can the **NEEDLES CHAMBER OF COMMERCE** (100 G St; 760/326-2050). **NEEDLES MUSEUM** (on the city park at 929 Front St; 760/326-5678) will fill you in on local history. They're currently trying to restore the old block-long Harvey House hotel and restaurant nearby, which served Santa Fe Railroad passengers before the days of the interstates. The two-story cement building, noted for its many columns, has been vacant for over a decade.

Ridgecrest

Ridgecrest serves as the Death Valley gateway for visitors approaching from the western boundary. If you're interested in petroglyphs, some of them dating back 3,000 years, you'll find more than 100,000 ancient rock art drawings in Little Petroglyph Canyon on the China Lake Naval Weapons Center. One catch: most of the base is off-limits to visitors. Fortunately, **MATURANGO MUSEUM** (100 E Flores Ave; 760/375-6900; www.maturango.org) offers special docent-led tours up the canyon. Scraped into the dark desert "varnish" of sunburnt rocks, the artwork fairly dances in the shimmering desert sun. Other attractions near Ridgecrest include **FOSSIL FALLS**, a now-dry, water-sculpted chasm that once linked several massive lakes of the Pleistocene epoch; **PINNACLES NATIONAL NATURAL LANDMARK**, tufa spires created by geothermal springs in the depths of now-dry Searles Lake; the Randsburg and Johannesburg **MINING DISTRICTS,** where a few antique shops nestle in the midst of hundreds of abandoned mines; and the deeply eroded, color-banded cliffs and canyons of **RED ROCK CANYON STATE PARK.** Randsburg, with one main street, is a perfect example of a living ghost town; in 1895 three prospectors discovered gold at the base of Rand Mountain and the Yellow Aster mine turned the tiny town into a boom area with more than 4,000 residents.

For information on all these areas, contact **RIDGECREST VISITORS BUREAU** (760/375-8202 or 800/847-4830; www.visitdeserts.com). If you choose to make Ridgecrest your base for exploring, the small town has a handful of basic motels with familiar chain names. **THE HERITAGE INN & SUITES** (1050 N Norma; 760/446-6543 or 800/843-0693), just west of the U.S. Highway 395 business route, is better than most with some whirlpool tubs and suites; amenities include two heated pools, spas, an exercise room, coin laundry, and a free continental breakfast. Starve yourself for a day, then head over to the **TEXAS CATTLE COMPANY** (1429 N China Lake Blvd; 760-446-6602; www.texascattlecompany.com) for some Texas-size servings in a casual, country-style steak house.

THE SIERRA NEVADA NATIONAL PARKS

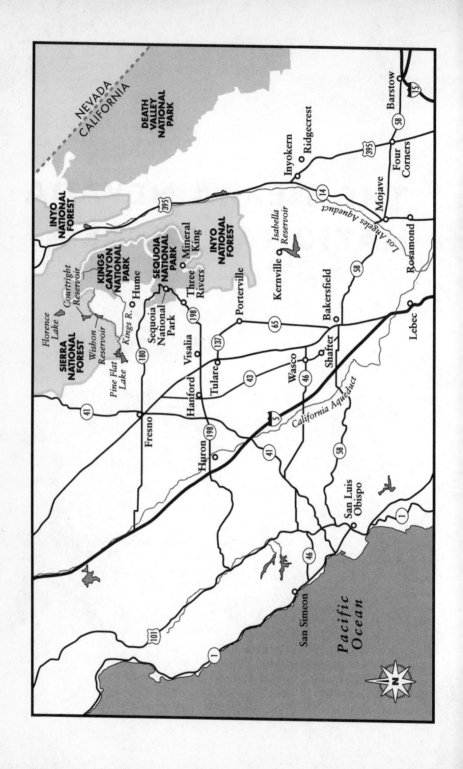

THE SIERRA NEVADA NATIONAL PARKS

The majestic Sierra Nevada mountain range stretches one-third the length of California, mostly hugging the state's border with Nevada. Most of the land is designated national forest. The range encompasses dozens—hundreds—of lakes, including scenic Lake Tahoe near Reno, Nevada. Of the four major national parks in the mountains, Yosemite is the largest and best known, but Sequoia and Kings Canyon National Parks are, in the words of naturalist and Sierra Club founder John Muir, "the gem of the Sierra" and "a rival to the Yosemite Valley."

California's Central Valley lies at the western base of the Sierra, a fertile agricultural region that also serves as gateway for the many visitors who travel from the densely populated coastal cities to visit the unspoiled wilderness in the Sierra. Once an arm of a vast inland sea 500 miles long and approximately 40 miles wide, the San Joaquin Valley draws its name from the San Joaquin River, which flows from the Sierra Nevada above Fresno into the great Sacramento River Delta and eventually out to sea through San Francisco Bay. This verdant region is surrounded by some of the state's largest mountain ranges: in addition to the Sierra Nevada to the east, you'll find the Tehachapis to the south, and the Diablo and Temblor coastal ranges to the west. The Spanish names Diablo (devil) and Temblor (earthquake) both refer to the presence of the devastating San Andreas Fault that is their geological mother.

Much to the delight of its residents, this lush and rural valley remains low-key. The tourist industry hasn't infiltrated the area the way it has other parts of the state, and the valley is predominantly known as one of the world's most productive farming regions. Its fertility stems greatly from the ancient sediments laid down here, where the former mud can be thousands of feet thick. Meanwhile, deep sedimentary rock produces natural gas and oil—which explains the grasshopper-like oil pumps that line the roadsides surrounding Bakersfield.

Valley towns such as Visalia and Bakersfield prosper, growing cotton, grapes, almonds, pistachios, roses, and a wide array of other crops. Because a cruise-control journey down Interstate 5 (the fastest way by far to traverse the state by automobile) misses much of the San Joaquin Valley's agricultural history, Highway 99, which runs north to south farther inland, justifiably attracts travelers with more time on their hands. It is along this route that the valley that gained wrenching fame in John Steinbeck's *The Grapes of Wrath* becomes more accessible. Amid the plight of Depression-era workers, Steinbeck also saw a place where blossoming groves spread like "fragrant pink and white waters in a shallow sea" and the land "quickens with produce" each spring. Though Steinbeck's observations still hold true, this is also a route that will satisfy any visitor's love for turn-of-the-20th-century architecture, old family-run restaurants—and one of the valley's popular pastimes, antiquing. Many of the valley towns boast some of the state's finest civic architecture from the late 1800s and early 1900s, as well as grand old Victorian and Craftsman houses.

Farther inland from Highway 99, a side trip into the Sierra Nevada to Sequoia and Kings Canyon National Parks highlights the famous "big trees" of the Giant Forest Village area as well as the immense, glacier-carved canyon of the Kings River at Cedar Grove. Back-country day hiking, backpacking, and horse-packing opportunities abound in these gateways to the wilderness. The area, because of its high crest of "fourteener" peaks (those 14,000 or more feet high, culminating in Mount Whitney at 14,494 feet), was a favorite of early explorers Joseph LeConte and John Muir. Muir called the Sierra Nevada "the range of light," and on a clear day its snowy crest is a gleaming beacon visible not only from mountain parks and roads but from the San Joaquin Valley itself.

ACCESS AND INFORMATION

From the north, **TWO MAJOR HIGHWAYS**, Interstate 5 and Highway 99, provide access from San Francisco and Sacramento. From the south, **INTERSTATE 5** ascends the long grade over the "Grapevine" above Los Angeles and drops down into the valley before splitting at **HIGHWAY 99**, which continues northward to Bakersfield. Both are intersected by **HIGHWAY 198** and **HIGHWAY 180**, which lead straight into Sequoia National Park and Kings Canyon National Park, respectively. Allow between four and five hours driving time from Los Angeles to the main visitors centers in the parks; Bakersfield is just under two hours, and Fresno about two hours beyond. From San Francisco, Fresno is about a three-hour drive; allow another one to two hours to reach most popular park sites from there.

Dense, low-lying ground fog (known locally as "tule fog") is a grave concern to drivers when it settles over any San Joaquin Valley road or highway. Interstate 5, because it skirts the hills slightly above the valley, is less prone to dense fog, but it, too, can be socked in. If you're caught in a fog, take the first exit immediately and wait it out at a coffee shop, motel, turnout, or rest stop. Do not attempt to drive; horrendous multiple-vehicle accidents are not uncommon under such conditions.

The most central airport is **FRESNO YOSEMITE INTERNATIONAL AIRPORT** (4995 E Clinton Wy; 559/498-4095; www.flyfresno.org), which is serviced by about nine airlines, including American Continental, Delta, and United Express. Nearby Bakersfield's **MEADOWS FIELD** (1401 Skyway Dr; 661/393-7990; www.meadows field.com) is served by America West and United Express. **AMTRAK** (800/USA-RAIL; www.amtrak.com) trains stop in Bakersfield, Wasco, and Hanford. **GREY-HOUND** (800/231-2222; www.greyhound.com) provides bus service to several regional stops, with main depots at Bakersfield and Visalia.

Sequoia National Park and Kings Canyon National Park

Although they were created by separate acts of Congress, Sequoia and Kings Canyon share miles of boundary and are managed as one park; Kings Canyon lies to the north, with Sequoia—the second national park designated in this country—to the south. Together they comprise over 1,300 square miles of incredible High Sierra terrain ranging in elevation from 1,300 feet to more than 14,000 feet. An automobile traveler gets only a small taste of these grand wilderness areas; for the most part, these are backcountry parks.

SIERRA NEVADA PARKS THREE-DAY TOUR

DAY 1. Enjoy an eye-opening cafe mocha or fruit frappé at **ART WORKS** in **HANFORD,** then explore the **HISTORIC BUILDINGS** in and around Civic Center Park. Don't miss having lunch and the town's signature sundae at **SUPERIOR DAIRY PRODUCTS COMPANY,** a little-changed creamery and fountain that's been in business since 1929. After lunch, head east on Highway 198 to **VISALIA,** checking in at historic **SPALDING HOUSE B&B** in time to enjoy the rosy sunset sky from its huge front porch. For dinner, make reservations at the **VINTAGE PRESS RESTAURANT.**

DAY 2. After breakfast, drive east through **THREE RIVERS** to **GIANT FOREST** and stroll through **SEQUOIA NATIONAL PARK'**s ancient groves of *Sequoia gigantea.* Be sure to visit the new **GIANT FOREST MUSEUM,** and take advantage of one of several short **HIKES** nearby. If you had extra days, you'd continue on to Kings Canyon, but to keep moving you'll need to backtrack to Three Rivers, where you can spend the night deep in the trees at **SEQUOIA VILLAGE INN** and dine overlooking the river at the **GATEWAY.**

DAY 3. Get an early start for the drive to **BAKERSFIELD** south via Highway 65, a scenic route through historic **PORTERVILLE,** where history buffs should make a quick stop at **ZALUD HOUSE** (393 N Hockett St; 559/782-7548) and **PORTERVILLE HISTORICAL MUSEUM** (257 N "D" St; 559/784-2053). Arrive in Bakersfield for a late lunch at **HAPPY JACK'S PIE 'N' BURGER** before spending the afternoon browsing for **ANTIQUES** downtown and along H Street. Spend the night at **FOUR POINTS SHERATON,** and don't miss trying a massive **BASQUE DINNER** at one of the city's several restaurants that have been serving the community since the turn of the century. Or, if you're a country music fan, make dinner reservations at **BUCK OWENS' CRYSTAL PALACE** and honky-tonk the night away.

Named for its large stands of trees, **SEQUOIA NATIONAL PARK** is best approached from Visalia via Lemon Cove and Three Rivers, a route that follows the robust Kaweah River as it drains off the Great Western Divide. Ash Mountain Entrance is not far past Three Rivers. Be sure your gas tank is over half full before leaving Three Rivers: at press time no gas was for sale in the national parks. The **FOOTHILLS VISITOR CENTER** (559/565-3341), at a 1,700-foot elevation, will acquaint you with both parks' main features and help you assay the campsite situation if you don't already have a reservation.

The 38-mile highway from Ash Mountain through Sequoia to the Kings Canyon National Park boundary is known as **GENERALS HIGHWAY.** Passable most of the year, in winter the highway may require chains or be closed for several days after a storm. Be prepared for hot weather in summer, as well as occasional delays as road crews work to repair the historic road—an ongoing process much needed in recent years after damaging winter storms.

Located in and around Giant Forest and Lodgepole Village are the **MAJOR VIS-ITOR ATTRACTIONS** for the parks. Four of the parks' five largest trees thrive in **GIANT FOREST.** Most of these Methuselahs are between 1,800 and 2,700 years old, about 250 feet tall, and close to 100 feet in circumference (picture a tree's base wide enough to block a two-lane street!) In fact, the **GENERAL SHERMAN TREE** is the world's largest living organism at 274 feet tall and 102 feet around. Despite its age—estimated to be 21,000 to 27,000 years—the tree is still growing! From here you'll have access to many invigorating **HIKING TRAILS,** such as **CONGRESS TRAIL.** This 2-mile stroll begins at the Sherman Tree and follows a paved trail through the heart of the sequoia forest. It is recommended for first-time visitors to the Giant Forest, as well as visitors with limited time. The **HAZELWOOD NATURE TRAIL** begins on the south side of the Generals Highway, adjacent to the Giant Forest Lodge. Along this gentle 1-mile loop, signs tell the story of humanity's relationship to the Big Trees. Shorter hikes lead to nearby **MEADOWS,** like Crescent Meadow (closed in winter), which boasts a stream and the unique sight of Tharp's Log, a fallen sequoia that provided a rustic summer home for the Giant Forest's first Caucasian resident, Hale Tharp. **HUCKLEBERRY MEADOW** is another option, totally immersed in wildflowers each summer. Probably one of your most memorable activities here will be exploring **CRYSTAL CAVE,** the only cave open to the public in the parks. Well worth the steep half-hour hike from the parking area, mesmerizing stalagmite and stalactite formations abound inside various "rooms" just beyond the entrance to the cave. Hours of operation vary for the season and there is a charge for entrance, along with rules for safety; check with the visitors center for specific requirements. In 2001, the area welcomed a new interpretive center, the **GIANT FOREST MUSEUM** (559/565-4480), open daily from 9am to 4:30pm (longer in summer). Following a historically sensitive renovation, this 1928 structure—designed by the same architect responsible for Yosemite's Ahwahnee Hotel—manages to showcase its own "national park rustic" style along with state-of-the-art visitor exhibits. The museum's theater, composed of a replica of a giant sequoia, explains the life cycle of the trees in the face of nature.

Continuing on to **KINGS CANYON NATIONAL PARK,** you pass into the former General Grant National Park, now included in the Kings Canyon boundaries. This section is now known as Grant Grove, whose highlight is the **GENERAL GRANT TREE,** also known as the "Nation's Christmas Tree." It's the third largest tree in the world, and has also been designated a national living memorial to Americans who died in war.

From Grant Grove, Highway 180 threads 30 miles northeast into the Grand Canyon of the south fork of the Kings River and a park site known as **CEDAR GROVE.** This road is closed in winter (and with it, the entire valley). Cedar Grove and the Grand Canyon area, where summer temperatures may climb into the 90s, are well-forested, with granite sentinels rising high on all sides. Cedar Grove Visitor Center (559/565-3793) and a permit station at Road's End (6 miles east of Cedar Grove Village) can help out with information and permits. One small hotel, Cedar Grove Lodge (559/565-0100) offers overnight accommodations along with a cafe. This is real back trail country, but a few attractions are more reachable and a must-see for their natural beauty. **BOYDEN CAVERN,** open May through September, can be viewed on a 45-minute tour of its unusual marble formations. The **ROARING RIVER FALLS,** its viewpoint reachable with a tranquil and shady 5-minute walk, is a spectacular water display boasting a final 80-foot river drop into a deep pool below.

At the southern end of Sequoia National Park lie the tiny communities of **SILVER CITY** and **MINERAL KING.** Driving to historic Mineral King isn't easy, but it's the only way to get there unless you're a backpacker. A narrow (mostly one-lane), 25-mile-long road snakes into the valley, climbing from Highway 198 near Three Rivers into the high country of Silver City until it dead-ends against the Great Western Divide. Along the way you'll be comin' round the mountain 698 times (sometimes blindly). Navigate this stretch slowly—take an hour or longer if you really want to play it safe—and enjoy the scenery, which ranges from oak woodland to giant sequoia groves. By the time you emerge at Silver City, the valley is classic Sierra high country, with great stands of pine and fir beneath towering snow-laden granite peaks and bowl-shaped cirques.

A failed **SILVER-MINING REGION** after the 1870s, Mineral King drifted quietly along until it almost became a ski resort in the early 1970s. After a pitched court battle between environmental interests and a private developer (ol' Walt Disney himself), President Carter signed over 12,600 acres of Forest Service–administered wilderness to Sequoia National Park in 1978. The valley floor, however, is definitely not wilderness.

Privately owned rustic cabins and a cabin resort/cafe/general store may eventually be phased out, but for now they help create an ideal destination for those who love being near enough to alpine high country to explore it on day hikes, yet return to a snug cabin each night (see Lodgings, below).

Favored destinations for hikers include several lakes tucked high on the south face of the canyon. Best known are **WHITE CHIEF LAKE** and **EAGLE LAKE,** both about 4 miles in, one way—a long, steep day hike, or a more leisurely overnight backpacking trip. The trail to White Chief crosses one of the Sierra Nevada's most unusual natural features: here extensive marble veins course through the mountainside, hollowed by streams into low-roofed caverns (best explored by experienced spelunkers only). The White Chief trail passes right by one **OLD MINE TUNNEL,** however, that leads straight into the mountain. Unlike most dangerous remnant workings around the West, where the risk of cave-in or getting lost is alarmingly real, the White Chief shaft has been left open by rangers so that hikers can safely take a short walk into the darkness. Overnight trips in the backcountry require a permit, and it's often best to obtain one in advance because trailhead quotas can be limited during the short summer season. Write or fax Wilderness Permit Reservations (HCR 89 Box 60, Three Rivers, CA 93271; 559/565-3708; fax 565-4239). For campsite reservations in the valley, call 800/365-2267 or log on to http://reservations.nps.gov. The road into Mineral King closes each winter, usually from the first snow (November) through the end of May.

A wide assortment of **CAMPFIRE PROGRAMS,** presented by ranger/naturalists, is offered year-round in Sequoia. **GUIDED TOURS** are conducted during summer months. To learn more about backpacking or horse packing in the parks' wilderness, or to join a guided trip, call the information numbers given above for help in hooking up with a reputable guide service. Additional information about Sequoia and Kings Canyon is available on the parks' Web page at **WWW.NPS.GOV/SEKI**.

LODGINGS

Grant Grove Village / ★★

HWY 180, KINGS CANYON NATIONAL PARK; 559/335-5500 After many years of the status quo, accommodations at Kings Canyon National Park changed dramatically for the millennium with the expansion of Grant Grove Village. The Village's new John Muir Lodge, operated by park concessionaire Sequoia Kings Canyon Park Services Company, offers 30 rooms and six suites in a woodsy two-story building hidden in the forest behind the village. (This concessionaire also operates the clean, basic lodge deep in Kings Canyon called Cedar Grove Lodge; it's only open May–October, and reservations can be made via the same phone number above.) One of the challenges along the year-round highway through the big trees of Kings Canyon used to be winter lodging: most of this resort's tent-style, "rustic," or "bath cabin" Meadow Camp cabins had to be closed during snowy months. Now the newer John Muir Lodge hosts year-round visitors in hotel-style comfort. Deluxe rooms come with private baths and are priced well over $100—a far cry from some of Grant Grove Village's classic tent cabins, which still go for about $35 a night. Many guests here are weeklong visitors; some have been coming for generations. Those who like a more rustic experience often choose the Meadow Camp cabins. Those equipped with baths rent for a little more than $100. Others have no running water, no bath, and no heat other than a woodstove and are priced accordingly: about $50 to $60. Snow closes the road from Grant Grove Village into Kings Canyon each winter. *$–$$; DIS, MC, V; checks OK for deposit only; www.sequoia-kingscanyon.com; 65 miles east of Fresno on Hwy 180.* ♿

Silver City Mountain Resort / ★★

NORTH SIDE OF MINERAL KING RD, SEQUOIA NATIONAL PARK; 559/561-3223 SUMMER; 805/528-2730 WINTER Once there were dozens of rustic cabin and tent-cabin resorts like this one in the Sierra Nevada. Now Silver City has become one of the last nostalgic holdouts in a busier world where travelers usually demand large full baths and electricity. That's right, these cabins and "chalets" have no power other than kerosene and propane. Many of Silver City's accommodations, however, still qualify as downright luxurious in these parts. They range from tiny 12-foot-by-12-foot sleeper cabins, adorned with knotty pine paneling, an upholstered easy chair or couch, and a kitchen table, on up to fully stocked chalets, which might have a queen bed and are so popular they should be reserved about six months in advance for holidays and weekends. Most have nicely stocked kitchenettes so you can prepare your own meals (the resort's restaurant is open only five days a week), and all have housekeeping, providing the ultimate luxury in the mountains: cool, clean sheets and pillowcases. At night you'll warm your cabin with a woodstove after sitting out front around a campfire and counting stars with other travelers who share your love of a simpler inn experience. *$–$$; MC, V; checks OK; silvercity@the grid.net; www.silvercityresort.com; 21 miles up Mineral King Rd from Hwy 198.*

Wuksachi Village & Lodge / ★★

64740 WUKSACHI WY NEAR LODGEPOLE, SEQUOIA NATIONAL PARK; 559/565-4070 OR 888/252-5757 Wuksachi Village & Lodge, opened in 1999, features 102 hotel-style rooms ranging from economy to deluxe. Rooms are thoughtfully flexible in furnishings and layout: most have two queen beds and a queen-size sofa bed, so you can really fit in a crowd. Many of your fellow visitors will be spending at least several days here, and a friendly, community feel soon develops as you see familiar faces. Nicely decorated, the lodge has an upscale feeling, with Native American motifs, mission-style furniture, and stonework in the public areas. A crackling fire in a woodstove greets you in the lobby. Steps away, the Lodge's restaurant has a "walk-in" fireplace. Other than a pizza place in Lodgepole, this Wuksachi eatery is the only casual, sit-down dining option around. *$$; AE, DIS, MC, V; checks OK; www.visitsequoia.com; 30 miles from Ash Mountain park entrance.* &

Bakersfield

Bakersfield is a tough, gritty city with a soft heart. Just when you think it consists of nothing more than a confusing tangle of streets and railroad tracks, industrial districts and a still-struggling (but greatly revitalized) downtown, you stumble upon a pocket of vibrancy—and, most important, authenticity—that's missing in many cities. And the farther east you get from Highway 99 into downtown, the better it gets.

Named for early landowner Colonel Thomas Baker, who planned a canal that would link Kern Lake with the San Francisco Bay, and incorporated in 1873, Bakersfield thrives on oil, natural gas, cotton, and other agriculture. Bakersfield is considered the Okie capital of California; country singer Merle Haggard, who is known for his hit "I'm Proud to Be an Okie from Muskogee," hails from the Bakersfield suburb of Oildale. However, when it comes to leisure, residents love good food and antiques—and the city has plenty of both. Drive by a city park on the weekend and your nose may well lead you to a **BASQUE BARBECUE** (the city claims a population of more than 3,500 Basque residents) where an entire lamb, redolent of its garlic marinade, turns slowly on a spit above a white-hot oak fire. Poke around downtown, or on 19th Street east of Chester, or on H Street between Brundage Lane and California Avenue, and you'll find great antique shops and emporiums. Bakersfield must be the valley's storehouse of knickknacks: whatever disappeared from your grandmother's attic seems to have ended up here. Most items are reasonably priced, and it's not uncommon for a charter busload of antique hunters to arrive from Los Angeles for a look around. Downtown's **FIVE AND DIME ANTIQUE MALL** (1400 19th St, at K St; 661/323-8048) took over an old Woolworth building some time ago; its luncheonette area hasn't changed a whit since the 1940s, and it's still open if you want a Coke and a grilled cheese sandwich. As they say in the collectibles

TRAILS OF THE BASQUE SHEEPHERDERS

Hiking deep in a side canyon of the Sierra Nevada, you come across evidence of their passing. Perhaps a rusted kettle. Or even their names. Some immortalized themselves with florid script lightly carved into the growing bark of aspen trees, names like Arrieta and Carrica. It's still possible to find such names preserved in the living bark, and even an occasional date such as 1904—or earlier.

Who were they?

Basque sheepherders. They immigrated as young men from the western end of the Pyrenees to herd sheep in the United States, especially during the years from the 1850s (the California gold rush) to about 1960. Most came just after the turn of the century. With them they brought one of Europe's oldest (and most mysterious) cultures, eventually setting up colonies throughout California, Nevada, and on up into Idaho. The camp life was hard, lonely, nomadic. Town beckoned, and eventually the days of the West's open range were gone.

Today you can still experience their proud role in the West's history, especially in the southern half of the Central Valley, but the opportunity is fading. Older family members keep the old-country ways alive by holding grand festivals at which strong men toss 250-pound weights or play pelote (handball), and beautiful dark-haired girls dance in swirling red dresses and black-aproned vests. Everyone tries a swig or two from the bota—a kidney-shaped leather bag held at arm's length to squirt a thin stream of acrid red wine directly into pursed lips (or all over an amateur's shirt!). Some bakeries in towns like Bakersfield still turn out distinctive "sheepherder's bread"—the high-domed round loaves that herders originally baked in cast-iron pots buried in coals.

And always the lamb sizzles over a white-hot bed of coals, lovingly turned and brushed with a garlicky marinade by men in red berets. Accompanying the lamb are side dishes such as beans with ham or chorizo, hot sauce (not unlike a fresh salsa), salad, pasta dishes, pig's feet, and sliced beef tongue. Many Basque "family-style" restaurants are still located in the very hotels that once housed single men who were between jobs out on that lonely range.

Once in a rare while, if you look across an open field along California's Interstate 5 around Kettleman City and spot a herd of sheep, you may see a sheepherder's trademark home: the curious canvas-sided (or more often, bent-plywood-sided) wagon on wheels. A few are still around, but a way of life—a lonely life that helped feed the West—is all but gone.

—*Peter Jensen*

business: it's mint! The two best **ANTIQUE MALLS** are Great American (625 19th St; 661/322-1776) and Central Park Antique Mall (701 19th St; 661/633-1143); you can easily budget a couple of hours for each. On H Street, shop owners have taken over about two long blocks of Craftsman-era bungalows and turned them into tea shops and one Martha Stewart–esque haven after another. One of the best is Grandma's Trunk (1115 H St; 661/323-2730); be sure to work your way through the house all the way to the back garden and garage.

For even more history, visit **KERN COUNTY MUSEUM AND PIONEER VILLAGE** (3801 Chester Ave, at 34th St; 661/852-5000; www.kcmuseum.org), a cluster of vintage and architecturally significant houses on a site in the fairgrounds. In all, more than 50 original buildings have been moved here from other parts of the city and county, making it a "living museum" of life in the mid-1850s in the area. Adjacent to the museum is the Lori Brock Children's Discovery Center (661/852-5000), a hands-on experience museum for children or all ages. For general tourist information visit or call the **GREATER BAKERSFIELD CHAMBER OF COMMERCE** (1725 I St; 661/327-4421; www.bakersfieldchamber.org) or the **CONVENTION & VISITORS BUREAU** (1325 P St; 661/325-5051; www.visitbfield.com).

BASEBALL fans who've grown tired of the Big League hustle of big ticket prices and Grand Canyon–scale stadiums should attend a game at Sam Lynn Ball Park (4009 Chester Ave, next to the Kern County Museum; 661/322-1363). Here the Bakersfield Blaze, a Class A farm team of the San Francisco Giants, battles other up-and-coming ball players April through August. Tickets are $4 to $6 at the ballpark ticket office—that'll take you back!

Several of the town's best **RESTAURANTS** are located near the original train station, in the vicinity of E 21st Street and Baker Street (the old Southern Pacific line). Basques gathered here in the early 1900s before heading out for sheep camps as far away as the Owens Valley in the eastern Sierra, and they continue to gather here today. You'll still hear Basque spoken at the area's famed Basque bars and family-style restaurants such as the Noriega Hotel or the Wool Growers Restaurant (see below). Although this neighborhood can feel a little deserted and spooky at night, don't shy away; popular restaurants have their own well-lighted parking lots, and incidents are rare.

RESTAURANTS

Bill Lee's Bamboo Chopsticks / ★

1203 18TH ST, BAKERSFIELD; 661/324-9441 Bring a big appetite to Bill Lee's, an institution in Bakersfield since 1938. The decor here is postmodern sophisticated and spacious, with an entry foyer guarded by a terra-cotta tomb warrior statue and beautiful carved-wood panels in the dining rooms. Portions are huge and inexpensive. Dinner often begins with a bowl of wonton soup loaded with slices of cured pork, vegetables, and plump dumplings (although on a recent visit the broth was not quite hot enough and the dumplings a little tough). Fried rice and various chow meins can feed a hungry family for little more than $5 each, while more sophisticated dishes such as a delicious shrimp Cantonese in a garlic–black bean sauce are still priced well under $10. As each dish stacks up in the middle of your table atop odd little stainless steel toadstool-shaped stands, you'll find yourself wondering why you ordered so much. To take some home, of course. *$; AE, DC, DIS, MC, V; checks OK; lunch, dinner every day; full bar; reservations recommended; comments@bill lees.com; www.billlees.com; from 99 N, off the Chester exit on 178 E.* &

The Bistro / ★★

5101 CALIFORNIA AVE, BAKERSFIELD; 661/323-3905 Geared to the well-heeled oil executive and business-traveler crowd, the Bistro—in the Four Points by Sheraton hotel—has also won the hearts of Bakersfield residents, who treat it like their own high-end club whenever it's time for a graduation or anniversary dinner. Designed by a San Francisco firm imported expressly to give it a big-city look, the restaurant features elegant mahogany paneling and trim in the big high-back bar area. In the main rooms the style's a bit lighter, with cedar trim and cases displaying a superb collection of contemporary Native American craft pieces. In short, the Bistro feels good, and despite the valley's generally casual tone, you'll feel good here too, in a nice dress or a sport coat for dinner. Chef Mike Kelly, presiding over the line since the early 1990s, changes the menu seasonally, often incorporating traditional continental themes with plenty of Pacific Rim interlopers. A favorite starter is the tempura artichoke hearts drizzled with a honey-mustard sauce. Entrees may include sea bass with a peanut crust that cracks open to reveal a steamy, fragrant fillet. Oven-fried prawns wrapped in sweet crab-meat sizzle in lemon-garlic butter. Rack of lamb, baked with a tamarind barbecue sauce, pays tribute to Basques and their love of a good leg or chop. Meat lovers relish the chateaubriand, a massive, succulent cut that is typical of the Bistro's undainty portions. Dinners include soup or salad, helping to keep the prices a pleasant surprise for this quality and quantity. For dessert, the crème brûlée just might be the best north of the Tehachapis. At lunchtime, big salads like the cobb or the crackling chicken are first-rate. *$$; AE, DC, MC, V; no checks; breakfast, lunch, dinner every day; full bar; reservations recommended; www.four points.com; take California Ave exit off Hwy 99 and head southwest.* &

Buck Owens' Crystal Palace / ★★

2800 BUCK OWENS BLVD, BAKERSFIELD; 661/328-7500 "They're going to put me in the movies," sings Buck as he steps to the mike on the Crystal Palace's porchlike stage. The country music and television *(Hee-Haw)* legend, still belting them out at age 70, often takes the stage here Friday and Saturday nights to let the crowd know this is his joint and he's there to have as much fun as they are. Fashioned after a Wild West town whose false storefronts surround the stage as in an Elizabethan theatre, Crystal Palace is a great honky-tonk—without some of the honkier elements like cigarette smoke, tossed beer bottles, and chicken wire between the performers and the crowd. In fact, you can feel comfortable bringing your young'uns and your grandma here. Buck's kitchen serves hearty, well-prepared burger-and-potato-skins-type fare, plus more upscale selections such as Buck's Cowboy Steak, a 32-ounce mesquite-grilled extravaganza; shrimp kabobs; or catfish broiled with Cajun spices. The cold beer arrives in mugs big enough to dunk a softball. But the heart of the experience is Buck or the other acts onstage: great music seven nights a week, exemplifying the days when Owens and Merle Haggard put

Bakersfield on the country music map. *$; AE, MC, V; no checks; dinner Mon–Sat, brunch Sun; full bar; reservations recommended on weekends; crystalpalace@atg. com; www.buckowens.com; Buck Owens Blvd exit off Hwy 99.* &

Happy Jack's Pie 'n' Burger / ★

1800 20TH ST, BAKERSFIELD; 661/323-1661 Waiting for your burger, your eye drifts to a photo of the local high school's Driller Wrestling Team. An elderly lady next to you, surely a regular customer, says sadly to no one in particular, "It's nice to know that life's eternal." Ennui settles in like a low-lying tule fog. And then it arrives: the best hamburger in the valley. At Happy Jack's, the fry guy constructs a burger so carefully he could almost be a food stylist for some Ansel Adams of food photography. Stacked high, perhaps with a spicy Anaheim green chile and Russian dressing joining the usual tomato-lettuce-onion tucked inside, a Happy Jack burger needs its white jacket of tissue paper just to keep it all together. No french fries sully the simplicity of Happy Jack's menu—they're not available, probably because the chef's too busy attempting perfection at one thing and one thing only. Desserts feature the unforgettable "Rudy"—a peanut butter and chocolate cream pie with a thin, very flaky crust. Not big. Just good—real good. Full and happy, you take one last look backward at this bizarre little place with its varnished wood siding as you totter into the blazing heat of downtown Bakersfield. *$; Cash only; lunch, dinner, Mon–Fri; no alcohol; reservations not necessary; behind the Fox Theatre, downtown.*

Luigi's / ★★

725 E 19TH ST, BAKERSFIELD; 661/322-0926 Bakersfield's Italian community (and seemingly everyone else in town) has been piling into this noisy storefront since 1911, when it started as a small grocery that also served fresh pasta, stews, and minestrone. Today this crowded, informal deli, bar, and dining hall hosts a brief but lively lunch hour at picnic-style tables covered with red-checkered cloths. The Luigi sandwich is a hefty engineering feat of dry salami, cotto salami, mortadella, provolone, Swiss, mustard, Luigi's special sandwich sauce, lettuce, and onion. Pasta bolognese features a rich sauce recipe that has been in the family (and made fresh daily) since 1911, when Emilia Lemucchi first lovingly stirred up a batch. Team photos from over 50 years of local high school football, baseball, and other sports cover the walls. Two of the waitresses in the front room have worked side by side for more than 20 years; regular patrons look forward to their quick wit and a friendly shoulder rub when they tie on a customer's pasta bib. Lunch specials include a different pasta daily, baked stuffed chicken breast, baby back ribs with rigatoni pasta, and a special New York steak on Fridays. *$; AE, MC, V; checks OK; lunch Tues–Sat; full bar; reservations not accepted; near railroad tracks just south of E Truxton Ave.* &

Noriega Hotel / ★★

525 SUMNER ST, BAKERSFIELD; 661/322-8419 Founded by Faustino Noriega in 1893 and taken over by the Elizalde family in 1931, Noriega's still honors its boardinghouse traditions and proudly proclaims itself *Eskualdunen Etchea*—"the Basque People's House." Step through the door of this historic hotel before 7pm and you may think you've come to the wrong place. In classic Basque fashion, the front room is a large and lively bar, but there's no dining room in sight. Promptly at 7pm the bar clears, and everyone goes into the back room for dinner. Noriega's serves hearty fixed-price family-style meals, and dinner courses arrive in unending waves: salad, soup, beans, pickled tongue, cottage cheese (a unique garlicky mixture that is almost like a dip), salsa, pasta (often spaghetti), two entrees for everybody (that's right, two!), hot, greasy french fries, vegetables, a chunk of blue cheese just before dessert, and ice cream or flan. The beef stew and baked chicken are excellent, but the roast leg of lamb with garlic, served on Friday nights, is the hands-down winner with longtime customers. What makes this place different from other Basque restaurants? Better-than-average cooking and the variety of courses. Red wine—jug variety, but almost perversely tart and delicious—arrives at the table in a screw-top bottle. They decant it, no doubt, from some vast tank in the back room. For real Basque tradition, this is the place. *$$; AE, MC, V; checks OK; breakfast, lunch, dinner Tues–Sun; full bar; reservations recommended; near Baker St.* &

24th St Cafe / ★★

1415 24TH ST, BAKERSFIELD; 661/323-8801 So crowded on a weekend morning that dozens of people sit in chairs on the sidewalk sipping coffee while they wait, 24th St deserves its popularity. Breakfast sweeps you away like some long-lost lover; you just can't remember when you've had one this good. The extensive menu has all sorts of creative yet somehow fundamentally right dishes such as a grilled sourdough egg sandwich, layered with melted Swiss cheese, ham, chopped jalapeño pepper, grilled and lightly caramelized red onion, one fried egg over easy, mayo, and mustard. Homemade hash comes to the table with a thin, spectacularly well-browned crust and steaming insides. Pancakes are big and light. Scrambles include sautéed scallops with scrambled eggs, green onions, and garlic. The wide-ranging menu also includes fresh trout, pan-fried or poached with eggs. Full yet? While breakfast is served all day, lunch is equally well prepared with such selections as a tri-tip sandwich with corn and pinto beans, chili, or meat loaf. Service is efficient and friendly. Decor is a mix of antique bicycles, toys, and other collectibles: a diner look, yet very "today." No one who's in Bakersfield for more than half a day should miss this place. *$; No credit cards; checks OK; breakfast, lunch every day; beer and wine; reservations not accepted; at 24th St (Hwy 178) and K St.* &

Wool Growers Restaurant / ★★

620 E 19TH ST, BAKERSFIELD; 661/327-9584 Bakersfield has many good Basque restaurants, so it's almost a disservice to the community to pick one over the other. Perhaps loyal Basques make the rounds from one to the next. If that's the case, there must be a lot of Basques in Bakersfield, for Wool Growers is jammed on weekend nights. Owned by Jenny Maitia, the restaurant has been redecorated in recent years; consequently, it doesn't feel quite as authentic as some others. Wool Growers has become civilized, but that's a good thing: you can bring your skittish Auntie Doris here and she'll love it. Dinners run the gamut: plenty of bread, pickled beef tongue, steaming hot soup (we had a hearty spicy cabbage that turned absolutely sublime with a good dollop of the house salsa), salad, pasta, entrees (such as lamb chops, oxtail stew, or scampi), vegetables, mounds of french fries. These all come in wondrously large, hot, fresh helpings from a huge kitchen at the back of the main room, served family style at your party's own booth or table. *$; AE, DIS, MC, V; no checks; lunch, dinner, Mon–Sat; full bar; reservations recommended; just before Baker Ave.* &

LODGINGS

Four Points Hotel by Sheraton / ★★

5101 CALIFORNIA AVE, BAKERSFIELD; 661/325-9700 Think again if your image of Bakersfield is still one of a sleepy little farm and railroad town. Big Oil spurred much of Bakersfield's recent growth, and industry executives from around the country pour in here weekly to visit various corporate headquarters. In response to this gusher of business travelers, Sheraton has built one of the most sophisticated yet unpretentious hotels in the Central Valley. Six two-story wings cluster around a lushly landscaped courtyard full of fountains, streams, and ponds, as well as a near-Olympic-length pool with a trellis-shaded seating area cooled by misters. Of the 198 rooms, 58 have patios adjacent to the courtyard. Rooms are furnished with cherry-wood pieces in a continental style or in a lighter, whitewashed look with peach-colored draperies. At least three telephones, all with data ports, are in each room, and the 27-inch televisions are larger than those in most homes. A full buffet breakfast in the restaurant, the Bistro (see review), is included with all room rates over a certain very-reasonable price point; lower-priced rooms still get a continental breakfast. *$–$$; AE, CB, DIS, MC, V; checks OK; www.fourpoints.com; take California Ave exit off Hwy 99 and go southwest.* &

Visalia

Islands of trees rise above oceans of tilled earth around Visalia, an urban center set in a busy agricultural landscape. Located on the eastern edge of the valley, this gateway city to Sequoia National Park (46 miles away) has a mild, warm climate that attracted early settlers because it promised abundant crops as well as good health. Boosters once touted its "pure air"; that's not quite as true today, but on a clear morning after a winter storm, the ragged scarp of the Sierra Nevada—rising like a white wave of granite surf—seems close indeed.

Located about 11 miles off Highway 99, Visalia is often bypassed by travelers. To make matters worse, Highway 198 running through town thoroughly cuts the city in two. But pull off, and you'll be rewarded with the discovery of a vintage downtown, historic houses turned inns, and some of the best dining in the valley.

While in the downtown area, take note of the 1,200-seat 1928 **VISALIA FOX THEATRE** at Main and Encina Streets. Like the Fox Theatre in Hanford, its Spanish Colonial style evokes a massive Andalusian wedding cake with hints of Moorish influence—perfect for a Hoot Gibson or Errol Flynn movie. An old sign that says "The Coolest Spot in Town" dates back to the days when that claim referred to temperature, not hipness. On a hot day you, too, may want to experience the "cool breezes of the Alaska air-washer." Movies, concerts, and special events will soon take place here again; after a period of decline, the Fox is being restored through a community-wide fund-raising effort. Several Main Street restaurants and businesses are also part of the street's comeback. **ANTIQUE SHOPPING** can be rewarding in Visalia. Two worthy venues are the Showcase Mall (26644 S Mooney Blvd; 559/685-1125) and Carriage House Antique Mall (1584 E Mineral King Ave; 559/635-8818). To take in the historical charm of Visalia's neighborhoods, request or pick up one or all three of the city-produced *Heritage Tour* brochures available at the **CONVENTION AND VISITORS BUREAU** (301 East Acequia St; 559/713-4000; www.cbvisalia.com). For those wanting an up-close look or U-Pick opportunities from the city's agricultural offerings, the visitors bureau also hands out an *Ag Trail Tour* brochure, with the 25-mile tour beginning at the visitors bureau and heading west on Mineral King Street.

Once blanketed by oak trees, Visalia has preserved its original landscape in its 1906 parkland, **MOONEY GROVE PARK** (5 miles south of Visalia off Hwy 63 at 27000 S Mooney Blvd; 559/733-6796) and has preserved some of its buildings as well in the park's requisite **PIONEER VILLAGE,** including an unusual cast-iron facade from an 1873 Masonic and Odd Fellows Hall. Don't miss the log-built boathouse set on the edge of a quiet, mirrored lake, which provides pedal boats and rowboats for leisurely cruises. **TULARE COUNTY MOONEY GROVE MUSEUM** (2700 S Mooney Blvd; 559/733-6616) has a classic selection of historical artifacts.

RESTAURANTS

Mearle's College Drive-In / ★

604 S MOONEY BLVD, VISALIA; 559/734-4447 Patsy Cline is crooning "I Fall to Pieces" on the jukebox, the grill's sizzlin', and a tall, cold, curvaceous glass of Coke just arrived at your table. Welcome to Mearle's, where the 1940s and 1950s are alive and well. This basically unchanged vestige of drive-in culture opened in 1940, and three generations of Visalians have celebrated dates, grad nights, and weddings with its famous hamburgers. Today Mearle's fry cook still fills a bun just fine—classic airbread, drippy melted cheese, pickles, lettuce, onion, tomato—with heaps of french fries on the side. Try the Chili Size to sample their fresh-made chili, and don't miss indulging in an old-fashioned fountain milk shake or a "mud slide" sundae. During summer, classic-car owners gather here on the last Saturday night of every month. Lamentably, Mearle's no longer has carhops, the metal awning over the parking places looks like it's about to fall down, and the bathroom will remind you of an old gas station on Route 66. But hey, if you want new, there's a McDonald's down the street. *$; AE, DIS, MC, V; local checks only; breakfast, lunch, dinner every day; no alcohol; reservations not necessary; College of Sequoias exit off Hwy 198.*

The Vintage Press Restaurant / ★★★

216 N WILLIS ST, VISALIA; 559/733-3033 How fitting that one of the oldest towns in the Central Valley should have a restaurant steeped in history, art objects, and antiques. A love of fine California cuisine has brought Valleyites in from a 100-mile-plus radius since 1966 for every special occasion. Vintage Press fairly squeezes a rich, comforting ambience from its setting: a homelike suite of dining rooms and lounges that includes a large, flower-bowered outdoor patio. Owner John Vartanian and family (including chef/son David) pour all their efforts into finding the freshest ingredients, and local growers pull their trucks in each morning with just-picked lettuces and other row crops. Local mushroom foragers and cheese makers contribute to the famous puff pastry wild mushroom appetizer (sautéed with Cognac) and the good slab of white cheddar that's laid over a thick, sizzling lunchtime hamburger. Popular dinner entrees include a savory, garlic-fragrant rack of lamb in a red wine sauce and what is perhaps the restaurant's best-known showcase dish: bacon-wrapped certified Angus filet mignon with mushroom duxelles in a cabernet-shallot sauce spiral. For dessert it's hard to pass up a pecan tart with house-made cinnamon ice cream, or the chocolate Grand Marnier cake. An award-winning wine list includes over 900 selections from a 9,000-bottle cellar, fairly priced, with many "wines of the month" offered at the top of the list so you don't have to feel overwhelmed. Don't miss the Hole in the Wall saloon bar where you can sample one of over 60 single-malt Scotches. Or the 300-square-foot 1910 oil painting of cherubs and angels in a bevy of clouds. By the end of a meal, you'll have experienced the valley's best version of culinary heaven. *$$$; AE, DC, MC, V; checks OK; lunch, dinner every day, brunch Sun; full bar; reservations recommended; www.thevintagepress.com; near Center St in downtown Old Visalia.* &

LODGINGS

Ben Maddox House / ★★☆

601 N ENCINA ST, VISALIA; 559/739-0721 OR 800/401-9800 Sleep inside a sequoia tree? Only in a sense: carpenters built Ben Maddox House in 1876 out of lumber cut from the "big tree" sequoia groves in the Sierra Nevada. Ben Maddox was part owner of the Mt. Whitney Power Co., which brought the first electricity to the valley. He and other citizens also spearheaded efforts to preserve the redwoods, riding on horseback into the mountains with a delegation from Washington, D.C. Today this stately yellow Victorian with its white-columned portico and four guest bedrooms is a sweet reminder of his local contributions. Some guests prefer the spacious Ben Maddox bedroom with its large Italian marble bathroom. Others may choose the Rose Room for its floral motif and its more private location at the side of the house. In summer, a swimming pool offers a cool escape from valley heat. Another big attraction is owner Diane Muro's cooking. Unlike most B&B hosts, she lets guests choose from a full breakfast menu. Be sure to ask for her homemade jams—a bitter-cherry tree out front provides a mother lode of fruit each year. On warm mornings you can take breakfast outdoors on a deck. *$; AE, DIS, MC, V; checks OK; www. benmaddoxhouse.com; 5 blocks north of Main St at Race St.* &

The Spalding House Bed & Breakfast Inn / ★★★

631 N ENCINA ST, VISALIA; 559/739-7877 Few houses in California boast a porch as grand as Spalding House's. The mansion's wide, low-roofed outdoor "room" sweeps down one side facing east (toward the snowcapped Sierra Nevada, visible on a clear day) and offers guests a seat in a Craftsman-style swing. A fine example of Colonial Revival style, built in 1901, Spalding House was a lumberman's dream home. The public rooms still give evidence of a gracious ease that once cosseted a prominent family. The three suites are sedate and of the period: no wild wallpaper or "theme rooms" here. What you will find is accommodations tastefully decorated with antiques, white linens, and gauzy curtains. One touch of whimsy is in the Aviary Room, where a beautiful little sitting porch has been fashioned from a former colorful tiled aviary. The Cutler Suite used to be a sleeping porch, and the Spalding Suite has a large sitting area off the bedroom. Owners Wayne and Peggy Davidson are gracious hosts, and Wayne cooks a great complimentary breakfast in the house's vast kitchen. *$$; AE, MC, V; checks OK; www. spaldinghouse.com; 6 blocks north of downtown at Grove Ave.*

Three Rivers

More than just a place to gas up the car before heading into Sequoia National Park, Three Rivers has long attracted artists, writers, and other free spirits. A group called the Kaweah Colony settled here in 1885 (six years after the town's founding), hoping to create an egalitarian, self-sustaining community based on harvesting timber from the giant redwoods nearby. For six years they met with some success, but the shift in public mood toward preservation of the mountains' scenic resources (rather than more plundering) doomed the Kaweahans' venture. Now with a population of about 3,000, Three Rivers has become a resort town at the confluence of the north, middle, and south forks of the Kaweah River. It's a good place to stretch your legs and spend the night, for lodging, always limited in national parks, is quite possibly unavailable if you venture into Sequoia-Kings without a hotel reservation. Three Rivers's lodgings, on the other hand, are numerous and vary from comfortable bed-and-breakfasts to sizable chain motels.

Art galleries and shops in town are few, but you might stop in **REIMER'S** (559/561-4576), an almost edible-looking gingerbread-bedecked store that from the outside greatly resembles its contents of homemade candies and ice cream, unique gifts, Christmas goodies, and home decorations. Spring wildflowers are another attraction, and in early May the **RED BUD ARTS AND CRAFTS FESTIVAL** (at the Lions Club Roping Arena on N Fork Dr, about 1½ miles up-canyon from Hwy 198) celebrates their return before the 90-plus temperatures of summer—and the waves of park-bound tourists—arrive once more. A business association called the **RESERVATION CENTRE** (559/561-0410; www.rescentre.com) can provide you with local event and lodging information for not only Three Rivers/Lemon Cove but also all of the nearby national parks. For specific information on the area, go to www.three rivers.com.

RESTAURANTS

The Gateway / ★☆

45978 SIERRA DR, THREE RIVERS; 559/561-4133 It's hard to be far from water in the Sierra foothills below Sequoia-Kings, but the land still seems parched and thirsty until you get to higher elevations. Built on the gurgling Kaweah, a river fed by melting snow, with panoramic views of the canyon from both its open-air veranda and its dining room, the Gateway straddles this world between wet and dry, hot and cold, especially if you have an icy beer in one hand and a juicy rib in the other. Along with the view, ribs made the Gateway famous. A rack of baby back pork glistens in a glaze of beery-spicy tomato sauce before making a heavenly mess of your chin, fingers, and napkin—a mountain-man kind of experience if there ever was one. The fork-tender charbroiled filet mignon (cut on the premises) is one of the best in the mountains, and a lobster and steak dinner will make you think you're back in the big city (with both its fine steak house quality and its price). The Gateway makes its own salad dressings, and offers alternative fare such as fish so you don't have to feel adrift in a den of carnivores. While you're dining, you might be lucky enough to glimpse bears down along the river. $$; AE, DC, DIS, MC, V; no checks; breakfast Sat–Sun, lunch, dinner Tues–Sun; full bar; reservations recommended; 6 miles east of Three Rivers on Hwy 198.

LODGINGS

Buckeye Tree Lodge / ★

46000 SIERRA DR, THREE RIVERS; 559/561-5900 Although the Buckeye definitely has an up-in-the-mountains feel, you're only at 1,300 feet. During the spring, the Kaweah River, which runs right beside the nicely landscaped 2-acre property, rages along through its canyon like an angry white horse. By summer it has calmed down and taken on lazy-stream status, perfect for sitting on a boulder and dangling your toes, or casting a line in search of trout. Eleven rooms in the main lodge are clean and modern with handmade oak furnishings. Natural colors provide the predominant scheme for everything from walls to spreads—a refreshing break from the aggressively "country" theme of most mountain lodgings. The two-story lodge features verandas that double as walkways to the rooms, so each unit's deck is somewhat communal. Escape instead to the pool, which is large and well sited in the sun, or to the lawns and walks shaded by oaks. The lodge's most interesting accommodation is the Redbud Cottage, a small house with a king bedroom, a half-bedroom with twin bed, and a living room with queen bed and sofa sleeper, plus a kitchen and a wood-burning fireplace to take the chill off those cool mountain nights. $–$$; AE, CB, DC, DIS, MC, V; no checks; info@buckeyetree.com; www.buckeyetree.com; 6 miles NE of town on Hwy 198 (1/2 mile from park entrance).

Sequoia Village Inn / ★

45971 SIERRA DR (HWY 198), THREE RIVERS; 559/561-3652 Innkeeper Curt Nutter is well known in these parts as an inveterate hiker, and he'll bend your ear about the best places to tramp in the Sierra Nevada. In addition to being a walking guidebook, he runs a neat and quiet little inn in a deep canyon adjacent to historic Pumpkin Hollow Bridge. The first cabins here were built in the 1940s to house park rangers, so they have a little more room than most typical tourist cabins or motel rooms. The decor is homey, and much of the clientele consists of families looking for a quiet retreat after a day in the national park. Smallest accommodations still have a queen bed, while two newer more spacious chalet-style cabins are for families or groups: one sleeps 9, the other 12. Both chalets have a California Craftsman style and boast views up the canyon. Amenities include pool and hot tub, French roast coffee, and popcorn (microwave in room). On clear nights Nutter will occasionally bring out a big reflecting telescope for some stargazing. $; AE, MC, V; California checks OK; 5 miles past Three Rivers, take immediate left after Pumpkin Hollow Bridge.

Fresno

Fresno dates back to 1872, when the town was founded as a water stop for the Southern Pacific Railroad. After the gold rush, many unsuccessful miners turned to agriculture to make a living. Today, farming remains the region's leading business, with more than 250 commercial crops grown annually.

However, the town itself is an endless stretch of strip malls, apartment complexes, and ranch-style homes. Just about every chain store and fast-food restaurant known to man can be found along its streets. Downtown, with its conglomeration of government buildings, may be the only part of Fresno with buildings more than four stories high, but on weekends and evenings it becomes a virtual ghost town.

One place where you will find activity—and a bit of history as well—is Fresno's **TOWER DISTRICT.** Built around the restored Tower Theater, a 1939 art deco movie house that was renovated in 1990, this trendy neighborhood is teeming with stylish restaurants, theaters such as Roger Rocka's Dinner Theater (1226 N Wishon Ave; 559/266-9494) and the Second Space Theater (928 E Olive Ave; 559/266-0660), and lively watering holes such as Avalon Billiard Club (1064 N Fulton Ave; 559/495-0852). The Tower Theater (815 E Olive Ave; 559/485-9050) itself, with its dramatically backlit etched glass panels and Italian terrazzo foyer, hosts concerts by performers like George Winston and Diana Krall.

History buffs can tour the elegant homes of several of Fresno's founders, like the **KEARNEY MANSION MUSEUM** (7160 W Kearney Blvd; 559/441-0862) or the **MEUX HOME MUSEUM** (1007 R St; 559/233-8007; www.meux.mus.ca.us). Those who want to take a pleasant stroll outdoors can head to the **CHAFFEE ZOOLOGICAL GARDENS,** set in Roeding Park (894 W Belmont Ave; 559/498-2671; www.chaffeezoo.org). With more than 600 mammals, birds, and reptiles, this local zoo boasts a tropical rain forest exhibit and reptile house. The park offers picnic areas, lakes, tennis courts, and recreational areas for kids.

The **FRESNO FAIRGROUNDS** (1121 S Chance Ave; 559/650-3247; www.fresno fair.com) is home of the annual Big Fresno Fair each October, but it offers more than just that event: other events include live and satellite horse racing, the AgFRESNO agricultural show in November, and home and garden shows in spring and summer. Fresno has a new visitors center that is quite impressive. The former water tower, built in 1894, was patterned after a medieval German water tower and stands 100 feet high. The **FRESNO CONVENTION & VISITORS BUREAU** spent two years and more than $500,000 to renovate the tower and place it on the National Register of Historic Places. The tower, now the city's main tourism information hub, is located at 2430 Fresno Street (559/237-0988; www.fresnocvb.org).

RESTAURANTS

The Daily Planet / ★★

1211 N WISHON AVE, FRESNO; 559/266-4259 Mahogany paneling, velvet drapes, art deco wall sconces, and a period mural on the ceiling take diners back to an era long past in this alluring eatery situated next to the historic Tower Theater. The menu, atmosphere, and bar also reflect the decadence of an earlier time, before we discovered cholesterol and the adverse effects of smoking and drinking. Here, as the faint strains of a piano player echo over the crowd, patrons swill cocktails like the Daily Planet's signature Stockholm 75 (citrus vodka, lemon juice, and champagne), sip Glenmorangie's single malt, smoke cigars, and sup on entrees with fat-gram counts in the triple digits. Start with oyster shooters with a zesty chipotle cream sauce, a bowl of fresh corn bisque with basil, or shrimp spiedini, tender skewered shrimp and prosciutto glazed with a tangy balsamic vinaigrette. For the main course, the hearty rack of lamb with a light basil-honey marinade and the homey pot roast with creamy garlic mashed potatoes take comfort food to new levels. If you can't decide what to order, go with the prix-fixe menu, which changes every three weeks to make the most of seasonal ingredients. Be sure, however, to save room for the decadent chocolate praline taco stuffed with white chocolate mousse and fresh fruit, or the chocolate apricot torte served with a rich brandy whipped cream. *$$$; MC, V; local checks only; lunch Mon–Fri, dinner every day; full bar; reservations recommended; www.tower2000.com; corner of Olive Ave.* &

Echo Restaurant / ★★★

609 E OLIVE AVE, FRESNO; 559/442-3246 Opened in 1995, this charming French-California eatery changes its menu daily to make the most of chef Tim Woods's daily shopping trips to local farms and ranches in the neighboring San Joaquin Valley. Once he has selected the freshest seasonal ingredients possible, Woods returns to the kitchen to create such specialties as grilled Madera County quail marinated in Dijon mustard and herbs, creamy summer squash and garlic soup, savory roasted pork loin with a fennel-seed-and-black-pepper crust, and succulent grilled fillet of Harris Ranch beef with applewood-smoked bacon and rosemary. Enjoy a glass of wine from the restaurant's impressive wine list, lauded with an award of excellence from *Wine Spectator,* sink into the comfy Frank Lloyd Wright–designed chairs at your white linen–covered table, and watch the action in the open kitchen—it's all a part of the dining experience here. Chocolate lovers shouldn't skip a slice of dense, moist bittersweet chocolate cake, but McGuinness strawberries with a rich white chocolate cream and champagne also score points on the decadence scale. *$$$; AE, DIS, MC, V; checks OK; dinner Tues–Sat; beer and wine; reservations recommended; www.echomenu.com; corner of Echo St.* &

LODGINGS

Radisson Hotel & Conference Center Fresno / ★★

2233 VENTURA ST, FRESNO; 559/268-1000 OR 800/333-3333 Just across the street from Fresno Convention Center, this 321-room hotel is built around an eight-story central atrium, with a three-story waterfall and faux ivy dripping down from each floor. Formerly a Holiday Inn, the place was extensively remodeled when Radisson took over in early 1999, with upgrades to the furnishings, remodeled bathrooms, a new fitness center, and an extensive game room that would keep any kid entertained. Rooms have coffeemakers, data ports, and irons and ironing boards, while deluxe suites give travelers an additional living room area to spread out in. Conventioneers and business travelers appreciate the hotel's extensive banquet facilities and 18 meeting rooms. A small but well-kept indoor-outdoor pool and whirlpool, a gift shop, and a full-service hair salon add to the hotel's list of amenities. The spacious lobby boasts the International Cafe for a quick, convenient meal and the Atrium Lounge, where guests can savor a cocktail and enjoy live piano music nightly. A complimentary shuttle transports guests to and from Fresno Yosemite International Airport. *$$; AE, DC, DIS, JCB, MC, V; checks OK; www.radisson.com/fresnoca; between Van Ness Ave and M St.* ♿

The San Joaquin Hotel / ★★

1309 W SHAW AVE, FRESNO; 559/225-1309 OR 800/775-1309 This three-story apartment-complex-turned-all-suites-hotel boasts one-, two-, and three-bedroom suites all overlooking an immaculately kept garden courtyard with rosebushes, an Italian fountain, and a small pool and whirlpool spa. With six different floor plans (three of which include a full kitchen), the spacious suites are individually decorated and run the gamut in style—from art deco moderne to austere Oriental. Even the smallest, the Squire, features a separate living room, bedroom, and huge bathroom, with such homey extras as full-length mirror, coffeemaker, medicine cabinet, and tons of closet space. Though there's no restaurant, room service is available from a neighboring Italian restaurant. A complimentary continental breakfast is served in a nondescript nook off the lobby each morning, featuring fruit, bagels, cereal, coffee, and juices. *$$; AE, DC, DIS, MC, V; no checks; www.sjhotel. com; west of Palm Ave.* ♿

Hanford

Visitors to Sequoia National Park learned Hanford's secret over 75 years ago. This small valley city, located halfway between Interstate 5 and Highway 99, has a prosperous charm exemplified in a classic downtown built around a shaded courthouse square. The local economy of Hanford, established in 1887 by the Southern Pacific Railroad, was originally based on the railroad, crops, and dairies. But as auto travel became the preferred means of reaching the valley and the Sierra Nevada, Hanford languished. Even Highway 198 now bypasses the town by a half mile. Oddly enough, from the 1950s to the 1980s it was best known for its improbably huge, popular continental-Chinese restaurant, **IMPERIAL DYNASTY**—which is still open, although a bit quieter nowadays (see review). Located in China Alley, on the east edge of town, are several interesting buildings that were established by the Chinese immigrants who moved to the San Joaquin Valley in the late 1800s.

Today Hanford easily warrants an overnight stay for its historic appeal. Many visitors arrive by train from the San Francisco Bay area, and you can pick up tour information at **HANFORD VISITOR AGENCY** (200 Santa Fe Ave; 559/582-0483; visithanford.com), inside the 1898 railroad station.

Courthouse Square's magnificent **COUNTY OF KINGS COURTHOUSE** (on 8th St between Irwin and Douty Sts), built in 1896, is worth a visit (note the see-through cast-iron stairs inside), although it's occupied by businesses these days. The jail building next door (113 Court St; 559/582-9741), built in 1898, has a castlelike tower and a great arched stone entry; it's now a restaurant known as the Bastille, where the decor is the main attraction. Other buildings of interest around the square include the **CIVIC AUDITORIUM** (in Civic Center Park, 400 N Douty St), dating back to 1924; the former post office (218 Douty St), built in 1914; and the **HANFORD FOX THEATRE** (Irwin and 8th Sts; 559/584-7423), a 1929 Spanish Colonial temple for the early talkies, which now hosts concerts and special events. Restored to its 1929 elegance, the theater is one of only 33 remaining atmospheric theaters in the nation; the ceiling twinkles with "stars" and a crescent moon lights the European "sky." In short, Hanford is a treasure box of civic architecture. Residential streets fan out through equally historic neighborhoods, although these have seen more incursion by the modern world. For the best look at the area's history, visit the stone **HANFORD CARNEGIE MUSEUM** (109 E 8th St; 559/584-1367). Architecture scholars consider this 1905 structure the finest example of a Carnegie-built free public library in the state.

Parched from all that meandering around the square? If you don't fancy a milk shake at Superior Dairy Products Company, one of the world's great soda fountains (see review), wander a few blocks from the square to **ART WORKS** (120 W 6th St; 559/583-8790), in the 1893 Arcade Building facing the railroad tracks; this hip little gallery and coffeehouse is a fine place to shop for enticing, inexpensive gifts. The **CHINA ALLEY** district preserves the turn-of-the-20th-century business district, when Hanford's population of Chinese railroad laborers and their families was one of the state's largest. The centerpiece of China Alley is a **TAOIST TEMPLE** built in 1893—one of the country's oldest Chinese temples—and on the National Register of Historic Places; at one time the temple housed a school. Tours of the brick building with original teakwood and marble are conducted by appointment only; call 559/582-4508 for information. The portion of the temple that once housed the school is now the **TEMPLE THEATRE**, the home of the King's Players, a live theater group. The theater's history is apparent in its huge Chinese calligraphy and restored golden dragons. Show tickets may be obtained by calling 559/584-7241.

RESTAURANTS

Imperial Dynasty / ★★☆

2 CHINA ALLEY, HANFORD; 559/582-0196 Located in a windowless brick building on a historic Chinatown alley, Imperial Dynasty traces its roots back to 1883, when the Wing family first began serving meals in town. Over the years the menu evolved from Chinese to continental, with steak, seafood, and even escargots sharing the bill of fare. One seems caught in a time warp here: the back page of the menu features a photocopy of an award won in 1960 for "Best Dinner," bestowed by the Wine and Food Society of Pasadena, like a royal decree that still holds weight. Twin dining rooms up front feature pagodalike roofs sheltering a wondrous art collection; a jade-museum room downstairs is used mostly for parties. After an appetizer of escargots à la bourguignonne (in Dijon mustard, Chablis, and butter sauce) or *fonds d' artichauts Monselet* (five small artichoke hearts and about 10 oysters doing laps in a steamy pool of lemony butter), you'll think France has fully taken over the kitchen. Then comes a navy bean soup. Then a hot little patty of egg foo yung beneath a salty onion sauce. The eclecticism continues, with a huge serving of lamb shanks, perhaps, for an entree. You begin to realize that Imperial Dynasty embraces the big portion/multicourse ethic as strenuously as the Basque restaurants of other valley towns. Overall, this restaurant is very 1960s; it was undoubtedly worthy of its acclaim at a time when American tastes were just warming up to Europe, but now it's noteworthy mostly for its longevity, grand history, and odd location. And, yes, for its excellent service proferred by a grandmotherly Chinese waitress. *$$; AE, DIS, MC, V; checks OK; dinner Tues–Sun; full bar; reservations recommended; at Green St.*

Superior Dairy Products Company / ★★

325 N DOUTY ST, HANFORD; 559/582-0481 Take a seat at the counter in this 1929 fountain to watch soda queen Ruby turn out one gargantuan shake or sundae after another, each topped with an Everest of whipped cream from a chrome nozzle leading to some hidden, endless reservoir. Superior has a movie-set feel, but it's all real and unaffected, from the pressed-tin ceiling right down to the black-and-chrome napkin holders. Waitresses wearing hot-pink shirts move efficiently from booths to counter and back, pitching the popular tri-tip combo (beef sliced and served on a split buttered-and-grilled French roll) or the other satisfyingly simple sandwiches that read like a throwback to your parents' or grandparents' eras: liverwurst, deviled egg, Swiss cheese, ham, tuna. The homemade ice cream is as spectacular as the setting. Served in huge quantities, fresh and creamy, it's rich and irresistible enough to seize up your arteries on the spot. As you eat, watch the world drift by through big picture windows overlooking Hanford's courthouse and jail—a classic small-town valley experience. *$; No credit cards; local checks only; lunch, dinner every day; no alcohol; reservations not accepted; corner of 9th St on Civic Center Park.* &

LODGINGS

The Irwin Street Inn / ★★

522 N IRWIN ST, HANFORD; 559/583-8000 Capturing the charm of the nostalgic town square area of Hanford is this group of restored Victorian residences that make up the Irwin Street Inn, hotel, and restaurant. Overnight accommodations feature individually decorated period decor with four-poster beds, private bathrooms with oak-trimmed tubs and pull-chain toilets, Oriental rugs and leaded glass windows. Guest room selections range from doubles to two doubles to suites. The restaurant offers delicious homemade breakfasts (don't pass on the homemade muffins) and soup and sandwich lunches in the antique-filled parlor dining areas or on the graceful terrace; romantic dinners are offered on Friday and Saturday nights only. *$$; AE, DC, DIS, MC, V; local or corporate checks only; www.irwinstreetinn.com; corner of Porter St.*

Index

425

We Stand By Our Reviews

Sasquatch Books is proud of *Best Places Southern California*. Our editors and contributors go to great lengths and expense to see that all of the restaurant and lodging reviews are as accurate, up-to-date, and honest as possible. If we have disappointed you, please accept our apologies; however, if a recommendation in this 2nd edition of *Best Places Southern California* has seriously misled you, Sasquatch Books would like to refund your purchase price. To receive your refund:

1. Tell us where and when you purchased your book and return the book and the book-purchase receipt to the address below.
2. Enclose the original restaurant or lodging receipt from the establishment in question, including date of visit.
3. Write a full explanation of your stay or meal and how *Best Places Southern California* misled you.
4. Include your name, address, and phone number.

Refund is valid only while this 2nd edition of *Best Places Southern California* is in print. If the ownership, management, or chef has changed since publication, Sasquatch Books cannot be held responsible. Tax and postage on the returned book is your responsibility. Please allow six to eight weeks for processing.

Please address to Satisfaction Guaranteed, *Best Places Southern California*, and send to:
Sasquatch Books
119 South Main Street, Suite 400
Seattle, WA 98104

Best Places Southern California Report Form

Based on my personal experience, I wish to nominate the following restaurant, place of lodging, shop, nightclub, sight, or other as a "Best Place"; or confirm/correct/disagree with the current review.

_____

_____

_____

_____

(Please include address and telephone number of establishment, if convenient.)

REPORT

Please describe food, service, style, comfort, value, date of visit, and other aspects of your experience; continue on another piece of paper if necessary.

_____

_____

_____

_____

_____

_____

_____

I am not concerned, directly or indirectly, with the management or ownership of this establishment.

_____

SIGNED

_____

ADDRESS

_____

_____

PHONE DATE

Please address to _Best Places Southern California_ and send to:
SASQUATCH BOOKS
119 SOUTH MAIN STREET, SUITE 400
SEATTLE, WA 98104
Feel free to email feedback as well: **BESTPLACES@SASQUATCHBOOKS.COM**